D0017619

Guatemala

John Noble
Susan Forsyth

Contents

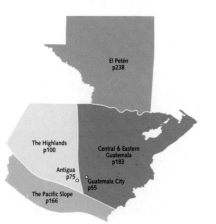

El Petén
p238

The Highlands
p100

Central & Eastern
Guatemala
p183

Antigua
p75

Guatemala City
p55

The Pacific Slope
p166

Destination: Guatemala

Guatemala is a rare destination that rewards even the most jaded travelers with revelatory experiences – a place where indigenous life endures much as it did before Europeans first arrived, and where no superlatives can capture the grandeur of the landscape. In the highlands it seems there's always a volcano looming over your shoulder, and beautiful lakes large and small are scattered among pine, cloud and rain forests all over the country. This fabulous geography means travelers can hike, bike, dive, ride, cave and kayak ad infinitum.

Wildlife viewing is popular too, especially in the rain forests of the northern Petén region. But El Petén is also synonymous with the awesome temples of Tikal. Peerless among Classic Mayan cities, Tikal is a must-see for any visitor. Mayan sites such as El Mirador in the extreme jungle depths can be even more exciting because reaching them is an adventure in its own right!

Studying Spanish has long served as a traveler's gateway to Guatemalan life, and language schools have now been set up in almost every town travelers like to linger in. Whether you prefer the international scene of Antigua or the mountain seclusion of Todos Santos Cuchumatán, odds are there's a school and setting for you.

But the most striking feature of Guatemala is its people. A visit to the raucously colorful markets in towns like Chichicastenango or Sololá will give you a feel for the palpable living culture of Guatemala's indigenous population. You'll rarely get a brusque reception from any Guatemalan, and with their infectiously amicable and helpful demeanor, it's the Guatemalans themselves who, more than anything, really make traveling in Guatemala special.

JEFFREY N BECOM

TIKAL (p257)
Marvel at lofty temples rising above jungle full of wildlife

YAXHA (p267)
Climb to the top of ancient temples with superb vistas over two lakes

RÍO DULCE (p234)
Speed down a jungle-fringed tropical river to the fascinating Caribbean enclave of Livingston

EL MIRADOR (p273)
Walk two days through jungle to reach the tallest of all Mayan pyramids

FLORES (p242)
Stroll the tranquil streets of an age-old island town

SAYAXCHÉ AREA SITES (p269)
Travel by boat along jungle-lined rivers to Mayan ruins at Ceibal, Dos Pilas and Aguateca

GRUTAS DE LANQUÍN & SEMUC CHAMPEY (p196)
Explore spectacular caves, cool off in gorgeous turquoise lagoons

NEBAJ (p136)
Walk the beautiful hill country of the traditional, colorful Ixil Maya

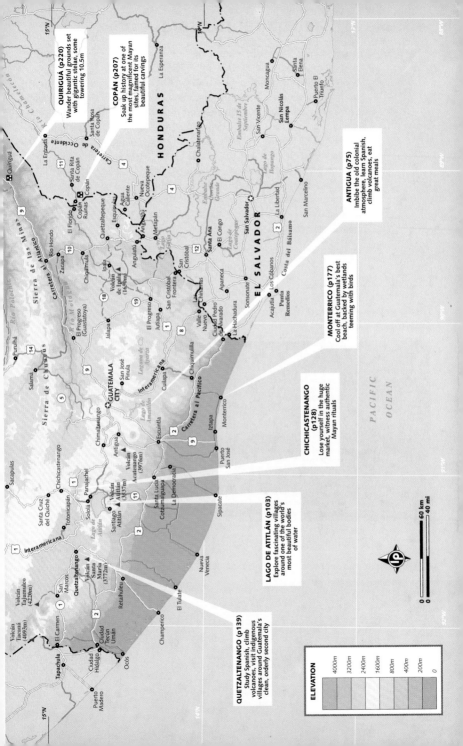

QUIRIGUA (p220)
Wander beautiful grounds set with gigantic stelae, some towering 10.5m

COPÁN (p207)
Soak up history at one of the most magnificent Mayan sites, famed for its beautiful carvings

ANTIGUA (p75)
Imbibe the old colonial atmosphere, learn Spanish, climb volcanoes, eat great meals

MONTERRICO (p177)
Cool off at Guatemala's best beach, backed by wetlands teeming with birds

CHICHICASTENANGO (p128)
Lose yourself in the huge market, witness authentic Mayan rituals

LAGO DE ATITLÁN (p103)
Explore fascinating villages around one of the world's most beautiful bodies of water

QUETZALTENANGO (p139)
Study Spanish, climb volcanoes, visit indigenous villages around Guatemala's clean, orderly second city

HONDURAS

EL SALVADOR

PACIFIC OCEAN

Sierra de las Minas

Sierra de Chuacús

ELEVATION

4000m
3200m
2400m
1600m
800m
400m
200m
0

60 km
40 mi

The magnificent temples, palaces and sculptures of the ancient Maya, mostly constructed between AD 250 and AD 900, are for many the country's biggest attraction. Many of the ancient sites still have romantic jungle settings. Supreme among Guatemala's magnificent relics of ancient Mayan civilization is **Tikal** (p257), where awesome temples rise above the jungle canopy. The surrounding Petén forests harbor **Yaxhá** (p267), **Uaxactún** (p265), **Ceibal** (p269), **Aguateca** (p271) and the remote, unrestored **El Perú** (p272) and **El Mirador** (p273). In southeastern Guatemala, the sculptures of **Quiriguá** (p220) are outstanding, and those at **Copán** (p207), a short detour into Honduras, are even more so. In Guatemala City don't miss the **Museo Popol Vuh** (p63) or the **Museo Nacional de Arqueología y Etnología** (p64).

GREG JOHNSTON

Detour to the splendid ancient city of **Copán** (p207)

ALFREDO MAIQUEZ

Admire the outstanding Mayan stelae at **Quiriguá** (p220)

Behold Guatemala's supreme relic of ancient Mayan civilsation: **Tikal** (p257)

JOHN ELK II

RICHARD I'ANSON

Fall in love with **Lago de Atitlán** (p103), one of the world's most beautiful lakes

GREG JOHNSTON

Refresh your senses among the waterfalls and turquoise lagoons of **Semuc Champey** (p197)

Spot the magnificent scarlet macaw near **El Perú** (p272)

TOM BOYDEN

HIGHLIGHTS Natural Wonders

Guatemala's landscapes – from its 30 volcanoes to its rivers, lakes and waterfalls – are truly spectacular. They shelter abundant wildlife, especially in the northern jungles and central cloud forests. Its volcanoes include active **Pacaya** (p85) and dormant but higher **Acatenango** (p85), **Santa María** (p143) and **Tajumulco** (p143). The banks of the dramatic **Río Dulce** (p234) are jungle-lined, while **Laguna Petexbatún** (p270) and **Laguna Lachuá** (p199) harbor plentiful wildlife. Ancient **Tikal** (p264) is hard to beat for animal and bird abundance, but wildlife spotters shouldn't miss the **Bocas del Polochic** (p227), **Biotopo del Quetzal** (p188) and **Parque Nacional Laguna del Tigre** (p272).

All over the country, you will encounter the colorful crafts, vivid markets and ritualistic religion of the Maya – especially in the Highlands. Soak up the atmosphere and barter for handicrafts at the indigenous markets in **Chichicastenango** (p128) and **Sololá** (p104). Admire the colorful clothes in towns like **Todos Santos Cuchumatán** (p161) and **Nebaj** (p136). Witness traditional rituals at Chichicastenango's **Iglesia de Santo Tomás** (p129) and nearby **Pascual Abaj** (p130), or the shrines to the deity Maximón in **Zunil** (p151) or **Santiago Atitlán** (p117). Don't miss the collection of fine Mayan weaving at Guatemala City's **Museo Ixchel** (p63).

Admire the skill that goes into **weaving** traditional clothes (p41)

ERIC L WHEATER

Barter with stallholders for intricate **textiles** (p282)

RICHARD I'ANSON

RICHARD I'ANSON

Soak up the atmosphere of the indigenous market in **Chichicastenango** (p128)

Getting Started

Traveling in Guatemala requires little detailed planning. Bus transport around the country is plentiful (if rarely comfortable!). For many trips all you need to do is show up at the bus station and hop on the next bus. Accommodations are equally easy to find: unless you have your heart and mind set on one chosen hotel, booking ahead isn't usually necessary. The major exception to all this is Semana Santa (Easter week), when the whole country takes a holiday and you need to book rooms, and often transport, in advance.

Guatemala is a country for any budget. It's popular with backpackers because you can survive on a few dollars a day, but it also has many mid-range lodgings and restaurants offering comfort and quality at good prices.

See the Directory (p274) for more details on climate, festivals and events.

WHEN TO GO

There is really no bad time for visiting Guatemala, though the rainy season – called *invierno* (winter) – makes access off paved roads more difficult from mid-May to mid-October, and on into November and even December in the north and east of the country. In the lowland jungles of El Petén, the mud at this time will be a bummer, guaranteed. Humidity – never low on the coasts or in El Petén – increases during the rainy season, too. In the highlands things can get very cold and damp during the rainy season, especially at night. It doesn't rain all day every day during the rainy season, but you can expect daily showers (downpours in the north) at the very least. The dry season – *verano* (summer) – is from about November to April, and this means sweltering heat in El Petén and along the coasts and comfortably warm days in the highlands. In the eastern parts of the country, rain is actually possible at any time.

The height of the foreign tourist season is from Christmas to Easter. Things become acute around Christmas, New Year's and Easter, when Guatemalans too take holidays and in many places you need to book ahead for rooms or transportation. A secondary high season lasts from June to August when throngs of North Americans and Europeans descend on Guatemala to study Spanish and travel about.

LP INDEX

Liter of gas (petrol) US$0.55

Liter of bottled water US$0.60

Bottle of Gallo US$1.50

Souvenir T-shirt US$6

Chuchito (Corn dough filled with a spicy meat and served in a corn husk) US$0.50

COSTS & MONEY

Prices in Guatemala are among the best in Central America. Beds in *hospedaje*s (budget hotels) normally cost US$3 to US$4 per person. Markets sell fruit and snacks for pennies, cheap eateries called *comedores* offer one- or two-course meals for US$2 to US$3, and bus trips cost less than US$1 per hour. It's completely realistic to spend less than US$15 a day in Guatemala without too much hardship. If you want more comfort, you can readily move up to nice rooms with private hot-water bathrooms and eat well-prepared food in pleasant surroundings and still pay only US$30 per person for a room and two – or even three – meals. Add in transport, admission fees, a bit of shopping and a few beers and you're looking at a total budget around US$50 a day for fairly comfortable mid-range traveling.

Unfortunately, there are few bargains here for solo travelers, as there often isn't much price difference between a single and a double room. If it's practical, hook up with some other folks to defray room costs. Many places have rooms for three or four people where the per-person price is much less than for one or two. In restaurants, you can save money by opting for set two- or three-course meals, often called the *menú del día*, costing no more than one single à la carte main dish. On the road, public buses are far cheaper than the more comfortable shuttle minibuses put on for tourists.

TRAVEL LITERATURE

Ronald Wright's *Time among the Maya* (p22) is a story of travels through the whole Mayan region – Guatemala, Mexico, Belize and Honduras – delving into the glorious past and exploited present of the Maya and examining their obsession with time. Wright visits many of the places you'll visit, and his book is a fascinating read, even though written in the troubled 1980s.

Guatemalan Journey by Stephen Benz is another one to enjoy while you're in Guatemala. It casts an honest and funny modern traveler's eye on the country. So does Anthony Daniels' *Sweet Waist of America*, also published as *South of the Border: Guatemalan Days*, where the medic author pinpoints some of the country's quirky contradictions.

In *Sacred Monkey River* Christopher Shaw explores by canoe the jungle-clad basin of the Río Usumacinta, a cradle of ancient Mayan civilization along the Mexico–Guatemala border – a great read.

Bird of Life, Bird of Death, by Jonathan Evan Maslow, subtitled *A Naturalist's Journey Through a Land of Political Turmoil,* tells of the author's searches for the resplendent quetzal (the 'bird of life') – which he found to be increasingly endangered, while the zopilote (vulture; the 'bird of death') flourished.

The 19th-century classic *Incidents of Travel in Central America, Chiapas and Yucatan*, by John L Stephens (illustrated by Frederick Catherwood), was the first extensive and serious look at many Mayan archaeological sites. This tome is a laborious but interesting read.

INTERNET RESOURCES

Gringo's Guide (www.thegringosguide.com) Useful info on the country's main travel destinations.
Guatemala (www.mayaspirit.com.gt) Moderately interesting official site of Inguat, the national tourism institute.
Lanic Guatemala (lanic.utexas.edu/la/ca/guatemala) The University of Texas' magnificent set of Guatemala links.
La Ruta Maya Online (www.larutamayaonline.com) Reasonably useful mixed bag.
Lonely Planet (www.lonelyplanet.com) Succinct summaries on Guatemala travel; the popular Thorn Tree bulletin board; travel news; and the SubWWWay section, which has links to the most useful travel resources elsewhere on the Web.

HOW MUCH?

Three-hour 2nd-class bus ride US$2

A week of Spanish classes with homestay US$90-200

Admission to Tikal US$6.50

Taxi from Guatemala City airport to city center US$8

Comfortable lakeside double with bathroom, Lago de Atitlán US$25-35

DON'T LEAVE HOME WITHOUT...

- Checking the visa situation (p284).
- Checking governments' travel advice (p277).
- Warm clothes for chilly highland nights – at least a sweater or light jacket and a pair of fairly warm pants (eg denim).
- A flashlight (torch) for exploring caves, ruins, and your room when the electricity fails (as it often does).
- A mosquito net, if you're planning an extended jungle adventure or will be sleeping in cheap rooms without screens.
- Insect repellent containing DEET (p297), for wet-season travels. You may want to take medication against malaria, too (p295).
- A small towel, for rooms without one.

TOP TENS
OUR FAVORITE FIESTAS

You don't have to go looking for festivals in Guatemala. You'll run into parades, fireworks, music and dancing in towns and villages all over the country. But some extra-special events are worth planning for:

- Fiesta de El Cristo de Esquipulas, January 15, Esquipulas (p203)
- Fiesta de San Pedro, January 19–25, Rabinal
- Semana Santa (Easter Week), March or April, Antigua (p88) and Santiago Atitlán (p117)
- Feria de San Felipe, end April/early May, El Castillo de San Felipe (p226)
- Rabin Ajau Folkloric Festival, late July/early August, Cobán (p189)
- Fiesta de Rilaj Maam (Maximón), October 28, San Andrés Itzapa (p119) and Zunil (p119)
- Día de Todos los Santos (All Saints' Day), November 1, Todos Santos Cuchumatán (p163) and San José (p254)
- Feria del Barrilete Gigante (Giant Kite Festival), November 1, Santiago Sacatepéquez (p98) and Sumpango (p98)
- Quema del Diablo (Burning of the Devil), December 7, Chichicastenango (p131)
- Fiesta de Santo Tomás, December 21, Chichicastenango (p131)

BEST MAYAN READS

The Maya, past and present, are the theme of whole libraries of writing. Here are our 10 favorite books on them:

- *The Maya,* Michael D Coe (p19)
- *The Blood of Kings: Dynasty & Ritual in Maya Art,* Linda Schele and Mary Ellen Miller (p21)
- *Scandals in the House of Birds: Shamans and Priests on Lake Atitlán,* Nathaniel Tarn (p37)
- *I, Rigoberta Menchú: An Indian Woman in Guatemala,* Rigoberta Menchú (p29)
- *Maya of Guatemala – Life and Dress,* Carmen L Pettersen (p42)
- *Chronicle of the Maya Kings and Queens,* Simon Martin and Nikolai Grube (p24)
- *Unfinished Conquest: The Guatemalan Tragedy,* Víctor Perera (p24)
- *The Maya Textile Tradition,* Margot Blum Schevill (editor) (p42)
- *Breaking the Maya Code,* Michael D Coe (p19)
- *The Ancient Maya,* Robert J Sharer (p19)

LAND OF ETERNAL SPRING

This is what they call Guatemala in the tourist blurbs. Of course it isn't, but it *is* a natural wonderland. Here are our 10 select sites for experiencing the country's animal, vegetable, geological and scenic marvels.

- Tikal (p257)
- Lago de Atitlán (p103)
- Ixil Triangle (p136)
- the Río Dulce (p234)
- Volcán Tajumulco (p143)
- Semuc Champey (p197)
- Volcán Acatenango (p85)
- Laguna Petexbatún (p270)
- Laguna Lachuá (p199)
- the Cuchumatanes mountains north of Huehuetenango (p157)

Itineraries

CLASSIC ROUTES

HIGHLAND FLING
10 days / Guatemala City to Quetzaltenango

Guatemala's most spectacular scenery and strongest Mayan traditions await you along this well-traveled route.

From the capital head first to gorgeous **Antigua** (p75), enjoying the country's finest colonial architecture, the great restaurants and the big traveler and language-student scene. Several volcanoes wait to be climbed here. From Antigua move on to **Panajachel** (p105) on volcano-ringed **Lago de Atitlán** (p103). Hop in a boat to check out some of the quieter, more traditional Mayan villages around the lake such as **Santiago Atitlán** (p117), **San Pedro La Laguna** (p121), **San Marcos La Laguna** (p125) or **Santa Cruz La Laguna** (p127). Now head north to **Chichicastenango** (p128) for its huge Thursday and Sunday market. If you have extra time, detour north to **Nebaj** (p136), where you'll find great walking and a strong Mayan way of life amid stunning scenery.

From Chichicastenango follow the Interamericana Highway west along the mountain ridges to **Quetzaltenango** (p140), Guatemala's clean, orderly, second city, with a host of intriguing villages, markets and natural wonders waiting within short bus rides. From Quetzaltenango you can head south, or on to Mexico – perhaps via **Todos Santos Cuchumatán** (p161), a fascinating Mayan mountain town with great walking possibilities.

This 320km jaunt could take a few months if you stop off to learn some Spanish in Antigua, Panajachel, San Pedro La Laguna or Quetzaltenango, and you could more than double the distance with detours to Nebaj and Todos Santos Cuchumatán.

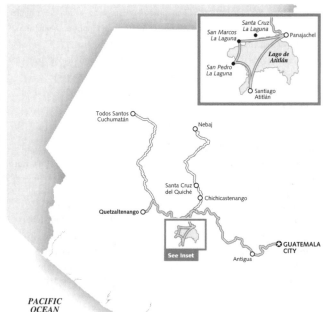

THE BIG LOOP   3 weeks

This trip takes you to the best of Guatemala's Mayan ruins, into its dense jungles and to some of its spectacular natural marvels.

Start out northeastward from Guatemala City and detour south into Honduras to see the great Mayan site of **Copán** (p207). Return to Guatemala and continue northeastward to another fine Mayan site, **Quiriguá** (p220), and on to the curious Garífuna enclave of **Lívingston** (p232) on the sweaty Caribbean coast. Take a boat up the jungle-lined **Río Dulce** (p234) to **Río Dulce town** (p232), then turn north up Highway 13 to stay and chill out at **Finca Ixobel** (p240) before continuing to **Flores** (p242), a quaint small town on an island in the Lago de Petén Itzá. From Flores, head for **Tikal** (p257), the most majestic of all Mayan sites. Spend a night at Tikal itself or nearby **El Remate** (p254). While in the Flores-Tikal area, you should have time to take in further impressive Mayan sites such as **Yaxhá** (p267) and **Uaxactún** (p265).

From Flores head southwest to the relaxed riverside town of **Sayaxché** (p268), which is at the center of another group of intriguing Mayan sites – **Ceibal** (p271), **Aguateca** (p269) and **Dos Pilas** (p270). The road south from Sayaxché is now nearly all paved to **Chisec** (p198) and **Cobán** (p189), jumping-off points for a whole series of pristine natural wonders such as jungle-ringed **Laguna Lachuá** (p199), the **Grutas de Lanquín** (p196) and the turquoise lagoons and waterfalls of **Semuc Champey** (p197).

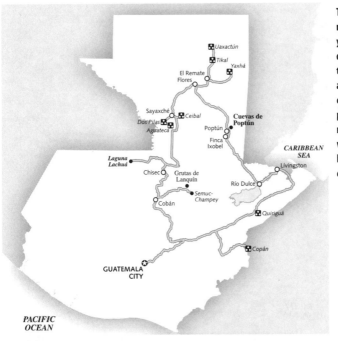

This 1900km round trip takes you to all the top destinations in the center, east and north of the country. Really pushing, you might do it in two weeks, but if you have four, you'll enjoy it more.

ROADS LESS TRAVELED

ACROSS THE CUCHUMATANES   2 days / Huehuetenango to Cobán

The road from Huehuetenango to Cobán is almost all unpaved and always inspiring, with stunning, endlessly changing scenery and varied tableaux of indigenous mountain life. From the northern end of the highlands, it takes hardy trippers straight into the center of the country.

Buses are not too common on some stretches of the route, and sometimes you may need to resort to pickups or trucks – which at least afford unimpeded 360° views. Starting high in the Cuchumatanes mountain range, you climb out of **Huehuetenango** (p157) en route to **Aguacatán** (p164), where you're treated to panoramic views of pine-studded slopes and the fertile valleys below.

From Aguacatán the road snakes down through the Río Blanco valley to **Sacapulas** (p135) on the Río Negro. (If you want to detour to **Nebaj,** p136, for a spot of hiking amid gorgeous Cuchumatanes scenery, you can get a Nebaj bus here.) From Sacapulas the road starts climbing again, up precipitous slopes, then winds down and up again to the neat, clean town of **Uspantán** (p136), where you may need to spend the night. From Uspantán it's a direct shot down through beautifully forested countryside and the Mayan village of **San Cristóbal Verapaz** (p196) to **Cobán** (p189). Sit on the right for views.

The 142km between Huehue and Cobán are not quite so difficult to traverse as they were a few years ago, but they still represent a challenging trip of one or two days (depending on your connections and your karma!). You'll find full practical travel details for this route in the relevant town sections.

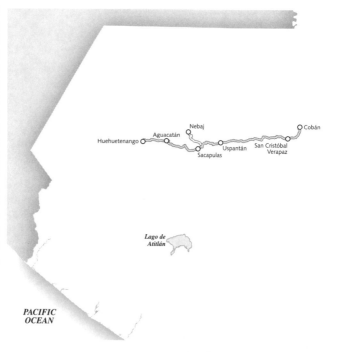

TAILORED TRIPS

THE MAYA THEN & NOW

In **Guatemala City** (p55), your start and finish, don't miss the museums dedicated to Mayan archaeology and textiles. Head west to the **Iximché** ruins (p103), and on to **Lago de Atitlán** (p103), surrounded by traditional villages such as **Santiago Atitlán** (p117). Don't miss the big Mayan markets at **Sololá** (p104) and at **Chichicastenango** (p128), also the scene of unique religious practices. Northward, visit the old K'iche' Mayan capital **K'umarcaaj** (p134), still an important center for Mayan rites. Westward, **Quetzaltenango** (p140) is a base for visiting many traditional villages (for example, **Zunil**, p151) and the sacred **Laguna Chicabal** (p157). Further north, see the old Mam Mayan capital, **Zaculeu** (p158), en route to **Todos Santos Cuchumatán** (p161), a mountain village with strong traditions and uniquely striking costumes.

Next, head east along mountain roads to **Nebaj** (p136), a center of the colorful Ixil Maya, and to **San Cristóbal Verapaz** (p196). Head north through Cobán to **Sayaxché** (p268), close to the ancient Mayan sites **Ceibal** (p271), **Aguateca** (p271) and **Dos Pilas** (p270), then on to **Flores** (p242) and the mother of all Mayan cities, **Tikal** (p257). In the Petén jungles, you can explore remoter archaeological sites such as **Yaxhá** (p267), **Uaxactún** (p265), **El Zotz** (p272) and (if you have stamina for four or five days' walking) **El Mirador** (p273).

Head back to Guatemala City via **Quiriguá** (p220) and, just over the Honduras border, **Copán** (p207).

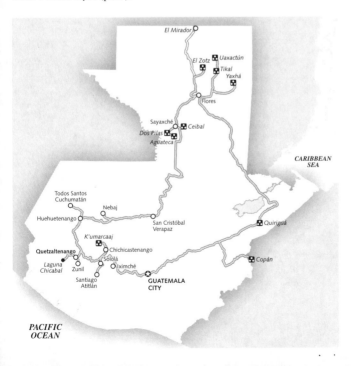

NATURAL WONDERS

Tone up your muscles by climbing a couple of the volcanoes around Antigua: the active **Pacaya** (p85) and the mighty **Acatenango** (p85). Move on to **Lago de Atitlán** (p103), certainly one of the most beautiful lakes in the world. Continue westward to bag more volcanoes around Quetzaltenango – say, **Santa María** (p143) and **Tajumulco** (p143), the highest peak in Central America. Head north to experience the beauty of the Cuchumatanes mountains around **Todos Santos Cuchumatán** (p161) and **Nebaj** (p136). East from Nebaj is **Cobán** (p189), stepping stone for the lovely lagoons and waterfalls of **Semuc Champey** (p197), the extensive cave system of the **Grutas de Lanquín** (p196), the forest trails of the **Biotopo del Quetzal** (p188) and the jungle-surrounded **Laguna Lachuá** (p199). Move north to the thick jungles of El Petén, exploring the rich bird and plant life of **Laguna Petexbatún** (p270). The magnificent ancient Mayan city **Tikal** (p257) and the area around **El Perú** ruins (p272) are two of the finest spots in the country for observing tropical wildlife. On your way back south, pause for cave exploration at **Finca Ixobel** (p240), a boat ride along the beautiful, jungle-shrouded **Río Dulce** (p234) and a side trip to the **Bocas del Polochic** reserve (p227), which supports over 300 bird species.

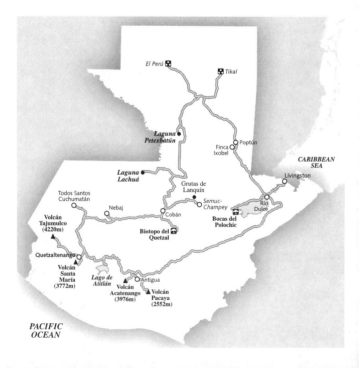

The Authors

JOHN NOBLE
Coordinating Author

John has been fascinated by Guatemala ever since his first backpacking trip at a time when Panajachel's Calle Santander was a dusty lane lined with a few houses and a lot of empty space. He has since taken every opportunity to visit and revisit as many Mayan archaeological sites as he can, and soak up all possible aspects of contemporary Mayan culture. Writing this book provided the perfect opportunity to deepen his knowledge of all his favorite spots in Guatemala and to get to know a few new ones. John is English but lives in Spain with his wife and co-author Susan Forsyth and their children. He has written or co-written many other Lonely Planet guides including several editions of *Mexico*.

Our Coordinating Author's Favorite Trip

I'm hooked on the romance of jungle-shrouded Mayan ruins and my favorite way to enter Guatemala is across the Río Usumacinta (p289) from Mexico's Chiapas state (having visited the Mexican Mayan sites of Palenque, Bonampak and Yaxchilán en route). Inside Guatemala, the sites around Sayaxché – Ceibal (p269), Aguateca (p270), Dos Pilas (p270) – are the first goal and the dream way to reach them (though not cheap) is by boat up the Río de la Pasión (p268). Then it's a bus hop to the beautiful island town of Flores (p242) and on to peerless Tikal (p257), the ultimate goal of any Maya fan in Guatemala – but just the beginning for anyone who's into investigating El Petén's many remoter Mayan sites!

SUSAN FORSYTH
Co-author

Susan has been exploring the Mayan world for over a decade on travel and work assignments in southern Mexico and Guatemala. It was a trip along the jungle-clad Río Usumacinta to visit the ruins of Mexico's Yaxchilán that first whetted her appetite for exploring the country on the river's far side, Guatemala. Today it's her passion for colorful handicrafts that particularly draws her to Guatemala. She finds the reds and pinks used in weaving traditional fabrics here intoxicating. Cloth from Zunil near Quetzaltenango is her favorite. Susan, an Australian, has lived in Spain for many years and finds herself increasingly fascinated, and perplexed, by Spain's colonial history and its legacy.

CONTRIBUTING AUTHOR

Dr David Goldberg MD wrote the Health chapter (p292). David completed his training in internal medicine and infectious diseases at Columbia-Presbyterian Medical Center in New York City, where he has also served as voluntary faculty. At present, he is an infectious diseases specialist in Scarsdale, New York state, and the editor-in-chief of the website MDTravelHealth.com.

Snapshot

Guatemala stands at a crossroads. The 1996 Peace Accords, which ended 36 years of vicious, traumatic civil war, contained the seeds of a brighter future for a country where repression of the indigenous Mayan majority by the colonial minority has been the rule for almost 500 years. With agreements on improving the rights of women and indigenous people, on improving education and health care, and on accountability for human-rights violations during the war, the Peace Accords gave cause for hope that a just, humane and democratic society might finally arise from the ashes of the civil war nightmare.

FAST FACTS

Population: 11.2 million

Life expectancy at birth: 65 (US: 77)

Adult literacy: 69% (US: 99%)

Female adult literacy: 61% (US: 99%)

Percentage of population living on less than US$2 a day: 34%

Fertility rate: 4.9 (US: 2.0)

Infant mortality per 1000 live births: 44 (US: 7)

Annual cigarette consumption per adult: 442 (US: 2193)

Annual electricity consumption per person (kilowatt hours): 341 (US: 11,994)

Annual carbon dioxide emissions per person (tons): 0.9 (US: 19.9)

But nearing the end of the four-year presidency of Alfonso Portillo in 2004, little has been done. It was clear that the same old militaristic ruling class remained in charge of Guatemala – literally so, since Portillo's party leader was General Efraín Ríos Montt, who was dictator back in 1982-83 during the worst campaigns of civil war atrocities (some say genocide against the Maya) had been carried out. International bodies from the United Nations to the Interamerican Human Rights Commission reported very negatively in 2002 and 2003 on the state of indigenous rights, women's rights and human rights in Guatemala. Guatemalans who campaigned for such rights were often the victims of threats, attacks and murders. *El Periódico* newspaper printed an article in 2003 arguing that a 'parallel power structure' involving Efraín Ríos Montt had effectively run Guatemala ever since he had been ousted as president 20 years previously. Within days, the paper's publisher and his family were attacked in their home by an armed gang of 12. Days later, Ríos Montt himself was, incredibly, granted permission by Guatemala's constitutional court to stand in the elections for Portillo's successor in late 2003, despite the fact that the constitution banned presidents who had in the past taken power by coup, as Ríos Montt had in 1982. In the end Guatemala's voters dealt Ríos Montt a resounding defeat, electing Oscar Berger, of the moderately conservative Gran Alianza Nacional, as president till 2008.

Guatemalans of all stripes feel threatened by the alarming level of crime and violence in the country. The country's role in the international drugs trade, and the private security forces that go with that, may bear much of the blame. Whatever the causes, the official security forces seem powerless and unwilling to contain crime, which touches almost everybody – from Guatemala City bus drivers who are forced to provide local gangs with protection money, to the magistrates, human rights campaigners, journalists and environmentalists who receive death threats when their work makes life difficult for the powerful and corrupt, and to the tourists who are robbed at gunpoint while walking empty country paths.

With official channels so ineffective, much of the best work for indigenous and women's rights, for improving health, education and housing, for protecting Guatemala's priceless natural heritage and for giving hope to the poor and needy is being done by countless non-governmental groups, local and international. Volunteers are much in demand by many of these organizations, giving foreigners a great opportunity to make a contribution.

History

ARCHAIC PERIOD (UP TO 2000 BC)

It's accepted that, barring a few Vikings in the north and conceivable direct transpacific contact with Southeast Asia, the pre-Hispanic inhabitants of the Americas arrived from Siberia. They came in several migrations between perhaps 60,000 and 8000 BC, during the last ice age, crossing land that is now submerged beneath the Bering Strait, then gradually moving southward.

These early inhabitants hunted mammoths, fished and gathered wild foods. The ice age was followed by a hot, dry period in which the mammoths' natural pastureland disappeared and the wild nuts and berries became scarce. The primitive inhabitants had to find some other way to survive, so they sought out favorable microclimates and invented agriculture, in which maize (corn) became king. The inhabitants of what are now Guatemala and Mexico successfully hybridized this native grass and planted it alongside beans, tomatoes, chili peppers and squash (marrow). They wove baskets to carry in the harvest, and they domesticated turkeys and dogs for food. These early homebodies used crude stone tools and primitive pottery, and shaped simple clay fertility figurines.

The Ancient Maya, by Robert J Sharer, is a 1990s update of Sylvanus G Morley's classic 1940s tome of the same name. The first half of the book treats the Mayan story chronologically; the second half discusses different aspects of their culture. The book is admirably clear and uncomplicated.

PRECLASSIC PERIOD (2000 BC–AD 250)

The improvement in the food supply led to an increase in population, a higher standard of living and more time to experiment with agricultural techniques and artistic niceties. Decorative pots and healthier, fatter corn strains were produced. Even at the beginning of the Preclassic period, people in Guatemala spoke an early form of the Mayan language. These early Maya also decided that living in caves and under palm fronds was passé, so they invented the *na*, or thatched Mayan hut – still used today throuhout much of the country. Where spring floods were a problem, a family would build its *na* on a mound of earth. When a family member died, burial took place right there in the living room, after which the deceased attained the rank of honored ancestor.

The Copán Valley (in present-day Honduras) had its first proto-Mayan settlers by about 1100 BC, and a century later settlements on the Guatemalan Pacific coast were developing a hierarchical society.

By the middle Preclassic period (800–300 BC) there were rich villages in the Copán Valley, and villages had been founded at what came to be the majestic city (and modern Guatemala's number one tourist attraction) of Tikal, amid the jungles of El Petén, northern Guatemala. Trade routes developed, with coastal peoples exchanging salt and seashells for highland tribes' tool-grade obsidian. A brisk trade in ceramic pots and vessels flourished throughout the region.

As the Maya honed their agricultural techniques, including using fertilizer and elevated fields to boost production, a rich, noble class emerged that indulged in such extravagances as resident scribes and artists – and temples, which consisted of raised platforms of earth topped by a thatch-roofed shelter very much like a normal *na*. The local potentate was buried

The Maya, by Michael D Coe, is probably the best single-volume, not-too-long telling of the ancient Maya story – learned and careful, yet readable and well illustrated. Coe's *Breaking the Maya Code* recounts the modern decipherment of ancient Mayan writing, and his *Reading the Maya Glyphs* will help you read ancient inscriptions.

TIMELINE	11,000 BC or earlier	Around 250 BC to AD 100
	First human occupation of Guatemala.	Early Mayan cities El Mirador and Kaminaljuyú flourish.

DECORATION & RECREATION

The ancient Maya considered flat foreheads and crossed eyes beautiful. To achieve these effects, children would have boards bound tight to their heads and wax beads tied to dangle before their eyes. Both men and women made cuts in their skin to gain much-desired scar markings, and women sharpened their teeth to points, another mark of beauty – which may also have helped them to keep their men in line!

The recreation most favored by the Maya was a ball game *(juego de pelota)*, courts for which can still be seen at many archaeological sites. It's thought that the players had to try to keep a hard rubber ball airborne using any part of their body other than their hands, head or feet. A wooden bat may also have been used. In some regions, a team was victorious if one of its players hit the ball through stone rings with holes little larger than the ball itself.

The ball game was taken very seriously and was often used to settle disputes between rival communities. On occasion, it is thought, the captain of the losing team was punished by execution.

beneath the shelter, increasing the site's sacred power. Pyramid E-VII-sub at Uaxactún, 23km north of Tikal, was a good example of this; others have been found at Tikal itself and El Mirador, another Petén site that flourished during the late Preclassic period (300 BC–AD 250). Kaminaljuyú, in Guatemala City, reached its peak from about 400 BC to AD 100, with thousands of inhabitants and scores of temples built on earth mounds.

Mesoweb (www.mesoweb.com) is a great resource on the Maya, past and present.

In El Petén, where limestone was abundant, the Maya began to build platform temples from stone. As each succeeding local potentate had to have a bigger temple, larger and larger platforms were built over existing platforms, eventually forming huge pyramids with a *na*-style shelter on top. The potentate was buried deep within the stack of platforms. El Tigre pyramid at El Mirador, 18 stories high, is believed to be the largest ever built by the Maya. More and more pyramids were built around large plazas, in much the same way that the common people clustered their thatched houses in family compounds facing a communal open space. The stage was set for the flowering of classic Mayan civilization.

CLASSIC PERIOD (AD 250–900)

During the Classic period the Maya produced pre-Hispanic America's most brilliant civilization in an area stretching from Copán, in modern Honduras, through Guatemala and Belize to Mexico's Yucatán Peninsula.

DID YOU KNOW?

El Mirador, in far northern Guatemala near the Mexican border, represents the greatest challenge to travelers of any ancient Mayan site, requiring visitors to walk four or five days through jungles.

The great ceremonial and cultural centers included Copán; Quiriguá in southern Guatemala; Kaminaljuyú; Tikal, Uaxactún, Río Azul, El Perú, Yaxhá, Dos Pilas and Piedras Negras, all in El Petén; Caracol in Belize; Yaxchilán and Palenque in Chiapas, Mexico; and Calakmul, Uxmal and Chichén Itzá on the Yucatán Peninsula. All these sites can be visited, with varying degrees of difficulty, today. Around the beginning of the Classic period, Mayan astronomers began using the elaborate Long Count calendar to date all of human history (pp23-3).

While Tikal began to assume a primary role in Guatemalan history around AD 250, El Mirador had been mysteriously abandoned about a century earlier. Some scholars believe a severe drought hastened this great city's demise.

AD 230	562
King Yax Moch Xoc of Tikal establishes the dynasty that will make Tikal the dominant city of the southern Mayan world.	Leading Mayan city Tikal defeated by rivals Calakmul and Caracol.

The Classic Maya were organized into numerous city-states. Each city-state had its noble house, headed by a priestly king who placated the gods by shedding his blood in ceremonies during which he pierced his tongue, penis or ears with sharp objects. For more on these rites and other Mayan beliefs, see p38. As sacred head of his community, the king also had to lead his soldiers into battle against rival cities, capturing prisoners for use in human sacrifices. Many a king perished in a battle he was too old to fight. A typical Mayan city functioned as the religious, political and market hub for the surrounding farming hamlets. Its ceremonial center focused on plazas surrounded by tall temple pyramids and lower buildings – so-called palaces – with warrens of small rooms. Stelae and altars were carved with dates, histories and elaborate human and divine figures. Stone causeways called *sacbeob*, probably built for ceremonial use, led out from the plazas.

The Blood of Kings: Dynasty & Ritual in Maya Art, by Linda Schele and Mary Ellen Miller, is a heavily and fascinatingly illustrated guide to the art and culture of the ancient Maya, with particular emphasis on sacrifices, bloodletting, the ball game, torture of captives and other macabre aspects of Mayan culture.

In the first part of the Classic period, most of the city-states were probably grouped into two loose military alliances centered on Calakmul, in Mexico's Campeche state, and Tikal. Like Kaminaljuyú and Copán, Tikal had strong connections with the powerful city of Teotihuacán, near modern Mexico City. When Teotihuacán declined, Tikal's rival Calakmul allied with Caracol to defeat a weakened Tikal in 562. However, Tikal returned to prominence under a resolute and militarily successful king named Moon Double Comb, also known as Ah Cacau (Lord Chocolate), who ruled from 682 to 734. Tikal conquered Calakmul in 695.

In the late 8th century, trade between Mayan states started to shrink and conflict began to grow. By the early 10th century the cities of Tikal, Yaxchilán, Copán, Quiriguá and Piedras Negras had reverted to little more than minor towns or even villages, and much of El Petén was abandoned. Many explanations, including population pressure and ecological damage, have been offered for the Classic Mayan collapse. Current theories point to three droughts, each lasting several years, around 810, 860 and 910, as major culprits.

POSTCLASSIC PERIOD (900–1524)

Some of the Maya who abandoned El Petén must have moved southwest into the highlands of Guatemala. In the 13th and 14th centuries they were joined by Maya-Toltec migrants or invaders from the Tabasco or Yucatán

---

Mayan Counting System

The ancient Mayan counting system was elegantly simple: dots were used to count from one to four; a horizontal bar signified five; a bar with one dot above it was six, a bar with two dots was seven, and so forth. Two bars signified 10, three bars 15. Nineteen, the highest common number, was three bars stacked up and topped by four dots.

To signify larger numbers the Maya stacked numbers from zero to 19 on top of each other. Thus the lowest number in the stack showed values from one to 19, the next position up signified 20 times its face value, the third position up signified 20 times 20 times its face value. The three positions together could signify numbers up to 7999. By adding more positions one could count as high as needed. Zero was represented by a stylized picture of a shell or some other object.

The Mayan counting system's most important use – and the one you will encounter during your travels – was in writing dates.

King Moon Double Comb, or Lord Chocolate, ascends Tikal's throne, launching a revival for Tikal.

Tikal conquers Calakmul.

THE MAYAN CALENDAR

The ancient Maya's astronomical observations and calculations were uncannily accurate. They could pinpoint eclipses and their Venus cycle erred by only two hours for periods covering 500 years.

Time was, in fact, the basis of the Mayan religion. They believed the current world to be just one of a succession of worlds, each destined to end in cataclysm and be succeeded by another. This cyclicity enabled the future to be predicted by looking at the past. Most Mayan cities were constructed in strict accordance with celestial movements, and observatories were not uncommon.

Perhaps the best analog to the Mayan calendar is the gears of a mechanical watch, where small wheels mesh with larger wheels, which in turn mesh with other sets of wheels to record the passage of time.

Tzolkin or Cholq'ij or Tonalamatl

The two smallest wheels in this Mayan calendar 'watch' were two cycles of 13 days and 20 days. Each of the 13 days bore a number from one to 13; each of the 20 days bore a name such as Imix, Ik, Akbal or Xan. As these two 'wheels' meshed, the passing days received unique names. For example, when day one of the 13-day cycle fell on the day named Imix in the 20-day cycle, the day was called 1 Imix. Next came 2 Ik, then 3 Akbal etc. After 13 days, the first cycle began again at one, even though the 20-day name cycle still had seven days to run, so the 14th day was 1 Ix, followed by 2 Men, 3 Cib etc. When the 20-day name cycle was finished, it began again with 8 Imix, 9 Ik, 10 Akbal etc. The permutations continued for a total of 260 days, ending on 13 Ahau, before beginning again on 1 Imix.

The two small 'wheels' of 13 and 20 days thus created a larger 'wheel' of 260 days, called a *tzolkin, cholq'ij* or *tonalamatl*.

Visitors interested in Mayan culture might want to head to one of the towns still observing the *tzolkin* calendar (such as Momostenango or Todos Santos Cuchumatán) for Wajshakib Batz, the start of the *tzolkin* year. It falls on May 28, 2004; February 12, 2005; October 30, 2005; July 17, 2006; and April 3, 2007. Outsiders are not necessarily invited to join in the ceremonies, as they tend to be sacred affairs, but it's still a good time to be in one of these traditional towns.

Vague Year (Haab)

Another set of wheels in the Mayan calendar watch comprised 18 'months' of 20 days each, which formed the basis of the solar year or *haab* (or *ab'*). Each month had a name – Pop, Uo, Zip, Zotz, Tzec etc – and each day had a number from zero (the first day, or 'seating,' of the month) to 19. So the month Pop ran from 0 Pop (the 'seating' of the month Pop), 1 Pop, 2 Pop and so forth to 19 Pop, and was followed by 0 Uo, 1 Uo and so on.

Eighteen months, each of 20 days, equals 360 days, a period known as a *tun*; the Maya added a special omen-filled five-day period called the *uayeb* at the end of this cycle in order to produce a solar calendar of 365 days. Anthropologists today call this the Vague Year, its vagueness coming from the fact that the solar year is actually 365.24 days long (the reason for the extra day in leap years of our Gregorian calendar).

Calendar Round

The huge wheels of the *tzolkin* and the *haab* also meshed, so that each day actually had a *tzolkin* name-and-number and a *haab* name-and-number used together: 1 Imix 5 Pop, 2 Ik 6 Pop, 3 Akbal 7 Pop and so on – a total of 18,980 day-name permutations. These repeated every 52 solar years,

9th century	13th & 14th centuries
The collapse of Classic Mayan civilization.	Toltec-Maya migrants from southeast Mexico establish kingdoms in the Guatemalan highlands.

a period called the Calendar Round. The Calendar Round was the dating system used not only by the Maya but by the Olmecs, Aztecs and Zapotecs of ancient Mexico. It's still in use in some traditional Guatemalan villages, and you can see why a special Mayan elder has to be designated to keep track of it and alert his community to important days in this complex system.

Long Count

For a people as obsessed with counting time as the Maya, the Calendar Round has one serious limitation: it only lasts 52 years. After that, it starts again, and there is no way to distinguish a day named 1 Imix 5 Pop in one 52-year Calendar Round cycle from the identically named day in the next cycle.

Thus the Long Count, which the Maya developed around the start of the Classic period (about AD 250). The Long Count uses the *tun*, the year of 18 20-day months, but ignores the *uayeb*, the final five-day period that follows the *tun* in the Vague Year. In Long Count terminology, a day was a *kin* (meaning 'sun'). A 20-*kin* 'month' is called a *uinal*, and 18 *uinals* make a *tun*. Twenty *tuns* make a *katun* (7200 days, nearly 20 of our Gregorian solar years), and 20 *katuns* make a *baktun* (144,000 days, about 394 years). Further gigantic units above *baktun* were only used for grandiose effect, as when a very self-important king wanted to note exactly when his extremely important reign took place in the awesome expanse of time. Curiously for us today, 13 *baktuns* (1,872,000 days, or 5125 Gregorian solar years) form something called a Great Cycle, and the first Great Cycle began on August 11, 3114 BC (some authorities say August 13) – which means it will end on December 23 (or 25), AD 2012. The end of a Great Cycle was a time fraught with great significance – usually fearsome. Stay tuned around Christmas 2012.

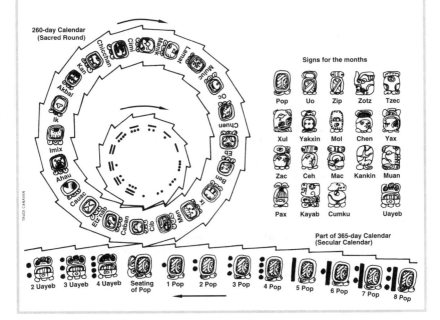

1524
Spaniards under Pedro de Alvarado conquer Guatemala.

1527
Alvarado establishes his capital at Santiago de los Caballeros (modern Ciudad Vieja, near Antigua).

areas of Mexico (the Toltecs were a militaristic culture from central Mexico with powerful, wide-ranging influence). Groups of these newcomers set up a series of rival states in the Guatemalan highlands: the most prominent were the K'iche' (or Quiché; capital: K'umarcaaj, near modern Santa Cruz del Quiché), the Kaqchiquels (capital: Iximché, near Tecpán); the Mam (capital: Zaculeu, near Huehuetenango); the Tz'utujil (capital: Chuitinamit, near Santiago Atitlán); and the Poqomam (capital: Mixco Viejo, north of Guatemala City). All these sites can be visited today. Another group from the Yucatán, the Itzáes, wound up at Lago Petén Itzá in the Petén region, settling in part on the island that is today called Flores.

Chronicle of the Maya Kings and Queens, by Simon Martin and Nikolai Grube (2000), tells in superbly illustrated detail the histories of 11 of the most important Mayan city-states and their rulers.

SPANISH CONQUEST

Spaniards under Hernán Cortés defeated the Aztec Empire based at Tenochtitlán (modern Mexico City) in 1521. It only took a couple of years for the conquistadors to turn to Guatemala in their search for wealth. Pedro de Alvarado, one of Cortés' most brutal lieutenants, entered Guatemala in 1524 with about 600 Spanish and Mexican soldiers and the unanswerable advantages of firearms and horses. Alvarado defeated a small K'iche' force on the Pacific Slope and then the much larger main K'iche' army near Xelajú (modern Quetzaltenango) soon afterwards – killing the K'iche' leader Tecún Umán in hand-to-hand combat, or so legend has it. Alvarado then sacked the K'iche' capital, K'umarcaaj. The K'iche' had failed to persuade their traditional local enemies, the Kaqchiquels, to join forces against the invaders. Instead, the Kaqchiquels allied with the Spanish against the K'iche' and Tz'utujils, and so the Spanish set up their first Guatemalan headquarters next door to the Kaqchiquel capital Iximché. The name Guatemala is a Spanish corruption of Quauhtlemallan, the name Alvarado's Mexican allies gave to Iximché (Land of Many Trees).

The romance between the Spanish and the Kaqchiquels soured when the latter couldn't meet the ever-increasing demands for gold, and Alvarado – not surprisingly – turned on them, burning Iximché to the ground. And so it went throughout Guatemala as the megalomaniacal Alvarado sought fortune and renown by murdering and subjugating the Mayan population. The one notable exception was the Rabinal of present-day Baja Verapaz, who survived with their preconquest identity intact and remain one of Guatemala's most traditional groups to this day.

Unfinished Conquest: The Guatemalan Tragedy, by Guatemalan Víctor Perera, interweaves personal experiences with an exploration of the current situation of the Guatemalan Maya and the long history preceding it.

Alvarado moved his base from Tecpán to Santiago de los Caballeros (now called Ciudad Vieja) in 1527, but shortly after his death while in Mexico in 1541, Ciudad Vieja was destroyed by a flood. The Spanish capital was relocated under the same name to a new site nearby, known today as Antigua.

COLONIAL PERIOD (1524–1821)

The Spanish effectively enslaved Guatemala's indigenous people to work what had been their own land for the benefit of the invaders, just as they did throughout the hemisphere. Refusal to work the land meant death. With the most fertile land and a labor force to work it firmly in hand, the colonists believed themselves omnipotent and behaved accordingly. That is to say, badly.

1541	1542
Santiago de los Caballeros destroyed by flood; a new city (now Antigua) is founded.	Spain enacts the New Laws, officially banning forced labor in its colonies.

Enter the Catholic Church and Dominican friar Bartolomé de Las Casas. Las Casas had been in the Caribbean and Latin America since 1502 and had witnessed firsthand the near complete genocide of the indigenous populations of Cuba and Hispaniola. Convinced he could catch more flies with honey than vinegar and horrified at what he saw in the Indies, Las Casas appealed to Carlos V of Spain to stop the violence. Las Casas described the fatal treatment of the population in his influential tract *A Very Brief Account of the Destruction of the Indies*. The king agreed with Las Casas that the indigenous people should no longer be regarded as chattels and should be considered vassals of the king (in this way they could also pay taxes). Carlos V immediately enacted the New Laws of 1542, which technically ended the system of forced labor. In reality, forced labor continued, but wanton waste of Mayan lives ceased. Las Casas and other Dominican, Franciscan and Augustinian friars went about converting the Maya to Christianity – a Christianity that became imbued with many aspects of animism and ceremony from the indigenous belief system.

A large portion of the Church's conversion 'success' can be attributed to the pacifism with which it approached Mayan communities, the relative respect it extended to traditional beliefs, and the education it provided in indigenous languages. In short, the Catholic Church became extremely powerful in Guatemala quite quickly. No clearer evidence existed of this than the 38 houses of worship (including a cathedral) built in Antigua, which became the colonial capital of all Central America from Chiapas to Costa Rica. But Antigua was razed by a devastating earthquake on July 29, 1773. The capital was moved 25km east to its present site, Guatemala City.

INDEPENDENCE

By the time thoughts of independence from Spain began stirring among Guatemalans, society was already rigidly stratified. At the very top of the colonial hierarchy were the European-born Spaniards; next were the *criollos*, people born in Guatemala of Spanish blood; below them were the ladinos or *mestizos*, people of mixed Spanish and Mayan blood; and at the bottom were the Maya and black slaves. Only the European-born Spaniards had any real power, but the *criollos* lorded it over the ladinos, who in turn exploited the indigenous population, who, as you read this, still remain on the bottom rung of the socioeconomic ladder.

Angered at being repeatedly passed over for advancement, Guatemalan *criollos* took advantage of Spanish weakness following a Napoleonic invasion in 1808, and in 1821 successfully rose in revolt. Unfortunately, independence changed little for Guatemala's indigenous communities, who remained under the control of the Church and the landowning elite. Despite cuddly-sounding democratic institutions and constitutions, Guatemalan politics has continued to this day to be dominated almost without pause by corrupt, brutal strongmen in the Pedro de Alvarado tradition, for the benefit of the commercial, military, landowning and bureaucratic ruling classes. While the niceties of democracy are observed, real government often takes place by means of intimidation and secret military activities.

DID YOU KNOW?

In their remote hideaway at Flores, the Itzáes managed to remain unconquered by the Spanish until 1697, far later than any other people in Guatemala or Mexico.

Guatemala in the Spanish Colonial Period, by Oakah L Jones Jr, is a comprehensive assessment of the 300 years of Spanish dominance. Where this book leaves off, Paul Dosal's *Doing Business with the Dictators: A Political History of United Fruit in Guatemala, 1899–1944* takes over.

1773	1821
Antigua destroyed by earthquake; new capital founded at Guatemala City.	Guatemala wins independence from Spain.

Mexico, which was recently independent, quickly annexed Guatemala, but in 1823 Guatemala reasserted its independence and led the formation of the United Provinces of Central America (July 1, 1823), along with El Salvador, Nicaragua, Honduras and Costa Rica. Their union, torn by civil strife from the start, lasted only until 1840 before breaking up into its constituent states. This era brought prosperity to the *criollos* but worsened the lot of the Guatemalan Maya. The end of Spanish rule meant that the Crown's few liberal safeguards, which had afforded the Maya a minimal protection, were abandoned. Mayan claims to ancestral lands were largely ignored and huge tobacco, sugarcane and henequen (agave rope fiber) plantations were set up. The Maya, though technically and legally free, were enslaved by debt peonage to the big landowners.

THE LIBERALS & CARRERA

The ruling classes of independent Central America split into two camps: the elite conservatives, including the Catholic Church and the large landowners, and the liberals, who had been the first to advocate independence and who opposed the vested interests of the conservatives.

During the short existence of the United Provinces of Central America, liberal president Francisco Morazán (1830–39) from Honduras instituted reforms aimed at ending the overwhelming power of the Church, the division of society into a *criollo* upper class and an indigenous lower class, and the region's impotence in world markets. This liberal program was echoed by Guatemalan chief of state Mariano Gálvez (1831–38).

But unpopular economic policies, heavy taxes and a cholera epidemic led to an indigenous uprising that brought its leader, a conservative ladino pig farmer, Rafael Carrera, to power. Carrera held power from 1844 to 1865 and undid much of what Morazán and Gálvez had achieved. He also naively allowed Britain to take control of Belize in exchange for construction of a road between Guatemala City and Belize City. The road was never built, and Guatemala's claims for compensation were never resolved, leading to a quarrel that festers to this day.

LIBERAL REFORMS OF BARRIOS

The liberals returned to power in the 1870s, first under Miguel García Granados, next under Justo Rufino Barrios, a rich young coffee plantation owner who held the title of president, but ruled as a dictator (1873–79). Under Barrios Guatemala made strides toward modernization, with construction of roads, railways, schools and a modern banking system. Everything possible was done to stimulate coffee production. Peasants in good coffee-growing areas (up to a 1400m altitude on the Pacific Slope) were forced off their lands to make way for new coffee *fincas* (plantations), while those living above 1400m (mostly Maya) were forced to work on the *fincas*. This created migrant labor patterns that still exist among some highland groups. Under Barrios' successors a small group of landowning and commercial families came to control the economy, foreign companies were given generous concessions, and political opponents were censored, imprisoned or exiled by the extensive police force.

1823–40	1870s
Guatemala is part of the United Provinces of Central America.	Liberal governments modernize Guatemala but turn indigenous lands over to coffee plantations.

ESTRADA CABRERA & MINERVA

Manuel Estrada Cabrera ruled from 1898 to 1920, and his dictatorial style, while bringing progress in technical matters, placed a heavy burden on all but the ruling oligarchy. He fancied himself a bringer of light and culture to a backward land, styling himself the 'Teacher and Protector of Guatemalan Youth.'

He sponsored Fiestas de Minerva (Festivals of Minerva) in the cities, inspired by the Roman goddess of wisdom, invention and technology, and ordered construction of temples to Minerva, some of which still stand (as in Quetzaltenango). Guatemala was to become a 'tropical Athens.' At the same time, however, Estrada Cabrera looted the treasury, ignored the schools and spent extravagantly to beef up the armed forces. He was also responsible for courting the US-owned United Fruit Company, a business of gross hegemonic proportions that set up shop in Guatemala in 1901.

JORGE UBICO

When Estrada Cabrera was overthrown in 1920, Guatemala entered a period of instability, which ended in 1931 with the election of General Jorge Ubico as president. Ubico had a Napoleon complex and ruled as Estrada Cabrera had, but more efficiently. He insisted on honesty in government, and modernized the country's health and social welfare infrastructure. Debt peonage was outlawed, but a new bondage of compulsory labor contributions to the government road-building program was established in its place. His reign ended when he was forced into exile in 1944.

ARÉVALO & ARBENZ

Just when it appeared that Guatemala was doomed to a succession of harsh dictators, the elections of 1945 brought a philosopher – Juan José Arévalo – to the presidential palace. Arévalo, in power from 1945 to 1951, established the nation's social security system, a government bureau to look after indigenous concerns, a modern public health system and liberal labor laws. He also survived 25 coup attempts by conservative military forces.

Arévalo was succeeded by Colonel Jacobo Arbenz, who continued Arévalo's policies, instituting an agrarian reform law that was meant to break up the large estates and foster high productivity on small, individually owned farms. He also expropriated vast lands conceded to the United Fruit Company during the Estrada Cabrera and Ubico years that were being held fallow. Compensation was paid at the value that the company had declared for tax purposes (far below its real value), and Arbenz announced that the lands were to be redistributed to peasants and put into cultivation for food. But the expropriation set off alarms in Washington, which (surprise! surprise!) supported United Fruit. In 1954, the US, in one of the first documented covert operations by the Central Intelligence Agency (CIA), orchestrated an invasion from Honduras led by two exiled Guatemalan military officers. Arbenz was forced to step down, and the land reform never took place.

Arbenz was succeeded by a series of military presidents elected with the support of the officer corps, business leaders, compliant political par-

'The elections of 1945 brought a philosopher – Juan José Arévalo – to the presidential palace'

1945–54	1954
Enlightened, progressive government by presidents Juan José Arévalo and Jacobo Arbenz.	Arbenz appropriates Guatemalan lands of the US-owned United Fruit Company and is deposed in US-orchestrated coup.

ties and the Catholic Church. Violence became a staple of political life. Opponents of the government regularly turned up dead or not at all. Land reform measures were reversed, voting was made dependent on literacy (which disenfranchised around 75% of the population), the secret police force was revived and military repression was common.

In 1960, left-wing guerrilla groups began to form.

1960s & 1970s

Guatemalan industry developed fast, but the social fabric became increasingly stressed as most profits from the boom flowed upwards, labor unions organized, and migration to the cities, especially the capital, produced urban sprawl and slums. A cycle of violent repression and protest took hold, leading to the total politicization of society. Everyone took sides; usually it was the poorer classes in the rural areas versus the power elite in the cities. By 1979, Amnesty International estimated that 50,000 to 60,000 people had been killed during the political violence of the 1970s alone.

A severe earthquake in 1976 killed about 22,000 people and left around a million homeless. Most of the aid sent for the people in need never reached them.

1980s

In the early 1980s, military suppression of antigovernment elements in the countryside reached a peak, especially under the presidency of General Efraín Ríos Montt, an evangelical Christian who came to power by coup in March 1982. Huge numbers of people, mostly indigenous men, were murdered in the name of anti-insurgency, stabilization and anticommunism. Guatemalans refer to this scorched-earth strategy as *la escoba*, the broom, because of the way the reign of terror swept over the country. While officials did not know the identities of the rebels, they did know which areas were bases of rebel activity – chiefly poor, rural, indigenous areas – so the government decided to terrorize the populations of those areas to kill off support for the rebels. Over 400 villages were razed, and most of their inhabitants massacred (often tortured as well).

It was later estimated that 15,000 civilian deaths occurred as a result of counter-insurgency operations during Ríos Montt's term of office alone, not to mention the estimated 100,000 refugees (again, mostly Maya) who fled to Mexico. The government forced villagers to form Patrullas de Autodefensa Civil (PACs; Civil Defense Patrols) to do much of the army's dirty work: the PACs were ultimately responsible for some of the worst human-rights abuses during Ríos Montt's rule.

In February 1982 four powerful guerrilla organizations had united to form the URNG (Guatemalan National Revolutionary Unity). Perhaps half a million people, mostly peasants in the western and central highlands and El Petén, actively supported the guerrilla movement, but as the civil war dragged on and both sides committed atrocities, more and more rural people came to feel caught in the crossfire. They were damned if they supported the insurgents and damned if they didn't.

In August 1983 Ríos Montt was deposed by General Oscar Humberto Mejía Victores, but the abuses continued. It was estimated that over

Daniel Wilkinson, in *Silence on the Mountain*, uncovers in microcosm the social background to the civil war as he delves into the reasons for the burning of a coffee estate by guerrillas.

1960s

Left-wing guerrilla groups form in opposition to military governments; civil war starts.

1976

Earthquake kills 22,000 in Guatemala.

RIGOBERTA MENCHÚ TUM

Rigoberta Menchú was born in 1959 near Uspantán in the highlands of Quiché department and lived the life of a typical young Mayan woman until the late 1970s, when the country's civil war affected her tragically and drove her into the left-wing guerrilla camp. Her father, mother and brother were killed in the slaughter carried out by the Guatemalan military in the name of 'pacification' of the countryside and repression of communism.

Menchú fled to exile in Mexico, where her story, *I, Rigoberta Menchú: An Indian Woman in Guatemala*, based on a series of interviews, was published and translated throughout the world, bringing the plight of Guatemala's indigenous population to international attention. In 1992 Rigoberta Menchú was awarded the Nobel Prize for peace, which provided her and her cause with international stature and support. The Rigoberta Menchú Tum Foundation, which she founded with the US$1.2 million Nobel Prize money, works for conflict resolution, plurality, and human, indigenous and women's rights in Guatemala and internationally.

Guatemalans, especially the Maya, were proud that one of their own had been recognized by the Nobel committee. In the circles of power, however, Menchú's renown was unwelcome, as she was seen as a troublemaker.

Anthropologist David Stoll's book *Rigoberta Menchú and the Story of All Poor Guatemalans* (1999) contested the truth of many aspects of Menchú's book, but has not seriously dented her reputation.

In 1999, before a Spanish court, the Rigoberta Menchú Tum Foundation formally accused former dictators General Oscar Humberto Mejía Victores (1983–86) and Efraín Ríos Montt (1982–83) of genocide. Menchú pressed for extradition proceedings. As of this writing, however, the Spanish courts had not accepted any obligation to pursue the matter. Menchú was still living in exile in Mexico, saying that she would not return to Guatemala unless true peace was brought to her country.

100 political assassinations and 40 abductions occurred each and every month under his rule. Survivors of *la escoba* were herded into remote 'model villages' known as *polos de desarrollo* (poles of development) surrounded by army encampments. The bloodbath led the US to cut off military assistance to Guatemala, which in turn resulted in the 1986 election of a civilian president, Marco Vinicio Cerezo Arévalo of the Christian Democratic Party.

Before turning over its power to the civilians, the military established formal mechanisms for its continued control of the countryside. There was hope that Cerezo Arévalo's administration would temper the excesses of the power elite and the military and establish a basis for true democracy. But armed conflict festered on in remote areas and when Cerezo Arévalo's term ended in 1990, many people wondered whether any real progress had been made.

Searching for Everardo, by US attorney Jennifer K Harbury, tells how she fell in love with and married a URNG guerrilla leader who then disappeared in combat, and of her dedicated and internationally publicized struggles with the US and Guatemalan governments – including a hunger strike outside the White House – to discover his fate.

EARLY 1990s

President Jorge Serrano (1990–93) was an evangelical Christian representing the conservative Movimiento de Acción Solidaria (Solidarity Action Movement). Serrano reopened a dialogue with the URNG, hoping to bring the decades-long civil war to an end. When the talks collapsed, the mediator from the Catholic Church blamed both sides for intransigence.

Massacres and other human-rights abuses continued during this period despite the country's return to democratic rule. In one dra-

1982–83	1992
State terror against rural indigenous communities peaks during the rule of General Efraín Ríos Montt.	Guatemalan Maya Rigoberta Menchú awarded the Nobel Prize for peace.

matic case in 1990, Guatemalan anthropologist Myrna Mack, who had documented army violence against the rural Maya, was fatally wounded after being stabbed dozens of times by a military death squad. Later that same year, the army massacred 13 Tz'utujil Maya (including three children) in Santiago Atitlán. Outraged, the people of Santiago fought back, becoming the first town to succeed in expelling the army by popular demand. That unprecedented success was a watershed event for the Mayan and human-rights cause in Guatemala.

Serrano's presidency came to depend more on the army for support. In 1993 he tried to seize absolute power, but after a tense few days was forced to flee into exile. Congress elected Ramiro de León Carpio, an outspoken critic of the army's strong-arm tactics, as president to complete Serrano's term.

La Hija del Puma (The Daughter of the Puma), directed by Ulf Hultberg, is a powerful 1995 film, based on a true story, about a K'iche' Mayan girl who survives the army massacre of her fellow-villagers and sees her brother captured. She escapes to Mexico but then returns to Guatemala in search of her brother.

PEACE ACCORDS

President de León's elected successor, Álvaro Arzú of the center-right PAN (Partido de Avanzada Nacional), took office in 1996. Arzú continued negotiations with the URNG, and finally, on December 29, 1996, 'A Firm and Lasting Peace Agreement' was signed at the National Palace in Guatemala City. During the 36 years of civil war, an estimated 200,000 Guatemalans had been killed, a million made homeless, and untold thousands had disappeared. The Peace Accords, as the agreement is known, contained provisions for accountability for the human-rights violations perpetrated by the armed forces during the war and the resettlement of Guatemala's one million displaced people. They also addressed the rights of indigenous peoples and women, health care, education and other basic social services, and the abolition of obligatory military service. Many of these provisions remain unfulfilled.

GUATEMALA SINCE THE PEACE ACCORDS

Any hopes that Guatemala might become a truly just and democratic society have looked increasingly frayed as the years have passed since 1996. A national referendum in 1999 (in which only 18% of registered voters turned out) voted down constitutional reforms formally legislating the rights of indigenous people, adding checks and balances to the executive office and retooling the national security apparatus.

The single most notorious and tragic flouting of peace, justice and democracy came in 1998 when Bishop Juan Gerardi, coordinator of the Guatemalan Archbishop's Human Rights Office (Odhag), was beaten to death outside his home. Two days previously, Bishop Gerardi had announced Odhag's findings that the army was responsible for most of the 200,000 civil war deaths and many other atrocities.

The 1999 presidential elections were won by Alfonso Portillo of the conservative Frente Republicano Guatemalteco (FRG, colloquially known as the Mano Azul – Blue Hand – for its symbol daubed on lampposts, rocks and trees countrywide). Portillo was just a front man for the FRG leader, ex-president General Efraín Ríos Montt, author of the early 1980s scorched-earth state terror campaign. As one common jibe had it, when the two men discussed important decisions, civilian president Portillo always had the last word – 'Yes, general.'

DID YOU KNOW?

Three soldiers were jailed in 2001 for the murder of Bishop Juan Gerardi, but two of them had their convictions annulled in 2002 (the third had already been killed in jail). The army colonel who was finally jailed in 2002 for ordering the 1990 murder of anthropologist Myrna Mack was freed on appeal in 2003.

1996	1998
Peace Accords are signed to end the 36-year civil war in which an estimated 200,000 Guatemalans died.	Odhag declares the army responsible for most civil war deaths; two days later Odhag's coordinator, Bishop Gerardi, is murdered.

President Portillo did pay out $1.8 million in compensation in 2001 to the families of 226 men, women and children killed by soldiers and paramilitaries in the northern village of Las Dos Erres in 1982, but implementation of the Peace Accords stalled and then went into reverse. In 2002 the United Nations representative for indigenous peoples, after an 11-day Guatemalan tour, stated that 60% of Guatemalan Maya were still marginalized by discrimination and violence. The United Nations' human development index for 2002, comparing countries on criteria such as income, life expectancy, school enrolment and literacy, ranked Guatemala 120th of the world's 173 countries, the lowest of any North, Central or South American country. Poverty, illiteracy, lack of education and poor medical facilities are all much more common in rural areas, where the Mayan population is concentrated.

International organizations, from the European Parliament to the Inter-American Commission on Human Rights, queued up to criticize the state of human rights in Guatemala. Those brave souls who tried to protect human rights and expose abuses were being subjected to threats and killings, the perpetrators of which seemed able to act with impunity. The URNG guerrillas had disarmed in compliance with the Peace Accords, but President Portillo failed to carry out a promise to disband the presidential guard (whose soldiers killed Bishop Gerardi and whose chief had ordered the 1990 Myrna Mack killing), and he doubled the defense budget, taking it beyond the maximum level fixed in the Peace Accords.

Lawlessness and violent crime increased horrifyingly. The US 'decertified' Guatemala – meaning it no longer considered it an ally in the battle against the drugs trade – in 2002. The same year, Amnesty International reported that criminals were colluding with sectors of the police and military and local affiliates of multinational corporations to flout human rights. According to police figures, 3630 people died violent deaths in 2002. Lynchings were not uncommon as people increasingly took the law into their own hands.

The national anticorruption prosecutor, Karen Fischer, fled the country in 2003 in the face of threats received when she investigated Panamanian bank accounts allegedly opened for President Portillo. Most worryingly of all, Ríos Montt himself was named FRG candidate for the late-2003 presidential elections, and then, incredibly, was given the go-ahead to stand by the country's constitutional court – despite a constitutional ban on presidents who had in the past taken power by coup (which Ríos Montt did in 1982). The FRG showed its colors fairly blatantly in the run-up to the election by making sizeable 'compensation' payments to the former members of the PACs, Civil Defense Patrols, who had carried out many atrocities during the civil war. At the time of writing, opinion polls were predicting an electoral win for less extreme right-winger Oscar Berger, of the so-called Gran Alianza Nacional.

For the latest on the progress (or otherwise) of human rights in Guatemala, visit the Guatemala Human Rights Commission/USA website (www.ghrc-usa.org) or click on 'Human Rights' on the website of the US embassy in Guatemala City (usembassy.state.gov /guatemala).

See www.amnesty.org for Amnesty International reports on Guatemala.

The Culture

THE NATIONAL PSYCHE

You will be amazed when you first reach Guatemala by just how helpful, polite and unhurried Guatemalans are. Everyone has time to stop and chat and explain what you want to know. This is apparent even if you've just crossed the border from Mexico, where things aren't exactly rushed either. Most Guatemalans like to get to know other people without haste, feeling for common ground and things to agree on, rather than making blunt assertions and engaging in adversarial dialectic. Some observers explain this mild manner as a reaction to centuries of repression and violence by the ruling class, but whatever the truth of that, it makes most Guatemalans a pleasure to deal with.

What goes on behind this outward politeness is harder to encapsulate. Few Guatemalans exhibit the stress, worry and hurry of the 'developed' nations, but this obviously isn't because they don't have to worry about money or employment. They're a long-suffering people who don't expect wealth or good government but make the best of what comes their way – friendship, their family, a good meal, a bit of good company. Families, on the whole, are strong and family members very supportive of each other. Religion, too, is a source of great strength to most Guatemalans – whether the orthodox Catholicism of the ladinos, or the animist-Catholic syncretism of the traditional Maya, or the evangelical Protestantism of increasing numbers of converts, mainly but not only Maya. People's faiths give them hope, not only of better things in the life to come but also of improvements in the here and now – whether through answered prayers or, in the evangelicals' case, of a more sober, more gainful and happier existence without alcohol, gambling or domestic violence.

'The Mayan villagers' strengths lie in their strong family and community ties, and their traditions'

The tales of violence – domestic violence, civil-war violence, criminal violence – that one inevitably hears in Guatemala sit strangely with the mild-mannered approach you will encounter from nearly everybody. Whatever the explanation, it helps to show why a little caution is in order when strangers meet.

It has been said that Guatemala has no middle class, that it just has a ruling class and an exploited class. It's true that Guatemala has a small, rich, ladino ruling elite whose main goal seems to be to maintain wealth and power at almost any cost. It also has an indigenous Mayan population, comprising more than half the people in the country, that tends to be poor, poorly educated and poorly provided for and has always been kept in a secondary role by the ruling elite. The Mayan villagers' strengths lie in their strong family and community ties, and their traditions. Those who do break out of the poverty cycle, through business or education, do not turn their backs on their communities. But as well as these two groups at the extremes, there is also a large group of working-class and middle-class ladinos, typically Catholic and family-oriented but with aspirations influenced by education, TV, international popular music and North America (of which many Guatemalans have direct experience as migrant workers) – and maybe by liberal ideas of equality and social tolerance. This segment of society has its bohemian/student/artist circles whose overlap with educated, forward-looking Maya may hold the greatest hope for progress toward an equitable society.

LIFESTYLE

The majority of Guatemalans live in one-room houses of brick, concrete blocks or traditional *bajareque* (a construction of stones, wooden poles and mud), with roofs of tin, tiles or thatch. They have earth floors, a fireplace (but usually no chimney) and minimal possessions – often just a couple of bare beds and a few pots. These small homes are often grouped in compounds with several others, all housing members of one extended family. Thus live most of Guatemala's great Mayan majority, in the countryside, in villages and in towns.

The few wealthier Maya and most ladino families have larger houses in towns and the bigger villages, but their homes may still not be much

GETTING ALONG WITH GUATEMALANS

Politeness is a very important aspect of social interaction in Guatemala. When beginning to talk with someone, even in such routine situations as in a store or on the bus, it's polite to begin with a greeting – a simple *'buenos días'* (good morning) or *'buenas tardes'* (good afternoon) and a smile will get conversations off to a positive start. The same holds true when you enter a room, including public places such as a restaurant or waiting room; make a general greeting to everyone in the room – the requisite *'buenos días'* or *'buenas tardes'* will do. When leaving a restaurant, it is common to wish the other diners *'buen provecho'* ('bon appétit'). Handshakes are another friendly gesture and are used frequently.

Note that many Maya, especially the further off the beaten track you venture, speak only their indigenous language. It's futile to try to engage these people in Spanish conversation, though sign and body language are always viable options.

In recent years, stories circulated in Guatemala that some foreign visitors (particularly white women) were kidnapping Mayan children, perhaps to raise them as their own, or even for the grisly purpose of selling their bodily organs. Some local people are extremely suspicious of foreigners who make friendly overtures toward children, especially foreigners who photograph indigenous children. Women traveling alone are treated most distrustfully in this regard, but in 2000 two men (a Japanese tourist and his Guatemalan driver) were beaten to death by a mob in Todos Santos Cuchumatán after the tourist started taking photos of children.

Many Maya are *very* touchy about having their photo taken. Always ask permission before taking pictures. Sometimes your request will be denied, often you'll be asked for a quetzal or two, and maybe in a few special instances you'll make new friends.

Many Mayan women prefer to avoid contact with foreign men; in their culture, talking with strange men is not something that a virtuous woman does. Male travelers in need of directions or information should try to find another man to ask. In general the Maya are a fairly private people, and outsiders need to treat them with sensitivity. Some Mayan communities are still very much in a recovery phase from the nightmare of the civil war. Once you get to know someone, they may be willing to share their war stories, which are probably horrific – but don't dig for information, let your hosts offer it. On the language front, using the term *indio* (Indian) to refer to a Mayan person carries racist undertones. The preferred term is *indígena*.

Pay attention to your appearance. It's difficult for Guatemalans to understand why a foreign traveler, who is naturally assumed to be rich, would go around looking scruffy when even poor Guatemalans do their best to look neat. When dealing with officialdom (police, border officials, immigration officers), it's a good idea to appear as conservative and respectable as possible.

General standards of modesty in dress have relaxed somewhat; some women wear miniskirts in towns and cities, where formerly this would have been unthinkable. Nevertheless, not all locals appreciate this type of attire. Dress modestly when entering churches. Shorts are usually worn, by men or women, only at the beach and in coastal towns, or where there are plenty of foreign tourists. Also think about safety in connection with your appearance. Particularly in the capital, locals will warn you against wearing even cheap imitation jewelry: you could be mugged for it. If you have any wealth, take care not to flaunt it.

EXPATS

About one in every 10 Guatemalans – 1.17 million people – lives in the US, according to research published in 2003 by the International Migration Organization. There has been a steady northward flow of Guatemalans since the 1980s, peaking in 2000 when 177,000 of them moved to the US. Money sent home by these expatriates amounts to US$1.2 billion a year, that's US$1,200 million, more than the combined value of traditional exports, including coffee, sugar and bananas. Los Angeles is Guatemalans' favorite US city: 380,000 of them live there. The next biggest Guatemalan colony is in New York (120,000), followed by Miami (91,000).

more than one or two bedrooms and a kitchen that also serves as a living area. Possessions, adornments and decorations may be sparse. Of course, some families have bigger, more comfortable and impressive homes. Middle-class families in the wealthier suburbs of Guatemala City live in good-sized one- or two-story houses with gardens. The most select residences will have their gardens walled for security and privacy. The elite few possess rural as well as urban properties – for example, a coffee *finca* (ranch) on the Pacific Slope with a comfortable farmhouse, or a seaside villa on the Pacific or Caribbean coast.

DID YOU KNOW?

Ángel González, a Mexican, has a near-monopoly on ownership of Guatemala's private TV stations.

Despite modernizing influences – education, cable TV, contact with foreign travelers in Guatemala, international popular music, time spent as migrant workers in the USA – traditional family ties remain strong at all levels of society. Large extended-family groups gather for weekend meals and holidays. Old-fashioned gender roles are strong too: many women have jobs to increase the family income but relatively few have positions of much responsibility. Homosexuality barely raises its head above the parapet: only in Guatemala City is there anything approaching an open gay scene, and that is pretty much for men only.

Traveling in Guatemala you will encounter a much wider cross-section of Guatemalans than many Guatemalans ever do as they live their lives within relatively narrow worlds. The Guatemalans you'll meet will also tend to be among the most worldly and open-minded, as a result of their contact with tourists and travelers from around the globe. Guatemala has a broad web of people, often young, who are interested in learning, in other cultures, in human rights, in music and the arts, in improving the position of women, the indigenous and the poor, in helping others. You only need to peel away one or two layers of the onion to uncover them.

Gregory Nava's tragic film *El Norte* (The North) brings home not only the tragedy of Guatemala's civil war but also the illusory nature of many Guatemalans' 'American dream' as it follows an orphaned brother and sister who head north to the US to look for a living.

By United Nations figures, 6.4 million Guatemalans – more than half the population – live in poverty. The official national minimum wage is only US$130 a month in urban areas and US$120 in rural areas – and not everyone is entitled even to this. A typical school teacher earns around US$180 a month. Poverty is most prevalent in rural, indigenous areas, especially the highlands. Wealth, industry and commerce are concentrated overwhelmingly in sprawling, polluted Guatemala City, the country's only large city, and home to about 18% of its people.

POPULATION

Of the 11.2 million people counted by Guatemala's 2002 census, some 50 to 60% are indigenous. Nearly all of this indigenous population is Mayan, although there is a very small population of non-Mayan indigenous people called the Chinka' (Xinca) in the southeastern corner of the country. The rest of Guatemala's population are nearly all

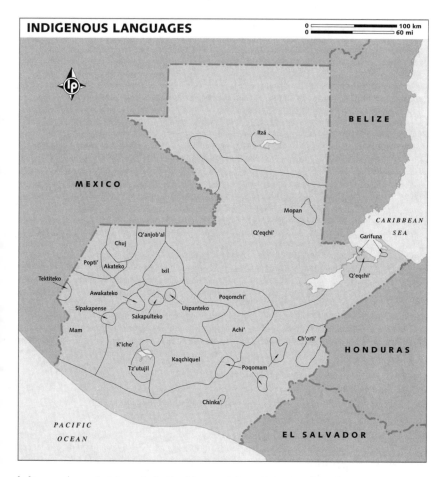

INDIGENOUS LANGUAGES

ladinos – descended from both the Maya and from European (mostly Spanish) settlers. There are also a few thousand Garífuna (descended from Caribbean islanders and shipwrecked African slaves) around the Caribbean town of Lívingston.

The Maya are spread throughout the country but are most densely concentrated in the highlands, which are home to the four biggest Mayan groups, the K'iche' (Quiché), Mam, Q'eqchi' (Kekchí) and Kaqchiquel (Cakchiquel). Mayan languages are still the way most Maya communicate, with approximately 20 separate (and often mutually unintelligible) Mayan languages spoken in different regions of the country. It's language that primarily defines which Mayan people someone belongs to. Though many Maya speak some Spanish, it's always a second language to them – and there are many who don't speak any Spanish.

The population as a whole is densest in the highland strip from Guatemala City to Quetzaltenango, the country's two biggest cities. Many towns and large villages are dotted around this region. Some 40% of the population lives in towns and cities, and 44% are aged under 15.

DID YOU KNOW?

Izabal in the east and El Petén in the north are the most sparsely populated of Guatemala's 22 departments, with 35 and 10 people per square kilometer respectively. The national average density is 103 people per square kilometer.

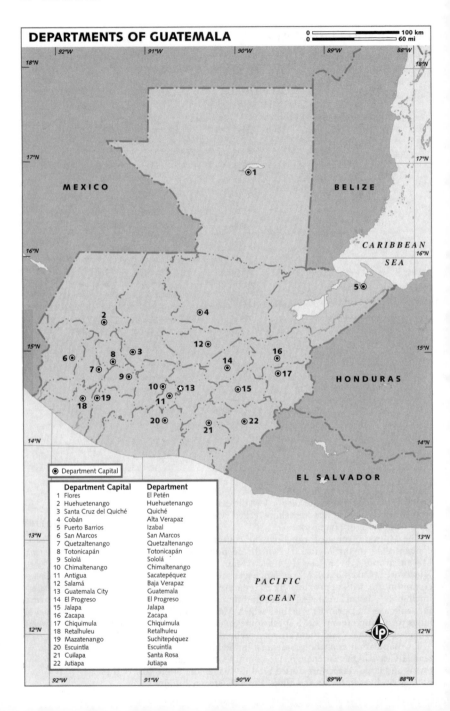

DEPARTMENTS OF GUATEMALA

Department Capital	Department
1 Flores	El Petén
2 Huehuetenango	Huehuetenango
3 Santa Cruz del Quiché	Quiché
4 Cobán	Alta Verapaz
5 Puerto Barrios	Izabal
6 San Marcos	San Marcos
7 Quetzaltenango	Quetzaltenango
8 Totonicapán	Totonicapán
9 Sololá	Sololá
10 Chimaltenango	Chimaltenango
11 Antigua	Sacatepéquez
12 Salamá	Baja Verapaz
13 Guatemala City	Guatemala
14 El Progreso	El Progreso
15 Jalapa	Jalapa
16 Zacapa	Zacapa
17 Chiquimula	Chiquimula
18 Retalhuleu	Retalhuleu
19 Mazatenango	Suchitepéquez
20 Escuintla	Escuintla
21 Cuilapa	Santa Rosa
22 Jutiapa	Jutiapa

SPORT

The sport that most ignites Guatemalans' passion and enthusiasm is football (soccer). Though Guatemalan teams always flop in international competition, the 10-club Liga Mayor (Major League) is keenly followed by reasonably large crowds. Two seasons are played each year: the Torneo de Apertura (Opening Tournament) from July to November and the Torneo de Clausura (Closing Tournament) from January to May. The two big clubs are Municipal and Comunicaciones, both from Guatemala City. The national press always has details on upcoming games: most matches kick off at 11am on Sunday. Admission to games runs from US$2 to US$3.50 for the cheapest areas and US$12 to US$20 for the best seats.

DID YOU KNOW?

Municipal, nicknamed Los Rojos (the Reds), tends to nurture young Guatemalan talents, while Comunicaciones (Las Cremas, the Creams) likes to import players from other countries.

RELIGION

Roman Catholicism is the predominant religion in Guatemala, but it is not the only religion by any stretch of the imagination. Since the 1980s, evangelical Protestant sects, around 75% of them Pentecostal, have surged in popularity, and it is estimated that 30% to 40% of Guatemalans are now evangelicals. These numbers continue to grow as evangelical churches compete hard for further souls. The number of new churches in some towns and villages, especially indigenous Mayan villages, is astonishing. You will undoubtedly hear loud Guatemalan versions of gospel music pouring out of some of them as you walk around, and in some places loudspeakers broadcast the music and its accompanying preaching across entire towns. One reason for the evangelicals' success is their opposition to alcohol, gambling and domestic violence: many women find that husbands who join evangelical churches become more reliable providers.

Catholicism is fighting back with messages about economic and racial justice, papal visits and new saints – Guatemala's most venerated local Christian figure, the 17th-century Antigua-hospital-founder Hermano Pedro de San José de Betancurt, was canonized in 2002 when Pope John Paul II visited Guatemala. Catholicism in the Mayan areas has never been exactly orthodox. The missionaries who brought Catholicism to the Maya in the 16th century wisely permitted aspects of the existing animistic, shamanistic Mayan religion to continue alongside Christian rites and beliefs. Syncretism was aided by the identification of certain Mayan deities with certain Christian saints, and survives to this day. A notable example is the deity known as Maximón in Santiago Atitlán, San Simón in Zunil and Rilaj Maam in San Andrés Itzapa near Antigua, who seems to be a combination of Mayan gods, the Spanish conquistador Pedro de Alvarado and Judas Iscariot (see the boxed text, p119).

Many sites of ancient Mayan ruins – among them Tikal, Kaminaljuyú and K'umarcaaj – still have altars where prayers, offerings and ceremonies take place today. Fertility rites, healing ceremonies and sacred observances to ring in the various Mayan new years are still practiced with gusto. These types of ceremony are directed or overseen by a Mayan priest known as a *tzahorín* and usually involve burning candles and copal (a natural incense from the bark of various tropical trees), making offerings to the gods and praying for whatever the desired outcome may be – a good harvest, a healthy child or a prosperous new year, for example. Some ceremonies involve chicken sacrifices as well. Each place has its own set of gods – or at least different names for similar gods.

Visitors may also be able observe traditional Mayan ceremonies in places such as the Pascual Abaj shrine at Chichicastenango (p129), the

To get a handle on Maximón and shamanism around Lago de Atitlán, check out *Scandals in the House of Birds: Shamans and Priests on Lake Atitlán* by anthropologist and poet Nathaniel Tarn.

ANCIENT MAYAN RELIGION

For the ancient Maya, the world, the heavens and the mysterious underworld called Xibalba were one great, unified structure that operated according to the laws of astrology, cyclical time and ancestor worship (for more on astrology and the calendar, see The Mayan Calendar, pp22-3). The towering, sacred ceiba tree symbolized the world-tree, which united the heavens (represented by the tree's branches and foliage), the earth (the trunk) and the nine levels of Xibalba (the roots). The heavens, the earth and the underworld were also all aspects of the single supreme creator, called Itzamná or Hunab Ku or Lizard House. The world-tree had a sort of cruciform shape and was associated with the color green. In the 16th century, when the Franciscan friars came bearing a cross and required the Indians to venerate it, the symbolism meshed easily with the established Maya belief in the ceiba or world-tree.

Points of the Compass

Each point of the compass had a color and a special religious significance. East, where the sun was reborn each day, was most important; its color was red. West, where the sun disappeared, was black. North, where the all-important rains came from, was white. South, the 'sunniest' point of the compass, was yellow. Everything in the Mayan world was seen in relation to these cardinal points, with the world-tree at the center.

Bloodletting & Human Sacrifice

Just as the great cosmic dragon shed its blood, which fell as rain to the earth, so humans had to shed blood to link themselves with Xibalba. Bloodletting ceremonies were the most important religious ceremonies, and the blood of kings was seen as the most acceptable for these rituals. Mayan kings often initiated bloodletting rites to heighten the responsiveness of the gods. Thus, when the Christian friars said that the blood of Jesus, the King of the Jews, had been spilled for the common people, the Maya could easily understand and embrace the symbolism.

Sacred Places

Mayan ceremonies were performed in natural sacred places as well as their human-made equivalents. Mountains, caves, lakes, cenotes (natural limestone cavern pools), rivers and fields were and still are sacred. Pyramids and temples were thought of as stylized mountains. A cave was the mouth of the creature that represented Xibalba, and to enter it was to enter the spirit of the secret world. This is why some Mayan temples have doorways surrounded by huge masks: as you enter the door of this 'cave' you are entering the mouth of Xibalba.

Ancestor worship was very important to the ancient Maya, and when they buried a king beneath a pyramid or a commoner beneath the floor or courtyard of a *na* (thatched Mayan hut), the sacredness of the location was increased.

altars on the shore of Laguna Chicabal outside Quetzaltenango (p157), or El Baúl near Santa Lucía Cotzumalguapa (p173), but a lot of traditional rites are off-limits to foreigners.

WOMEN IN GUATEMALA

One of the goals of the 1996 Peace Accords was to improve women's rights in Guatemala. By 2003 the Inter-American Commission on Human Rights had to report that laws discriminating against women had yet to be repealed. Women got the vote and the right to stand for election in 1946, but by 2003 only eight of the 113 congressional deputies were women. Women's leaders repeatedly criticize Guatemala's *machista* culture, which believes a woman's place is in the home (unless she's out washing the clothes or at the market or collecting firewood). The situation is, if anything, worse for indigenous women in rural areas, who also have to live with most of the country's direst poverty.

The international organization Human Rights Watch reported in 2002 that women working in private households were persistently discriminated against. Domestic workers, many of whom are from Mayan communities, lack certain basic rights of other workers, including the rights to be paid the minimum wage and to work an eight-hour day and a 48-hour week. Many domestic workers begin working as young adolescents, but Guatemalan labor laws do not provide adequate protection for domestic workers under the age of 18.

For information on Guatemalan women's organizations (and much, much more) visit EntreMundos (www.entremundos.org).

ARTS
Literature
A great source of national pride is the Nobel Prize for Literature that was bestowed on Guatemalan Miguel Ángel Asturias (1899–1974) in 1967. Best known for *Men of Maize*, his magical realist epic on the theme of European conquest and the Maya, and for his thinly veiled vilification of Latin American dictators in *The President*, Asturias also wrote poetry (collected in the early volume *Sien de Alondra*, published in English as *Temple of the Lark*) and served in various diplomatic capacities for the Guatemalan government. Other celebrated Guatemalan authors include short-story master Augusto Monterroso (1921–2003) – look for his *The Black Sheep and Other Fables* – and Luis Cardoza y Aragón (1901–92), principally known for his poetry and for fighting in the revolutionary movement that deposed dictator Jorge Ubico in 1944.

DID YOU KNOW?

Despite men taking the lead in Guatemala's *machista* culture, women live longer, averaging 68 years against 62 for men.

Music
The marimba is considered the national instrument, although scholars cannot agree whether this xylophone-type instrument already existed in Africa before slaves brought it to Guatemala. Marimbas can be heard throughout the country, often in restaurants or in plazas in the cool of an evening. The very earliest marimbas used a succession of increasingly large gourds as the resonator pipes, but modern marimbas are more commonly outfitted with wooden pipes, though you may see the former type in more traditional settings. The instrument is usually played by three men and there is a carnival-like quality to its sound and traditional compositions.

Guatemalan festivals provide great opportunities for hearing traditional music featuring instruments such as cane flutes, square drums and the *chirimía*, a reed instrument of Moorish roots related to the oboe.

Guatemalan tastes in pop music are much influenced by the products of other Latin American countries. The Mexican group Maná may be the one you'll hear more than any other. The Guatemalan most admired by Guatemalan youth is rock singer Ricardo Arjona, according to one recent survey.

Maya Cosmos – Three Thousand Years of the Shaman's Path, by David Freidel, Linda Schele and Joy Parker, traces Mayan creation myths from the past to the present with a dose of lively personal experience.

Architecture
Modern Guatemalan architecture, apart from a few flashy bank and office buildings along Av La Reforma in Guatemala City, is chiefly characterized by expanses of drab concrete. Some humbler rural dwellings still use a traditional wall construction known as *bajareque*, where a core of stones is held in place by poles of bamboo or other wood, which is faced with stucco or mud. Village houses are increasingly roofed with sheets of tin instead of tiles or thatch – less aesthetic but also less expensive.

EDUCATION IN GUATEMALA

Education is free and in theory compulsory between the ages of seven and 14. Primary education lasts for six years, but in reality only 50% of children reach grade five, according to 2002 United Nations figures. Secondary school begins at age 13 and comprises two cycles of three years each, called *básico* and *magisterio*. Not all secondary education is free – a major deterrent for many. Some people continue studying for their *magisterio* well into adulthood. Completing *magisterio* qualifies you to become a school teacher yourself. It's estimated that only about 23% of children of the 13-to-18 age group are in secondary school. Guatemala has five universities. The Universidad de San Carlos, founded in 1676 in Antigua (later moved to Guatemala City), was the first university in Central America.

Overall, adult literacy is around 69% in Guatemala, but it's lower among women (61%) and rural people. Mayan children who do seasonal migrant work with their families are least likely to get an education, as the time the families go away to work falls during the school year. A limited amount of school teaching is done in Mayan languages – chiefly the big four, K'iche', Mam, Kaqchiquel and Q'eqchi' – but this rarely goes beyond the first couple of years of primary school. Spanish remains the necessary tongue for anyone who wants to get ahead in life.

MAYAN ARCHITECTURE

Ancient Mayan architecture is a mixed bag of incredible accomplishments and severe limitations. The Maya's great buildings are both awesome and beautiful, with their aesthetic attention to intricately patterned facades, delicate 'combs' on temple roofs, and sinuous carvings. These magnificent structures, such as the ones found in the sophisticated urban centers of Tikal, El Mirador and Copán, were created without beasts of burden (except for humans) or the luxury of the wheel. Nor did Mayan builders ever devise the arch: instead, they used what is known as a corbeled arch, consisting of two walls leaning toward one another, nearly meeting at the top and surmounted by a capstone. This created a triangular rather than rounded arch and did not allow any great width or make for much strength. Instead, the building's foundations and substructure needed to be very strong. Once structures were completed, experts hypothesize, they were covered with stucco and painted red with a mixture of hematite and most probably water.

Mary Ellen Miller's well illustrated *Maya Art and Architecture* paints the full picture from gigantic temples to intricately painted ceramics.

Although formal studies and excavations of Mayan sites in Guatemala have been ongoing for more than a century, much of their architectural how and why remains a mystery. For example, the purpose of *chultunes*, underground chambers carved from bedrock and filled with offerings, continues to baffle scholars. And while we know that the Maya habitually built one temple on top of another to bury successive leaders, we have little idea how they actually erected these symbols of power. All the limestone used to erect the great Mayan cities had to be moved and set in place by hand – an engineering feat that must have demanded astronomical amounts of human labor. Try to imagine mining, shaping, transporting and hefting two million cubic meters of limestone blocks: this is the amount of rock scholars estimate was used in the construction of the Danta complex at El Mirador.

COLONIAL ARCHITECTURE

During the colonial period (the early 16th to early 19th centuries) churches, convents, mansions and palaces were all built in the Spanish styles of the day, chiefly Renaissance, Baroque and Neoclassical. But while the architectural concepts were European-inspired, the labor used to realize them was strictly indigenous. Thus, Mayan

RICHARD I'ANSON

Sunday market, **Chichicastenango** (p128)

Mayan man in colorful **traje** (p118)

KRAIG LIEB

RICHARD I'ANSON

A young woman selling woven
textiles (p282)

Selecting beans at a **coffee farm** (p187)

ALFREDO MAIQUEZ

Masks for sale, **Sunday market** (p128), Chichicastenango

Masked dancers (p131)

Semana Santa parade (p88), Antigua

One of Guatemala's many **fiestas** (p11)

embellishments – such as the lily blossoms and vegetable motifs that adorn Antigua's La Merced – can be found on many colonial buildings, serving as testament to the countless laborers forced to make the architectural dreams of Guatemala's newcomers a reality. Churches were built high and strong to protect the elite from lower classes in revolt.

Guatemala does not have the great colonial architectural heritage of neighboring Mexico, partly because earthquakes destroyed many of its finest buildings. But the architecture of Antigua is particularly striking, as new styles and engineering techniques developed following each successive earthquake. Columns became lower and thicker to provide more stability. Some Antigua buildings, including the Palacio de los Capitanes and Palacio del Ayuntamiento on the central plaza, were given a double-arch construction to strengthen them. With so many colonial buildings in different states of grandeur and decay, from nearly crumbled to completely restored, Antigua was designated a World Heritage Site by Unesco in 1979.

After the 1776 earthquake, which prompted the relocation of the capital from Antigua to Guatemala City, the Neoclassical architecture of the day came to emphasize durability. Decorative flourishes were saved for the interiors of buildings, with elaborate altars and furniture adorning churches and homes. By this time, Guatemalan architects were hell-bent on seeing their buildings stay upright, no matter how powerful the next earthquake. Even though several serious quakes have hit Guatemala City since then, many colonial buildings (such as the city's cathedral) have survived. The same cannot be said for the humble abodes of the city's residents, who suffered terribly when the devastating quake of 1976 reduced their homes to rubble.

Weaving

Guatemalans make many traditional handicrafts, both for everyday use and to sell to tourists and collectors. Crafts include basketry, ceramics and wood carving, but the most prominent are weaving, embroidery and other textile arts practiced by Mayan women. The beautiful *traje* (traditional clothing) made and worn by these women is one of the most awe-inspiring expressions of Mayan culture.

The most arresting feature of these costumes is their highly colorful weaving and embroidery, which makes many garments true works of art. It's the woman's *huipil*, a long, sleeveless tunic, that receives the most painstaking loving care in its creation. Often entire *huipiles* are covered in a multicolored web of stylized animal, human, plant and mythological shapes that can take months to complete. Each garment identifies the village from which its wearer hails (the Spanish colonists allotted each village a different design in order to distinguish their inhabitants from each other) and within the village style there can be variations according to social status, as well as the creative individual touches that make each garment unique.

The *huipil* is one of several types of garment that have been in use since pre-Hispanic times. Other colorful types include the *tocoyal*, a woven head-covering often decorated with bright tassels; the *corte*, a piece of material 7m or 10m long that is used as a wraparound skirt; and the *faja*, a long, woven waist sash that can be folded to hold what other people might put in pockets. Blouses are colonial innovations. Mayan men's garments owe more to Spanish influence; nudity was discouraged by the church, so shirts, hats and *calzones*, long baggy shorts that evolved into full-length pants in most regions, were introduced in

For a wonderful collection of photos of *huipiles* and other Mayan textiles, see the website of Nim Po't (www.nimpot.com).

Well-illustrated books on Mayan textiles will help you to start identifying their wearers' villages. Two fine works are *Maya of Guatemala – Life and Dress* by Carmen L Pettersen and *The Maya Textile Tradition*, edited by Margot Blum Schevill.

colonial times. Mayan men now generally wear dull Western clothing, however, except in places such as Sololá and Todos Santos Cuchumatán where they still sport colorful *traje*. For more on the various types of traditional garment, see p118.

Materials and techniques are changing, but the pre-Hispanic backstrap loom is still widely used. The warp (long) threads are stretched between two horizontal bars, one of which is fixed to a post or tree, while the other is attached to a strap that goes round the weaver's lower back. The weft (cross) threads are then woven in. Throughout the highlands you can see women weaving in this manner outside the entrance to their homes. Nowadays, some *huipiles* and *fajas* are machine made, as this method is faster and easier than hand weaving.

Yarn is still hand-spun in many villages. For the well-to-do, silk threads are used to embroider bridal *huipiles* and other important garments. Vegetable dyes are not yet totally out of use, and red dye from cochineal insects and natural indigo are employed in several areas. Modern luminescent dyes go down very well with the Maya, who are happily addicted to bright colors, as you will see.

It's generally in the highlands, which are heavily populated by Maya, that colorful traditional dress is still most in evidence, though you will see it in all parts of the country. The variety of techniques, materials, styles and designs is bewildering to the newcomer, but you'll see some of the most colorful, intricate, eye-catching and widely worn designs in Sololá and Santiago Atitlán, near the Lago de Atitlán, Nebaj in the Ixil Triangle, Zunil near Quetzaltenango, and Todos Santos and San Mateo Ixtatán in the Cuchumatanes mountains.

To see large collections of fine weaving, don't miss the Museo Ixchel in Guatemala City (p63) or the shop Nim Po't in Antigua (p96).

Environment

THE LAND

Guatemala covers an area of 109,000 sq km – a little less than the US state of Louisiana, a little more than England. Geologically, most of the country lies atop the North American tectonic plate, but this abuts the Cocos plate along Guatemala's Pacific coast and the Caribbean plate in the far south of the country. When any of these plates gets frisky, earthquakes and volcanic eruptions ensue. Hence the major quakes of 1773, 1917 and 1976 and the spectacular chain of 30 volcanoes – some of them active – running parallel to the Pacific coast from the Mexican border to the Salvadoran border. North of the volcanic chain rises the Cuchumatanes range.

North of Guatemala City, the highlands of Alta Verapaz gradually decline to the lowland of El Petén, occupying northern Guatemala. El Petén is hot and humid or hot and dry, depending on the season. Central America's largest tracts of virgin rain forest straddle El Petén's borders with Mexico and Belize, although this may cease to be true if conservation efforts are not successful.

Northeast of Guatemala City the valley of the Río Motagua, dry in some areas, moist in others, runs down to Guatemala's short, very hot Caribbean coast. Bananas and sugarcane thrive in the Motagua valley.

Between the volcanic chain and the Pacific Ocean is the Pacific Slope, with rich coffee, cotton, rubber, fruit and sugar plantations, cattle ranches, beaches of black volcanic sand and a sweltering climate.

Guatemala's unique geology also includes tremendous systems of caves. Water coursing for eons over a limestone base created aquifers and conduits that eventually gave way to subterranean caves, rivers and sinkholes when the surface water drained into underground caverns and streams. This type of terrain (known as karst) is found throughout the Verapaces region and makes Guatemala a killer spelunking destination.

WILDLIFE

Guatemala's natural beauty, from volcanoes and lakes to jungles and wetlands, is one of its great attractions. With 19 different ecosystems, the variety of fauna and flora is great – and if you know where to go, opportunities for seeing exciting species are plentiful.

Animals

Estimates point to 250 species of mammals, 600 species of birds, 200 species of reptiles and amphibians and many species of butterflies and other insects.

The national bird, the resplendent quetzal (for which the national currency is named), is small but exceptionally beautiful. The male sports a bright-red breast, brilliant blue-green neck, head, back and wings, and a blue-green tail several times as long as the body, which stands only around 15cm tall. The female has far duller plumage. The quetzal's main habitat is the cloud forests of Alta Verapaz.

Exotic birds of the lowland jungles include toucans, macaws and parrots. If you visit Tikal, you can't miss the ocellated turkey, also called the Petén turkey, a large, multicolored bird reminiscent of a peacock. Tikal is an all-round wildlife hot spot: you stand a good chance of spotting howler and spider monkeys, coatis (locally called *pisotes*) and other mammals, plus toucans, parrots and many other birds. Some 300 endemic and

DID YOU KNOW?

Guatemala sits at the confluence of three tectonic plates – hence its 30 volcanoes and frequent earthquakes.

DID YOU KNOW?

Tajumulco (4220m), west of Quetzaltenango, is the highest peak in Central America. La Torre (3837m), north of Huehuetenango, is the highest nonvolcanic peak in Central America.

DID YOU KNOW?

To see rare scarlet macaws in the wild, the place to head is La Ruta Guacamaya (the Scarlet Macaw Trail) to El Perú ruins in El Petén (p272).

TWO YOU DON'T WANT TO MEET

The Central American or common lancehead, also called the fer-de-lance (locally known as *barba amarilla*, yellow beard) is a highly poisonous viper with a diamond-pattern back and an arrow-shaped head. The tropical rattlesnake *(cascabel)* is the most poisonous of all rattlers. Both inhabit jungles and savanna.

---

migratory bird species have been recorded at Tikal, among them nine hummingbirds and four trogons. Good areas for sighting waterfowl, including the jabiru stork, the biggest flying bird in the western hemisphere, are Laguna Petexbatún and the lakes near Yaxhá ruins, both in El Petén, and the Río Dulce between the Lago de Izabal and Lívingston.

Guatemala's forests still host many mammal and reptile species. Petén residents include jaguars, ocelots, pumas, two species of peccary, opossums, tapirs, kinkajous, agoutis (*tepescuintles*, rodents 60–70cm long), white-tailed and red brocket deer, and armadillos. Guatemala is home to at least five species of sea turtle (the loggerhead, hawksbill and green ridley on the Caribbean coast, and the leatherback and olive ridley on the Pacific) and at least two species of crocodile (one found in El Petén, the other in the Río Dulce). Manatees exist in the Río Dulce, though they're notoriously hard to spot.

> Bird-lovers must get hold of either *The Birds of Tikal: An Annotated Checklist*, by Randell A Beavers, or *The Birds of Tikal*, by Frank B Smythe. If you can't find them elsewhere, at least one should be on sale at Tikal itself, and both are useful much further afield.

Plants

Guatemala has more than 8000 species of plants in 19 different ecosystems ranging from mangrove forests and wetlands on both coasts to the tropical rain forest of El Petén and the pine forests, open grasslands and cloud forests of the mountains. The cloud forests, with their epiphytes, bromeliads and dangling old-man's-beard, are most abundant in Alta Verapaz department. Trees of El Petén include the sapodilla, wild rubber trees, mahogany, several useful palms and the ceiba (Guatemala's national tree for its manifold symbolism to the Maya, also called the kapok or silk-cotton tree in English).

The national flower, the *monja blanca* (white nun orchid), is said to have been picked so much that it's now rarely seen in the wild; nevertheless, with 550 species of orchid (one-third of them endemic to Guatemala), you shouldn't have any trouble spotting some. If you're interested in orchids, be sure to visit the Vivero Verapaz orchid nursery at Cobán (p189).

Domesticated plants, of course, contribute at least as much to the landscape as wild ones. The *milpa* (maize field) is the backbone of agricultural subsistence everywhere. *Milpas* are, however, usually cleared by the slash-and-burn method, which is a major factor in the diminution of Guatemala's forests. Cities such as Antigua become glorious with the lilac blooms of jacaranda trees in the early months of the year.

PARKS & PROTECTED AREAS

Guatemala has 92 protected areas, including *reservas de biosfera* (biosphere reserves), *parques nacionales* (national parks), *biotopos protegidos* (protected biotopes), *refugios de vida silvestre* (wildlife refuges) and *reservas naturales privadas* (private nature reserves). Even though some areas are contained within other, larger ones, they amount to 28% of the national territory. Many of the protected areas are remote and hard of access to the independent traveler; the table shows those that are easiest to reach and/or most interesting to visitors (but excludes volcanoes, nearly all of which are protected, and areas of mainly archaeological interest).

> Ecotravels in Guatemala (www.planeta.com /guatemala.html) has arresting articles, good reference material and numerous links.

Protected Area	Features	Activities	Best Time to Visit	Page
Reserva de Biosfera Maya	21,000 sq km area across northern Petén; includes four national parks	jungle treks, wildlife spotting	any, drier November-May	p242
Reserva de Biosfera Sierra de las Mina	cloud-forest reserve of great biodiversity; key quetzal habitat	hiking, wildlife spotting	any	p227
Parque Nacional Tikal	diverse jungle wildlife among Guatemala's most magnificent Mayan ruins	wildlife spotting, seeing Mayan city	any, drier November-May	p261
Parque Nacional Laguna del Tigre	remote, large park within Reserva Maya; freshwater wetlands, Petén flora and fauna	wildlife spotting; visiting El Perú archaeological site; volunteer opportunities at Las Guacamayas biological station	any, drier November-May	p246
Parque Nacional Mirador-Río Azul	national park within Reserva Maya; Petén flora and fauna	jungle treks to El Mirador archaeological site	any, drier November-May	p273
Parque Nacional Río Dulce	Beautiful jungle-lined lower Río Dulce between Lago de Izabal and the Caribbean; manatee refuge	boat trips	any	p224
Parque Nacional Laguna Lachuá	circular, jungle-surrounded, turquoise lake, 220m deep; many fish, occasional jaguars and tapir	camping, swimming, guided walks	any	p199
Parque Nacional Grutas de Lanquín	large cave system 61km from Cobán	visiting caves, swimming, seeing bats; don't miss the nearby Semuc Champey lagoons and waterfalls	any	p196
Biotopo del Quetzal (Biotopo Mario Dary Rivera)	easy-access cloud-forest reserve; howler monkeys, birds' nature trails	bird-watching, possible quetzal sightings	any	p188
Biotopo Cerro Cahuí	forest reserve beside Lago de Petén Itzá	spotting Petén wildlife including monkeys, walking trails	any	p255
Biotopo San Miguel La Palotada	adjoins Parque Nacional Tikal; dense Petén forest with millions of bats	jungle walks, visits to El Zotz archaeological site and bat caves	any, drier November-May	p272
Refugio de Vida Silvestre Petexbatún	lake near Sayaxché; waterbirds	boat trips, fishing, visiting several archaeological sites	any	p270
Refugio de Vida Silvestre Bocas del Polochic	delta of Río Polochic at western end of Lago de Izabal; Guatemala's second-largest freshwater wetlands	bird-watching (more than 300 species), howler monkey observation	any	p227
Reserva Natural Monterrico	Pacific beaches and wetlands; birdlife, turtles	boat tours, bird- and turtle-watching	June-November (turtle nesting)	p177

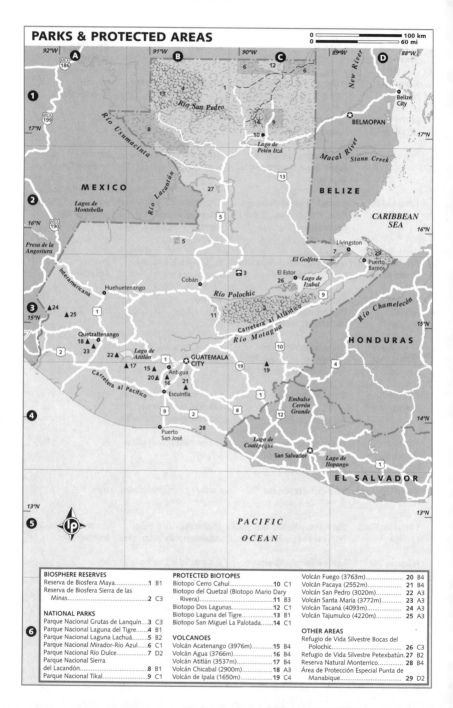

PARKS & PROTECTED AREAS

ENVIRONMENTAL ISSUES

Environmental consciousness is not enormously developed in Guatemala, as the vast amounts of garbage strewn across the country and the choking clouds of diesel gas pumped out by its buses and trucks will quickly tell you. Despite the impressive list of parks and protected areas, genuine protection for those areas is harder to achieve, partly because of official collusion to ignore the regulations and partly because of pressure from poor Guatemalans in need of land. Deforestation is a problem in many areas, especially El Petén, where jungle is being felled at an alarming rate not just for timber but also to make way for cattle ranches, oil pipelines, clandestine airstrips, new settlements and new maize fields cleared by the slash-and-burn method.

On the Pacific side of the country, where most of the population of Guatemala lives, the land is mostly agricultural or given over to industrial interests. The remaining forests in the Pacific coastal and highland areas are not long for this world, as local communities cut down the remaining trees for heating and cooking.

Nevertheless a number of Guatemalan organizations are doing valiant work to protect their country's environment and biodiversity. The following are good resources for finding out more about Guatemala's natural and protected areas:

Alianza Verde (www.alianzaverde.org in Spanish; Parque Central, Flores, Petén) Association of organizations, businesses and people involved in conservation and tourism in El Petén; provides information services such as Destination Petén magazine, the website www.peten.net (in Spanish), and Cincap, the Centro de Información Sobre la Naturaleza, Cultura y Artesanía de Petén, in Flores.

Arcas (Asociación de Rescate y Conservación de Vida Silvestre; ☎ /fax 476-6001; www.arcas guatemala.com; 21a Calle 9-44A, Zona 11, Mariscal, Guatemala City) Nongovernmental organization (NGO) working with volunteers in sea turtle conservation and rehabilitation of Petén wildlife (see also p253 and p178).

Asociación Ak' Tenamit (☎ Guatemala City 254-1560, 254-3346; Río Dulce 908-3392; www.aktenamit.org; 11a Av A 9-39, Zona 2, Guatemala City) Mayan-run NGO working to reduce poverty and promote conservation and ecotourism in the rain forests of eastern Guatemala.

Cecon (Centro de Estudios Conservacionistas de la Universidad de San Carlos; ☎ 361-5450, 331-0904; www.usac.edu.gt/cecon/INDEX%20CECON.htm in Spanish; Av La Reforma 0-63, Zona 10, Guatemala City) Manages six public *biotopos* and one *reserva natural*.

Conap (Consejo Nacional de Áreas Protegidas; ☎ 238-0000, 253-5579; conap.online.fr; Edificio IPM, 5a Av 6-06, Zona 1, Guatemala City) The government arm in charge of protected areas.

Fundación Defensores de la Naturaleza (☎ 440-8138, 445-0332; www.defensores.org.gt in Spanish; 7a Av 7-09, Zona 13, Guatemala City) NGO that owns and administers several protected areas.

ProPetén (☎ 926-1370, 926-1141; www.propeten.org; Calle Central, Flores, Petén) Works in conservation in Parque Nacional Laguna del Tigre.

Proyecto Ecoquetzal (☎ /fax 952-1047; bidaspeq@guate.net; 2a Calle 14-36, Zona 1, Cobán, Alta Verapaz) Works in forest conservation and ecotourism.

Les D Beletsky's *Belize & Northern Guatemala: The Ecotravellers' Wildlife Guide* provides detailed, almost encyclopedic information on the area's flora and fauna.

Timber, Tourists, and Temples, edited by Richard Primack and others, brings together experts on the Mayan forests of Guatemala, Mexico and Belize for an in-depth look at the problems of balancing conservation with local people's aspirations.

Food & Drink

What you eat in Guatemala will be a mixture of Guatemalan food, which is nutritious and filling without often sending your taste buds into ecstasy, and international traveler-and-tourist food that's available wherever travelers and tourists hang out. Your most satisfying meals in both cases will probably be in smaller eateries where the boss is in the kitchen him or herself. Guatemalan cuisine reflects both the old foodstuffs of the Maya, such as corn (maize), beans, squashes, potatoes, avocados, chilies and turkey, and the influence of the Spanish – bread, greater amounts of meat, rice, European vegetables. Modern international cuisine comes in considerable variety in places like Antigua, Guatemala City, Panajachel and Quetzaltenango. In villages and ordinary towns off the tourist trail, food will be strictly Guatemalan.

STAPLES & SPECIALTIES

DID YOU KNOW?

A woman feeding a family of eight (not unusual in Guatemala) makes around 170 tortillas a day.

The fundamental staple is the tortilla – a thin round patty of corn dough cooked on a griddle called a *comal*. Tortillas can accompany any meal: if you know Mexican tortillas, you'll find that Guatemalan ones are smaller and a little plumper – except when they appear on a menu under the heading 'Tortillas' (with chicken or meat or eggs etc), when they'll be bigger and performing a vaguely pizza-base-like function. Fresh handmade tortillas can be delicious. Tortillas are the exclusive domain of women and you'll see and hear women making them in every corner of the country. Fresh machine-made ones are sold at a *tortillería*. The tortillas sold in restaurants are fairly fresh and kept warm in a hot, moist cloth. These are all right, but will eventually become rubbery. Tortillas accompanying meals are unlimited; if you run out, just ask for more.

The second staple is *frijoles* (fri-*hoh*-les) or black beans. These can be eaten boiled, fried, refried, in soups, spread on tortillas or with eggs. *Frijoles* may be served in their own dark sauce, as a runny mass on a plate, or as a thick and almost black paste. No matter how they come, they can be delicious and are always nutritious. The third Mayan staple is the squash.

Bread (*pan*, sold in *panaderías*) replaces tortillas in some tourist restaurants and for some Guatemalans who prefer not to eat *a la indígena*.

The above staples accompany all sorts of things at meal times. There's always a hot sauce on hand, either bottled or homemade: the extra kick it provides can make the difference between a so-so and a tasty meal.

Be careful with salads and fruit: if they have been washed in dodgy water or cut with a dirty knife, they can cause you problems. Salads are so common that it can be hard *not* to eat them. If the establishment you're eating in impresses with its cleanliness, the salad is likely to be safe. If vegetables, salads and the like are washed in purified water, then you're home and dry.

The Recipe Archives website has fine Guatemalan recipes at http://recipes2.alastra.com/ethnic/guatemalan.html.

Breakfast

Desayuno chapín, or Guatemalan breakfast, is a large affair involving (at the least) eggs, beans, fried plantains, tortillas and coffee. This will be on offer in any *comedor* (basic eatery). It may be augmented with rice, cheese or *mosh,* an oatmeal/porridge concoction. Scrambled eggs are often made with chopped tomatoes and onions.

TRAVEL YOUR TASTE BUDS

Guatemala's most sensational flavors can be sampled on the Caribbean coast where the specialty is *tapado*, a mouth-watering casserole of seafood, plantain, coconut milk, spices and a few vegetables. Yummmmm!

Less tongue-tingling but filling and warming on chilly mountain mornings is *mosh,* a breakfast dish that sounds just like what it is, an oatmeal/porridge that ranges from sloppy to glutinous.

More flavorsome, and found widely around the country, is *pepián* – chicken or turkey in a spicy sesame-seed and tomato sauce. Keep your fingers crossed that the bird under the sauce has some flesh on it. *Jocón* is a green stew of chicken or pork with green vegetables and herbs.

In Cobán and the Alta Verapaz department, try *kac-cik* (*kak-ik* or *sack'ik*), a turkey soup-cum-stew with ingredients such as pepper (capsicum), garlic, tomato and chili.

In the Ixil Triangle the local favorite is *boxbol* – maize dough and chopped meat or chicken, wrapped tightly in leaves of the *güisquil* squash and boiled. It's served with salsa.

Anywhere tourists go, you'll also find a range of other breakfasts on offer, from light continental-style affairs to US-style bacon, eggs, *panqueques* (pancakes), cereals, fruit juice and coffee. Breakfast is usually eaten between 6am and 10am.

DID YOU KNOW?

Most Guatemalans who eat cornflakes like them with hot milk. Specify *leche fría* (cold milk) if you don't fancy this!

Lunch

This is the biggest meal of the day and is eaten between noon and 2pm. Eateries usually offer a fixed-price meal of several courses called an *almuerzo* or *menú del día*, which may include from one to four courses and is usually great value. A simple *almuerzo* may consist of soup and a main course featuring meat with rice or potatoes and a little salad or vegetables, or just a *plato típico*: meat or chicken, rice, beans, cheese, salad and tortillas. More expensive versions may have a fancy soup or *ceviche*, a choice main course such as steak or fish, salad, dessert and coffee. You can also choose à la carte from the restaurant's menu, but it will be more expensive.

Dinner/Supper

La cena is, for Guatemalans, a lighter version of lunch, usually eaten between 7pm and 9pm. Even in cities, few restaurants will serve you after 10pm. In rural areas, sit down no later than 8pm to avoid disappointment. In local and village eateries, supper may be the same as breakfast: eggs, beans and plantains. In restaurants catering to tourists, dinner might be anything from pepper steak to vegetarian Thai curry.

To find out more about Guatemalan food on the Internet, visit 1try.com's links at www.1try.com /recipes_g/guatemalan _cuisine.html.

DRINKS
Coffee, Tea & Chocolate

While Guatemala grows some of the world's richest coffee, a good cup is only generally available in top-end and some tourist restaurants and cafés, because most of the quality beans are exported. Black tea *(té negro)*, usually made from bags, can be disappointing. Herbal teas are much better. Chamomile tea *(té de manzanilla)*, common on restaurant and café menus, is a good remedy for a queasy gut.

Hot chocolate or cocoa was the royal stimulant during the Classic period of Mayan civilization, being drunk on ceremonial occasions by the kings and nobility. Their version was unsweetened and dreadfully bitter. Today it's sweetened and, if less authentic, at least more palatable. Hot chocolate can be ordered *simple* (with water) or *con leche* (with milk).

ONES TO AVOID

You may come across armadillo, *venado* (venison), *paca* or *tepescuintle* (agouti), *tortuga* or *caguama* (turtle), and *iguana* (lizard) on some menus. Don't order them: they may well be endangered species. The same applies here to the humble *conejo* (rabbit).

Juices & Licuados

Fresh fruit and vegetable juices *(jugos)*, milkshakes *(licuados)* and long, cool, fruit-flavored water drinks *(aguas de frutas)* are wildly popular. Many cafés and eateries offer them and almost every village market and bus station has a stand with a battalion of blenders. The basic *licuado* is a blend of fruit or juice with water and sugar. A *licuado con leche* uses milk instead of water.

Limonada is a delicious thirst-quencher made with lime juice, water and sugar. Try a *limonada con soda,* which adds a fizzy dimension, and you may have a new drink of choice. *Naranjada* is the same thing made with orange juice.

Alcoholic Drinks

Breweries were established in Guatemala by German immigrants in the late 19th century, but they didn't bring a heap of flavor with them. The two nationally distributed beers are Gallo (pronounced 'gah-yoh,' rooster) and Cabro. The distribution prize goes to Gallo – you'll find it everywhere – but Cabro is darker and more flavorful. Moza is the darkest local beer, but its distribution is limited.

Rum *(ron)* is one of Guatemala's favorite strong drinks, and though most is cheap in price and taste, some local products are exceptionally fine. Zacapa Centenario is a smooth, aged Guatemalan rum made in Zacapa. It should be sipped slowly and neat, like fine cognac. Ron Botrán Añejo, another dark rum, is also good. Cheaper rums like Venado are often mixed with soft drinks to make potent but cooling drinks such as the *Cuba libre* of rum and Coke. On the coast you'll find *cocos locos,* green coconuts with the top sliced off and rum mixed with the coconut water.

Aguardiente is a sugarcane firewater that flows in cantinas and on the streets. Look for the signs advertising Quetzalteca Especial. This is the *aguardiente* of choice.

Ponche is a potent potable made from pineapple or coconut juice and rum and served hot.

Water & Soft Drinks

Purified water *(agua pura)* is widely available in hotels, shops and restaurants (p298). Salvavida is a universally trusted brand. You can order safe-to-drink carbonated water by saying '*soda.*'

Soft drinks are known as *aguas* (waters). If you want straight unflavored water, say '*agua pura,*' or you may be asked '*¿Qué sabor?*' ('What flavor?').

WHERE TO EAT & DRINK

A *comedor* is a basic, no-fuss eatery serving straightforward local food in plain surroundings for low prices. If the place looks clean and busy, it will likely be hygienic and a good value: the best *comedor* food is equivalent to good home cooking. There is unlikely to be a printed or written menu or even much choice: the staple fare is set breakfasts, set lunches and set suppers, each for around US$1.50 to US$3. The cheapest *comedores* of all are tables and benches set up in markets, with the cooking done on the spot.

A *restaurante* is at least a little fancier than a *comedor*. It will have pretensions (at least) to decor, staff might wear some kind of uniform, and there'll be a menu – a selection from soups, salads, sandwiches, *antojitos* (snacks), burgers, pasta, pizza, chicken, meat and fish dishes, and desserts. A typical set meal in a decent restaurant costs US$3 to US$6, à la carte a little more. In Guatemala City, Antigua, Panajachel and Quetzaltenango you can eat at specialist and ethnic restaurants and some quite classy, moderately expensive establishments. But even in the capital's most exclusive spots you'll find it hard to leave more than US$30 lighter.

Comedores and *restaurantes* typically open from 7am to 9pm, but the hours can vary by up to a couple of hours either way. Places close earlier in small towns and villages, later in cities and tourist destinations. A few fancier city places may not open until 11am or noon and close from 3pm to 6pm. If a restaurant has a closing day, it is usually Sunday.

A *café* or *cafetería* will offer, apart from the coffee, food of some kind. This might be light snacks or it might be a fuller range akin to a restaurant. A *pastelería* is a cake shop, and often it will provide tables and chairs where you can sit down and enjoy its baked goods with a drink.

Guatemala has plenty of fast-food restaurants, but most ubiquitous is the local chicken franchise, Pollo Campero.

Bars are open long hours, typically from 10am or 11am to 10pm or 11pm. If they have a closing day, it's usually Sunday. Officially, no alcohol may be served in public bars or eateries after 8pm Sunday but the only places we found this law observed were Antigua, Panajachel and Lívingston.

You'll find a further nine recipes at www.recipehound.com /recipes/guatemala.html.

Quick Eats

Bus snacks can become an important part of your Guatemalan diet, as long bus rides with early departures are not uncommon. Women and girls come on the bus proclaiming '¡*Hay comida!*' ('I got food!'). This is usually a small meal of tortillas smeared with beans, accompanied by a piece of chicken or a hard-boiled egg. Other snacks include fried plantains, ice cream, peanuts, *chocobananos* (chocolate-covered bananas), *hocotes* (a tropical fruit eaten with salt, lime and nutmeg) and *chuchitos* (small parcels of corn dough filled with meat or beans and steamed inside a corn husk). *Elotes* are grilled ears of corn on the cob eaten with salt and lime.

Much the same cheap fare is doled out by street stalls around bus stations, markets, street corners and so on. It's rare for any of these items to cost as much as US$1, and if you're on a tight budget you may do quite a lot of your eating at street stalls. On buses and streets alike, take a good look at the cleanliness of the vendor and stall: this is a good indication of how hygienic the food will be.

The biggest Internet collection of Guatemalan recipes is for readers of Spanish only, at www.quetzalnet.com /recetas.

VEGETARIANS & VEGANS

Given that meat is a bit of a luxury for many Guatemalans, it's not too hard to get by without it. The basic Mayan combination of tortillas, beans and vegetables is fairly nutritious. If you request a set lunch or *plato típico* without meat at a *comedor* you'll still get soup, rice, beans, cheese, salad and tortillas. Indeed some restaurants offer just this combination of items under the name *plato vegetariano*. Be careful with soups: even if they contain no pieces of meat, they may be made with

---

DOS & DON'TS

- When you sit down to eat, it's polite to say *'buenos días'* or *'buenas tardes'* (as appropriate) to the people at the next table.

- When you leave a restaurant it's polite to say *'buen provecho'* (bon appetit) to those near you. They may say the same to you, which is a way of wishing you good digestion!

- Always tip, around 10%: the wages of the people who cook and serve your food are often pitifully low.

For more Guatemalan recipes, log on to Guatemala – Recipes at expedition.bensenville .lib.il.us/centralamerica /guatemala/recipes.htm.

meat stock. Beans, if fried, may have been fried in lard. If you eat eggs, dairy products or fish, you can eat more or less the same breakfast as anyone else, and your options for other meals increase greatly. In most places that travelers go, many restaurants – especially ethnic ones – have nonmeat items on the menu. There are even a few dedicated vegetarian restaurants in cities and tourist haunts. Chinese restaurants are also a good bet for nonmeat food. Plenty of fruit, vegetables and nuts are always available in markets.

EAT YOUR WORDS
Communicating successfully with restaurant staff is halfway to eating well. For further guidance on pronouncing Spanish words, see pp301-9.

Useful Phrases

Do you have a menu (in English)?   *¿Hay una carta (en inglés)?*
ai *oo*-na *kar*-ta (en een-*gles*)?

What is there for breakfast/lunch/dinner?   *¿Qué hay para el desayuno/el almuerzo/la cena?*
ke ai *pa*-ra el de-sa-*yoo*-no/el al-*mwer*-so/la *se*-na?

Is this water purified?   *¿Ésta agua es purificada?*
es-ta *a*-gwa es poo-ree-fee-*ka*-da?

I'm a vegetarian.   *Soy vegetariano/a.*
soy ve-khe-te-*rya*-no/a

I don't eat meat or chicken or fish or eggs.   *No como carne ni pollo ni pescado ni huevos.*
no *ko*-mo *kar*-ne nee *po*-yo nee pes-*ka*-do nee *we*-vos

I'd like the set lunch.   *Quisiera el menú del día.*
kee-sye-*ra* el me-*noo* del *dee*-a

Is it spicy-hot?   *¿Es picante?*
es pee-*kan*-te?

The bill, please.   *La cuenta, por favor.*
la *kwen*-ta, por fa-*vor*

Menu Decoder

aguacate – avocado
ajo – garlic
a la parrilla – grilled, perhaps over charcoal
a la plancha – grilled on a hotplate
antojitos – literally 'little whims,' these are snacks or light dishes such as burritos, *chiles rellenos*, *chuchitos*, enchiladas, quesadillas, tacos and tamales. They can be eaten at any time, on their own or as part of a larger meal.
arroz – rice
atole – a hot gruel made with maize, milk, cinnamon and sugar
aves – poultry
banano – banana

bistec or **bistec de res** – beefsteak
burrito – any combination of beans, cheese, meat, chicken or seafood, seasoned with salsa or chili and wrapped in a wheat-flour tortilla
café (negro/con leche) – coffee (black/with milk)
calabaza – squash, marrow or pumpkin
caldo – broth, often meat-based
camarones – shrimps
camarones gigantes – prawns
carne – meat
carne asada – tough but tasty grilled beef
cebolla – onion
cerveza – beer
ceviche – raw seafood marinated in lime juice and mixed with onions, chilies, garlic, tomatoes and cilantro (coriander leaf)
chicharrón – pork crackling
chile relleno – a large chili stuffed with cheese, meat, rice or other foods, dipped in egg whites, fried and baked in sauce
chuchito – small *tamal*
chuletas (de puerco) – (pork) chops
churrasco – slab of grilled meat
coco – coconut
enchilada – ingredients similar to those in a *burrito* rolled up in a tortilla, dipped in sauce and then baked or partly fried
ensalada – salad
fajita – grilled meat served on a flour tortilla with condiments
filete de pescado – fish fillet
flan – custard, crème caramel
fresas – strawberries
frijoles – black beans
frutas – fruit
guacamole – avocados mashed with onion, chili sauce, lemon and tomato
guajolote – turkey
güisquil – type of squash
hamburguesa – hamburger
helado – ice cream
huachinango – red snapper
huevos fritos/revueltos – fried/scrambled eggs
jamón – ham
jícama – a popular root vegetable resembling a potato crossed with an apple; eaten fresh with a sprinkling of lime, chili and salt, or cooked like a potato
jocón – green stew of chicken or pork with green vegetables and herbs
lechuga – lettuce
legumbres – root vegetables
licuado – milkshake made with fresh fruit, sugar and milk or water
limón – lime or lemon
limonada – drink made from lime juice; limonada con soda is made with carbonated water
mariscos – seafood
melocotón – peach
miel – honey
milanesa – crumbed, breaded
mojarra – perch
mosh – hot oatmeal/porridge
naranja – orange
naranjada – drink made from orange juice and fizzy water
pacaya – a squash-like staple

papa – potato
papaya – pawpaw
pastel – cake
pato – duck
pavo – turkey
pepián – chicken and vegetables in a piquant sesame and pumpkin seed sauce
pescado (al mojo de ajo) – fish (fried in butter and garlic)
piña – pineapple
plátano – plantain (green banana), edible when cooked (usually fried)
plato típico – meat or chicken, rice, beans, cheese, salad, tortillas and maybe a soup to start
pollo (asado/frito) – (grilled/fried) chicken
postre – dessert
puerco – pork
puyaso – a choice cut of steak
quesadilla – flour tortilla topped or filled with cheese and occasionally other ingredients and then heated
queso – cheese
refacciones – light meals; see *antojitos*
salchicha – sausage
salsa – sauce made with chilies, onion, tomato, lemon or lime juice and spices
sopa – soup
taco – a soft or crisp corn tortilla wrapped or folded around the same filling as a burrito
tamal – corn dough stuffed with meat, beans, chilies or nothing at all, wrapped in banana leaf or corn husks and steamed
tapado – a seafood, coconut milk and plantain casserole
tarta – cake
tocino – bacon or salt pork
tomate – tomato
tostada – flat, crisp tortilla topped with meat or cheese, tomatoes, beans and lettuce
verduras – green vegetables
zanahoria – carrot

English–Spanish Glossary

butter	*mantequilla*	man-te-*kee*-yah
cup	*taza*	*ta*-sa
drink	*bebida*	be-*bee*-da
fork	*tenedor*	te-ne-*dor*
glass	*vaso*	*va*-so
knife	*cuchillo*	koo-*chee*-yo
lunch	*almuerzo*	al-*mwer*-so
margarine	*margarina*	mar-ga-*ree*-na
milk	*leche*	*le*-che
pepper (black)	*pimienta*	pee-*myen*-ta
plate	*plato*	*pla*-to
salt	*sal*	sal
spoon	*cuchara*	koo-*cha*-ra
sugar	*azúcar*	a-*soo*-kar
table	*mesa*	*me*-sa
tip	*propina*	pro-*pee*-na

Guatemala City

CONTENTS

Guatemala's capital city, the largest urban agglomeration in Central America, spreads across a flattened mountain range run through by deep ravines. It's not a pretty site.

Initially, the sprawl and smog may remind you of Mexico City, that mighty Latin megalopolis to the north. But Guatemala City (or Guate as it's referred to locally) has a distinct flavor. There's the huge and chaotic market cum bus terminal, bursting with enough sounds, colors and odors to stun even the well-initiated. There are the rickety urban buses roaring along in thick black clouds of diesel, trawling for ever more passengers. There's the shocking contrast between the glitzy Zona Viva, home to luxury hotels, gourmet restaurants and trendy nightclubs, and the poverty-stricken outlying shantytowns overflowing with migrants from the countryside (many of them displaced civil-war victims).

Few colonial buildings prettify Guate, a fairly young city. The colonial monuments are all in nearby Antigua, the former capital. Little architecture in Guatemala City is notable, but at least most buildings are only five or six stories high, allowing light to flood the narrow streets.

The interesting sights in Guatemala City may be seen in a day or two. Many travelers skip the city altogether, preferring to make Antigua their base. Still, you may want, or need, to get acquainted with the capital because this is the hub of the country, where all transportation lines meet and all services are available.

TOP FIVE

- Visiting the country's best **museums** (p64) and **zoo** (p64)
- Dining fine in **Zona 10's Zona Viva** (p66 and p70)
- Connecting with the bohemian culture of Zona 1 **bars** (p70) and **clubs** (p71)
- Gazing on Guatemala from above at the **Mapa en Relieve** (p63)
- Leaving

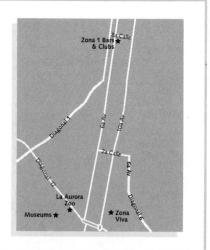

- ELEVATION: 1500M
- POPULATION: 2 MILLION

HISTORY

Kaminaljuyú, one of the first important cities in the Mayan region, flourished in what's now the western part of Guatemala City two millennia ago. By the time Spanish conquistadors arrived in the 16th century, only overgrown mounds were left. The site remained insignificant until the earthquake of July 29, 1773, razed much of the then Spanish colonial capital, Antigua. The authorities decided to move their headquarters to La Ermita valley, hoping to escape further destruction, and on September 27, 1775, King Carlos III of Spain signed a royal charter for the founding of La Nueva Guatemala de la Asunción. Guatemala City was officially born.

Unfortunately, the colonial powers didn't move the capital far enough, for earthquakes in 1917, 1918 and 1976 rocked the capital and beyond, reducing buildings to rubble. The 1976 quake killed nearly 23,000, injured another 75,000 and left an estimated one million homeless.

ORIENTATION

The formal and ceremonial center of Guatemala City is the Parque Central at the heart of Zona 1, which is home to most of the city's better budget and mid-range hotels, many of its bus stations and a lot of commerce. South down 6a or 7a Av from Zona 1 is Zona 4. Straddling the border of the two zones is the Centro Cívico (Civic Center), with several large, modern government and institutional buildings, including the main tourist information office. Southwestern Zona 4 is a chaotic area where the city's major market district and the biggest 2nd-class bus station, the Terminal de Autobuses, fuse into one overcrowded mess.

South from the southeast corner of Zona 4 runs Av La Reforma, a broad boulevard forming the boundary between Zonas 9 and 10. These zones are among the city's poshest residential and office areas, especially Zona 10 with its Zona Viva (Lively Zone) where deluxe hotels, fancy restaurants and nightclubs, and glitzy malls all congregate.

The city's airport, Aeropuerto La Aurora, is in Zona 13, just south of Zona 9 and a 6km drive or bus ride from the heart of Zona 1. Zona 13 has several museums and the parklike La Aurora Zoo.

Maps

Intelimapas' *Mapa Turístico Guatemala*, Inguat's *Mapa Vial Turístico* and International Travel Maps' *Guatemala* (p281) all contain useful maps of Guatemala City. **Sophos** (p57) is one of the most reliable sources of maps. The **Instituto Geográfico Nacional** (IGN; ☎ 332-2611; www.ign.gob.gt in Spanish; Av Las Américas 5-76, Zona 13; ☼ 9am-5pm Mon-Fri) sells 1:50,000 and 1:250,000 topographical sheets of all parts of Guatemala, costing US$6 each.

INFORMATION
Airline Offices

American Airlines Guatemala City Marriott Hotel (☎ 337-1177; www.aa.com; 7a Av 15-45, Zona 9)
Continental Airlines Edificio Unicentro (☎ 366-9985; www.continental.com; 18a Calle 5-56, Zona 10); Guatemala City Marriott Hotel (☎ 331-2051/2; 7a Av 15-45, Zona 9)

KNOWING EXACTLY WHERE YOU ARE

Guatemala City, like (almost) all Guatemalan towns, is laid out on a logical street grid. Avenidas run north–south; calles run east–west. Each avenida and calle has a number, with the numbers usually rising as you move from west to east and north to south. Addresses enable you to pinpoint exactly which block a building is in, and which side of the street it's on. The address 9a Av 15-24 means building No 24 on 9a Av in the block after 15a Calle; 9a Av 16-19 refers to building No 19 on 9a Av in the block after 16a Calle; 4a Calle 7-3 is building No 3 on 4a Calle in the block after 7a Av. Odd-numbered buildings are on the left-hand side as you move in the rising-numbers direction; even numbers are on the right.

In addition, most cities and towns are divided into a number of zonas – 21 in Guatemala City, fewer in other places. You need to know the zona as well as the street address, for in some places the numbers of avenidas and calles are repeated in more than one zona. Beware, too, a couple of other minor wrinkles in the system. Short streets may be suffixed 'A,' as in 14a Calle A, which will be found between 14a Calle and 15a Calle. In some smaller towns and villages no-one uses street names, even when they're posted on signs.

GUATEMALA CITY

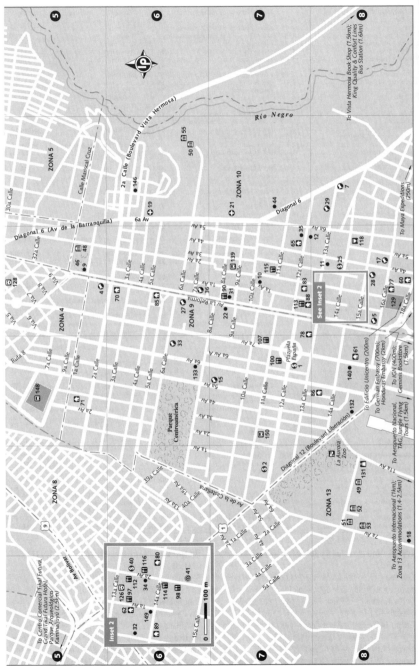

ZONA 5

Calle Mariscal Cruz

2a Calle (Boulevard Vista Hermosa)

Río Negro

To Vista Hermosa Book Shop (1.5km);
King Quality & Comfort Lines
Bus Station (1.6km)

50 ■ 🔢 55

146 ●

19 🔵

ZONA 10

21 🔵

44 ●

Diagonal 6

29 🔵

7 🔵

To Maya Expeditions
(250m)

30a Calle

Diagonal 6 (Av de la Barranquilla)

32a Calle

ZONA 4

128 🔢

46 ● 48 🔢
9 ●

70 🔵

Vía 8
Vía 9
Vía 6
Vía 5

4 🔵

3a Calle
4a Calle
5a Calle

6a Calle

2a Av
4a Av
5a Av

6a Av

85 🔵

139 🔵
115

90 🔵 83

36 🔵
31

10 🔵

65 🔵 35
12

13a Calle

11 ● 25 🔵

17 🔵

28 🔵

118 🔢

5a Av
6a Av

See Inset 2

27 🔵

22 🔵

113 🔵
88 🔵

14a Calle

15a Calle

5 🔵

129 🔢

77 🔵
60 🔵
16a Calle
18a Calle

33 🔵

107
📷

Plazuela
España
1 🔵

78 🔵

140 ●

61 🔵

To Edificio Unicentro (200m)

To Germán Embassy (700m);
Honduras Embassy (2km)

To IGN (400m);
Geminis Bookstore
(1.5km)

Ruta 8

7a Calle
9a Calle
3a Calle
2a Calle

148 🔢

71 🔵

133 🔵
15 🔵

100 🔵

3a Calle
4a Calle
5a Calle
6a Calle

5a Av
6a Av

10a Calle

11a Calle

12a Calle

13a Calle

14a Calle

86 🔵

132 ●

Parque
Centroamérica

ZONA 8

39a Calle

Av de la Castellana

ZONA 13

150
📷

2 🔵

Diagonal 12 (Boulevard Liberación)

La Aurora
Zoo

To Aeropuerto Nacional;
TAG; Jungle Flying
Tours (1.5km)

49 🔢 131

52 🔢

51 🔢
93

18 ●

To Aeropuerto Internacional (1km);
Zona 13 Accommodations (1–4.2.5km)

9 🔵

To Centro Comercial Tikal Futura,
Grand Tikal Futura Hotel,
Parque Arqueológico
Kaminaljuyú (2.5km)

Av Bolívar

1 🔵

7a Av
11a Av

0   100 m
0 _____ 500 ft

Inset 2

13a Calle

40 🔵
116

126 🔢
97 🔢
112

34 🔵
114 🔢
98 🔢

80 🔵

41 📷

32 ●

149 🔵
89 ●

14a Calle

15a Calle

GUATEMALA CITY

Copa Airlines Zona 10 (☎ 385-5500; www.copaair.com; 1a Av 10-17)

Cubana Edificio Atlantis (☎ 367-2288/89/90; www.cubana.cu; Local 29; 13a Calle 3-40, Zona 10)

Delta Airlines Edificio Centro Ejecutivo (☎ 1-800-300-0005; 15a Calle 3-20, Zona 10)

Grupo TACA Hotel Real Inter-Continental Guatemala (☎ 470-8222; www.taca.com; 14a Calle 2-51, Zona 10); Aeropuerto Internacional La Aurora (☎ 361-5784) This group comprises Aviateca, Inter, LACSA, Nica and TACA airlines.

Iberia Edificio Galerías Reforma (☎ 331-1012, 332-0911, 332-3913; www.iberia.com; Local 204; Av La Reforma 8-60, Zona 9); Aeropuerto Internacional La Aurora (☎ 332-5517/8)

Jungle Flying Tours Zona 13 (☎ 339-0502; www.aereorutamaya.com; cnr Av Hincapié & 18a Calle Final, Hángar L-22)

Mexicana Edificio Edyma Plaza (☎ 333-6001; www.mexicana.com; Local 104, 13a Calle 8-44, Zona 10); Aeropuerto Internacional La Aurora (☎ 331-3291)

RACSA Aeropuerto Internacional La Aurora (☎ 361-5703/4; www.racsair.com)

TAG Zona 13 (☎ 360-3038; tagsa@intelnett.com; cnr Av Hincapié & 18a Calle, Hángar 15)

Tikal Airlines Aeropuerto Internacional La Aurora (Tikal Jets; ☎ 334-6855; www.tikaljets.com)

United Airlines Edificio El Reformador (☎ 336-9923/ 4/5/6; www.unitedguatemala.com; Oficina 201, Av La Reforma 1-50, Zona 9); Aeropuerto Internacional La Aurora (☎ 332-1994/5)

Bookstores

Geminis Bookstore (☎ 366-1031; Casa Alta, 3a Av 17-05, Zona 14) Good range of books in English, but rather far from the center of things.

Sophos (☎ 334-6797; Av La Reforma 13-89, Zona 10) Relaxed place to have a coffee and read while in the Zona Viva, with a good selection of books in English on Guatemala and the Maya, including Lonely Planet guides, and maps.

Vista Hermosa Book Shop (☎ 369-1003; 2a Calle 18-50, Zona 15) Ditto.

Internet Access

Zona 1 is thronged with inexpensive cyber-cafés. Elsewhere, rates tend to be higher.

Café Internet Navigator (14a Calle east of 6a Av, Zona 1; ☻ 8am-8pm) US$0.80 an hour.

Carambolo Café Internet (14a Calle east of 7a Av, Zona 1; ☻ 8:30am-8:30pm) US$1.30 an hour.

Internet (Local 5, 6a Av 9-27, Zona 1; ☻ 8am-7pm) US$0.65 an hour.

Web Station (2a Av 14-63, Zona 10; ☻ 10am-midnight Mon-Sat, noon-midnight Sun) US$2.60 an hour. One of the cheapest in the Zona Viva.

Laundry

Lavandería El Siglo (12a Calle 3-42, Zona 1; ☻ 8am-6pm Mon-Sat) Charges US$4 to wash and dry up to 12lb (5.5kg).

Medical Services

Guatemala City has many private hospitals and clinics. Public hospitals and clinics provide free consultations but can be busy: to reduce waiting time, get there before 7am.

Clínica Cruz Roja (Red Cross Clinic; 3a Calle 8-40, Zona 1; ☻ 8am-5:30pm Mon-Fri, 8am-noon Sat) This public clinic charges for consultations but is inexpensive.

Farmacia del Ejecutivo (☎ 238-1447; 7a Av 15-01, Zona 1) Public pharmacy. Open 24 hours and accepts Visa and MasterCard.

Hospital Centro Médico (☎ 332-3555, 334-2157; 6a Av 3-47, Zona 10) Recommended. This private hospital has some English-speaking doctors.

Hospital General San Juan de Dios (☎ 253-0443/7; 1a Av at 10a Calle, Zona 1) One of the city's best public hospitals.

Hospital Herrera Llerandi (☎ 334-5959, emergencies 334-5955; 6a Av 8-71, Zona 10) Another recommended private hospital with some English-speaking doctors.

Money

Take normal precautions when using ATMs here; see p281.

ABM Zona 9 (☎ 361-5602; Plazuela España) This shop changes cash euros into quetzals.

American Express Zona 9 (☎ 331-7422; Centro Comercial Montufar, 12a Calle 0-93; ☻ 8am-5pm Mon-Fri, 8am-noon Sat) This is in an office of Clark Tours.

Banco Agromercantil Zona 1 (8a Calle facing Parque Centenario; ☻ 9am-7pm Mon-Fri, 9am-1pm Sat) Changes US dollars cash (not traveler's checks).

Banco Uno Zona 10 (☎ 366-2191; Edificio Unicentro, 18a Calle 5-56) Changes cash euros into quetzals.

Banquetzal Airport arrivals hall (☻ 6am-9pm) Changes US dollars cash and American Express traveler's checks into quetzals, and has a MasterCard and American Express ATM; Airport departures level (☻ 6am-8pm Mon-Fri, 6am-6pm Sat & Sun) Has currency exchange services and a MasterCard ATM.

Edificio Testa Zona 1 (cnr 5a Av & 11a Calle) Has Visa, MasterCard and American Express ATMs (on the 5a Av side of the building). Credomatic gives cash advances on Visa and MasterCard – take your passport. There's another Visa ATM across the street.

Lloyds TSB Zona 10 (14a Calle 3-51) Changes euro traveler's checks.

MasterCard ATM Zona 10 (Hotel Stofella, 2a Av 12-28)

Visa ATMs Zona 1 (cnr 5a Av & 6a Calle opposite Parque Centenario); Zona 10 (2a Av south of 13a Calle); Zona 10 (Edificio Unicentro 18a Calle 5-56); Zona 9 (Guatemala City Marriott Hotel, 7a Av 15-45); Airport arrivals hall There's a Visa ATM by the exit doors.

Post

DHL (☎ 332-7547; www.dhl.com; 12a Calle 5-12, Zona 10) Courier service.

Main post office (7a Av 11-67, Zona 1; ☻ 8:30am-5pm Mon-Fri, 8:30am-1pm Sat) In a huge pink building at the Palacio de Correos. There's a small post office at the airport.

UPS (☎ 360-6460; www.ups.com; 12a Calle 5-53, Zona 10) Courier service.

Telephone

Telgua These street card phones are plentiful.

Telefónica office (2a Av btwn 13a & 14a Calles, Zona 10) Telefónica street card phones are fairly common too; cards can be bought at the Telefónica office.

Tourist Information

Inguat Main tourist office (☎ 331-1333, 331-1347; fax 331-2369; informacion@inguat.gob.gt; 7a Av 1-17, Zona 4; ⏰ 8am-4pm Mon-Fri) Located in the lobby of the Inguat (Guatemala Tourism Institute) headquarters in the Centro Cívico; the office has limited handout material, but staff are extremely friendly and helpful; Aeropuerto Internacional La Aurora (☎ 331-4256; ⏰ 6am-9pm) In the arrivals hall; Palacio de Correos (Main Post Office; ☎ 251-1898; 7a Av 11-67, Zona 1; ⏰ 9am-5pm Mon-Fri); Palacio Nacional de la Cultura (☎ 253-0748; 6a Calle facing Parque Central, Zona 1; ⏰ 9-11:45am & 2-4:45pm Mon-Fri, 9-10:45am & 2-3:45pm Sat & Sun)

Travel Agencies

Servisa (☎ /fax 332-7526; Av La Reforma 8-33, Zona 10) An efficient agency.

Viajes Tivoli (☎ 238-4771/2/3; centro@tivoli.com.gt; 12a Calle 4-55, Edificio Herrera, Zona 1) Housed in a building with several other travel agencies; take your pick.

DANGERS & ANNOYANCES

Street crime, including armed robbery, has increased in recent years. Use normal urban caution (behaving as you would in, say, Manhattan or Rome): don't walk down the street with your wallet bulging out of your back pocket, and avoid walking downtown alone late at night. Work out your route before you start so that you're not standing on corners looking lost or peering at a map. It's safe to walk downtown in early evening, as long as you stick to streets with plenty of lighting and people. Stay alert and leave your valuables in your hotel. Don't flaunt anything of value, and be aware that women and children swell the ranks of thieves here. The incidence of robbery increases around the 15th and the end of each month, when workers get paid.

The area around 18a Calle in Zona 1 has many bus stations, and hosts the lowlife and hustlers who tend to lurk around them. Nearly half of Zona 1 robberies happen here, the worst black spots being the intersections with 4a, 6a and 9a Avs. This part of town (also a red-light district) is notoriously dangerous at night; if you are arriving by bus at night or must go someplace on 18a Calle at night, take a taxi.

The more affluent sections of the city – Zona 9 and Zona 10, for example – are much safer. The Zona Viva, in Zona 10, has police patrols at night. But even here, going in pairs is better than going alone.

All buses are the turf of adroit pickpockets. Some armed robberies happen on buses, too, though mainly in the city's outlying zones.

Never try to resist if you are confronted by a robber.

SIGHTS

The major sights are in Zona 1 (the historic center) and Zonas 10 and 13, where the museums are grouped.

Zona 1

The main sights here are grouped around the **Parque Central** (officially the Plaza de la Constitución). The standard colonial urban-planning scheme required every town in the New World to have a large plaza for military exercises and ceremonies. On the north side of the plaza was usually the *palacio de gobierno* (colonial government headquarters). On another side, preferably the east, would be a church (or cathedral). On the other sides of the square there could be additional civic buildings or the imposing mansions of wealthy citizens. Guatemala City's Parque Central is a classic example of the plan.

The Parque Central and adjoining Parque Centenario are never empty during daylight hours, with shoeshine boys, ice cream vendors and sometimes open-air political meetings adding to the general bustle.

On the north side of the Parque Central is the imposing **Palacio Nacional de la Cultura** (☎ 253-0748; 6a Calle; ⏰ 9-11:45am & 2-4:45pm Mon-Fri, 9-10:45am & 2-3:45pm Sat & Sun), built as a presidential palace between 1936 and 1943 during the dictatorial rule of General Jorge Ubico at enormous cost in the lives of the prisoners who were forced to labor here. It's the third palace to stand on the site. Despite its tragic background, architecturally the palace is one of the country's most interesting constructions, a mélange of multiple earlier styles from Spanish Renaissance to Neoclassical. Today, most government offices have been removed from here and it's open as a museum and for a few ceremonial events.

Visits are by guided tour (available in English), lasting about 45 minutes – the tours are free, but a tip to your guide is a good idea. You pass through a labyrinth of gleaming brass, polished wood, carved stone and frescoed arches. Features include an optimistic mural of Guatemalan history by Alberto Gálvez Suárez above the main stairway, and a two-ton gold, bronze and Bohemian-crystal chandelier in the reception hall. The banqueting hall sports stained-glass panels depicting – with delicious irony – the virtues of good government. From here your guide will probably take you out onto the presidential balcony, where you can imagine yourself a banana-republic dictator reviewing your troops. In the western courtyard, the Patio de la Paz, a monument depicting two hands stands where Guatemala's Peace Accords were signed in 1996; each day at 11am the rose held by the hands is changed by a military guard and tossed to a woman among the spectators.

The **Catedral Metropolitana** (7a Av facing Parque Central; ☼ 6am-noon & 2-7pm daily) was constructed between 1782 and 1815 (the towers were finished in 1867). It has survived earthquake and fire well, though the quake of 1917 did substantial damage and the one in 1976 did even more. Its heavy proportions and sparse ornamentation don't make for a particularly beautiful building, but it does have a certain stateliness, and the altars are worth a look.

The **Mercado Central**, behind the cathedral, was one of the city's major markets for food and other daily necessities until the building was destroyed by the 1976 earthquake. Reconstructed in the late 1970s, it now specializes in tourist-oriented handicrafts (p71).

The **Museo Nacional de Historia** (☎ 253-6149; 9a Calle 9-70; US$1.30; ☼ 8:30am-4pm Mon-Fri) is a jumble of historical relics with an emphasis on photography and portraits. Check the carefully manicured hairstyles of the 19th-century generals and politicos.

Zona 2

North of Zona 1, Zona 2 is mostly a middle-class residential district, but it's worth venturing along to Parque Minerva to see the **Mapa en Relieve** (Relief Map; US$2; ☼ 9am-5pm), a huge open-air map of Guatemala showing the country at a scale of 1:10,000. The vertical scale is exaggerated to 1:2000 to make the volcanoes and mountains appear dramatically higher and steeper than they really are. Constructed in 1905 under the direction of Francisco Vela, the Mapa was fully restored and repainted in 1999. Viewing towers afford a panoramic view. This is an odd but fun place, and it's curious to

observe that Belize is still represented as part of Guatemala. To get there take bus No V-21 northbound on 7a Av just north or south of the Parque Central.

Zona 4

Pride of Zona 4 (actually straddling its borders with Zonas 1 and 5) is the **Centro Cívico**, a set of large government and institutional buildings constructed during the 1950s and '60s. One is the headquarters of **Inguat** (Instituto Guatemalteco de Turismo), housing the city's main tourist office (p62). Nearby are the **Palacio de Justicia** (High Court; cnr 7a Av & 21a Calle, Zona 1), the **Banco de Guatemala** (7a Av, Zona 1) and the **Municipalidad de Guatemala** (City Hall; 22a Calle, Zona 1). The bank building bears relief sculptures by Dagoberto Vásquez depicting his country's history; the city hall contains a huge mosaic by Carlos Mérida, completed in 1959.

Behind Inguat is the national stadium, **Estadio Nacional Mateo Flores** (10a Av, Zona 5), and on a hilltop west across the street from the Centro Cívico is the **Centro Cultural Miguel Ángel Asturias** (p71), housing several theaters.

Zona 10

Two of the country's best museums are housed in large, modern buildings at the Universidad Francisco Marroquín, 1km east of Av La Reforma.

The **Museo Ixchel** (☎ 331-3634/8; 6a Calle Final; US$2.50; ☼ 9am-5pm Mon-Fri, 9am-1pm Sat) is named for the Mayan goddess of the moon, women, reproduction and, of course, textiles. Photographs and exhibits of indigenous costumes and other crafts show the incredible richness of traditional arts in Guatemala's highland towns. If you enjoy Guatemalan textiles at all, you must visit this museum. It has disabled access, a section for children, a café, a shop and a library, and guided tours are available in English or Spanish.

Behind it is **Museo Popol Vuh** (☎ 361-2301; www.popolvuh.ufm.edu; 6a Calle Final; adult/child/student with ID US$2.50/0.75/1; ☼ 9am-5pm Mon-Fri, 9am-1pm Sat), where well-displayed pre-Hispanic figurines, incense burners and burial urns, plus carved wooden masks and traditional textiles, fill several rooms. Other rooms hold colonial paintings and gilded wood and silver artifacts. A faithful copy of the Dresden Codex, one of the precious 'painted books' of the Maya, is among the most interesting pieces, and there's a colorful display of animals in Mayan art.

The Universidad de San Carlos has a large, lush **Jardín Botánico** (Botanical Garden; Calle Mariscal Cruz 1-56; US$1.30; ☼ 8am-3:30pm Mon-Fri) on the northern edge of Zona 10. The admission includes the university's **Museo de Historia Natural** (Natural History Museum) at the site.

Zona 13

The attractions here in the city's southern reaches are all ranged along 5a Calle in the Finca Aurora area, northwest of the airport. While here, you can also drop into the **Mercado de Artesanías** (p71).

La Aurora Zoo (☎ 472-0894; 5a Calle; adult/child US$1.30/0.65; ☼ 9am-5pm Tue-Sun) is not badly kept as zoos go, and the lovely, parklike grounds alone are worth the admission fee.

Almost opposite the zoo entrance is the **Museo de los Niños** (Children's Museum; ☎ 475-5076; 5a Calle 10-00; US$4.50; ☼ 8am-noon & 1-5pm Tue-Thu, 8am-noon & 2-6pm Fri, 10am-1:30pm & 2:30-6pm Sat & Sun), a hands-on affair that is a sure success if you have kids to keep happy. The fun ranges from a giant jigsaw-map of Guatemala to a Lego room and, most popular of all, a room of original and entertaining ball games.

The **Museo Nacional de Arqueología y Etnología** (☎ 472-0489; Sala 5, Finca La Aurora; US$4; ☼ 9am-4pm Tue-Fri, 9am-noon & 1:30-4pm Sat & Sun) has the country's biggest collection of ancient Mayan artifacts, but explanatory information is very sparse. There's a great wealth of monumental stone sculpture, including Classic-period stelae from Tikal, Uaxactún and Piedras Negras, a superb throne from Piedras Negras and animal representations from Preclassic Kaminaljuyú. Also here are rare wooden lintels from temples at Tikal and El Zotz, and a room of beautiful jade necklaces and masks. Don't miss the large-scale model of Tikal. The ethnology section has displays on the languages, costumes, dances, masks and homes of Guatemala's indigenous peoples.

Next door is the **Museo Nacional de Arte Moderno** (☎ 472-0467; Sala 6, Finca La Aurora; US$1.30; ☼ 9am-4pm Tue-Fri, 9am-noon & 2-4pm Sat & Sun), with a collection of 20th-century Guatemalan art including works by well-known Guatemalan artists such as Carlos Mérida, Carlos Valente and Humberto Gavarito. Behind the archaeology museum is the

Museo Nacional de Historia Natural Jorge Ibarra (☎ 472-0468; 6a Calle 7-30; US$1.30; ☼ 9am-4pm Tue-Fri, 9am-noon & 2-4pm Sat & Sun), renowned for its large collection of dissected animals.

Zona 7

The **Parque Arqueológico Kaminaljuyú** (☎ 253-1570; 11a Calle just west of 23a Av, Zona 7; US$3.25; ☼ 9am-4pm), with remnants of one of the first important cities in the Maya region, is some 4km west of the city center. At its peak, from about 400 BC to AD 100, ancient Kaminaljuyú had thousands of inhabitants and scores of temples built on earth mounds, and probably dominated most of highland Guatemala. Large-scale carvings found here were the forerunners of Classic Maya carving, and Kaminaljuyú had a literate elite before anywhere else in the Maya world. The city fell into ruin before being reoccupied around AD 400 by invaders from Teotihuacán in central Mexico, who rebuilt it in Teotihuacán's talud-tablero style, with buildings stepped in alternating vertical (tablero) and sloping (talud) sections. Unfortunately most of Kaminaljuyú has been covered by urban sprawl: the parque arqueológico is but a small portion of the ancient city and even here the remnants consist chiefly of grassy mounds. To the left from the entrance is La Acrópolis, where you can inspect excavations of a ball court and talud-tablero buildings from AD 450 to 550. The best carvings from the site are in the Museo Nacional de Arqueología y Etnología (p64).

You can get here by bus No 35 from 4a Av, Zona 1, but check that the bus is going to the ruinas de Kaminaljuyú (kah-mih-nahl-huh-yuh) – not all do. A taxi from Zona 1 costs around US$3.50.

GUATEMALA CITY FOR CHILDREN

Guatemala City has enough children's attractions to make it worth considering as an outing from Antigua if you have kids to please. The **Museo de los Niños** (p64) and **La Aurora Zoo** (p64), conveniently over the road from each other in Zona 13, top the list. Kids might also relish the dead animals in various states of preservation at the nearby **Museo Nacional de Historia Natural Jorge Ibarra** (p64). It shouldn't be too hard to find some food that the littl'uns are willing to eat at the food courts in the **Centro Comercial Los Próceres** or **Centro Comercial Tikal**

Futura malls (p71), where everyone can also enjoy a little air-conditioning and shopping (window or otherwise). The **Mapa en Relieve** (p63), too, amuses most ages, and there are a few swings and climbing frames in the adjacent park.

TOURS

Clark Tours (☎ 337-7777; www.clarktours.com.gt; Torre II, Centro Gerencial Las Margaritas, Diagonal 6 No 10-01, Zona 10) Guatemala's longest-established tour operator offers morning and full-day city tours. The morning tour (US$26 per person, daily except Thursday and Sunday) visits the Palacio Nacional de la Cultura, cathedral, Mapa en Relieve and Centro Cívico. The day tour (US$240 to US$260 for up to four people) adds three of the city's best museums and Kaminaljuyú. Clark tours also has branches at the Westin Camino Real (p68), Holiday Inn (p68) and Guatemala City Marriott Hotel (p68).

SLEEPING

For budget and many mid-range hotels, make a beeline for Zona 1. For top-end establishments, Zonas 10 and 9 provide most of the options. If you have just flown in or are about to fly out, a few guesthouses near the airport are as convenient as you could get.

Budget

ZONA 1

Many of the city's cheaper lodgings are clustered in the area between 6a and 9a Avs and 14a and 17a Calles, 10 to 15 minutes' walk south from the Parque Central. Keep street noise in mind as you look for a room.

Hotel Spring (☎ 230-2858; hotelspring@hotmail.com; 8a Av 12-65; s/d/tr with shared bathroom US$12/17/22, with bathroom US$17/22/26 or US$25/31/37; P 🖳) The Spring combines sunny patios and 43 tall, spacious, clean rooms with fair prices – though the rooms with shared bathrooms are often full. There's no fancy decoration and many carpets are well past their prime, but that's a quibble. All rooms have cable TV; some of the more expensive ones are wheelchair accessible. It's worth booking ahead. A cafetería serves meals from 6:30am to 1:30pm; Internet is available till 3pm.

Hotel Fenix (☎ 251-6625; 7a Av 15-81; s & d US$6, with bathroom & TV US$10) This is one of the best budget bets in town, thanks to its friendly family atmosphere, clean rooms and good security, despite the somewhat dodgy locale. The rooms with a shared bathroom are quieter, being upstairs. The hotel has a café and spacious hang out areas.

Pensión Meza (☎ 232-3177; 10a Calle 10-17; dm US$4, s/d US$6/7, d with bathroom US$12) Relaxed, friendly and cheap, the Meza has been a gathering ground for savvy budget travelers for decades. The English-speaking owner, Mario, was born here in the 1920s. Mario remains an amiable host to travelers many decades younger than himself. The rooms are dilapidated and adorned with travelers' murals and graffiti but come with mostly firm beds. The Meza also has a sunny courtyard, table tennis, a book exchange and a big notice board. Conveniently next door are a cheap restaurant and Jonathan's Bar, serving beer.

Hotel Quality Service (☎ 251-8005/6/7; quality service@intelnet.net.gt; 8a Calle 3-18; s/d/tr/q US$17/23/29/45; P 🖳) This curiously named establishment provides 22 reasonably sized rooms with cable TV, private bathroom and colorful accoutrements. You can enjoy fresh air and plants along the semi-open corridor. Rates include parking and breakfast.

Hotel Capri (☎ 232-8191, 251-3737; 9a Av 15-63; s/d US$8/13, with bathroom US$14/20; P) The Capri is popular with Guatemalan businesspeople and families, who gather in the pleasant, clean lobby. All rooms have cable TV, hot water, windows, tile floors and bright pink flowery bedspreads.

Zona 1 has plenty of other budget hotels:

Hotel Excel (☎ 253-2709; 9a Av 15-12; s/d US$20/24) Bright, modern, three-level hotel.

Hotel Clariss (☎ 232-1113; 8a Av 15-14; s/d US$16/19; P 🖳) Friendly place next to the Cobán bus terminal.

Hotel Ajau (☎ 232-0488; 8a Av 15-62; s/d US$8/10, with bathroom US$13/14; 🖳) Dingy but reasonably quiet 44-room hotel.

Hotel Gran Central (☎ 232-9514; 9a Av 15-31; s/d/tr US$5/6/8, s or d with bathroom US$8) Dark, noisy and very cheap.

ZONA 9

Hotel del Istmo (☎ 332-4389; 3a Av 1-38; s/d without TV US$16/20, s/d/tr with TV US$18/22/27) If you are arriving by Melva bus from San Salvador,

THE AUTHOR'S CHOICE

Hotel Pan American (☎ 232-6807/8/9; www.hotelpanamerican.com; 9a Calle 5-63, Zona 1; s/d/tr/q US$54/60/65/70; P 💻) Guatemala City's luxury hotel before WWII, the Pan American is still run by its founding family and is one of the few hotels in the city with any air of history. It's welcoming and comfortable with polished service. In the fine, tall Art Deco lobby a tinkling fountain and colorful weavings provide colonial and Mayan touches. The 52 rooms follow the same themes and sport attractively tiled floors, cable TV, telephone, bathroom (with tub) and fan. Avoid rooms facing the noisy street. There's a restaurant serving all meals (p69), and guests have access to email.

Hotel Casa Santa Clara (☎ 339-1811; www.hotelcasasantaclara.com; 12a Calle 4-51, Zona 10; s/d/tr US$75/80/90; P 💻) This charming 14-room hotel offers many of the same comforts as the Zona Viva giants a block or two away, but with much more personalized attention and an intimate atmosphere. Reading lamps, cable TV, phone, fan, wooden furnishings and attractive paintings and prints of Guatemalan life give the amply sized rooms comfort and character, and there's a garden restaurant/café out front. Book ahead.

Hotel Colonial (☎ 232-6722, 232-2955; www.hotelcolonial.net; 7a Av 14-19, Zona 1; s/d/tr US$17/22/27, with bathroom US$25/30/35; P) This is a large old house in a convenient location converted to a hotel with spacious communal areas and heavy, dark, colonial decor. It's a very well-run establishment whose 42 rooms are clean, good-sized and adequately furnished. Nearly all have a bathroom and TV. The restaurant serves breakfast (US$3 to US$5) from 6:30am to 2pm.

Hotel Chalet Suizo (☎ 251-3786; fax 232-0429; 14a Calle 6-82, Zona 1; s/d/tr with shared bathroom US$13/20/24, with bathroom US$22/29/34) This friendly, spotless and well-managed hotel has been a travelers' favorite for decades. It has an excellent central location; the 47 rooms around airy courtyards are bare but comfortable. The hotel has a safe and luggage storage.

Radisson Hotel & Suites (☎ 332-9797, in the US 800-333-3333; www.radissonguatemala.com; 1a Av 12-46, Zona 10; ste US$117; P ✂ 🎾 💻) The Radisson boasts a floor for women (with a beauty salon and pink towels!) and one for families (with newly adopted Guatemalan children in mind). The 99 suites vary widely in size and facilities but not in price. All have kitchen, safe, minibar and big windows with views that get better the higher you go. Free Internet, coffee and snacks are available on all floors, and the rooms have US$5-a-day data ports. Other facilities include restaurant, bar, business center, gym and sauna.

---

this hotel at the terminal is clean, comfortable and convenient. All of the rooms have a hot-water bathroom and a cable television.

ZONA 13 (NEAR THE AIRPORT)

Four dependable guesthouses in a middle-class residential area in Zona 13 are very convenient for the airport. All their room rates include breakfast and airport transfers (call from the airport on arrival). See the Mid-Range section (below) for the details of the two slightly more expensive guesthouses.

Dos Lunas (☎ /fax 334-5264; www.xelapages.com/doslunas; 21a Calle 10-92; per person with small/big breakfast US$10/12; P 💻) Cleanliness, security, and friendly, helpful, English-speaking hosts make Dos Lunas an excellent value. Six of the pink-painted rooms share bathrooms and there's one double with a private bathroom for US$25. Dos Lunas also offers

onward-travel packages and Flores flights at good prices.

Economy Dorms (☎ 331-8029; 8a Av 17-74; s & d US$20) Despite the name, this guesthouse offers four serviceable, fan-cooled rooms but no dormitories. Breakfast is continental minimalist.

Mid-Range

Mid-range lodgings are liberally scattered around town. All the following are comfortable and some are even charming.

ZONA 1

Hotel Royal Palace (☎ 232-5125, 220-8970; www.hotelroyalpalace.com; 6a Av 12-66; s & d US$55; P 🎾) At the heart of bustling 6a Av, this colonial hotel has had a major facelift. Rooms are large, sparkling clean and wheelchair-accessible, with good wooden furniture and flowery bedspreads. They have fans and white tiled floors, except on the fourth floor which is carpeted, air-conditioned and costs US$67. Exterior rooms mostly have small balconies, but interior ones avoid street noise. Facilities include a restaurant (p69), bar, gym, sauna, and free airport transfers.

Hotel Fortuna Royal (☎ 238-2484; hotelfortunaroyal@yahoo.com; 12a Calle 8-42; s/d/tr US$26/32/36; P) The 21 rooms are large, with good tiled bathrooms and big mirrors and wardrobes. Cable TV, phone, and touches such as oriental-style reading lamps, alarm clock and minibar help make it one of the best downtown deals in this range. There's a restaurant too.

Other adequate choices:

Hotel Centenario (☎ 238-0381/2/3; 6a Calle 5-33; s/d with hot-water bathroom US$28/36) Drab but clean hotel overlooking Parque Centenario.

Hotel Tally (☎ 232-9845; 7a Av 15-24; s/d US$26/31; P 🔀) Pink rooms with bathtubs face the hotel's leafy parking lot.

ZONA 9

Howard Johnson Inn (☎ 360-7188; www.hojo.com; Av La Reforma 4-22; s/d/tr US$61/67/79; P 🔀) The Hojo's 36 comfy, carpeted rooms sport air-conditioning and fan, solid wooden furniture, phone, TV and attractive tiled bathrooms. Only outside rooms have windows of any size, however. Room rates include a full breakfast and airport transfers, and there's a good little restaurant.

Mi Casa (☎ 709-4466, 339-2247; hotelmicasa@intelnett.com; 5a Av A 13-51; dm per person US$15, s/d US$30/40; P 🖳) This friendly B&B offers four good-sized rooms with private bathrooms, lino floors, standard acrylic paintings, fans and reading lamps. The four-person dorm and one smaller single/double (US$25/35) share bathrooms. All rates include a good continental breakfast. Occupants of private bathrooms qualify for free airport transfers. Internet is available for US$1/1.50 per 30/60 minutes.

Hotel Cortijo Reforma (☎ 332-0712; fax 331-8876; Av La Reforma 2-18; s/d/tr US$55/60/66; P) The 130 suites here, though far from modern or flashy, each feature a large living room, bedroom, good tiled bathroom, phone and TV. Some (a little costlier) also have kitchens.

ZONA 10

Eco Hotel los Próceres (☎ 337-3250; ecoproceres@hotmail.com; 18a Calle 3-03; s/d/tr US$35/45/59; P 🔀) The 20 brightly decorated rooms, each

with attractive tiled bathroom, phone, clock, cable TV, wooden furniture and air-conditioning, are a very good value for the location on the edge of the Zona Viva. Rates include a light breakfast.

Hotel Posada de los Próceres (☎ 363-0744/46; posadazv@gua.net; 16a Calle 2-40; P 🖳 🔀) This hotel, only a block away, and with the same ownership and prices, is older and a little less attractive, with fans instead of air-conditioning in some rooms, but it offers Internet access for US$2.60 an hour.

ZONA 13 (NEAR THE AIRPORT)

Rates at both these places include breakfast and airport transfers (call from the airport on arrival).

Aeropuerto Guest House (☎ 332-3086; www.hotelaeropuerto.centroamerica.com; 15a Calle A 7-32; s/d US$25/30, with bathroom US$30/35; P 🖳) Just 350m from the airport door, this guesthouse has nine comfy rooms and a friendly atmosphere. English is spoken and this guesthouse offers luggage storage, cable TV in the living room, and Internet (US$2 per half-hour). Breakfast is continental.

Hostal Los Volcanes (☎ 360-3232; www.hostallosvolcanes.com; 16a Calle 8-00; per person US$15, s/d with bathroom & TV US$25/40; 🖳) The Volcanes has nine cheerful rooms, each with a fan, and offers luggage storage and deals incorporating onward transportation. Breakfast here is juice, eggs, toast and coffee.

Top End

Many top-end hotels have desks in the airport arrivals area, where you can book a room and/or obtain transportation (often free) to the hotel.

Hotel Stofella (☎ 338-5600; www.bestwestern.com; 2a Av 12-28, Zona 10; s/d US$73/79; P 🔀 🔀 🖳) This pleasant medium-sized Zona Viva hotel is part of the international Best Western chain, and provides quality rooms – with air-conditioning, safes, and phones in bedroom and bathroom – at reasonable prices. Rates include breakfast and one hour of free Internet usage daily. You can hook up a computer in your room for US$5 a day.

Hotel Princess Reforma (☎ 334-4545; www.hotelesprincess.com; 13a Calle 7-65, Zona 9; s & d US$117; P 🔀 🖳) Larger than it looks from outside, the Princess still has a pleasantly soothing ambience and is prettily decorated with old-fashioned prints. It boasts a pool, gym, restaurant, English-pub-style bar, and air-conditioning and 'no-hands' phones in the 110 rooms. Check the website for special deals.

Holiday Inn (☎ 332-2555; www.holidayinn.com.gt; 1a Av 13-22, Zona 10; s & d Mon-Thu US$140, Fri-Sun US$79; P ✕ ☯ ☐ ☮) Rooms are spacious, carpeted and solidly furnished, with plenty of top-end facilities, including data port and even phone in the bathroom. The hotel has a pool, gym, business center and disabled-access rooms. Airport transfers are included in the rates.

Grand Tikal Futura Hotel (☎ 439-1234; www.grandtikalfutura.com.gt; Calzada Roosevelt 22-43, Zona 11; s & d Mon-Thu US$117, Fri-Sun US$79; P ☯ ☐ ☮) The towering glass architecture here is a contemporary reinterpretation of the grandiose concepts of ancient Tikal. The 205 luxurious rooms and suites all enjoy spectacular views and have their own safes. On the lower levels of the complex, you'll find one the city's biggest shopping malls, 10 cinemas and a bowling alley. It's in the west of the city on the road to Antigua, 3km from Zona 1, Zona 10 or the airport.

Guatemala City has other lavish, top-of-the-top-end establishments:

Hotel Real Inter-Continental Guatemala (☎ 379-4444; www.interconti.com; 14a Calle 2-51, Zona 10; s & d US$129; P ✕ ☯ ☐ ☮)

Westin Camino Real (☎ 333-3000; www.caminoreal.com.gt; cnr 14a Calle & Av La Reforma, Zona 10; s & d US$140; P ✕ ☯ ☐ ☮)

Guatemala City Marriott Hotel (☎ 339-7777; www.marriott.com; 7a Av 15-45, Zona 9; s & d US$122; P ✕ ☯ ☐ ☮)

EATING

Cheap eats are easy to find in Zona 1. Fine dining focuses on Zona 10.

Budget
ZONA 1

Dozens of restaurants and fast-food shops are strung along and just off 6a Av between 8a and 15a Calles. American fast-food chains like McDonald's and Burger King are sprinkled liberally throughout Zona 1 and the rest of the city. They're open long hours, often from 7am to 10pm. Pollo Campero is Guatemala's KFC clone: a serve of chicken, fries, Pepsi and bread costs around US$4.

Bar-Restaurante Europa (☎ 253-4929; Local 201, Edificio Testa, 11a Calle 5-16; mains US$2.50-5; ☯ 8am-8:30pm Mon-Sat) The Europa is a comfortable, relaxed, 11-table restaurant, bar and gathering place for locals and foreigners alike (the bar stays open till midnight). A sign on the door says 'English spoken, but not understood.' It has international cable TV and good-value food – try chicken cordon bleu for dinner, or eggs, hash browns, bacon and toast for breakfast.

Café-Restaurante Hamburgo (☎ 238-4029; 15a Calle 5-34; set lunch or dinner US$2.25-3.25; ☯ 7am-9:30pm) This bustling spot facing the south side of Parque Concordia serves good Guatemalan food to grateful diners, with chefs at work along one side and orange-aproned waitresses scurrying about. At weekends a marimba adds atmosphere. Prices range from around US$1 for some salads or breakfast items up to US$6 for some à la carte seafood or meat.

Cafetería Patsy (☎ 232-6703; 14a Calle 4-73; burgers, subs & salads US$2-4; ☯ 7:30am-8pm) This is a fine place to sit down for a breather with a drink and a pastry or sandwich. Breakfasts cost around US$2.50 and a set lunch US$3.

Restaurante Cantón (☎ 251-6331; 6a Av 14-29; dishes US$4.50-8; ☯ 9am -10pm) The Cantón will never win culinary awards, but it's about the best of several Chinese restaurants along 6a Av, providing ample portions of straightforward food.

Restaurante Long Wah (☎ 232-6611; 6a Calle 3-70; dishes US$4-6; ☯ 11am-10pm) With friendly service and decorative red-painted arches, the Long Wah is a good choice from Zona 1's other concentration of Chinese eateries, in the blocks west of Parque Centenario.

Zona 1 has several other reasonable budget eateries:

Cafetín El Rinconcito (9a Av 15-74; mains US$2.50-4.50) Simple neighborhood restaurant in the cheap hotel area.

Restaurante Rey Sol (11a Calle 5-51; meals around US$4; ☯ 8am-5pm Mon-Sat) Vegetarian restaurant.

ZONA 10
Cafetería Patsy (☎ 331-2435; Av La Reforma 8-01) A bright, cheerful place popular with local office workers, this has the same menu and hours as Patsy's Zona 1 branch (p68). The prices are especially good for this location.

THE AUTHOR'S CHOICE

Tre Fratelli (☎ 366-2678; 2a Av 13-25, Zona 10; pasta & pizza US$5-10; ☺ 12:30pm-1am) For good Italian food and a fun atmosphere, don't miss this large Zona Viva restaurant. It's immensely popular with all comers, thanks to an unmatchable recipe of good food in ample portions, thumping background music, sparkling lights and sports on TV.

San Martín & Company (13a Calle 1-62, Zona 10; light meals US$2-4; ☺ 6am-8pm Mon-Sat) Cool and clean, with ceiling fans inside and a small terrace outside, this Zona Viva café and bakery is great at any time of day. For breakfast try a scrumptious omelette and croissant (the former arrives *inside* the latter). Later there are tempting and original sandwiches, soups and salads. The entrance is on 2a Av.

Los Cebollines (mains US$6-13; ☺ 7am-10pm Sun-Thu, 7am-11pm Fri & Sat); Zona 1 (6a Av 9-75); Zona 9 (12a Calle 6-17, Plazuela España) Casual, clean and spacious, though not exactly cheap, the two branches of Los Cebollines serve up excellent Mexican food, from enchiladas or salads to sizzling meat grills, plus huge, thirst-quenching *naranjadas* (orange juice and soda water). TVs show cable sport.

Hacienda Real (☎ 333-5408; 13a Calle 1-10, Zona 10; steaks US$9.75-18; ☺ lunch & dinner daily) For carnivores, nowhere beats the Hacienda Real, where the service is good but the atmosphere relaxed as you dine by candlelight around the fountain in the patio or under a wooden roof. Guatemalan steaks cost US$9.75 to US$12.25; imported ones are dearer. The entrance is on 1a Av.

Café Sebastián (☎ 232-1646; 5a Calle 6-81, Zona 1; set lunch US$2; ☺ lunch Mon-Fri) A friendly and inexpensive little spot with just five tables, in the street behind the Palacio Nacional de la Cultura, Café Sebastián makes a great lunchtime retreat from the noise and heat of the city. Cool jazz plays and the jolly color scheme make you feel good. The set lunch – for example, soup followed by beef stroganoff with rice, melon, guacamole and tortillas – is good value.

Ta'Contento (cnr 14a Calle & 2a Av; around US$1 per taco) One of the few establishments in the Zona Viva where you can eat for under US$5, bright Ta'Contento serves up a wide variety of tacos with lots of Mexican sauces.

Mid-Range

ZONA 1

Hotel Pan American (☎ 232-6807; 9a Calle 5-63; breakfast US$6-10, lunch US$8-12; ☺ 6am-9pm) The restaurant at this venerable hotel (p66) is high on ambience. It has highly experienced and polished waiters sporting traditional Mayan regalia. The food (Guatemalan, Italian and American) is fine, although it is a little on the expensive side.

Hotel Royal Palace (☎ 232-5125; 6a Av 12-66; breakfast US$3-7) The restaurant at this hotel (p66) provides good-value breakfasts in calm surroundings.

El Gran Pavo de Don Neto (☎ 232-9912; 13a Calle 4-41; mains US$8-11; ☺ 7am-11pm) Big and bright, the Gran Pavo serves almost every Mexican dish imaginable. The *birria*, a spicy-hot soup of meat, onions, peppers and *cilantro* (coriander leaf), served with tortillas, is a meal in itself for US$4.

ZONA 4

Cuatro Grados Norte, situated on Vía 5 between Rutas 1 and 3, is the name for a two-block pedestrianised strip of restaurants and cafés with sidewalk tables and relaxed café society. Inaugurated in 2002, and the only place of its kind in Guatemala City, it is conveniently close to the main Inguat tourist office. It is lively in the evening. You can choose from a dozen or so establishments, some of which double as galleries, bookstores or music venues.

Del Paseo (☎ 385-9047; Vía 5 1-81, Cuatro Grados Norte; dishes US$5-8.50) This spacious, artsy, Mediterranean-style bistro is one of Cuatro Grados Norte's most popular spots. Relaxed jazz plays in the background unless there's a live band (try Thursdays from 9pm). You might select roast chicken breast with tropical fruits and grated coconut – or how about spinach-and-ricotta filo pastry parcels? Wine goes for US$3 a glass.

L'Osteria (☎ 360-1816; Vía 5, Cuatro Grados Norte; one-person pizza & pasta US$4-7; ☺ noon-3pm & 6-10:30pm Tue-Thu, noon-3pm & 6pm-midnight Fri & Sat, noon-8pm Sun) You can come here for Italian fare.

ZONA 10

Inka Grill (☎ 363-3013; 2a Av 14-22; mains US$6.50-10.50) Peruvian artifacts adorn the pink and yellow walls; tasty Peruvian food makes the tables a treat. Try the specialty *arroz con mariscos* (rice with seafood). There's a good international wine list too.

Top End

ZONA 1

Restaurante Altuna (☎ 232-0669; 5a Av 12-31; mains US$9-13; ☺ noon-10:30pm Tue-Sat, noon-4:30pm Sun) This large and classy restaurant has the atmosphere of a private club. It has tables in several rooms that are off a skylighted patio. The specialties are seafood and Spanish dishes; service is both professional and welcoming.

ZONA 10

Tamarindos (☎ 360-2815; 11a Calle 2-19A; meals around US$15-20 including drinks; ☺ lunch Mon-Fri, dinner Mon-Sat) A chic and delicious Thai and Italian restaurant with a Guatemalan twist. The four-cheese gnocchi is irresistible, and the vegetarian pad Thai blends a thousand flavors. The stylish decor recalls New York – but the prices are Guatemalan.

Siriacos (☎ 334-6316; 1a Av 12-16; mains US$9.50-15; ☺ noon-3pm & 6-11pm Mon-Fri, 6-11pm Sat) Very near the Radisson Hotel, Siriacos is flashy but informal, with a sunken dining room and bar, a skylighted patio courtyard and a menu of continental specialties.

ZONA 9

Puerto Barrios (☎ 334-1302; 7a Av 10-65; mains US$12-16; ☺ noon-3pm & 7-11pm) The Puerto Barrios specializes in tasty prawn and fish dishes and is awash in nautical themes – paintings of buccaneers, portholes for windows, a big compass by the door. The waiters are no doubt thankful to have exchanged their former knee breeches and frogged coats for plain white shirts and bow ties, however.

DRINKING

Zona 1

Staggering from bar to bar about the darkened streets of Zona 1 is not recommended, but fortunately there's a clutch of good drinking places all within half a block of each other just south of the Parque Central.

Las Cien Puertas (Pasaje Aycinena 8-44, 9a Calle 6-45) This super-hip (but not studiously so) little watering hole is a gathering place for all manner of local creative types (and a few travelers) who may be debating politics, strumming a guitar or refining the graffiti when you show up. Tasty snacks such as tacos and quesadillas are served. It's in a shabby colonial arcade that's said to have a hundred doors (hence the name) and is sometimes closed off for live bands.

Cafe Kumbala (Pasaje Aycinena 8-51) Across the arcade, this is a neater bar with a big screen showing mellow music videos and sometimes movies.

El Portal (Portal del Comercio, 6a Av; ☺ 10am-10pm Mon-Sat) This atmospheric old drinking den serves fine draft beer (around US$2 a mug) and free tapas. Ché Guevara was once a patron. Sit at the long wooden bar or one of the wooden tables. Clients are mostly, but not exclusively, men. To find it, enter the Portal del Comercio arcade from 6a Av a few steps south of the Parque Central.

El Rincón del Centro (9a Calle 6-37) In every way a halfway house between El Portal and Pasaje Aycinena, this bar attracts a mixed crowd, from students to 30- and 40-somethings, all enjoying a few beers to recorded rock.

Zona 4

Several eateries in Cuatro Grados Norte (p69) double as bars and you'll find a lively, informal atmosphere in the second half of the week.

Zona 10

El Establo (14a Calle 5-08) This mellow watering hole attracts both foreigners and locals with its pub-style layout, three-sided, brass-topped bar, good pub food and enormous range of music spun by the German owners. Not cheap, though, at US$3 a Gallo.

ENTERTAINMENT

Wining and dining the night away in the Zona Viva is what many visitors do. Otherwise, consider taking in a movie at one of the multiscreen cinema complexes such as **Cines Tikal Futura** (Centro Comercial Tikal Futura; ☎ 440-3297; Calzada Roosevelt 22-43, Zona 11) or **Cines Próceres** (Centro Comercial Los Próceres; ☎ 332-8508; 16a Calle, Zona 10). Tickets cost between US$2 and US$4. Or check out the cultural events at the **Centro Cultural Miguel Ángel Asturias** (☎ 232-4042/3/4/5; 24a Calle 3-81, Zona 1). You'll find movie and some other listings in *Prensa Libre* newspaper. The Ministerio de Cultura y Deportes publishes a monthly what's-on bulletin, available free at the Palacio Nacional de la Cultura (p62).

Gay Venues

Don't get too excited about this heading: there are only a couple of places worthy of mention for men, and nothing much for women.

Pandora's Box (☎ 332-2823; Ruta 3 No 3-08, Zona 4; ☺ 9pm-1am Fri & Sat, 8am-1pm Sun) Has been hosting Guatemala's gay crowd since the '70s. Modernized a few years ago, it has two dance floors, a rooftop patio and a relaxed atmosphere with a mainly under-30 crowd. There's no entry charge. Zona 4 isn't the city's best section, so don't go a-wandering unaccompanied or late at night.

Ephebus (☎ 253-4119; 4a Calle 5-30, Zona 1; ☺ 9pm-3am Thu-Sat) A well-established gay disco-bar in a former private house near the city center, often with strippers.

El Encuentro (☎ 230-4459; Local 229, Centro Capitol, 6a Av 12-51, Zona 1; ☺ 5pm-midnight Mon-Sat) This quiet bar in the back of a noisy downtown mall is another gay meeting place.

Live Music

La Bodeguita del Centro (☎ 230-2976; 12a Calle 3-55, Zona 1) There's a hopping, creative local scene in Guatemala City, and this large, bohemian hangout is one of the best places to connect with it. Posters featuring the likes of Ché, Marley, Lennon, Victor Jara, Van Gogh and Pablo Neruda cover the walls from floor to ceiling. There's live music of some kind almost every night from Tuesday to Saturday, usually starting at 9pm, plus occasional poetry readings, films or forums. Entry is usually free Tuesday to Thursday, with a charge of US$2.50 to US$5 on Friday and Saturday nights. Food and drinks are served. Pick up a monthly schedule of events: local group Unicornio brews up a great party atmosphere for a varied crowd the last Friday and Saturday nights of each month.

Blue Town Cafe Bar (11a Calle 4-51, Zona 1) If La Bodeguita doesn't suit you, check out this nearby bar. It's a youthful spot with live bands.

TrovaJazz (Vía 6 No 3-55, Zona 4) Jazz and folk fans should look into what's happening at this establishment.

Nightclubs

Zona 10 has a bunch of clubs attracting 20-something local crowds along 13a Calle and adjacent streets such as 1a Av. For salsa and merengue, head for **Mr Jerry** (☎ 368-0101; 13a Calle 1-26, Zona 10).

SHOPPING

Mercado Central (9a Av btwn 6a & 8a Calles; ☺ 9am-6pm Mon-Sat, 9am-noon Sun) Until the quake of 1976, Mercado Central, behind the cathedral, was where locals shopped for food and other necessities. Reconstructed after the earthquake, it now deals in colorful Guatemalan handicrafts such as textiles, carved wood, metalwork, pottery, leather goods and basketry, and is a pretty good place to shop for these kinds of things, with reasonable prices.

Mercado de Artesanías (Crafts Market; ☎ 472-0208; cnr 5a Calle & 11a Av, Zona 13; ☺ 9:30am-6pm) This sleepy official market near the museums and zoo sells similar goods in less-crowded conditions.

For fashion boutiques, electronic goods and other first-world paraphernalia, head for the large shopping malls such as **Centro Comercial Los Próceres** (16a Calle, Zona 10) or **Centro Comercial Tikal Futura** (Calzada Roosevelt 22-43, Zona 11).

For a more everyday Guatemalan experience, take a walk along 6a Av between 8a and 16a Calles in Zona 1. This street is always choked with street stalls noisily hawking everything from cheap copied CDs to shoes, underwear and overalls.

GETTING THERE & AWAY
Air

Guatemala City's **Aeropuerto La Aurora** (☎ 334-7680, 331-7241/3, 334-7689) is the country's major airport. Nearly all international flights land and take off here. At the time of writing, the country's only scheduled domestic flights were between Guatemala City and Flores – a route operated daily by five airlines. The major carrier, Grupo TACA, makes two return flights daily (one in the morning, one in the afternoon), plus an extra flight four mornings a week that continues from

Flores to Cancún (Mexico) and returns from there via Flores in the afternoon. Tikal Airlines (Tikal Jets), Jungle Flying Tours, RACSA and TAG all fly from Guatemala to Flores in the morning (6am or 7am) and return in the afternoon. See p57 for contact details.

Tickets to Flores cost around US$90/125 one-way/round trip with Grupo TACA, US$90/112 with Tikal Airlines and US$70/100 with the others, but some travel agencies, especially in Antigua, offer large discounts on these prices.

Tikal Airlines goes from La Aurora's main terminal, known as the 'Aeropuerto Internacional' and set on the west side of the runways with its entrance on 11a Av, while the other three airlines go from the east side of the aerodrome, the so-called Aeropuerto Nacional, entered from Av Hincapié.

Bus

Buses from here run all over Guatemala and into Mexico, Belize, Honduras, El Salvador and beyond. Most bus companies have their own terminals, many of which are in Zona 1. The Terminal de Autobuses, in Zona 4, is used only by some 2nd-class buses. Here are details on services to domestic and international destinations:

Antigua (US$0.65, 1¼hr, 45km, departs every few minutes, 5am-9pm) Departs from the lot at 18a Calle and 4a Av, Zona 1.

Belize City, Belize Take a bus to Flores/Santa Elena and an onward bus from there.

Biotopo del Quetzal (US$4, 3½hr, 156km); Escobar y Monja Blanca (☎ 238-1409; 8a Av 15-16, Zona 1; departs hourly, 4am-5pm, via El Rancho and Purulhá)

Chetumal, Mexico Take a bus to Flores/Santa Elena, where daily buses depart for Chetumal; see p252.

Chichicastenango (US$1.55, 3hr, 145km, departs every 15-20min, 5am-5pm) Departs from the Terminal de Autobuses. Some buses also depart from the corner of 20a Calle and Av Bolívar, Zona 1.

Chiquimula (US$2.60, 3hr, 170km); Rutas Orientales (☎ 253-7282; 19 Calle 8-18, Zona 1; departs every 30min 4:30am-6pm); Transportes Guerra (☎ 238-2917; 19a Calle 8-39, Zona 1; departs every 30min 7am-6pm)

Ciudad Pedro de Alvarado/La Hachadura, El Salvador border Take a bus to Taxisco; some of these continue to the border; otherwise change at Taxisco. Buses leave Taxisco for the border about every 15min until about 5pm.

Ciudad Tecún Umán/Ciudad Hidalgo, Mexican border (US$5.25, 6hr, 250km); Fortaleza del Sur (☎ 230-

3390; 19a Calle 8-70, Zona 1; departs 20 times daily 12:15am-6:30pm)

Cobán (US$4.25, 4½hr, 213km); Escobar y Monja Blanca (☎ 238-1409; 8a Av 15-16, Zona 1; departs hourly 4am-5pm) Buses stop at El Rancho and the Biotopo del Quetzal.

Copán, Honduras (US$35, 5hr, 238km); Hedman Alas (☎ 362-5072/3/4; 2a Av 8-73, Zona 10; departs at 5am daily) First-class buses, which continue to San Pedro Sula and La Ceiba. It's cheaper, and slower, to take a bus to Chiquimula, then another to the border at El Florido, then another on to Copán.

El Carmen/Talismán, Mexican border (US$5.75, 7hr, 290km); Fortaleza del Sur (☎ 230-3390; 19a Calle 8-70, Zona 1; departs 20 times daily 12:15am-6:30pm)

Escuintla (US$1.25, 1hr, 57km) Various companies run about every 15min, 5am-6pm, from the Terminal de Autobuses.

Esquipulas (US$4, 4½hr, 222km); Rutas Orientales (☎ 253-7282; 19 Calle 8-18, Zona 1; departs every 30min, 4:30am-6pm)

Flores/Santa Elena (8-10hr, 500km); Fuente del Norte (☎ 251-3817; 17a Calle 8-46, Zona 1; departs 18 times daily, US$9-17 depending on the service); Línea Dorada (☎ 232-5506, 201-2710; 16a Calle 10-03, Zona 1; departs at 10am, US$23; 9pm, US$23; 10pm, US$12; and 10:30pm, US$17)

Huehuetenango (5hr, 266km); Los Halcones (☎ 238-1929; 7a Av 15-27, Zona 1; US$4, departs at 7am, 2pm and 5pm); Transportes Velásquez (☎ 221-1084; 20a Calle 1-37, Zona 1; US$2.60) All go by the Interamericana.

Jalapa (US$2, 3½hr, 167km); Transportes Melva (every 30min 4:15am-5:15pm) Via Cuilapa and Jutiapa. Departs from the Terminal de Autobuses.

La Democracia (US$1.50, 2hr, 92km); Chatía Gomerana (every 30min, 6am-4:30pm) Stops at Escuintla. Departs from the Terminal de Autobuses.

La Mesilla/Ciudad Cuauhtémoc, Mexican border (US$5.25, 8hr, 345km); Transportes Velásquez (☎ 221-1084; 20a Calle 1-37, Zona 1; every 2hr, 5:30am-1:30pm) From Ciudad Cuauhtémoc there are fairly frequent buses and vans on to Comitán and San Cristóbal de Las Casas.

Lívingston See Puerto Barrios and Río Dulce; from either place, you can reach Lívingston by boat (p237).

Melchor de Mencos, Belize border (US$10.50, 11hr, 600km); Fuente del Norte (☎ 251-3817; 17a Calle 8-46, Zona 1; departs 4 times daily) There's a special Maya de Oro service, US$17, at 10:30pm every two days.

Monterrico Take a bus to Taxisco, change there for a bus to La Avellana, and from La Avellana take a boat (p180).

Nebaj Take a bus to Santa Cruz del Quiché, and another from there.

Panajachel (US$2.10, 3½hr, 150km); Transportes Rébuli (☎ 230-2748; 21a Calle 1-34, Zona 1; departs hourly 7am-4pm) There's a Pullman service, US$3.25, at 9:30am.

ALFREDO MAIQUEZ

Palacio Nacional de la Cultura (p62), Guatemala City

ALFREDO MAIQUEZ

Postcard stand, **Zona 1** (p62), Guatemala City

High-rises, **Zona 10** (p57), Guatemala City

GREG JOHNSTON

View over Antigua to **Volcán Agua** (p85)

Looking through the **Arco de Santa Catalina** (p83) toward **La Merced church** (p83), Antigua

Streetscape, **Antigua** (p76)

Catedral de Santiago (p81), Antigua

Poptún ($US7-10.50, 6-7hr, 387km) Take a Fuente del Norte bus headed to Flores.

Puerto Barrios (US$5.25, 5hr, 295km); Litegua (☎ 232-7578; 15a Calle 10-40, Zona 1; departs 16 times daily 5am-5pm)

Puerto San José (US$2, 2½hr, 90km) Via Escuintla. Various companies run about every 15min, 5am-6pm, from the Terminal de Autobuses.

Quetzaltenango (US$4, 4hr, 205km); Transportes Álamo (☎ 251-4838; 21a Calle 0-14, Zona 1; departs 6 times daily btwn 8am and 5:30pm) Líneas América (☎ 232-1432; 2a Av 18-47, Zona 1; departs 7 times daily, 5am-7:30pm); Transportes Galgos (☎ 253-4868; 7a Av 19-44, Zona 1; departs 7 times daily, 5:30am-7pm); Transportes Marquensita (☎ 230-0067; 1a Av 21-31, Zona 1; departs 8 times daily, 6:30am-5pm) All these are Pullman services.

Quiriguá Take a Puerto Barrios bus. (For details on getting from the highway to the Quiriguá ruins, see p222)

Retalhuleu (US$4, 3hr, 196km); Fortaleza del Sur (☎ 230-3390; 19 Calle 8-70, Zona 1; departs 20 times daily 12:15am-6:30pm)

Río Dulce (US$5.25, 6hr, 280km); Litegua (☎ 232-7578; 15a Calle 10-40, Zona 1; departs 6am, 9am, 11:30am and 1pm) Flores-bound buses stop at Río Dulce too.

Salamá (US$2-2.50, 3hr, 150km); Transportes Dulce María (☎ 253-4318; 17a Calle 11-32, Zona 1; departs every 30min 5am-5pm)

San Salvador, El Salvador (5-6hr, 240km) Melva Internacional (☎ 331-0874; 3a Av 1-38, Zona 9; via the border at Valle Nuevo; US$8, departs hourly 5am-4pm; and especiales, US$10, at 6:45am, 9am and 3pm); Tica Bus (☎ 331-4279, 361-1773; 11a Calle 2-74, Zona 9; US$9.50, departs at 1pm); King Quality & Confort Lines (☎ 369-0404/56; 18a Av 1-96, Zona 15; US$19.50, luxury bus departs 6:30am, 8am, 2pm and 3:30pm); Pullmantur (☎ 367-4746; Holiday Inn, 1a Av 13-22, Zona 10; US$28/45 ejecutiva/primera clase, luxury bus departures at 7am, 8:30am Sunday, and 3pm)

Santa Cruz del Quiché (US$2.10, 3½hr, 163km, departs every 15-20min, 5am-5pm) Departs from the Terminal de Autobuses. Some buses also depart from the corner of 20a Calle and Av Bolívar, Zona 1.

Santa Elena See Flores/Santa Elena.

Santa Lucía Cotzumalguapa Take a bus to Escuintla and another from there.

Santiago Atitlán (US$2.60, 4hr, 165km) Buses from the Atitlán and Esmeralda companies depart hourly 4am-2pm from the corner of 20a Calle and 8a Av, Zona 1.

Sayaxché Fuente del Norte (☎ 251-3817; 17a Calle 8-46, Zona 1) Via Río Dulce and Flores (departs at 4pm, US$10.50, and 7pm, US$13, 11hr, 560km) Via Cobán (US$10.50, 10hr, 420km, departs 5.30pm)

Tapachula, Mexico (6-7hr, 290km); Transportes Galgos (☎ 253-4868, 232-3661; 7a Av 19-44, Zona 1; US$21.50, departs 7:30am and 2pm); Línea Dorada

(☎ 232-5506; 16a Calle 10-03, Zona 1; US$18, departs 8am); Tica Bus (☎ 331-4279; 11a Calle 2-74, Zona 9; US$17.50, departs noon)

Taxisco (US$2, 2hr, every 30min 5am-4pm) Departs from Terminal de Autobuses.

Tecpán (US$1, 2hr, 92km) Veloz Poaquileña (cnr 20a Calle & Av Bolívar, Zona 1; departs every 30min, 5:30am-7pm)

Tegucigalpa, Honduras (US$52, 12hr, 700km) Hedman Alas (☎ 362-5072/3/4; 2a Av 8-73, Zona 10; departs 5am)

Tikal Take a bus to Flores/Santa Elena, and onward transport from there.

Car

Most major rental companies have offices both at La Aurora airport (in the arrivals area) and in Zona 9 or 10. Companies include the following:

Ahorrent (www.ahorrent.com) Zona 9 (☎ 361-5661; Boulevard Liberación 4-83); Aeropuerto Internacional La Aurora (☎ 362-8921/2)

Avis (www.avisenlinea.com in Spanish) Zona 9 ☎ 339-3249; 6a Av 7-64); Aeropuerto Internacional La Aurora (☎ 331-0017)

Dollar (www.dollarguatemala.com) Zona 10 (☎ 332-7525; Av La Reforma 8-33); Aeropuerto Internacional La Aurora (☎ 339-4724)

Hertz (www.hertz.com.gt) Zona 9 (☎ 332-2242; 7a Av 14-76); Westin Camino Real (☎ 368-0107); Holiday Inn (☎ 332-2555); Guatemala City Marriott Hotel (☎ 339-7777); Hotel Real Inter-Continental Guatemala (☎ 379-4444); Aeropuerto Internacional La Aurora (☎ 331-1711, 339-2631)

Tabarini (www.tabarini.com) Zona 10 (☎ 331-6108; 2a Calle A 7-30); Aeropuerto Internacional La Aurora (☎ 331-4755)

Tally Renta Autos (www.tallyrentaautos.com) Zona 1 ☎ 232-0421/3327; 7a Av 14-60); Aeropuerto Internacional La Aurora (☎ 332-6063)

Thrifty (☎ 333-7444; thrifty@intelnet.gt; 1a Av 13-74, Zona 10)

Shuttle Minibus

Shuttle services from Guatemala City to popular destinations such as Panajachel and Chichicastenango (both around US$20) are offered by travel agencies in Antigua such as Sin Fronteras and Adventure Travel Center (p79).

GETTING AROUND
To/From the Airport

Aeropuerto La Aurora is in Zona 13, in the southern part of the city, 10 to 15 minutes from Zona 1 by taxi, half an hour by bus.

For the city bus, cross the road outside the arrivals exit and climb the steps. At the top, with your back to the terminal building, walk to the left down the approach road (about 100m), then turn right to the bus stop. Bus No 83 'Terminal' and No 83 'Bolívar' go to the Parque Central in Zona 1, passing through Zonas 9 and 4 en route: you can get off at any corner along the way. No 83 'Terminal' goes up 7a Av through Zonas 9, 4 and 1; No 83 'Bolívar' goes via Av Bolívar and then 5a Av. Both run about every 15 minutes, 6am to 9pm, and cost US$0.15. Going from the city center to the airport, No 83 'Aeropuerto' goes south through Zona 1 on 10a Av, south through Zonas 4 and 9 on 6a Av, passes by the west end of La Aurora Zoo and the Zona 13 museums and stops right in front of the international terminal. It then continues southward passing close to all the Zona 13 guesthouses.

Door-to-door shuttle minibuses run from the airport to any address in Antigua (usually US$10 per person, one hour). Look for signs in the airport exit hall or people holding up 'Antigua Shuttle' signs. The first shuttle leaves for Antigua about 7am and the last around 8pm or 9pm.

Taxis wait outside the airport's arrivals exit. Official fares are posted on a sign here (US$6 to US$7 to Zona 9 or 10, US$8 to Zona 1, US$25 to Antigua), but in reality you may have to pay a bit more – US$8 to US$9 to Zona 1, US$30 to Antigua. Be sure to establish the destination and price before getting in. A tip is expected. Prices for taxis *to* the airport, hailed on the street, are likely to be lower – around US$6 from Zona 1. For Antigua, shuttle minibuses are more economical than taxis if there's only one or two of you

Bus & Jitney

If you spend any time out and about in Guatemala City, especially Zona 1, its buses will become a major feature of your existence as they roar along in large numbers belching great clouds of black smoke. Jets flying low

over the city center intermittently intensify the cacophony. Still, Guatemala City buses are cheap, frequent and, though often very crowded, useful. They are not, however, always safe. Theft and robbery are not unusual; there have even been murders on board. Buses cost US$0.15 per ride: you pay the driver as you get on.

To get from Zona 1 to Zona 10, take bus No 82 or 101 southbound on 10a Av between 8a and 13a Calles. These buses swing west to travel south down 6a Av for 1km or so before swinging southeast along Ruta 6 (Zona 4) then south along Av La Reforma. For the main Inguat tourist office, get off on 6a Av at 22a Calle (Zona 1) and walk east along 22a Calle, then south down the far (east) side of 7a Av.

Traveling north *to* Zona 1, bus Nos 82 and 101 go along Av La Reforma then 7a Av, Zona 4 (passing right by Inguat) and 9a Av, Zona 1.

To get to the Terminal de Autobuses in Zona 4 by city bus, it makes sense simply to get any bus that's going south through Zona 4 on 6a Av (such as No 83 'Aeropuerto' – above) or north through Zona 4 on 7a Av (such as No 83 'Terminal' – above), then walk a few blocks west to the terminal. This saves you getting caught in the snarl-ups around the terminal itself. The same holds true in reverse if you want to get away from the Terminal de Autobuses by city bus.

City buses stop running about 9pm, and *ruteleros* (jitneys) begin to run up and down the main avenues. Jitneys run all night, until the buses resume their rattling rides at 5am. Hold up your hand at a street corner to stop a jitney or bus.

Taxi

Plenty of taxis cruise most parts of the city. Fares are negotiable: always establish your destination and fare before getting in. Zona 1 to Zona 10, or vice-versa, costs around US$4 to US$5. If you want to phone for a taxi, **Taxi Amarillo Express** (☎ 332-1515, 470-1515) has metered cabs that often work out cheaper than others.

Antigua

With its cobblestone streets, sprays of bougainvillea bursting from crumbling ruins, and pastel facades under terracotta roofs, Antigua Guatemala is one of the oldest and most beautiful cities in the Americas. Its setting, beneath three dramatic volcanoes, Agua (3766m), Fuego (3763m) and Acatenango (3976m), is majestic. Fuego erupted most recently in 2002, providing spectacular light shows, and was still smoking merrily in 2003.

Many seasoned Guatemala travelers head straight to Antigua from Guatemala City airport. The city has a pan-international feel, being among the most popular Latin American cities for studying Spanish, with around 75 schools. It's particularly thronged with gringos from June to August, and you can dine in French restaurants or watch football from home on TV any day. But Antigua is still, in its own way, Guatemalan. Check out market days (Monday, Thursday and Saturday) or go for a sunrise stroll through the sleepy streets and you'll see.

Perhaps the most exciting time to visit Antigua is Semana Santa (Easter week), especially on Good Friday. This takes some advance planning, however, as this is the busiest week of the year for tourism: make hotel reservations at least two months prior. The quietest months, though not drastically so, are May, June, September and October. Antigua is cold after sunset, especially between September and March, so bring warm clothes.

Antigua residents are known by the nickname *panza verde* (green belly), as they are said to eat lots of avocados, which grow abundantly here.

TOP FIVE

- Looking down on active Volcán Fuego from the 3976m summit of **Acatenango** (p85)
- **Studying Spanish** (p86) with well-trained teachers at one of Guatemala's best language schools
- Sampling the broadest range of good **restaurants** (p92) and **bars** (p94) Guatemala has to offer
- Soaking up **history** (p81) in Antigua's museums and lovely colonial monasteries, mansions, churches and convents
- **Shopping** (p96) for Mayan crafts, fine jewelry or fruit and nuts

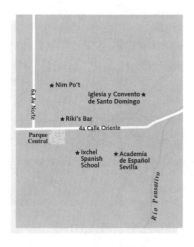

- ELEVATION: 1530M
- POPULATION: 40,000

HISTORY

Antigua was founded on March 10, 1543, as La muy Noble y muy Leal Ciudad de Santiago de los Caballeros de Goathemala, the Spanish colonial capital of Guatemala, after the 1541 flooding of the previous capital, which was at present-day Ciudad Vieja (p98) on the flanks of Volcán Agua. During the 17th and 18th centuries, little expense was spared on the city's magnificent architecture. At its peak Antigua had no fewer than 38 churches, including a cathedral. In 1776, after the great earthquake of July 29, 1773, destroyed Antigua (which had already suffered considerable damage from earlier quakes), the capital was transferred again, this time to Guatemala City. Antigua was evacuated and plundered for building materials, but it never completely emptied of people, and began to grow again around 1830, by then known as La Antigua Guatemala (Old Guatemala). Renovation of battered old buildings helped maintain the city's colonial character. In 1944 President Jorge Ubico declared Antigua a national monument, and in 1979 Unesco designated it a World Heritage Site.

ORIENTATION

Volcán Agua is south of the city and visible from most points within it; Volcán Fuego and Volcán Acatenango are to the southwest (Acatenango is the more northerly of the two). These three volcanoes provide easy reference points.

Antigua's focal point is the broad and beautiful Parque Central. Few places in town are more than 15 minutes' walk from here. The city's street-naming system is unusual in that it has no *zonas* (zones), and compass points are added to the numbered Calles and Avs, indicating whether an address is *Norte* (north), *Sur* (south), *Poniente* (west) or *Oriente* (east) of the Parque Central.

Another famous Antigua landmark is the Arco de Santa Catalina, an arch spanning 5a Av Norte 2½ blocks north of the Parque Central, on the way to La Merced church. This is one of the few Antigua constructions that withstood the 1773 earthquake.

Buses arrive at and depart from the streets around the market, about 400m west of the Parque Central.

INFORMATION
Bookstores

El Cofre (6a Calle Poniente 26) Second-hand books, mainly in English.

Hamlin y White (☎ 832-7075; 4a Calle Oriente 12A) New and used books in several languages, including many Lonely Planet titles.

Librería Casa del Conde (Portal del Comercio 4) This store has new books on Guatemala and the Maya in several languages; carries International Travel Maps and some used books.

Rainbow Reading Room (7a Av Sur 8) Thousands of used books in English and Spanish for sale, rent or trade.

Un Poco de Todo (☎ 832-4676; 5a Av Norte 10A) New books in English and Spanish.

ANTIGUA IN...

Two Days

Start with breakfast in colonial surroundings at **Café Condesa**, then drop by one of our recommended agencies to set up a volcano trip for tomorrow – Acatenango if you can afford it, Pacaya otherwise. Spend the day exploring some of Antigua's colonial buildings – the **cathedral**, **Santo Domingo**, **Las Capuchinas**, **La Merced** – with a light lunch along the way. Eat a great Italian dinner at **El Punto** then check out **Riki's Bar**. Don't stay out too late: in the morning you leave early for your **volcano**. Afterwards enjoy the dinner you've earned at **Mesón Panza Verde** (or **Helas** or **Cafe La Escudilla** for tighter budgets), followed by a couple of drinks at **Monoloco** or **Reilly's** or **Fridas**. Round things off, if you still can, with a shimmy at **La Casbah**.

Four Days

Follow the two-day itinerary, then visit the **Centro Cultural La Azotea** at Jocotenango on day three. At night take in tacos at **Tacool**, the best **movie** you can find, and a drink at **Onis** (in any order!). On day four reactivate with an out-of-town **guided walk** or **bike ride** or **horse ride**. Watch the sun go down from **Café Sky** before enjoying food and the lounge scene at **Perú Café**. Then revisit your favorite bar…

Emergency

Bomberos Municipales (Municipal Firefighters; ☎ 831-0049)

Bomberos Voluntarios (Volunteer Firefighters; ☎ 832-0234)

Policía Municipal de Turismo (Municipal Tourism Police; ☎ 832-7290; Palacio del Ayuntamiento, 4a Av Norte; ☉ 24hr). The helpful tourism police will go with you to the national police and assist with the formalities including any translating that needs to be done.

Policía Nacional Civil (National Civil Police; ☎ 832-0251; Palacio de los Capitanes, Parque Central) Formal reports to the police about a crime or loss should be made to the Policía Nacional Civil.

Internet Access

Antigua has many affordable Internet services. Among the best for price, connection quality and convenience are the following:

Aló Internet (5a Calle Poniente 28) US$1 an hour.

Cafe Internet de Telgua (6a Av Norte 21B; ☉ 9am-8pm Mon-Fri, 9am-5pm Sat, 11am-5pm Sun)

Conexion (☎ 832-3768; fax 832-0082; users@conexion .com.gt; Centro Comercial La Fuente, 4a Calle Oriente 14; ☉ 8:30am-7:30pm) All-purpose communications center with Internet access for US$1.30 an hour (US$2 an hour to hook up your laptop) plus printing, photocopying and CD-burning services. Can set up dial-in Internet access for those with a phone line, computer and modem (see p280).

El Cofre (6a Calle Poniente 26) US$1 an hour.

El Naufrago (5a Av Norte 30A; ☉ 8:30am-10pm) US$1.30 an hour.

Enlaces (☎ 832-5555; 6a Av Norte 1; ☉ 8am-7:30pm Mon-Sat, 8am-1pm Sun) Internet US$1.30 an hour; good connections, smoking & nonsmoking areas.

Enlínea (5a Av Sur 12) US$1 an hour.

Funky Monkey (Pasaje El Corregidor, 5a Av Sur 6) US$1 an hour.

Internet Cafe (Hotel Convento Santa Catalina Mártir, 5a Av Norte 28; ☉ 8am-10pm) US$1.60 an hour; some of the most reliable connections in town.

Nueva Er@ (6a Av Norte 34 & 39) US$1.30 an hour.

Laundry

Laundries are everywhere, especially along 6a Calle Poniente.

Lavandería Dry Clean (6a Calle Poniente 49; ☉ 7am-7pm Mon-Sat, 9am-6pm Sun) Charges US$3.75 a load.

Quick Laundry (☎ 832-2937; 6a Calle Poniente 14; ☉ 8am-5pm Mon-Sat) Fast and reliable and charges US$3.25 to wash and dry a 5lb (2.25kg) load.

Medical Services

Casa de los Nahuales (☎ 832-0068; 3a Av Sur 6) Offers alternative medical and spiritual services, including Mayan horoscopes, massages, aromatherapy and Bach flower remedies.

Casa de Salud Santa Lucía (☎ 832-3122; Calzada de Santa Lucía Sur 7) If possible, you're probably best going to a private hospital such as Casa de Salud Santa Lucía.

Hospital Nacional Pedro de Betancourth (☎ 832-2801) This public hospital in San Felipe, 2km north of the center, has an emergency service.

Hospital Reina de los Ángeles (☎ 832-2258; Calle Ancha de los Herreros 59) Another private hospital.

Ixmucane (☎ 832-5539; womanway@aol.com; 4a Av Norte 32) Provides a complete range of gynecological and obstetrical services, from dispensing birth control to delivering babies. Herbal supplements, treatment and information are available here too, in English and Spanish.

Obras Sociales de Hermano Pedro (Hospital San Pedro; ☎ 832-0883; 6a Calle Oriente 20) This is the more central of Antigua's two public hospitals, but it has no emergency service. It's primarily a refuge for the handicapped, elderly and abused, but does give medical consultations.

Money

Bancafé (4a Calle Poniente 22) Has a Visa ATM.

Banco Industrial (5a Av Sur 4; ☉ 9am-7pm Mon-Fri, 9am-5pm Sat) Has a Visa ATM and changes US dollars (cash and traveler's checks).

Banco del Quetzal (4a Calle facing Parque Central; ☉ 8:30am-7pm Mon-Fri, 9am-1pm Sat & Sun) Often has the best rates and has a MasterCard ATM outside. Also changes US dollars (cash and traveler's checks).

Credomatic (Portal del Comercio; ☉ 9am-7pm Mon-Fri, 9am-1pm Sat) Gives Visa and MasterCard cash advances. Changes US dollars (cash and traveler's checks).

LAX Travel (☎ /fax 832-1621, 832-2674; laxantigua@ intelnet.net.gt; 3a Calle Poniente 12) You can change cash euros here.

Lloyds TSB (cnr 4a Calle Oriente & 4a Av Norte; ☉ 9am-3:30pm Mon-Fri, 9:30am-12:30pm Sat) Gives Visa and MasterCard cash advances. Changes US dollars (cash and traveler's checks).

Visa & MasterCard ATM (5a Av Norte) Facing Parque Central.

Post

Post office (cnr 4a Calle Poniente & Calzada de Santa Lucía) West of the Parque Central, near the market.

If you want to ship packages, the following offer door-to-door service:

Airborne Express (☎ 832-1696; 6a Av Sur 12)

Envíos Etc (2a Calle Poniente 3)

Federal Express (2a Calle Poniente 3)

Quickbox (☎ 832-3825; 6a Calle Poniente 7)

UPS (☎ 832-0073; 6a Calle Poniente 34)

Telephone & Fax

Many businesses, including several cyber-cafés, offer cut-rate international calls. Some of these are by Internet telephone – very cheap, but line quality is unpredictable.

Nueva Er@, **Funky Monkey** and **Internet Cafe** (Hotel Convento Santa Catalina Mártir, 5a Av Norte 28; 8am-10pm) These three cybercafés offer Internet calls anywhere in the world for US$0.15 to US$0.40 a minute (p78).

Conexion (☎ 832-3768; fax 832-0082; users@conexion .com.gt; Centro Comercial La Fuente, 4a Calle Oriente 14; 8:30am-7:30pm) Charges US$0.40 a minute to the USA or Canada and US$0.80 to Europe.

Enlaces (☎ 832-5555; 6a Av Norte 1; 8am-7:30pm Mon-Sat, 8am-1pm Sun) Calls from here are a little more expensive than at other places; faxes sent from here cost US$1.30 to US$2.60 per page.

Guatemala Ventures (☎ /fax 832-3383; 1a Av Sur 15) Rents cell phones, on which you can call the US for US$0.10 a minute or Europe for US$0.20, for US$10 a week (with a US$50 deposit).

Western Union Kall Shop (6a Av Sur 12; Mon-Fri 8:30am-6pm, Sat 8:30am-4pm) You pay US$0.45 a minute to call the US or Canada, US$0.65 to Mexico, Central America or Europe, US$0.75 to South America and US$0.90 to anywhere else.

Tourist Information

Inguat (☎ 832-0763; Palacio de los Capitanes, Parque Central; 8am-12:30pm & 2:30-5pm Mon-Fri, 9am-12:30pm & 2:30-5pm Sat & Sun) This tourist office has free city maps, bus information and schedules of Semana Santa events, and the staff will try to find the answers to any poser you might throw at them.

Antigua Guatemala: The City and Its Heritage This book, by long-time Antigua resident Elizabeth Bell, is well worth picking up at a bookstore: it describes all the city's important buildings and museums, and neatly encapsulates Antigua's history and fiestas.

Travel Agencies

Everywhere you go in Antigua, you'll come across travel agencies. These agencies offer international flights, shuttle minibuses, tours to interesting sites around Antigua and elsewhere in Guatemala, and more. Reputable travel agencies include the following:

Adventure Travel Center (☎ /fax 832-0162; viareal@ guate.net; 5a Av Norte 25B)

Antigua Tours (☎ /fax 832-5821; www.antiguatours .net; Portal de Santo Domingo, 3a Calle Oriente 28) Inside the Casa Santo Domingo Hotel.

Atitrans (☎ 832-3371; www.mundo-guatemala.com; 6a Av Sur 8)

Aviatur (☎ /fax 832-5989; aviaturfer@yahoo.com.mx; 5a Av Norte 34)

El Condor Expeditions (☎ 498-9812, 496-9567; 4a Calle Poniente 34)

LAX Travel (☎ /fax 832-1621, 832-2674; laxantigua@ intelnet.net.gt; 3a Calle Poniente 12) An international flight specialist.

Monarcas Travel (☎ 832-1939; Calzada de Santa Lucía 7) Operates shuttles to Copán and elsewhere.

National Travel (☎ 832-8383; antigua@nationalgua .com; 6a Av Sur 1A) Offers one-way flights, including student and teacher fares.

Rainbow Travel Center (☎ /fax 832-4202; rainbow travel@gua.gbm.net; 7a Av Sur 8) A specialty here is student and teacher air fares.

Sin Fronteras (☎ 832-1017; www.sinfront.com; 5a Av Norte 15A) Sells one-way international air tickets; issues student and youth cards for US$8; sells International Travel Maps; runs tours to Cuba among other destinations.

STA Travel (☎ 832-3985; istranti@intelnet.net.gt; 6a Calle Poniente 25) Offers student and teacher air fares and a change-of-date and lost-ticket-replacement service for tickets issued by student/youth travel agencies; issues student, teacher and youth cards for US$8.

Viajes Tivoli (☎ 832-1370, 832-4274; antigua@tivoli .com.gt; 4a Calle Oriente 10, local 3)

Vision Travel & Information Services (☎ 832-3293, 832-1962; fax 832-1955; www.guatemalainfo.com; Casa de Mito, 3a Av Norte 3) Tours ranging from Tikal to local coffee *fincas* (plantations) are offered here, as are shuttle services and many guidebooks (including Lonely Planet titles) to buy or simply read on the spot.

Voyageur Tours (☎ 832-4237; www.travel.net.gt; Centro Comercial La Fuente, 4a Calle Oriente 14) Operates some good-value shuttle minibus services.

Volunteer Work

AmeriSpan Guatemala (☎ 832-0164; fax 832-1896; www.amerispan.com; 6a Av Norte 40A) Can hook you up with volunteer opportunities all over Guatemala. It charges a US$60 registration fee.

Proyecto Mosaico Guatemala (☎ /fax 932-0955; www.pmg.dk; Casa de Mito, 3a Av Norte 3; 2-4pm Mon-Fri) This is a nonprofit organization providing volunteers and resources to over 60 projects in Guatemala. Its resource center in the Casa de Mito has information on these projects and matches up volunteers with projects. It's very interested in people with medical experience but there's work for periods from one week to one year doing things as varied as carpentry, teaching, environmental protection, helping HIV-positive kids and organic farming. You need to be at least 18 and fit.

DANGERS & ANNOYANCES

Though you'll probably never have a problem, be wary when walking empty streets late

ANTIGUA

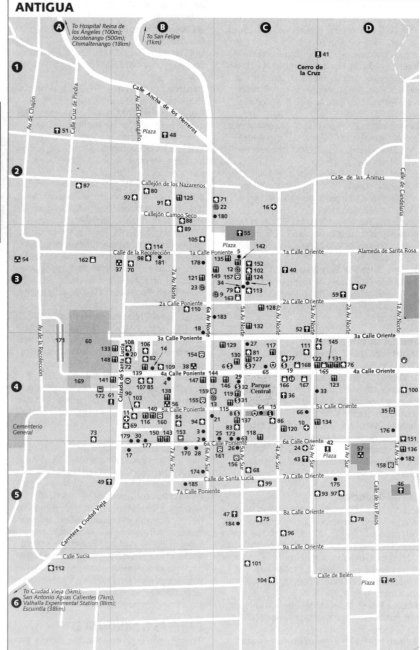

ANTIGUA

A To Hospital Reina de los Ángeles (100m); Jocotenango (500m); Chimaltenango (18km)

B To San Felipe (1km)

C

D

1

41

Cerro de la Cruz

Calle Ancha de los Herreros

Av de Chajón

Calle Cruz de Piedra

Av del Desengaño

2

51

Plaza

48

Calle de las Ánimas

Calle de Candelaria

87

Callejón de los Nazarenos

80

92

91

125

71

@ 22

● 180

16 **✚**

Callejón Campo Seco

88

89

105

55

Plaza

142

3

54

162

114

Calle de la Recolección

1a Calle Poniente

178 ●

5

135

152

1a Calle Oriente

Alameda de Santa Rosa

98

181

37 **70**

12 @

102

124

40

67

Av de la Recolección

7a Av Norte

121

23 @

149 **157**

34

79

9

163

1

113

59

2a Calle Poniente

110

6a Av Norte

● **183**

5a Av Norte

128

4a Av Norte

3a Av Norte

2a Calle Oriente

132

52

2a Av Norte

1a Av Norte

3a Calle Poniente

18

129

● **27**

117

74

145

3a Calle Oriente

171

60

108

106

14

133

20

148

82

72

139

109

154

130

81

7

6 **S**

77

19

111

122 **131**

168

165

76

4a Calle Oriente

Calzada de Santa Lucía

4a Calle Poniente

144

38

147

29

146

159

119

13

32

Parque Central

166

167

33

123

169

141

107 **85**

4

138

56

36

90

103

● **33**

100

172 **61**

5a Calle Poniente

115

8

64 **15**

66 ●

5a Calle Oriente

35

11

140

116 **160**

84

94

21

137

86

10

120

134

176 ●

69

73

179 **30**

150 **143** **153**

3

25 **173**

83

63

118

6a Calle Oriente

24

42

57

151

136

17

177

170 **28**

2

6a Calle Poniente

26

161

43

Plaza

158

182

174 ●

156

68

7a Calle Oriente

175

46

49

185

7a Calle Poniente

99

93 **97**

Calle de los Pasos

5

Cementerio General

47

184 ●

75

8a Calle Oriente

78

96

9a Calle Oriente

Calle Sucia

112

101

104

Calle de Belén

Plaza

45

6 To Ciudad Vieja (5km); San Antonio Aguas Calientes (7km); Valhalla Experimental Station (8km); Escuintla (38km)

Carretera a Ciudad Vieja

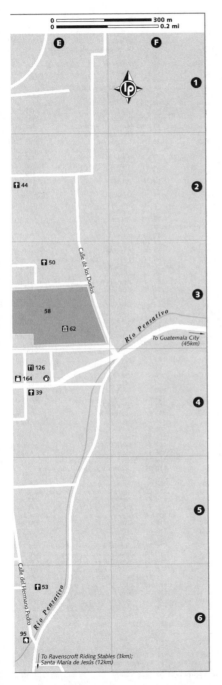

at night, especially away from the center, as robberies have taken place. Pickpocketing is rife during Semana Santa: even more than at other times of year, don't carry anything you don't immediately need. Armed robberies have occurred in the past on Cerro de la Cruz and in the Cementerio General, but crime in these places has effectively ceased since the formation in 1996 of the Policía Municipal de Turismo (p78), who provide free escorts to both sites and to some of the ruins around town. Some of the volcanoes visited from Antigua, especially Pacaya and Agua (p85), have also been the scene of robberies.

SIGHTS
Parque Central
This broad and beautiful plaza, easily the loveliest in the country, is the gathering place for *Antigüeños* and visitors alike – a fine, verdant place to sit or stroll and observe Antigua happening around you, from hawkers and shoe-shiners to school kids and groups of tourists. The famous central fountain is a 1936 reconstruction of the original 1738 version.

PALACIO DE LOS CAPITANES
Dating from 1558, the **Captain-Generals' Palace** was the governmental center of all Central America from Chiapas to Costa Rica until 1773. It didn't gain its stately double-arcaded facade, which marches proudly along the southern side of the park, until the early 1760s, however. Today the palace houses the Inguat tourist office, the national police and the office of the governor of Sacatepéquez department.

CATHEDRAL
On the east side of the park, **Catedral de Santiago** (admission US$0.40; ☺ 9am-5pm) was begun in 1542, demolished in 1668, rebuilt between 1669 and 1680, repeatedly damaged by earthquakes, wrecked in 1773, and only partly rebuilt between 1780 and 1820. The present cathedral, without its expensive original decoration, occupies only the entrance hall of the 17th-century edifice, and strictly speaking is not a cathedral but the Parroquia (Parish Church) de San José. It's most striking at night when it is tastefully lit. More interesting by day are the remains of the main part of the

ANTIGUA

cathedral, entered from 5a Calle Oriente, with massive columns, tall arches and underground crypts. Conquistador Pedro de Alvarado, his wife Beatriz de la Cueva, their daughter Leonora de Alvarado, Guatemala's first bishop Francisco Marroquín, and the conquistador (and historian of the Spanish conquest) Bernal Díaz del Castillo were all buried beneath the main altar, though their bones went astray at some stage in history. Behind the main altar, steps lead down to a former crypt now serving as a chapel, with a smoke-blackened Christ.

PALACIO DEL AYUNTAMIENTO

The **City Hall**, on the north side of the park, dates mostly from 1743. In addition to town offices, it houses the **Museo de Santiago** (☎ 832-2868; admission US$1.30; ☺ 9am-4pm Tue-Fri, 9am-noon & 2-4pm Sat & Sun), in the former town jail, exhibiting furnishings, artifacts and weapons mainly from colonial times. Next door is the **Museo del Libro Antiguo** (Old Book Museum; ☎ 832-5511; admission US$1.30; ☺ 9am-4pm Tue-Fri, 9am-noon & 2-4pm Sat & Sun), which has exhibits of colonial printing and binding, including a replica of Guatemala's first printing press, which began work here in the 1660s.

UNIVERSIDAD DE SAN CARLOS

The **San Carlos University**, now in Guatemala City, was founded in Antigua in 1676; what used to be its main building (built in 1763), half a block east of the park, houses the **Museo de Arte Colonial** (☎ 832-0429; 5a Calle Oriente 5; admission US$3.25; ☺ 9am-4pm Tue-Fri, 9am-noon & 2-4pm Sat & Sun), with some expressive sculptures of saints and paintings by leading Mexican artists of the colonial era, such as Miguel Cabrera and Juan de Correa.

Churches & Monasteries

Once glorious in their gilded baroque finery, Antigua's churches have suffered indignities from both nature and humankind. Rebuilding after earthquakes gave the churches thicker walls, lower towers and belfries and unembellished interiors, and moving the capital to Guatemala City deprived Antigua of the population needed to maintain the churches in their traditional richness. Still, they are impressive. In addition to those churches mentioned below, you'll find many others scattered around town in various states of decay. The Policía Municipal de Turismo (see Emergency, p78) will provide free escorts to some of the outlying monuments, where robberies have sometimes occurred.

IGLESIA Y CONVENTO DE NUESTRA SEÑORA DE LA MERCED

From the Parque Central, walk three long blocks along 5a Av Norte, passing beneath the **Arco de Santa Catalina**, which was built in 1694 (to enable nuns to cross the street without being seen) and rebuilt with its clock tower in the 19th century. At the northern end of 5a Av is La Merced – Antigua's most striking colonial church.

La Merced's construction began in 1548. The most recent of its several bouts of rebuilding has taken place since the 1976 earthquake. Inside the **monastery ruins** (admission US$0.40; ☺ 9am-6:30pm) is a fountain 27m in diameter, said to be the largest in Hispanic America. It's in the shape of a water lily (traditionally a symbol of power for Mayan lords), and lily motifs also appear on the church's entrance arch, suggesting the influence of indigenous laborers used to construct La Merced. There are pretty views from the upper level of the monastery. A candlelit procession, accompanied by much bell ringing and firecrackers, starts and ends here on the last Thursday evening of each month.

IGLESIA DE SAN FRANCISCO

Little of the original 16th-century **Iglesia de San Francisco** (east end of 8a Calle) remains, but reconstruction and restoration over the centuries have produced a handsome structure. In the north transept is the tomb of Santo Hermano Pedro de San José de Betancurt (1626–67), a Franciscan monk who founded a hospital for the poor in Antigua and earned the gratitude of generations. He's Guatemala's most venerated local Christian figure, and was made a saint in 2002 when Pope John Paul II visited Guatemala. His intercession is still sought by the ill, who pray fervently by the tomb. On the south side of the church are the **Museo del Hermano Pedro** and the ruins of the adjoining **monastery** (joint admission US$0.40; ☺ 8am-5pm): the museum houses relics from the church and the Santo Hermano's curiously well-preserved personal belongings.

ANTIGUA

LAS CAPUCHINAS

Inaugurated in 1736 by nuns from Madrid, **Las Capuchinas** (Iglesia y Convento de Nuestra Señora del Pilar de Zaragoza; cnr 2a Av Norte & 2a Calle Oriente; students/others US$2/4; 9am-5pm) was seriously damaged by the 1773 earthquake and thereafter abandoned. Restoration began in 1943 and continues today. The building has many unusual features, including a unique tower-like building of 18 nuns' cells built around a circular patio.

IGLESIA Y CONVENTO DE LA RECOLECCIÓN

The massive **La Recolección** (La Recolección; Av de la Recolección; students/others US$2/4; 9am-5pm) is among Antigua's most impressive monuments. Built between 1701 and 1715, the church was inaugurated in 1717, but suffered considerable damage from an earthquake that same year. The buildings were destroyed in the earthquake of 1773: enormous chunks of masonry still lie jumbled around the ruined church.

COLEGIO DE SAN JERÓNIMO

Built in 1757, the **Colegio de San Jerónimo** (Real Aduana; cnr Calzada de Santa Lucía & 1a Calle Poniente; students/others US$2/4; 9am-5pm) was used as a school by friars of the Merced order. But because it did not have royal authorization, it was taken over in 1761 by Spain's Carlos III, and in 1765 designated for use as the Real Aduana (Royal Customs House). The handsome cloister centers on a lovely octagonal fountain – an evocative setting for various dance and other cultural performances.

IGLESIA Y CONVENTO DE SANTA CLARA

First completed in 1702, **Santa Clara's** (2a Av Sur 27; students/others US$2/4; 9am-5pm) existing construction, inaugurated in 1734, was wrecked in 1773 but remains large and impressive.

In front of the church is a plaza with public clothes-washing sinks, where some women still come to do their wash, spreading their laundry out on the ground to dry. Also in the plaza stands a gift made to Antigua (formally Santiago de los Caballeros de Guatemala) in 1988 by the city of Santiago de Compostela in Galicia, Spain: a *cruceiro*, a typically Galician stone cross carved with biblical scenes.

IGLESIA Y CONVENTO DE SANTO DOMINGO

Founded in 1542, **Santo Domingo** (832-0140; 3a Calle Oriente 28; archaeological area nonguests/guests US$1.30/free; archaeological area 9am-6pm Mon-Sat, 10am-6pm Sun) became the biggest and richest monastery in Antigua. Its large church was completed in 1666. Damaged by three 18th-century earthquakes, the buildings were further depleted when pillaged for construction material in the 20th century. The site is currently occupied by the Hotel Casa Santo Domingo. You can visit the hotel's public spaces, which are tastefully dotted with colonial statuary and archaeological pieces, any time. The archaeological areas (*áreas arqueológicas*) in the hotel grounds include the very picturesque ruined monastery church (cleared of a 5m layer of rubble in the 1990s and now used for Mass and weddings), the adjacent cloister with its large fountain created in 1618, and two crypts discovered in the 1990s – one, the Cripta del Calvario, boasts a pristine mural of the Crucifixion; the other holds two graves with human bones. Also in the archaeological areas are a museum of colonial art and a small archaeological museum. In addition the **Museo Colección 2000**, a fascinating juxtaposition of ancient Mayan artifacts and modern international glassware, was in process of being transferred to the hotel as we researched this edition.

Casa Popenoe

The beautiful **Casa Popenoe** (832-3087; 1a Av Sur 2; admission US$1.30; 2-4pm Mon-Sat) was built in 1636 by Don Luis de las Infantas Mendoza. After the 1773 earthquake, the house stood desolate for 150 years until it was bought in 1929 by agricultural scientist William Popenoe and his wife Dorothy. Their painstaking, authentic restoration yields a fascinating glimpse into how a royal official lived in 17th-century Antigua.

Monumento a Landívar

Commemorating Jesuit priest and poet Rafael Landívar (1731–93), **Monumento a Landívar** (cnr Calzada de Santa Lucía & 5a Calle Poniente) is a structure of five colonial-style arches set in a pristine little park. Landívar lived and wrote in Antigua for some time, and his poetry is esteemed as the best of the colonial period, even though much of it was written in Italy after the Jesuits were expelled from Guatemala. Landívar's ruined house is behind the monument.

Market

Antigua's **market** (btwn Calzada de Santa Lucía & Av de la Recolección; ☯ Mon, Thu & Sat) – chaotic, colorful and always busy – sprawls north of 4a Calle. Morning, when villagers from the Antigua vicinity are actively buying and selling, is the best time to come. On the official market days, Mayan women spread their wares over open-air areas north and west of the covered market area. Like many Guatemalan markets, Antigua market is cheek-by-jowl with the bus station, adding to the crowds, noise and dirt.

Cementerio General

Antigua's **Cementerio General** (☯ 7am-noon & 2-6pm), southwest of the market and bus terminal, is a beautiful conglomeration of tombs and mausoleums decked with wreaths, exotic flowers and other signs of mourning. There have been robberies here, so go with the free escort from the Policía Municipal de Turismo (see Emergency, p78).

Cerro de la Cruz

Overlooking Antigua from the north is Cerro de la Cruz (Hill of the Cross), which provides fine views looking south over town toward Volcán Agua. In the past this hill was famous for muggers waiting to pounce on unsuspecting visitors, and Antigua's tourism police were formed precisely to counter this threat. The Policía Municipal de Turismo (see Emergency, p78) offer a free escort, and it's still best to go with them.

ACTIVITIES

Two professional, established and friendly outfits offering a big range of activities are **Old Town Outfitters** (☎ /fax 832-4171; www .bikeguatemala.com; 5a Av Sur 12C) and **Guatemala Ventures/Mayan Bike Tours** (☎ /fax 832-3383; www .guatemalaventures.com; 1a Av Sur 15). Drop by either or both places to chat about possibilities.

Volcano Ascents

All three volcanoes overlooking Antigua are tempting challenges but how close you can get to **Fuego** depends on recent levels of activity. In 2003 it was still unsafe to go up on Fuego's cone. In many ways the twin-peaked Acatenango, the highest of the three and overlooking Fuego, is the most exhilarating summit. For an active-volcano experience many people take tours to **Pacaya** (2552m), 25km southeast of Antigua (a 1½-hour drive). In general the weather and the views on all the volcanoes are better in the morning. In the rainy season (May to October) thunderstorms are possible in the afternoon. Get reliable advice about safety before you climb, for example from the Inguat tourist office, or from your embassy in Guatemala City if need be. Take sensible precautions: wear adequate footwear (volcanic rock can be very rough on shoes), warm clothing (it can be very cold up there) and, in the rainy season, some sort of rain gear. Carry a flashlight (torch) in case the weather changes; it can get as dark as night when it rains on the mountain – though it's better not to go at all if rain is expected. Don't neglect food and water.

In view of the possible dangers not only from volcanic activity and the elements but also from armed robbers preying on tourists on some volcano trails, it's safest to go with a reputable agency. People like Old Town Outfitters and Guatemala Ventures know what's happening on the mountains and will keep you clear of trouble. **Agua** trips with Guatemala Ventures (US$39) drive to the end of the dirt road well beyond the village of Santa María de Jesús, in whose vicinity hikers have been robbed. The summit is about two hours' walk from the end of the road (against five hours from the village).

Trips of varying difficulty are available. Guatemala Ventures will drive you by 4WD to within two hours' walk of the top of **Acatenango** (US$59 one day, US$99 with a night camping on the mountain), or you can make a longer foot ascent of five to six hours (with Old Town Outfitters this costs US$45 for a one-day trip, US$65 if you camp overnight on the volcano).

One-day Pacaya trips, with 1½ to two hours' walking uphill and one to 1½ hours down, cost US$30 with Old Town Outfitters (US$25 with four or more people) and US$39 with Guatemala Ventures. With luck you'll be able to look down into the crater of this active volcano. **Gran Jaguar Travel Agency** (☎ /fax 832-2712; g_jaguar@yahoo.com; 4a Calle Poniente 30) runs bargain-basement seven-hour Pacaya trips daily for US$7 (leaving Antigua at 6am) or US$5 (leaving at 1pm). Extra costs include food, drinks, and US$3.25 admission to the Pacaya protected area. Other operators around town offering similarly priced Pacaya trips will probably be acting as agents for Gran Jaguar. The installation of park rangers on Pacaya has made this volcano, once notorious for robberies of tourists, much more secure.

Another possibility is hike-and-bike trips (below).

Other Hikes

Old Town Outfitters (☎ /fax 832-4171; www.bike guatemala.com; 5a Av Sur 12C) has a popular range of guided day (US$30) and half-day (US$20) walks in the hills around Antigua. It can also take you to any summit in the country or on a three-day trek through eastern Guatemala's Sierra de las Minas, with its cloud forests. It rents out and sells camping gear too. **Guatemala Ventures/Mayan Bike Tours** (☎ /fax 832-3383; www.guatemalaventures.com; 1a Av Sur 15) offers a range of hikes including some interesting cloud-forest, bird-watching and ridge-hiking options.

Cycling

Old Town Outfitters (☎ /fax 832-4171; www.bike guatemala.com; 5a Av Sur 12C) rents out quality bikes with gloves, helmets and maps for US$13/20 per half/whole day. It also does a great range of mountain bike tours at all levels of difficulty, from the gentle Sip & Cycle Coffee Tour (US$25) or the exhilarating one-day Cielo Grande Ridge Ride (US$45) to the two-day Pedal & Paddle Tour (US$140 to US$175), which includes kayaking and hiking at the Lago de Atitlán.

Guatemala Ventures/Mayan Bike Tours (☎ /fax 832-3383; www.guatemalaventures.com; 1a Av Sur 15) also rents out good mountain bikes for US$1.50 an hour and offers some tasty bike tours from intermediate to expert levels. It does hike-and-bike tours to Acatenango volcano (US$49 to US$109, one to two days) and bike-and-kayak trips to Lago de Atitlán and Monterrico (US$129, both two days).

El Coyote (☎ 832-8383; National Travel, 6a Av Sur 1A) is another place that rents out mountain bikes and offers tours.

Horse Riding

Ravenscroft Riding Stables (☎ 832-6229; 2a Av Sur 3, San Juan del Obispo), 3km south of Antigua

on the road to Santa María de Jesús, offers English-style riding, with scenic rides of three, four or five hours in the valleys and hills around Antigua, for US$15 per hour per person. You need to be fairly fit. Reservations and information are available through the **Hotel San Jorge** (☎ 832-3132; 4a Av Sur 13). You can reach the stables on a bus bound for Santa María de Jesús (p96).

Guatemala Ventures/Mayan Bike Tours (☎ /fax 832-3383; www.guatemalaventures.com; 1a Av Sur 15) offers half-day rides on trails around Volcán Agua for US$69.

You can also ride at La Azotea in Jocotenango (p97).

LANGUAGE COURSES

Antigua's famous Spanish-language schools attract students from around the world. There are around 75 schools to choose from.

The price, quality of teaching and student satisfaction varies greatly from one school to another. Often the quality of instruction depends upon the particular teacher, and thus may vary even within a single school. Visit a few schools before you choose one, and if possible, talk to people who have studied recently at schools you like the look of – you'll have no trouble running into lots of Spanish students in Antigua. The Inguat tourist office has a list of authorized schools. They include the following:

Academia de Español Guatemala (☎ 832-5057/60; www.travellog.com/guatemala/antigua/acadespanol/school.html; 7a Calle Oriente 15)

Academia de Español Sevilla (☎ /fax 832-5101; www.sevillantigua.com; 1a Av Sur 8) This school has a good, free activity program, and offers a shared student house as an accommodation option.

Academia de Español Tecún Umán (☎ /fax 832-2792; www.escuelatecun.com; 6a Calle Poniente 34A) Also has school on Lago de Atitlán.

AmeriSpan Guatemala (☎ 832-0164; www.amerispan.com; 6a Av Norte 40A) Not a school, but has information on some of the best schools in Antigua and around the country.

APPE (Academia de Profesores Privados de Español; ☎ /fax 832-0720; www.appeschool.com; 6a Calle Poniente 40)

Casa de Lenguas Guatemala (☎ 832-4846; guatemala@casadelenguas.com; 6a Av Norte 40) This school has group classes (US$65 a week) as well as individual classes (US$95).

Centro de Español Don Pedro de Alvarado
(☎ /fax 832-4180; www.guacalling.com/donpedroschool;
6a Av Norte 39)
Centro Lingüístico De La Fuente (☎ 832-2711;
www.delafuenteschool.com; 1a Calle Poniente 27)
Centro Lingüístico La Unión (☎ /fax 832-7337;
www.launion.conexion.com; 1a Av Sur 21) Many classes
take place in the school's pretty patio. It gives discounts for
good test results!
Christian Spanish Academy (☎ 832-3922; www.learn
csa.com; 6a Av Norte 15) Very professional outfit where
students get to report on teachers weekly.
Escuela de Español San José el Viejo (☎ 832-3028;
www.sanjoseelviejo.com; 5a Av Sur 34) Professional, 30-
teacher school with pool, superb gardens, tennis court and
own tasteful accommodation.
Ixchel Spanish School (☎ /fax 832-7137; www.ixchel
school.com; 3a Av Sur 6) Comfortable, welcoming school
with enjoyable group activities and lush garden.
Proyecto Lingüístico Francisco Marroquín
(☎ /fax 832-2886; www.plfm-antigua.org; 7a Calle
Poniente 31) Antigua's oldest Spanish school, founded
in 1971; it's run by a nonprofit foundation working to
preserve Maya languages and culture, and courses in some
of these are also available.

Classes start every Monday at most schools,
though you can usually be placed with a
teacher any day of the week. Most schools
cater for all levels and allow you to stay as
long as you like. Three or four weeks is
typical, though it's perfectly OK to do just
one week. The busiest seasons are January and from April to August, and some
schools request advance reservations for
these times.

Instruction is nearly always one-on-one
and costs US$65 to US$115 per week for
four hours of classes daily, five days a
week. You can enroll for up to 10 hours
a day of instruction. Most schools offer to
arrange room and board with local families, where you'll usually have your own
room, often with shared bathrooms, for
around US$55 per week (including three
meals daily except Sunday). Some schools
may offer accommodation in guesthouses
or their own hostels for similar or slightly
higher prices.

Homestays are supposed to promote the
total immersion concept of language learning, but often there are several foreigners
staying with one family. This can make
it more like a hotel than a family atmosphere. Often there are separate mealtimes

for students and the family. Make a point
of inquiring about such details if you really
want to be totally immersed.

Antigua is not for everyone who wants
to study Spanish; there are so many foreigners about, it takes some real discipline
to converse in Spanish rather than your
native tongue. Many enjoy this social
scene, but if you think it will bother you,
consider studying in Xela, the Petén or
elsewhere, where there are fewer foreign
students and more opportunities to dive
into Spanish.

Questions to think about when you're
looking at schools:

▪ Where do the classes take place – on a
quiet, shaded patio or in hot classrooms
with buses roaring along the street outside?
▪ What experience and qualifications do
the teachers have in teaching Spanish as
a second language?
▪ What afternoon and evening activities are
available (many schools offer activities
like salsa classes, movies and excursions –
some of them free)?
▪ Can the school provide opportunities for
voluntary work in your free time – for
example assisting in local schools, visiting hospitals or playing with children at
orphanages?

TOURS

Elizabeth Bell, author of books on Antigua,
leads three-hour cultural walking tours of
the town (in English and/or Spanish) on
Tuesday, Wednesday, Friday and Saturday
at 9:30am. On Monday and Thursday, the
tours are led by her colleague Roberto
Spillari and start at 2pm. The cost is US$18
(US$15 for Spanish students and project
volunteers). Reservations are suggested and
can be made at **Antigua Tours** (p79). The
Adventure Travel Center, **Vision Travel**, **El Condor
Expeditions** and **Sin Fronteras** (p79) also offer
daily city walking tours, visiting a variety of
convents, ruins and museums. These firms
also do interesting tours of assorted villages
and coffee or macadamia plantations for
US$20 to US$30.

Numerous travel agencies offer tours
to far-flung destinations such as Tikal,
Copán, Río Dulce, the Cobán area, Monterrico, Chichicastenango, Guatemala City and

Panajachel. Two-day trips to Tikal, flying from Guatemala City to Flores and back, cost between US$150 and US$300, largely depending on where you choose to stay. A hectic one-day return trip to Tikal costs US$150 to US$180. Two-day land tours to Copán (some also including Quiriguá and Río Dulce) cost US$115 to US$150.

On long-distance tours be sure what you are paying for – some of the cheaper tours simply amount to shuttling you to Guatemala City then popping you on a public bus.

FESTIVALS & EVENTS

The most exciting time to be in Antigua is **Semana Santa** (Easter Week), when hundreds of people dress in deep purple robes to accompany the most revered sculptural images from the city's churches in daily street processions remembering Christ's Crucifixion and the events surrounding it. Dense clouds of incense envelop the parades and the streets are covered in breathtakingly elaborate *alfombras* (carpets) of colored sawdust and flower petals. These beautiful but fragile works of art are destroyed as the processions shuffle over them, but are re-created the next morning for another day of parades.

The fervor and the crowds peak on Good Friday, when an early morning procession departs from La Merced, and a late afternoon one leaves from the Escuela de Cristo. There may also be an enactment of the crucifixion in the Parque Central. Have ironclad Antigua room reservations well in advance of Semana Santa, or plan to stay in Guatemala City or another town and commute to the festivities.

Processions, *velaciones* (vigils) and other events actually go on every weekend through Lent, the 40-day period prior to Semana Santa. Antigua's tourist office has schedules of everything, and the booklet *Lent and Holy Week in Antigua* by Elizabeth Bell gives explanations.

On a secular note, beware of pickpockets. It seems that Guatemala City's entire population of pickpockets (numbering perhaps in the hundreds) decamps to Antigua for Semana Santa. In the press of the emotion-filled crowds lining the processional routes, they target foreign tourists especially.

SLEEPING

Antigua's climate, combined with the plaster and cement used in construction, means some hotel rooms can be damp and musty, and this holds true for all price ranges, not just the budget places. Rooms on the ground floor and/or with carpet seem to fare worst, so avoid the mildew funk by going for an upstairs room, preferably with wood or tile floors. Upper floors generally get more air and more light.

Book as far ahead as you can for accommodations during Semana Santa, and be prepared for rates to double then.

Some Antigua hotels have desks in the Guatemala City airport arrivals area, where you can book a room and/or obtain transportation (often free) to the hotel.

Budget

When checking a budget establishment, look at several rooms, as some are much better than others. Where hot water is indicated, expect an electric unit taped to the shower head; feel especially blessed if there's actually a separate hot-water tap.

Hotel Mochilero's Place (☎ 832-7743; 4a Calle Poniente 27; s/d/tr US$10/12/15, s/d with bathroom US$12/14) This friendly, conveniently located place has 10 clean, spacious rooms and comfortable beds. Facilities include free coffee and tea, free luggage storage, and sinks and lines for your washing. Try to get a room facing south for killer views of Volcán Agua.

Yellow House (☎ 832-6646; main@granjaguar.com; 1a Calle Poniente 24; s/d US$6/11; ✗ ▣) This popular little newcomer, run by a local couple, has a particularly friendly atmosphere. Rooms are simple but very clean and nonsmoking, with comfy beds, wooden furniture, pastel walls and big mosquito-netted windows. The shared bathrooms are immaculate. Rates include use of the guest kitchen, unlimited free Internet and drinking water.

Posada Don Diego (☎ 832-1401; posadadon_diego@hotmail.com; 6a Av Norte 52; s/d US$10/17; ▣) Run by a friendly young Guatemalan couple, this is another popular small place. The handful of rooms – set beside a pretty little patio with wooden pillars, a patch of lawn and a stone fountain – are pleasingly decorated in yellow and blue and include private bath, cable TV, furniture and reading lamp. Prices include morning coffee and 30 minutes' Internet daily.

Hotel la Casa de Don Ismael (☎ /fax 832-1932; www.casadonismael.com; 3a Calle Poniente, Lotificación Cofiño, 20 Callejón 6; s/d/tr US$8/12/15) Safe, friendly Don Ismael's, hidden down a small side-street, fills up fast. The seven cheerful, comfy rooms share three hot-water bathrooms. There's a pleasant roof terrace, washing sinks, drinking water and breakfast available.

Posada Don Tono (3a Calle Poniente, Lotificación Cofiño, 2o Callejón 4; s/d/tr/q US$7/9/14/16) Next door to Don Ismael, this is another friendly little spot with six simple, clean rooms alongside a small patio, free drinking water, and use of a kitchen.

Casa Santa Lucía No 2 (☎ 832-6189; Calzada de Santa Lucía Norte 21; s/d/tr US$13/13/20; P) This is an attractive option. The 12 good-sized, clean rooms have wood-beam ceilings, hot-water bathrooms and comfy beds. There's drinking water in the hall.

Casa Santa Lucía No 4 (☎ 832-3302; Calzada de Santa Lucía Norte 5; s & d US$13) Two blocks down the street from Casa Santa Lucía No 2, the bigger No 4 occupies a remodeled, century-old, three-story building. The 30 rooms are moderate-sized but quite OK, with dark wood ceilings and furniture. All have hot-water bathrooms.

Casa Santa Lucía No 3 (☎ 832-1386; 6a Av Norte; s/d/tr US$11/13/20) This third member of the Santa Lucía group is in colonial style, with 20 rooms, again all with hot-water bathrooms. Casa Santa Lucía No 1 (Calzada de Santa Lucía Sur 9; d US$13) and Casa Santa Lucía No 5 (6a Calle Poniente 58; d with/without bathroom US$13/11) are only open during very busy periods or when booked by large groups.

Hotel Posada San Vicente (☎ /fax 832-3311; hotel_san_vicente@yahoo.com.mx; 6a Av Sur 6; s/d/tr US$15/20/25) Clean, colorful rooms, all with bathroom, on two stories around a wide patio, combined with a roof terrace and an in-house travel agency, make this 20-room hotel a good deal. The upstairs rooms are a bit bigger.

Internacional Mochilero Guesthouse (☎ 832-0520; 1a Calle Poniente 33; dm/s/d US$5/6/9, s/d/tr with bathroom US$16/16/16; 🖳) Geared to mochileros (backpackers) this friendly hostel provides an open-air kitchen, several small sitting areas, and Internet for US$1.30 an hour. Rooms are smallish but clean and quite cheerful, with firm mattresses.

Posada Refugio (☎ 832-7433; 4a Calle Poniente 30; s/d/tr US$4/7/10, with bathroom US$5/8/12) Rooms are mostly small and gloomy, and there's a 1am curfew, but it's cheap, and the roof terrace has fine views.

Posada Ruiz 2 (2a Calle Poniente 25; s/d US$4/5) The small rooms here share bathrooms opening on the courtyard, but it's a fair deal for the price, and some budget travelers stay here, congregating in the courtyard in the evening.

If none of the establishments above are suitable, Antigua has many other decent budget places:

Posada de Don Valentino (☎ 832-0384; 5a Calle Poniente 28; s/d/tr US$15/22/25; P 🖳) Fifteen rooms with hot-water bathrooms; two top-floor triples have volcano views.

Hotel Posada Doña Olga (☎ 832-0623; Callejón Campo Seco 3A; s/d US$11/13) Quiet 13-room place with café and roof terrace.

Hotel Cristal (☎ 832-4177; Av El Desengaño 25; s/d/tr US$10/12/16, with bathroom US$11/14/18; P) Smallish, dull rooms around a pretty patio.

Posada Doña Angelina (☎ 832-5173; 4a Calle Poniente 33; s/d/tr US$6/12/16, with bathroom US$12/18/24) Wacky owner and large-ish rooms make up for generic decor.

Mid-Range

Some of Antigua's mid-range hotels allow you to wallow in the city's colonial charms for a moderate outlay of cash.

Hotel Quinta de las Flores (☎ 832-3721; www.quintadelasflores.com; Calle del Hermano Pedro 6; s/d/tr/q US$54/66/120/120; P 🐾) This is a special place, aptly named for its flores (flowers). The large, beautiful gardens here are tastefully strewn with old paraphernalia like carts and boats. The gardens incorporate fountains, a play area, pool, sitting areas and restaurant. There are eight large, luxurious rooms, most with a fireplace, plus five rustic-style, two-story houses each with two bedrooms, a kitchen and living room. Considerable discounts are offered for stays by the week.

Posada Asjemenou (☎ 832-2670; 5a Av Norte 31; s/d/tr US$20/26/32, with bathroom US$26/33/40) Just north of the Arco de Santa Catalina, the Asjemenou is built around two patios, the front one being a lovely grassy courtyard with a fountain. Rooms are sizable and clean, with drinking water provided and little safe boxes built into the wall. Rates include breakfast in the front patio. In quieter seasons prices can be slashed by almost half.

ANTIGUA

THE AUTHORS' CHOICE

Casa Santo Domingo Hotel (☎ 832-0140; www.casasantodomingo.com.gt; 3a Calle Oriente 28; s/d/tr Mon-Fri US$122/122/140, Sat & Sun US$144/144/162; P ⊑ ⌂) This wonderful luxury hotel is set amid the beautiful remains of the Santo Domingo monastery. The 97 rooms and suites are of an international five-star standard, but the public spaces are wonderfully colonial, dotted with antiques and archaeological relics, and include a large swimming pool, fine restaurant, shops and three museums. The Dominican friars never had it so good. A fine place to spend a lot of money; the prices go down from September to November.

Mesón Panza Verde (☎ 832-2925; www.panzaverde.com; 5a Av Sur 19; d US$75-200; P ⌂) The stunning Panza Verde is an elegant American-owned guesthouse with four rooms and eight suites. It's decked out with sumptuous furniture and fittings, some pieces are ever so fashionably tatty due to being semi-outdoors. Upstairs there is an art gallery that is reached by a staircase with a beautiful iron balustrade. The atmosphere and restaurant here are among the most appealing in Antigua.

Hotel Casa Azul (☎ 832-0961/2; www.casazul.guate.com; 4a Av Norte 5; d with breakfast US$89-101; P ⌂) The Casa Azul is a designer's gem with communal spaces, courtyard, garden and rooms all working together in seamless harmony. The upstairs units are spectacular, with sweeping views, luxurious baths, telephones and minibars. The cheaper downstairs rooms are just as impressive, but without views. Still, they give better access to the pool, Jacuzzi and sauna. It's a fine spot for honeymooners!

Hotel Aurora (☎ /fax 832-0217, 832-5155; www.hotelauroraantigua.com; 4a Calle Oriente 16; s/d/tr/q with breakfast US$43/50/56/65; P) The Aurora is a beautiful old-fashioned mid-range hotel with 17 rooms around a grassy courtyard graced by a fountain and many flowers.

Posada Juma Ocag (☎ 832-3109; Calzada de Santa Lucía 13; s/d/tr US$13/13/18) Everything you could want in a budget hotel. The seven spotless, comfortable rooms have high-quality mattresses and traditional appointments including wrought-iron bedheads, reading lamps and mirrors made by your friendly, attentive host, Juan Ramón. Each room has a private hot shower; there's also a rooftop patio and well-tended little garden. Touches like drinking water and decorative ceramic masks make this great value. It's peaceful, despite the location on a busy street. Reservations are accepted in person only.

Hotel Posada Landívar (☎ /fax 832-2962; posada_landivar@hotmail.com; 5a Calle Poniente 23; s/d/tr US$14/24/31; P) This is a friendly little place with five of its seven rooms set round a pretty little patio with a fountain. Rooms (all with hot-water bathrooms) are decent-sized, with flowery bedspreads and in some cases fans. Colorful weavings and paintings, drinking water, baggage storage and a little roof garden add to the appeal.

Hotel Posada San Pedro (☎ 832-3594; 3a Av Sur 15; s/d US$22/30) The 10 rooms here are super-clean and inviting, with pink and white paint, good wooden furniture, cable TV and tiled bathrooms. Two spacious sitting areas and two terraces with great views add to the comfortable, friendly atmosphere.

Hotel La Sin Ventura (☎ 832-0581, 832-4888; www.lasinventura.com; 5a Av Sur 8; s/d/tr US$20/35/50) This friendly place sports 34 sparkling clean rooms, in a color combination of yellow, blue and white. It's just half a block from the Parque Central and the views from

the small roof terrace are superb. One-bed doubles cost just US$25, but these, like the singles, are on the lowest and darkest of the three floors.

Posada San Sebastián (☎ /fax 832-2621, 832-6952; snsebast@hotmail.com; 3a Av Norte 4; s/d/tr US$46/56/66) Staying here is like spending the night in a museum. Each of the nine terracotta-tiled rooms is unique and richly packed with fascinating Guatemalan antiques. All have hot-water bathroom and cable TV, and you have use of a kitchen, roof terrace and a pretty little courtyard garden.

Hotel San Jorge (☎ /fax 832-3132; 4a Av Sur 13; s/d/tr with breakfast US$39/46/53; P) Though in a modern building, this hotel has a rustic reception area and all 14 rooms share a long balcony and overlook a beautiful flower-filled garden complete with tinkling fountain and chirping birds. The rooms have a fireplace, cable TV, pretty tiles and a bathroom with a tub. Guests can use the swimming pool of the posh Hotel Antigua nearby. The English-speaking local host is very welcoming. Ask about discounts in low season.

Hotel Posada Los Búcaros (☎ /fax 832-2346; www.hotelosbucaros.com; 7a Av Norte 94; s/d/tr US$25/30/35; P) This hotel in the northwest of town provides 13 plain but well-kept rooms, many of them with wood-beam roofs and red-tile floors. It's set around two patios and guests have the use of a sitting room with fireplace and a large, clean, equipped kitchen with free coffee. Staff will pick you up for free from Guatemala City airport.

Hotel Santa Clara (☎ /fax 832-0342; 2a Av Sur 20; s/d/tr/q US$21/26/29/32) In a quiet area south of the center, the 19-room Santa Clara has some older rooms with character featuring tiling and brickwork, set around a pretty patio. It also has newer, mostly brighter rooms on two levels at the rear. It's clean and popular with small groups. The hot showers are terrific.

Hotel Posada La Merced (☎ 832-3197; www .merced-landivar.com; 7a Av Norte 43, s/d/tr/q US$ 25/37/49/61; P ⊠) This sprawling, fairly plain hotel has been jazzed up by the travel-wise, pleasant New Zealander who runs it. The 25 good clean rooms have comfortable beds, most with attached hot-water bathrooms. Hammocks are hung in a couple of interior patios. Flowers and bright local fabrics add a cheery tone, while candles create a relaxed mood at night. Guests can use a well-equipped communal kitchen. Baggage storage is available.

Hotel Palacio Chico (☎ 832-0406; palaciochico@ hotmail.com; 4a Av Sur 4; s/d/tr with breakfast US$15/30/45) Close to Parque Central and with a friendly reception, this hotel is a good value. Rooms are spacious, attractively painted with that sponged-over technique that is so fetching in Antigua, and have lots of wood.

There are plenty of other good mid-range choices in Antigua:

Hotel Posada del Sol (☎ 832-6838; Calle de los Nazarenos 17; s/d/tr/q US$20/25/30/34; P) Attractive and spacious six-room hotel in a peaceful leafy part of town.

Hotel El Descanso (☎ 832-0142; 5a Av Norte 9; s/d/tr/q with breakfast US$26/28/38/50) Friendly, spotless, very central, four-room hotel.

Hotel La Tatuana (☎ 832-1223; 7a Av Sur 3; s/d/tr/q US$14/24/36/40) Attractive, modernized, five-room hotel with small roof terrace.

El Carmen Hotel (☎ /fax 832-3850, 832-3847; 3a Av Norte 9; s/d/tr US$44/50/56) Plain, clean, comfortable

central hotel, featuring a fine view from its roof terrace, and rooms around a covered patio .

Hotel Posada Real (☎ 832-4597; Av del Desengaño 24; s/d/tr US$20/25/30; P) This moderately priced hotel has nine clean, mostly large rooms but lacks atmosphere and suffers traffic noise.

Top End

Cloister (☎ /fax 832-0712; www.thecloister.com; 5a Av Norte 23; s/d/tr/ste with breakfast US$90/90/100/110; P ⊠) A romantic option is this renovated cloister from the 16th century, one of the most exclusive hotels in Antigua. Bubbling fountains highlight the horticultural triumph that is the Cloister's garden courtyard, and guests will likely spend a lot of time relaxing here. All seven rooms and suites have antique furniture, fireplace and library. Prices include breakfast. Credit cards are not accepted.

Casa Capuchinas (☎ /fax 832-0121, 832-7941; www .casacapuchinas.com; 2a Av Norte 7; s/d/tr with breakfast US$79/79/98). The five rooms at this lovely B&B are furnished in old-fashioned yet uncluttered and very comfortable styles, with soothing yellow and blue tones. There's a beautifully tended garden with neat patches of lawn.

Hotel Casa Noble (☎ 832-0864; kasanoble@infovia .com.gt; 2a Av Sur 29; s/d/tr with breakfast US$92/92/147) Though buses pass by this beautiful, re-modeled, 18th-century mansion, the 11 rooms are set well back and don't suffer undue noise. They have a fireplace and TV and are decorated in subtle harmony with the buildings' many wooden features and the foliage of the garden. This is a house with a romantic history – discover the origin of the fountain dedicated to the Virgin Mary. Upstairs rooms have volcano views. Prices include breakfast.

Posada del Ángel (☎ 832-5303, ☎ /fax 832-0260; www.posadadelangel.com; 4a Av Sur 24A; d Sun-Thu US$150-200, Fri & Sat US$175-225; P ⊠ ⌾) The Posada became Antigua's most celebrated B&B when Bill Clinton bedded down here in 1999. The three rooms and one suite all have fireplaces, fresh flowers, gorgeous furnishings and highly polished tile floors. The pool is a lap pool – long and skinny, just for doing laps.

Hotel Convento Santa Catalina Mártir (☎ 832-3080; www.convento.com; 5a Av Norte 28; s/d/tr US$79/92/104; P ⌨) The Arco de Santa Catalina (right outside the front door) was built for the nuns of this ex-convent. Nicely renovated, the hotel has some rooms around the former cloister – a leafy affair with a fountain – and others behind its car park with their own little lawn areas. The hotel's 17 rooms are traditional in style; they are also very comfortable.

Antigua has no shortage of charming and/or luxurious accommodations:

La Casa de la Música (☎ 832-3684; www.lacasadelamusica.centramerica.com; 7a Calle Poniente 3; s US$36-54; d US$42-90) Charming, five-room, kid-friendly B&B with patios, fountains, triple volcano views and a fabulous breakfast.

Casa de los Cántaros B&B (☎ 832-0674; www.travellog.com/guatemala/casa/cantaros.html; 5a Av Sur 5; s US$68-79, d US$79-98) Colonial mansion groaning with antiques – another gem of a place to stay.

Hotel Antigua (☎ 832-2801; www.portahotels.com; 8a Calle Poniente 1; s/d/tr US$90/100/117; ℗ ☎) Large, colonial, country-club-style hotel.

La Casa de los Sueños (☎ 832-0802; www.lacasadelossuenos.com; 1a Av Norte 1; s/d/tr US$92/92/110; ℗ ☎) Lovely, verdant B&B with large rooms, large gardens and large pool.

Radisson Villa Antigua Resort (☎ 832-0011; www.villaantigua.com; cnr Calle Sucia & Carretera a Ciudad Vieja; s/d/tr US$104/104/122; ℗ ☎) This 175-room, five-star hotel is the biggest and most modern in town, with every amenity.

EATING

Within 10 minutes' walk of the Parque Central you can dine well and inexpensively on Italian, Spanish, French, Greek, Thai, Indonesian, Vietnamese, Irish, Austrian, German, US, Chinese, Peruvian, Mexican and even Guatemalan food.

Budget

Cafe La Escudilla (4a Av Norte 4; pasta US$2.50-3.25, meat dishes US$3.50-5.50; ☯ 7am-midnight) Hugely popular with travelers and language students, La Escudilla is an inexpensive patio restaurant with a tinkling fountain, lush foliage and tables under the open sky. The food is simple but well prepared and there are plenty of vegetarian options, as well as economical breakfasts and a one-course set lunch or dinner for under US$2.40. At the back is Riki's Bar (p94).

Tacool (☎ 832-0287; 6a Av Norte 35B; 4 tacos US$3.25; ☯ 11am-midnight) Savor Antigua's best tacos in Tacool's two cozy upstairs rooms, one lounge-style.

Mi Destino (1a Av Sur 17; mains US$2-2.50) This casual café run by an amiable collection of happy-go-lucky young Guatemalans serves a variety of good-value eats; try the *quesadillas* (flour tortilla topped or filled with cheese) or the Greek salad with chicken breast.

Restaurante Big House (☎ 832-2856; 6a Av Norte 11; breakfasts US$2-3.25; ☯ 7am-10pm) Come here for some of the best-value breakfasts in town.

Rainbow Cafe (7a Av Sur 8; mains US$4-6; ☯ 7am-midnight) Fill up from an eclectic range of all-day breakfasts, curries, stir-fries, Cajun chicken, guacamole etc, and enjoy the relaxed patio atmosphere. The Rainbow has a bookshop and travel agency on the same premises.

Restaurante Doña Luisa Xicotencatl (☎ 832-2578; 4a Calle Oriente 12; sandwiches & breakfast dishes US$3-4; ☯ 7am-9:30pm) Probably Antigua's best-known restaurant, this is a place to enjoy the colonial patio ambience over breakfast or a light meal rather than a blow-out. The bakery here sells many kinds of breads, including whole grain. Check out the hot-from-the-oven banana bread daily at around 2pm.

La Fuente (4a Calle Oriente 14; mains US$4; ☯ 7am-7pm) Another pretty courtyard restaurant, tranquil La Fuente has lots of vegetarian selections, good breakfasts and desserts.

Restaurante La Estrella (☎ 832-7264; 4a Calle Poniente 3; mains US$2.50-4; ☯ noon-9:45pm) An efficient, friendly, economical Chinese restaurant, the Estrella has several tofu options.

Doña María Gordillo Dulces Típicos (4a Calle Oriente 11) This shop opposite Hotel Aurora is filled with traditional Guatemalan sweets, and there's often a crowd of *Antigüeños* lined up to buy them.

Panificadora Colombia (4a Calle Poniente 34; coffee & croissant US$1.80) Good for breakfast before the 7am pullman bus to Panajachel (p96). Probably the cheapest eating in town is the good, clean, tasty food served from **street stalls** (cnr 4a Calle Poniente & 6a Av Norte), a block west of the Parque Central, in the early evening.

Fancy an Austrian meal for something different? At **Restaurante Wiener** (☎ 832-1244; Calzada de Santa Lucía Portal 8; breakfast dishes US$1.50-2.50; ☯ closed Tue) the Wiener Schnitzel costs US$4. Wiener also serves decent breakfasts.

Jardín Bavaria (7a Av Norte 49; breakfast dishes US$2.20, mains US$2.20-4.50; ☯ 7-1am Mon-Sat, 9am-3pm Sun high season, 1pm-1am Mon-Sat, 9am-3pm Sun low season) is a bar/restaurant with a verdant patio and spacious roof terrace, offering a mixed

THE AUTHORS' CHOICE

La Repostería (Calzada de Santa Lucía Portal 13; snacks US$0.35) Fresh off the bus? Need to stop and get your bearings? Do it over a coffee and a delicious little *chile relleno* (p53) in a soft bread roll here, just round the corner from the Guatemala City bus stop.

   Café Condesa (Portal del Comercio 4; snacks US$2.50-5) Walk through the Librería Case del Conde on the west side of the Parque Central to this delightful restaurant around the patio of a 16th-century mansion. On the menu are excellent breakfasts, coffee, salads, sandwiches, quiches, cakes and pies. The Sunday buffet, from 10am to 2pm, a lavish spread for US$7, is an Antigua institution.

   Helas (4a Av Norte 4; mains US$3-6; ☽ 6pm-1am Tue-Fri, 1pm-1am Sat & Sun) Tucked into a separate room off Cafe La Escudilla, Helas is a little sky-blue corner of the Aegean with all your Greek favorites (except *retsina*). The *meze helas* (US$6) brings you a bit of everything – fabulous!

   El Punto (7a Av Norte 8A; pizza & pasta US$5-6.50; ☽ 6:30-10:30pm Tue-Thu, noon-3pm & 6:30-10:30pm Fri & Sat, noon-5pm Sun) Highly popular El Punto serves probably Antigua's best Italian food in a neat but animated setting of three adjoining rooms and a patio, each with three or four tables – and some particularly interesting posters on Italian and Guatemalan themes.

   Mesón Panza Verde (☎ 832-2925; 5a Av Sur 19; mains US$5-18) This guesthouse restaurant provides divine Continental cuisine in an appealing Antiguan atmosphere. Two courses should cost you about US$20. If you don't have the budget for a full meal but want to check out the great ambience and gorgeous patio, have a drink or snack at the Panza Verde's Café Terraza.

   La Cocina de Lola (2a Calle Poniente 3; mains US$7.50-11; ☽ noon-3pm & 6-10pm Tue-Sat, noon-9pm Sun) This relaxed and pretty Spanish restaurant, with rooms around a patio, specializes in fish, seafood and paella. The food is delicious and the service excellent. You won't go wrong if you order something *a la plancha* (grilled on a hotplate). Some days there are lunch deals such as paella and *sangría* for two at US$12.

Guatemalan/German menu and US$4.50 Sunday lunches.

The Bagel Barn (5a Calle Poniente 2; bagels US$2-3.25; ☽ 7am-10pm), just off the Parque Central, is popular for its breakfasts, coffee, and bagels with almost anything. **Cookies Etc** (3a Av Norte 7; breakfasts & sandwiches US$1.30-2; ☽ 8am-6pm) is a good spot for something sweet, and at breakfast it treats diners to bottomless cups of coffee. **La Cenicienta Pasteles** (5a Av Norte 7) serves a range of tempting cakes at US$1 a slice.

Some of Antigua's liveliest bars (p94) have great-value food. **Monoloco** (5a Av Sur 6, Pasaje El Corregidor; dishes US$2.50-4) has tasty Tex-Mex and pizza, while **Onis** (7a Av Norte 2; dishes US$2.50-4) is good for stuffed potatoes, pasta and chicken. English-run **Los Arcos** (1a Calle Poniente 3; mains US$4-10) has the longest menu in town, from all-day breakfasts to Thai stir-fries, and does a decent job of most of it.

Mid-Range

Fridas (☎ 832-0504; 5a Av Norte 29; snacks US$2.50-4, mains US$6-8; ☽ 12:30pm-midnight) Dedicated to Ms Kahlo, this bright bar-cum-restaurant serves tasty, if not cheap, Mexican fare and is always busy.

Queso y Vino (☎ 832-7785; 5a Av Norte 32A; salads US$3-10, pizzas from US$4.50; ☽ noon-3pm & 6-10pm Wed-Mon) This popular little spot is a fine choice for Italian food. There's a wide range of pizzas, pastas, sauces and cheeses plus Chilean wines and Spanish reds to accompany the food. It's usually full around 8:30pm.

Caffé Mediterráneo (☎ 832-7180; 6a Calle Poniente 6A; mains US$5-6; ☽ noon-3pm & 6-10pm Mon & Wed-Sat, noon-4:30pm & 6:30-9pm Sun) A refined little restaurant with just seven tables spaced around a large room adorned with tasteful pasta prints, Caffé Mediterráneo serves well-prepared Italian food. A satisfying three-course meal will cost US$10 to US$12, plus drinks.

Perú Café (☎ 832-2147; 5a Calle Poniente 15B; mains US$4-6.50; ☽ 11am-midnight Wed-Mon) Enjoy tasty Peruvian specialties at this pretty patio restaurant. The excellent *causas* are like burgers with layers of mashed potato instead of bread; *ají de gallina* is chicken in yellow chile sauce with baked potatoes, parmesan and rice.

Tre Fratelli (☎ 832-7730; 6a Calle Poniente 30; pizza & pasta US$5-10; ☽ noon-9:30pm Sun-Thu, noon-10:30pm Fri & Sat) Antigua's branch of one of Guatemala city's best restaurants has the

ANTIGUA

same animated atmosphere and a pretty, verdant courtyard. The food is good quality Italian cuisine, with fish, chicken and steaks too for US$9 to US$11.

Café Flor (4a Av Sur 1; mains US$4-8; 11am-11pm) The Flor makes a good stab at Thai, Indonesian and Chinese food. Dishes come in generous quantities.

Cafe Beijing (5a Calle Poniente 15C; mains US$4-6) Perú Café's neighbor, another pretty courtyard restaurant, has food from several Asian countries. There are plenty of vegetarian options and a set lunch of soup, fried rice and salad costs US$3 to US$4.

Café Rocío (832-1871; 6a Av Norte 34; mains US$5-7; 7am-11pm) Another pan-Asian locale, and with a romantic little garden area, this restaurant offers you *gado-gado* (the famous Indonesian vegetarian dish with peanut sauce), Thai satay, yellow Thai curry and a range of tofu dishes.

Restaurante Las Palmas (832-0376; 6a Av Norte 14; mains US$4-6) Twinkling lights and gentle guitar music make this a popularly romantic dinner spot. The staples are chicken, seafood, steaks and pasta; try the fettuccine with goat's cheese, shrimps, herbs and garlic.

La Fonda de la Calle Real (mains US$5-8.50) 3a Calle Poniente 7 (832-0507; noon-10pm); 5a Av Norte 5 (832-2629; noon-10pm); 5a Av Norte 12 (832-3749; 8am-10pm) This restaurant with three spacious branches, all in appealing colonial style, has a good, varied menu ranging from generous salads and sandwiches (US$3) to grilled meats (up to US$8.50). The specialty *caldo real*, a hearty chicken soup, makes a good meal. The 5a Av Norte 12 branch is a little cheaper than the others but 3a Calle Poniente 7 is the most attractive, with several rooms and patios.

Top End

La Casserole (832-0219; Callejón de la Concepción 7; 2-course meals US$13-16; noon-3pm & 7-10pm Tue-Sat, noon-4pm Sun) This French restaurant with friendly but smooth service is one of Antigua's best. It's great for steak and dessert lovers. There are just a dozen tables in a patio and one side room.

Las Antorchas (832-0806; 3a Av Sur 1; steaks US$8.50-15; 11am-3pm & 6-10pm Mon-Sat, 11am-5pm Sun) This place has a beautiful courtyard to go with its sumptuous steaks.

Casa Santo Domingo Hotel (832-0140; 3a Calle Oriente 28; 2-course meals US$13-25) The restaurant at this luxurious hotel is another beautiful spot for a splurge, with mixed Guatemalan and international delights served inside or out in the garden.

Posada de Don Rodrigo (832-0291; 5a Av Norte 17; plato chapín US$11) The indoor/outdoor restaurant in this hotel is one of the city's most charming and popular places for lunch or dinner. You can dine to the strains of a live *marimba* (xylophone-like music). Order the house favorite, *plato chapín*, a platter of Guatemalan specialties.

DRINKING

Antigua's bar scene has bounced back after many establishments were closed down by a mayor trying to smarten up the city's image in 2001 and 2002. You can choose from a bunch of buzzing drinking places – except Sunday, when no alcohol is served after 8pm. Many people roll in from Guatemala City for a spot of Antigua-style revelry on Friday and Saturday.

Riki's Bar (4a Av Norte 4; until midnight) At the back of Cafe La Escudilla, this is the hippest bar in town, packed every evening with Antigua's young, international scene of locals, travelers and language students. For quieter moments, slip through to the low-key **Paris Bar** in the rear.

Monoloco (Crazy Monkey; 5a Av Sur 6, Pasaje El Corregidor) The Crazy Monkey can be the most fun bar in Antigua – it has a real party atmosphere. It's a two-level place (partly open-air upstairs, with benches and long tables), with sports on TV and good-value food.

Reilly's (5a Av Norte 31; 1:30pm-1am) Guatemala's only Irish bar (so far), Reilly's is sociable and relaxed, with a young international crowd. Sadly, small bottles of Guinness are US$4.50 – more than double the cost of local beers! The Sunday evening quiz is one of Antigua's most enjoyable events.

Onis (832-6812; 7a Av Norte 2; until 1am) With a back terrace overlooking the illuminated ruins of San Agustín church, Onis is another travelers' and students' haunt. Unlike some Antigua bars, it has a liquor license: shots and cocktails cost US$2 to US$3, but rum, vodka or gin are just US$0.15 for women from 7pm to 10pm on Thursday. There's good, economical food too.

Café Sky (1a Av Sur 15) On the rooftop above the Guatemala Ventures/Mayan Bike Tours office, this is a very popular place for sunset drinks.

Perú Café (5a Calle Poniente 15B; ☽ 6pm-midnight Wed-Mon) The lounge here, run by amiable Peruvian Guille, has chilled electronic background music, often with a DJ or live music Wednesday to Friday.

Los Arcos (☎ 400-0377; 1a Calle Poniente 3; ☽ 8-1am) Come here for pool, draft beer and all-drinks-one-price offers.

For a quick caffeine fix, hit **Café Condesa Express** (Portal del Comercio 4; ☽ 6:45am-6:45pm) on the west side of the Parque Central. Antigua's best coffee is at **Tostaduría Antigua** (6a Calle Poniente 26).

ENTERTAINMENT

Proyecto Cultural El Sitio (☎ 832-3037; www .elsitiocultural.org; 5a Calle Poniente 15) This arts center has lots going on, from music, dance and theater events (including plays in English) to exhibition openings most Saturdays (usually all are welcome).

Classical concerts happen in the **Museo de Arte Colonial** (p81) and the **Antiguo Colegio de la Compañía de Jesús** (6a Av Norte btwn 3a & 4a Calles).

Cinema, TV & Slide Shows

Several cinema houses show a wide range of Latin American, art-house and general-release movies, some in English, some in Spanish, usually for US$1.25 to US$2. Check the programs of the following:

Bagel Barn (5a Calle Poniente 2) Café with movies at 8pm daily.

Cafe 2000 (☎ 832-2981; 6a Av Norte 2) Café showing free movies on big screen.

Cinema Bistro (5a Av Sur 14) Four screenings a day, three films each time; movie-and-meal deals cost US$4 to US$5.

Maya Moon (6a Av Norte 1A) Three screens that each show three films a day.

Mi Destino (1a Av Sur 17) This is a café too and the nightly movies are free with any consumption.

Proyecto Cultural El Sitio (☎ 832-3037; www.elsitiocultural.org; 5a Calle Poniente 15) Movies usually on Tuesday evening.

For North American and European sports on TV, check the programs that are posted at **Cafe 2000** (above) and **Los Arcos** and **Monoloco** (p94).

Writer Elizabeth Bell gives a fascinating one-hour English-language **slide show** (admission US$3) about Antigua called *Behind the Walls* at 6pm on Tuesday in the Christian Spanish Academy (p86).

Dancing

La Casbah (☎ 832-2640; 5a Av Norte 30; admission including 1 drink US$2.50-4; ☽ 9pm-1am Mon-Sat) This two-level disco near the Santa Catalina arch has a warm atmosphere and is gay-friendly and quite a party most nights – especially on Thursday (ladies' night), when women who arrive before 11pm get two drinks free.

Torero's Discoteque (Av de la Recolección) Some emboldened salsa-lovers head out here, west of the market, for a local experience after a few drinks at weekends.

You can learn to salsa at several places including **Latinos** (1a Av Sur 22) and **Salsa Buena**

TRUE JADE

Jade, beloved of the ancient Maya, isn't always green. It can be lilac, yellow, pink, white or even black. On the other hand a lot of stones passed off as jade are not the real thing. There are two main forms of genuine jade: nephrite, found in Asia, and jadeite, found in Guatemala. Albite, serpentine, chrysoprase, diopside, chrysolite and aventurine – none of these are true jade. It seems that the ancient Mayans themselves had a hard time telling the difference. Many items of Mayan 'jade' in museums have been revealed, on testing, to be one or other of these inferior stones.

Several Antigua shops specialize in jade, including **La Casa del Jade** (www.lacasadeljade.com; 4a Calle Oriente 10), **Jades SA** (www.centramerica.com/jades; 4a Calle Oriente 1, 12 & 34 Hotel Casa Santo Domingo, 3a Calle Oriente 28) and **El Reino del Jade** (cnr 5a Av Norte & 2a Calle Poniente). At La Casa del Jade and Jades SA's 4a Oriente 34 branch, you can visit the workshops in the rear of the showrooms. Jades SA's jade comes from a rediscovered ancient Mayan jade mine in Guatemala's Motagua valley. You should ask about prices at a few places before making any purchase.

To discern quality jade, look for translucency, purity and intensity of color and absence of flaws – and ask if you can scratch the stone with a pocket knife: if it scratches, it's not true jadeite but an inferior stone.

(6a Calle Poniente 19). Ask around to find the current hottest spot.

SHOPPING

Nim Po't (www.nimpot.com; 5a Av Norte 29) Boasting a huge collection of Mayan dress, as well as hundreds of masks and other woodcarvings, this sprawling space is packed with *huipiles*, (tunics) *cortes* (skirts), *fajas* (belts) and more, all arranged according to region. It makes for a fascinating visit whether you're in the market or not.

Colibri (4a Calle Oriente) This has beautiful basketwork from El Petén and top-quality woven fabric from a Mayan women's co-operative. Prices are moderate. There are other classy craft shops like this on 4a Calle Oriente and on 5a Av Norte around the Santa Catalina arch.

Mercado de Artesanías (Handicrafts Market; 4a Calle Poniente; ☼ 8am-8pm) At the west end of town by the main market, this market sells masses of Guatemalan handicrafts. While not at the top end of the quality range, it has a variety of colorful masks, blankets, jewelry, purses and so on. Don't be afraid to bargain.

There are also a number of craft shops on 4a Calle Poniente, between the Parque Central and the market. Vendors will also approach you in the Parque Central, or while you are drinking a coffee or eating breakfast in a casual dining place. Prices for handicrafts can be much higher in Antigua than elsewhere in Guatemala. Always bargain for a fair price.

Casa del Tejido Antiguo (www.casadeltejido.com; 1a Calle Poniente 51; admission US$0.70; ☼ 9am-5:30pm Mon-Sat) This is another intriguing place for textiles; it's like a museum, market and workshop rolled into one.

Antigua has some excellent but pricey jewelry and clothes shops. If you're not flush, stay away from these places, but if you have the cash and see something you like, grab it as you probably won't find the same quality elsewhere in Guatemala.

Joyería del Ángel (4a Calle Oriente 5A) This shop has exquisite pieces of imaginative, up-to-the-minute exotic jewelry using shells, semiprecious stones, bone and classy clasps. Many pieces are large and flamboyant; others are daintier with unusual combinations like jade and rose garnets. Some pieces are moderately priced but on the whole this place is quite expensive.

Casa de Arte Popular (4a Calle Oriente 10) One of the interesting art galleries along 4a Calle Oriente, it's in the same building as La Casa del Jade. For information on the distinctive style of art exhibited here, see Tz'utujil Oil Painting (p122).

Tostaduría Antigua (6a Calle Poniente 26) The place to head for coffee, where 500g of beans, freshly roasted to your specifications, will cost about US$3. Add a bag made from traditional material scraps for US$1.

GETTING THERE & AROUND
Bus

Buses to Guatemala City, Ciudad Vieja and San Miguel Dueñas arrive and depart from a street just south of the market. Buses to Chimaltenango, Escuintla, San Antonio Aguas Calientes and Santa María de Jesús go from the street outside the west side of the market. If you're heading out to local villages, it's best to go early in the morning and return by mid-afternoon, as bus services drop off dramatically as evening approaches.

To reach highland towns such as Chichicastenango, Quetzaltenango, Huehuetenango or Panajachel (except for the one direct daily bus to Panajachel – see below), take one of the frequent buses to Chimaltenango, on the Interamericana Highway, and catch an onward bus from there. Making connections in Chimaltenango is easy, as many friendly folks will jump to your aid as you alight from one bus looking for another. But stay alert and don't leave your pack unattended, as bag slashing isn't unheard of in Chimal. Alternatively you can take a bus from Antigua heading toward Guatemala City, get off at San Lucas Sacatepéquez and change buses there – this takes a little longer, but you'll be boarding the bus closer to the capital so you're more likely to get a seat.

Chimaltenango (US$0.30, 30min, 19km, every 15min 5am-7pm)

Ciudad Vieja (US$0.15, 15min, 7km) Take a San Miguel Dueñas bus.

Escuintla (US$0.65, 1hr, 39km, 16 a day 5:30am-5pm)

Guatemala City (US$0.65, 1¼hr, 45km, every few mins 6am-7pm)

Panajachel (US$4.50, 2½hr, 146km, 1 daily 7am) Departs from El Condor Expeditions (☎ 498-9812; 4a Calle Poniente 34)
San Antonio Aguas Calientes (US$0.15, 30min, 9km, every 20min 6:30am-7pm)
San Miguel Dueñas (US$0.20, 30min, 10km, every few mins 6am-7pm) The placards just say 'Dueñas.'
Santa María de Jesús (US$0.15, 30min, 12km, every 45min 6am-7:30pm)

Shuttle Minibus

Numerous travel agencies and tourist minibus operators offer frequent and convenient shuttle services to places tourists go, including Guatemala City and its airport, Panajachel and Chichicastenango. They go less frequently (usually on weekends) to places further afield. These services cost a lot more than buses, but they are comfortable and convenient, with door-to-door service at both ends. Typical one-way prices:

Chichicastenango	US$10-12
Copán (Honduras)	US$15-25
Guatemala City	US$7-10
Monterrico	US$9-15
Panajachel	US$10-12
Quetzaltenango	US$25
Río Dulce	US$25-40

Pin down shuttle operators about departure times and whether their trip requires a minimum number of passengers. Be careful of 'shuttles' to Flores or Tikal. This service may just consist of taking you to Guatemala City and putting you on a public bus there.

Car & Motorcycle

Rental companies include the following:
Ahorrent (☎ 832-0968; 6a Calle Poniente 29)
Ceiba Rent (☎ 511-9592; www.ceibarent.com; 6a Calle Poniente 6) Has motorcycles from US$29 a day as well as cars from US$39.
Dollar (☎ 219-6848; www.dollarguatemala.com; 5a Av Norte 15)
Tabarini (www.tabarini.com); Av Sur (☎ 832-8107; 6a Av Sur 22); Radisson Villa Antigua Resort (☎ 832-7460; Radisson Villa Antigua Resort)

Taxi

Taxis wait where the Guatemala City buses stop and on the east side of Parque Central. A ride in town costs around US$1.60. A taxi to/from Guatemala City usually costs US$30 (US$40 after midnight).

AROUND ANTIGUA

JOCOTENANGO

This village just northwest of Antigua (effectively a suburb) gives you a taste of more typical Guatemalan life than downtown Antigua. Storefronts are occupied by tailors at their sewing machines, school kids throng the streets in the middle of the day, and women linger over their purchases to chat.

Sights

Jocotenango's **Centro Cultural La Azotea** (☎ 832-0907; www.centroazotea.org; Calle del Cementerio, Final; adult/child US$3.25/0.65; ⏰ 8:30am-4pm Mon-Fri, 8:30am-2pm Sat) is an excellent three-in-one coffee, music and costume museum. The coffee section includes a 19th-century water-wheel-powered processing plant: you get a free cup to drink at the end of the tour. Part two of the center is the Casa K'ojom, a top-class collection of traditional Mayan musical instruments, masks, paintings and other artifacts amassed by dedicated cultural conservationist Samuel Franco. The displays set the objects in the context of the many ceremonies and customs in which they are used, with a particularly interesting section on Maximón, the semipagan deity revered by many highland Maya (see p119). A good audiovisual show illustrating the musical instruments in action is part of the visit. The third exhibit is the Rincón de Sacatepéquez, displaying the colorful costumes and crafts of the Antigua valley. Free tours to all this are available in English and Spanish.

Also at La Azotea are two shops selling quality coffee, local crafts, Mayan instruments and recordings and videos of them, a restaurant with good, moderately priced Guatemalan food, and the **Establo La Ronda**, where you can take a one-hour morning horse ride round the grounds for US$2 (ring two days ahead).

The **church** dominating the main square is a marvel of crumbling pink stucco that still holds services. About 100m along the street toward Antigua from the square, the **Fraternidad Naturista Antigua** (☎ 831-0379; Calle Real 30; ⏰ 7am-6pm Sun-Thu, 7am-1pm Fri) offers massages, saunas and chiropractic services. It also sells an amazing variety of medicinal herbs. A 45-minute massage with unlimited sauna time costs US$6.50; a sauna alone is

US$5; there are separate, very clean, facilities for men and women. The massages can be strenuous, some say rough, and men should be especially careful here as the masseurs are wicked strong!

Getting There & Away

You can also use local buses (US$0.15, 10 minutes) between Jocotenango and Antigua. They run about every 15 minutes during daylight from behind Antigua market and from Jocotenango's square. It's also quite possible to walk: it's less than 1km along Calle Ancha de los Herreros from the north end of Antigua's 6a Av to Jocotenango's square.

Free minibuses to La Azotea leave from Antigua's Parque Central hourly from 9am to 2pm, returning from La Azotea hourly from 10:30am to 2:30pm and at 4pm. You're quite free to explore the village before hopping back on the bus. From La Azotea's ticket office, walk 350m back along the driveway then 350m straight on along the street ahead (1a Calle) to reach Jocotenango's main square.

CIUDAD VIEJA

Seven kilometers southwest of Antigua along the Escuintla road is **Ciudad Vieja** (Old City), site of the first capital of the Captaincy General of Guatemala. Founded in 1527, it was destroyed in 1541 when Volcán Agua loosed a flood of water penned up in its crater. The water deluged the town with tons of rock and mud, leaving only a few ruins of La Concepción church.

Java junkies in this neck of the woods will want to check out the coffee plantation **Finca los Nietos** (☎ 831-5438; www.geocities.com/losnietosfinca; 🕙 8-11am Mon-Fri) for a tour and a taste. The hour-long tour (US$5.25 per person; minimum two people) will answer all your nitty-gritty coffee questions, from how seedlings are propagated to how beans are roasted. The price includes a bag of coffee. Phone for an appointment and mention then if you want to roast your own beans (minimum 2.5kg or 5lb). The *finca* is 7km from Antigua, just off the bus route to San Antonio Aguas Calientes: you go through Ciudad Vieja and San Lorenzo El Cubo, then get off the bus at the crossroads before the textile shop called Carolina's (bus drivers know this intersection). This is before

the road goes downhill to San Antonio. Walk two blocks to the right (toward Volcán Agua) until you come to a white wall with bougainvillea and pine trees showing above it. Ring the bell and you're in.

SAN ANTONIO AGUAS CALIENTES

If you continue on to **San Antonio Aguas Calientes**, you'll see why this village is noted for its textiles as soon as you enter its plaza. Stalls in the plaza sell local woven and embroidered goods, as do shops on side streets (walk to the left of the church to find them). Bargaining is expected.

Valhalla Experimental Station (☎ 831-5799; exvalhalla@yahoo.com; 🕙 8am-4:40pm), a macadamia farm raising 300 species of this delicious nut, is near the village of San Miguel Dueñas, 4km west of Ciudad Vieja. You can tour this organic, sustainable agriculture project and sample nuts, oils and cosmetics made from the harvest. Bring a picnic and save some room for the stellar, hand-dipped chocolate-covered macadamia nuts for sale at the shop here. To get there take a San Miguel Dueñas bus from Antigua or, if under your own steam, follow the Escuintla road past Ciudad Vieja and turn right at a large cemetery on the right-hand side. From here, the farm is about a 15-minute walk or five-minute drive downhill. This road goes on to San Miguel Dueñas. To continue round to San Antonio Aguas Calientes from here, take the first street on the right – between two houses – after coming to the concrete-block paving in Dueñas (if you reach the Texaco station in the village center, you've missed the road). The road winds through coffee *fincas,* farming hamlets and little vegetable fields.

For information on buses to these villages, see p96.

SANTIAGO SACATEPÉQUEZ & SUMPANGO

Throughout Latin America, All Saints' Day (November 1) is a spectacle. In parts of Guatemala they celebrate with the **Feria del Barrilete Gigante** (Festival of the Giant Kite). The two biggest parties happen in Santiago Sacatepéquez and Sumpango, about 20km and 25km north of Antigua respectively. These kites are giants: made from tissue paper with wood or bamboo braces, and with guide ropes as thick as a human arm, most are more than 13m wide and have intricate, colorful designs. They're flown over the cemetery to speak with the souls of the dead. Judges rank the kites according to size, design, color, originality and elevation. Part of the fun is watching the crowd flee when a giant kite takes a nose dive!

Unfortunately, the wind is sometimes insufficient to lift these giant kites, which makes for an anticlimactic festival, despite the plethora of fantastic street food. *Fiambre,* a traditional dish made from meat, seafood and vegetables served cold in vinaigrette, is typically eaten on this day. It's a labor of love to make a decent *fiambre,* and women take pride in their prowess at preparing it. It is, however, an acquired taste.

Many agencies run day trips from Antigua to Santiago Sacatepéquez on November 1 for around US$8 per person, though you can easily get there on your own by taking any Guatemala City–bound bus and getting off with the throngs at the junction for Santiago. From here, take one of the scores of buses covering the last few kilometers. The fastest way to Sumpango is to take a bus to Chimaltenango and backtrack to Sumpango; this will bypass all of the Santiago-bound traffic, which is bumper to bumper on fair day.

ANTIGUA

The Highlands

The Highlands encompass not only the great chain of volcanoes running from the Antigua area to Tacaná on the Mexican border but also the 3000m-plus Cordillera de los Cuchumatanes north of Huehuetenango. This rugged topography creates Guatemala's most dramatic scenery, intensified by mountain lakes such as the magical Lago de Atitlán. The often remote, sometimes inhospitable landscape is home and refuge to a high percentage of Guatemala's indigenous Maya people, who maintain their traditional customs, rites, beliefs and costumes most strongly in these mountain fastnesses. Mayan languages are the mother tongues here, Spanish a distant second.

In among this countryside of scattered villages surrounded by *milpas* (maize fields) – plenty of them still without vehicle access – are urban or cosmopolitan pockets such as Quetzaltenango, Guatemala's second city with its many language schools, and Panajachel, the international tourist resort beside the Lago de Atitlán. Life in smaller places can be somewhat *triste* (sad, boring), so it's a good idea to visit them on one of their ebullient market or festival days.

Most towns here were already populated by the Maya when the Spanish arrived. History turned bloody and inhumane with the beginning of the civil war in 1960, when the Highlands were targeted heavily by guerrillas and the army alike. During the 36-year war, merciless death squads killed with impunity, villages were razed and tens of thousands of refugees fled to Mexico. Reconstruction and recovery from that nightmare are ongoing.

THE HIGHLANDS

TOP FIVE

- Village-hopping and chilling out around sublime **Lago de Atitlán** (p103)
- Browsing the bustling, colorful, indigenous markets at **Chichicastenango** (p128) and **Sololá** (p104)
- Learning Spanish and climbing volcanoes around **Quetzaltenango** (p139)
- Walking amid the beautiful Cuchumatanes scenery around **Nebaj** (p136) or **Todos Santos Cuchumatán** (p161)
- Admiring the colorful costumes in towns like **Santiago Atitlán** (p117), **Todos Santos Cuchumatán** (p161) and **Nebaj** (p136), and tuning into age-old **Mayan culture** in small towns and villages everywhere

CLIMATE

The emerald-green grass, tall fields of yellow maize (corn) and towering stands of pine that characterize the Highlands all depend on the abundant rain that falls between May and October. If you visit during this rainy season, be prepared for some dreary, chilly, damp days. At high altitudes it can get cold at night at any time of year. But when the sun comes out, this land is stunning to behold.

GETTING AROUND

The meandering Interamericana (Highway CA-1), running 345km along the mountain ridges between Guatemala City and the Mexican border at La Mesilla, passes close to all the region's most important places and countless buses roar up and down it all day, every day. Two key intersections act as major bus interchanges – Los Encuentros for Panajachel and Chichicastenango, and Cuatro Caminos for Quetzaltenango. If you can't find a bus going all the way to your destination, simply get one to Los Encuentros or Cuatro Caminos and change there. These transfers are usually seamless, with not-too-frustrating waiting times and locals that are always ready to help travelers to find the right bus.

Travel is easiest in the morning and, for smaller places, on market days. By mid- or late afternoon, buses may be difficult to find, and it's not generally a good idea to

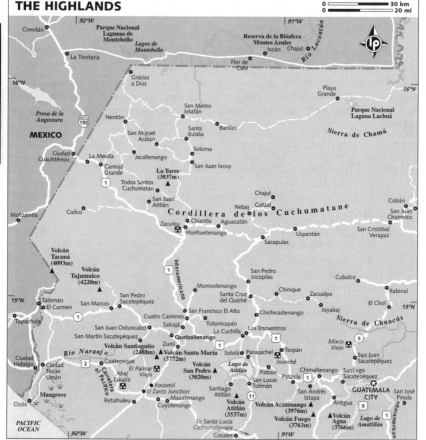

THE HIGHLANDS

be out on the roads after dark. On more remote routes further off the beaten track, you may be relying more on pickups or trucks than buses for transport.

Shuttle minibuses ferry tourists between the major destinations of the region and beyond. They travel faster, more comfortably and more expensively than buses. There's a belief that shuttles are more vulnerable to highway robbery, because a vanload of *gringos* (Westerners) is such a tempting target. However, in reality the percentage of shuttles that gets held up is minuscule, but you have to make up your own mind.

LAGO DE ATITLÁN

Surrounded by volcanoes, steep hillsides and villages where traditional Mayan culture meets the international travel scene, the Lago de Atitlán – 8km across from north to south, 18km from east to west, and averaging around 300m deep – is one of the world's most beautiful and fascinating bodies of water. Many travelers have fallen in love with it and made their homes here. It's a three-hour bus ride west from Guatemala City or Antigua. The main lakeside town is Panajachel, or Gringotenango as it is sometimes unkindly called, and most people initially head here to launch their Atitlán explorations.

The Maya around the north and northeast sides of the lake are mostly Kaqchiquel, while those on the west, south and southeast are Tz'utujil. When the Spanish arrived in 1524 the Kaqchiquels allied with them against the Tz'utujils, who were defeated in a bloody battle at Tzanajuyú. The Kaqchiquels subsequently rebelled against the Spanish and were themselves subjugated by 1531.

There is an ersatz town at the highway junction of Los Encuentros, based on the presence of throngs of people changing buses. From La Cuchilla junction, 2km further west along the Interamericana, a road descends 12km southward to Sololá, and then a sinuous 8km more, losing 500m in altitude, through pine forests to Panajachel. Sit on the right-hand side of the bus for breathtaking views of the lake and its surrounding volcanoes.

Dangers & Annoyances

One of the best things about Lago de Atitlán is – or should be – the many spectacular walks you can take up the volcanoes, along the lakeshore from village to village and elsewhere. Sadly, foreigners walking isolated paths have become an all-too-easy target for robbers (often armed) and even rapists. At the time of writing several trails in the lake area are simply unsafe to walk unless in a large group or with a police escort (which you will sometimes be able to obtain for free). The ascent of Volcán San Pedro and the Santiago–San Pedro and San Marcos–Jaibalito trails are the most notoriously risky routes, and you should seek advice from people who know before venturing out on any walk.

Stay out of the lake in the first couple of weeks of the rainy season, when many months' worth of dry-season garbage and excreta is washed down into it.

TECPÁN

Founded as a Spanish military base during the conquest, Tecpán today is a somewhat dusty town with a couple of small hotels. The ruins of the Kaqchiquel Maya capital, Iximché (ish-im-*che*), make it worth a visit for history fans.

Overlooking the more northerly of Tecpán's twin central plazas is a fine colonial church, the **Parroquia de San Francisco de Asís**. Tecpán honors San Francisco de Asís (St Francis of Assisi) in its annual **festival** in the first week of October. Market day is Thursday.

Iximché

Founded in 1463 on a flat promontory surrounded by ravines, Iximché was well sited to be the Kaqchiquel capital. At that time, the Kaqchiquel were at war with the K'iche' Maya, and the city's natural defenses served them well.

The Spanish, who arrived in 1524, set up their first Guatemalan headquarters at Tecpán. However, the demands of the Spanish for gold and other loot soon put an end to their alliance with the Kaqchiquel, who were defeated in the ensuing guerrilla war.

Entering the **archaeological site** (admission US$3.25; ⏲ 8am-4:30pm), first visit the small museum on the right, then continue to the four ceremonial plazas, which are

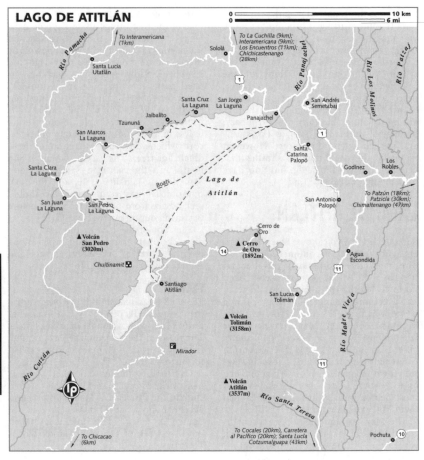

LAGO DE ATITLÁN

surrounded by temple structures up to 10m high and ball courts. Some structures have been uncovered: on a few the original plaster coating is still in place.

Ruinas buses to the site (US$0.15, 15 minutes) leave the north side of the more southerly of Tecpán's plazas at least every hour till 4pm. The last bus back leaves the site no later than 4:30pm.

Sleeping & Eating

Hotel Iximché (☎ 840-3495; 1a Av 1-38, Zona 2; s/d US$4/8, with bathroom US$7/13) This hotel will put you up in pink-painted, decent-sized, adequately clean rooms. It's just off the southern plaza.

There are various eateries around the twin plazas.

Getting There & Away

Veloz Poaquileña runs buses to Guatemala City (US$1, two hours) about every 30 minutes, 5:30am to 7pm, from in front of the church. Few buses traveling to or from Los Encuentros (US$0.70, 40 minutes), or anywhere else northwest along the Interamericana, go into central Tecpán. It's about a 1km walk (or, if you're lucky, a short ride on a yellow urban bus) to the center from the Tecpán turnoff on the Interamericana.

SOLOLÁ

pop 9000 / elevation 2110m

There was a Kaqchiquel town (called Tzoloyá) here long before the Spanish showed up. Sololá's importance comes from its location on trade routes between the *tierra caliente* (hot lands of the Pacific Slope) and *tierra fría* (the chilly highlands). All the traders meet here, and Sololá's terrific **market** (☿ Tue & Fri) is one of the most authentic in the Highlands. On market mornings the plaza next to the cathedral is ablaze with the colorful costumes of people from a dozen surrounding villages and towns. Displays of meat, vegetables, fruit, housewares and clothing are neatly arranged in every available space, with tides of buyers ebbing and flowing around the vendors. Elaborate stands are well stocked with brightly colored yarn for making the traditional costumes you see around you. This is a local rather than a tourist market.

Every Sunday morning the officers of the traditional religious brotherhoods *(cofradías)* parade ceremoniously to the cathedral. On other days, Sololá sleeps.

You can make a very pleasant walk from Sololá down to the lake, whether taking the highway to Panajachel (8km) or the walking track to Santa Cruz La Laguna (10km), but ask around about safety before starting out.

Virtually everyone stays in Panajachel, but if you need a bed in Sololá, **Hotel Belén** (☎ 762-3105; 10a Calle 4-36, Zona 1; s/d US$5/9; **P**) has eight clean upstairs rooms with hot-water bathrooms. It's a block uphill behind the clock tower that overlooks the main square.

All buses between Panajachel and Los Encuentros stop at Sololá. It's US$0.20 and 20 minutes to either place.

PANAJACHEL
pop 14,000 / elevation 1560m
In the hippie heyday of the 1960s and '70s Pana, as it's widely known, was a haunt of laid-back travelers in semipermanent exile. When the civil war of the late '70s and early '80s made Panajachel a dangerous – or at least unpleasant – place to be, many moved on. But the town's tourist industry is booming again and has spread to several lakeside villages.

Pana is not a particularly beautiful place – it has developed haphazardly according to the demands of the tourist trade. But you need only to head down to the shore of the lake to understand why it attracts so many visitors. Lago de Atitlán is one of the world's most spectacular locales, period. Diamond splatters dance across the water, fertile hills dot the landscape with color, and over everything loom the volcanoes, permeating the entire area with a mysterious beauty. The place never looks the same twice.

Lago de Atitlán is often placid and beautiful early in the day, which is the best time for swimming – though Pana's shores aren't the cleanest. (Note that since the lake is a volcanic crater filled with water, the lake bed often drops off sharply very near the shore.) By noon the Xocomil, a southeasterly wind, may have risen to ruffle the water's surface, sometimes violently, making it a tough crossing for the small boats plying between the lakeside villages. This is particularly true between November and February, a time known as the windy season in these parts. It's always good to get your traveling done in the morning, when weather conditions are better and there is more traffic.

Many cultures mingle on the dusty streets of Panajachel. Ladinos and *gringos* control the tourist industry. The Kaqchiquel and Tz'utujil Maya from surrounding villages come to sell their handicrafts to tourists.

THE HIGHLANDS

HOW ATITLÁN WAS BORN

The first volcanoes in the Atitlán region popped up 150,000 years ago, but today's landscape has its origins in the massive Los Chocoyos eruption of 85,000 years ago, which blew volcanic ash as far as Florida and Panama. The quantity of magma expelled from below the earth's crust caused the surface terrain to collapse, forming a huge, roughly circular hollow that soon filled with water – the Lago de Atitlán. Smaller volcanoes rose out of the lake's southern waters thousands of years later: Volcán San Pedro (today 3020m above sea level) about 60,000 years ago, followed by Volcán Atitlán (3537m) and Volcán Tolimán (3158m) some 40,000 to 30,000 years ago. These reduced the lake's surface area but at the same time created the dramatic volcano vistas that make Atitlán what it is. The lake today is around 300m deep and has a surface area of 128 sq km. Its water level fluctuates curiously from year to year.

The lakeside villa owners drive up on weekends from Guatemala City. Groups of tourists descend on the town from buses for a few hours, a day or an overnight. And still there are the 'traditional' hippies, with long hair, local dress and Volkswagen minibuses.

Orientation

Calle Principal (also called Calle Real) is Pana's main street. Many establishments here don't use street addresses.

Most buses stop at the intersection of Calle Principal and Calle Santander, the main road to the lake. Calle Santander is lined with restaurants, shops, accommodations, cybercafés, travel agencies and other tourist services. Beyond the Calle Santander corner, Calle Principal continues 400m to 500m northeast to the town center, where you'll find the market (busiest on Sunday and Thursday, but in action daily), church, town hall and a further smattering of places to sleep and eat.

Calle Rancho Grande (also called Calle del Balneario) is the other main road to the beach; it's parallel to, and east of, Calle Santander. The pedestrian Calle del Lago runs along the lakeside between Calle Santander and Calle Rancho Grande. It's a pretty place for strolling.

Information

BOOKSTORES

Gallery Bookstore (Comercial El Pueblito, Av Los Árboles) Sells and exchanges used books, plus sells a few new ones including some Lonely Planet guides.

Libros del Lago (Calle Santander) Has an excellent stock of books in English and other tongues on Guatemala, the Maya and Mesoamerica, plus maps, English and Latin American literature in English, and Lonely Planet and other guidebooks.

EMERGENCY

Policía de Turismo (Tourist Police) Main branch (☎ 762-1120; Municipalidad, Calle Principal); Inguat tourist office (☻ 9am-5pm) English-speaking; have their main office in the town hall.

INTERNET ACCESS

As you'd expect, Pana has plenty of places to check your email and surf the Web. The standard price is US$1.30 an hour; typical hours are 9am to 10pm, perhaps slightly shorter on Sunday.

Gallery Bookstore (Comercial El Pueblito, Av Los Árboles)
Jade Internet (Centro Comercial San Rafael, Calle Santander) One of several cybercafés on Calle Santander.
MayaNet (Calle Santander 3-62)
Planet Internet (Calle Santander) Has good connections.
Pulcinella (Calle Principal 0-62)

LAUNDRY

Lavandería Viajero (Edificio Rincón Sai, Calle Santander; ☻ 8am-7pm) Reliable place; charges US$0.45 per pound.

MEDICAL SERVICES

The nearest hospital is at Sololá.
Centro de Salud (Clinic; Calle Principal; ☻ 8am-6pm Mon-Fri, 8am-1pm Sat)

MONEY

Banco Agromercantil (cnr Calles Principal & Santander; ☻ 9am-6pm Mon-Fri, 9am-1pm Sat) Changes US-dollar cash and traveler's checks, and has a MasterCard ATM.
Banco de Comercio (Calle Principal; ☻ 9am-5pm Mon-Fri, 9am-1pm Sat) Changes US-dollar cash and traveler's checks; next door are a Visa ATM and Banco Agromercantil.
Banco Industrial (Comercial Los Pinos, Calle Santander; ☻ 9am-4pm Mon-Fri, 9am-1pm Sat) Changes cash US dollars, offers Visa-card cash advances and has a Visa ATM.
Credomatic (Centro Comercial San Rafael, Calle Santander) Visa and MasterCard cash advances and changes cash US dollars.

Some of the travel agencies, restaurants and hotels along Calle Santander will change US dollars or euros cash but not at the best rates.

Americo's Tours Does Visa and MasterCard cash advances, but charges a 10% commission.
Circus Bar (Av Los Árboles) Changes euros.

POST

Post Office (cnr Calles Santander & 15 de Febrero)
DHL (Edificio Rincón Sai, Calle Santander) Courier service.
Get Guated Out (☎ /fax 762-0595; gguated@c.net.gt; Comercial El Pueblito, Av Los Árboles) English-speaking outfit that can ship your important letters and parcels by air freight or international courier. It will also buy handicrafts for you and ship them for export – handy if you can't come to Panajachel yourself.

TELEPHONE

Some cybercafés and travel agencies located on Calle Santander offer moderately cheap phone calls – around US$0.70 a minute to North America or Central America and US$1.30 a minute to Europe. Try **Jade Internet** or **Planet Internet**. For local calls

THE HIGHLANDS

there is a line of card phones outside **Telgua** (Calle Santander).

TOURIST INFORMATION
Inguat (☎ 762-1392, ☎ /fax 762-1106; Calle del Lago; ☽ 9am-5pm) By the lakeside, this tourist office has little material available although staff can answer straightforward questions.

TRAVEL AGENCIES
Many of the full-service travel agencies located in Panajachel are scattered along Calle Santander. These establishments offer trips, tours and shuttle services to other destinations around Guatemala. Included among these travel agencies are the following businesses:

Americo's Tours (☎ 762-2021; Calle Santander)
Atitrans (☎ 762-2336, 762-0146; Edificio Rincón Sai)
San Nicolás Agencia de Viajes (☎ 762-0382; fax 762-0391; Calle Santander 1-71)
Tolimán Excursions (☎ /fax 762-2455, 762-0334; Calle Santander 1-77)
Union Travel (☎ 762-2426; Local 2, Comercial Los Pinos)

Sights
MUSEUMS
Pana has two very worthwhile museums. The **Museo Lacustre Atitlán** (Hotel Posada de Don Rodrigo; Calle Santander; admission US$4.50; ☽ 8am-6pm Sun-Fri, 8am-7pm Sat) has fascinating displays on the history of the Atitlán region and the volcanic eruptions that created its majestic landscape, and a collection of ancient Mayan artifacts recovered from the lake. The **Museo Raúl Vasquéz** (5a Calle Peatonal, Calle Principal; admission US$1.30; ☽ 10am-6pm) is the home, studio, and sculpture and meditation garden of the quirky Panajachel artist for which it is named. The garden is filled with Vásquez's sculptures of an eclectic selection of deities, from Jesus Christ to Shiva; indoors, you can browse his colorful, abstract paintings. To get there follow Calle Principal 700m northeast from the market, and follow the museum sign pointing down an alley: it's 120m off the road.

RESERVA NATURAL ATITLÁN
A former coffee plantation being retaken by natural vegetation, **Reserva Natural Atitlán** (☎ 762-2565; adult/child US$5/3; ☽ 8am-5pm) is 200m past the Hotel Atitlán on the northern outskirts of town. It makes a good outing on foot or bicycle. You can walk the main trail at a leisurely pace in an hour: it leads up over swing bridges to a waterfall then down to a platform for viewing the local population of spider monkeys. You should also see coatis *(pisotes)*, relatives of the raccoon with long snouts and long, upright, furry tails. The reserve also includes a herb garden and butterfly enclosure.

Activities
CYCLING, HIKING & HORSE RIDING
Lago de Atitlán is a cycling, hiking and riding wonderland, with hill and dale spread among a fantastic setting. You can take a bike by boat to Santiago, San Pedro or another village to start a cycling tour around the lake. A few places in Panajachel rent out bikes: equipment varies, so check out a bike before renting it. **Alquiler de Motos y Bicicletas Emanuel** (☎ 762-2790; Calle 14 de Febrero; ☽ 8am-6pm Mon-Fri, 8am-1pm Sun) rents out decent bikes for US$0.70/4.50/6.50 per one/eight/24 hours. **Maco** (☎ 762-0883; Calle Santander) has similar prices.

See Santiago Atitlán (p117) and following sections for information on walks around Lago de Atitlán, and Santiago Atitlán for horse-riding opportunities.

Make inquiries about safety before setting out for any hike or ride, and keep asking as you go (p103). In some cases it's better to go with a guide, and some travel agencies in Panajachel, such as **Tolimán Excursions** (p107), offer guided hikes and rides in the lake area.

A one-day walking trip from Panajachel to the top of Volcán San Pedro and back (crossing the lake by boat) should cost around US$20 per person.

DIVING
British-and-American-run **ATI Divers** (☎ 762-2621, outside normal opening hours 706-4117; laiguana perdida@itelgua.com; Plaza Los Patios, Calle Santander; ☽ 9:30am-1pm Mon-Sat) leads dive trips from Santa Cruz La Laguna (p127). Professional Association of Diving Instructors (PADI) beginning certification is a four-day affair costing US$175. ATI also offers advanced certification, fun dives for certified divers (US$25/45 for one/two dives), and specialty courses including a two-dive altitude course (US$65). Lago de Atitlán is an interesting dive site because it's a collapsed volcanic cone with bizarre geological formations, but there is not much aquatic

PANAJACHEL

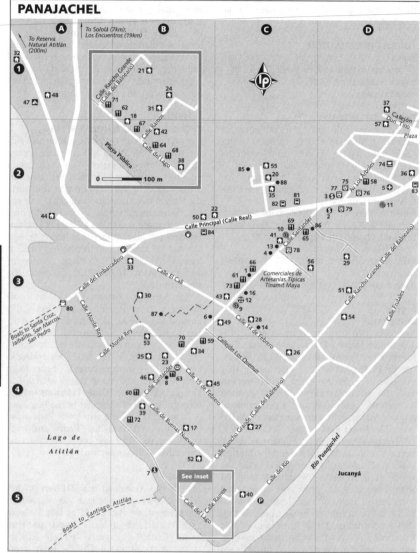

flora or fauna here. During the rainy season the water clouds up, so the best time to dive is between October and May (in the morning).

ATI Divers also organize the annual garbage cleanup of the lake, during which several tons of trash are collected. This event, typically held in September, is a great opportunity to give something back to the community and make new friends.

Language Courses

Panajachel has a niche in the language school scene. Two well set-up schools are **Jardín de América** (☎ /fax 762-2637; www.jardindeamerica.com; Calle 14 de Febrero, 3a Av Peatonal 4-44) and **Jabel**

THE HIGHLANDS

0 _____ 300 m
0 _____ 0.2 mi

To Museo Raúl Vásquez (350m);
San Lucas Tolimán (24km)

Market

INFORMATION
Americo's Tours.......................... **1** C3
Atitrans....................................(see 65)
Banco Agromercantil...................**2** D2
Banco de Comercio.....................**3** D2
Banco Industrial.........................(see 6)
Centro Comercial San Rafael.......**4** C3
Centro de Salud..........................**5** D2
Comercial El Pueblito..............(see 58)
Comercial Los Pinos...................**6** B3
Credomatic................................(see 4)
DHL...(see 65)
Edificio Rincón Sai....................(see 65)
Gallery Bookstore.....................(see 58)
Get Guated Out........................(see 58)
Inguat Tourist Office...................**7** B5
Jade Internet..............................(see 4)
Lavandería Viajero....................(see 65)
Libros del Lago..........................**8** B4
MayaNet....................................**9** C3
Planet Internet.........................**10** C3
Police Station...........................(see 89)
Pulcinella.................................**11** D2
San Nicolás Agencia de Viajes...(see 13)
Telgua.....................................**12** C3
Tolimán Excursions...................**13** C3
Union Travel..............................(see 6)
Visa ATM...................................(see 3)

SIGHTS & ACTIVITIES   pp107–8
Alquiler de Motos y Bicicletas
  Emanuel................................**14** C3
ATI Divers................................(see 66)
Church....................................**15** E2
Maco.......................................**16** C3
Museo Lacustre Atitlán............(see 39)

SLEEPING   pp110–13
Bungalows El Aguacatal.............**17** B4
Bungalows El Rosario.................**18** B2
Campana Campground................**19** F5
Casa de Huéspedes Las
  Hermanas..............................**20** C2
Casa Loma...............................**21** B1

Grand Hotel..............................**22** C2
Hospedaje Anexo Santa Elena....**23** B4
Hospedaje Contemporáneo........**24** B1
Hospedaje El Viajero..................**25** B4
Hospedaje García.......................**26** C4
Hospedaje Jere..........................**27** C4
Hospedaje Mi Chosita................**28** C3
Hospedaje Montúfar..................**29** D3
Hospedaje Ramos 2................(see 42)
Hospedaje Santo Domingo.........**30** B3
Hospedaje Sueño Real...............**31** B1
Hotel Atitlán............................**32** A1
Hotel Cacique Inn......................**33** B3
Hotel Dos Mundos.....................**34** B4
Hotel El Viajero.........................**35** C2
Hotel Maya-Kanek.....................**36** D2
Hotel Montana...........................**37** D1
Hotel Playa Linda......................**38** B2
Hotel Posada de Don Rodrigo.....**39** B4
Hotel Posada K'amol B'ey...........**40** C5
Hotel Primavera........................**41** C3
Hotel Ramos.............................**42** B2
Hotel Regis...............................**43** C3
Hotel Tzanjuyú..........................**44** A2
Hotel Utz-Jay............................**45** B4
Hotel Villa Martita.....................**46** B4
Hotel Visión Azul Campground....**47** A1
Hotel Visión Azul.......................**48** A1
Mario's Rooms...........................**49** C3
Mini Hotel Riva Bella.................**50** B2
Müller's Guest House.................**51** D3
Porta Hotel del Lago..................**52** B5
Posada de los Volcanes...........(see 46)
Posada Monte Rosa....................**53** B4
Rancho Grande Inn....................**54** D3
Rooms Santa Elena.....................**55** C2
Rooms Santander.......................**56** C3
Villa Lupita...............................**57** D2

EATING   pp113–14
Al Chisme..................................**58** D2
Brisas de Lago........................(see 68)
Cafe Bombay............................**59** B4
Deli Jasmín...............................**60** B4

Deli Llama de Fuego...................**61** C3
Don Neto..................................(see 70)
El Bambú...................................**62** B1
El Pescador...............................(see 64)
El Pájaro Azul...........................**63** B4
El Xocomil................................**64** B2
Guajimbo's...............................(see 61)
La Terraza................................**65** C3
Las Chinitas..............................**66** C3
Las Palmeras..........................(see 73)
Los Alpes.................................**67** B2
Los Pumpos..............................**68** B2
Pana Pan..................................**69** C2
Restaurante Emilio...................(see 68)
Restaurante Los Cayucos...........**70** B4
Restaurante Mario...................(see 49)
Restaurante Taly.....................(see 62)
Restaurante Tocoyal.................**71** A1
Ristorante La Lanterna..........(see 34)
Sunset Cafe..............................**72** B4
Tacos 3xQ10............................**73** C3

DRINKING   p114
Crossroads Café.........................**74** D2
Pana Arte.................................(see 78)
Ubu's Bar.................................(see 58)

ENTERTAINMENT   pp114–15
Chapiteau.................................**75** D2
Circus Bar.................................**76** D2
El Aleph...................................**77** D2
Pana Rock................................**78** C3
Socrates...................................**79** D2
Turquoise Buffalo...................(see 58)

TRANSPORT   pp115–16
Embarcadero Tzanjuyú...............**80** A3
Main Bus Stop...........................**81** C2
Oficina de Microbuses y Taxis San
  Francisco...............................**82** C2
Pickups to Santa Catarina Palopó &
  San Antonio Palopó.................**83** D2
Transportes Rébuli Office............**84** B3

OTHER
Centro de Tutoría e Idiomas.....**85** C2
Jabel Tinamit...........................**86** C2
Jardín de América.....................**87** B3
Middle Path Herbs.................(see 66)
Plaza Los Patios.....................(see 66)
Spanish School Mayan...............**88** C2
Town Hall.................................**89** E2

To Santa Catarina Palopó (4km);
San Antonio Palopó (9km)

Tinamit (☎ 762-0238; www.jabeltinamit.com; Calle Santander). Both have ample gardens and good atmospheres. Four hours of one-on-one study five days a week, including a homestay with a local family, will cost around US$120 a week at either place. Other schools include **Centro de Tutoría e Idiomas** (CTI; ☎ 762-0259, 762-1005; 2a Av Peatonal 1-84, Zona 2) and **Spanish School Mayan** (☎ 810-7196; Callejón Santa Elena), both of which teach some Mayan languages as well as Spanish.

Tours

If you're pressed for time, a boat tour of the lake, stopping at a few villages, is a fine idea. Boats leave the Playa Pública quay daily at

8:30am and 9:30am for tours to San Pedro La Laguna (where you stop for about 1½ hours), Santiago Atitlán (1½ hours) and San Antonio Palopó (one hour). Both get back at 3:30pm so you get a little less shore time on the 9:30am departure. Cost is US$6.50 on either tour. Many travel agencies (p107) offer more expensive boat tours (around US$25 per person), which may include weaving demonstrations, visits to the shrine of Maximón in Santiago and so on.

Festivals & Events
The **festival of San Francisco de Asís**, October 4, is celebrated with massive drinking and fireworks in Panajachel.

Sleeping
BUDGET
Panajachel has many little family-run *hospedajes* (pensions): you'll see their signs along Calle Santander. They're as simple as they come – perhaps two plain beds, a small table and a light bulb in a room of bare boards. Most provide clean-enough toilets, and some have hot showers. There are also plenty of more upscale establishments still in the budget price bracket.

Hotel Visión Azul (☎ 762-1419, ☎ /fax 762-1426; person/vehicle/tent US$2/2/4) This has a picturesque but less secure campground on an open grassy area right by the lake. Rates include electricity and cold showers.

Hotel Utz-Jay (☎ 762-0217, ☎ /fax 762-1358; utzjay_garcia@yahoo.com; Calle 15 de Febrero 2-50; s/d/tr/q US$19/22/26/30; P ✕) This excellent-value small hotel, a short distance from the lake and Calle Santander, has eight cozily furnished, nonsmoking rooms in cottages around a grassy garden. They have traditional fabrics, a hot-water bathroom, fan and nice touches like candles and drinking water. Good breakfasts and laundry service are available and there's a traditional Mayan sauna called a *chuj*. The owners speak Spanish, French and English, have lots of information about the area, and run hiking and camping trips around the lake.

Posada Monte Rosa (☎ 762-0055; Calle Monte Rey; s/d/tr US$13/20/26; P) A short distance off Calle Santander, the 10 rooms here are sizeable and bright, with hot-water bathrooms and colorful Mayan-style curtains, and fronted by little patches of lawn.

Hospedaje Santo Domingo (☎ 762-0236; Calle Monte Rey; s/d US$3/5, s/d/tr with bathroom US$9/13/16) This amicable, tranquil establishment has a variety of rooms. The cheapest are very basic wood-plank affairs, but there are also better shared-bathroom doubles for US$7 in a newer, two-story block. There's a grassy hangout area here that makes this place.

Hospedaje El Viajero (☎ 762-0128; off Calle Santander; s/d/tr/q US$8/12/16/20; P) The eight bare, simple rooms at this welcoming, family-run place have hot-water bathrooms. Upstairs rooms are a bit bigger, brighter and airier. El Viajero is at the end of a short lane off lower Calle Santander, making it quiet and peaceful, yet you're near everything. You can use a cooker, microwave and fridge, and there's laundry service and free drinking water.

Hospedaje Montúfar (☎ 762-0406; Callejón El Capulín, Primera Calle Peatonal 2-52, Zona 2; s/d US$6/7, d/tr/q with 2 double beds US$9/12/16) Off northern Calle Santander, the Montúfar is spotless, friendly and family-run, with a little greenery-hung patio. Beds are firm and the shared bathrooms clean, with hot showers. A great choice for peace and quiet at budget prices.

Mario's Rooms (☎ 762-2370, 762-1313; Calle Santander; s/d/tr US$6/8/10, with bathroom US$9/11/16) The 24 clean, simple rooms are ranged on two floors beside a long patio with plants. This is a good value, even if the bathrooms are just cubicles built into the corner of the room and shared-bathroom customers have to pay US$0.25 for a hot shower.

Villa Lupita (☎ 762-1201; Callejón Don Tino; s/d US$4/7; P) Family-run Lupita is great value if you feel like staying in the town center. The 18 clean, secure rooms have comfortable beds, reading lamps and colorful carpets, and there's free coffee and drinking water. The shared hot-water bathrooms are clean, and the roof terrace affords good views.

Hospedaje Jere (☎ 762-2781; jere_armando@yahoo .com; Calle Rancho Grande; s/d/tr US$7/11/13; P) The Jere, 250m from the lake, has nine pleasant rooms with hot-water bathroom and bright, woven-cotton bedspreads. Everything is enlivened by textiles, photos, maps and informative posters, and you can book shuttle buses and lake tours on the spot.

Casa Loma (☎ 762-1447; soniaazurdia@hotmail .com; Calle Rancho Grande; s US$7-8, d US$8-11, s/d with bathroom US$20/25) Two friendly Pana-bred sisters who now live much of the year in Canada are the owners of this seven-room guesthouse. Most rooms are in a two-story wooden building overlooking a big garden and with good, firm beds. The two bathrooms boast TV and tile floors and were brand new in 2003. There are also two attractive large apartments available from April to December for US$350 to US$450 a month. For bookings you can call the sisters in Canada: ☎ 416-493-7935 (Sonia), ☎ 905-737-5090 (Neca).

Casa de Huéspedes Las Hermanas (☎ 762-0673; Callejón Santa Elena; s/d US$4/8, with bathroom US$5/9) An excellent small cheapie along a lane off Calle Principal, Las Hermanas has just four rooms around a pleasant little patio. Rooms have floor rugs, woven bedspreads and paintings on the walls, and there's a café serving all meals. Bathrooms have hot water. Round the corner is **Hotel El Viajero** (s/d/tr/q US$8/12/16/20), whose eight rooms all have kitchen and hot-water bathroom, and along the lane is **Rooms Santa Elena** (Callejón Santa Elena; s/d/tr US$3/6/8), with spongy beds and cold showers but appealing to some travelers for its very low prices.

Rooms Santander (☎ 762-1304; off Calle Santander; s/d US$5/7, with bathroom US$8/11) One of Pana's longest-running budget hostelries, the Santander is still going strong with clean rooms on two levels around a small patio full of trees.

Hotel Maya-Kanek (☎ /fax 762-1104; Calle Principal; s/d US$8/16; P) A town-center hotel with friendly management, the Maya-Kanek has rooms around a cobbled parking courtyard with a small garden. The 20 rooms, though small and simple, are a bit more comfortable than at a *hospedaje*, and they come with hot-water bathroom. Ask for a discount if you stay more than one night.

Grand Hotel (☎ 762-2940/1; granhotel@amigo.com .gt; Calle Principal; s/d/tr/q US$17/20/24/30; P 🐾) The Grand looks grungy from the street, but inside is a garden with lawns, plants and fountains. The 30 rooms are a little tired but adequately clean, with cheery colored bedspreads. Get one at the back for quietness. All rooms have TV and hot-water bathroom, and there's a pool and restaurant, so it's a good place to stay if you're traveling with kids.

Campana Campground (☎ 762-2479; Carretera a Santa Catarina Palopó; rooms per person US$4) The North

American owner has traveled a lot himself. He provides good security, a kitchen, clean bathrooms (US$0.60 for a hot shower), electrical hookups (US$0.20), free drinking water, basketball, darts and inexpensive international phone calls, all in a pleasant, tree-surrounded setting. To get there, follow the Palopó road 1km from Calle Principal and turn left opposite Calle Cementerio. If need be, you can rent camping gear for around US$1.30 a night. Three clean little rooms in wooden cabins are available too.

Hospedaje Sueño Real (☎ 762-0608; fax 762-1097; Calle Ramos; s/d/tr US$9/20/20, with bathroom US$11/24/ 24) The Sueño Real is the best of four fairly popular budget places up Calle Ramos, a short lane off Calle del Lago. It provides tasteful, clean rooms with TV, fan and hot-water bathroom. The 2nd-floor terrace with chairs, tables and lake view is a plus. It has international phone services and it also rents out bicycles.

Also on Calle Ramos are three cheaper but clean and acceptable places, all offering rooms with bathroom:

Hospedaje Contemporáneo (☎ 762-2214; s/d US$7/12) Hospitable place to stay.

Hotel Ramos (☎ 762-0413; Calle Ramos; s/d US$7/11; P) Has been recently spruced-up.

Hospedaje Ramos 2 (☎ 762-0389; Calle Ramos; s/d US$6/9 to US$10/13; P) Three-story place near Hotel Ramos.

Pana has plenty of very plain but acceptable *hospedajes* with shared bathrooms:

Hospedaje García (☎ 762-2187; Calle 14 de Febrero 2-24; s/d/tr US$4/8/12) Rooms are set along walkways around a leafy garden that's also home to Stereo Pentecostés, the local Pentecostal radio station.

Hospedaje Mi Chosita (Calle 14 de Febrero; d US$4) Absolutely no frills but certainly cheap, and run by a large Mayan family.

Hotel Villa Martita (Calle Santander 5-51; s/d/tr US$6/ 8/12) Friendly three-room place two blocks from the lake.

Hospedaje Anexo Santa Elena (☎ 762-1114; Calle Monte Rey 3-06; s/d US$4/7) Clean eight-room lodging just off lower Santander.

MID-RANGE

Mid-range lodgings are busiest on weekends. From Sunday to Thursday you may get a discount. All provide bathrooms with hot showers.

Hotel Dos Mundos (☎ 762-2078, 762-2140; dosmundos@atitlan.com; Calle Santander 4-72; s/d/tr

US$36/45/55; (P) (R)) Italian-owned Dos Mundos has a great location towards the lake end of Calle Santander, but its installations are set well away from the street. The 22 bungalows, all with terracotta floors, woven bedspreads, Italian fittings, cable TV and at least one double and one single bed, are set around tropical gardens with a large pool. Also here are a good Italian restaurant (p114), an in-house travel agency and a clean-cut continental-style bar fronting the street.

Hotel Primavera (☎ 762-2052; www.primaveratitlan.com; Calle Santander; s/d/tr US$20/30/40) The 10 rooms, nine of them upstairs above a green garden-patio, are clean, uncluttered and appealing, with Spanish tile floors and cypress-wood fittings. Rates go up about 50% for July, August, Semana Santa and the Christmas–New Year holidays.

Posada de los Volcanes (☎ 762-0244; www.posadadelosvolcanes.com; Calle Santander 5-51; s/d/tr/q US$25/32/42/50) This is a comfortable little hotel with 12 rooms on four floors. Some have two double beds, some have one; all are brightened by paintings and mirrors.

Hotel Playa Linda (☎ 762-0097; fax 762-1159; akennedy@gua.gbm.net; Calle del Lago; s/d/tr/q with lake view US$30/35/40/45, without lake view US$25/30/35/40; (P)) The Playa Linda has 17 assorted rooms, mostly good-sized, and welcoming owners and staff. Rooms 1–5 and 26 have large balconies with tables, chairs and wonderful lake views. All the rooms have a bathroom, most have fireplaces and some have a TV. Rates go up US$5 on Friday and Saturday, and by around 50% (with view) or around 35% (without view) for July, August, Semana Santa and the Christmas–New Year holidays.

Müller's Guest House (☎ /fax 762-2442; atmuller@amigonet.gt; Calle Rancho Grande; s/d/tr US$35/45/50; (P)) Just three attractive rooms with wood floors and ceilings and white-tiled bathrooms, around well-tended gardens, comprise the accommodations here. But there's plenty of comfortable communal space, and rates include breakfast.

Rancho Grande Inn (☎ 762-1554, 762-2255; www.ranchograndeinn.com; Calle Rancho Grande; d US$40-70; (P) (R)) Founded in the 1940s, the Rancho Grande has a dozen varied rooms, suites and *cabañas* (cabins) in perfectly maintained German country-style villas, all in a tropical Guatemalan setting with bright green lawns and a large pool. Some rooms sleep up to five people (US$115). All have TV, phone and carpets, and rates include a filling, delicious breakfast featuring original pancakes and home-grown honey and coffee.

Hotel Montana (☎ 762-0326; fax 762-2180; Callejón Don Tino; s/d/tr US$16/29/43; (P)) Down a narrow street near the church, the Montana has 23 clean, bright rooms with cable TV ranged along a fine, green, parking courtyard full of birdsong.

Mini Hotel Riva Bella (☎ 762-1348; fax 762-1353; Calle Principal 2-21; s/d/tr/q US$27/32/37/42; (P)) This collection of neat two-room bungalows, each with cable TV and its own parking place, is set around lush gardens.

Bungalows El Aguacatal (☎ 762-1482; fax 476-1582; Calle de Buenas Nuevas; s/d/tr/q US$26/26/45/45, with kitchen US$33/33/58/58; (P)) One block from the lake, El Aguacatal is aimed at weekenders from the capital, and you may get a few dollars' discount midweek. Each bungalow has two bedrooms and salon. Under the same management and sporting the same bright blue paint is the nearby **Bungalows El Rosario** (☎ 762-1491; Calle del Lago; s/d/tr/q US$13/26/33/39; (P)), with nine rooms around a courtyard-cum-parking area. Nos 1-4, with stone walls, are the most appealing.

Hotel Cacique Inn (☎ /fax 762-2053; Calle El Cali 3-82; s/d/tr US$54/61/69; (P) (R)) Near Embarcadero Tzanjuyú, where boats leave for the lake's western villages, the Cacique is an assemblage of pseudo-rustic red-roofed buildings around verdant gardens with lots of birds and a swimming pool. The 34 comfortable rooms have double beds, fireplaces and weavings.

Hotel Posada K'amol B'ey (☎ 762-0215; Calle Ramos; s/d US$18/24; (P)) This motel-style place, up a lane off Calle del Lago, provides clean, bright rooms along lovely grassy lawns. It's popular with vacationing and weekending Guatemalan families. This hotel abuts onion fields, which at times emit a powerful aroma.

Hotel Regis (☎ /fax 762-1152; www.atitlan.com; Calle Santander 3-47; s/d/tr/q US$42/50/55/60; (P) (R)) The Regis is a group of semicolonial-style villas among palm-shaded lawns. Its 25 large rooms have pleasing Frederick Crocker prints of Mayan costume. Guests can enjoy two natural thermal pools in the grounds. Rates rise to US$61/61/71/81 for July, August, Semana Santa and the Christmas–New Year holidays.

Hotel Visión Azul (Blue Vision; ☎ /fax 762-1426; on Hotel Atitlán road; s/d/tr/q US$39/39/50/57; P ☒) The Blue Vision has a quiet location just outside town looking toward the lake. The big, bright rooms in the main building have spacious terraces festooned with bougainvillea and ivy. Modern bungalows along the road provide more privacy but security may not be the greatest there. The hotel has a swimming pool. Out of season it can be empty and ghostly.

Hotel Tzanjuyú (☎ 762-1318; Calle Principal 4-96; s/d/tr US$35/35/39; P ☒) Set right on the lakeshore, with large gardens, this is another hotel that comes alive at holiday times. Out of season it can feel pretty desolate. All 36 rooms open onto small balconies with a superb lake view and are large and bright, with tile floors. The hotel has a swimming pool and restaurant.

TOP END

Hotel Atitlán (☎ /fax 762-1416/29; www.hotelatitlan .com; Finca San Buenaventura; s/d/tr with breakfast US$132/132/147; P ☐ ☒) Pana's loveliest hotel is on the lakeshore 1.5km northwest of the town center. It's a rambling, three-story, semicolonial-style affair surrounded by large and gorgeous gardens. Inside are gleaming tile floors, antique wood carvings and exquisite handicraft decorations. The patio has views across the swimming pools to the lake. The 65 rooms all have lake-facing balconies, and the hotel has a restaurant (see p114), bar and an outstanding gift shop.

Hotel Posada de Don Rodrigo (☎ 762-2326/29; chotelera@c.net.gt; Calle Santander; s/d/tr US$85/95/105; P ☒) This is another fine luxury hotel, with a pool and terrace overlooking the lake. The 39 rooms are good-sized, with fireplaces and large beds. Only eight have lake views, however, and these cost US$12 extra.

Porta Hotel del Lago (☎ 762-1555/56/57; www .portahotels.com; cnr Calle Rancho Grande & Calle de Buenas Nuevas; full board & drinks s/d/tr/q US$92/134/177/219; P ☒) This six-story resort hotel overlooking the lake seems a little out of place in low-rise Panajachel. It has two swimming pools (one for children) in nice gardens, plus gym, disco and games. All 100 rooms have two double beds.

Eating
BUDGET

Deli Jasmín (☎ 762-2586; lower Calle Santander; items US$2-3.50; ☺ 7am-6pm Wed-Mon) This tranquil garden restaurant serves a great range of healthy foods and drinks to the strains of soft classical music. Breakfast is served all day, and you can buy wholewheat or pita bread, hummus or mango chutney to take away. **Deli Llama de Fuego** (☎ 762-2585; upper Calle Santander; ☺ 7am-6pm Thu-Tue) has the same excellent menu in only slightly less peaceful surroundings.

Las Chinitas (Plaza Los Patios, Calle Santander; mains or set lunch US$3-6) Las Chinitas serves up unbelievably delicious, moderately priced Asian food. Try the Malaysian curry with coconut milk or the satay, both with rice, tropical salad and your choice of tofu, tempeh, chicken, pork or prawns.

Guajimbo's (Calle Santander; mains US$4-6) A few doors south from Las Chinitas, this Uruguayan grill is another of Pana's best eateries, serving up generous meat and chicken dishes with vegetables, salad, garlic bread and either rice or boiled potatoes. You won't leave hungry. Try the *chivita Hernandarias* – tenderloin cooked with bacon, mozzarella, peppers (capsicums) and olives. There are vegetarian dishes, good-value breakfasts and bottomless cups of coffee for US$0.70.

Cafe Bombay (☎ 762-0611; Calle Santander; dishes US$2.50-4; ☺ 5-10pm Mon, noon-10pm Tue-Sun) Little, street-side Bombay turns out all sorts of inexpensive but carefully prepared vegetarian goodies ranging from a plate of hummus, mushroom pate, olives and pita bread to stir-fry veggies with brown rice and ginger-soy-cashew sauce.

Pana Pan (Calle Santander 1-61; pastries US$0.80) Great cinnamon rolls, banana and chocolate muffins and wholewheat bread make a call here obligatory. Take away or sit down with a coffee.

El Pájaro Azul (lower Calle Santander; mains US$2.25-5) This clean-cut spot with wrought-iron chairs at square wood tables is good for a wide range of needs from crepes to steak *a la pimienta*.

Tacos 3xQ10 (Calle Santander; 3 tacos US$1.30; ☺ 8am-10pm Sun-Thu, 8am-11pm Fri & Sat) Try the yummy *hawaiiano*, with chicken, onion, chile and pineapple.

Las Palmeras (☎ 762-0058; Calle Santander; mains US$2.50-4) A popular little travelers' eatery on

THE HIGHLANDS

mid-Santander, Las Palmeras serves a range of chicken, fish and meat dishes. The *plato típico de Panajachel* is a good deal.

Sunset Cafe (cnr Calles Santander & del Lago; mains US$4-6; 🕙 11am-midnight) This open-air eatery has a great lake vista and serves meat, fish and vegetarian dishes. With a bar and live music nightly, it can get quite chirpy at weekends and holidays.

Among the cheapest places to eat are many of the tourist restaurants overlooking the lake at the east end of Calle del Lago, such as **El Bambú** and **Restaurante Taly** (both with breezy upper floors), **Los Alpes, El Xocomil, El Pescador, Los Pumpos, Restaurante Emilio** and **Brisas de Lago**. Most of these places will do you breakfast for US$1.50 to US$2 or quite acceptable lunch or dinner mains for US$4.

Al Chisme (🕿 762-2063; Comercial El Pueblito, Av Los Árboles; mains US$3-5; 🕙 7am-10:30pm) Al Chisme offers Tex-Mex, vegetarian and pasta dishes, and more expensive meat and fish. Its street-side patio is most popular in the evening, especially when there's live music.

Cheap meals on Calle Santander? Several places offer bargain set meals:

Restaurante Los Cayucos (breakfast mains US$1-1.50; mains from US$1.70) The food is standard, but the prices bring in the customers.

Don Neto (mains US$2-3.25) The US$2 lunch or dinner gives you a choice of eight or nine meat or fish selections, with fries, salad, rice, tortilla and a soft drink.

Restaurante Mario (lunch US$4) The lunch includes soup, a main dish with rice or steamed veggies, and coffee.

MID-RANGE & TOP END

Ristorante La Lanterna (Hotel Dos Mundos, Calle Santander 4-72; mains US$4.50-6.50; 🕙 7am-3pm & 6-10pm) This is a good, authentic Italian restaurant with both inside and garden tables; you're welcome to use the swimming pool if you eat here.

La Terraza (🕿 762-0041; Edificio Rincón Sai, Calle Santander; mains US$5-10; 🕙 daily) This airy upstairs terrace restaurant has French, Mexican and Asian offerings in its wide-ranging and reliable menu.

Restaurante Tocoyal (Calle del Lago; mains US$8-11; 🕙 8:30am-5pm Sun-Fri, 8:30am-8pm Sat) The Tocoyal is a cut above the other Calle del Lago eateries. Staples are meat, chicken and fish, but there are cheaper vegetarian dishes and *chiles rellenos* (chile stuffed with cheese, meat or rice).

Porta Hotel del Lago (🕿 762-1555; cnr Calle Rancho Grande & Calle de Buenas Nuevas; breakfast/dinner buffet US$5.75/11.50) This luxury hotel offers lavish Sunday buffets when it's fully occupied, which happens on weekends and holidays.

Hotel Atitlán (🕿 762-1416/029/41; Finca San Buenaventura; lunch or dinner buffet US$15) This hotel, on the northern outskirts of town, is even more luxurious and has a beautiful restaurant with some outdoor tables and magnificent lake views. If you come to eat here, you can use the swimming pool and gardens for free. The Sunday breakfast buffet is US$9. Lunch or dinner buffets are offered when occupancy is high: call ahead. Otherwise, ample set meals are always available for similar prices.

Drinking

Pana's best places to drink are generally the places that also have live music (p115). Other locales handily close to music spots are **Pana Arte** (Calle Santander), above Pana Rock, with a popular happy hour, and the lounge-style **Ubu's Bar** (Comercial El Pueblito, Av Los Árboles).

Crossroads Café (Calle del Campanario 0-27; coffee US$0.80-1; 🕙 9am-1pm & 4-8pm Tue-Sat) If your beverage of choice is coffee, make for this café. Try the espresso or the good *café con leche* made with local organic beans.

Entertainment

Panajachel's miniature Zona Viva focuses on Av Los Árboles. Things can be quiet from Sunday to Wednesday.

CINEMA

Turquoise Buffalo (Comercial El Pueblito; admission US$2) This cinema shows two movies each evening. If you go earlier in the day, you can choose your own film (minimum: two people).

DANCING

After the music stops at the Circus Bar or Al Chisme (see p115), many folk simply cross the street to **Chapiteau** (Av Los Árboles; 🕙 until 3am), a disco-bar with billiards upstairs – it can be fun. A couple of doors down is **El Aleph** (Av Los Árboles; 🕙 until 3am), with occasional trance and hip-hop DJ sessions or live music.

Socrates (Calle Principal) Opposite the start of Av Los Árboles, this large disco-bar plays thumping Latin pop, highly popular with the

Guatemalan teens and 20s who descend on Pana at weekends and holidays (and a smattering of *gringos*). The assorted folk pictured on the walls run the gamut from Albert Einstein to Jerry García of Grateful Dead.

LIVE MUSIC

Circus Bar (☎ 762-2056; Av Los Árboles; ☺ noon-midnight) With walls hung with old circus posters, smooth drinks service and food, Circus Bar has live music (normally a Latin combo of some kind) from 8pm to 11pm nightly. An interestingly mixed crowd usually assembles.

Al Chisme (Comercial El Pueblito; Av Los Árboles) Along the street, this bar/restaurant often serves up neat jazz or piano music on Friday or Saturday nights.

Pana Rock (Calle Santander) This bar hosts varied live music from about 7pm to midnight nightly. The band might just be playing Marley, Lennon and Eagles covers, but it can be fun, often with quite a crowd of *gringos* and young Guatemalans, aided by a two-shots-for-US$2 happy hour lasting most of the evening.

Sunset Cafe (cnr Calles Santander & del Lago; ☺ 11am-midnight) For sunset (and later) drinks overlooking the lake, head for this popular café, with great views, food, a bar and live music nightly.

Shopping

Calle Santander is lined with booths, stores and complexes that sell (among other things) traditional Mayan clothing, jade, Rasta berets with built-in dreadlocks, colorful blankets, leather goods and wood carvings. Freelance vendors and artisans also set up tables or blankets, especially on weekends. Among this is **Comerciales de Artesanías Típicas Tinamit Maya** (☺ 7am-7pm), an extensive handicrafts market, with an impressive variety at dozens of stalls. You can make good buys here if you bargain and take your time. **Middle Path Herbs** (Plaza Los Patios, Calle Santander) sells medicinal herbs and health foods (and can put you in touch with an acupuncturist or masseur).

Some travelers prefer the Pana shopping scene to the well-known market at Chichicastenango because the atmosphere is low key and you're not bumping into tour groups with video cameras at every turn. The beach end of Calle Rancho Grande is also adorned with booths.

There are also wholesalers in Pana if you want to buy in bulk (if you're interested, check www.panajachel.info for some contacts). There are even companies that will do the shopping and shipping for you (p106).

Getting There & Away

BOAT

Slow ferries to Santiago Atitlán depart from the Playa Pública, east of the tourist office, at 5:45am, 8:30am, 9:30am, 10:30am, 11:30am, 1pm, 3pm and 4:30pm. The one-hour crossing costs US$1.30. Boats leave Santiago for Panajachel at 6am, 7am, 11:45am, 12:30pm, 1:30pm, 3pm and 4:30pm. Schedules may vary a little but the overall frequency is fairly reliable.

For Santa Cruz La Laguna, Jaibalito, San Marcos La Laguna and San Pedro La Laguna, zippy fiberglass *lanchas* (outboard launches) leave about every half-hour, approximately 7am to 6pm, from Embarcadero Tzanjuyú at the foot of Calle del Embarcadero. Some boats go straight to San Pedro (30 minutes), others call at other villages on the way (taking about one hour to San Pedro). The fare from Panajachel to San Pedro is officially US$2 but in practice tourists are usually charged US$2.60. From Pana to the other villages, or between one village and another, it's US$1.30. *Lanchas* are also available for private hire from the Playa Pública or Embarcadero Tzanjuyú: you could expect to pay around US$23 to San Pedro.

To the villages along the lake's eastern shore, there are no public boat services. A privately hired *lancha* from the Playa Pública costs around US$13 to Santa Catarina Palopó, US$23 to San Antonio Palopó and US$40 to San Lucas Tolimán. It's better to go by bus or pickup (see below).

BUS

Panajachel's main bus stop is at the junction of Calle Santander and Calle Principal, across from Banco Agromercantil. The taxi and shuttle bus booth nearby on Calle Principal can usually give you the general picture on bus schedules, but this is not an exact science. Transportes Rébuli, running buses to Guatemala City, has an office further down Calle Principal, but its buses still usually depart from the Principal/Santander corner. Departures –

approximately and subject to change – are as follows:

Antigua (US$4.50, 2½hr, 146km) A direct pullman bus leaves from the Rébuli office at 10:45am, Monday to Saturday. Or take a Guatemala City bus and change at Chimaltenango.

Chichicastenango (US$1.30, 1½hr, 37km, 8 daily 7am-4pm) Or take any bus heading to Los Encuentros and change buses there.

Ciudad Tecún Umán (via Cocales US$4, 6½hr, 210km; via Quetzaltenango US$3.55, 210km, 7hr)

Cocales (US$1, 2½hr, 70km, 8 daily 6:30am-2:30pm)

Guatemala City (US$2.10, 3½hr, 150km, 10 daily 5am-2:30pm) Or take a bus to Los Encuentros and change there.

Huehuetenango (3½hr, 140km) Bus to Los Encuentros and wait there for a bus bound for Huehue or La Mesilla. Or catch a bus heading to Quetzaltenango, alight at Cuatro Caminos and change buses there. There are buses at least hourly from these junctions.

La Mesilla (6hr, 225km) See Huehuetenango, p160.

Los Encuentros (US$0.70, 35min, 20km) Take any bus heading toward Guatemala City, Chichicastenango, Quetzaltenango or the Interamericana.

Quetzaltenango (US$1.55, 2½hr, 90km, 6 daily 5am-4pm) Or bus to Los Encuentros and change there.

San Lucas Tolimán (US$1, 1½hr, 28km, 1 daily 4pm) Or take any bus heading for Cocales, get off at the San Lucas turnoff and walk about 1km into town.

Sololá (US$0.20, 20min, 8km) There are frequent direct local buses. Or take any bus heading to Guatemala City, Chichicastenango, Quetzaltenango or Los Encuentros.

CAR & MOTORCYCLE

Alquiler de Motos y Bicicletas Emanuel (☎ 762-2790; Calle 14 de Febrero; ☽ 8am-6pm Mon-Fri, 8am-1pm Sun) and **Maco** (☎ 762-0883; Calle Santander) both businesses rent out motorcycles for around US$6/23/30 per one/eight/24 hours. Emanuel also offers better, modern, automatic machines for US$9/45/58. Maco has cars for US$39 for eight hours, US$61 a day or US$250 a week.

SHUTTLE MINIBUS & TAXI

Tourist shuttle buses take half the time of buses, for several times the price. You can book at a number of travel agencies on Calle Santander (p107). The **Oficina de Microbuses y Taxis San Francisco booth** (Calle Principal near cnr Calle Santander) also sells shuttle bus seats (or can call you a taxi). Despite impressive advertised lists of departures, real shuttle schedules depend on how many customers there are, so try to establish a firm departure time before parting with money. Typical fares: Antigua US$10; Chichicastenango US$7 to US$8; Guatemala City US$20; La Mesilla US$35; Quetzaltenango US$20; and Ciudad Tecún Umán US$35.

On Chichicastenago's market days, Thursday and Sunday, shuttles run from Panajachel to Chichi for US$4/7 one way/return.

AROUND PANAJACHEL

East of Pana, 5km and 10km respectively along a winding road, lie the lakeside villages of Santa Catarina Palopó and San Antonio Palopó – picturesque places of narrow streets paved in stone blocks and adobe houses with roofs of thatch or tin. Some villagers still go about daily life dressed in their beautiful traditional clothing. There's little in the way of sightseeing, but these are good places to buy the luminescent indigo weavings you see all around Lago de Atitlán. Also out here is a surprising little clutch of mid-range and top-end places to stay.

Santa Catarina Palopó

On weekends and holidays, young textile vendors may line the path to the lakeside at Santa Catarina Palopó with their wares, and any day you can step into wooden storefronts hung thick with bright cloth.

Villa Santa Catarina (☎ 762-1291, 762-2827; www.villasdeguatemala.com; s/d/tr US$61/69/73; ⓟ ⓢ) If your budget allows, this is a treat for a drink or a meal. The dining room serves moderately priced table d'hôte meals and the hotel has a big swimming pool and lovely gardens almost on the lakeshore. The 36 neat rooms have wood-beam ceilings, colorful weavings and lake views. Rooms 24, 25, 26, 27 (partly) and the two suites (US$104) face across the lake to Volcán San Pedro. Two children under 12 can share with two adults for free.

Hospedaje 5-Ajpu (☎ 762-2981; s/d US$4/7) Up the hillside a bit, a local family provides a few plain rooms (some with lake view) with a clean shared bathroom.

Hotel Casa Palopó (☎ 762-2270; www.casapalopo.com; s or d US$153-208; ⓟ ▢ ⓢ) One kilometer past Santa Catarina, on the hillside above the road to San Antonio Palopó, is a luxury retreat for the moneyed. It has just seven rooms, furnished in tasteful modern style with Mayan touches, super views, pool and classy restaurant.

San Tomás Bella Vista Ecolodge (☎ 762-1566; www.hotelsantomas.0catch.com; s/d/tr/q US$45/60/75/ 90; P ♠) This place, a further 2km along, has vast grounds running down to the lakeshore, with walking trails and even a sandy beach. The 14 rooms, in bungalows, are bright and spacious. Rates include breakfast; main dishes at lunch and dinner cost US$5 to US$10. This is one of those places that is best at weekends and holidays: midweek, with no one around, it can seem desolate.

Restaurante Laguna Azul (mains US$3.25-5) This open-air place on the lakeshore below the Villa Santa Catarina serves reasonably priced chicken, fish and meat dishes.

San Antonio Palopó

San Antonio Palopó is a larger but similar village. Entire families clean mountains of scallions by the lakeshore and tend their terraced fields in bursts of color provided by their traditional dress. Up the hillside, the gleaming white church forms the center of attention. **Cerámica Palopó Atitlán** (☎ 762-2606), to the right along the street just before the lake as you descend from the church, sells attractive blue stoneware pottery.

Hotel Terrazas del Lago (☎ 762-0157; fax 762-0037; s/d/tr US$24/31/36) This excellent hotel, almost on the lakeshore, has 15 attractive stone-walled rooms with Frederick Crocker prints, small terraces and hot-water bathrooms, and serves good, inexpensive meals on a terrace looking straight across to Volcán Tolimán.

Getting There & Away

Pickups to both villages leave about every half-hour from the corner of Calles Principal and El Amate in Panajachel. It takes 20 minutes to Santa Catarina (US$0.30) and 45 minutes to San Antonio (US$0.50). Frequency is less after about noon, and the last pickup back to Pana leaves San Antonio about 5pm.

San Lucas Tolimán

elevation 1590m

Further around the lake from San Antonio Palopó, but reached by a different, higher-level road, San Lucas Tolimán is busier and more commercial than most lakeside villages. Set at the foot of the dramatic Volcán Tolimán, it's a coffee-growing town and a transport point on a route between the Interamericana and the Carretera al Pacífico.

Market days are Sunday and Thursday. The 16th-century **Parroquia de San Lucas** parish church has a beautiful children's folk choir, which sings at 10:30am Mass most Sundays. The parish, aided by Catholic missionaries from the USA and volunteers from North America and Europe, has been active in redistributing coffee-plantation land, setting up the Juan-Ana fair-trade coffee co-op and founding schools, a clinic and a reforestation program. For visits to the co-op, guided volcano hikes and information on volunteering, contact the **parish office** (☎ 722-0112; sanlucas@pronet.net.gt).

From San Lucas, a paved road goes west around Volcán Tolimán to Santiago Atitlán.

Hotel Tolimán (☎ 722-0033; www.atitlanhotel.com; Final de Calle Principal; s/d with breakfast US$49/59; P ♠) This hotel has 22 rooms and suites in a rustic but comfortable style with hot-water bathroom, and a restaurant, bar and a pool in lush gardens on the lake shore.

For details on bus and boat transport, see p115.

SANTIAGO ATITLÁN

elevation 1590m

South across the lake from Panajachel, beside an inlet squeezed between the towering volcanoes of Tolimán and San Pedro, lies Santiago Atitlán. Though Santiago is the most touristed lakeside settlement outside Panajachel, many *atitecos* (as its people are known) cling to a traditional Tz'utujil Maya lifestyle. Women weave and wear *huipiles* embroidered with brilliantly colored flocks of birds and bouquets of flowers, and the town's *cofradías* (Mayan religious brotherhoods) maintain the ceremonies and rituals of *la costumbre*, the syncretic traditions and practices of Mayan Catholicism. There's a large art and crafts scene here, too. The best days to visit are Friday and Sunday, the main market days, but in fact any day will do.

Santiago is also a curiosity because of its reverence for the highland deity Maximón (mah-shee-*mohn*). Maximón is paraded about triumphantly during Semana Santa – a time of much activity by the *cofradías* – but the rest of the year he resides with his caretakers, receiving offerings of candles, cigars, food, beer and rum when asked to cure the sick, make crops grow, bring harm to enemies and so on. Local children will

TRADITIONAL CLOTHING

Anyone visiting the Highlands can delight in the beautiful *traje indígena*, traditional Mayan clothing. The styles, patterns and colors used by each village – originally devised by the Spanish colonists to distinguish one village from another – are unique, and each garment is the creation of its weaver, with subtle individual differences.

The basic elements of the traditional wardrobe are the *tocoyal* (head-covering), *huipil* (tunic), *corte* or *refago* (skirt), *calzones* (trousers), *tzut* or *kaperraj* (cloth), *paz* or *faja* (sash) and *caïtes* or *xajáp* (sandals).

Women's head coverings are beautiful and elaborate bands of cloth up to several meters long, wound about the head and often decorated with tassels, pom-poms and silver ornaments. In some places they are now only worn on ceremonial occasions and for tourist photos.

Women's *huipiles* are worn proudly every day. Though some machine-made fabrics are now being used, many *huipiles* are still made completely by hand. The white blouse is woven on a backstrap loom, then decorated with appliqué and embroidery designs and motifs common to the weaver's village. Many of the motifs are traditional symbols. No doubt all motifs originally had religious or historical significance, but today that meaning is often lost to memory.

Cortes (refagos) are pieces of cloth 7m to 10m long that are wrapped around the body. Traditionally, girls wear theirs above the knee, married women at the knee and old women below the knee, though the style can differ markedly from region to region.

Both men and women wear *fajas*, long strips of backstrap-loom-woven cloth wrapped around the midriff as belts. When they're wrapped with folds upward like a cummerbund, the folds serve as pockets.

Tzutes (for men) or *kaperraj* (for women) are the all-purpose cloths carried by local people and used as head coverings, baby slings, produce sacks, basket covers and shawls. There are also shawls for women called *perraj*.

Before the coming of the Spaniards, the leather thong sandals known as *caïtes* or *xajáp* were commonly only worn by men. Even today, many Highland women and children go barefoot, while others wear more elaborate *huarache*-style sandals or modern shoes.

offer to take you to see him for a small tip. See the boxed text opposite for more on this strange figure.

In the 1980s left-wing guerrillas had a strong presence in the Santiago area, leading to the killings or disappearance of hundreds of villagers at the hands of the Guatemalan army. Santiago became the first village in the country to succeed in expelling the army, following a notorious massacre of 13 villagers on December 1, 1990.

Orientation & Information

The street straight ahead from the dock leads up to the town center. Every tourist walks up and down this street, so it's lined with craft shops and art galleries. A short distance ahead from the dock you'll see a small **Oficina de Información Turística** (🕒 9am-5pm), run by local guide Martín Tzina Sicay. Martín can set you up with guided trips to most places of interest in the area and put you in touch with almost anyone in Santiago, as well as provide straightforward information and a useful town map (US$0.30).

You'll find a lot of fascinating information about Santiago, in English, at www .santiagoatitlan.com.

About 500m up from the dock, turn left past the Hotel Tzutuhil to reach the central plaza and, behind it, the Catholic church. You can change US-dollar cash and traveler's checks at **Banrural** (🕒 8:30am-5pm Mon-Fri, 9am-1pm Sat) on the plaza.

Dangers & Annoyances

Santiago children may greet you as you disembark at the dock, selling small souvenirs or offering to act as guides. If you hire them, agree on the price beforehand or, as one sage traveler put it, you'll 'be amazed at the bad language some charming little girls can haul out.' Santiago kids have been known to pick tourist pockets. If a few of them start to crowd you in, watch out.

Muggings of tourists have reportedly occurred, mostly at night, on the outskirts of

Santiago, such as the trail between the dock and the Hotel Bambú or the road out to the Posada de Santiago. Take care.

Sights
The huge parish church, the **Iglesia Parroquial Santiago Apóstol**, was built between 1572 and 1581. A memorial plaque on your right just inside the entrance commemorates Father Stanley Francis Rother, a missionary priest from Oklahoma: Beloved by the local people, he was hated by ultrarightist 'death squads,' who murdered him in his study at the church during the troubled year of 1981. Along the walls are wooden statues of the saints, each of whom has new clothes made by local women every year. On the carved wooden pulpit, note the figures of corn (from which humans were formed, according to Mayan religion) and of the angel, quetzal bird, lion and horse (symbols of the four evangelists, with the quetzal replacing the more traditional eagle). Mayanist Allen Christenson writes that in the center of the nave is a hole called the R'muxux Ruchiliew, which traditionalist Tz'utujils believe is an entrance to the underworld. The hole is uncovered only on Good Friday, when a large cross bearing a statue of Christ is lowered into it. At the far end of the church stand three sacred colonial altarpieces which were renovated between 1976 and 1981 by brothers Diego Chávez Petzey and Nicolás Chávez Sojuel. The brothers subtly changed the central altarpiece from a traditional European vision of Heaven to a more Mayan vision representing a sacred mountain with two Santiago *cofradía* members climbing towards a sacred cave. The three altarpieces together symbolize the three volcanoes around Santiago, which are believed to protect the town and also, in a local creation myth, to have been the first dry land that rose out of the

---

A GOD IS A GOD IS A GOD
The Spanish called him San Simón, the *ladinos* (persons of mixed indigenous and European race) named him Maximón and the Maya know him as Rilaj Maam (ree-lah-*mahm*). By any name, he's a deity revered throughout the Guatemalan highlands. Assumed to be a combination of Mayan gods, Pedro de Alvarado (the Spanish conquistador of Guatemala) and the biblical Judas, San Simón is an effigy to which Guatemalans of every stripe go to make offerings and ask for blessings. The effigy is usually housed by a member of a *cofradía* (Mayan Catholic brotherhood), moving from one place to another from year to year, a custom anthropologists believe was established to maintain the local balance of power. The name, shape and ceremonies associated with this deity vary from town to town, but a visit will be memorable no matter where you encounter him. For a small fee, photography is usually permitted, and offerings of cigarettes, liquor or candles are always appreciated.

In Santiago Atitlán, Maximón is a wooden figure draped in colorful silk scarves and smoking a fat cigar. Locals guard and worship him, singing and managing the offerings made to him (including your US$0.25 entry fee). His favorite gifts are Payaso cigarettes and Venado rum, but he often has to settle for the cheaper firewater Quetzalteca Especial. Fruits and gaudy, flashing electric lights decorate his chamber; effigies of Jesus Christ and Christian saints lie or stand either side of Maximón and his guardians. Fires may be burning in the courtyard outside as offerings are made to him.

In Nahualá, between Los Encuentros and Quetzaltenango, the Maximón effigy is à la Picasso: a simple wooden box with a cigarette protruding from it. Still, the same offerings are made and the same sort of blessings asked for. In Zunil, near Quetzaltenango, the deity is called San Simón but is similar to Santiago's Maximón in custom and form.

San Jorge La Laguna on Lake Atitlán is a very spiritual place for the highland Maya; here they worship Rilaj Maam. It is possible that the first effigy was made near here, carved from the *palo de pito* tree that spoke to the ancient shamans and told them to preserve their culture, language and traditions by carving Rilaj Maam (*palo de pito* flowers can be smoked to induce hallucinations). The effigy in San Jorge looks like a joker, with an absurdly long tongue.

In San Andrés Itzapa near Antigua, Rilaj Maam has a permanent home, and is brought out on October 28 and paraded about in an unparalleled pagan festival. This is an all-night, hedonistic party where dancers grab the staff of Rilaj Maam to harness his power and receive magical visions. San Andrés is less than 10km south of Chimaltenango, so you can easily make the party from Antigua.

primordial waters. You can read a version of Allen Christenson's interpretation at www.mesoweb.com.

On the subject of religion, you can't fail to notice while wandering around Santiago just how many evangelical churches are now competing with Catholicism and traditional Mayan *costumbre* for the villagers' faith.

The site of the 1990 massacre is now the **Parque de Paz** (Peace Park), about 500m beyond the Posada de Santiago.

Activities

There are several rewarding **day hikes** around Santiago. Unfortunately, owing to robberies and attacks on tourists in the Atitlán area, it's highly advisable to go with a guide and tourist police escort. Martín Tzina Sicay (p118) will take you with two tourist police up any of the three **volcanoes** (US$78 per group); or to the **Mirador de Tepepul**, about 4km south of Santiago (US$26 for two); or to **Cerro de Oro**, some 8km northeast (US$26 for two). The Mirador trip, four to five hours roundtrip, goes through cloud forest populated with many birds, including parakeets, curassows, swifts, boat-tailed grackles and tucanets (if you're lucky you might even glimpse a quetzal), and on to a lookout point with beautiful views all the way to the coast. Cerro de Oro is a small village beneath a hill of the same name (1892m), about halfway between Santiago and San Lucas Tolimán. The climb up the hill yields great views, and there's a pretty church in town. You could travel at least one way by one of the pickups running between Santiago and San Lucas Tolimán. Another destination from Santiago is **Chuitinamit**, a small hill across the inlet from Santiago with the ruins of the pre-Hispanic Tz'utujil capital and the site of the Santiago area's first church and Franciscan monastery, founded about 1540. Walking to San Pedro La Laguna is not recommended, unless the security situation improves, since this remote route has a robbery risk.

Jim and Nancy Matison (☎ 811-5516; wildwest@amigo.net.gt) offer well-recommended **horse rides** to the Mirador de Tepepul and elsewhere, for US$45 to US$60. Most rides include a meal. They do guided hikes, too.

Dolores Ratzan Pablo is an accomplished guide specializing in **Mayan ceremonies**. This charming, funny Tz'utujil woman can introduce you to the wonders of Mayan birthing and healing ceremonies or take you to weaving demonstrations and art galleries. Dolores speaks English, Spanish, Kaqchiquel and of course, Tz'utujil. Tours typically last between one and three hours, for US$15 an hour. Contact her through the Posada de Santiago or Oficina de Información Turística.

Language Courses

Recommended **Spanish classes** are offered for US$3.25 an hour from 7am to noon, Monday to Friday, by villager Rosa Archile. Ask at the Oficina de Información Turística.

Sleeping & Eating

Hotel & Restaurant Bambú (☎ 721-7332/3; www.ecobambu.com; s/d/tr US$39/48/53; P) The Bambú is a fine hotel with lovely lakeside gardens run by amiable Spaniard José de Castro, a veteran Latin American traveler. It's 600m from the dock: walk to the left (north) along a path through lakeside vegetable gardens – the hotel's large grass-roofed restaurant building is visible from the dock. The 10 spacious rooms are in grass- or bamboo-roofed buildings, with cypress wood fittings, colorful paint and earthy tile floors. All have bathroom. The excellent restaurant, with big picture windows, serves an international array of very well prepared pasta, meat, seafood and vegetarian main dishes for US$6 to US$11. For those with vehicles, the hotel has an entrance from the Cerro de Oro road on the edge of Santiago.

Posada de Santiago (☎ 721-7366, 721-7167; www.posadadesantiago.com; s/d/tr US$38/50/60; P) This is another of the most charming hotels around Lago de Atitlán. Seven cottages and two suites, all with stone walls, fireplaces, porches, hammocks and folk art, are set around beautiful gardens stretching up from the lake. There are also a few budget rooms for US$11 per person, sharing hot-water bathrooms, and two suites for US$70 and US$80. The restaurant has well-prepared Asian, continental and American food and a very cozy ambience. The Posada can set you up with hikes and biking trips. It's 1.5km from the dock. Walk up the street ahead all the way to its end, turn left, go to the end of the street, and turn right on to a paved road, which almost immediately becomes dirt. Alternatively you can arrange for the Posada to pick you up by *lancha* at the Santiago dock (US$3 to US$4) or at Panajachel (US$20).

Hotel Chi-Nim-Yá (☎ 721-7131; s/d US$4/8, with bathroom US$6/11) This simple hotel is 30m to the left from the first crossroads as you walk up from the dock. The 22 rooms, around a central courtyard, are bare and clean, with concrete floors. The nicest is No 6 on the upper floor, which is large and airy, with lots of windows and lake views.

Hotel Tzutuhil (☎ 721-7174; s/d US$4/7, with bathroom US$5/9) Go four blocks uphill from the dock then turn left to this hotel, whose reception is in the *ferretería* (hardware store) next door. It's a modern five-story building, rather an anomaly in this little town. Rooms are bland but mostly bright, many having large windows with decent views. Go up on the rooftop for great sunsets.

El Pescador (set lunch US$4) Two blocks up the street straight ahead from the dock, this is a good, clean restaurant with big windows, white-shirted waiters and neatly laid tables. A typical *menú del día* (set lunch) might bring you chicken, rice, salad, guacamole, tortillas and a drink.

Shopping
The street leading up from the dock to the town center is lined with shops selling leather belts and hats, carved wooden animals, colorful textiles, masks and paintings.

Getting There & Away
Subject to change (of course!), boats leave Santiago for San Pedro La Laguna (US$1.30, 45 minutes) at 7am, 9am, 10am, 11am, noon, 1pm, 2pm, 3:30pm and 5pm. Pickups to San Pedro, Cerro de Oro and San Lucas Tolimán start outside the Hotel Chi-Nim-Yá. Buses to Guatemala City (US$2.60, four hours) leave about hourly, 4am to 2pm, from the main plaza. For transport from Panajachel, see p115.

SAN PEDRO LA LAGUNA
elevation 1610m
San Pedro is the most popular lakeside town among budget travelers thanks to its super-cheap accommodation, super-cheap language schools and hip *gringo* scene. It's a scruffier, untidier place than many other lakeside settlements, but that doesn't deter some travelers from hanging out here for quite some time. A few liked it here so much that they stayed on and started their own restaurants or businesses.

Like Santiago Atitlán, San Pedro has a lot of evangelical churches, is home to some talented Tz'utujil artists, and suffered badly during the civil war. Coffee is an important local crop. You'll see beans being picked and spread out to dry on wide platforms at the beginning of the dry season. Marijuana is another widely cultivated crop in San Pedro.

Orientation & Information
San Pedro has two docks, about 1km apart. The one on the southeast side of town serves boats going to and from Santiago Atitlán. The other, around on the northwest side of town, serves boats going to and from Panajachel. From each dock, streets run ahead to meet outside the market in the town center, a few hundred meters uphill. Most of the interest for travelers is in the lower part of town, between the two docks and either side of them. Various minor streets, tracks and paths enable you to walk around this lower area without going up to the town center. To work your way across this lower area from the Panajachel dock, turn left immediately before the Hotel Mansión del Lago, then right opposite Casa Elena, then left at the top of that street. From the Santiago dock, turn right immediately before the Hotel Villasol. No one much uses street names or numbers in San Pedro, even though they do officially exist. We give them where it has been possible to discover them.

You can change US-dollar cash and traveler's checks at **Banrural** (☯ 8:30am-5pm Mon-Fri, 9am-1pm Sat), in the town center. There's Internet access at **D'Noz**, **Casa Verde Internet** and the **Internet Cafe**, all just up the street from the Panajachel dock, and **Planetoutreach** above Restaurant Tin-Tin. The typical rate is US$1 an hour. You can call North America/Europe for US$0.65/0.90 at **D'Noz**, or anywhere in the world for US$0.65 a minute at **Hotel Mansión del Lago**, 100m further up the street.

Activities
ASCENDING VOLCÁN SAN PEDRO
Looming above the village, Volcán San Pedro almost asks to be climbed by anyone

THE HIGHLANDS

THE HIGHLANDS

TZ'UTUJIL OIL PAINTING

Although many of the paintings on display in Santiago's tourist galleries – landscapes, portraits, scenes of local life – use lurid acrylic colors and look very similar to each other, some works by finer Santiago artists such as Martín Reanda Quieju, Nicolás Reanda Quieju, Pedro Miguel Reanda, Miguel Chávez and Martín Ratzan Reanda exude a special energy and talent. Good Tz'utujil painting has a distinctive primitivist style, depicting rural life in vibrant colors. Centered on San Pedro La Laguna and Santiago Atitlán, the style is distinctly Mayan and has been the theme of shows the world over.

Legend has it that Tz'utujil art began one day when Rafael González y González from San Pedro La Laguna noticed some dye that had dripped and mixed with the sap of a tree; he made a paintbrush from his hair and began creating the type of canvases still popular today. His relatives Pedro Rafael González Chavajay, Lorenzo González Chavajay and Mariano González Chavajay are leading exponents of the Tz'utujil style.

The grandfather of Santiago painting was Juan Sisay; success at an international art exhibition in 1969 sparked an explosion of painters working in his style. Juan Sisay was assassinated in 1989, but his sons Manuel, Diego and Juan Francisco carry his banner, chiefly working in photographic-style portraits.

For more on Mayan oil painting, visit the website **Arte Maya Tz'utuhil** (www.artemaya.com).

---

with a bit of energy and adventurous spirit. Unfortunately the trails have been the scene of robberies, and without a dramatic improvement in the situation we suggest that you do not climb the volcano without a responsible guide who can convince you that the risk when you go will be minimal.

Excursion Big Foot (7a Av, Zona 2), 50m to the left at the first crossroads up from San Pedro's Panajachel dock, has a track record of responsibility in this respect and goes at 6am when there are at least four people (US$4 each). The ascent is through fields of maize, beans and squash, followed by primary cloud forest. You'll be back in San Pedro about 1pm. Take water, snacks, a hat and sunblock.

OTHER ACTIVITIES

A worthy alternative climb to Volcán San Pedro that still has (at the time of writing) an unblemished security record is the hill to the west of the village that is generally referred to as **Indian Nose**. (Its skyline resembles the profile of an ancient Mayan dignitary.) **Excursion Big Foot** (see above) will guide a minimum of four people up there for US$4 each.

Walking from San Pedro to other lakeside villages is, sadly, potentially risky. In recent years there have been robberies, at least one armed attack and at least one rape at various places between San Pedro and Jaibalito, and robberies between San Pedro

and Santiago. Hopefully this will change, but meanwhile we don't recommend these walks except with a responsible guide who can give convincing safety assurances. It takes about four hours from San Pedro to Santiago, 1½ hours to San Pablo, three hours to San Marcos and six hours to Santa Cruz.

You can rent a local **kayak** for a paddle on the lake from various people including Excursion Big Foot, which charges US$0.65 an hour.

Language Courses

San Pedro is making quite a name for itself in the language game with ultra-economical rates at its Spanish schools, whose numbers are now approaching double figures. Check out a couple of schools before deciding. Some of them are distinctly rustic, rather amateurish affairs; others are professional enterprises with good reputations. Optional extras can range from volcano hikes and dance classes to Mayan culture seminars and volunteer work opportunities. The standard price for four hours of one-on-one classes, five days a week, is US$50 to US$55. Accommodation with a local family, with three meals daily (except Sunday) usually costs US$40. Schools can also organize other accommodation options. Schools include:

Casa Rosario (☎ 613-6401; www.casarosario.com) Run by respected brothers and teachers Samuel and Vicente

Cumes; holds classes in gardens near the lake; office is along first street to left as you walk up from Santiago dock.

Corazón Maya (☎ 721-8160; www.corazonmaya.com) Turn first left as you go up from Santiago dock to reach this well established school.

Escuela de Español Casa América (☎ 767-7718, 816-5143; casaamerica@hotmail.com) Set in gardens near the lake, between the two docks; teaches Tz'utujil and Spanish.

Mayab' Spanish School (☎ 815-7722; www.mayab spanishschool.com) Set in gardens near lake, between the two docks; has library and collection of Guatemalan videos.

San Pedro Spanish School (☎ 721-8176; www.san pedrospanishschool.org) Well organized school on street between the two docks, with classes held under shelters in artistically designed gardens; consistently gets good reviews.

Sol de Oro Spanish School (☎ 614-9618, 802-8977; geocities.com/soldeorospanish) Enthusiastic young school with attached accommodations, along first street to left as you walk up from Santiago dock.

Sleeping

Although San Pedro has a lot of places to stay, you may still find that your first choices are full.

Hotel Mansión del Lago (☎ 811-8172, 721-8041; s/d/tr US$10/10/16; P) The first place you find going uphill from the Panajachel dock is San Pedro's smartest (which is not saying much). The 15 or so rooms are clean and bare, with hot-water bathrooms. The upper floors have views.

Hotel Restaurant Maritza (s/d US$3/6) Go 200m to the right from the crossroads just below Hotel Mansión del Lago to reach this basic family-run place, with four small rooms and a garden overlooking the lake. The price includes use of a kitchen and hot showers.

Casa Elena (☎ 310-9243; 7a Av 8-61, Zona 2; s/d US$2/4, with bathroom US$4/8) Go 200m to the left from the Mansión del Lago corner to find Casa Elena, which has good, clean rooms, some of them large with big windows overlooking the lake. The Elena has its own dock. The location is excellent.

Hotel Xocomil (s/d US$2/4) Up the lane opposite Casa Elena is a hotel with quiet rooms around a cement courtyard. To reach further cheapies, continue along 7a Av past Casa Elena and take the second path to the right (after Hotel Villa del Lago). The path soon passes the very basic **Posada Casa Domingo** (s/d US$2/4) and comes out at the better **Posada Xetawal** (6a Calle B 7-22, Zona 2; s/d US$3/4), which has clean, sizeable rooms with firm beds, hot

showers and a kitchen for guests. Turn right at the Xetawal, then left along a wider street after 100m to **Hospedaje the Island** (7a Av A 6-11, Zona 2; s/d US$2/4), with reasonably sized, bare, clean rooms.

Past Hospedaje the Island, the street wanders along past a few language schools and travelers' eateries to reach another cluster of accommodations nearer to the Santiago dock.

Hotelito El Amanecer Sak'cari (☎ 812-1113, 721-8096; 7a Av 2-12, Zona 2; s/d US$6/10; P) On the left just after San Pedro Spanish School, the Sak'cari has clean, tangerine-colored rooms with a bathroom. It's the eastward lake views from the 10 front rooms that make it a little special.

Hospedaje Tika'aaj (7a Av, Zona 2; s/d/tr US$2/4/5) This popular budget place is 150m along the street past the Sak'cari. Rooms are generic but the hammocks around the gardens help create a relaxed atmosphere. The shared showers have hot water.

Past Hospedaje Tika'aaj, 7a Av ends at Calle Principal, the street running up from the Santiago dock towards the town center.

Hospedaje Villasol (☎ 334-0327; cnr 7a Av & Calle Principal; s/d US$3/4, with bathroom US$5/8; P) The 45 rooms here, just 200m from the Santiago dock, are bare but clean; those with a bathroom look onto a grassy courtyard.

Hotel San Francisco (☎ 721-8016; 5a Av 2-32, Zona 3; s & d US$4, s/d with bathroom US$5/6) Most rooms at this popular place have a small terrace, lake view and hot-water bathroom. All have a kitchen, which makes it a good deal for language students not staying with families. To find it, go 80m up Calle Principal from Hotel Villasol, then along the street to the left.

Hotel Posada de Don Manuel Tá (☎ 810-1939, 416-2123; s/d US$6/8; P) The 10 agreeably clean, tile-floored rooms, on two floors, are in shades of pink and tangerine, with hot-water bathrooms. It's a few steps along the street off Calle Principal opposite Hospedaje Villasol (coming from the Santiago dock, the first street on the left).

Hotel Punta d'Oro (☎ 614-9618, 802-8977; s/d/tr US$7/7/9) This hotel shares premises and management with the Sol de Oro Spanish School. Rooms are plain, with a hot-water bathroom and a communal kitchen and eating area. It also has bungalows for four with a kitchen (US$200 a month, pro rata

THE HIGHLANDS

for shorter periods). To get here, go 600m along the street past Hotel Posada de Don Manuel Tá, then 200m down a path to the left.

In many places in San Pedro it's possible to negotiate deals for longer stays and during the off-season. For longer stays, it's also possible to rent a room or an entire house in town. Ask around.

Eating

Restaurante Nick's Place (breakfast mains US$1.60, mains US$2.50) Arriving at San Pedro's Panajachel dock you can't miss (straight in front of you) the travelers' favorite, serving generous portions inside or out on its terrace overlooking the lake. Upstairs above Nick's is another popular hangout, **D'Noz**, with a global menu, board games and lending library.

Clark's Café Luna Azul (breakfast US$2-2.50, lunch US$2.50-3.50; ⏱ 9am-3pm) The Luna Azul has no serious rivals for the accolade of Guatemala's best three-egg omelet and hash brown breakfast for under US$2. You can see it from the Panajachel dock, and most arriving boats will drop you there if you ask. Otherwise go 300m to the right from the crossroads just below Hotel Mansión del Lago, then 50m down a stone-paved path to the right, then left along an earth path through a cornfield.

To find the main cluster of popular eateries, walk to the left from the Hotel Mansión del Lago corner and head towards Hospedaje The Island and Hotelito El Amanecer Sak'cari.

Restaurante Italiano Pinocchio (breakfast mains US$1.50-2, pasta US$3) About 200m past Hospedaje The Island is this restaurant, which serves good, homemade pastas and cakes; the breakfast is decent value too.

Café Munchie's (curries US$3.25) Next door is the good, vegetarian Munchie's, adorned with floral-cum-cosmic murals. Soups, salads and sandwiches on homemade wholewheat bread will set you back US$1.50 to US$2. A few meters further on, **El Otro Lado** is primarily a nocturnal hangout but also makes burgers, sandwiches and the like at moderate prices.

Restaurant Tin-Tin (mains US$4-5.25; ⏱ 8am-2:40pm & 5-8:40pm) Concocting inexpensive vegetarian and Asian food, Tin-Tin has a nice garden to sit in.

Past the San Pedro Spanish School, **Arte Libre** serves teas, breakfasts, waffles, pancakes and main dishes such as yogurt chicken curry (US$3) in a pretty little garden with cane chairs.

It's 150m on from Arte Libre to the next cluster of places – the straightforward **Comedor Mata Hari** and **Restaurante Brenda's** (mains US$2-3), popular for its cheap chicken and pasta, and the large, upper-floor **Restaurante Ti-Kaaj** (burgers, pizza & pasta US$2.25-3.25), with a slightly more elaborate travelers' menu.

Restaurante Pacha Mama/Rosalinda (2a Calle, Zona 2; mains US$1.30-2) On the street leading up to the center from the Santiago dock (fork right 150m past Hotel Villasol), this friendly place serves good, cheap food in a small courtyard. Crepes with fruit, yoghurt, granola and honey, or beans, rice, vegetables and guacamole, cost US$1.30 each.

Entertainment

El Otro Lado (7a Av, Zona 2) This is the nocturnal hotspot. With a bar, lounge and roof garden, two happy hours nightly, cocktails from US$1.30, nightly movies, darts, board games, big-screen TV with English-language news and sports, and techno and trance to gyrate to, you couldn't ask for much more.

At the Panajachel dock, **D'Noz** shows movies nightly, while you can dance to salsa and merengue and watch more TV at the **Alegre Lounge**, just up the street.

Shopping

About 100m uphill from Hotel Mansión del Lago is **Caza Sueños**, a leather shop owned by brothers Fernando and Pedro González. They handcraft custom leather goods, including vests, boots, bags and whatever else you may want in hide. For an incredibly reasonable US$35 the brothers will craft a pair of shoes to your specifications of size, color, fringe, trim and lace style; allow a few days. **Galería de Arte**, on the road leading uphill from the Santiago dock, is operated by the family of celebrated primitivist artist Pedro Rafael González Chavajay. Some of his paintings and those of many of his family and students are exhibited and sold here.

Getting There & Away

Passenger boats arrive here from Panajachel (p115) and Santiago Atitlán (p121). Boats from San Pedro to Santiago (US$1.30, 45 minutes) leave hourly from 6am to 2pm.

The last *lancha* from San Pedro to San Marcos, Jaibalito, Santa Cruz and Panajachel usually leaves around 5pm.

San Pedro is connected by paved roads to Santiago Atitlán (18km, a route served by pickups) and to the Interamericana at Km 148 (about 20km west of Los Encuentros). A paved branch off the San Pedro–Interamericana road runs along the northwest side of the lake from Santa Clara to San Marcos. Veloz San Pedro buses leave for Quetzaltenango (US$2, 2½ hours) from San Pedro's Catholic parish church, up in the town center, at 4:45am, 6am and 7am.

SAN MARCOS LA LAGUNA
pop 2000 / elevation 1640m

San Marcos is a very peaceful place, with houses set among shady coffee trees near the shore. Some believe it has a special spiritual vibe, so it's not surprising that it has become a center for meditation, holistic therapies, massage, Reiki and other spiritually oriented activities. It's certainly a tranquil place for anyone to kick back and distance the everyday world for a spell. Lago de Atitlán is beautiful and clean here, with several little docks you can swim from.

Boats usually put in at a central dock just below Posada Schumann. The path leading up to the village center from here, and a parallel one about 100m west, are San Marcos' main axes for most visitors.

Sights & Activities

The village's greatest claim to fame is the meditation center **Las Pirámides** (☎ 205-7302, 205-7151; www.laspiramides.com.gt). You can enter from the path that passes Posada Schumann, or walk a short distance to the left (west) from the dock below Posada Schumann. A one-month personal development course begins every full moon, with three sessions daily, Monday to Saturday: one of Hatha yoga, one of meditation, and one of introduction to the spiritual life (first week), Shaluha-Ka therapy (second week), metaphysics and astral travel (third week) and retreat (fourth week). The final week requires fasting and silence by participants, so is not recommended for novice spiritualists. If you can stay for a month to do the whole course, come in time for full moon. Most sessions are held in English, though occasionally they'll be translated from Spanish. There's also a three-month

solar course running from each equinox to the following solstice, with a whole month's silence at the end.

Other experiences available here include yoga, aura work, massage (US$20) and Tarot readings. Monday through Saturday, nonguests can come for the meditation (5pm to 6pm) or Hatha yoga (7am to 8:30am) sessions for US$4.

Most structures on the property are pyramidal in shape and oriented to the four cardinal points, including the two temples where sessions are held. Accommodations are available in little pyramid-shaped houses for US$12/11/10 per day by the day/week/month. Included in this price are the course, use of the sauna, and access to a fascinating library with books in several languages. There's also a great vegetarian restaurant here and room to wander about in the medicinal herb garden.

Next door to Hotel Unicornio, **San Marcos Holistic Centre** (www.sanmholisticcentre.com; ☯ 10am-5pm Mon-Sat), run by Briton Louise Rothwell with various resident and visiting practitioners, provides a whole range of massages, holistic therapies and training courses in fields such as Bach flower remedies, Reiki, shiatsu, massage and reflexology. The approach is relaxed and you're welcome to discuss possibilities before committing to anything. English, Spanish, French and German are spoken. Most massages and therapies cost around US$13 an hour.

The walks along the lake west to Santa Clara La Laguna and east to Jaibalito and Santa Cruz La Laguna are breathtaking, but attacks and robberies have made it essential to take local advice before setting out. The section between San Marcos and Jaibalito is particularly notorious and you may be advised only to try it in a large group, or not at all.

Sleeping & Eating

Hotel La Paz (☎ 702-9168; per person US$5) Along a side path off the track behind Posada Schumann, the mellow La Paz has rambling grounds holding two doubles and five dormitory-style rooms. All are in bungalows of traditional *bajareque* (a stone, bamboo and mud construction) with thatch roofs, and some have loft beds. Antiques, art works, the organic gardens and vegetarian restaurant, the traditional

Mayan sauna and the music and book room above the restaurant all contribute to making this place a little bit special. You can join Hatha yoga sessions (US$2) in a special pavilion at 8am, or take a massage.

Hotel El Unicornio (www.hotelunicornio.com; s/d US$5/9) A favorite with the budget-conscious, El Unicornio has eight rooms in small, thatch-roofed A-frame bungalows among verdant gardens, sharing hot showers, nice hangout areas, a sauna and an equipped kitchen. Mexican owner Chus is a musician and enjoys playing with guests and making fun recordings in his little domed studio. To get there turn left past Hotel La Paz, or walk along the lakeside path and turn right after Las Pirámides.

Aaculaax (niecolass@hotmail.com; rooms per person US$7-11) An ecological fantasy come true, the new, German-owned Aaculaax is a five- to 10-minute walk to the left (west) along the lakeside path from the Posada Schumann dock. It's built around the living rock of the hillside, also using lots of recycled glass and plastic (plastic bottles stuffed hard with empty plastic bags form the core of many walls). Each of the seven double rooms is unique, with terrace, lake views, hot-water bathroom and compost toilets, and four have kitchens. A bar and restaurant should be open by the time you get there.

Hotel Jinava (www.jinava.de; s/d/tr US$13/13/20) The Jinava rambles up lovely hillside gardens from its own little beach on the western edge of San Marcos. Five pretty rooms in tile-roofed *casitas* have hot-water bathroom, small terrace, tile floors and ethnic textiles. The restaurant/bar serves an eclectic menu running from burritos (US$2.40) to Thai curry (US$5.25) and plays *son,* reggae, blues and salsa. Lancheros should be able to drop you at the Jinava's own dock; otherwise walk up past Posada Schumann to the main street, then go about 250m up to the left.

Posada Schumann (☎ 202-2216, 299-4711; hotel schumann@hotmail.com; s US$11-17, d US$22-33) Set in gardens that stretch right down to the lakeside, popular Posada Schumann has neat rooms in stone or wooden cottages, some with kitchen, most with bathroom and some with an upper floor and extra bed. There's also a restaurant and sauna.

Hotel Paco Real (☎ 891-1025; agutknecht54@hot mail.com; s/d/tr US$6/11/15) Along the same side-path as Hotel La Paz, the Paco Real has simple but tasteful rooms in thatched cottages, with shared bathrooms. Also here is a good restaurant with some Mexican choices (mains US$3.50 to US$4.50).

Il Giardino (☎ 804-0186; mains US$2.75-5.25) This excellent vegetarian restaurant, owned by a Costa Rican/Italian couple, is set in a tranquil, spacious garden reached just before Hotel Paco Real. Main dishes include pizzas, spaghetti and fondues. The burritos with salsa and melted mozzarella are a treat.

Hotel San Marcos (s/d US$4/7) Almost opposite Il Giardino, this has four plain rooms each with two single beds, and shared baths with hot showers.

Getting There & Away

The last dependable boat back to Jaibalito, Santa Cruz and Panajachel usually goes about 5pm. For information on boats from Panajachel, see p115.

A paved road runs east from San Marcos to Tzununá and west to San Pablo and Santa Clara, where it meets the road running from the Interamericana to San Pedro. You can travel between San Marcos and San Pedro by pickup, with a transfer at San Pablo.

JAIBALITO
pop 360

This small village, only accessible by boat or on foot, has two marvelous places to stay. Unfortunately the picturesque hike to San Marcos (three hours) is not recommended at the time of writing, except perhaps for large groups, because of attacks on walkers in the Tzununá area. The equally picturesque 45-minute path to Santa Cruz is, however, currently safe.

Sleeping & Eating

La Casa del Mundo (☎ 218-5332, 204-5558; www.lacasa delmundo.com; s US$11-20, d US$13-20, d with bathroom US$33-37, tr with bathroom US$40-44; ✗) Perched on a secluded cliff facing the three volcanoes, this is one of Guatemala's most spectacular hotels. Designed and built by husband and wife team Bill and Rosie Fogarty, it has beautiful gardens, good lake swimming and even a wood-fired hot tub overhanging the lake (US$33 for up to 10 people). Every room has privacy and views and is impeccably outfitted with comfortable beds, Guatemalan fabrics and fresh flowers. The best rooms seem to be floating above the water, with no land visible beneath. All rooms are nonsmoking. The excellent restaurant is open to the public; dinner (US$9) is four courses of seriously tasty food. You can rent kayaks (US$3.50 to US$7 an hour) for exploring the lake. Room reservations (by phone only) are advisable.

Vulcano Lodge (☎ 410-2237; vulcanolodge@hotmail .com; www.atitlan.com; d US$16-26, tr US$31) Towards the back of the village, Norwegian-owned-and-built Vulcano Lodge doesn't enjoy La Casa del Mundo's views, but its handful of trim and spotless Scandinavian-cum-Guatemalan rooms are just as appealing and its gardens just as lovely. As well as the two doubles and two triples, there's a spacious two-bedroom suite costing US$33/45/53/58 for two/three/four/five people. There's also a fine restaurant with mainly European food (US$9 for the all-you-can-eat four-course dinner). The owners, Terje and Monica, are well versed in local walking routes.

Getting There & Away
Jaibalito is a 20-minute *lancha* ride from Panajachel or San Pedro. As well as the public dock roughly in the center of the village, the Casa del Mundo has a pier.

SANTA CRUZ LA LAGUNA
elevation 1665m
Santa Cruz La Laguna is another serene little lakeside village. The vibe here is somewhere between the international party scene of San Pedro and the therapeutic, spiritual feel of San Marcos. The main part of the village is up the hill a bit; the hotels are on the lakeside, right beside the dock.

ATI Divers (p107) is based at La Iguana Perdida here. You can also take some good **walks** from Santa Cruz. The 45-minute path to Jaibalito is spectacular. Continuing from Jaibalito to San Marcos has been dangerous because of attacks on tourists, but the Santa Cruz police will often provide a free escort. Another walk goes up the hill to Sololá (or down the hill *from* Sololá!), which is three to 3½ hours one-way.

Sleeping & Eating
Three welcoming lakeside places provide beds and meals.

El Arca de Noé (☎ 306-4352; thearca@yahoo.com; www.atitlan.com/arcadenoe.htm; s/d US$11/16, with bathroom US$24/26, 4-person bungalows US$31-44) The

European-run Arca has a variety of rooms, all with lake views, in stone cottages in beautiful waterside gardens. Solar energy provides some hot water and electric light. It has a welcoming, sociable atmosphere and great food: the large candlelit set dinner, always with a vegetarian option, is US$8.50. For breakfast try the filling, tasty Western omelette (US$3).

La Iguana Perdida (☎ 762-2621, 706-4117; laig uanaperdida@itelgua.com; dm US$3, s US$6-10, d US$8-15, tr US$12-16) The Iguana Perdida has a young, fun atmosphere and a variety of accommodations from an open-air dorm to a triple with terrace. There's no electricity and the showers in the bathrooms (all shared) are lovely and cold! Meals are served family-style, with everyone eating together; a three-course dinner is US$5.50. You always have a vegetarian choice, and everything here is on the honor system: your tab is totaled up when you leave. Don't miss the Saturday night cross-dressing, fire and music barbecues!

Casa Rosa Hotel (☎ 390-4702, 416-1251; la_casa _rosa@hotmail.com; dm US$5, s US$10-19, d US$15-29) With gardens running down to the lake but a little removed from the action of the other hotels, Casa Rosa is a nice, quiet place with varied, clean, plain rooms with shared or private bathroom, and also stone-and-wood bungalows costing US$24/33/40/48 for one/two/three/four people. There's good food in the restaurant, which so far is the only part of the establishment to have electricity. The owner, Rosa Lubia García, offers Spanish classes and there's a sauna in the nicely maintained gardens.

Getting There & Away
For details of boats to Santa Cruz, see Panajachel (p115) and San Pedro La Laguna (p124).

QUICHÉ

The Departamento del Quiché, homeland of most of the K'iche' Maya, is best known for the town of Chichicastenango, with its big markets on Thursday and Sunday. North of Chichi is Santa Cruz del Quiché, the capital of the department. On its outskirts lie the ruins of K'umarcaaj, the last capital city of the K'iche' Maya. Further north, the town of Nebaj in the Ixil Triangle area, which suffered terribly during the civil war, is attracting increasing numbers of travelers.

The road into Quiché leaves the Interamericana at Los Encuentros, winding northward through pine forests and cornfields. Women sit in front of their little roadside houses weaving gorgeous pieces of cloth on backstrap looms. From Los Encuentros, it takes about half an hour to travel the 17km to Chichicastenango.

CHICHICASTENANGO

pop 23,000 / elevation 2030m

Surrounded by valleys, with mountains serrating the horizons, Chichicastenango can seem isolated in time and space from the rest of Guatemala. When its narrow cobbled streets and red-tiled roofs are enveloped in mist, as they often are, it can seem magical. The crowds of crafts vendors and tour groups who flock in for the huge Thursday and Sunday markets give the place a much worldlier, commercial atmosphere, but Chichi remains beautiful and interesting, with lots of shamanistic and ceremonial overtones. *Masheños* (citizens of Chichicastenango) are famous for their adherence to pre-Christian religious beliefs and ceremonies. If you have a choice of days, come for the Sunday market rather than the Thursday one, as the *cofradías* (Mayan religious brotherhoods) often hold processions in and around the church of Santo Tomás on Sunday.

Chichi has two religious and governmental establishments. On the one hand, the Catholic Church and the Republic of Guatemala appoint priests and town officials; on the other, the indigenous people elect their own religious and civil officers to manage local matters, with a separate council and mayor, and a court that decides cases involving only local indigenous people.

Once called Chaviar, Chichi was an important Kaqchiquel trading town long before the Spanish conquest. In the 15th century the Kaqchiquel and the K'iche' (based at K'umarcaaj near present-day Santa Cruz del Quiché, 20km north) went to war. The Kaqchiquel abandoned Chaviar and moved their headquarters to the more defensible Iximché. When the Spanish conquered K'umarcaaj in 1524, many of its residents fled to Chaviar, which they renamed Chugüilá (Above the Nettles) and Tziguan Tinamit (Surrounded by Canyons). These are the names still used by the K'iche' Maya, although everyone else calls the place Chichicastenango, a name given by the Spaniards' Mexican allies.

Information

Chichi's many banks all stay open on Sunday, taking their day off (if any) on some other day of the week. Most banks change US-dollar cash and traveler's checks.

ACSES (6a Calle east of 5a Av) Charges US$1.60 an hour for Internet use.

Banco Industrial (⏰ 10am-2pm Mon, 10am-5pm Wed & Fri, 9am-5pm Thu & Sun, 10am-3pm Sat) Almost

---

THE MAYAN 'BIBLE'

One of the most important Mayan texts, the *Popol Vuh*, was written down after the Spanish conquest in K'iche' Maya, using Latin script. The K'iche' scribes showed their book to Francisco Ximénez, a Dominican who lived and worked in Chichicastenango from 1701 to 1703. Friar Ximénez copied the K'iche's book word for word, then translated it into Spanish. Both his copy and the Spanish translation survive, but the Mayan original has been lost. The *Popol Vuh* deals with the dawn of life and the glories of gods and kings. You'll find copies on sale throughout Guatemala. The definitive English translation is by Dennis Tedlock. Its tale is somewhat cyclical and not always consistent, but its gist is as follows: the great god K'ucumatz created humankind first from earth (mud), but these earthlings were weak and dissolved in water. The god tried again, using wood. The wood people had no hearts or minds and could not praise their creator. These too were destroyed, all except the monkeys of the forest, who are the descendants of the wood people. The creator tried once again, this time successfully, using material recommended by four animals – the grey fox, the coyote, the parrot and the crow. The substance was white and yellow corn, ground into meal to form the flesh and stirred into water to make the blood. Thus do Guatemalans think of themselves with pride as *hombres de maíz*, men of corn.

next door to Banrural; changes US-dollar cash and traveler's checks.

Banrural (6a Calle east of 5a Av; ☺ 9am-5pm Sun-Fri, 9am-1pm Sat) Changes US-dollar cash and traveler's checks; has a MasterCard ATM.

Hotel Santo Tomás (p132) Has a good selection of books for sale in its lobby.

Internet Digital (5a Av 5-60) Charges US$1.60 an hour for Internet use.

Visa ATM (cnr 5a Av & 6a Calle) On the street.

Dangers & Annoyances

The cemetery on the western edge of town is an unwise place to wander, even in groups. Tourists have been robbed at gunpoint there.

Crowded markets are the favorite haunts of pickpockets, so be alert while you wander in the labyrinth of stalls here.

When you arrive in Chichi, you may be approached by touts offering guide services and assistance in finding a hotel. Showing up at a hotel with a tout in tow means you'll be quoted a higher price for a room, as the hotel has to give them a kickback – and this on top of your tip! In fact, you don't need their 'help,' because there's no difficulty finding lodgings. In fact, touts won't take you to some of the best-value hotels because the owners refuse to provide kickbacks.

Sights

MARKET

In the past villagers would walk for many hours carrying their wares to participate in Chichi market, one of Guatemala's largest indigenous markets. Some still do, and when they reach Chichi on the night before the market, they lay down their loads in one of the arcades or spaces around the plaza, cook some supper, spread out a blanket and go to sleep.

At dawn on Thursday and Sunday they spread out their vegetables, fruits, chunks of chalk (ground to a powder, mixed with water and used to soften dried maize), balls of wax, handmade harnesses and other merchandise and wait for customers. The plaza is now the territory of more full-time traders, with stalls covered in unsightly black plastic sheeting, but many more traders fill the streets for several blocks around the plaza on Sunday and Thursday. Tourist-oriented handicraft stalls selling masks, textiles, pottery and so on now occupy much of the plaza and the streets

to the north. Things the villagers need – vegetables, fruit, baked goods, macaroni, soap, clothing, spices, sewing notions, toys – cluster at the north end of the square, in the *centro comercial* off the north side, and in streets to the south.

The market starts winding down around 3pm. Prices are best just before it breaks up, as tired traders would rather sell than carry goods away with them. By this time you'll also notice quite a few drunks staggering around or lying comatose in the street.

IGLESIA DE SANTO TOMÁS

This **church** on the east side of the plaza dates from about 1540 and is often the scene of rituals that are only slightly Catholic and more distinctly Mayan. The front steps of the church serve much the same purpose as did the great flights of stairs leading up to Mayan pyramids. For much of the day (especially on Sunday), they smolder with incense of copal resin, while indigenous prayer leaders called *chuchkajaues* (mother-fathers) swing censers (usually tin cans poked with holes) and chant magic words marking the days of the ancient Maya calendar and in honor of their ancestors.

It's customary for the front steps and door of the church to be used only by important church officials and by the *chuchkajaues,* so you should go around to the right and enter by the side door.

Inside, the floor of the church may be spread with pine boughs and dotted with offerings of maize kernels, flowers, bottles of liquor wrapped in corn husks, and candles. Many local families can trace their lineage back centuries, some even to the ancient kings of the K'iche'. The candles and offerings on the floor are in remembrance of those ancestors, many of whom are buried beneath the church floor just as Maya kings were buried beneath pyramids. Photography is not permitted in this church.

On the west side of the plaza is another whitewashed church, the **Capilla del Calvario**, which is similar in form and function to Santo Tomás, but smaller.

MUSEO REGIONAL

Chichi's **Museo Regional** (5a Av 4-47; admission US$0.15; ☺ 8am-noon & 2-4pm Tue-Wed & Fri-Sat, 8am-4pm Thu, 8am-2pm Sun), entered from the south side of the main square, has a collection of

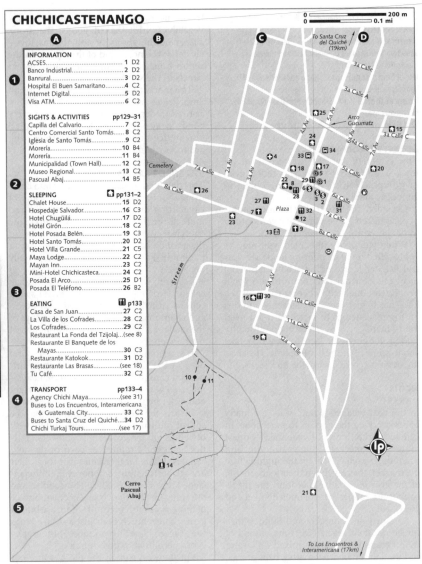

CHICHICASTENANGO

0 — 200 m
0 — 0.1 mi

INFORMATION
ACSES..................................... 1 D2
Banco Industrial..................... 2 D2
Banrural................................. 3 D2
Hospital El Buen Samaritano......... 4 C2
Internet Digital........................ 5 D2
Visa ATM................................ 6 C2

SIGHTS & ACTIVITIES pp129–31
Capilla del Calvario.................. 7 C2
Centro Comercial Santo Tomás...... 8 C2
Iglesia de Santo Tomás.............. 9 C2
Morería.................................. 10 B4
Morería.................................. 11 B4
Municipalidad (Town Hall)......... 12 C2
Museo Regional....................... 13 C2
Pascual Abaj........................... 14 B5

SLEEPING pp131–2
Chalet House.......................... 15 D2
Hospedaje Salvador.................. 16 C3
Hotel Chugüilá........................ 17 D2
Hotel Girón............................. 18 C2
Hotel Posada Belén................... 19 C3
Hotel Santo Tomás................... 20 D2
Hotel Villa Grande................... 21 C5
Maya Lodge............................ 22 C2
Mayan Inn.............................. 23 C2
Mini-Hotel Chichicasteca.......... 24 C2
Posada El Arco........................ 25 D1
Posada El Teléfono................... 26 B2

EATING p133
Casa de San Juan..................... 27 C2
La Villa de los Cofrades............. 28 C2
Los Cofrades........................... 29 C2
Restaurant La Fonda del Tzijolaj...(see 8)
Restaurante El Banquete de los
   Mayas................................. 30 C3
Restaurante Katokok................ 31 D2
Restaurante Las Brasas.............(see 18)
Tu Café.................................. 32 C2

TRANSPORT pp133–4
Agency Chichi Maya..................(see 31)
Buses to Los Encuentros, Interamericana
   & Guatemala City............... 33 C2
Buses to Santa Cruz del Quiché... 34 D2
Chichi Turkaj Tours..................(see 17)

To Santa Cruz
del Quiché
(19km)

To Los Encuentros &
Interamericana (17km)

Cerro
Pascual
Abaj

---

ceremonial masks, copper axheads, obsidian spearheads, incense burners, figurines and *metates* (grindstones for maize). The museum also holds the Rossbach jade collection, with some beautiful necklaces and figurines. Hugo Rossbach, from Germany, served as Chichi's Catholic priest for many years until his death in 1944.

PASCUAL ABAJ

On a hilltop south of the town, **Pascual Abaj** (Sacrifice Stone) is a shrine to the Mayan earth god Huyup Tak'ah (Mountain Plain). Said to be hundreds – perhaps thousands – of years old, the stone-faced idol has suffered numerous indignities at the hands of outsiders, but local people still revere it. *Chuchkajaues* come regularly to offer incense, food, cigarettes, flowers, liquor, Coca-Cola, and perhaps even to sacrifice a chicken, in thanks and hope for the Earth's continuing fertility.

Sacrifices do not take place at regular hours. If you're in luck, you may witness one. The worshipers will not mind if you watch, but be sure to request permission before taking any photos and don't assume it will be granted. You may be asked if you want to make an offering (of a few *quetzals*) yourself. If there is no ceremony, you can still see the idol and enjoy the walk up the pine-clad hill. Tourists walking to visit Pascual Abaj have on occasions been robbed, so the best plan is to join with others and go not too late in the afternoon.

Walk downhill on 5a Av from the main plaza, turn right into 9a Calle and follow it downhill. At the bottom of the hill, bear left along a path and head up through either of the **morerías** (ceremonial mask workshops, worth a visit on the way up or way back) that are signposted here. From the back of either *morería*, follow the path uphill through the trees to the top of the hill. You'll find the idol in its rocky, smoke-blackened shrine in a clearing, looking a little like something from Easter Island. The squat stone crosses nearby have many significances for the Maya, only one of which pertains to Christ. The area is littered with past offerings.

Festivals & Events
Holidays and special events here can offer a more intriguing experience than the usual

dancing, drinking and fireworks typical of Guatemalan fiestas. December 7 sees the **Quema del Diablo** (Burning of the Devil), when residents burn their garbage in the streets and usher a statue of the Virgin Mary to the steps of the Iglesia de Santo Tomás. There's lots of incense and candles, a *marimba* band and an ingenious and daring fireworks display that has observers running for cover. The following day is the **Feast of the Immaculate Conception**; don't miss the early morning dance of the giant, drunken cartoon characters in the plaza.

The **fiesta of Santo Tomás** starts on December 13 and culminates on December 21 when pairs of brave (some would say mad) men fly about at high speeds suspended from a tall, vertical pole in the *palo volador* (fliers' pole) extravaganza. Traditional dances and parades also feature.

Sleeping
Chichi does not have a lot of accommodations, and it's a good idea to arrive fairly early on Wednesday or Saturday if you want to secure a room the night before the Thursday or Sunday market.

BUDGET
Posada El Arco (☎ 756-1255; 4a Calle 4-36; s/d US$16/ 20) This winner guesthouse, near the Arco Gucumatz, is the best accommodation for the price in Chichi. All seven rooms are spacious and spotless, with attractive decor, fireplace and hot-water bathroom. You can sit in lawn chairs in the garden and enjoy a

THE HIGHLANDS

COFRADÍAS

Chichi's religious life is centered in traditional religious brotherhoods known as *cofradías*. Membership in the brotherhood is an honorable civic duty, and election as leader is the greatest honor. Leaders must provide banquets and pay for festivities for the *cofradía* throughout his term. Though it is very expensive, a *cofrade* (brotherhood member) happily accepts the burden, even going into debt if necessary.

Each of Chichi's 14 *cofradías* has a patron saint. Most notable is the *cofradía* of Santo Tomás, Chichicastenango's patron saint. *Cofradías* march in procession to church every Sunday morning and during religious festivals, with the officers dressed in costumes showing their rank. Before them is carried a ceremonial staff topped by a silver crucifix or sun-badge that signifies the *cofradía's* patron saint. A drum and a flute, and perhaps a few more modern instruments such as a trumpet, may accompany the procession, as do fireworks.

During major church festivals, effigies of the saints are carried in grand processions, and richly costumed dancers wearing traditional wooden masks act out legends of the ancient Maya and of the Spanish conquest. For the rest of the year, these masks and costumes are kept in storehouses-cum-workshops called *morerías*; you'll see them, marked by signs, around the town.

great northward view of the mountains of Quiché. The friendly owners, Emilsa and Pedro Macario, speak English and Spanish. Reservations are a good idea.

Chalet House (☎ 756-1360; 3a Calle C No 7-44; s/d US$13/16) The cozy Chalet House is run by another friendly, English-speaking husband-and-wife team. Rooms have good beds, homey touches and hot-water bathroom. Rates rise to around US$16/20 in July, August and September.

Hotel Girón (☎ 756-1156; 6a Calle 4-52; s/d/tr with bathroom US$9/13/17; P) This two-story hotel, set around a courtyard/car park with some trees, is reasonably clean and OK value for the money. You can sit out on the broad walkways in front of the rooms. There are also two rooms that share one bathroom and these cost US$6/8/10 for s/d/tr.

Posada El Teléfono (8a Calle A 1-64; s/d US$4/7) This family-run budget *posada* (guesthouse) has half a dozen clean rooms with firm beds, a few homey decorative touches and shared hot-water baths. The rooftop rooms have plenty of light and air.

Hotel Posada Belén (☎ 756-1244; 12a Calle 5-55; s/d US$5/8, with bathroom US$7/11) Up on a hill away from the chaos of the market area, the Belén has 18 fairly clean rooms. The showers aren't the greatest, but the top-floor rooms have killer views.

Mini-Hotel Chichicasteca (☎ 756-2111; 5a Calle 4-42; s/d US$5/9) This hotel's adequately clean rooms with bare brick walls and shared bathrooms are a decent budget choice.

Hospedaje Salvador (☎ 756-1329; 5a Av 10-09; s/d/tr US$4/7/10, with bathroom US$7/10/12) This large, maze-like building, two blocks south of the square, is the biggest of the cheapies, with 52 rooms that are almost clean. They get better as you go higher: Nos 49 to 52 on the top floor are light and airy, with good views. Try negotiating for reduced prices. The entrance is an unmarked blue door on 10a Calle and there's a US$0.65 key deposit.

MID-RANGE

Hotel Chugüilá (☎ 756-1134; chuguila@intelnet.net.gt; 5a Av 5-24; s/d/tr US$32/37/42; P) All 36 colonial-style rooms have a bathroom, and some have a fireplace, but check a few before settling in as they vary and mildew has beset some. They're set around a large, pretty courtyard providing ample parking – overall, it's decent value.

Maya Lodge (☎ 756-1167; 6a Calle A 4-08; s/d/tr US$25/31/39; P) Located right on the main plaza, this hotel has a slightly colonial atmosphere. The 10 rooms have wooden ceilings, three with a fireplace and all with a hot-water bathroom, are set along a pillared patio and adorned with woven rugs and Mayan-style bedspreads. The hotel has a restaurant.

Hotel Villa Grande (☎ 756-1053; www.villasde guatemala.com; s US$37-49, d US$43-61, tr US$71; P ☎) This modern 75-room hotel is 1km south of the center, in low tile-roofed buildings set into a hillside. The walk to or from town can make a nice stroll, though it might not be the safest at night. The Villa Grande has good views, a swimming pool and a restaurant, but there's zilch atmosphere unless a few other guests are in. The regular rooms are rather stark, and half of them look out on nothing but a rear wall. The suites all have patio, sitting area, fireplace and large bathroom.

TOP END

Mayan Inn (☎ 756-1176; www.mayaninn.com.gt; 8a Calle A 1-91; s/d/tr US$80/92/110) A lovely old inn on a quiet street, the Mayan Inn was founded in 1932 by Alfred S Clark of Clark Tours and is the best hotel in town. It has grown to include several restored colonial houses, their courtyards planted with exuberant tropical flora and their walls covered with bright indigenous textiles. Not all of the 30 rooms are equally charming, so look before choosing. Each has a fireplace and interesting antique furnishings. The bathrooms (many with tubs) may be old-fashioned, but they are decently maintained. A staff member is assigned to answer your questions and serve you in the dining room (see p133), as well as to look after your room – there are no door locks.

Hotel Santo Tomás (☎ 756-1316; hst@itelgua.com; 7a Av 5-32; s/d/tr US$82/97/119; P ☎) Colonial in architecture and decoration but modern in construction and facilities, the Santo Tomás is very attractive and a favorite with tour operators. Each of the 43 rooms (with 30 more due to open in 2004) has a bathroom (with tub) and a fireplace; all are grouped around pretty courtyards with colonial fountains. There's a swimming pool, Jacuzzi and a good bar and dining room (see p133).

Eating

BUDGET

Casa de San Juan (4a Av, main plaza; dishes US$1-3) The San Juan is one of the few eateries in town with style – art on the walls, jugs of lilies, wrought-iron chairs – and its food is great too, ranging from burgers and tortillas to a *churrasco* or a *plato vegetariano*. We recommend the nicely presented *chile relleno*, with guacamole, rice, salad and tortillas.

La Villa de los Cofrades (6a Calle A, main plaza; dishes US$2.50-4) You can't beat this location in the arcade on the north side of the plaza. This is a fine café for breakfast, crepes or larger meals, and a throw of backgammon if you like.

Tu Café (5a Av, main plaza; mains US$2.50-4) The *plato vegetariano* here is soup, rice, beans, cheese, salad and tortillas, for a reasonable US$2.50. Add *lomito* (a pork fillet) and it becomes a *plato típico* (US$4).

Restaurant La Fonda del Tzijolaj (Centro Comercial Santo Tomás; breakfast US$2-3.50, lunch & dinner mains US$3.50-6) Upstairs overlooking the plaza, this restaurant combines reasonable food with lowish prices.

Los Cofrades (cnr 6a Calle & 5a Av; lunch & dinner mains US$4.50-6.50) This bright upstairs restaurant (enter from 6a Calle) with excellent food has tables out on the balcony and inside between brick arches. The set lunch or dinner is substantial; simpler fare is available too. Along the street is the similar **Restaurante Katokok** (6a Calle 6-45; pasta & meat dishes US$5.25-6.25).

Restaurante El Banquete de los Mayas (cnr 5a Av & 10a Calle; lunch or dinner US$2-5.50; 🕑 6:30am-10:30pm) Big breakfasts are served at this brightly decorated restaurant for US$2.25 to US$4.50. For lunch or dinner, straightforward meat, rice, veggies and beans goes for US$2.

Restaurante Las Brasas (6a Calle 4-52; mains US$4.25-6.25) Above the entrance to Hotel Girón, Las Brasas serves meat dishes at reasonable prices. Its breakfasts (US$2.20 to US$3.75) are a good deal.

MID-RANGE

Mayan Inn (8a Calle A 1-91; set breakfast/lunch/dinner with drinks US$6/12/12) The three dining rooms at the Chichi's classiest hotel have beamed ceilings, red-tiled floors, colonial-style tables and chairs, and decorations of colorful local cloth. Waiters wear traditional costumes evolved from the dress of Spanish colonial farmers: colorful headdress, sash, black embroidered tunic, half-length trousers and squeaky leather sandals called *caïtes*. The food may not be as stellar as the costuming, however.

Hotel Santo Tomás (7a Av 5-32; 3-course dinner US$12) Chichi's other top-end hotel has a good dining room, but you might find it crowded with tour groups. Try to get one of the courtyard tables, where you can enjoy the sun and the *marimba* band that plays at market-day lunchtimes and on the evenings before.

Getting There & Away

Buses heading south to Los Encuentros, Panajachel, Quetzaltenango, Guatemala City and all other points reached from the Interamericana normally arrive and depart from the corner of 5a Calle and 5a Av, one block south (uphill) from the Arco Gucumatz arch. Buses heading north to Santa Cruz del Quiché stop half a block north (downhill) on the same street. On market days, however, buses to or from the south may stop at the corner of 7a Av and 9a Calle, to avoid the congested central streets.

Antigua (3½hr, 108km) Take any bus heading for Guatemala City and change at Chimaltenango.

Guatemala City (US$1.55, 3hr, 145km, every 20min 4am-5pm)

Los Encuentros (US$0.65, 30min, 17km) Take any bus heading south for Guatemala City, Panajachel, Quetzaltenango and so on.

Nebaj (103km) Take a bus to Santa Cruz del Quiché and change there.

Panajachel (US$1.30, 1½hr, 37km, 8 daily 5am-2pm) Or take any southbound bus and change at Los Encuentros.

Quetzaltenango (US$1.50, 3hr, 94km) Seven buses run daily, mostly in the morning; or take any southbound bus and change at Los Encuentros.

Santa Cruz del Quiché (US$0.40, 30min, 19km, every 20min 5am-8pm)

On market days, shuttle buses arrive en masse mid-morning, bringing tourists from Panajachel, Antigua, Guatemala City and Quetzaltenango. They depart for the return trip around 2pm. If you're looking to leave Chichi, you can usually catch a ride out on one of these.

Chichi Turkaj Tours (☎ 293-5480; Hotel Chugüilá, 5a Av 5-24) and **Agency Chichi Maya** (☎ 756-1008; 6a Calle 6-45) provide shuttles to the same places and elsewhere including Huehuetenango, the

Mexican border and the ruins of K'umarcaaj near Santa Cruz del Quiché. In most cases they need four or five customers unless you're prepared to rent the whole vehicle (which costs around US$25 to Panajachel, or US$60 to Antigua or Quetzaltenango).

SANTA CRUZ DEL QUICHÉ
pop 13,000 / elevation 2020m

The capital of Quiché department is 19km north of Chichicastenango. As you leave Chichi heading north along 5a Av, you pass beneath the Arco Gucumatz, an arched bridge named for Ku'ucumatz, the founder of the old K'iche' Maya capital K'umarcaaj, near Santa Cruz.

Without Chichi's big market and attendant tourism, Santa Cruz – usually called El Quiché or simply Quiché – is quieter and more typical of Guatemalan towns. Travelers who come here usually do so to visit K'umarcaaj or to change buses en route further north (for Nebaj, for example).

The main market day is Saturday, making things slightly more interesting and way more crowded.

Orientation & Information

Everything you need is within a few short blocks of the central plaza, called the Parque Central. From the bus station, walk three bocks north on 1a Av (Zona 5), then two blocks to the left (west), then one to the right (north) to reach the plaza's southeast corner. The church rises on the east side of the plaza, with the market behind it.

Bancafé (9am-7pm Mon-Fri, 9am-1pm Sat) and **Banrural** (8:30am-6pm Mon-Fri, 9am-1pm Sat), both at the plaza's northwest corner, change US-dollar cash and traveler's checks too. Bancafé has a Visa ATM, Banrural has a MasterCard ATM. You can access the Internet at **Occitel** on the west side of the plaza.

Sights
MUSEO MILITAR

Should you want to know the Guatemalan army's version of the civil war in Quiché department, have a look at the **Military Museum** (admission US$0.25; 9am-noon & 2-6pm Mon-Fri) in the northeast corner of the plaza. Displays cover uniforms and weapons, the struggle against communism, and social work now being done by the military. No comment.

K'UMARCAAJ

The ruins of the ancient K'iche' Maya capital (also called Gumarcaaj or Utatlán) are 3km west of El Quiché along an unpaved road. Take a flashlight (torch) if you have one. Head west along 11a Calle, opposite the bus station, and follow this all the way to **K'umarcaaj** (admission US$1.30; 8am-5pm). A taxi there and back from the bus station, including waiting time, costs around US$8.

The kingdom of K'iche' was established in late post-Classic times (about the 14th century) by a mixture of indigenous people and invaders from the Tabasco/Campeche border area in Mexico. Around 1400, King Ku'ucumatz founded K'umarcaaj and conquered many neighboring settlements. During the long reign of his successor Q'uik'ab (1425–75), the K'iche' kingdom extended its borders to Huehuetenango, Nebaj, Rabinal and the Pacific Slope. At the same time the Kaqchiquel, a vassal people who once fought alongside the K'iche', rebelled, establishing an independent capital at Iximché.

When Pedro de Alvarado and his Spanish conquistadors hit Guatemala in 1524, it was the K'iche', under their king Tecún Umán, who led the resistance to them. In the decisive battle fought near Quetzaltenango on February 12, 1524, Alvarado and Tecún locked in mortal combat. Alvarado prevailed. The defeated K'iche' invited Alvarado to visit K'umarcaaj, secretly planning to kill him. Smelling a rat, Alvarado enlisted the aid of his Mexican auxiliaries and the anti-K'iche' Kaqchiquel, and together they captured the K'iche' leaders, burnt them alive in K'umarcaaj's main plaza and then destroyed the city.

The ruins have a fine setting, shaded by tall trees and surrounded by ravines, which failed to defend it against the conquistadors. Archaeologists have identified 100 or so large structures here, but only limited restoration or clearing has been done. The **museum** at the entrance will help orientate you. The tallest of the structures round the central plaza, the Templo de Tohil (a sky god), is blackened by smoke and has a niche where contemporary prayer-men regularly make offerings to Mayan gods. K'umarcaaj is still very much a sacred site for the Maya.

Down the hillside to the right of the plaza is the entrance to a long tunnel known as the *cueva*. Legend has it that the K'iche' dug the tunnel as a refuge for their women and children in preparation for Pedro de Alvarado's coming, and that a K'iche' princess was later buried in a deep shaft off this tunnel. Revered as the place where the K'iche' kingdom died, the *cueva* is sacred to highland Maya and is an important location for prayers, candle burning, offerings and chicken sacrifices.

If there's anyone around the entrance, ask permission before entering. Inside, the long tunnel (perhaps 100m long) is blackened with smoke and incense and littered with candles and flower petals. Use your flashlight and watch your footing: there are several side tunnels and at least one of them, on the right near the end, contains a deep, black shaft.

Sleeping & Eating

Hotel Rey K'iche (☎ 755-0827; 8a Calle 0-39, Zona 5; s/d/tr US$11/19/27; P) Between bus station and plaza, the Rey K'iche has 24 good, clean, modern rooms with brick and/or whitewash walls, cable TV and hot-water bathroom. There's free drinking water and a decent restaurant open 24 hours daily.

Hotel San Pascual (☎ 755-1107; 7a Calle 0-43, Zona 1; s/d US$5/10, with bathroom US$8/13; P) Also between the bus station and plaza, this is a clean and friendly hotel with plants in its two courtyards.

Posada Calle Real (2a Av 7-36, Zona 1; s/d US$5/8) Opposite Pollo Campero two blocks south of the Parque Central, this relative cheapie is set around three courtyards. It has bare and basic rooms with clean bathrooms.

Comedor Fliper (1a Av 7-31, Zona 1; mains US$2; ✆ lunch & dinner) This small, friendly, inexpensive diner is around the corner from Hotel San Pascual, 1½ blocks south of the plaza.

El Torito (3a Av 4-35, Zona 1; set lunch US$3) One real bull's head and several leather imitations gaze down on diners here, one block west of the plaza. The good-value set lunch will normally bring you soup and a meat dish with tortillas. The house specialty, filet mignon, is US$5.50.

Pollo Campero (2a Av 7-35, Zona 1; meals US$3-4; ✆) This chain restaurant two blocks south of the Parque Central is by far the most popular eatery in town. The air-conditioning may have something to do with this.

Getting There & Away

Many buses from Guatemala City to Chichicastenango continue to El Quiché. The last bus from El Quiché headed south to Chichicastenango and Los Encuentros leaves mid-afternoon.

El Quiché is the jumping-off point for the somewhat remote reaches of northern Quiché, which extend all the way to the Mexican border. Departures from the bus station include:

Chichicastenango (US$0.40, 30min, 19km) Take any bus heading for Guatemala City.

Guatemala City (US$2.10, 3½hr, 163km, every 20min 3am-5pm)

Los Encuentros (US$0.80, 1hr, 36km) Take any bus heading for Guatemala City.

Nebaj (US$1.70, 2½hr, 75km, 8 daily 8:30am-5pm)

Sacapulas (US$1, 1hr, 45km, hourly 8:30am-5pm) Or take any bus heading for Nebaj or Uspantán.

Uspantán (US$2, 3hr, 75km, 5 daily 9:30am, 10:30am, 1:30pm, 3pm & 3:30pm)

SACAPULAS

This small, friendly town on the Río Negro is where the El Quiché–Nebaj road meets the Huehuetenango–Cobán road and so is a place where you may need to change buses or possibly stay a night. **Banrural** (✆ 8am-5pm Mon-Fri, 8am-noon Sat) on the plaza, up the hill from the bridge, changes cash US dollars.

There's a Cruz Roja (Red Cross) post on the southern bank of the river, next door to the friendly **Hospedaje Black River** (rooms per person US$2.60). The rooms here are basic but clean and secure, with shared, cold-water bathroom. Meals in the restaurant are tasty, filling and cheap: a breakfast of *mosh*, eggs, beans, cheese, tortillas and coffee costs just US$1.30.

Getting There & Away

The 45km road from El Quiché is paved; the spectacular mountain roads to Huehue, Nebaj and Cobán are unpaved but in reasonable condition. Bus schedules from Sacapulas are imprecise:

Cobán (US$3, 5hr, 100km) Transportes Mejía's Aguacatán-Cobán bus stops at the north end of Sacapulas bridge at about 7:30am on Saturday and Tuesday (only). Otherwise, head to Uspantán and either spend the night there or try to get through in one day by pickups (most frequent in the morning).

El Quiché (US$1, 1hr, 45km, 12 daily 1:30am-5:30pm) Buses stop at the south end of the bridge at erratic hours: the greatest frequency is between about 6am and 10am.

Huehuetenango (US$2, 2½hr, 42km, 2 daily 4am & 5:30am) Buses go from the north end of the bridge: later in the day, occasional pickups and other vehicles can take you as far as Aguacatán, from where buses leave for Huehue a dozen times between 4:45am and 4pm.

Nebaj (US$1, 1½hr, 26km, 8 daily 9:30am-6pm) Catch these at the south end of the bridge.

Uspantán (US$1.20, 1¾hr, 30km, 5 daily 10:30am, 11:30am, 2:30pm, 4pm & 4:30pm) Catch them at the south end of the bridge.

Pickups and some other vehicles provide extra transport at fares equivalent to those of buses. Traffic is extremely light by late afternoon, so the earlier you're up in this part of Guatemala, the better.

USPANTÁN
pop 3500
Uspantán is where you'll probably spend the night while traveling between Nebaj/Sacapulas/Huehuetenango and Cobán, unless you get right through in one day. It's a benevolent and clean town, with wide paved avenues, though it can seem distinctly eerie if you arrive after dark during one of the frequent power outages and the place is enveloped in fog! It can get very cold here, so don't hesitate to ask for extra blankets.

Rigoberta Menchú (p29) grew up a five-hour walk through the mountains from Uspantán. She is not loved by all her former neighbors, however, so don't be shocked if you get a chilly reaction on this front.

Banrural (7a Av, Zona 4; ☺ 8:30am-5pm Mon-Fri, 9am-1pm Sat), 2½ blocks from the central plaza, will change cash US dollars.

Sleeping & Eating
Pensión Galindo (5a Calle 2-09; s/d US$3/6) About three blocks from the plaza, Galindo has a dozen tiny, clean rooms round a neat little patio open to the stars. The showers are cold and you need to bring your own toilet paper, but it's a fine place to stay.

Hotel La Uspanteka (4a Calle 5-18; s/d US$2/4) Just off the plaza, this is another decent option, with 17 cleanish rooms.

The simple **comedor** on the plaza, opposite the Municopaz office (which is next to the church), will grill slices of meat over hot coals and serve it up with rice, avocado, tortillas and hot chocolate for US$1.60. There are several other *comedores* around the center: **Comedor Central** (6a Calle, Zona 1), 1½ blocks from the plaza, and **Comedor Kevin** (7a Calle 5-28, Zona 3), 2½ blocks from the plaza, are both OK.

Getting There & Away
Five or six buses daily leave Uspantán for Quiché (US$2, three hours) via Sacapulas, the first two at about 3am and 5am, the last at 4pm. For Cobán (US$2, three to four hours), buses go at 3am and 5am. On Saturday and Tuesday (only) there's also Transportes Mejía's Aguacatán–Cobán bus, at about 9am. Get to the plaza in good time for the early buses as they fill up fast with sleepy locals. For Nebaj get a Sacapulas bus and change either at the *entronque de Nebaj* (Nebaj turnoff), about 8km before Sacapulas, or at Sacapulas itself where you might be more likely to get a seat.

Uspantán to Cobán is one of the most gorgeous rides in Guatemala (see Itineraries, p14) and epitomizes the chicken bus experience, as it's a difficult ride in a crowded bus on an unpaved road. You may find yourself praying to higher powers as the bus loses its grip on muddy mountain passes in the pitch black of night, but try to be awake when the sun pushes over the tops of the mountains, burning off the fog clinging to the valley below. Sit on the right for views.

NEBAJ
pop 11,000 / elevation 1900m
Hidden in a remote fold of the Cuchumatanes mountains north of Sacapulas is the Triángulo Ixil (Ixil Triangle), comprising the towns of Nebaj, Cotzal and Chajul and dozens of outlying villages and hamlets. The scenery is breathtakingly beautiful, and the local Ixil Maya people, though they suffered perhaps more than anybody in Guatemala's civil war and are still very impoverished, cling proudly to many of their old traditions. Nebaj women are celebrated for their beautiful purple, green and yellow pom-pommed hair braids, and for their *huipiles* and *rebozos* (shawls) of the same colors, with many bird and animal motifs. This is a fascinating area to explore and free (to date) of crime against tourists and of the trails of trash that disfigure so much of the Guatemalan countryside.

Living in this beautiful mountain fastness has long been both a blessing and a curse. The Spaniards found it difficult to conquer and laid waste to the inhabitants when they did. The area suffered terribly during the Guatemalan civil war, especially during the brutal reign of Efraín Ríos Montt (1982–83), when the local people became the chief victims of the army's merciless measures to dislodge guerrillas from the area. Massacres and disappearances were rife, and more than two dozen villages were destroyed. The horror touched every family, and many people fled to Guatemala City, Mexico or simply to the forests. Some were settled in *polos de desarrollo* (poles of development), supposed 'strategic hamlets' whose real purpose was to enable the army to keep their inhabitants under close control. You may hear some appalling personal experiences from locals while you are here. For a horrifying report and analysis of massacres in and around Nebaj, see the website http://shr.aaas.org/guatemala/ciidh/dts/toc.html.

The people of the Ixil Triangle are making a heroic effort to build a new future. Development organizations and nongovernment organizations (NGOs) have contributed to this and you'll likely encounter some of their workers too. One project of special interest to visitors, carried out with the help of the Spanish NGO Solidaridad Internacional, has been the establishment of a network of signed walking routes and *posadas comunitarias,* simple village lodgings with meals and guides available, to make it easier for travelers to hike some of the beautiful Ixil countryside and experience village life.

Orientation & Information

Coming from the south, your first view of Nebaj, set neatly at the foot of a bowl ringed by green mountains, makes the rough bus ride worthwhile. Nebaj's central plaza, known as the Parque, has a large church on its south side. From the southeast corner of the Parque, the market (daily but busiest on Sunday) is one block east, and the Terminal de Buses (Bus Station) is one longish block south then 1½ blocks east. Calzada 15 de Septiembre, sometimes simply called the Salida a Chajul, runs northeast from the Parque to become the road to Cotzal and Chajul.

The restaurant **El Descanso** (☎ 801-5087, 418-3940; www.nebaj.com; 3a Calle, Zona 1; ☼ 6am-10pm) is a focal point for travelers, development workers and locals. To reach it, walk two blocks north along 5a Av from the northwest corner of the Parque, then half a block to the left. **Tetz Chemol** in the El Descanso building sells 1:50,000 area maps for US$8.50.

Bancafé (2a Av 46; ☼ 9am-4pm Mon-Fri, 9am-1pm Sat), one block east from the northeast corner of the Parque, then half a block north, changes US-dollar cash and traveler's checks and has a Visa ATM. The **post office** (5a Av 4-37) is one block north of the Parque. **La Red** (El Descanso Bldg, 3a Calle, Zona 1) has Nebaj's fastest Internet connections, for US$1.30 per hour (US$0.90 with its discount card). **Centro de Internet Cámara de Comercio** (2a Av; ☼ 8am-9pm), in the same block as Bancafé, charges US$0.50 per 20 minutes online.

There's a heap of fascinating and helpful information about Nebaj in Spanish at www.nebaj.org. If you can't understand Spanish, the maps and listings are still useful.

Activities

Guias Ixil (☎ 801-5087, 418-3940; www.nebaj.com; 3a Calle, Zona 1), in the El Descanso building, offers hikes with informative young local guides. Like all the other enterprises in this building, a portion of Guias Ixil's profits goes to a community project. Short one-day hikes, costing US$5.25 for one person, plus US$2.60 for each extra person, go to **Las Cataratas** (a series of waterfalls on the Río Las Cataratas north of town), or around town with visits to the **sacred sites** of the *costumbristas* (people who still practice non-Christian Mayan rites). Las Cataratas is actually easy enough to reach on your own: walk 1.25km past the Hotel Ilebal Tenam along the Chajul road to a bridge over a small river. Immediately before the bridge, turn left (north) onto a gravel road and follow the river. Walking downriver for 45 minutes to an hour, you'll pass several small waterfalls before reaching a larger waterfall about 25m high.

Longer day hikes with Guias Ixil, costing US$6.50 for one person, plus US$2.60 for each extra, go across the mountains to **Cocop** (one of the worst hit of all villages in the civil war, 4km east of Nebaj as the crow flies), **Acul** (founded as the first *polo de desarrollo* in 1983; 4km west) or **Ak' Txumb'al**, also called La Pista, about 5km north (also founded as a *polo de desarrollo*). Ak' Txumb'al means New Mentality in the Ixil language, a name given by its military founders; La Pista (Spanish for Airstrip) refers to a civil-war landing strip where you can still see bomb craters. A three-day hike to **Xeo** and **Cotzol** (northwest of Nebaj) and back to Nebaj through Ak' Txumb'al costs US$8.50 per day for one person, plus US$5.80 for each extra. As this book went to press, Guias Ixiles was inaugurating two- to three-day treks over the Cuchumatanes to Todos Santos Cuchumatán north of Huehuetenango – a route also covered by Quetzaltenango-based Quetzaltrekkers (p143).

In Cocop, Xeo and Cotzol you can stay in **posadas comunitarias** (dm US$2; veg/meat meals US$1.30/2) – community-run lodges with wooden-board beds, bedding, drinking water, toilets and solar electricity. Just north of Acul, in a beautiful, tranquil valley along the road leading to the Nebaj–Salquil Grande road, **Hospedaje San Antonio** (☎ 439-3352; rooms per person US$8; meals US$4.50) has neat, wood-roofed and wood-floored rooms, some with a hot-water bathroom. This place makes its own cheese.

Guias Ixil sells a very useful booklet, *Trekking en la Región Ixil,* full of maps and information on the above village walks, for US$2.

Pablo's Tours (☎ 755-8287; pablostours@hotmail .com; 3a Calle 3-20, Zona 1), next door to El Descanso, also provides guided walks of up to two days, plus horse rides. It's run by a young local guy and gets good reports. Drop in to see its program and photos.

If you prefer to hike without a guide, take a copy of *Trekking en la Región Ixil* with you and organize lodging and food on arrival in villages. There are further *posadas comunitarias* at Xexocom, Chortiz and Parramos Grande, west of Nebaj, on a possible four-day hike route.

Language Courses

Nebaj Language School (☎ 801-5087, 418-3940; www .nebaj.com; El Descanso Bldg, 3a Calle, Zona 1) charges US$75 for 20 hours a week of one-to-one Spanish lessons, including some hiking and cultural activities, or US$3.25 per hour. Staying with a local family, with two meals a day, costs US$36 a week.

Festivals & Events

Nebaj's annual **festival** runs from August 12 to 15.

Sleeping

Hotel Ilebal Tenam (☎ 755-8039; Calzada 15 de Septiembre; s/d/tr US$3/6/7, s/d with bathroom US$7/12; P) A friendly hotel with spotless, good-sized rooms, most looking onto a central courtyard, the Ilebal Tenam is 500m from the Parque and a good deal.

Anexo Hotel Ixil (☎ 756-0036; cnr 2a Av & 9a Calle, Zona 5; s/d US$7/13; P) This is the best place in town, just one block south of the bus station. The clean, bright, good-sized rooms, on two levels round a garden courtyard with parking, have cable TV and a hot-water bathroom. Good breakfasts cost US$2.50.

Hotel Ixil (☎ 756-0036; 10a Calle, Zona 4; rooms per person US$3) Hotel Ixil is a friendly budget spot with bare, clean rooms with shared hot-water bathrooms around two courtyards. Rooms sleep up to four. It's four blocks south of the Parque along 5a Av. Buses from the south come into town up 5a Av and almost pass the door.

Hotel Turansa (☎ 755-8219; cnr 5a Calle & 6a Av; s US$7-9, d US$10-13; P) The 16 clean, green-and-white rooms with cable TV and a hot-water bathroom are set on two levels around a parking courtyard. The cheaper rooms, downstairs, are smaller and have smaller beds. It's one block west of the Parque.

Hotel Shalom (☎ 755-8031; cnr Calzada 15 de Septiembre & 4a Calle, Zona 1; s/d/tr US$7/13/18; P) The large, clean rooms here, one block from the Parque, have cable TV, gas-fired hot water and decent-quality wooden furniture – it's expensive for Nebaj, though.

Hospedaje Las Clavellinas (0 Calle, Zona 1; r per person US$2) With wooden beds and wooden roofs in quite big rooms round a yard, and sometimes hot water in the showers, this is friendly and not bad for the money. Walk north up 4a Av from the Parque: 0 Calle is the fifth street on the right. Knock on a black door on your right.

Hospedaje La Esperanza (☎ 756-0098; 6a Av 2-36, Zona 1; rooms per person US$3) This reasonably friendly place has basic wooden rooms with pink walls. There's hot water in the shared showers. Upstairs rooms provide more light and air, but some beds sag.

Hotel Villa Nebaj (Av 15 de Septiembre) This larger, mid-range hotel under construction two blocks from the Parque will likely provide the most comfortable lodgings in town (when completed).

Eating

El Descanso (☎ 801-5087, 418-3940; 3a Calle, Zona 1; items US$2-3.25; ☼ 6am-10pm) El Descanso is a two-floor café with bar and lounge areas, good music and board games. Friendly young staff will serve you anything from a salad or sandwich to a *churrasco*. El Descanso shares its building with Guias Ixil, Tetz Chemol shop and the Nebaj Language School, and a portion of the profits from all these businesses goes to fund a lending library in town for children and young adults.

Restaurante Maya-Inca (☎ 756-0058; 5a Calle 1-90; lunch & dinner meals US$3; ☼ 7am-9pm) This is a very clean little restaurant, with posters of Peru and great-value food, 1½ blocks east of the Parque. Your US$3 dinner could be Peruvian *papas rellenas* (baked potatoes with a minced-meat, raisins and egg filling), accompanied by beans, avocado, soup, a drink, bread, butter, jam, fruit salad and honey. Large and excellent breakfasts cost US$2.30. Also here is a roomful of quality weavings done by widows of the Ixil Triangle.

Comedor Dámaris (Av 15 de Septiembre; lunch & dinner meals US$1.70) A large room with six long tables, the Dámaris has such *típico* Guatemalan adornments as plastic flowers, strings of leftover Christmas decorations and stacks of Coke crates. The set lunch might be a tasty *caldo de res* (a broth with large chunks of meat and veggies), half an avocado, tortillas and a soft drink. It's one block from the Parque.

Pizza del César (☎ 755-8095; 2a Av; medium/small pizzas US$6/7, slices US$0.70-1.40) The pizza is average, but it's pizza. From the northeast corner of the Parque, go one block east then half a block north.

Shopping
You can buy local textiles at stalls on and around the Parque, or at Restaurante Maya-Inca, or at Tetz Chemol in the El Descanso building. A *huipil* costs anywhere from US$30 to US$170, depending on quality. A *rebozo* is US$15 to US$20, and a *cinta* (the pom-pommed braid woven into Ixil women's hair) around US$20.

Getting There & Away
About eight daily buses run to/from Santa Cruz del Quiché (US$1.70, 2½ hours), via Sacapulas (US$1, 1½ hours). The best time to get one is between 5am and 8am, and the last departure may be no later than noon. There's an 11pm bus all the way

to Guatemala City via Chichicastenango. To head west to Huehuetenango or east to Cobán, change at Sacapulas (p135). It's a matter of luck whether you make Cobán in one day from Nebaj.

WESTERN HIGHLANDS

The departments of Quetzaltenango, Totonicapán and Huehuetenango are more mountainous and generally less frequented by tourists than regions closer to Guatemala City. The scenery here is incredibly beautiful, and the indigenous culture vibrant, colorful and fascinating. Highlights of a visit to this area include Quetzaltenango, Guatemala's second-largest city, with an ever-growing language-school and volunteer-work scene; the pretty nearby town of Zunil, with its Fuentes Georginas hot springs; ascents of the volcanoes around Quetzaltenango; and the remote mountain village of Todos Santos, north of Huehuetenango, with a strong traditional culture and excellent walking possibilities.

CUATRO CAMINOS
Westward from Los Encuentros, the Interamericana twists and turns ever higher into the mountains, bringing still more dramatic scenery and cooler temperatures. It reaches its highest point, 3670m, after the village of Nahualá, some 42km from Los Encuentros. After a further 17km, you come to another dusty and important highway junction, Cuatro Caminos (Four Ways). You'll know the place by the many parked buses and people milling about as they change buses. The road to the southwest leads to Quetzaltenango (13km). To the east is Totonicapán (12km). Northward, the Interamericana continues to Huehuetenango (77km) and La Mesilla on the Mexican border (160km).

QUETZALTENANGO
pop 119,000 / elevation 2335m
Quetzaltenango is the commercial center of western Guatemala and the center of the K'iche' Mayan people, who form about half of the city's population. Almost everyone calls the city Xelajú – the original K'iche' name for the site where the Spanish conquistadors built their town – or simply Xela (*shay*-lah).

Towering on the southern skyline is the 3772m Volcán Santa María, with the active 2488m Santiaguito on its southwestern flank.

Xela has a lively cultural scene, a good selection of hotels and is a base for many inspiring trips out to indigenous villages, volcanoes, lakes and hot springs. It has also become a major center for Spanish-language learning, now almost rivaling Antigua in this respect. Some students prefer the Spanish schools in Xela because the environment here more closely approaches the total immersion ideal of language study. The scene is also enlivened by the foreign volunteer workers who come here to participate in a wide variety of projects. Many language schools and volunteer projects are closely connected with each other and it's quite possible to participate in both at once.

Xela is big, but by Guatemalan standards, it is an orderly, clean and safe city. It helps that the bus terminal is far removed from the center.

History

Quetzaltenango came under the sway of the K'iche' Maya of K'umarcaaj when they began their great expansion in the 14th century. Before that it had been a Mam Maya town. It was near here that the K'iche' leader Tecún Umán was defeated and killed by the Spanish conquistador Pedro de Alvarado in 1524 (p134).

Quetzaltenango prospered in the late-19th-century coffee boom, with brokers opening warehouses here and *finca* (plantation) owners coming to the city to buy supplies. The boom was shattered by a combined earthquake and eruption of Santa María in 1902, which brought mass destruction. Still, the city's position at the intersection of roads to the Pacific Slope, Mexico and Guatemala City guaranteed it some degree of prosperity. Today it's again busy with commerce, of the indigenous, foreign and ladino varieties.

Orientation

The heart of Xela is the Parque Centroamérica, shaded by old trees, graced with neoclassical monuments and surrounded by the city's important buildings. Most accommodations are within a few blocks of the park.

The main bus station is Terminal Minerva, on 7a Calle, Zona 3, on the western outskirts and next to one of the city's main markets. First-class bus lines have their own terminals (p150).

Information
BOOKSTORES
El Libro Abierto (Map p141; 15a Av A 1-56, Zona 1) Great selection of books in English and Spanish on Guatemala and the Maya, plus Lonely Planet guides, fiction, dictionaries, language textbooks and maps; will buy used books.
Vrisa Bookshop (Map p141; 15a Av 3-64, Zona 1) Has an excellent range of secondhand books in English.

EMERGENCY
Bomberos (firefighters; ☎ 761-2002)
Cruz Roja (Red Cross; ☎ 761-2746)
Policía Nacional (national police; ☎ 765-4991/2)
Policía Municipal (municipal police; ☎ 761-5805)

INTERNET ACCESS
Email access is among the cheapest in Guatemala at around US$0.80 to US$0.90 an hour. These are just some of the places available:
Celas Maya (Map p141; 6a Calle 14-55, Zona 1) Language school with public internet room; lots of computers.
Enl@ces.com (Map p141; 7a Calle 13-29, Zona 1)
Infinito Internet (Map p146; 7a Calle 15-16, Zona 1)
Internet (Map p141; cnr 5a Calle & 4a Av)
S@turno Internet (Map p141; 15a Av 3-51, Zona 1) Scanning and printing services available here too.
Salon Tecún (Map p141; Pasaje Enríquez, just off Parque Centroamérica; ☼ 9am-10pm)

INTERNET RESOURCES
Xela Pages (www.xelapages.com) is packed with information, though not all is fully up-to-date.

LAUNDRY
It costs around US$0.50 to wash and dry 1kg loads at a laundry. You may have to pay a bit more for detergent.
Lavandería El Centro (Map p141; 15a Av 3-51, Zona 1; ☼ 8:30am-6pm Mon-Fri, 8:30am-5pm Sat)
Lavandería Mini-Max (Map p141; 14a Av C47)
Rapi-Servicio Laundromat (Map p141; 7a Calle 13-25A, Zona 1; ☼ 8am-6pm Mon-Sat)

MEDICAL SERVICES
Hospital Privado Quetzaltenango (Map p146; ☎ 761-4381; Calle Rodolfo Robles 23-51)
Hospital San Rafael (Map p146; ☎ 761-4414, 761-2956, 9a Calle 10-41, Zona 1) This hospital has a 24-hour emergency service.

CENTRAL QUETZALTENANGO

0 — 100 m
0 — 0.1 mi

THE HIGHLANDS

INFORMATION	
ATMs..................................(see 3)	
Banco de Occidente........................**1** B3	
Banco Industrial..........................**2** B3	
Banrural...................................**3** B3	
DHL......................................**4** C1	
El Libro Abierto..........................**5** A1	
Enl@ces.com..........................(see 53)	
Guatemala Intercultural....................**6** A3	
Inguat Tourist Office......................**7** B4	
Internet..................................**8** E4	
Lavandería El Centro......................**9** A2	
Lavandería Mini-Max.....................**10** B1	
Megatel.................................**11** B1	
Rapi-Servicio Laundromat................**12** A3	
S#turno Internet.........................**13** A2	
Telgua..................................**14** A2	
Viajes SAB..............................**15** B1	
Vrisa Bookshop..........................**16** A2	
Xela Sin Límites.........................**17** C1	

SIGHTS & ACTIVITIES	pp142-3
Adrenalina Tours........................**18** A4	
Cathedral...............................**19** B4	
Municipalidad............................**20** B3	
Museo de Arte.........................(see 22)	
Museo de Historia Natural................**21** B4	
Museo del Ferrocarril de los Altos......**22** B3	

SLEEPING	pp145-8
Anexo Hotel Modelo......................**23** A2	
Casa Iximulew...........................**24** A2	
Casa Kaehler............................**25** B2	
Casa Mañen B&B.........................**26** C3	
Gran Hotel Americano....................**27** A2	
Guest House El Puente...................**28** A3	
Guest House.............................**29** B1	
Hotel Casa Florencia.....................**30** B2	
Hotel Kiktem-Ja.........................**31** A3	
Hotel Modelo............................**32** A4	
Hotel Occidental.........................**33** B4	
Hotel Quetzalteco.......................**34** B2	
Hotel Radar 99..........................**35** B2	
Hotel Río Azul...........................**36** B2	
Hotel Villa Real Plaza....................**37** A4	
La Casa de l@s Amig@s...................**38** E4	
Los Olivos...............................**39** B2	
Pensión Bonifaz.........................**40** B3	
Pensión/Hotel Horiani....................**41** B2	

EATING	pp148-9
Cafe Baviera............................**42** A4	
Café El Árabe............................**43** A4	
Café Enano's............................**44** C3	
Café La Luna............................**45** C3	
Casa Babilón............................**46** A4	
El Rincón de los Antojitos................**47** A2	
Giuseppe's Gourmet Pizza................**48** A2	
Maxim's.................................**49** A2	
Pizza Cardinali..........................**50** B2	
Restaurant El Kopetin....................**51** B2	
Restaurante Las Calas...................**52** A2	
Royal Paris..............................**53** A2	

DRINKING	p149
Iq.......................................**54** A1	
King and Queen Taberna.................**55** A3	
Salón Tecún.............................**56** A4	

ENTERTAINMENT	p149-50
Bar La Cueva............................**57** A4	
Casa de la Cultura......................(see 21)	
Casa Verde.............................**58** B1	
Cinema Paraíso..........................**59** B1	
La Fratta................................**60** A1	
Teatro Municipal.........................**61** B1	
Teatro Roma............................**62** A1	

TRANSPORT	pp150-1
Minibuses to Terminal Minerva...........**63** A4	
Minibuses to Terminal Minerva...........**64** B1	
Minibuses to Terminal Minerva...........**65** A4	
Taxi Stand..............................**66** B3	

OTHER	
Asotrama...............................**67** B2	
Celas Maya.............................**68** A3	
EntreMundos...........................**69** C4	
Escuela de Baile Tropicalatina...........**70** A3	
Escuela de Español Sakribal.............**71** C4	
Eureka Language School.................**72** B2	
Inepas...............................(see 24)	
Proyecto Lingüístico Quetzalteco de Español.............................**73** E4	
Ulew Tinimit............................**74** D3	
Utatlán Spanish School..................**75** A4	

MONEY

Parque Centroamérica is the place to go when you're looking for banks. **Banco de Occidente** (Map p141; 8:30am-7pm Mon-Fri, 8:30am-1:30pm Sat), in the beautiful building on the northern side of the plaza, changes US-dollars cash and traveler' checks and gives advances on Visa. **Banco Industrial** (Map p141; 9:30am-5pm Mon-Fri, 9:30am-1:30pm Sat), on the east side of the plaza, changes US-dollar cash and traveler's checks, and has a Visa ATM. A MasterCard ATM and another Visa ATM are next to **Banrural** on the west side of the plaza.

POST

DHL (cnr 12a Av & 1a Calle) For shipping packages.
Main post office (Map p141; 4a Calle 15-07, Zona 1) Central location.

TELEPHONE

You'll find plenty of card phones outside Telgua (cnr 15a Av & 4a Calle).

Several other places offer international telephone services, including:
Infinito Internet (Map p146; 7a Calle 15-16, Zona 1) US$0.20/0.25/0.40 a minute to USA/Canada/Europe.
Megatel (Map p141; 1a Calle 14-35, Zona 1; 8am-8pm Mon-Sat, 8am-6pm Sun) US$0.45/0.55/0.60 a minute to USA/Canada/Europe.

TOURIST INFORMATION

Inguat (Map p141; /fax 761-4931; 8am-1pm & 2-5pm Mon-Fri, 8am-1pm Sat) Next door to the Museo de Historia Natural at the southern end of Parque Centroamérica, this tourist office offers free maps and information about the town and the area in Spanish, English and Italian.

TRAVEL AGENCIES

Guatemaya Intercultural (Map p141; 765-0040; guatmain@quetzal.net; 14a Av A 3-06, Zona 1) Sells student, youth, teacher and discounted air fares; issues student, youth and teacher cards (US$9); and offers deals to Tikal and other tours within Guatemala, and to Cuba and South America.
Viajes SAB (Map p141; 765-0965, 763-6402; 1a Calle 12-35, Zona 1) Make plane reservations, reconfirm flights and attend to other niggling travel details here.
Xela Sin Límites (Map p141; /fax 761-6043; www.xelapages.com/xelasinlimites; 12a Av C-35, Zona 1) Does tours locally and around Guatemala and can make international travel arrangements.

Sights

PARQUE CENTROAMÉRICA

The park and the buildings surrounding it are pretty much what there is to see in Xela

itself. The Casa de la Cultura at the southern end holds the funky **Museo de Historia Natural** (Map p141; admission US$0.80; 8am-noon & 2-6pm Mon-Fri, 9am -1pm Sat), which has a fascinating collection including exhibits on the Maya, the liberal revolution in Central American politics and the Estado de Los Altos, of which Quetzaltenango was the capital. *Marimbas,* the weaving industry, stuffed birds (frightening eagles and owls) and animals (some scary members of the cat family) and other local artifacts also claim places here.

The once-crumbling **cathedral** has been rebuilt in recent decades: The facade of the colonial building has been preserved, and a modern church built behind it.

The **Municipalidad** (City Hall; Map p141), at the northeastern end of the park, was rebuilt after the 1902 earthquake in the grandiose neoclassical style so favored as a symbol of culture and refinement in this wild mountain country.

On the west side of the park between 4a and 5a Calles is **Pasaje Enríquez**, an imposing arcade built to be lined with elegant shops – but as Quetzaltenango has few elegant shoppers, it stands half-empty.

At the southwest corner of the park is the **Museo del Ferrocarril de los Altos** (Map p141; admission US$0.80; 8am-noon & 2-6pm Mon-Fri, 9am-1pm Sat), which focuses on the railroad that once connected Xela with Retalhuleu. Upstairs is the **Museo de Arte** (Map p141; admission US$0.80; 8am-noon & 2-6pm Mon-Fri, 9am-1pm Sat) exhibiting mostly modern art, along with schools of art, dance and *marimba.*

OTHER SIGHTS

Walk north on 14a Av to 1a Calle to see the impressive neoclassical **Teatro Municipal** (Map p141; 1a Calle), which holds regular, recommended performances. Inside are three tiers of seating, the lower two with private boxes for prominent families; each is equipped with a vanity.

Mercado La Democracia (Map p141; 1a Calle, Zona 3), about 10 blocks north of Parque Centroamérica, is an authentic Guatemalan city market with food and other necessities for city dweller and villager alike.

About 3km northwest of Parque Centroamérica, near the Terminal Minerva bus station and another big market, is the **Parque Zoológico Minerva** (Map p146; admission free;

🕑 9am-5pm Tue-Sun), a zoo-park with a few monkeys, coyotes, raccoons, deer, Barbary sheep and a sad, solitary lion, plus a few rides for children. Outside the zoo on an island in the middle of 4a Calle stands the neoclassical **Templo de Minerva** (Map p146), built by dictator Estrada Cabrera to honor the Roman goddess of education and to inspire Guatemalans to new heights of learning.

Activities
VOLCANO ASCENTS & TREKS
There are many exciting walks and climbs to be done from Xela. **Volcán Tajumulco** (4220m), 50km northwest, is the highest point in Central America and a challenging trip of one long day from the city or two days with a night camping on the mountain. This includes about five hours' walking up from the starting point, Huitán, and three to four hours down. Huitán is about three hours by bus from Xela.

With early starts, **Volcán Santa María** (3772m), towering to the south of the city, and the active **Santiaguito** (2488m), on Santa María's southwest flank, can both be done in long mornings from Xela. You start walking at the village of Llanos del Pinal, 5km south of Xela (US$6.50 by taxi from Xela, or US$0.25 by bus), from which it's about four hours up to the summit of Santa María (then three hours down). Getting too close to Santiaguito is dangerous, so people usually just look at it from a *mirador* (lookout point) about 1½ hours' walk from Llanos del Pinal.

Quetzaltrekkers (Map p146; ☎ 761-5865; www .quetzaltrekkers.com; Casa Argentina's, Diagonal 12 8-37, Zona 1) is a well-run outfit specializing in volcano ascents and other great-value hikes, with camping along the way on some trips. Two-day Tajumulco trips (US$43) start every Saturday. Quetzaltrekkers also offers full-moon ascents of Santa María (US$13) and unusual two-day Santiaguito trips (US$53) starting from the ghost town of El Palmar Viejo, south of the mountain. A three-day Quetzaltenango–Lago de Atitlán trek, starting every Saturday, is US$66, and a five-day Nebaj–Todos Santos jaunt across the Cuchumatanes mountains is US$120. Prices include transport, food, equipment and a guide (who is usually a foreign volunteer). Quetzaltrekkers is a nonprofit organization that exists to fund the Escuela de la Calle, a free school in a poor neighborhood of Xela, and a dormitory for street children.

Adrenalina Tours (p145), another recommended agency, offers a whole range of volcano trips. A nine-hour Volcán Santa María outing from Xela costs US$50 to US$60 for up to four people including transport and breakfast, or US$27 to US$30 if you can organize your own transport and food. Adrenalina can also take you up Tajumulco or the less climbed Volcán Zunil or to Laguna Chicabal via an unusual route over Volcán Siete Orejas.

DANCE CLASSES
Salsa and merengue lessons are popular in Xela. The hot school at the time of writing was **Escuela de Baile Tropicalatina** (Map p141; 7a Calle 13-31, Zona 1), offering one-hour group classes for US$2.60 per person at 6pm Monday to Friday, and private classes for US$6.50, 9am to 6pm Monday to Friday.

Language Courses
Xela's many language schools attract students from around the world. Unlike Antigua, which has had a similar reputation for quite a bit longer, Xela is not overrun with foreigners, though there is a growing social scene revolving around language students and volunteer workers.

Xela seems to attract altruistic types, and most of the Spanish schools here provide opportunities to get involved in social action programs working with the local K'iche' Maya. Prices for the schools vary a little but not by much; the standard price is US$110/125 per week for four/five hours of instruction per day, Monday to Friday, including room and board with a local family, or around US$80/95 per week without homestay. Some schools charge up to 20% more for tuition during the high season from June to August, and many require nonrefundable registration fees. College students may be able to take classes for academic credit.

Most schools are lively and have plenty going on. Extras (some free, some not) range from movies and free Internet to dancing and cooking classes, trips out and lectures and discussions on Guatemalan politics and culture.

THE HIGHLANDS

Reputable language schools (there are more!) include the following:

Celas Maya (Map p141; ☎ /fax 761-4342; www.celas maya.edu.gt; 6a Calle 14-55, Zona 1) Set around a pleasant garden-courtyard; also offers classes in K'iche.

Centro Bilingüe Amerindia (CBA; Map p146; ☎ 761-1613; www.xelapages.com/cba; 7a Av 9-05, Zona 1) Classes in Mayan languages as well.

Centro de Estudios de Español Pop Wuj (Map p146; ☎ /fax 761-8286; www.pop-wuj.org; 1a Calle 17-72, Zona 1) Pop Wuj's profits go to development projects in nearby villages, in which students can participate. The school also offers medical and social work specialist-language programs. There's a party at the end of each week.

Centro Maya de Idiomas (CMI; Map p146; ☎ 767-0352; www.centromaya.org; 21 Av 5-69, Zona 3) Classes in Spanish, K'iche', Mam, Q'anjob'al and Tz'utujil. A Mayan teachers' cooperative; charges slightly more than most other schools. Sponsors female indigenous university students and has an English-language program for village children.

Escuela de Español Sakribal (Map p141; ☎ /fax 763-0717; www.sakribal.com; 6a Calle 7-42, Zona 1) Founded and directed by women.

Escuela Minerva (Map p141; ☎ /fax 767-4427; www.xelapages.com/minerva; 24 Av 4-39) Warm, welcoming staff here; plenty of activities, recommended.

Eureka Language School (Map p141; ☎ /fax 765-1424; www.eurekaxela.com; 12 Av 3-35, Zona 1) Has own transport for trips and a house on a farm where students can stay; lots of activities offered.

Inepas (Instituto de Estudios de Español y Participación en Ayuda Social; Map p141; ☎ 765-1308; www.inepas .org; 15a Av 4-59) Offers a range of cheap accommodation other than living with a family. Inepas also organizes worthy projects in which students are invited to participate.

Juan Sisay Spanish School (Map p146; ☎ /fax 765-1318; www.juansisay.com; 15a Av 8-38, Zona 1) Named for the Tz'utujil artist from Lake Atitlán, this is a teachers' collective involved in worthy projects. Recommended.

Kie-Balam Spanish School (Map p146; ☎ 761-1636; www.super-highway.net/users/moebius; Diagonal 12 No 4-46, Zona 1) This school can set up internships in community literacy projects and rural libraries.

Proyecto Lingüístico Quetzalteco de Español (Map p141; ☎ /fax 763-1061; www.hermandad.com; 5a Calle 2-42, Zona 1) This very professional and politically minded school also runs the Escuela de la Montaña, a language school with a maximum enrollment of eight, located on an organic coffee *finca* in the mountains near Xela. Participation in local culture and volunteering are strongly encouraged.

VOLUNTEERING IN XELA

The Quetzaltenango area has many nonprofit organizations working on social projects with the local K'iche' Maya people and others that need volunteers. Volunteer jobs can range from teaching math to village children, to designing websites for indigenous organizations, to developing sustainable agriculture, to medical work in clinics to working in orphanages for disabled children, to leading hikes for Quetzaltrekkers. For anyone in a giving frame of mind, the possibilities are endless. You can volunteer part-time for a week or two while also studying Spanish, or you can live and work in a close-knit indigenous village for a year. Obviously, the more Spanish you speak the better, but you can learn enough to be effective in a few weeks at one of Xela's schools. Indeed, many schools are intimately connected with particular social projects – some in fact exist primarily to generate funds for them – and can help students to participate in their free time. Skills in fields like medicine, nursing, teaching, youth work and computers are prized but there are possibilities for anyone with the will to help. Volunteers must normally meet all their own costs and be willing to commit to a project for a specified minimum time. Three months is fairly typical for full-time posts, though the minimum can be as little as a week or as long as a year.

EntreMundos (Map p141; ☎ 761-2179; www.entremundos.org; El Espacio, 6a Calle 7-31, Zona 1) is a forum for social projects in Xela. Its website has details on over 100 nonprofit projects all over Guatemala, many of which need volunteers, and its magazine, *EntreMundos,* comes out every couple of months with articles and ads about volunteering, volunteer opportunities and some completely unrelated interesting stuff!

Guatemaya Intercultural (p142) can place volunteers in any of 15 projects including human rights and ecological organizations, medical clinics, schools and old people's homes.

A major meeting point and melting pot of the volunteer scene in Xela is the monthly benefit dinner hosted by Quetzaltrekkers at Casa Argentina's to raise funds for the Escuela de la Calle. The three-course vegetarian meal is US$4.50, usually well over 100 people attend and it's quite a party. Keep your eye open for leaflets early in the month.

Ulew Tinimit (Map p141; ☎ /fax 761-6242; www
.intworkshop.com/spanishschool; 7a Av 3-18, Zona 1)
Mayan language classes also offered.
Utatlán Spanish School (Map p141; ☎ 763-0446;
www.xelapages.com/utatlan; Pasaje Enríquez, 12a Av
4-32, Zona 1)

Tours
Adrenalina Tours (Map p141; ☎ 761-4509; www
.adrenalinatours.com; Pasaje Enríquez, Zona 1), run by
energetic Belgian Patrick Vercoutere, is a
professional, knowledgeable and amiable
outfit providing a whole range of trips in
the Xela area. A half-day tour to Zunil and
Fuentes Georginas costs US$12 per person
(minimum two people); and a fascinating
all-day outing to El Palmar Viejo, Abaj
Takalik and a coffee/rubber/sugarcane *finca*
is US$42. It also rents out camping gear,
offers horse riding to San Andrés Xecul
and other places, and does a whole range
of volcano trips (p143).

Both **Inepas** (p144) and **Casa Iximulew** (see
below) do day tours to Fuentes Georginas,
San Francisco El Alto (US$25 per person)
and other spots, plus camping trips of two
or three days that visit the Santa María and
Santiaguito volcanoes. Inepas co-founder
Thierry Roquet (☎ 761-5057; www.mayaexplor.com)
now offers his own adventure and thematic
tours and still works with Inepas on its
longer and large-group trips. Between the
two outfits, there are English-, Spanish- and
French-speaking guides.

Quetzalventures (☎ 761-4520; www.quetzalvent
ures.com) offers a range of Guatemala-wide
tours focusing on the country's classic destinations – some involving camping and jungle hiking, others more luxurious. One-week
trips are mostly in the US$800 range. It can
also arrange Spanish classes and volunteer
opportunities. Profits go to community
projects such as Xela's Escuela de la Calle.

Festivals & Events
Xela's big annual party is the **Feria de la Virgen
del Rosario**, also called the Feria Centroameri-
cana de Independencia, in the week from
September 15. Residents kick up their heels
at a fairground on the city's perimeter and
there's plenty of entertainment in the Parque
Centroamérica too. The prizes in the **Juegos
Florales Centroamericanos**, an international
Spanish-language literary competition hosted
by the city, are awarded at this time too.

Sleeping
BUDGET
Cheap accommodations are scattered
around the central area with a concentration just north of Parque Centroamérica.

Casa Argentina's (Map p146; ☎ 761-2470, 761-
0010; Diagonal 12 8-37; dm US$3, s US$4-6, d US$7) A
hot budget choice and with good cause,
this unpretentious, mellow place is about a
10-minute walk west from Parque Centroamérica. There are 18 rooms – spacious
enough, and clean – on two levels; the
upper level has a large sitting-out area with
views. The dormitory has 20 beds and a TV.
There's a communal kitchen, filtered drinking water and security boxes for valuables.
Readers have mentioned that the water supply (hot and cold) can be erratic. Quetzaltrekkers (see above) is based here.

La Casa de l@s Amig@s (Map p146; ☎ 763-0014;
5a Calle 2-59, Zona 1; rooms per person US$4, with bath-
room US$5) Run by a cooperative of teachers
from the Proyecto Lingüístico language
school across the street, this place has six
simple rooms, each with two or three beds;
only one has bathroom. There's a clean
communal kitchen, hot water for showers
and a small patio for catching some fresh
air. It's a 15-minute walk east from Parque
Centroamérica.

Hostal Don Diego (Map p146; ☎ 761-6497; dondie
goxela@hotmail.com; 7a Calle 15-20; dm/s US$5/6) This
friendly place has a large, sociable courtyard
area and small rooms with shared bathrooms. Check the cleanliness of the sheets.
Rates include a small breakfast and half an
hour online at Infinito Internet next door. It
offers reduced rates for weekly or monthly
stays, with or without kitchen use.

Casa Kaehler (Map p141; ☎ 761-2091; 13a Av 3-33,
Zona 1; s/d/tr US$10/12/16, d with bathroom US$17) This
is an old-fashioned European-style family
pension with seven rooms of various shapes
and sizes on two levels around a geranium-
filled courtyard. Room 7 is the biggest and
the only one with bathroom. The rooms are
all old and basic with wooden floorboards
but they're scrupulously clean. It's an excellent, safe place for women travelers; ring
the bell to gain entry.

Casa Iximulew (Map p141; ☎ 765-1308; info@
inepas.org; 15a Av 4-59; s US$5-6, d US$10) The building containing this establishment also
houses the Inepas language school and
aid and volunteer program. There are only

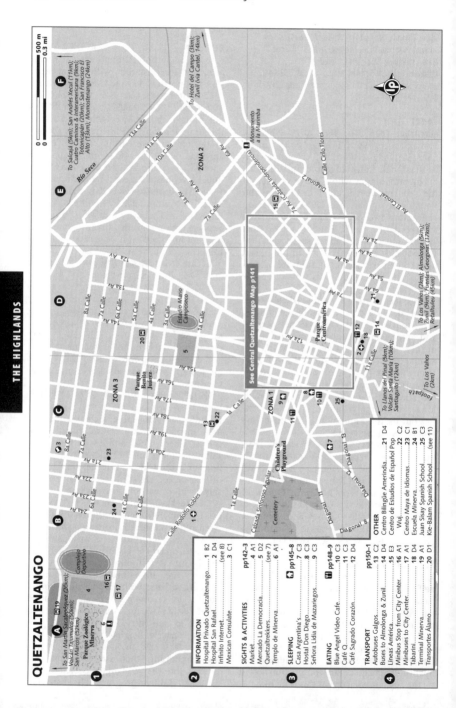

QUETZALTENANGO

THE HIGHLANDS

See Central Quetzaltenango Map p141

ZONA 2

ZONA 3

ZONA 1

To Salcajá (5km); San Andrés Xecul (11km); Cuatro Caminos & Interamericana (9km); Totonicapán (20km); San Francisco El Alto (13km), Momostenango (24km)

To Hotel del Campo (3km); Zunil (via Cantel, 14km)

Monumento a la Marimba

To San Martin Sacatepéquez (20km); Volcán Tajumulco (30km); San Marcos (52km)

Estadio Mario Camposeco

Parque Benito Juárez

Parque Centroamérica

Parque Zoológico Minerva

Complejo Deportivo

Children's Playground

Cemetery

Calzada Sinforoso Aguilar

Río Seco

To Llanos del Pinal (5km); Volcán Santa María (10km); Santiaguito (12km)

To Los Vahos (2km); Almolonga (5km); Zunil (9km); Fuentes Georginas (17km); Retalhuleu (45km)

To Los Vahos (2km)

500 m
0.3 mi

two rooms for rent, with shared warm bath – one single, and one double with two beds. It also rents out apartments about a 10-minute walk from the city center for US$75/225 by the week/month; each has two bedrooms, fully equipped kitchen, living room, courtyard and cable TV. It arranges homestays too, and provides tours (p145) and other services for travelers. French, English and Spanish are spoken.

Los Olivos (Map p141; ☎ 761-0215; 13a Av 3-32; s/d/tr US$17/22/26; **P**) Here you can enjoy one of 26 rooms set around a covered courtyard, with hot-water bathroom, cable TV and nice extras such as towels, soap and drinking water.

Gran Hotel Americano (Map p141; ☎ 761-8118; fax 761-8219; 14a Av 3-45; s/d US$11/17; **P**) On the busy 14a Av strip, the 13 comfortable rooms here have a hot-water bathroom, cable TV and telephone. There's a restaurant.

Guest House El Puente (Map p141; 15a Av 6-75; rooms per person US$3-5) Formerly a language school, this simple old place has a lovely big green garden to sit in. Room prices depend on the number of beds in each room: a double is US$10. There are two hot-water bathrooms shared between the half-dozen rooms.

Hotel Kiktem-Ja (Map p141; ☎ 761-4304; 13a Av 7-18; s/d/tr US$13/17/21; **P**) West of Parque Centroamérica is this huge old hotel in the colonial-style Edificio Fuentes. The 20 darkish rooms, all with a bathroom and eight with fireplace, are on two levels around the flowery courtyard, which also serves as a car park.

Hotel Occidental (Map p141; ☎ 765-4065; 7a Calle 12-23; s/d US$6/9, with bathroom US$9/13) Just a few steps from Parque Centroamérica, the large, bare, high-ceilinged rooms here are clean and quiet, and have comfy beds, but the atmosphere can be gloomy.

Pensión/Hotel Horiani (Map p141; ☎ 763-5228; 12a Av 2-23; d US$6) A simple but clean little family-run *hospedaje*, this has six rooms, with shared hot-water bathroom, on a couple of levels. Enter on 2a Calle.

Hotel Río Azul (Map p141; ☎ /fax 763-0654; 2a Calle 12-15, Zona 1; s/d/tr US$9/13/17) This family-run option offers pseudoluxury and cleanliness compared to other accommodations nearby. All rooms have squishy foam beds and a bathroom. Prices are high for what you get, though.

Hotel Quetzalteco (Map p141; 12a Av, a block north of Parque Centroamérica; s/d US$4/8, d with bathroom US$12) This serviceable cheapie has basic, fairly clean rooms; choose one upstairs, as those downstairs are dark. There's hot water. Amiable-enough folk run the place.

Hotel Radar 99 (Map p141; 13a Av; s/d/tr US$5/7, d with bathroom US$8) Next door to Casa Kaehler, the Radar gets mixed reviews. The rooms are upstairs and well-worn but clean enough. There's hot water.

Guest House (Map p141; 1a Calle 12-35; d US$5) Tucked around behind Viajes SAB, this is a newish budget alternative. The rooms, with shared bathroom, are tiny and super-basic but there's an appealing communal sitting area.

For long-term stays, an option is renting an apartment. Read all the fine print and know the terms for deposits, gas and electricity charges before plunking down your cash.

Señora Lidia de Mazariegos (Map p146; ☎ 761-2166; silvia@hotmail.com; 4a Calle 15-34; apt per week/month US$59/179) Rents out fully furnished apartments with cable TV and free gas for the first month.

MID-RANGE & TOP END

Casa Mañen B & B (Map p141; ☎ 765-0786; www.comeseeit.com; 9a Av 4-11; s/d/ste US$67/80/122) Most tourist towns in Guatemala have at least one hotel fit for honeymooning couples – a quiet place with romantic atmosphere, beautifully and comfortably outfitted rooms, tranquil gardens and a distinguishing style. In Xela, Casa Mañen is it. All nine rooms have traditional appointments (hand-woven woolen rugs, bed throws and wall hangings), hand-carved furniture, tiled floors, TV and a hot-water bathroom, even toweling dressing gowns folded on the beds. Upstairs units have balconies and views, there's a roof terrace, and the breakfast is great (see p148).

Pensión Bonifaz (Map p141; ☎ 765-1111; bonifaz@intel.net.gt; 4a Calle 10-50, Zona 1; s/d/tr US$55/68/77; **P**) Though a bit on the stuffy side, this four-star hotel near the northeast corner of Parque Centroamérica is Xela's best known. Some of the 73 comfortably old-fashioned rooms have cable TV and phone; all have private bathrooms, some with tubs. The 30 rooms in the original colonial-style building (the one you enter) are preferable to those in the adjoining, modernized building. The hotel has a good dining room (see below) and a cheery bar.

Hotel del Campo (Map p141; ☎ 763-1665; Km 224, Camino a Cantel; s/d/tr US$37/47/57; [P] [⛱]) This is Xela's largest and most modern hotel. Its 96 rooms have showers and TV and are decorated in natural wood and red brick, and there's an all-weather swimming pool. Rooms on the lowest floor can be dark, so get a room numbered in the 50s. The hotel is 4.5km (a 10-minute drive) east of the town center, off the main road between Quetzaltenango and Cuatro Caminos; watch for signs for the hotel and for the road to Cantel.

Hotel Modelo (Map p141; ☎ 761-2529, 763-0216; 14a Av A 2-31, Zona 1; s/d/tr/q US$30/34/37/40; [P]) This friendly family-run hotel has good wood-floored rooms with bathroom, cable TV and phone. Some are along a pretty patio at one side but tend to be noisier because they front the street. It has a good restaurant (see below)

Anexo Hotel Modelo (Map p141; ☎ 765-1271; s/d/tr/q US$21/26/29/32) Just down the street, this hotel's rooms, with tile floors, are almost as comfortable as at the main hotel.

Hotel Villa Real Plaza (Map p141; ☎ 761-4045; 4a Calle 12-22, Zona 1; s/d/tr US$43/49/55; [P]) Only half a block west of Parque Centroamérica, this is a comfortable hotel with young, vivacious management. The 60 large, airy rooms all have a bathroom, cable TV, phone and false chimney. There's a courtyard restaurant, bar and sauna.

Hotel Casa Florencia (Map p141; ☎ 761-2326; www.hotelcasaflorencia.com; 12a Av 3-61, Zona 1; s/d/tr US$25/38/43; [P]) This hotel, just a few steps up the hill from the plaza, is run by a pleasant *señora* who keeps everything spotless. There are nine spacious rooms, all with bathroom, cable TV and carpet, but mostly without an exterior window. Breakfast is available in the dining room. Be absolutely sure of your arrangements if you book by phone.

Eating

As with hotels, Quetzaltenango has a good selection of places to eat in all price ranges. Cheapest are the **food stalls** in and around the small market to the left of the Casa de la Cultura, where snacks and main-course plates are sold for US$1 or less.

Pensión Bonifaz (Map p141; 4a Calle 10-50, Zona 1; mains US$8-9) The dining room of this hotel off the northeast corner of Parque Centroamérica is the best in town. This is where the local social set comes to dine and be seen. Food is good, and prices, though high by Guatemalan standards, are not outrageous. Two courses might run to US$15.

Café El Árabe (Map p141; ☎ 761-7889; 4a Calle 12-22, Zona 1; mains US$4-9) Fans of Middle Eastern food will be thrilled to find such an authentic place here, just off Parque Centroamérica. The Arabic bread is made on the premises and all the ingredients for all dishes are lovely and fresh. You can fill up on meat dishes but there are plenty of vegetarian choices. The falafel and dips are wonderful.

Pizza Cardinali (Map p141; ☎ 761-0924; 14a Av 3-41, Zona 1; mains US$6.50-7.50; [☺] daily) This Italian-owned restaurant has all the Mediterranean-style decor to conjure the ambience. The menu of pastas, pizza and dishes like *scaloppine* is equally authentic. *Ravioli al ricotta* is a tasty choice. Portions are large, the wine is good and classical music helps the digestion.

Royal París (Map p141; 14a Av A 3-06, Zona 1; mains US$6-8; [☺] 11am-3pm & 6-11pm Mon-Sat, noon-11pm Sun) This classy French restaurant, in a long upstairs room with cool jazz in the background and a few balcony tables, is just the place for a splurge. It's good on fish and meat – try the *sabroso de res al roquefort* (steak filet with blue cheese). There's plenty of wine (from US$4.50 a half-liter), and you can start with soup (US$2.50), salad (US$3.50), snails (US$5) or baked Camembert (US$5), and round things off with a crepe (US$1.50).

Casa Babilón (Map p141; cnr 5a Calle & 13a Av; mains US$3-9) There's French influence, too, at this smaller eatery, where good *churrascos* are served simply with fried mushrooms and garlic bread. Or choose more economical burgers, tacos, sandwiches – or some pretty good crepes. French wine starts at US$19 a bottle, but there's Italian too, from US$1.50 a glass.

Hotel Modelo (Map p141; 14a Av A 2-31; set lunch or dinner US$4.50) The international restaurant here serves breakfast and has good set-price lunches and dinners.

Casa Mañen B&B (Map p141; ☎ 765-0786; www.comeseeit.com; 9a Av 4-11; breakfast mains US$5) The folks here serve up a mean breakfast, including Belgian waffles, smoked pork chops, fruit and eggs. Anyone can stop by.

Restaurante Las Calas (Map p141; 14a Av A 3-21; mains US$4-5; ☺ 7am-9:30pm Mon-Sat) An artistic sort of place with lilies growing in the patio and lily-theme art on the walls (and a gallery in the back), Las Calas serves good medium-priced meals. Satisfying portions of chicken, fish or beef are creatively prepared and served with a unique *salsa picante*. This restaurant also features paella and cheaper vegetarian dishes.

El Rincón de los Antojitos (Map p141; ☎ 765-1308; 15a Av 4-59; mains US$3.25-4.50; ☺ 8am-8pm) This is a tiny but popular spot with good Guatemalan and French food including a variety of vegetarian dishes. The specialties include *pepián* (chicken or pork in a special sesame sauce, a typical indigenous Guatemalan dish) and chicken in mushroom-and-cream sauce. It offers a range of cheeses and wines. From 3pm to 6pm only hot drinks are served – the idea is to use the place as a study space for the students at the school to which it's attached.

Café Sagrado Corazón (Map p146; cnr 9a Av & 9a Calle, Zona 1; lunch plates US$2-2.60; ☺ 9am-9pm Mon-Sat) This is an excellent place for Guatemalan home cooking. The gregarious mother-daughter team of Guadalupe and Miriam serves delicious breakfast, lunch and dinner, and there's always a vegetarian option.

Giuseppe's Gourmet Pizza (Map p141; 15a Av 3-68; medium pizza US$6-9; ☺ noon-10pm) Come here for yummy, filling pizza and pasta at reasonable prices. Locals flock to Giuseppe's, and it's usually packed by 7pm.

Cafe Baviera (Map p141; 5a Calle 13-14; dishes US$2-3; ☺ 7am-8:30pm) This European-style café has good coffee, roasted on the premises, and is a decent place for breakfast or for a snack at any time. The wooden walls are hung with countless photos and clippings on Xela and international themes.

Café La Luna (Map p141; 8a Av 4-11; snacks US$2; ☺ 9:30am-9pm Mon-Fri, 4-9pm Sat & Sun) La Luna is a comfortable, relaxed place to hang out, drink coffee, write letters and socialize. Choose any of several rooms: decor is in a similar vein to Cafe Baviera but the music is classical instead of jazz.

Blue Angel Video Cafe (Map p141; 7a Calle, Zona 1) This economical café with excellent, healthy foods and an awesome tea selection, popular with language students, was closed at the

time of writing, pending a move across the street – look for it in its new location opposite Hostal Don Diego.

Salón Tecún (Map p141; Pasaje Enríquez, west side Parque Centroamérica, Zona 1; meals US$2.25-3.25; ☺ 8am-1am) The Tecún, consistently Xela's busiest bar (see below), serves good food too. The pizzas (US$4 to US$5) are fine.

Café Q (Map p146; Diagonal 12 4-46; mains US$2.50-3; ☺ 7-10pm Mon-Fri) The Q's varied international flavors include interesting vegetarian options like falafel, soy burgers and chickpea soup.

Restaurant El Kopetin (Map p141; 14a Av 3-51; meals US$5-11.50; ☺ daily) This has red tablecloths, natural wood and a family atmosphere. Its long and varied menu ranges from Cuban-style sandwiches to filet mignon. A full meal costs around US$9. Alcohol is served.

Maxim's (Map p141; 4a Calle 14-25; mains US$2.60-12) This recently renovated restaurant serves Chinese food and *churrascos*. The decor is eastern and quite bright, and prices are very reasonable.

Café Enano's (Map p141; meals US$1.90-2.60) Just off Parque Centroamérica, this little eatery serves cheap Guatemalan breakfast, lunch and dinner.

Drinking

Salón Tecún (Map p141; Pasaje Enríquez, west side Parque Centroamérica, Zona 1; ☺ 8am-1am) Busy all day and night with a healthy crowd of Guatemalans and foreigners, the Tecún claims to be the country's longest-running bar (since 1935). Don't miss it.

King and Queen Taberna (Map p141; 7a Calle 13-27, Zona 1) Popular with a language student/volunteer crowd, this is a fine place for a few beers and a snack.

Iq' (Map p141; 14a Av A 1-37) This long thin bar plays good rock music and specializes in varied beers and Middle Eastern and Greek snacks such as *paklava*.

The bar at Pensión Bonifaz (see p148) is the place for more highbrow socializing.

Entertainment

It gets chilly when the sun goes down, so you won't want to sit out in the Parque Centroamérica enjoying the balmy breezes – there aren't any. Nevertheless, it's softly lit and still a pleasant place for an evening stroll.

Casa Verde (Map p141; ☎/fax 763-0271; www .spanishgua.com/casaverde.html; 12a Av 1-40, Zona 1; ☺ 4pm-midnight Tue-Sat) This is a happening venue for concerts, theater, poetry readings, films, open-mike nights and other evening activities. Thursday night features salsa dancing, Friday night *trova* (Latin American protest folk). Casa Verde also has billiards, chess, backgammon and other games and a restaurant/bar.

La Fratta (Map p141; 14a Av A A-80) This is the salsa hotspot on Wednesday nights until about 1am.

Bar La Cueva (Map p141; Pasaje Colonial, 13a Av 6-20, Zona 1) It's worth checking out this establishment on Friday and Saturday nights. It has space for dancing and a cave-like bar out back.

Cultural performances are presented at the beautiful **Teatro Municipal** (Map p141; 1a Calle) and the **Casa de la Cultura** (Map p141; ☎ 761-6427) on Parque Centroamérica. The **Teatro Roma** (Map p141; 14a Av A facing Teatro Municipal) sometimes screens interesting movies.

Blue Angel Video Cafe (Map p146; 7a Calle, Zona 1) Videos are shown every night here – although it's closed at the time of writing pending a move across the street.

Cinema Paraíso (Map p141; ☎ 408-1963; 1a Calle 12-20, Zona 1; admission US$1.30) Also showing nightly videos is Paraíso, which is a café too.

Shopping

Asotrama (Map p141; ☎ 763-0823; 12a Av 3-39) Check out the shop belonging to this association of Mayan women weavers. It's just uphill from the park. It runs backstrap-loom courses from here too. For course details see www.xelapages.com.

Getting There & Away

BUS

For 2nd-class buses, head out to the Terminal Minerva, a dusty, noisy, crowded yard on 7a Calle, Zona 3, in the west of town. Buses leave frequently for many Highland destinations. Leaving or entering town, some buses make a stop east of the center at the Rotonda, a traffic circle on Calzada Independencia, marked by the Monumento a la Marimba. Getting off here when you're coming into Xela saves the 10 to 15 minutes it will take your bus to cross town to Terminal Minerva.

First-class companies operating between Quetzaltenango and Guatemala City have their own terminals.

All the following buses depart from Terminal Minerva, unless otherwise indicated.

Almolonga (US$0.25, 15min, 6km, every 15 min 5:30am-5pm) It stops for additional passengers at the corner of 9a Av and 10a Calle, southeast of Parque Centroamérica.

Antigua (170km) Take any bus heading to Guatemala City by the Interamericana and change at Chimaltenango.

Chichicastenango (US$1.20, 3hr, 94km, 8 daily 5am, 6am, 9:30am, 10:45am, 11am, 1pm, 2pm & 3:30pm) If you don't get one of these, take a bus heading to Guatemala City by the Interamericana and change at Los Encuentros.

Ciudad Tecún Umán, Mexican border (US$2, 3½hr, 129km, hourly 5am-2pm)

Cuatro Caminos (US$0.25, 30min, 11km) Take any bus heading for Huehuetenango, Momostenango, Totonicapán, San Francisco El Alto etc.

El Carmen/Talismán (Mexican border) Take a bus to Coatepeque (US$1.45, 2 hours, every half-hour), and change there to a direct bus to El Carmen (US$1.65, 2hr).

Guatemala City (US$4, 4hr, 205km); Transportes Álamo (☎ 761-7117; 4a Calle 14-04, Zona 3; 5 daily 4:30am-2:30pm); Líneas América (☎ 761-2063; 7a Av 3-33, Zona 2; 7 daily 5:15am-8pm); Transportes Galgos (☎ 761-2248; Calle Rodolfo Robles 17-43, Zona 1; 5-8 daily 3am-4:15pm) Cheaper 2nd-class buses go from Terminal Minerva every half-hour, 3am to 4:30pm, but they make many stops and take longer.

Huehuetenango (US$1, 2hr, 90km, every 30min 5am-5:30pm)

La Mesilla, Mexican border (US$1.55, 3½hr, 170km, 6 daily 5am, 6am, 7am, 8am, 1pm & 4pm) Alternatively, take a bus to Huehuetenango and change there.

Momostenango (US$0.50, 1¼hr, 26km, every 30min 6am-5pm)

Panajachel (US$1.55, 2½hr, 90km, 6 daily 5am, 6am, 8am, 10am, noon & 3pm) Alternatively, take any bus bound for Guatemala City by the Interamericana and change at Los Encuentros.

Retalhuleu (US$1, 1hr, 46km, every 30min 4:30am-6pm) Look for 'Reu' on the bus; 'Retalhuleu' won't be spelled out.

San Andrés Xecul (US$0.25, 4min, every 1hr-2hr 6am-3pm) Or take any bus to San Francisco El Alto or Totonicapán, get out at the Esso station at the Moreiria junction and flag a pickup.

San Francisco El Alto (US$0.25, 1hr, 15km, every 15min 6am-6pm)

San Martín Sacatepéquez (US$0.40, 45min, 22km) Various companies have buses that leave when full. Placards may say 'Colomba' or 'El Rincón.' Minibuses also serve this route.

Totonicapán (US$0.40, 1hr, 22km, every 20min 6am-5pm) Departing from the Rotonda on Calzada Independencia. Placards generally say 'Toto.'

Zunil (US$0.25, 20min, 10km, every 30min 7am-7pm) Has an additional stop at the corner of 9a Av and 10a Calle, southeast of Parque Centroamérica.

SHUTTLE MINIBUS

Adrenalina Tours (p145) runs shuttles to many destinations including Guatemala City (US$36 per person), Antigua (US$32), Chichicastenango (US$23), Panajachel (US$23), Monterrico (US$60), Ciudad Tecún Umán (US$30) and La Mesilla (US$50). Prices assume a minimum of two people: there's 20% off for four people. Pensión Enriquez, beside Pasaje Enríquez, facing Parque Centroamérica, also does shuttles.

CAR & MOTORCYCLE

Rental companies in Xela include:

Adrenalina Tours (p145) Rents out motorcycles as well as cars.

Econorent (☎ 765-0592, 215-7160; cnr 4a Calle & 14a Av, Zona 3)

Tabarini (☎ /fax 763-0418; 9a Calle 9-21, Zona 1)

Getting Around

Terminal Minerva is linked to the city center by minibuses known as *microbuses,* charging US$0.15 for the 10- to 15-minute ride. From the terminal, walk south through the market to the intersection by the Templo de Minerva, where you'll see the vehicles waiting on the south side of 4a Calle. Going from the center to the terminal, you can catch the *microbuses* on 13a Av at the corner of 7a or 4a Calle, or on 14a Av north of 1a Calle. A taxi from Terminal Minerva to the city center costs around US$3. The Rotonda bus stop on Calzada Independencia is also served by Parque microbuses running to the center and by taxis.

There's a taxi stand at the north end of Parque Centroamérica.

Cycling is a great, efficient way to explore the countryside or commute to Spanish class. Among other places, Zunil, Fuentes Georginas and San Andrés Xecul are all attainable in day trips by bike. American-run **Vrisa Bookshop** (☎ 761-3237; 15a Av 3-64, Zona 1; ☉ 9am-7pm Mon-Sat) rents good-quality mountain and cross-country bikes for US$4/10/20 per day/week/month. It provides free maps for self-guided tours.

AROUND QUETZALTENANGO

The beautiful volcanic country around Quetzaltenango makes for many exciting day trips. For many, the volcanoes themselves pose irresistible challenges (p143).

The steam baths at Almolonga are basic but cheap and accessible. The hot springs at Fuentes Georginas are idyllic. You can feast your eyes and soul on the wild church at San Andrés Xecul, or hike to the ceremonial shores of Laguna Chicabal. Or simply hop on a bus and explore the myriad small traditional villages that pepper this part of the Highlands. Market days are great opportunities to observe locals in action, so Sunday and Wednesday in Momostenango, Monday in Zunil, Tuesday and Saturday in Totonicapán and Friday in San Francisco El Alto are good days to visit these surrounding towns.

Los Vahos

If you're a hiker and the weather is good, you'll enjoy a trip to the rough-and-ready sauna/steam baths at **Los Vahos** (The Vapors; admission US$2; ☉ 8am-6pm), 3.5km from Parque Centroamérica. Take a bus headed for Almolonga and ask to get out at the road to Los Vahos, which is marked with a small sign reading 'A Los Vahos.' From here it's a 2.3km uphill walk (around 1½ hours) to Los Vahos. As you climb, the views of the city on a clear day are remarkable. But, better still, walk south straight out of the city center along 13a Av to its end where you'll see the little, yellow-and-red Monte Sinai evangelical church. Continue straight ahead on the road passing the right-hand side of the church. The road soon zigzags uphill becoming a dirt track and then a good footpath. Follow the path past the dairy and school to where it joins the main track to Los Vahos. From here you'll have 1km or so more to walk uphill to the steam baths.

At Los Vahos you can have a sauna/steam bath and a picnic if you're so inclined. The saunas are just two dark stone rooms behind plastic curtains. Occasionally, the vents are carpeted with eucalyptus leaves, giving the steam a herbal quality. Straight in front of the steam-bath entrance is a rocky hillside, which you can climb to some caves.

A taxi costs US$18 for the return trip.

Zunil

pop 6000 / elevation 2076m

Zunil is a pretty agricultural and market town in a lush valley framed by steep hills and dominated by a towering volcano. As you speed downhill toward Zunil on the road from Quetzaltenango, you will see it framed as if in a picture, with its white colonial church gleaming above the red-tiled and rusted tin roofs of the low houses.

On the way to Zunil the road passes through **Almolonga**, 6km from Quetzaltenango, an indigenous town become relatively wealthy from vegetable-growing (it exports veggies to El Salvador) and with a population that is more than 90% evangelical Christian. Market days are Tuesday, Thursday and Saturday when you'll see the most gorgeous vegetables ever. Almolonga celebrates its annual fair on June 27. Don't miss the **Iglesia de San Pedro**, which has a gilded altarpiece with a backdrop of incongruous neon lights, an inverted galleon ceiling and huge old paintings. At the lower end of the village the road passes through **Los Baños**, an area with natural hot sulfur springs. Several little places down here have bath installations; most are quite decrepit, but if a hot-water bath at low cost is your desire, you may want to stop. Rather tomb-like enclosed concrete tubs rent for US$2 to US$3 an hour. **El Recreo** and **Los Cirilos** are among the better setups.

Winding down the hill from Los Baños, the road skirts Zunil and its fertile gardens before a road on the left leads across a river bridge and, 1km further, to Zunil's plaza.

Zunil, founded in 1529, is a typical Guatemalan highland town. What makes it so beautiful is its setting in the mountains and the traditional indigenous agriculture practiced here. The cultivated plots, divided by stone fences, are irrigated by canals; you'll see the farmers scooping up water from the canals with a shovel-like instrument and throwing it over their plants. Women wash their clothes near the river bridge in pools of hot water that come out of the rocks. In Zunil, the centuries-old life cycle thrives.

SIGHTS

Another attraction of Zunil is its particularly striking **church**. Its ornate facade, with eight pairs of serpentine columns, is echoed inside by a richly worked altar of silver. On market day (Monday) the plaza in front of the church is bright with the predominantly red and pink traditional garb of the local K'iche' Maya people buying and selling.

Half a block downhill from the church plaza, the **Cooperativa Santa Ana** (7:30am-

6pm) is a handicrafts cooperative in which more than 500 local women participate. Handicrafts, mainly superbly woven-cloth, are displayed and sold here, and weaving lessons are offered.

While you're in Zunil, visit the image of **San Simón**, the name given here to the much-venerated non-Christian deity known elsewhere as Maximón. His effigy, propped up in a chair, is moved each year to a different house; ask any local where to find San Simón, everyone will know (local children will take you for a small tip). You'll be charged a few quetzals to visit him and US$0.65 for each photograph taken. For more on San Simón, see p119.

The **festival of San Simón** is held each year on October 28, after which he moves to a new house. The **festival of Santa Catarina Alejandrí**, official patron saint of Zunil, is celebrated on November 25. In between, November 1 sees lots of kites flying above the cemetery. If you want more of the natural-steam-bath-sauna experience, head to **Eco Saunas Las Cumbres**, which is about 500m south of Zunil village.

GETTING THERE & AWAY

From Zunil, which is 10km from Quetzaltenango, you can continue to Fuentes Georginas (8km), return to Quetzaltenango via the Cantel road (16km), or alternatively, take Highway 9S down through ever lusher countryside to El Zarco junction on the Carretera al Pacífico. Buses depart Zunil for Xela from the main road beside the bridge.

Fuentes Georginas

The prettiest, most popular natural spa in Guatemala is **Fuentes Georginas** (admission US$1.30; 8am-5pm Mon-Sat, 8am-4pm Sun). Four pools of varying temperatures are fed by hot sulfur springs and framed by a steep, high wall of tropical vines, ferns and flowers. Fans of Fuentes Georginas were dismayed when a massive landslide in 1998 destroyed several structures, filled the primary bathing pool with trees, mud and rubble and crushed the angelic Greek goddess that previously gazed upon the pools. But after the site was successfully restored, spa regulars realized that the landslide had opened a new vent that feeds the pools. As a result, the water here is hotter than ever. Though the setting is intensely tropical, the mountain air currents keep it deliciously cool through the day. There is a little 500m walk starting from beside the pool and worth doing to check out the birds and orchids. Bring a bathing suit, which is required.

Besides the **restaurant** (🕒 8am-6pm; meals US$6-8), which serves great *papas*, there are three sheltered picnic tables with cooking grills (you need to bring your own fuel). Big-time soakers will want to spend the night: down the valley a few dozen meters are seven rustic but cozy **cottages** (s/d/tr/q US$12/16/20/24), each with a shower, a BBQ area and a fireplace to ward off the mountain chill at night (wood and matches are provided; US$3.25 for extra wood). Included in the price of the cottages is access to the pools all day and all night, when rules are relaxed.

Trails here lead to two nearby volcanoes: **Volcán Zunil** (three hours one way) and **Volcán Santo Tomás** (five hours one way). Guides are essential if you don't want to get lost and are available for around US$10 for either trip. Ask at the restaurant.

GETTING THERE & AWAY
Take any bus to Zunil, where pickup trucks wait to give rides up the hill 8km to the springs, a half-hour away. Negotiate the price for the ride. It's very likely they'll tell you it's US$4.50 roundtrip, and when you arrive at the top, tell you it's US$4.50 each way – this is an annoying game the pickup drivers play. If there are many people in the group, they may charge US$1 per person. Unless you want to walk back down the hill, arrange a time for the pickup driver to return to pick you up. You can walk from Zunil to Fuentes Georginas in about two hours. If you're the mountain-goat type, you may enjoy this; it's a strenuous climb.

Hitchhiking is not good on the Fuentes Georginas access road, as there are few cars and they are often filled to capacity with large Guatemalan families. The best days to try for a ride are Saturday and Sunday, when the baths are busiest.

If you're driving, walking or hitching, go uphill from Zunil's plaza to the Cantel road (about 60m), turn right and go downhill 100m to a road on the left marked 'Turicentro Fuentes Georginas, 8km.' (This road is near the bus stop on the

Quetzaltenango–Retalhuleu road – note that there are three different bus stops in Zunil.) This road heads up to Fuentes Georginas. You'll know you're approaching the baths when you smell the sulfur in the air.

Alternatively, make it all simple and take a shuttle or a tour from Quetzaltenango. Adrenalina Tours (p145), runs a half-day transport-only shuttle service to Fuentes Georginas at 8am and 2pm for US$6.50 per person roundtrip.

El Palmar Viejo
The turnoff to El Palmar Viejo is signposted immediately before the Puente Samala III bridge, about 30km down the Retalhuleu road from Xela. It's 4km west from the main road to the village itself – or rather the overgrown remnants of the village, for El Palmar was destroyed by a mudslide and floods emanating from Santiaguito volcano at the time of Hurricane Mitch in the 1990s. Its inhabitants were resettled at a new village, El Palmar Nuevo, east of the main highway, but some still come here to tend plantations. A river has cut a deep ravine through the heart of the old village, slicing the **church** in two. A pair of **swing bridges** cross the ravine. Downstream, to the right of the river, you can see the top of the village cemetery **chapel** poking up through the trees – but beware, reaching the cemetery involves crossing an unstable bridge. Atop the hill behind the **cemetery** is a modern Mayan **altar**. Buses bound for Retalhuleu can drop you at the El Palmar Viejo turnoff, but it's probably best to come with a guide, as this is an isolated place. Adrenalina Tours (p145) is one agency that comes here.

Salcajá
Seven kilometers from Xela, this is an apparently unremarkable town that everyone passes through en route to all points north. However, behind all the traffic and dust lurk some special qualities to which Salcajá alone can lay claim.

Salcajá's **Iglesia de San Jacinto**, two blocks west on 3a Calle from the main road (3a Av, Zona 1), dates from 1524. It was the first Christian church in Central America. The facade retains some character, with carved lions and bunches of fruit, but the real treat (if you find the church open) is inside, where you'll find several original paintings and a pretty, ornate altar.

Salcajá is famed for its traditional *ikat*-style textiles, remarkable for the hand-tied and dyed threads that are laid out in the preferred pattern on a loom. Shops selling bolts of this fabric are ubiquitous in Salcajá, and you can usually visit their workshops before purchasing.

Salcajá is also known for its production of two alcoholic beverages that locals consider akin to magic elixirs. *Caldo de frutas* (literally, fruit soup) is like a high-octane sangría that will knock your socks off. It's made by combining *nances* (cherry-like fruits), apples, peaches, and pears and fermenting them for years. You can purchase fifths of it for around US$3 after viewing the production process. *Rompopo* is an entirely different type of potent potable, made from rum, egg yolks, sugar and spices. A sickly yellow *rompopo* costs around US$4 a fifth. Little liquor shops all over Salcajá peddle the stuff, but you may like to try the friendly **Rompopo Salcajá** (4a Calle 2-02), a block east of the main road along 4a Calle.

All buses headed north from Quetzaltenango pass through Salcajá, so it's easy to hop off here en route to other destinations.

San Andrés Xecul

A few kilometers past Salcajá and less than 1km before Cuatro Caminos, the road from Quetzaltenango passes the Morería crossroads, where the road to San Andrés Xecul branches off to the west. After about 3km on this uphill spur, you'll start seeing rainbow cascades of hand-dyed thread drying on the roofs and you'll know you have arrived in San Andrés Xecul. This small town is boxed in by fertile hills and boasts the most bizarre, stunning **church** imaginable. Technicolored saints, angels, flowers and climbing vines fight for space with whimsical tigers and frolicking monkeys on the shocking yellow facade. The red, blue and yellow cones on the bell tower are straight from the circus big top.

Sitting on the wall overlooking the entire Quetzaltenango valley and contemplating this wild combination of Catholic and Mayan iconography, it's hard to believe hallucinogenic substances didn't somehow figure in. Why and how this church came

to resemble the inside of a lunatic's mind has been lost, though the church doors are inscribed 1917. Inside, a carpet of candles illuminate bleeding effigies of Christ. These are unabashedly raffish, with slabs of thick makeup trying to make him look alive and boyish. In one especially campy display, a supine Jesus is surrounded by gold and satin trimmings that hang thick inside his glass coffin. The pews are generally packed with praying indigenous women. The outside of the church was vibrantly refurbished in late 1999.

Continue walking up the hill and you'll come to a smaller (and decidedly more sedate) **yellow church**. Mayan ceremonies are still held here, and the panoramic view across the valley is phenomenal. The **annual festival** is November 29 and 30 – a good time to visit this town. There are no facilities; the easiest way to get here is by taking any northbound bus from Xela, alighting at the Esso station at the Morería crossroads and hailing a pickup or walking the 3km uphill. Buses returning to Xela line up at the edge of the plaza and make the trip until about 5pm.

Totonicapán
pop 10,000 / elevation 2500m
If you want to visit a laid-back, pretty Guatemalan highland town with few other tourists in sight, San Miguel Totonicapán, 30km northeast of Xela via Cuatro Caminos, is the place to go.

The ride from Cuatro Caminos is along a pine-studded valley. From Totonicapán's bus station it's a 600m walk up 4a Calle to the twin main plazas. The lower plaza has a statue of Atanasio Tzul, leader of an indigenous rebellion that started here in 1820, while the upper one is home to the requisite large **colonial church** and a wonderful **municipal theater**, built in 1924 in neoclassical style and recently restored.

Market days are Tuesday and Saturday; it's a locals' market, not a tourist affair, and it winds down by late morning.

ACTIVITIES
The **Casa de la Cultura Totonicapense** (☎ 712-9817, 766-1575; kiche78@hotmail.com; www.larutama yaonline.com/aventura.html; 8a Av 2-17), next door to Hospedaje San Miguel 1½ blocks off the lower plaza, has displays of indigenous

culture and crafts and administers a fascinating 'Meet the Artisans' program to introduce tourists to some of the town's many artisans and local families. A one-day program, usually for a minimum of four people and requiring a week's advance booking, includes visits to various craft workshops (including potters, carvers of wooden masks and musical instruments, and weavers), a concert of traditional instruments and a traditional lunch in a private home. Prices range from US$49 per person for four people down to US$24 per person for 15 to 20 people. An alternative program, costing US$15/10/6 per person for two/six/10 people, takes you on foot to nearby villages to visit community development projects, natural medicine projects, schools, artisans' workshops and Mayan sacred sites. All tours are in Spanish. At the time of writing the Casa de la Cultura was in temporary premises at the back of the bus station, but it was due to return to its permanent building in April 2004, after renovations.

FESTIVALS & EVENTS
The festival of the **Apparition of the Archangel Michael** is on May 8, with fireworks and traditional dances. The **Feria Titular de San Miguel Arcángel** (Name-Day Festival of the Archangel Saint Michael) runs from September 24 to 30, peaking on the 29th. Totonicapán keeps traditional masked dances very much alive with its **Festival Tradicional de Danza** – dates vary but recently it was over a weekend in late October.

SLEEPING & EATING
Hospedaje San Miguel (☎ 766-1452; 8a Calle; s/d US$4/8, with bathroom US$8/16) This is a clean, tidy place, 1½ blocks off the lower plaza – not what you'd call Swiss-clean, but good for the price. The rooms with a bathroom are bigger and better, and have phone and TV. Casa de la Cultura clients can stay with local families for around US$18 per person including dinner and breakfast. For good-value eating head 100m down 3a Calle from the plaza to the **American Coffee Shop** (set lunches US$1.80; ⊗ 10am-10pm Mon-Sat), a clean local lunch spot.

GETTING THERE & AWAY
The last direct bus back to Quetzaltenango (US$0.40, one hour) leaves Totonicapán at 6:30pm.

San Francisco El Alto
pop 8000 / elevation 2630m
High on a hilltop overlooking Quetzaltenango (17km away) stands the town of San Francisco El Alto.

Banco de Comercio (2a Calle 2-64; ⊗ 8:30am-7pm Mon-Fri, 9am-1pm Sat) changes US-cash dollar and traveler's checks. Bancafé, at the same intersection, has a Visa ATM. San Francisco's big party is the **Fiesta de San Franciosco de Asís**, celebrated around October 4 with traditional dances such as La Danza de Conquista and La Danza de los Monos.

This whole town is Guatemala's garment district: Every inch is jammed with vendors selling sweaters, socks, blankets, jeans, scarves and more. Bolts of cloth spill from storefronts packed to the ceiling with miles of material, and this is on the quiet days! On Friday, the real market action kicks in. The large plaza in front of the 18th-century church is covered in goods. Stalls are crowded into neighboring streets, and the press of traffic is so great that a special system of one-way roads is established to avoid colossal traffic jams. Vehicles entering the town on market day must pay a small fee, and any bus ride within town is laborious.

San Francisco's market is regarded as the biggest, most authentic market in the country, and it's not nearly as heavy with handicrafts as those in Chichicastenango and Antigua. As in any crowded market, beware of pickpockets and stay alert.

Around mid-morning, when the clouds roll away, panoramic views can be had from throughout town, but especially from the roof of the **church**. The caretaker will let you go up (on the way through, have a look at the church's six elaborate gilded altarpieces and remains of what must once have been very colorful frescoes).

For food, **El Manantial** (☎ 738-4373; 2a Calle 2-42; mains US$2.50-3), a couple of blocks below the plaza, is surprisingly pleasant and clean, though your chicken burrito might come swimming in thousand-island dressing.

Momostenango
pop 8000 / elevation 2200m
Beyond San Francisco El Alto, 15km from Cuatro Caminos and 26km from Quetzaltenango, this town, set in a pretty mountain

THE HIGHLANDS

valley along a road through pine woods, is famous for the making of *chamarras,* or thick, heavy woolen blankets. The villagers also make ponchos and other woolen garments. The best days to look for these are Wednesday and Sunday, the main market day. A basic good blanket costs around US$13; it's perhaps twice as much for an extra-heavy 'matrimonial.'

Momostenango is also noted for its adherence to the ancient Mayan calendar and for its observance of traditional rites. Hills in the town are the scene of ceremonies enacted on the important dates of the calendar round. Visits on important celestial days – such as the summer solstice, the spring equinox, the start of the Mayan solar year (February 24), or Wajshakib Batz, the start of the 260-day *cholq'ij* or *tzolkin* year – can be particularly powerful and rewarding. But few Mayan ceremonies are open to outsiders, so don't assume showing up means you'll be able to participate. Should you be so fortunate as to observe a ceremony, be sure to treat altars and participants with the utmost respect.

Bancafé (1a Calle, Zona 2; 9am-4pm Mon-Fri, 9am-1pm Sun), a block south of the plaza, changes US-dollar cash and traveler's checks and has a Visa ATM.

SIGHTS & ACTIVITIES
Los Riscos, a set of strange geological formations on the edge of town, are worth the little walk it takes to see them. Technically eroded pumice, these bunches of tawny spires rising into the air look like something from Star Trek. To get there, head downhill on 3a Av, Zona 2, from beside Kikotemal shop, which is two blocks east along 1a Calle from Bancafé. Turn right after 100m at the bottom of the hill, go left at a fork (signed 'A Los Riscos'), then after 100m turn right along 2a Calle and walk 300m to Los Riscos.

Takiliben May Wajshakib Batz (736-5537; misionmaya@yahoo.com.mx; 3a Av A 6-85, Zona 3) is at the southern entrance to town – turn up a signed path just north of the Texaco station to find it. Ttakiliben May, a 'Maya Mission,' is dedicated to studying and teaching Mayan culture and sacred traditions. Its director, Rigoberto Itzep Chanchavac, is a *chuchkajau* (Mayan priest) responsible for advising the community on when special

days of the Mayan calendars fall. Rigoberto also does Mayan horoscopes (US$5) and leads day or half-day workshops where groups of around eight can gain an understanding of customs that usually remain hidden from outsiders. His *chuj* (traditional Mayan sauna; US$10 per person), is open on Tuesday and Thursday from 3pm to 6pm. Ideally, a week's notice is needed for these last two activities. The Takiliben May can also provide tourist guides for US$10 an hour.

FESTIVALS & EVENTS
Picturesque *diablo* (devil) **dances** are held here in the plaza a few times a year, notably on Christmas Eve and New Year's Eve. The homemade devil costumes can get quite campy and elaborate: all have masks and cardboard wings, and some go whole hog with fake fur suits and heavily sequined outfits. Dance groups gather in the plaza with a five- to 13-piece band, drinking alcoholic refreshments during the breaks. For entertainment, they are at their best around 3pm, but the festivities go on late into the night. The annual fair, **Octava de Santiago**, is celebrated from July 28 to August 2.

SLEEPING & EATING
Accommodations are very basic.

Posada de Doña Pelagia (736-5175; 2a Av 2-88, Zona 1; s/d US$2/3) Just off the second of Momos' twin plazas, this place has small rooms off a small, open-air patio. Some are moderately clean, some are grubby. A shower, hot or cold, is US$0.65.

Hospedaje y Comedor Paclom (cnr 2a Av & 1a Calle, Zona 2; d US$7) A block uphill from the first plaza, this serviceable place to stay has rooms facing a courtyard crammed with plants and birds.

Comedor Aracely (2a Av 3-02, Zona 1) Situated down the street from the church, friendly Aracely is one of the better of several cheap eateries.

GETTING THERE & AWAY
You can get buses to Momostenango from Quetzaltenango's Terminal Minerva, or Cuatro Caminos, or San Francisco El Alto. They run about every half-hour, with the last one back to Quetzaltenango normally leaving Momos at 4:30pm.

Laguna Chicabal

This magical, sublime lake is nestled in the crater of Volcán Chicabal (2712m) on the edge of a cloud forest. Laguna Chicabal is billed as the 'Center of Maya-Mam Cosmovision' on huge signs, both on the path leading out of town and at the crater itself. As such, it is a very sacred place and a hotbed of Mayan ceremonial activity. There are two active Mayan altars on its sandy shores, and Mayan priests and worshippers come from far and wide to perform ceremonies and make offerings here, especially on and around May 3. The lake is 575m wide and 331m deep.

Adding to the atmosphere of mystery, a veil of fog dances over the water, alternately revealing and hiding the lake's placid contours. Amid the thick, pretty vegetation are picnic tables and one of Guatemala's most inviting campsites, right on the lakeshore. Because the lake and grounds have great ceremonial significance, campers and hikers are asked to treat them with the utmost respect. In addition, Laguna Chicabal is pretty much off-limits to tourists during the entire first week of May, so that ceremonial traditions can be observed without interference.

Laguna Chicabal is a two-hour hike from San Martín Sacatepéquez (also known as San Martín Chile Verde), a friendly, interesting village about 22km from Xela. This place is notable for the elaborate traditional dress worn by the village men, who sport a white tunic with red pinstripes that hangs to mid-shin and has densely embroidered red, pink and orange sleeves. A thick, red sash serves as a belt. The tunic is worn over pants that nearly reach the ankles and are similarly embroidered.

To get to the lake, head down from the highway toward the purple-and-blue church and look for the Laguna Chicabal sign on your right (you can't miss it). Hike 45 minutes uphill through fields and past houses until you crest the hill. Continue hiking, going downhill for 15 minutes until you reach the rangers' station, where you pay the US$2 entrance fee. From here, it's another 30 minutes uphill to a *mirador* and then a whopping 615 steep steps down to the edge of the lake. Start early for best visibility. Coming back up, allow two hours.

For bus information, see p150. For the return, there are fairly frequent minibuses from San Martín or you can hail a pickup. There are a few basic cook shacks on the square in San Martín, though you may prefer to hop off in San Juan Ostuncalco for a meal. In this interesting town, half-way between San Martín and Xela, the artisans are renowned for their wicker furniture and fine handcrafted instruments. San Juan's market day is Sunday. A taxi from Quetzaltenango to San Martín Sacatepéquez costs around US$13.

HUEHUETENANGO

pop 40,000 / elevation 1902m

Distanced from Guatemala City by mountains and a long, twisting road, Huehuetenango (weh-weh-teh-*nahn*-go), has that bustling, self-sufficient air exuded by many larger provincial towns. Coffee growing, mining, sheep raising, light manufacturing and agriculture are the main activities in this region.

The lively market is filled every day with traders who come down from the lofty Sierra de los Cuchumatanes, which dominates the department of Huehuetenango. The market area is about the only place you'll see colorful traditional costumes in this town, as most of its citizens are *ladinos* who wear modern clothes.

Huehue (as it's often called) doesn't inspire many people to linger. Its streets are especially clogged with noisy and dirty traffic in the late afternoon. The late postclassic ruins of Zaculeu, just outside the town, are its only real tourist attraction. For travelers, Huehue is usually a leg on the journey to or from Mexico – it's a logical place to spend your last or first night in Guatemala – or the starting point for ventures up into the dramatic Cuchumatanes with their traditional Mayan hill villages.

History

Huehuetenango was a Mam Maya region until the 15th century, when the K'iche', expanding from their capital K'umarcaaj, which is near present-day Santa Cruz del Quiché, pushed them out. Many Mam fled into neighboring Chiapas, Mexico, which still has a large Mam population near its border with Guatemala. In the late 15th century, the weakness of K'iche' rule brought about civil war, which engulfed the Highlands and provided a chance

HUEHUETENANGO

0   200 m
0   0.1 mi

INFORMATION	
Bancafé.......................................1	B2
Banco Industrial........................2	B1
Centro de Información Turística........3	C1
Corpobanco...............................4	B2
Génesis Internet........................5	B1
Interhuehue..............................6	B2
Mexican Consulate......................7	C2
Telgua.....................................8	B1
Visa ATM...........................(see 2)	

SIGHTS & ACTIVITIES	
Church......................................9	C2
Gobernación Departamental........10	C1
Town Hall................................11	B1

SLEEPING	pp159–60
Hotel Casa Blanca......................12	B2
Hotel Central............................13	B1
Hotel Gobernador......................14	C1
Hotel La Sexta..........................15	B2
Hotel Mary...............................16	C1
Hotel San Luis de la Sierra..........17	A2
Hotel Vásquez..........................18	B2
Hotel Zaculeu...........................19	B1
Todos Santos Inn......................20	B1

EATING	pp160
Cafe Bougambilias.....................21	C2
La Cabaña del Café....................22	B1
La Fonda..................................23	B1
Mi Tierra.................................24	B2
Pastelería Monte Alto.................25	C1
Restaurante Las Brasas...............26	C1

DRINKING	pp160
Zafarrancho.............................27	B2

TRANSPORT	p160–1
Buses from Main Bus Station.......28	B2
Buses to Main Bus Station..........29	B2
Buses to Zaculeu......................30	A2
Los Halcones Bus Station...........31	B2
Taxis......................................32	C2

for Mam independence. The turmoil was still unresolved in 1525 when Gonzalo de Alvarado, the brother of Pedro, arrived to conquer Zaculeu, the Mam capital, for Spain.

Orientation & Information

The town center is 4km northeast of the Interamericana, and the bus station is off the road linking the two, about 2km from each. Almost every service of interest to tourists is in Zona 1 within a few blocks of the Parque Central.

Huehue's helpful, English-speaking **Centro de Información Turística** (☎ 694-9354; Edificio de Gobernación de Zona 1, 2a Calle; 8am–noon & 1:30-5pm Mon-Fri) can provide verbal and printed information on the city and the whole Huehuetenango department, which stretches to the Mexican borders north and west.

Bancafé (cnr 6a Av & 3a Calle; 9am-7pm Mon-Fri, 9am-1pm Sat) Changes US-dollar cash and traveler's checks; has a Visa ATM.

Banco Industrial A block further north of Corpobanco; has Visa ATMs.

Corpobanco (cnr 6a Av & 3a Calle; 8:30am-7pm Mon-Fri, 8:30am-12:30pm Sat) Changes US-dollar cash and traveler's checks.

Hotel La Sexta (6a Av 4-29) Has a call office where you can call North America for US$0.65 a minute or Europe for US$0.80.

Génesis Internet (2a Calle 6-37; 8:30am-1pm & 3-7pm Mon-Sat) Charges US$0.90 an hour.

Interhuehue (3a Calle 6-65B; 9am-12:30pm & 2-6pm) Charges US$0.90 an hour.

Mi Tierra (4a Calle 6-46; 9am-7pm) Provides Internet access for US$1.30 an hour.

Post office (2a Calle 3-54; 8:30am-5:30pm Mon-Fri, 9am-1pm Sat) Half a block east of the Parque. Next door, there's a line of Telgua card phones outside the Telgua office.

Zaculeu

With ravines on three sides, the late post-Classic religious center Zaculeu ('White Earth' in the Mam language) occupies a strategic defensive location that served its Mam Maya inhabitants well. It finally failed, however, in 1525 when Gonzalo de Alvarado and his conquistadors laid siege to the site for two months. It was starvation that ultimately defeated the Mam.

The parklike **Zaculeu archaeological zone** (admission US$3.25; ☺ 8am-6pm), about 200m square, is 4km west of Huehuetenango's main plaza. Cold soft drinks and snacks are available. A small museum at the site holds, among other things, skulls and grave goods found in a tomb beneath Estructura 1, the tallest structure at the site.

Restoration by the United Fruit Company in the 1940s has left Zaculeu's pyramids, ball courts and ceremonial platforms covered by a thick coat of graying plaster. It's oddly stark and clean. Some of the restoration methods were not authentic to the buildings, but the work goes further than others in making the site look as it might have done to the Mam priests and worshipers when it was still an active religious center. What is missing, however, is the painted decoration, which must have been applied to the wet plaster as in frescoes. The buildings show a great deal of Mexican influence and were probably designed and built originally with little innovation.

Buses to Zaculeu (US$0.15, 20 minutes) leave about every 30 minutes, 7am to 6pm, from in front of the school at the corner of 2a Calle and 7a Av. A taxi from the town center costs US$2.50 one way (US$3.25 from the bus station). One hour is plenty of time to look round the site and museum.

Tours

As this book went to press, the admirable folk from Quetzaltrekkers in Quetzaltenango (p143) were about to open a new trekking and tours outfit, Clearly Adventurous (www.clearlyadventurous.com), in central Huehuetenango. It will be well worth seeing what it offers: check the website for up-to-date contact details.

Sleeping
BUDGET
Hotel Mary (☎ 764-1618; 2a Calle 3-52; s/d/tr US$8/12/14) The 26 good, clean, medium-sized rooms here are painted in cheerful yellow and green tones, and all have a bathroom (hot water from 6am to 9am and 6pm to 9pm) and TV. It's a cut above other similar-priced places, and the ground-floor Cafetería Mary serves all meals.

Hotel Central (☎ 764-1202; 5a Av 1-33; s/d/tr/q US$3/4/6/7) This cheapie has 10 largish, simple and well-used rooms with shared

bathroom. Most are around a pillared wooden interior balcony, giving the place a modicum of antique charm.

Hotel La Sexta (☎ 764-1488; 6a Av 4-29; s/d/tr US$6/11/16, with bathroom US$9/13/20; **P**) The blue-and-yellow-painted parking courtyard is prettier than the rooms, which are drab if reasonably clean.

Hotel Gobernador (☎ /fax 769-0765; 4a Av 1-45; d/tr US$4/6/8, with bathroom US$6/9/13) The Gobernador is a solid budget choice, but compare a few rooms before choosing, as some are airier and less damp and dingy than others. The shared showers are hot and strong!

Hotel Vásquez (☎ 764-1338; 2a Calle 6-67; s/d US$6/7, d/tr with bathroom US$10/12; **P**) This place has a car park in the front and 18 boxlike, fairly cheerless but reasonably clean rooms at the back. The showers have hot water.

Todos Santos Inn (☎ 764-1241; 2a Calle 7-64; s/d US$5/8, with bathroom US$6/11) Rooms upstairs, with shared bathrooms, are more acceptable than those downstairs, with a bathroom, which tend to be damp, musty and dark. There's hot water but no towels.

MID-RANGE
Hotel Zaculeu (☎ 764-1086; fax 764-1575; 5a Av 1-14; s/d/tr/q ground floor US$15/22/29/26, upstairs US$28/36/45/54; **P**) Half a block north of the plaza, the colonial-style Zaculeu has a lovely garden courtyard, a good restaurant serving breakfast and dinner, laundry service and 37 large rooms, all with a hot-water bathroom, drinking water and TV. Ground-floor rooms are darker and some are damp-affected, unfortunately including some of those around the plant-filled front patio, which is the prettiest area.

Hotel Casa Blanca (☎ 769-0777/8/9; 7a Av 3-41; s/d/tr US$24/30/35; **P**) This bright, pleasant hotel is the best in the city center. The 15 rooms all come with hot-water bathroom, phone and cable TV, and there are two flowery patios, two restaurants (see p160), and parking.

Hotel San Luis de la Sierra (☎ 764-9216, ☎ /fax 764-9219; 2a Calle 7-00; s/d US$20/28; **P**) Another good choice. The clean, medium-sized rooms have pine furniture, TV, hot-water bathroom and nice touches like fan, reading lamp and shampoo. There's a restaurant here too.

There are plenty of hotels near the bus station: leave the east side of the station between the Díaz Álvarez and Transportes Fronterizos offices, and walk left up the street outside to come out on 3a Av, Zona 5. Within 300m or so in each direction here there's a total of at least seven hotels. Try **Hotel California** (☎ 769-0500; 3a Av 4-25; s US$9, s/d with bathroom US$16/32) or **Hotel Cascata** (☎ 764-1188; Lote 4 4-42; s/d US$8/16, with bathroom US$12/26).

Eating

Mi Tierra (4a Calle 6-46; mains US$3-5; ☉ 7am-9pm) An excellent, informal café/restaurant/cybercafé with Antigua-like ambience and mixed local and foreign clientele and food. Breakfast features almost any combination you like of croissants, muffins, omelets, hash browns, eggs, bacon, pancakes, tortillas, juices and good coffee. We sincerely recommend the bacon and egg muffins! Dinner choices range from baked potatoes to fajitas or *puyaso* (cut of steak).

La Fonda (2a Calle 5-35; mains US$3-5; ☉ 5:45am-10:30pm) A few steps from the Parque Central, this clean, reliable place serves varied Guatemalan and international fare including good-value pizzas.

Pastelería Monte Alto (2a Calle facing Parque Central; cakes & pastries US$0.50-0.80; ☉ 9am-9pm) With its ceiling fans and glittery lamps, this café is a soothing place to sit down over a coffee and cake (it has a fine range), doughnut or pie.

Hotel Casa Blanca (7a Av 3-41; set lunches US$2.50; ☉ 6am-10pm) For lovely surroundings, you can't beat the two restaurants at this classy hotel, one indoors, the other in the garden. Breakfasts cost US$2 to US$3.50 (on Sunday, from 8am to 11am, it's a big buffet for US$3.25), burgers and croissants are around US$2, and steaks (try filet mignon or cordon bleu) are around US$5.

Restaurante Las Brasas (4a Av 1-36; mains US$4.50-6; ☉ 8:30am-10pm) Half a block from the Parque Central, this is one of Huehue's best restaurants. The specialties are Chinese food and steaks.

Cafe Bougambilias (5a Av north of 4a Calle; breakfast mains US$2) One of three *comedors* in a line along the southern part of the Parque, the Bougambilias has a team of busy cooks preparing food on the ground floor, while the two upper floors have tables with views over the park and plenty of fresh air. It's good for all meals, with large serves of straightforward food.

La Cabaña del Café (2a Calle 6-50; dishes US$2-3; ☉ 8am-9pm) Come here for good coffee and reasonable pasta, salads, sandwiches and breakfasts, in a log-cabin-style interior.

Drinking

Zafarrancho (4a Calle 6-42) Downtown Huehue has few bright after-dark spots. An exception is this bar with free tapas next to Mi Tierra restaurant. Ché and Zapatista photos contribute to its slightly underground feel.

Getting There & Away

The bus station is 2km southwest of the center. Departures include:

Antigua (230km) Take a Guatemala City bus and change at Chimaltenango.

Aguacatán (US$1, 1hr, 22km, 12 daily 6am-7pm) Covered by the Mendoza and Rivas companies.

Barrillas (US$3.25, 7hr, 139km, 10 daily 2am to 10pm) Covered by Transportes Josué and Autobuses del Norte.

Cobán (142km) No direct service: Transportes Mejía has a bus from Aguacatán (see above) to Cobán at 6:30am Tuesday and Saturday, via Sacapulas and Uspantán. In general your best bet is to use whatever buses, pickups and other transport you can find to get to Uspantán, spend the night there and catch the 3am or 5am bus on to Cobán. For more information, see Sacapulas and Uspantán (p135). If you start very early you *might* get to Cobán in one day from Huehue.

Cuatro Caminos (US$1, 1½hr, 77km) Take any bus heading for Guatemala City or Quetzaltenango.

Gracias a Dios (US$2.20, 5hr, 145km) La Chiantlequita (4 daily 3:30am, 5am via Yalambojoch, 12:30pm & 1pm)

Guatemala City (5hr, 266km) Los Halcones pullman buses (US$4) leave at 4:30am, 7am and 2pm from its town-center terminal on 7a Av; from the main terminal, around 20 buses (US$2.50 to US$4) leave between 2am and 4pm by Transportes El Condor, Díaz Álvarez and Transportes Velásquez.

La Mesilla, Mexican border (US$1, 2hr, 84km, 20 daily 5:45am-6:30pm)

Nebaj (68km) Take a bus to Sacapulas, or a bus to Aguacatán and a pickup on to Sacapulas, then another bus from Sacapulas to Nebaj.

Nentón (US$1.70, 3hr, 102km, 6 daily 3:30am-1pm) La Paisanita and La Chiantlequita.

Panajachel (159km) Take a Guatemala City bus and change at Los Encuentros.

Quetzaltenango (US$1, 2hr, 90km, 14 daily 6am-2:30pm)

Sacapulas (US$2, 2½hr, 42km); Rutas García (11:30am); Transportes Rivas (12:45pm)

San Mateo Ixtatán (US$2.80, 6hr, 111km) Take a Barrillas bus.

Soloma (US$1.80, 3hr, 70km, 16 daily 2am-10pm)
Covered by Transportes Josué and Autobuses del Norte.
Todos Santos Cuchumatán (US$1.30, 3hr, 40km, 9
daily 3:45am, 5:30am, 11:30am, 12:45pm, 1:30pm,
1:45pm, 2pm, 2:45pm & 3:45pm) Covered by the Flor de
María, Mendoza, Pérez, Todosanterita, Concepcionerita and
Chicoyera companies; some buses do not run Saturday.

Tabarini (☎ 764-9356) has a car rental office in
Sector Brasilia in the west of town.

Getting Around

For city buses from the bus station to the
town center, leave the east side of the bus
station through the gap between the Díaz
Álvarez and Transportes Fronterizos offices. During hours of darkness until 11pm
and after 2am, 'Centro' buses (US$0.15)
go intermittently from the street outside;
in daylight hours, cross this street and
walk through the covered market opposite
to a second street, where 'Centro' buses
(US$0.10) depart every few minutes. To
return to the bus station from the center,
catch the buses outside Barbería Wilson
(6a Av 2-22).

A taxi between the bus terminal and
town center costs US$2.50.

AROUND HUEHUETENANGO

Except for Todos Santos Cuchumatán, the
mountainous far northwest of Guatemala
is little visited by travelers. The adventurous few will often be a novelty to the local
Mayan folks they meet. Spanish skills, pa-
tience and tact will pave the way in these
parts.

El Mirador

This is a lookout point up in the Cuchumatanes overlooking Huehuetenango, 12km
from town (one hour by bus). On a sunny
day it offers a great view of the entire region
and many volcanoes. A beautiful poem, *A
Los Cuchumatanes*, is mounted on plaques
here. Any bus from Huehue heading for
Todos Santos, Soloma or Barrillas comes
past here.

Unicornio Azul

This Guatemalan- and French-run **horse-
riding ranch** (☎ /fax 205-9328; www.unicornioazul.com)
at Chancol, about 25km by road northeast
of Huehuetenango, offers riding in the Cuchumatanes from one hour to one/three/

nine days (US$78/309/885). The nine-day
trip crosses the mountains to the Ixil Triangle and back.

Todos Santos Cuchumatán

pop 3000 / elevation 2450m
If you're interested in contemporary but
traditional Mayan life and dramatic mountain scenery, put the small town of Todos
Santos Cuchumatán, 40km northwest of
Huehuetenango, on your itinerary. Todos
Santos lies in the bottom of a deep valley,
and the last 1¼ hours of the approach by
bus are down a bone-shaking dirt road that
leaves the paved Huehuetenango–Soloma
road after a 1½-hour climb up from Huehue.

Traditional clothing is very much in use
here and unusually it's the male costume
that is the more eye-catching. Men wear
red-and-white-striped trousers, small flat
hats with blue ribbon around them, jackets
with multicolored stripes and thick woven
collars. Saturday is the main market day,
and by the end of it the main street is half-
full of inebriated *todosanteños* staggering
they know not where. There's a smaller
market on Wednesday.

Reasons to visit Todos Santos include
good walking in the hills, learning Spanish (there are three schools) and getting
to know a traditional and close-knit but
friendly community. Todos Santos suffered terribly during Guatemala's civil war
and is still very poor. To supplement their
subsistence from agriculture, families from
here still travel in the early part of the year
to work for meager wages in very tough
conditions on coffee, sugar and cotton
plantations on the Pacific Slope. Working in the US is however proving a more
lucrative alternative for some *todosanteños*
today, as the amount of new construction
in the valley demonstrates.

Todos Santos gained notoriety in 2000
when a Japanese tourist and his Guatemalan bus driver were murdered by a mob of
villagers after the tourist attempted to take
photos of a young village girl. By all accounts
this was an isolated incident sparked off by
rumors that child-sacrificing satanists were
in the area at the time. But it's confirma-
tion, if such were needed, that one should
never photograph Mayan people without
permission.

THE HIGHLANDS

If you're coming to Todos Santos in the wet season (mid-May to November), bring warm clothes, as it's cold up here, especially at night.

ORIENTATION & INFORMATION

Todos Santos' main street is about 500m long. Towards its west end are the church and market on the north side, with the central plaza raised above street level on the south side. Buses stop at this west end of the street. A side street going uphill beside the plaza leads to most of the accommodations. No street names are in common use, but businesses and sights are either well signposted or known by everyone.

To make **telephone calls** look for signs saying 'Se alquila teléfono' or 'Llamadas Nacionales y Internacionales' in the area around the church.

Banrural On the central plaza; changes US-dollar cash and traveler's checks.

Mountain Muse Also called Rebecca's Place, in the narrow street leading to the market, has a fine selection of used books in English for sale. It buys books too.

Post office (8:30am-5pm Mon-Fri, 8am-noon Sat) On the central plaza.

Todos Santos Internet (9am-9pm) 30m off the main street, 400m back towards Huehue from the church, charges US$1.60 an hour for Internet access.

SIGHTS & ACTIVITIES

A set of small ancient **ruins** is 500m up the uphill street beside the central plaza. Among trees on the left of the road, it consists of a few grassy mounds and two crosses with indications of contemporary Mayan offerings. Todos Santos' **Museo Cultural** (US$0.65 or larger donation) is in a two-story house, 125m down a dirt street off the main street. It comes to life when Fortunato, its creator and a community leader, is there to explain the assembled clothes, photos and antique artifacts.

Walking around Todos Santos provides superb opportunities to check out the rugged countryside. All the language schools offer guided walks – usually two or three mornings a week – which are free for students and usually US$1.30 for nonstudents. If you want to walk on your own, invest a few quetzals in the leaflets describing several of the best routes, with sketch maps, sold by Nuevo Amanecer language school. January to April are the best months for walking, with the best and warmest weather, but you can usually walk in the morning, before the weather closes in, year-round (except maybe in July).

One of the most spectacular destinations is **La Torre** (3837m), the highest nonvolcanic point in Central America. Start by taking a bus east up the valley to the hamlet of La Ventosa (US$0.60, about 50 minutes) from where it's a trail walk of about 1¼ hours through limestone and pines to the top. At the summit (marked by a radio mast), the southern horizon is dotted with almost a dozen volcanoes from Tacaná on the Mexican border to Volcán Agua near Antigua.

Las Letras, on a hillside above town, is a good morning walk (about 1½ to two hours roundtrip). The 'Letters' spell out Todos Santos, but may be illegible; it depends on when the stones were last rearranged. Still, it's a hale hike and affords beautiful views, especially in the morning after the fog lifts. You can continue up beyond Las Letras to the villages of **Tuicoy** and **Tzichim** (about five hours from Todos Santos). A bus leaves Tzichim for Todos Santos at noon on Thursday. From Tuicoy you can detour to the Puerta del Cielo, an outstanding lookout.

Other walk destinations include **Las Cuevas**, a sacred cave still used for Mayan rituals (this walk starts from 'La Maceta,' a tree growing out of rock, 30 minutes by bus up the Huehue road from Todos Santos), and the village of **San Juan Atitán**, over the mountains to the south of Todos Santos (about five hours one way).

Todos Santos' chilly climate makes it a great place to try the traditional **Mayan sauna** called a *chuj*. This is a small adobe building (traditionally with space for three small people) with wooden boards covering the entrance. A wood fire burns in a stone hearth inside, and water is sprinkled on the stones or heated in a ceramic jug to provide steam. Sometimes herbs are used to create aromatic vapors. A *chuj* can be claustrophobic, and the fire burning within the enclosed space is throat-tightening, so it's not an experience everyone will enjoy. Still, if you're into it, check out the large *chuj* at the Hotel Casa Familiar (p163).

LANGUAGE COURSES

Todos Santos' three language schools are controlled by villagers and all make major contributions to community projects – funding a library, medicines, school materials, scholarships for village kids to go to high school in Huehue, and so on. They are the following:

Academia Hispano Maya (opposite the Hotelito Todos Santos)

El Proyecto Lingüístico (elproyecto1@hotmail.com; on the main street)

Nuevo Amanecer (escuela_linguistica@yahoo.com; 150m down the main street opposite the church)

The standard weekly price for 25 hours' one-on-one Spanish tuition, with lodging and meals in a village home, is US$115. Included are usually guided walks, movies, seminars on local life and issues, and saunas. All three schools also offer classes in Mam and in Mayan weaving (weaving costs around US$1 an hour or US$35 for a week's course). Individual language classes are usually $4 an hour. The schools can put you in touch with volunteer work in reforestation and English teaching.

FESTIVALS & EVENTS
Todos Santos is famous for the annual **horse races** held on the morning of November 1 (El Día de Todos los Santos), which are the culmination of a week of festivities and an all-night male dancing and *aguardiente*-drinking spree on the eve of the races. Traditional foods are served throughout the day, and there are mask dances.

SLEEPING & EATING
Hotel Casa Familiar (dm/s/d US$2/3/6) About 50m up the hill from the plaza, Casa Familiar has bare wooden rooms adorned with past travelers' graffiti, and shared hot-water showers (US$0.90 for nonguests). The rooms are well cleaned, though, and have plenty of blankets, windows and fine views. There's a sauna too, and a restaurant where chicken dishes cost around US$2.60 and *mosh* (porridge), granola and banana costs US$1.60.

Hotelito Todos Santos (s/d US$4/7, with bathroom US$5/9) Along a side street that goes off to the left a few meters up the hill beside the plaza, this has Todos Santos' most comfortable rooms – bare but clean with tile floors and firm beds. Three of the four bathrooms open onto the street, separate from the main part of the hotel upstairs. The hotel

has a casual café, sinks for washing clothes, and some hot water.

Hotel Mam (s/d US$3/6) Next door to the Hotelito, this cheapie has five basic rooms (two opening onto the street, three upstairs). The mattresses are comfy and there are clothes-washing sinks, but water supplies are erratic.

Hospedaje El Viajero (s/d US$3/4) Turn right up the hill at the end of the street past Hotelito Todos Santos to reach this adequate option with bare, reasonably sized rooms along an upstairs terrace.

You can arrange **rooms with families** (rooms per person US$2-2.50, with 3 meals US$4.50) through the language schools irrespective of whether you're studying. You'll get your own bedroom, and share bathroom and meals with the family. A week's full board should cost US$25.

Comedor Martita (opposite Hotel Mam; lunch & dinner meals US$2.25) This simple family-run *comedor* serves the best food in town, prepared with fresh ingredients by friendly hosts. You walk through the kitchen to get to the eating area, which has a nice view over the town and valley. A typical US$2.25 meal might be boiled chicken, rice, vegetables, beans, a *refresco* and coffee.

Cafe Ixcanac (Restaurante Tzolkin; main st 200m east of church; pizzas US$4-4.50) The pizzas are not bad. Cheaper salads, sandwiches and breakfasts are served too.

Mountain Muse (mains US$3; ☾ 9am-11pm) Curries, stir-fry and chow mein are on the menu here. They might not be available on the day, but it's worth a try.

ENTERTAINMENT
All the language schools show movies on Guatemalan, Mayan and Latin American themes in the evening, with a small admission charge (usually US$0.65) for nonstudents. The English-language documentaries *Todos Santos* and *Todos Santos: The Survivors*, made in the 1980s by Olivia Carrescia, are particularly fascinating to see here on the spot. They deal with the traditional life of Todos Santos and with the devastation and terror of the civil war, when by some accounts 2000 people were killed in the area.

GETTING THERE & AWAY
Half a dozen buses leave for Huehuetenango (US$1.30, three hours) between 4:45am and

6:30am, then usually three others between noon and 1pm. Daily buses head northwest down to Concepción Huista, San Antonio Huista and Jacaltenango. Times are erratic, but the 5am departure is fairly reliable.

Soloma

This agricultural town, 70km north of Huehuetenango by paved road, is one of the biggest towns in the Cuchumatanes. The Maya here speak Q'anjob'al, but most of the *ladino* cowboys will greet you in English! The town's prosperity and its residents' language skills can be attributed to the migratory laborers who annually make the arduous trip to the United States, working as cowhands, auto detailers or landscapers. The populace is very gregarious here, and visitors will fast make friends. There's a Banrural on Soloma's plaza. For phone calls, use the international services at the Caucaso Hotel (see below). Market day is Sunday.

The **cemetery** south of town is worth a look, as most of the colorful tombs are bigger than the average Guatemalan home. You can make good day trips to nearby villages like **San Juan Ixcoy** (7km), where the women wear traditional white *huipiles* embroidered at the collar and hanging almost to their ankles.

Attesting to the town's prosperity is a fine choice of accommodations.

Caucaso Hotel (☎ 780-6178, 780-6113; 3a Calle 3A-37; s/d with bathroom US$7/11) Just beyond the church, this is a sweet budget hotel. Rooms with bath have TV, and there are also clean, simple singles with comfortable beds and shared hot-water bathroom for US$4. All rooms come with purified drinking water and complimentary coffee or tea. It has international phone and fax services here too, and there's a nice little patio out back.

Hotel San Antonio Also in this price range is this big architectural anomaly of blue glass at the entrance to town. Its rooms are clean, with hot-water bathroom, and cable TV.

Hospedaje Katy (s or d US$2) Perhaps the best cheapie is here, where basic rooms with shared bath are arranged around a concrete courtyard. Lots of local cowboys hang out here.

Restaurante Alma Latina (meals US$2) Head to this sprawling cafetería on the east side of the plaza for food.

See under Huehuetenango (p161) for details on buses to Soloma. Minivans serving San Juan Ixcoy and other nearby villages leave from beside the plaza.

San Mateo Ixtatán

The women of this small Chuj town, 42km north of Soloma, wear perhaps the most colorful *huipiles* in all Guatemala – gorgeous red-dominated affairs with large concentric star patterns. There's also a prettily painted **church** on the plaza, and two small archaeological sites, **Yolchunab** and **Lachepa**. San Mateo has a couple of simple *hospedajes*. Unpaved roads lead west to Nentón and east to Barrillas and Playa Grande. The section between Barrillas and Playa Grande is not always passable. For details on buses to San Mateo and Barrillas, see (p160).

Nentón, Los Huistas & Gracias a Dios

In a lower-lying, more lushly vegetated zone between the Cuchumatanes and the Mexican border, Nentón and the Los Huistas area to its south suffered grievously during the civil war, when murders and disappearances were rife. Reconstruction is happening, including a paved road to Nentón from the Interamericana, and the area has a few archaeological remains and a distinctive culture including the Popti' (Jakalteko) Mayan language. North of Nentón it's possible to cross into Mexico (near the Lagos de Montebello) at remote Gracias a Dios, but there are no border facilities there and you would have to head to Mexican immigration at Comitán or San Cristóbal de Las Casas to get your passport stamped. There are places to stay in Gracias a Díos if you get stuck. For details on buses to Nentón and Gracias a Dios, see p160.

Huehuetenango to Cobán

This spectacular and often rugged cross-country route on mostly unpaved roads is an exciting way of getting into the center of the country from the northwest highlands. It takes up to two days. You climb up out of Huehuetenango to **Aguacatán** (which has a bank and other services, including the Hospedaje Nuevo Amanecer, should you need them). Here you are treated to panoramic views of pine-studded slopes and the fertile valleys below. The trip continues via a snaking road down to Sacapulas (see p135) and climbs again to Uspantán (p136). Along the way you have the option of diverting to Nebaj (p136). Also see Itineraries (p14) for further information.

LA MESILLA

The Guatemalan and Mexican immigration posts at La Mesilla and Ciudad Cuauhtémoc are 4km apart, and you must take a collective taxi (US$0.50) between the two. The strip in La Mesilla leading to the border post has a variety of services, including a police station, post office and a bank. There are also moneychangers who will do the deal – at a good rate if you're changing dollars, a terrible one for pesos or quetzals.

With an early start from Huehuetenango (or from Comitán or San Cristóbal de Las Casas in Mexico) you should have no trouble getting through this border and well on into Mexico (or Guatemala) in one day. During daylight hours fairly frequent buses and combis run from Ciudad Cuauhtémoc to Comitán (US$3 to US$4, 1¼ hours) and San Cristóbal (US$7, 2½ hours). From La Mesilla buses leave for Huehuetenango (US$1, two hours) at least 20 times between 5:45am and 6pm. If you get marooned in La Mesilla, try **Hotel Mily's** (d US$15), which has rooms with fan, cable TV and hot-water bathroom; bargaining may be in order here. Further down the hill is the super-basic **Hotel El Pobre Simón** (rooms per person US$2).

166

The Pacific Slope

A hot, humid region of lush tropical verdure, Guatemala's Pacific Slope has rich volcanic soil that's good for growing coffee at higher elevations and palm oil seeds and sugarcane at lower ones. It's one of the country's most prosperous regions, with large plantations that generate a lot of jobs and commerce.

The Pacific shore is lined with endless spoiled beaches of dark volcanic sand, frighteningly polluted and marred by all manner of human abuse. The temperature and humidity along the shore are always uncomfortably high, day and night. The few small resorts attract mostly local – not foreign – beachgoers, though Monterrico, with its nature reserve and turtle preservation projects, buzzes with foreigners, who come from Antigua on weekends.

A fast highway, the Carretera al Pacífico (CA-2), roughly parallels the coast all the way from Ciudad Tecún Umán on the Mexican border to Ciudad Pedro de Alvarado on the El Salvador border. The 250km from Ciudad Tecún Umán to Guatemala City can be covered in five hours by bus – much less than the 345km of the Interamericana (CA-1) through the Highlands from La Mesilla. Most of the towns along the Carretera al Pacífico are muggy and somewhat chaotic and hold little interest. There are oases of interest and fun, though: the Xocomil water park and Xetulul theme park near Retalhuleu are Guatemala's biggest tourist attractions, while the fascinating archaeological relics at Abaj Takalik, Santa Lucía Cotzumalguapa and La Democracia tell the little-known story of Guatemala's non-Mayan archaeological heritage.

TOP FIVE

- Hanging out at **Monterrico** (p177), Guatemala's best beach scene, enjoying warm tropical waters, brilliant seafood and luscious fruit drinks

- Strolling the parklike **Parque Arqueológico Abaj Takalik** (p171), a bridge in history between the Olmec and the Maya

- Paddling along the mangrove-lined canal and lagoons of the **Reserva Natural Monterrico** (p177), looking for wildlife

- Exploring the impressive sculptural relics of the non-Mayan Pipil culture at **Santa Lucía Cotzumalguapa** (p174)

- Enjoying fun days out at **Parque Acuático Xocomil** (p171) and **Parque de Diversiones Xetulul** (p171) near Retalhuleu

Abaj Takalik ★
★ Xocomil & Xetulul
Santa Lucía ★ Cotzumalguapa
Monterrico ★ ★
Reserva Natural Monterrico

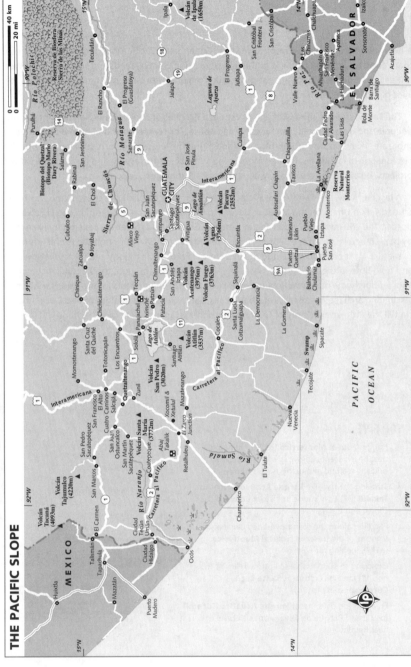

THE PACIFIC SLOPE

Mayan boys, **Todos Santos Cuchumatán** (p161)

JEFFREY N BECOM

Volcán San Pedro (p105), Lago de Atitlán

ANDREW MARSHALL & LEANNE WALKER

PASCALE BEROUJON

Buses (p289) go almost everywhere in Guatemala

Volcanoes (p105) surrounding Lago de Atitlán

AARON MCOY

Black-sand beach, **Monterrico** (p177)

Gallo beer (p50)

Endangered **sea turtle** (p178)

CIUDAD TECÚN UMÁN

This is the preferable and busier of the two Pacific Slope border crossings, having better transport connections with other places in Guatemala. A bridge links Ciudad Tecún Umán with Ciudad Hidalgo (Mexico). The border is open 24 hours daily, and several basic hotels and restaurants are available, but you should aim to be clear of the border well before dark. Banks here change US dollars and traveler's checks.

From Ciudad Tecún Umán frequent buses depart until about 6pm along the Carretera al Pacífico to Coatepeque, Retalhuleu, Mazatenango, Escuintla and Guatemala City. There are direct buses to Quetzaltenango (US$2, 3½ hours) up until about 2pm. If you don't find a bus to your destination, take one to Coatepeque or, better, Retalhuleu, and change buses there. On the Mexican side, buses run from Ciudad Hidalgo to the city of Tapachula (US$1.25, 45 minutes) every 20 minutes from 7am to 7:30pm.

EL CARMEN

A bridge across the Río Suchiate connects El Carmen with Talismán (Mexico). The border is open 24 hours daily. It's generally easier and more convenient to cross at Tecún Umán. There are few services at El Carmen, and those are very basic. Most buses between here and the rest of Guatemala go via Ciudad Tecún Umán, 39km south, and then along the Carretera al Pacífico through Coatepeque, Retalhuleu and Escuintla. On the way to Ciudad Tecún Umán, most stop at Malacatán on the road to San Marcos and Quetzaltenango, so you could try looking for a bus to Quetzaltenango there, but it's more dependable to change at Coatepeque (US$1.65, two hours from El Carmen) or Retalhuleu.

On the Mexican side, minibuses run frequently between Talismán and Tapachula (US$0.80, 30 minutes) until about 10pm.

COATEPEQUE

Set on a hill and surrounded by lush coffee plantations, Coatepeque is a brash, fairly ugly and chaotic commercial center, noisy and humid at all times. There is no reason to linger here.

Of the town's hotels, 35-room **Hotel Villa Real** (☎ 775-1308; 6a Calle 6-57, Zona 1; s/d US$15/20;

P) is among the best. On the highway, there's the 15-room **Hotel Virginia** (☎ 775-1801; Carretera al Pacífico Km 223; s/d US$40/50; P ⬛).

RETALHULEU

pop 40,000 / elevation 240m

The Pacific Slope is a rich agricultural region, and Retalhuleu is its clean, attractive capital – and proud of it. Most Guatemalans refer to Retalhuleu simply as Reu (*rey-oo*). As you speed downhill from Xela toward Reu, the pine trees and corn make way for coffee and bananas, eventually changing to coconuts, heliconia and other tropical flora partial to torrid conditions.

If Coatepeque is where the coffee traders conduct business, Retalhuleu is where they come to relax, splashing in hotel pools and sipping umbrella drinks in the bars. The rest of the citizens get their kicks strolling through the plaza with its whitewashed colonial church and wedding-cake government buildings shaded by royal palms. There's little to see in Retalhuleu proper, but there are some appealing attractions for adults and children not far away (p171).

Tourists are something of a curiosity in Reu and are treated well. The heat is fairly stifling, and if you can splurge for digs with a pool, you'll be happy for it; at the very least, make sure your room has a fan.

Orientation & Information

The town center is 4km southwest of the Carretera al Pacífico, along Calzada Las Palmas, a grand boulevard lined with towering palms. The bus terminal is on 10a Calle between 7a and 8a Avs, northeast of the plaza. To find the plaza, look for the twin church towers and walk toward them.

There is no official tourist office, but people in the Municipalidad (Town Hall), on 6a Av facing the east side of the church, will do their best to help.

Banco Industrial (cnr 6a Calle & 5a Av; ☷ 9am-7pm Mon-Fri, 10am-2pm Sat) and **Banco Occidente** (cnr 6a Calle & 6a Av) change US-dollar cash and traveler's checks and give cash advances on Visa cards. Banco Industrial has a Visa ATM. **Banco Agromercantil** (5a Av), facing the plaza, changes US-dollar cash and traveler's checks and has a MasterCard ATM.

Internet (cnr 5a Calle & 6a Av) charges US$1.30 for an hour online.

THE PACIFIC SLOPE

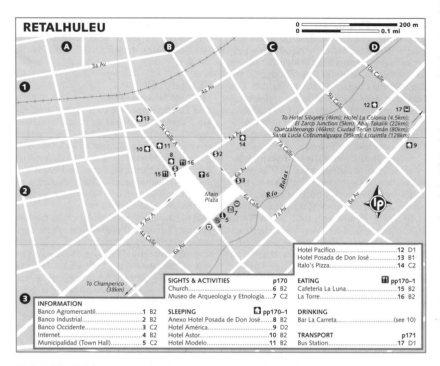

RETALHULEU

To Hotel Siboney (4km); Hotel La Colonia (4.5km);
El Zarco Junction (5km); Abaj Takalik (22km);
Quetzaltenango (46km); Ciudad Tecún Umán (80km);
Santa Lucía Cotzumalguapa (95km); Escuintla (128km);

To Champerico
(38km)

INFORMATION	
Banco Agromercantil	1 B2
Banco Industrial	2 B2
Banco Occidente	3 C2
Internet	4 B2
Municipalidad (Town Hall)	5 C2

SIGHTS & ACTIVITIES	p170
Church	6 B2
Museo de Arqueología y Etnología	7 C2

SLEEPING	pp170–1
Anexo Hotel Posada de Don José	8 B2
Hotel América	9 D2
Hotel Astor	10 B2
Hotel Modelo	11 B2

Hotel Pacífico	12 D1
Hotel Posada de Don José	13 B1
Italo's Pizza	14 C2

EATING	pp170–1
Cafetería La Luna	15 B2
La Torre	16 B2

DRINKING	
Bar La Carreta	(see 10)

TRANSPORT	p171
Bus Station	17 D1

Sights & Activities

The **Museo de Arqueología y Etnología** (6a Av 5-68; admission US$1.30; 8am-5:30pm Tue-Sat, 9am-noon Sun) is a small museum of archaeological relics. Upstairs are historical photos and a mural showing locations of 33 archaeological sites in Retalhuleu department.

You can **swim** at the Siboney and La Colonia hotels (p171) even if you're not staying there. The cost is US$1.30 at the Siboney and US$2 at La Colonia, where there's also a poolside bar.

Sleeping & Eating

Hotel Posada de Don José (771-0963; donjose@infovia.com.gt; 5a Calle 3-67, Zona 1; s/d US$35/42;) Two blocks northwest of the plaza, this is the nicest place in town. The 25 rooms, nearly all with air-con, are on two levels surrounding the large swimming pool, and the town's best restaurant (chicken, fish and steaks for US$5.50 to US$8.50) is set beneath an arcade beside the pool. Rooms have TV, telephone and a bathroom. The hotel has a less attractive annex a block along the street.

Hotel Astor (771-0475; hotelastor@terra.com.gt; 5a Calle 4-60, Zona 1; s/d/tr US$20/35/41;) Close to the plaza, this hotel, remodeled a few years ago, has a charming courtyard with a smaller pool and 26 very clean rooms, each with air-con, ceiling fan, phone, TV and hot-water bathroom. The upstairs rooms are new, but those downstairs around the courtyard have more atmosphere. Cocktails can be had in the hotel's air-conditioned **Bar La Carreta**.

Hotel América (771-1154; 8a Av 9-32, Zona 1; s/d US$11/15) A good-value cheaper place just down the street from the bus terminal, the América has spotless rooms with a bathroom, fan and TV.

Hotel Modelo (771-0256; 5a Calle 4-53, Zona 1; s & d US$16) The seven-room Modelo is friendly but much more basic and less attractive than the Astor across the street. Rooms have fan and bathroom but no hot water.

Hotel Pacífico (7a Av 9-29, Zona 1; s/d US$3/6) For a real cheapie, you'll have to endure the dank cells with lumpy beds at this somewhat creepy place near the bus station. The one room with a decrepit bathroom is US$7 for one or two people.

Out on the Carretera al Pacífico are several other hotels. These tend to be 'tropical motels' by design, with bungalows, swimming pools and restaurants. They are convenient if you have a car or can get a bus to drop you on the spot.

Hotel Siboney (☎ 771-0149; fax 771-0711; Cuatro Caminos, San Sebastián; s/d US$29/38; ⓟ ⓧ ⓡ) This 25-room hotel is 4km northeast of town where Calzada Las Palmas meets the Carretera al Pacífico.

Hotel La Colonia (☎ 771-6482; Carretera al Pacífico Km 178; s/d US$40/50; ⓟ ⓧ ⓡ) A few hundred meters east of the Siboney, La Colonia has a fairly luxurious layout – bungalows around the swimming pool – with 44 rooms.

Several *comedors* around the center provide economical meals.

Cafetería La Luna (5a Av 4-97; lunch mains including drink US$2.90) Opposite the west corner of the plaza, this is a town favorite.

Italo's Pizza (5a Av; small pizzas US$3.50-4) Half a block from the plaza, Italo's does reasonable pies.

La Torre (5a Av facing the plaza) You can hunt and gather for food supplies in this large supermarket; it's also air-conditioned, so browse away.

Getting There & Away
Most buses traveling along the Carretera al Pacífico detour into Reu. Departures include the following:

Champerico (US$0.40, 1hr, 38km, every few min 6am-7pm)
Ciudad Tecún Umán (US$1.65, 1½hr, 78km, every 20min 5am-10pm)
Guatemala City (US$4, 3hr, 196km, every 15min 2am-8:30pm)
Quetzaltenango (US$1, 1hr, 46km, every 30min 4am-6pm)
Santa Lucía Cotzumalguapa (US$1.70, 2hr, 97km)
Some Escuintla- or Guatemala City–bound buses may drop you at Santa Lucía; otherwise get a bus to Mazatenango (Mazate) and change there.

AROUND RETALHULEU
Parque Acuático Xocomil & Parque de Diversiones Xetulul
If you have children along, or simply if the heat is getting to you, head out to the **Parque Acuático Xocomil** (☎ 772-5763; Carretera CITO Km 180.5; adult/child US$9.75/6.50; ⏰ 9am-4pm Thu-Sun), a gigantic water park in the Disneyland

vein, but with a distinct Guatemalan theme. Among the 10 water slides, two swimming pools and two wave pools are re-creations of Mayan monuments from Tikal, Copán and Quiriguá. Visitors can bob along a river through canyons flanked with ancient temples and Mayan masks spewing water from the nose and mouth. Three real volcanoes – Santiaguito, Zunil and Santa María – can be seen from the grounds. Xocomil is very well executed and maintained, and kids love it. Xocomil is at San Martín Zapotitlán on the Quetzaltenango road, about 12km north of Reu.

Next door to Xocomil on the same road is the even more impressive **Parque de Diversiones Xetulul** (☎ 449-5480; adult/child US$26/13; ⏰ 10am-6pm Thu-Sun), a theme park with representations of a Tikal pyramid, historical Guatemalan buildings and famous buildings from many European cities, plus restaurants and many first-class rides. You need an extra US$6.50 ticket for the rides.

These two attractions are both run by Irtra, the Instituto de Recreación de los Trabajadores de la Empresa Privada de Guatemala (Guatemalan Private Enterprise Workers' Recreation Institute), which administers several fun sites around the country for workers and their families. Between them, Xocomil and Xetulul comprise the most popular tourist attraction in Guatemala, with over a million visitors a year.

Any bus heading from Retalhuleu toward Quetzaltenango will drop you at Xocomil or Xetulul.

Parque Arqueológico Abaj Takalik
About 30km west of Retalhuleu is the **Parque Arqueológico Abaj Takalik** (admission US$3.25; ⏰ 7am-5pm), a fascinating archaeological site set on land now occupied by coffee, rubber and sugarcane plantations. Abaj Takalik was an important trading center in the late Preclassic era, before AD 250, and forms a historical link between Mesoamerica's first civilization, the Olmecs, and the Maya. The Olmecs flourished from about 1200 to 600 BC on Mexico's southern Gulf coast, but their influence extended far and wide, and numerous Olmec-style sculptures have been found at Abaj Takalik.

The entire 6.5 sq km site spreads over nine natural terraces, which were adapted by its ancient inhabitants. Archaeological work is continuing outside the kernel of the site, which is the Grupo Central on terrace No 2, where the most important ceremonial and civic buildings were located. The largest and tallest building is Estructura 5, a pyramid 16m high and 115m square on terrace No 3, above No 2. This may have formed one side of a ball court. Estructura 7, east of Estructura 5, is thought to have been an observatory. What's most impressive as you move around the parklike grounds, with their temple mounds, ball courts and flights of steps paved with rounded river stones, is the quantity of stone sculpture dotted about, including numerous representations of animals and aquatic creatures (some in a curious pot-bellied style known as *barrigón*), miniature versions of the characteristic Olmec colossal heads, and early Mayan-style monuments depicting finely adorned personages carrying out religious ceremonies.

Abaj Takalik, which had strong connections with the city of Kaminaljuyú (in present-day Guatemala City), was sacked about AD 300 and its great monuments, especially those in Mayan style, were decapitated. Some monuments were rebuilt after AD 600 and the site retained a ceremonial and religious importance for the Maya, which it maintains to this day. Maya from the Guatemalan highlands regularly come here to perform ceremonies.

To reach Abaj Takalik by public transport, catch a bus from Retalhuleu to El Asintal (US$0.15, 30 minutes), which is 12km northwest of Reu and 5km north of the Carretera al Pacífico (Highway CA-2). The buses leave from a bus station on 5a Av A, 800m southwest of Reu plaza, about every half-hour, 6am to 6pm. Pickups at El Asintal provide transport on to Abaj Takalik, 4km further by paved road. You'll be shown round by a volunteer guide, whom you will probably want to tip. You can also visit Abaj Takalik on tours from Quetzaltenango (p145).

CHAMPERICO

Built as a shipping point for coffee during the boom of the late 19th century, Champerico, 38km southwest of Retalhuleu, is a tawdry, sweltering, dilapidated place that sees few tourists. Nevertheless it's one of the easiest ocean beaches to reach on a day trip from Quetzaltenango, and beach-starved students still try their luck here. Beware of strong waves and an undertow if you go in the ocean, and stay in the main, central part of the beach: if you stray too far in either direction you put yourself at risk from impoverished, potentially desperate shack dwellers who live towards the ends of the beach. Tourists have been victims of violent armed robberies here. Most beachgoers come only to spend the day, but there are several cheap hotels and restaurants. **Hotel Neptuno** (☎ 773-7206; s/d US$4/7), on the beachfront, is the best bet. The last bus back to Retalhuleu leaves at about 6:30pm.

MAZATENANGO

pop 38,000 / elevation 370m

Mazatenango, 23km east of Retalhuleu, is the capital of the department of Suchitepéquez. It's a center for the farmers, traders and shippers of the Pacific Slope's agricultural produce. There are a few serviceable hotels if you need to stop in an emergency. Otherwise just keep on keeping on.

SANTA LUCÍA COTZUMALGUAPA

pop 24,000 / elevation 356m

Another 71km eastward from Mazatenango is Santa Lucía Cotzumalguapa, an important stop for anyone interested in archaeology. In the fields and *fincas* (plantations) near the town stand great stone heads carved with grotesque faces and fine relief scenes, the product of the enigmatic Pipil culture that flourished here from about AD 500 to 700. In your explorations you may get to see a Guatemalan sugarcane *finca* in full operation.

The town, though benign enough, is unexciting. The local people around here are descended from the Pipil, an ancient culture that had linguistic and cultural links with the Nahuatl-speaking peoples of central Mexico. In Early Classic times, the Pipil who lived here grew cacao, the money of the age. They were obsessed with the ball game and with the rites and mysteries of death. Pipil art, unlike the flowery, almost romantic style of the Maya, is cold, grotesque and severe, but still very finely done. When these 'Mexicans' settled in this pocket of Guatemala, and where they came from, is not known, though connections with Mexico's Gulf Coast area, whose culture was also obsessed with the ball game, have been suggested.

Orientation & Information

Santa Lucía is now bypassed to the south by Highway CA-2, but the original highway running through the south of town is still known as the Carretera al Pacífico, and the best places to stay are on and just off it. The main plaza is 400m north from this, along 3a or 4a Av.

There are three main sites to visit, all outside town: El Baúl hilltop site, about 4.5km north; the museum at Finca El Baúl, 2.75km further north; and the Museo Cultura Cotzumalguapa, off the highway 2km northeast of town.

Taxi drivers in Santa Lucía's main square will take you round all three sites for about US$12. In this hot and muggy climate, riding at least part of the way is the least you can do to help yourself.

Bancafé (cnr 4a Av & 4a Calle), a block north of the plaza, changes US-dollar cash and traveler's checks and has a Visa ATM.

El Baúl Hilltop Site

This site has the additional fascination of being an active place of pagan worship for local people. Mayan people regularly, and especially on weekends, make offerings, light fires and candles and sacrifice chickens here. They will not mind if you visit as well, and may be happy to pose with the idols for photographs in exchange for a small contribution.

Of the two stones here, the great, grotesque, half-buried head is the most striking, with its elaborate headdress, beaklike nose and 'blind' eyes with big bags underneath. The head is stained with wax from candles, splashes of liquor and other drinks, and with the smoke and ashes of incense fires, all part of worship. People have been coming here to pay homage for more than 1400 years.

The other stone is a relief carving of a figure with an elaborate headdress, possibly a fire god, surrounded by circular motifs that may be date glyphs.

To get there you leave town northward on the road passing El Calvario church. From the intersection just past the church, go 2.7km to a fork in the road just beyond

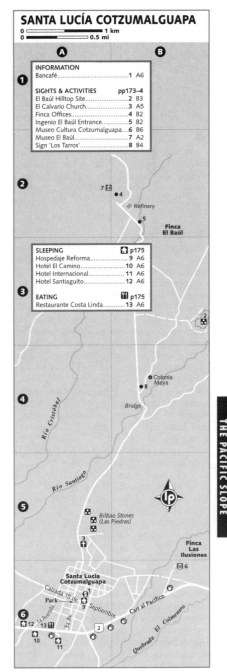

SANTA LUCÍA COTZUMALGUAPA

INFORMATION	
Bancafé.............................1 A6	

SIGHTS & ACTIVITIES	pp173–4
El Baúl Hilltop Site.....................2 B3	
El Calvario Church.....................3 A5	
Finca Offices............................4 B2	
Ingenio El Baúl Entrance...............5 B2	
Museo Cultura Cotzumalguapa....6 B6	
Museo El Baúl...........................7 A2	
Sign 'Los Tarros'........................8 B4	

SLEEPING	p175
Hospedaje Reforma...................9 A6	
Hotel El Camino.......................10 A6	
Hotel Internacional...................11 A6	
Hotel Santiaguito.....................12 A6	

EATING	p175
Restaurante Costa Linda............13 A6	

THE PACIFIC SLOPE

a bridge; the fork is marked by a sign saying 'Los Tarros'. Buses heading out to Finca El Baúl, the plantation headquarters, pass this sign. Take the right-hand fork, passing a settlement called Colonia Maya on your right. After you have gone 1.5km from the Los Tarros sign, a dirt track crosses the road: turn right here, between two concrete posts. Ahead now is a low mound topped by three large trees: this is the hilltop site. After about 250m fork right between two more identical concrete posts, and follow this track round in front of the mound to its end after some 150m, and take the path up on to the mound, which is actually a great ruined temple platform that has not been restored.

Museo El Baúl

About 2.75km on foot, or 5km by vehicle, from the hilltop site is **Museo El Baúl** (admission free; 8am-4pm Mon-Fri, 8am-noon Sat). It comprises a very fine open-air collection of Pipil stone sculpture collected from around Finca El Baúl's sugarcane fields. A large stone jaguar faces you at the entrance. Other figures include four humans or monkeys with arms folded across their chests, a grinning, blank-eyed head reminiscent of the one at the hilltop site, carvings of skulls, and at the back a stela showing a personage wearing an animal headdress standing over a similarly attired figure on the ground, seemingly winner and loser of a ball game. Unfortunately, nothing is labeled.

To get there, if driving, return to the fork with the Los Tarros sign. Take the other fork this time (what would be the left fork as you come from Santa Lucía), and follow the paved road 3km to the headquarters of the Finca El Baúl sugarcane plantation. Buses trundle along this road every few hours, shuttling workers between the refinery and the town center. (If you're on foot, you can walk from the hilltop site back to the crossroads with the paved road. Cross the road and continue along the dirt track. This will eventually bring you to the asphalt road that leads to the *finca* headquarters. When you reach the road, turn right.)

Approaching the *finca* headquarters (6km from Santa Lucía's main square), you cross a bridge at a curve. Continue uphill and you will see the entrance on the left, marked by a guard post and a sign 'Ingenio El Baúl Bienvenidos'. Tell the guards that you would like to visit the *museo,* and you should be admitted. Pass the sugar refinery buildings to arrive at the museum on the right.

Museo Cultura Cotzumalguapa

At the headquarters of another sugarcane plantation, Finca Las Ilusiones, is **Museo Cultura Cotzumalguapa** (admission US$1.30; 8am-4pm Mon-Fri, 8am-noon Sat). The collection here, of sculptures found around Las Ilusiones' lands, has some explanatory material and you'll probably be shown around by the caretaker. It includes a reconstruction of a sacrificial altar with the original stones, and photos of some fine stelae that were removed to the Dahlem Museum in Berlin in 1880. The most impressive exhibit, Monumento 21, is actually a glass-fiber copy of a stone that still stands in the fields of Finca Bilbao (part of Las Ilusiones' plantations), depicting what may be a shaman holding a sort of puppet on the left, a ball game player in the middle with a knife in one hand, and a king or priest on the right holding what may be a heart. Another copy of this stone, along with one of Monumento 19, lie on the ground across the street from the museum. Along the road just before the bridge to the *finca* house are copies of some of the sculptures from the El Baúl museum.

About 1.5km east of the town center on the Carretera al Pacífico, shortly before an Esso station on the left (not to be confused with other Esso stations on the right), take a side track 400m to the left (north) to find the museum.

Bilbao Stones

Monumento 21, whose copy is in the Museo Cultura Cotzumalguapa, still stands with three other fine sculpted stones dotted about the Finca Bilbao cane fields to the northeast of El Calvario church, on the north edge of Santa Lucía town. In the past, tourists have regularly visited these stones, often guided through the tall cane to *las piedras* by local boys. Unfortunately locals say it is now dangerous for tourists to go into these fields because of recent assaults. So unless you receive convincing information to the contrary, we don't recommend it.

Sleeping & Eating

Hotel Santiaguito (☎ 882-5435/6/7; fax 882-2287; Carretera al Pacífico Km 90.4; s/d/tr US$33/46/53; P ☒ ☒) On the highway on the west edge of town, the Santiaguito is fairly lavish for Guatemala's Pacific Slope, with spacious tree-shaded grounds and a nice swimming pool. The pool is open to non-guests for US$2.60. The large rooms have TV, phone, air-con and a bathroom. In the spacious restaurant cooled by ceiling fans, you can order a cheeseburger or salad for US$2.50, breakfasts for US$3 to US$4.50, or a fish, seafood or meat main dish for US$6 to US$9.

Hotel El Camino (☎ 882-5316; fax 882-5318; Carretera al Pacífico Km 90.5; s/d with fan US$14/23, with air-con US$16/26; P ☒) About 200m east along the highway from the Santiaguito, Hotel El Camino's air-con rooms are large and bright, with tiled floors, balconies, cable TV and large bathrooms with great showers – it's a good value. The fan rooms, downstairs, are less attractive.

Hotel Internacional (☎ 882-5504; s/d US$10/16; P) Down a short lane (signposted) a little east of Hotel El Camino is the Internacional. It has clean, good-sized rooms, with a fan, cold showers and a TV, around a courtyard providing ample parking. Rooms upstairs are airier and brighter.

Hospedaje Reforma (4a Av 4-71; s/d US$4/7) A block off the main plaza, this last-resort cheapie has dark, cell-like rooms (some with hay beds!). The rooms around the courtyard are better, but are only rented by the hour.

Restaurante Costa Linda, on the highway about 150m east of Hotel el Camino, is a friendly and clean place serving tasty meat and seafood at reasonable prices.

Getting There & Away

As the CA-2 now bypasses Santa Lucía, a lot of buses along it do not come into town. Coming to Santa Lucía from the east, you will almost certainly need to change buses at Escuintla (US$0.50, 30 minutes). From the west you will probably have to change at Mazatenango (US$1.30, 1¼ hours). At Cocales, 23km west of Santa Lucía, a road down from Lago de Atitlán meets Highway CA-2, providing a route to or from the highlands. Eight buses daily run from Cocales to Panajachel (US$1, 2½ hours, 70km), between about 6am and 2pm.

LA DEMOCRACIA

pop 4200 / elevation 165m

La Democracia, a nondescript Pacific Slope town 10km south of Siquinalá, is hot day and night, rainy season and dry season. During the late Preclassic period (300 BC to AD 250), this area, like Abaj Takalik to the northwest, was home to a culture showing influence from southern Mexico.

Sights

Facing the plaza, along with the church and the modest Palacio Municipal, is the small, modern **Museo Regional de Arqueología** (admission US$1.30; ☺ 8am-noon & 2-6pm), which houses some fascinating archaeological finds. The star of the show is an exquisite jade mask. Smaller figures, yokes used in the ball game, relief carvings and other objects make up the rest of this small but important collection.

At the archaeological site called Monte Alto, on the outskirts of La Democracia, huge basalt heads and pot-bellied sculptures have been discovered. These heads resemble crude versions of the colossal heads that were carved by the Olmecs on Mexico's southern gulf coast some centuries previously.

Today, these great **Olmecoid heads** are arranged around La Democracia's main plaza. As you come into town from the highway, follow signs to the Museo.

Sleeping & Eating

La Democracia has no places to stay and few places to eat. The eateries are very basic and ill-supplied; it's best to bring your own food and buy drinks at one of the shops facing the plaza. Café Maritza, right next to the museum, is a picture-perfect hot-tropics hangout with a rockola (jukebox) blasting music, and a crew of semisomnolent locals doing their thing and sweltering.

Getting There & Away

The Chatía Gomerana company runs buses every half-hour, 6am to 4:30pm, from Guatemala City's Terminal de Autobuses to La Democracia (US$1.50, two hours) via Escuintla. From Santa Lucía Cotzumalguapa, catch a bus 8km east to Siquinalá (8km) and change there.

ESCUINTLA

Surrounded by rich green foliage, Escuintla should be a tropical idyll where people swing languidly in hammocks and concoct pungent meals of readily available exotic fruits and vegetables. In fact, it's a hot, shabby commercial and industrial city that's integral to the Pacific Slope's economy but not at all important to travelers, except for making bus connections. **Bancafé** (cnr 4a Av & 12a Calle; 9am-6pm Mon-Fri, 9am-1pm Sat), two blocks north of the bus station, changes US-dollar cash and traveler's checks and has a Visa ATM. Escuintla has some marginal hotels and restaurants. If stranded, try the **Hotel Costa Sur** (☎ 888-1819; 12a Calle 4-13; s/d US$11/16), a couple of doors from Bancafé, which has well used but tolerable rooms with TV and fan but no hot water.

The main bus station is in the southern part of town, just off 4a Av, its entrance marked by a Scott 77 fuel station. Buses go to Antigua (US$0.65, one hour) about every half-hour, 5:30am to 4:30pm. Buses for Guatemala City (US$1.25, 1½ hours) go about every 20 minutes from the street outside, 5am to 6pm. Buses to Puerto San José (US$0.80, 45 minutes), some continuing to Iztapa, have similar frequency. Buses coming along the Carretera al Pacífico may drop you in the north of town, necessitating a sweaty walk through the hectic town center if you want to get to the main station.

AUTOSAFARI CHAPÍN

About 25km southeast of Escuintla, **Autosafari Chapín** (☎ 363-1105; Carretera al Pacífico Km 87.5) is a drive-through safari park and animal conservation project earning high marks for its sensitivity and success breeding animals in captivity. Species native to Guatemala here include white-tailed deer, tapir and macaws. Around the grounds also roam non-native species such as lions, rhinos and leopards. There is a restaurant and pool, and it makes a good day if you're traveling with kids. **Delta y Tropical** (cnr 1a Calle & 2a Av, Zona 4, Guatemala City) runs buses here from the capital (US$1.30, 1½ hours), every 30 minutes, 6am to 6:30pm, via Escuintla.

PUERTO SAN JOSÉ & LIKÍN

Guatemala's most important seaside resort leaves a lot to be desired. But if you're eager to get into the Pacific surf, head 50km south from Escuintla to Puerto San José and neighboring settlements.

Puerto San José (population 14,000) was Guatemala's most important Pacific port in the latter half of the 19th century and well into the 20th. Now superseded by the more modern Puerto Quetzal to the east, Puerto San José languishes and slumbers, except at weekends and holidays when thousands of Guatemalans pour into town. The beach, inconveniently located across the Canal de Chiquimulilla, is reached by boat.

It's smarter to head west along the coast 5km (by taxi or car) to **Balneario Chulamar**, which has a nicer beach and also a suitable hotel or two.

About 5km east of Puerto San José, just past Puerto Quetzal, is **Balneario Likín**, Guatemala's only upmarket Pacific resort. Likín is much beloved by well-to-do families from Guatemala City who have seaside houses on the tidy streets and canals of this planned development.

IZTAPA

About 12km east of Puerto San José is Iztapa, Guatemala's first Pacific port, used by none other than Pedro de Alvarado in the 16th century. When Puerto San José was built in 1853, Iztapa's reign as the port of the capital city came to an end, and it relaxed into a tropical torpor from which it has yet to emerge.

Iztapa has gained renown as one of the world's premier **deep-sea fishing** spots. World records have been set here, and enthusiasts can fish for marlin, sharks and yellowfin tuna, among others. November through June is typically the best time to angle for sailfish. **B&B Worldwide Fishing Adventures** (☎ 541-296-3962; www.wheretofish.com; 14161/2 E 10th Pl, Dalles, OR 97058), **Artmarina** (☎ 305-663-3553; www.artmarina.com; 1390 South Dixie Hwy, Ste 2221, Miami, FL 33146) and **Fishing International** (☎ 707-542-4242; www.fishinginternati onal.com; 184 S Fourth St, Santa Rosa, CA 95404) run all-inclusive deep-sea fishing tours to Iztapa from the USA. It is also possible to contract local boat owners for fishing trips, though equipment and comfort may be nonexistent and catch-and-release could prove a foreign concept. The boat owners hang out at the edge of the Río María Linda – bargain hard.

Yellowfin tuna will likely be out of reach for the local boats, as these fish inhabit the waters some 17km from Iztapa.

There's not much to do in Iztapa. The best thing to do is get a boat across the river to the sandbar fronting the ocean, where the waves pound and a line of palm-thatch restaurants offer food and beer.

Sleeping

Sol y Playa Tropical (☎ 881-4365/6; 1a Calle 5-48; s/d/tr US$12/22/28; ☒) Should you want to stay, the Tropical has tolerable rooms with fan and a bathroom on two floors around a swimming pool (which needed a clean when we were there).

Rancho Maracaibo (s & d US$2.50), on the beach, has very basic *cabañas*, with a bed and a reed mat on the floor.

Getting There & Away

You can catch a bus from the Zona 4 Terminal de Autobuses in Guatemala City all the way to Iztapa (US$2, three hours). They leave every half-hour, 5am to 6pm, traveling via Escuintla and Puerto San José. The last bus heading back from Iztapa goes around 5pm.

You can reach Monterrico by paved road from Iztapa: follow the street 1km east from Club Cervecero bar, where the buses terminate, and get a boat across the river to Pueblo Viejo (passenger *lanchas* per person US$0.30, vehicle ferry per vehicle US$2.20). From the far side buses leave for the pretty ride to Monterrico (US$0.80, one hour) at 8am, 11:30am, 2pm, 4pm and 6pm.

MONTERRICO

The coastal area around Monterrico is a totally different Guatemala. Life here is steeped with a sultry, tropical flavor – it's a place where hanging out in a hammock is both a major endeavor and goal. Among the main cash crops here is *pachete* (loofah), which get as big as a man's leg. In season, you see them everywhere growing on trellises and drying in the sun. The architecture, too, is different, with rustic wooden slat-and-thatched roofed houses instead of the dull cinderblock, corrugated-tin models common elsewhere. When the sky is clear, keep your eyes peeled for the awesome volcanoes that shimmer in the hinterland. This part of Guatemala is also treated to sensational lightning storms from around November to April.

Monterrico is a coastal village with a few small, inexpensive hotels right on the beach, a large wildlife reserve and two centers for the hatching and release of sea turtles and caymans. The beach here is dramatic, with powerful surf crashing onto black volcanic sand at odd angles. The odd-angled wave-print signals that there are rip tides; deaths have occurred at this beach, so swim with care. Strong swimmers, however, can probably handle and enjoy the waves. Behind the town is a large network of mangrove swamps and canals, part of the 190km Canal de Chiquimulilla.

Monterrico is probably the best spot for a weekend break at the beach if you're staying in Antigua or Guatemala City. It's fast becoming popular with foreigners. On weekdays it's relatively quiet, but on weekends and holidays it teems with Guatemalan families, and everything seems a bit harried. Monterrico has a real problem with trash, something that local businesses are trying to sort out.

Orientation & Information

From where you alight from the La Avellana boat, it's about 1km to the beach and the hotels. You pass through the village en route. From the *embarcadero* (jetty) walk straight ahead and then turn left. Pickups (US$0.25) meet scheduled boats or *lanchas*.

If you come by bus from Pueblo Viejo, from the stop walk about 300m toward the beach on Calle Principal. At the beach, head left to reach the cluster of hotels.

There is no bank, but there is a **post office** (Calle Principal) on the one real road in Monterrico. **Internet access** (☒ 8am-9pm; US$1.55/hr) is available on Calle Principal between Proyecto Lingüistico and the beach. Johnny's (p179) also has Internet access; ask at the restaurant.

Reserva Natural Monterrico

Sometimes called Biotopo Monterrico-Hawaii, the **Reserva Natural Monterrico**, administered by Cecon (Centro de Estudios Conservacionistas de la Universidad de San Carlos) is Monterrico's biggest attraction. This 20km-long nature reserve of coast and coastal mangrove swamps is bursting with avian and aquatic life. Its most famous denizens are the endangered leatherback and ridley turtles, which lay their eggs on the beach in many places along the coast. The mangrove swamps are a network of 25 lagoons, all connected by mangrove canals.

Boat tours of the reserve, passing through the mangrove swamps and visiting several lagoons, take around 1½ to two hours and cost US$5.25 per passenger. It's best to go just on sunrise, when you can see the most wildlife. If you have binoculars, bring them for bird-watching. January and February are the best months for bird-watching. To arrange a boat tour of the canal, stop by the Tortugario Monterrico (below). Local villagers, some tour companies (p179) and the Proyecto Lingüístico language school (p179) also do boat tours, but the guides who work at the Tortugario are particularly concerned with wildlife. Some travelers have griped about the use of motorboats (as opposed to the paddled varieties), because the sound of the motor scares off the wildlife. If you're under no time pressure, ask about arranging a paddled tour of the canal.

Tortugario Monterrico

The Cecon-run **Tortugario Monterrico** (admission US$1.20; ☻ 8am-noon & 2-5pm) is just a short walk east down the beach from the end of

Calle Principal and then a block inland. Several endangered species of animals are raised here, including leatherback, olive ridley and green sea turtles, caymans and iguanas. There's an interesting interpretative trail and a little museum with pickled displays in bottles. The staff offer lagoon trips (left) and will accept volunteers.

Parque Hawaii

This nature reserve operated by the **Arcas** (Asociación de Rescate y Conservación de Vida Silvestre, Wildlife Rescue & Conservation Association; www.arcasguatemala.com) comprises a sea-turtle hatchery with some caymans 8km east along the beach from Monterrico. It is separate from and rivals Cecon's work in the same field. Volunteers are welcome all year round, but the real sea turtle–nesting season is from June to November, with August and September being the peak months. Volunteers are charged US$50 a week for a room, with meals extra and homestay options with local families. A bus (US$0.50, 30 minutes) leaves the Monterrico jetty at 6am, 11am, 1:30pm and 3:30pm (and 6:30pm except Saturday) for the bumpy ride to the reserve. Pickups also operate on this route charging US$3.25 per person.

A RACE TO THE SEA

From September to January a delightful ritual takes place every Saturday at sunset in front of Monterrico's beachfront hotels. Workers from the Tortugario Monterrico walk out on the beach carrying big plastic tubs and two long ropes. They lay one rope out along the beach at a certain distance from the waterline, and the second one several meters away, parallel to the first, and tourists from the beach hotels gather around. Come up to see what's going on and you'll find that the plastic tubs are full of baby sea turtles!

Pick a likely looking turtle out of the tub, make a small donation (less than US$2) to support the *tortugario* (turtle hatchery) and line up behind the rope furthest from the waves. It's an amazing feeling, to hold a baby sea turtle in your hand. When everyone is ready, on the count of three, everyone releases their turtles, which make a frantic scramble toward the sea. Keep an eye on your turtle; if yours is the first to reach the rope closest to the waves, you'll win a free meal for two at one of the Monterrico hotels. Eventually, as the sun is sinking, all the turtles reach the water and are washed away by the waves.

The race is not only a fun chance to win a free dinner, it's also poignant, as you consider the fate of 'your' little sea turtle as you hold it in your hand. All the turtles have hatched within the past two to three days. They're released in a group to give them a better chance of survival. Scientists say that on their race across the sand to the sea, the tiny turtles are imprinted with information about their place of birth (the composition of the sand, the water etc) that will enable them to return from the sea to this exact spot to lay eggs when they are adults. Most of them won't make it to adulthood. But the efforts of conservation groups such as the Tortugario are giving this endangered species a better chance.

Language Courses

There are two Spanish language schools. **Proyecto Lingüistico Monterrico** (619-8200; www.espanol.netfirms.com; Calle Principal s/n), about 250m from the beach, is quite professional. Courses here run at US$85 per week with 20 hours of tuition, and accommodation with access to a kitchen, or US$65 for classes only. It has useful maps of the town. ALM Language School, on a little street parallel to Calle Principal, a couple of blocks east, charges the same. Both places have gardens for open-air classes but ALM is in a quieter location.

Tours

There are a couple of tour outfits – Don Quijote Travel and Iguana Tour, both with offices on Calle Principal. They'll take you horse riding, deep-sea fishing, boating on the canal and lagoons, and more. Most hotels offer trips too! (See also p178.)

Sleeping & Eating

Monterrico has several simple hotels, almost all of which are on the beach; the majority have restaurants serving whatever is fresh from the sea that day. Many accommodations offer discounts for stays of three nights or more. Reserve for weekends if you want to avoid a long hot walk on the scalding sand while you cruise around to ask for vacancies. Weekend prices are given here.

Johnny's (☎ 206-4702, 762-0015; johnnys@backpack americas.com; dm US$4.50, s & d US$16, with bathroom US$18, 4-person bungalows US$51; P 🖳 🅿) This American-and-Kiwi-owned hotel is the first substantial place you come to heading left from Calle Principal. It's popular with backpackers and is a favorite of vacationing Guatemalan families, particularly for the attractive bungalows, each with two bedrooms, living room, bathroom and fully equipped kitchen. Every pair of bungalows shares a BBQ and small swimming pool. There's also a larger general swimming pool. The rooms are not glamorous but have fans and screened windows. The dormitory has five beds. Its bar/restaurant overlooks the sea and is a popular hangout: the food is not gourmet but there are plenty of choices and imaginative *licuados* and other long cool drinks. Meals are US$3.50 to US$11.75. The mixed dips and nachos hit the spot.

El Kaiman (☎ 517-9285, 617-9880; rooms per person US$7; P 🅿) Next along the beach from Johnny's, El Kaiman has eight basic rooms, each with fan, mosquito nets and private bath. Rooms are for two to five people. The best are upstairs, though they're all a bit shabby. The restaurant, right on the beach, serves variable Italian cuisine and seafood. There's a brick oven for pizzas; it kicks on here at night!

Hotel Baule Beach (☎ 418-6155, 613-7719; rooms per person US$10-11; P 🅿) This establishment has a new swimming pool, but generally standards have slipped recently. Previously, when the Baule was a ludicrously popular hotel run by a former Peace Corps volunteer, throngs of students from Antigua would choke the place on weekends and party. Some colorful murals linger from this period. Now, the ragged rooms with a bathroom are not so clean; you'll find a mattress on a slab of concrete, underneath an ageing mosquito net. A pity, as it's right on the beach. Food prices are a bit high.

Hotel El Mangle (☎ 514-6517; s/d US$13/20; P 🅿) The next place along is a good value. It has individually decorated *cabañas* divided into clean, comfortable rooms with fans, bathrooms, quality beds and towels. There's a big open space, with a very pleasant pool, for hanging out and it's quiet. The seafront restaurant opens for breakfast and lunch only.

Hotel Pez de Oro (☎ 204-5249, ☎ /fax 368-3684; s/d/tr US$30/40/50; P 🅿) Further down the beach with a palm-shaded garden, this is Monterrico's most upscale hotel. Italian-owned, it has 11 pleasant, solid bungalows, each with a fan, mosquito nets and a hammock on the porch. The bathrooms are more inviting than elsewhere in the village. The excellent restaurant, with big sea views, serves up great Italian cuisine and seafood dishes. Pastas cost from US$5.25, whole fish from US$5.80.

Dulce y Salado (☎ 817-9046; www.dulceysalado.tk; La Curvina; s/d/tr US$13/20/26; P 🅿) You'll find this new Italian-owned place about a kilometer past the Pez de Oro. Walk towards the Italian flag. It's very quiet and much cleaner along here. It has eight attractive but simple, spacious, clean *cabañas* with a fan and bathroom, the latter with fresh blue and white tiles, all set around a sizable pool. The *cabañas* can take up to three people. Fulvio, one of the owners, is a chef so sample tasty homemade pastas with veg (US$4) or with prawns (US$6.50). He also prepares Guatemalan and Mexican dishes and some tempting desserts. The bus to/from the Parque Hawaii (p178) passes out the back.

Going in the opposite direction from these hotels, heading right from Calle Principal, are more options.

Hotel El Delfín (rooms per person US$6, bungalow with bathroom per person US$7; P) This place has a small not particularly inviting entrance with some hammocks. Things get better as you head in. The entrance leads to a huge building with a *palapa* (thatched palm-leaf) roof and simple darkish rooms, which are for one to three people and have a fan and mosquito net. Out back is a spacious area with pool, restaurant and bungalows with shower, fan and mosquito screens. The communal bathrooms for the interior rooms are clean. Management is welcoming and restaurant prices are moderate.

Café del Sol (☎ 810-0821; www.cafe-del-sol.com; d/tr Fri & Sat from US$18/24, s/d/tr Sun-Thu US$11/13/16; P) Carry on 200m or so past the Delfín to this great place with a sun theme. It's Swiss-and-Guatemalan-owned, with a warm, family atmosphere. You'll recognize it by the yellow paint, the expansive terrace and the tall palm trees. Most of the nine rooms are on ground level, some beachside and others behind the main building, close to the pool. All have a bathroom, mosquito net and fan. The best room, upstairs in a tall *palapa* structure, costs US$26/33 for doubles/triples on weekends. The restaurant's menu has some original dishes; try risotto with mushrooms (US$4) or fish fillet with tomatoes, peppers (capsicums) and olives (US$7). Eat on the terrace or in the big *palapa* dining area.

Eco Beach Place (☎ 611-6637; ecobeachplace@hotmail.com; d/tr US$20/24; P) This hotel owned by a friendly English-speaking Guatemalan is next door to Café del Sol. There are only four rooms, each for up to four people. All are wellkept and nicely decorated, with a bathroom, mosquito net and fan. The restaurant's specialty is grilled steak (US$6.50 to US$16). Apart from prawns, other choices, including breakfast, are reasonably priced.

Guest House (rooms per person US$5) This is a another place set back from the beach on a little path. It's a small hostel with four cozy and rustic rooms with mosquito nets, fans and shared bathroom. It's good value even though not directly on the beach. From the beach turn left at the first alley after Calle Principal. It's on the corner with the first lane parallel to the beach.

Taberna El Pelicano (mains US$8) This eatery, on the same inland street but further east, behind Johnny's, garners good reviews for the international fare prepared by its Swiss chef.

El Divino Maestro (Calle Principal) There are many simple seafood restaurants on Calle Principal. This restaurant, on the right as you head away from the beach, is a good choice; try its *caldo de mariscos* (seafood stew; US$4).

Drinking
El Animal Desconicido (8:01pm-late Thu-Sat) This is a real popular night spot both for its French owner's wide-ranging taste in music and for its decor, in which bright orange walls collide with moons, stars, suns, skeletons, iguanas and shells. Best from 11pm, it's on the beach near Hotel El Delfín.

Getting There & Away
There are two ways to get to Monterrico. The best way is to get to La Avellana, from where boats and car ferries depart for Monterrico – enabling you to get a taste for the relaxing and interesting launch trips on the area's waterways. The Cubanita company runs a handful of direct buses to/from Guatemala City (US$2.60, four hours, 124km), leaving the capital's Zona 4 Terminal de Autobuses at 10:30am, 12:30pm and 2:30pm, and starting back from La Avellana at 4pm and 6pm. A word of caution – a reader complained that the direct bus from Guatemala City to La Avellana went on from Taxisco to Chiquimulilla then returned to Taxisco where it waited for 30 minutes before continuing on its way to La Avellana. Ask the driver about the route before you start your journey. Alternatively you reach La Avellana by changing buses at Taxisco on Highway CA-2. Buses operate half-hourly from 5am to 4pm between Guatemala City and

Taxisco (US$1.50, 3½ hours) and roughly hourly from 7am to 6pm between Taxisco and La Avellana (US$0.50, 40 minutes). A taxi between Taxisco and La Avellana costs around US$4.

From La Avellana, catch a *lancha* or car ferry to Monterrico. The collective *lanchas* charge US$0.40 per passenger for the half-hour trip along the Canal de Chiquimulilla, a long mangrove canal. They start at 4:30am and run more or less every half-hour or hour until late afternoon. From Monterrico they leave at 3:30am, 5:30am, 7am, 8am, 9am, 10:30am, noon, 1pm, 2:30pm and 4pm. You can always pay more and charter your own boat. The car ferry costs US$6.50 per vehicle.

The second, longer route to Monterrico is via Iztapa and Pueblo Viejo. Only a few buses a day link Pueblo Viejo and Monterrico: they leave Monterrico for Pueblo Viejo (US$0.80, one hour) at 5:30am, 7:30am, 11am, 12:30pm, 2pm and 3pm.

Shuttle buses also serve La Avellana. You can take a round-trip from Antigua, coming on one day and returning the next, for around US$9 one way. From Antigua it's a 2½-hour trip. **Voyageur Tours** (in Antigua ☎ 832-4237; www.travel.net.gt; Centro Comercial La Fuente, 4a Calle Oriente 14) comes to La Avellana three or four times weekly in the low season, daily in peak periods, with a minimum of three passengers. On Saturday and Sunday, it picks up in Monterrico (not La Avellana) from outside Proyecto Lingüistico Monterrico at 3pm for the return trip. It charges only US$6.50 from Monterrico to Antigua, so it's best not to buy a return ticket in Antigua; the staff will take you on to Guatemala City (US$11) if you wish. Other shuttle services also make the Antigua–Monterrico trip.

AROUND MONTERRICO

East down the coast from Monterrico, near Las Lisas, is the Guatemalan Pacific coast's best-kept secret, **Isleta de Gaia** (☎ 885-0044; www.isleta-de-gaia.com; 2-/4-person bungalows US$64/148; 🖥 🐾), a bungalow-hotel built on a long island of sand and named for the Greek earth goddess. Overlooking the Pacific on one side and a romantic and silent lagoon with mangroves on the other, this small, friendly, ecological, French-owned resort is constructed from natural materials. There are 12 bungalows, on one and two levels, with sea, lagoon or pool views. Each has good beds, fan, a bathroom, balcony and hammock; decorations are Mexican and Costa Rican. The seafront restaurant offers Italian, Spanish and French cuisine with fresh fish naturally the star. It has boogie boards and kayaks for rent and a big boat for fishing trips (US$140 for two people). Reserve your stay in this little paradise by email four days in advance. The staff run a shuttle service to Guatemala City and Antigua. From Monterrico there is no road east along the coast beyond Hawaii, so you have to backtrack to Taxisco and take Highway CA-2 for about 35km to reach the turnoff for Las Lisas. From the turnoff, it's 20km to Las Lisas where you take a boat to Isleta de Gaia.

Chiquimulilla & the El Salvador Border
Surfers found in this part of Guatemala will likely be heading to or from La Libertad in El Salvador. Most people shoot straight through Escuintla and Taxisco to Chiquimulilla and on to the Salvadoran border at Ciudad Pedro de Alvarado/La Hachadura, from where it is about 110km along the coast of El Salvador to La Libertad. Be sure about whether or not you need a visa to enter El Salvador.

Buses leave Taxisco for the border every 15 minutes until 5pm. There are two serviceable *hospedajes* in La Hachadura on the El Salvador side of the border, but the *hostales* in Ciudad Pedro de Alvarado on the Guatemalan side are not recommended. Should you need to stop for the night before crossing the border, you could do worse than head to the friendly cowboy town of **Chiquimulilla**, some 12km east of Taxisco. There isn't much going on here, but it's a decent enough place to take care of errands and regroup. All the buses congregate in a central area of town just off the plaza. Nearby, you'll find several banks.

Hotel San Juan de Letrán (☎ 885-0831; cnr 2a Av & 2a Calle; s/d US$4/7; 🅿) This family-run hotel is a clean place offering fair-sized rooms with a fan and bathroom. There are also less attractive rooms with shared bath. Drinking water is provided and there are nice plantings. The cafetería attached serves some of the iciest drinks in Guatemala, which are very welcome in this sweltering heat, and big plates of tasty, cheap food. Buses run every hour between Taxisco and Chiquimulilla, and also hourly, until 6pm, from Chiquimulilla to the border (US$1.50, 45 minutes).

The other option for getting to El Salvador is to turn north from Chiquimulilla and take local buses through Cuilapa to the border at Valle Nuevo/Las Chinamas, traveling inland before veering south to La Libertad.

LAGO DE AMATITLÁN

Lago de Amatitlán is a placid lake backed by a looming volcano and situated a mere 25km south of Guatemala City. It should be a pretty and peaceful resort, but unfortunately it's not. The hourglass-shaped lake is divided by a railway line, and the lakeshore is lined with industry along some parts. On weekends, people from Guatemala City come to row boats on the lake (its waters are too polluted for swimming) or to rent a hot tub for a dip. Many people from the capital own second homes here.

There's little reason for you to spend time here. If you really want to have a look, head for the town of Amatitlán, just off the main Escuintla–Guatemala City highway. Amatitlán has a scruffy public beach area. If you have a car and some spare time, a drive around the lake offers some pretty scenery. Perhaps the lake will one day be restored to its beautiful, natural state.

Central & Eastern Guatemala

184

North and east of Guatemala City is a land of varied topography, from the misty, pine-covered mountains of Alta Verapaz to the hot, dry-tropic climate of the Río Motagua valley. The Carretera al Atlántico (CA-9) climbs northeast out of the capital before descending from the relative cool of the mountains to the dry heat of a valley where dinosaurs once roamed.

Reached from this highway are many intriguing destinations, including the beautiful highland scenery around Cobán; the paleontology museum at Estanzuela; the great basilica at Esquipulas, famous throughout Central America; the first-rate Mayan ruins at Copán, just across the border in Honduras; the marvelous Mayan stelae and zoomorphs at Quiriguá; the tropical lake of Izabal and the jungle waterway of the Río Dulce. The Carretera al Atlántico ends at Puerto Barrios, Guatemala's Caribbean port, from which you can take a boat to Livingston, peopled by the Garífuna.

Salamá and Cobán, the departmental capitals of Baja Verapaz and Alta Verapaz, are easily accessible along a smooth, fast, asphalt road that winds up from the hot, dry valley passing through long stretches of coffee-growing country and wonderful mountain scenery. Along the way to Cobán is one of Guatemala's premier nature reserves, the Biotopo del Quetzal. Beyond Cobán, along rough roads, are the country's most famous caverns, the Grutas de Lanquín, and the beautiful pools and cascades of Semuc Champey. Minibuses now ply the mostly paved route north from Cobán to Flores, El Petén. You can, however, still take back roads to El Petén if you're addicted to chicken buses and pickups. Plenty of other roads left to the whims of nature remain to satisfy adventurous types.

TOP FIVE

- Experiencing the natural wonders of **Semuc Champey** (p197) and the caves at **Grutas de Lanquín** (p196)
- Visiting the super-impressive Mayan sites at **Copán** (p207) and **Quiriguá** (p220) and hanging out in the relaxed town of **Copán Ruinas** (p213)
- Kicking back in the riverside town of **Río Dulce** (p222) and whizzing around the waterways by *lancha* (motor boat)
- Mixing with the Caribbean culture of the Garífuna in funky **Lívingston** (p232)
- Exploring little-visited protected areas such as **Parque Nacional Laguna Lachuá** (p199) or the wetlands of **Bocas del Polochic** (p227)

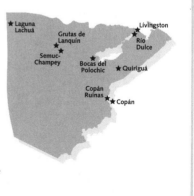

CENTRAL & EASTERN GUATEMALA

SALAMÁ

pop 11,000 / elevation 940m

Highway 14 (also marked CA-17) leaves the Carretera al Atlántico at El Rancho, 84km from Guatemala City. It heads west through a dry, desert-like lowland area, then turns north and starts climbing up into the forested hills. After 47km, at the junction called La Cumbre Santa Elena, Highway CA-17 to Salamá divides from Highway CA-14 for Cobán. Descending the other side of the ridge, Highway CA-17 winds down into the broad valley of the Río Salamá, and enters Salamá town, 17km from the Carretera.

Before the Spanish conquest, the mountainous departments of Baja Verapaz and Alta Verapaz were populated by the Rabinal Maya, noted for their warlike habits and merciless victories. They battled the powerful K'iche' Maya for a century but were never conquered.

When the conquistadors arrived, they too had trouble defeating the Rabinals. It was Fray Bartolomé de Las Casas who convinced the Spanish authorities to try peace where war had failed. Armed with an edict that forbade Spanish soldiers from entering the region for five years, the friar and his brethren pursued their religious mission, and succeeded in pacifying and converting the Rabinals. Their homeland thus was renamed Verapaz (True Peace) and is now divided into Baja Verapaz, with its capital at Salamá, and Alta Verapaz, centered on Cobán. The Rabinal have remained among the most dedicated and true to ancient Mayan customs, and there are many intriguing villages to visit in this part of Guatemala, including Rabinal itself (p187).

Information

Bancafé (🕘 9am-5pm Mon-Fri, 9am-1pm Sat) On the south side of the plaza (opposite the church), changes cash and traveler's checks and has a Visa and MasterCard ATM.

Banrural Next door to Bancafé; may offer better exchange rates and has a MasterCard ATM.

Cafe Deli-Donas (15a Calle 6-61) Has useful free maps of the town (without street names).

Police station One block west of the plaza.

Telgua (per hr US$1.30) Has Internet access. East of the plaza.

Tourist office (🕘 9am-1pm Mon-Fri) One block west of the plaza.

Sights

Salamá has some attractive reminders of colonial rule. The main plaza, for instance, boasts an ornate **church** with gold-encrusted altars and a carved pulpit, which is located just to the left before the altar. Be sure to check out Jesus lying in a glass coffin with cotton bunting in his stigmata and droplets of blood seeping from his hairline. His thick mascara and the silver lamé pillow where he rests his head complete the scene. The Salamá **market** is impressive for its colorful, local bustle, particularly on Sunday.

Tours

EcoVerapaz (☎ 940-0146, 610-3821; 8a Av 7-12, Zona 1) is in the shop Imprenta, Mi Terreno – a block west of the plaza on the road to La Cumbre. Its local, trained naturalists offer interesting tours throughout Baja Verapaz including caving, birding, hiking, horse riding and orchid trips. They also go to Rabinal to check out its museum and crafts. Guides speak some English. One-day tours start at US$25 per person for a group of 10 or more; it's US$40 per person for a group of five.

Sleeping

Hotel Real Legendario (☎ 940-0501; 8a Av 3-57, Zona 1; s/d/tr US$9/15/18; Ⓟ) Three blocks east of the plaza, you'll recognize this one by the stands of bamboo in the car park. The clean, secure rooms have fan, hot-water bathroom and cable TV.

Hotel Tezulutlán (☎ /fax 940-0141; s/d US$10/11; Ⓟ) This hotel, just east of the plaza and behind the Texaco fuel station, has five rooms around a leafy garden courtyard. All have cable TV and hot-water bathrooms.

Hotel San Ignacio (☎ 940-0186; 4a Calle 7-09; s/d/tr US$7/9/15) Opposite Hotel Tezulutlán is this clean family-run place with a big *palapa* (open-sided palm-leaf shelter) sitting area overlooking the street. The bright, fresh rooms are upstairs and have hot-water bathrooms.

Hospedaje Juárez (☎ 940-0055; 10a Av 5-55, Zona 1; s/d US$3/5, d/tr with bathroom US$8/11; Ⓟ) In the block directly behind the church, this is a good, clean, safe and friendly place to stay. There are 38 rooms; those on the top floor have hot-water bathrooms and are larger than those below.

CENTRAL & EASTERN GUATEMALA

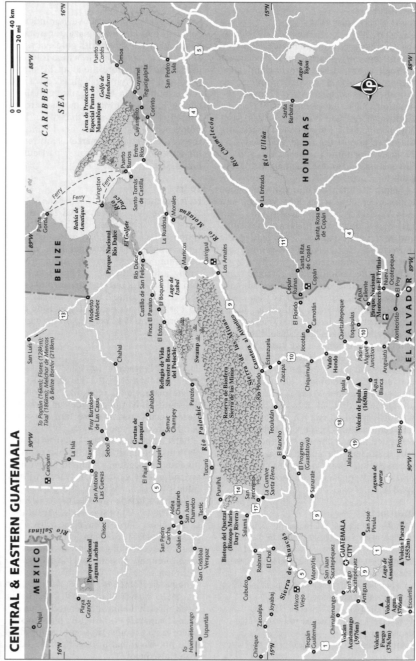

Turicentro las Orquídeas (☎ 940-1622; Carretera a Salamá Km 147; per tent US$4) Travelers with tents may want to check out this place, a few kilometers east of Salamá on Highway 17. They have a grassy area for camping plus a café, pool and open spaces slung with hammocks. You can use the pool (US$1.30 per person for the day) even if you're not camping there.

Eating

You don't have to step far from the plaza to eat well.

Cafe Deli-Donas (15a Calle 6-61; snacks US$1.40) This popular little café is just a few doors south of the plaza. Light meals, cakes (US$1.30) – the cheesecake is delectable – and Salamá's best coffee are served daily.

Cafetería Central (cnr 15a Calle & 9a Av; lunch US$2.40) Try the savory, filling lunches at this place a few doors back toward the plaza from Cafe Deli-Donas. The chicken broth followed by grilled chicken, rice and salad, with perhaps a mango to finish is a worthy feast.

Restaurante El Balcón de los Recuerdos (8a Av 6-28; mains US$4-6.50; ⏰ 8am-8:30pm Mon-Sat) This spacious restaurant, a half-block west of the plaza on the road to La Cumbre, is fan-cooled and has a central fountain. You can choose from a typical list of grilled meats, fish, prawns and seafood soup.

Pollo to Go (breakfast US$1.55-$2.60; mains US$4) Facing the west side of the plaza, this fast-food joint serves burgers and chicken in very clean and welcoming surroundings; you can take out or eat in.

Restaurante Caña Vieja (7a Av 4-41; light meals US$3) This friendly option is to the east of the plaza, just beyond Hotel San Ignacio. The chilled custard-apple juice is sensational.

Getting There & Away

Buses for Guatemala City (US$2.10 to US$2.60, three hours, 151km) depart hourly between 3am and 8pm from in front of Cafe Deli-Donas. There is a Pullman at 4am; arrive early for a seat. Buses coming from Guatemala City continue west from Salamá to Rabinal (US$1, 40 minutes, 19km) and then 15km further along to Cubulco. Buses for San Jerónimo leave from in front of the Municipalidad (east side of the plaza) every half hour from 6am to 5:30pm (US$0.20, 25 minutes).

Buses for La Cumbre (US$0.40, 25 minutes) and Cobán (US$1.70, 1½ to two hours) also leave from here about every 30 minutes from early morning to 4pm.

AROUND SALAMÁ

A few kilometers along the road to Salamá from highway CA-14, you come to the turnoff for **San Jerónimo**. Behind the town's beautiful church is a 16th-century sugar mill now used as a **museum** (admission free; ⏰ 8am-4pm Mon-Fri, 10am-noon & 1-4pm Sat & Sun) displaying a decent collection of artifacts and photographs, though none of the former are labeled. The grounds here are immaculate and there's a playground to keep the kids out of trouble. On the plaza are some large stones that were carved in ancient times.

About a five-minute walk from the town center are **Los Arcos**, a series of 124 arches, in various states of decay. These formed a sophisticated aqueduct system to power the sugar mill. To get there, take the main road heading east (away from Salamá), bear right and slightly downhill, where you'll see a 'Barrio El Calvario' sign. Keep an eye to your right along this road and you'll start to see the arches. A second set of arches can be seen by going right at the second dirt alley on this road. If you continue straight ahead for about 50m, rather than going right, you'll see more arches through gaps in the trees. Continue straight on this road to reach **Finca San Lorenzo**, a coffee farm open to the public. The last bus of the day returning to Salamá leaves San Jerónimo at 4pm.

Nine kilometers west of Salamá along Highway CA-5 is the village of **San Miguel Chicaj**, known for its weaving and for its traditional fiesta from September 25 to 29. Continue along the same road for another 10km to reach the colonial town of **Rabinal**, founded in 1537 by Fray Bartolomé de Las Casas as a base for his proselytizing. Rabinal has gained fame as a pottery-making center (look especially for the hand-painted chocolate cups), and for its citrus fruit harvest (November and December). Rabinal is also known for its adherence to pre-Columbian traditions, folklore and dance. If you can make it here for the annual fiesta of San Pedro, between January 19 and 25 (with things reaching a fevered pitch on January 21), or Corpus Cristi, do so. Market day here is Sunday. Rabinal also has the **Museo Comunitario Rabinal Achi'** (cnr 4a Av & 2a Calle, Zona 3), which is devoted to history, culture and the Achi' Maya who live in the district. Two small hotels, the **Pensión Motagua** and the **Hospedaje Caballeros**, can put you up.

It's possible to continue on from Rabinal another 15km to the village of **Cubulco**. Or, from Rabinal you can follow Highway CA-5 all the way to Guatemala City, a trip of about 100km passing through several small villages. Buses ply this mostly unpaved route, albeit very slowly. Along the way you could detour 16km north from Montúfar to the ruins of **Mixco Viejo** (US$3.25), which was the active capital of the Poqomam Maya when the Spaniards came and crashed the party. The location of this ceremonial and military center is awesome, wedged between deep ravines, with just one way in and one way out. To further fortify the site, the Poqomam built impressive rock walls around the city. It took Pedro de Alvarado and his troops more than a month of concerted attacks to conquer Mixco Viejo. When they finally succeeded, they furiously laid waste to this city, which scholars believe supported close to 10,000 people at its height. There are several temples and two ball courts here. Self-sufficient campers can overnight here for free. It's difficult to reach this site by public transport. From Guatemala City you need to get a Servicios Unidos San Juan bus from the Zona 4 Terminal de Autobuses to San Juan Sacatepéquez (US$0.35, one hour, departures every few minutes, 4am-6pm) then change to onward transport there. It's 12km north from San Juan to Montúfar.

BIOTOPO DEL QUETZAL

Along the main Cobán highway (CA-14), 34km beyond the La Cumbre turnoff for Salamá, you reach the Biotopo Mario Dary Rivera nature reserve, commonly called the **Biotopo del Quetzal** (US$3.25; ⏰7am-4pm) at Km 161, just east of the village of Purulhá.

If you stop here intent on seeing a quetzal, odds are you'll be disappointed – the birds are rare and elusive, and their habitat is almost destroyed. For more about the quetzal, see p43. You have the best chance

of seeing them from February to September. If you're really keen to see Guatemala's national bird in the wild, contact Proyecto EcoQuetzal in Cobán (p191).

Nevertheless it's well worth stopping to explore and enjoy this lush high-altitude cloud-forest ecosystem that is the quetzal's natural habitat – and you may get lucky! Early morning or early evening when the quetzals feed on *aguacatillo* trees are the best times to watch out for them – try around the Biotopín Restaurant and the Hotel y Comedor Ranchito del Quetzal (below).

Trail guide maps in English and Spanish (US$0.70) are available at the visitors center. They contain a checklist of 87 birds commonly seen here. Other animals include spider monkeys and *tigrillos*, which are similar to ocelots. Good luck spotting either of these.

Two excellent, well-maintained nature trails wind through the reserve: the 1800m Sendero los Helechos (Fern Trail) and the Sendero los Musgos (Moss Trail), which is twice as long. As you wander through the dense growth, treading on the rich, spongy humus and leaf-mold, you'll see many varieties of epiphytes (air plants), which thrive in the Biotopo's humid atmosphere.

Both trails pass by waterfalls, most of which cascade into small pools where you can take a dip; innumerable streams have their headwaters here, and the Río Colorado pours through the forest along a geological fault. Deep in the forest is **Xiu Gua Li Che** (Grandfather Tree), some 450 years old, which germinated around the time the Spanish fought the Rabinals in these mountains.

The reserve has a visitors center, a little shop for drinks and snacks, and a camping and barbecue area. The ruling on camping changes from time to time. Check by contacting Cecon in Guatemala City (p47), which administers this and other *biotopos*.

Sleeping & Eating

There are three lodging places close to the reserve.

Hotel y Comedor Ranchito del Quetzal (in Guatemala City ☎ 331-3579; s/d/tr US$5/8/12, with hot-water bathroom US$13/13/19; P) This rustic *hospedaje* with simple rooms is just beyond the Biotopo

CARDAMOM

The world's coffee drinkers know that high-quality coffee is important to Guatemala's export trade, but few know that Guatemala is the world's largest exporter of the spice cardamom. In Alta Verapaz, cardamom is more important to the local economy than coffee, providing livelihood for some 200,000 people. Cardamom *(Elettaria cardamomum)*, a herbaceous perennial of the ginger family native to the Malabar Coast of India, was brought to Alta Verapaz by German coffee-*finca* owners.

The plants grow to a height of between 1.5m and 6m and have coarse leaves up to 76cm long that are hairy on the underside. The flowers are white, and the fruit is a green, three-sided oval capsule holding 15 to 20 dark, hard, reddish-brown to brownish-black seeds. Though the cardamom plant grows readily, it is difficult to cultivate, pick and sort the best grades, so fragrant cardamom commands a high price. That does not seem to bother the people of Saudi Arabia and the Arabian Gulf states, who purchase more than 80% of the world supply. They pulverize the seeds and add the powder to the thick, syrupy, pungent coffee that is a social and personal necessity in that part of the world.

entrance, another 200m up the hill toward Purulhá and Cobán. Reasonably priced meals are served, and there are vegetarian options.

Posada Montaña del Quetzal (☎ 208-5958, in Guatemala City ☎ 367-1771/2; www.medianet.com.gt/quetzal; Carretera a Cobán Km 156.5; s/d/tr/q US$30/34/38/42, 2-bedroom bungalows US$42/48/52/64; (P)(⚓)) This comfortable place is 5km before the Biotopo del Quetzal if you're coming from Guatemala City. It has 18 attractive white-stucco, tile-roofed bungalows, each with a sitting room and fireplace, a bedroom with three beds and a hot-water bathroom. There are larger two-bedroom bungalows, and a restaurant. You can usually catch a shuttle between the Biotopo and the Posada.

Hotel Restaurant Ram Tzul (☎ 908-4066, in Guatemala City ☎ 335-1805; ramtzul@internet.net.gt; CA-14 Km 158; s/d/tr US$4/8/12, with hot-water bathroom US$13/13/20, s/d bungalows US$20/38; (P)) This eye-catching, tall, thatched-roof hotel is about halfway between the Posada Montaña del Quetzal and the *biotopo* entrance. It has a bar/restaurant where mains cost US$3 to US$4. The hotel property includes waterfalls and swimming spots.

Biotopín Restaurant (CA-14 Km 160.5) A half-kilometer before the *biotopo* entrance, this restaurant has decent meals at good prices.

Getting There & Away

Any bus to/from Guatemala City will set you down at the park entrance. Heading in the other direction, it's best to flag down a bus or microbus to El Rancho and change there for your next destination.

COBÁN

pop 20,000 / elevation 1320m

The asphalt road between the Biotopo and Cobán is good, smooth and fast, though curvy, with light traffic. Ascending into the evergreen forests, tropical flowers are still visible. As you enter Cobán, a sign says 'Bienvenidos a Cobán, Ciudad Imperial,' referring to the city charter granted in 1538 by Emperor Carlos V.

The town was once the center of Tezulutlán (Tierra de Guerra, or the 'Land of War'), a stronghold of the Rabinal Maya.

In the 19th century, when German immigrants moved in and founded vast coffee and cardamom *fincas* (plantations), Cobán took on the aspect of a German mountain town, as the *finca* owners built town residences. The era of German cultural and economic domination ended during WWII, when the USA prevailed upon the Guatemalan government to deport the powerful *finca* owners, many of whom actively supported the Nazis.

Today, Cobán is an interesting town to visit, though dreary weather can color your impression. Most of the year it is either rainy or overcast, dank and chill. You can count on sunny days in Cobán for only about three weeks in April. In the midst of the 'dry' season (January to March) it can be misty and sometimes rainy, or bright and sunny with marvelous clear mountain air.

Guatemala's most impressive festival of Indian traditions, the national folklore festival of **Rabin Ajau** with its traditional dance of the Paabanc, takes place in the latter part of July or in the first week of August. The **national orchid show** is hosted here every December.

There is not a lot to do in Cobán itself except enjoy the local color and mountain scenery, but the town is a base for marvelous side trips, including to the Grutas de Lanquín (p196) and the pools and cascades of Semuc Champey (p197).

Orientation

The main plaza *(el parque)* was under wraps in 2003; expect to find a revamped central square. Most of the services you'll need are within a few blocks of the plaza and the cathedral. The shopping district is around and behind the cathedral, and you'll smell the savory cardamom, which vendors come from the mountains to sell, before you see it.

The heart of Cobán is built on a rise, so unless what you're looking for is in the dead center, be ready to walk uphill and down.

Information

INTERNET ACCESS

At least four places offer Internet access. The going rate is US$1.55 an hour.

Access Computación (☎ 951-4040; 1a Calle 3-13; ❧ 9am-7pm Mon-Fri, 8am-6pm Sat)

Cybercobán (3a Av 1-11, Zona 4; ❧ 8:30am-7pm Mon-Sat) East (200m) of the plaza.

Cybernet Internet Café On the south side of the plaza.

Mayan Internet (6a Av 2-28; ❧ 8:30am-8pm Mon-Sat, 2:30-9pm Sun) Fast connections, 500m west of the plaza.

LAUNDRY

Casa D'Acuña (☎ 951-0482, 951-0484; uisa@amigo .net.gt; 4a Calle 3-11, Zona 2) US$4.40 to wash and dry a basket load.

Lavandería Providencia (❧ 8am-noon & 2-5pm Mon-Sat) On the south side of the plaza. A wash 7lb (3.2kg) costs US$1.20; drying costs US$2.20 per hour.

MONEY

The following banks change US-dollars cash and traveler's checks.

Bancafé (1a Av 2-66) Has a Visa ATM.

Banco G & T Continental (1a Calle) Opposite Hotel La Posada, has a MasterCard ATM.

Banco Industrial (1a Calle 4-36) Has another branch (cnr 1a Calle & 7a Av) with a Visa ATM.

POST & TELEPHONE

Post office (cnr 2a Av & 3a Calle) A block southeast from the plaza.

Telgua On the plaza; has plenty of card-phones outside.

TOURIST INFORMATION

Casa D'Acuña (☎ 951-0482, 951-0484; uisa@amigo .net.gt; 4a Calle 3-11, Zona 2) Can give you loads of information.

Hostal de Doña Victoria (☎ /fax 951-4213/4; 3a Calle 2-38, Zona 3) Ditto.

Municipalidad (Town Hall; ☎ 952-1305, 951-1148) Some switched-on, trained staff can answer inquiries from an office behind the police office.

Sights

TEMPLO EL CALVARIO

You can get a fine view over the town from this church atop a long flight of stairs at the north end of 7a Av. Indigenous people leave offerings at outdoor shrines and crosses in front of the church. You can walk around behind the church to enter the Parque Nacional Las Victorias, though this is not the park's main entrance. Don't linger here after 4pm!

The **Ermita de Santo Domingo de Guzmán**, a chapel dedicated to Cobán's patron saint, is 150m west of the bottom of the stairs leading to El Calvario.

PARQUE NACIONAL LAS VICTORIAS

This forested 0.82-sq-km **national park** (US$0.80; ❧ 8am-4:30pm, walking trails 9am-3pm), right in town, has ponds, barbeque, picnic areas, children's play areas, a lookout point, and kilometers of trails. The entrance is at 11a Av and 3a Calle, Zona 1.

VIVERO VERAPAZ

Orchid lovers mustn't miss the chance to see the many thousands of species at this famous **nursery** (☎ 952-1133; Carretera Antigua de Entrada a Cobán; US$1.30; ❧ 9am-noon & 2-4pm). The rare *monja blanca* (white nun orchid), Guatemala's national flower, can be seen here; there are also hundreds of species of miniature orchids, so small that you'll need the magnifying glass they will loan you to see them. Visits are by guided tour. The national orchid show is held here each December, and by all accounts, it's spectacular. Otherwise, try to visit between October and February when many flowers are in bloom.

Vivero Verapaz is about 2km from the town center – a 40-minute walk southwest from the plaza. You can hire a taxi for around US$2.

FINCA SANTA MARGARITA

A working coffee farm, **Finca Santa Margarita** (☎ 951-3067; 3a Calle 4-12, Zona 2; US$2; 🕑 guided tours 8am-12:30pm & 1:30-5pm Mon-Fri, 8am-noon Sat) offers stellar guided tours. From propagation and planting to roasting and exporting, the 45-minute tour will tell you all you ever wanted to know about these powerful beans. At tour's end, you're treated to a cup of coffee and can purchase beans straight from the roaster for US$2.60 to US$5 a pound (0.45kg). The talented guide speaks English and Spanish.

MUSEO EL PRÍNCIPE MAYA

This private **museum** (☎ 952-1541; 6a Av 4-26, Zona 3; US$1.30; 🕑 9am-6pm Mon-Sat) features a collection of pre-Columbian artifacts, with an emphasis on jewelry, other body adornments and pottery. The displays are well designed and maintained.

Language Courses

Not many people stop to study Spanish in Cobán. But you might consider the **Active Spanish School** (☎ 952-1432; www.guatemala365.com; 3a Calle 6-12, Zona 1), run by the dynamic Nirma Macz who can provide one-on-one teaching in Spanish and Q'eqchi'. Cost for 20 hours' tuition a week and a homestay with a local family including all meals is US$100. Nirma is an expert on the local dance/club scene so you're bound to have fun while you improve your Spanish.

Tours

Aventuras Turísticas (☎ /fax 951-4213; aventurasturisticas@terra.com; 3a Calle 2-38, Zona 3), in the Hostal de Doña Victoria, leads tours to Laguna Lachuá, the Grutas de Lanquín, Rey Marcos and Candelaria, Semuc Champey, Tikal, Ceibal and anywhere else you may want to go; they will customize itineraries. French-, English- and Spanish-speaking guides are available.

Casa D'Acuña (☎ 951-0484; fax 951-0482; 4a Calle 3-11, Zona 2) offers tours to Semuc Champey, the Grutas de Lanquín and other places further afield. Their guides are excellent.

Discovery Nature (☎ 951-0811; 3a Calle 1-46) operates out of Posada Don Matalbatz. This outfit offers day and overnight trips to Laguna Lachuá, excursions to other fantastic places around Cobán and rafting trips.

Proyecto EcoQuetzal (☎ /fax 952-1047; bidas peq@guate.net; 2a Calle 14-36, Zona 1; 🕑 8:30am-1pm & 2-5:30pm Mon-Fri) is an innovative project offering 'ethnotourism' trips in which participants hike to nearby villages nestled in the cloud forest and stay with a Q'eqchi' Maya family. To maximize the experience, travelers are encouraged to learn some Q'eqchi' words and stay with their host family for at least two days. For US$42 you'll get a guide for three days, lodging for two nights and six meals. Your guide will take you on hikes to interesting spots. The men of the family are the guides, providing them an alternative, sustainable way to make a living.

Reservations are required at least one day in advance. The Proyecto also rents boots, sleeping bags and binoculars at reasonable prices, so you need not worry if you haven't come prepared for such a rugged experience. Participants should speak at least a little Spanish. With a month's notice, this outfit also offers quetzal-viewing platforms; contact their office for full details.

Sleeping

When choosing a room in Cobán, you may want to ensure the showers have hot water because it can be cold in these parts.

BUDGET

Casa D'Acuña (☎ 951-0482, 951-0484; uisa@amigo.net.gt; 4a Calle 3-11, Zona 2; dm/d US$6/13) This clean, very comfortable European-style hostel is down a steep hill from the plaza. The four dormitories each have four beds and there are two private doubles, all with shared bathroom and good hot showers. The fabulous El Bistro restaurant (p194) is also here, along with a gift shop, laundry service and reasonably priced local tours.

Posada de Carlos V (☎ 952-3502; fax 951-3501; 1a Av 3-44, Zona 1; s/d/tr US$12/22/30; P) A bit removed from the center, this hotel has a lovely big garden and a bit of a rustic feel to it – some of the rooms are in sort-of a cottage, others in a more-modern block. All rooms have hot-water bathroom and cable TV. Amiable folk run the place.

COBÁN

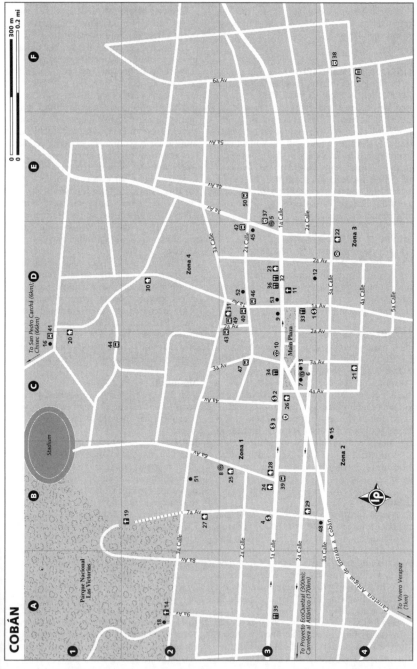

Hotel La Paz (☎ 952-1358; 6a Av 2-19, Zona 1; s US$4, s/d with bathroom US$6/10; **P**) This cheerful, clean hotel, 1½ blocks north and two blocks west of the plaza, is an excellent deal. It has many flowers, and a good cafetería next door. They claim to have hot water.

Posada Don Matalbatz (☎ /fax 951-0811; discov erynat@intelnet.net.gt; 3a Calle 1-46, Zona 1; dm US$6, rooms per person with shared bathroom US$7, s/d/tr with bathroom US$13/25/32; **P**) Conveniently located for odd-hour bus travel, this friendly place has a selection of rooms, including big, clean units facing a pretty courtyard with hot-water bathroom and cable TV. Upstairs, the attic room has the most light and character, and sleeps five. Also on this level are a couple of rooms with clean, shared bathroom and little balconies. It has the Café El Siguán (p194) and a pool table.

Hotel Central (☎ 952-1118; fax 952-1442; 1a Calle 1-79, Zona 1; s/d/tr with hot-water bathroom & TV US$11/17/24) The Central is clean and tidy, with rooms arranged a round a flowered courtyard. Smaller singles/doubles/triples are US$9/15/21 and without TVs. There's a touch of mold on the walls but the place is popular and staff are helpful. The Cafetería San Jorge is also here (p194).

Hotel Mansión Armenia (☎ 951-0978; www.ma yaninternet.com; 7a Av 2-18, Zona 1; s/d/tr with bathroom & TV US$21/24/31; **P**) This hotel, one block from Templo El Calvario, is comfortable, clean, quiet and modern, with courtyard parking and a cafetería (breakfast only). The owners are obliging.

Hotel Cobán Imperial (☎ 952-1131; 6a Av 1-12, Zona 1; s or d US$4-5, with bathroom & TV US$7; **P**) This hotel 250m west of the plaza has been remodeled to incorporate another that was behind it. It's a sprawling place with 23 rooms of varying degrees of comfort but it's clean, and is popular with Guatemalan families.

Hotel Rabin Ajau (☎ 951-4296; 1a Calle 5-37, Zona 1; s/d/tr US$13/16/20; **P**) This old-fashioned, plain hotel is well located but its disco is noisy. Rooms have hot-water bathroom and TV. There's also a restaurant.

MID-RANGE

Hostal de Doña Victoria (☎ /fax 951-4213/4; 3a Calle 2-38, Zona 3; s/d/tr US$20/26/54, low season US$12/20/26; **P**) This lovely hotel in a restored mansion more than 400 years old is jam-packed with eye-catching decorations varying from an old copper coffee machine to wooden masks to antique religious statues. Eight brightly painted comfortable rooms, with bathroom and TV, surround a central courtyard with lush plants and a restaurant/bar (p194).

Hotel La Posada (☎ 952-1495, 951-0588; laposa da@c.net.gt; 1a Calle 4-12, Zona 2; s/d/tr US$33/45/54) Just off the plaza, this colonial-style hotel is Cobán's best, though rooms streetside suffer from traffic noise. Its colonnaded porches are dripping with tropical flowers and furnished with easy chairs and hammocks from which you can enjoy the mountain views. The rooms have nice old furniture, fireplaces and wall hangings of local weaving, and a bathroom. TV costs US$3.50 daily. It has a restaurant and café (p194).

Pensión Monja Blanca (☎ 952-1712, 951-0531; fax 951-1899; 2a Calle 6-30, Zona 2; s/d US$7/14, with hot-water bathroom US$13/26) Run by a sweet older couple, this place is peaceful despite being on busy 2a Calle. After walking through two courtyards, you come to a lush garden packed with fruit and hibiscus trees around which the spotless rooms are arranged. Each room is furnished with two good-quality single beds with folksy covers, and has cable TV; the light switches are on the outside. This is a good place for solo women travelers.

Casa Alcázar Victoria (☎ 952-1143; fax 952-1389; 1a Av 5-34; s/d/tr US$20/26/54; P) This attractive new hotel about 600m north of the plaza is owned by the same people as the Doña Victoria but it's a different type of place. Set on two levels around a large interior patio, the building is a tasteful modern version of colonial style. Local weddings and parties are held here, so it's best to ask before you take a room if the patio will be used for a function during your stay. Rooms come with private hot-water bathroom and have pretty furnishings. There is a restaurant serving fresh Guatemalan fare.

Park Hotel (☎ 951-3388; parkhotel@guatemala travel.com; CA-14, Km 196.5, Santa Cruz Verapaz; s/d/tr from US$35/40/45; P 🐾) You'll find this place 14km from Cobán on the highway to Guatemala City. It has modern little bungalows and a restaurant set amid tropical forest and grassy grounds. The 54 regular rooms are in prefab duplex bungalows. There are more attractive, and more expensive, suites with living room, fireplace and cable TV.

Vivero Verapaz (p190; s or d US$32) The orchid nursery has three nice, quiet, fully equipped *cabañas* for rent.

Eating

Most of the hotels in Cobán come with their own restaurants.

El Bistro (4a Calle 3-11; mains US$8.50-13; 🕑 from 7am) Casa D'Acuña's restaurant is one of the best in town, with authentic Italian and other European-style dishes served in an attractive oasis of tranquility to a background of classical music. In addition to protein-oriented mains (fish, chicken and steak), there is a range of pastas (US$4-US$5.25), salads, homemade breads, cakes

and outstanding desserts. You can buy bread and cake to take on your day trips out of Cobán.

Hostal de Doña Victoria (3a Calle 2-38; breakfasts US$3, pasta US$4) The restaurant here is a good bet. The menu is not as elaborate as that of El Bistro but the setting is equally attractive, more Guatemalan than international. The food is fresh and enjoyable.

Café La Posada (1a Calle 4-12, Zona 2; snacks US$4; 🕑 1-9pm) This café at the west end of the plaza has tables on a veranda overlooking the square, and a comfortable sitting room inside with couches, coffee tables and a fireplace. All the usual café fare is served: nachos, tortillas, sandwiches, burgers, tacos, tostadas, fruit salad etc.

Hotel La Posada (1a Calle 4-12, Zona 2; breakfasts US$4-6, mains US$7-11) This hotel has a pleasant dining room overlooking a garden, with good food but slow service.

Café El Tirol (Oficinas Profesionales Fray Bartolomé de las Casas, 1a Calle 3-13; breakfasts US$2-4; 🕑 Mon-Sat) A good central café, the Tirol claims to have Cobán's 'best coffee' (try the specials) and offers several types of hot chocolate. It's a cozy little place in which to enjoy breakfasts, pastries and coffee or light meals, with a pleasant terrace away from the traffic.

Cafe El Siguán (3a Calle 1-46, Zona; breakfasts US$2-7; 🕑 6am-10pm) Part of the Posada Don Matalbatz, breakfasts, vegetarian food, salads, pastas and *licuados* are available. You might go for the *caldo de kac-cik*, a Q'eqchi' turkey stew (US$8).

Cafetería San Jorge (1a Calle 1-79, Zona 4; breakfasts from US$2, meat mains US$4) This place beside the Hotel Central has a varied menu and a dining room with large windows. The meat dishes are substantial and there are a variety of sandwiches (US$1 to US$2). Next door, **Yogurt Renee** makes delicious fruit yogurts and ice cream.

Cafetería Santa Rita (1a Calle; lunches US$3) Small, tidy and popular with locals, this eatery on the south side of the plaza offers good, simple Guatemalan breakfasts, lunches and dinners. A typical lunch plate might be stuffed peppers with rice and salad, while a typical breakfast comprises eggs, *frijoles*, fried bananas and tortillas.

Restaurant Kam Mun (1a Calle 8-12, Zona 2; mains US$5-11) Here you will find Chinese fare, served in a nice, clean atmosphere, 500m west of the plaza. Enjoy your meal surrounded by Chinese dragons, Buddhas and floral paintings.

In the evening, **food trucks** (kitchens on wheels) park around the plaza and offer some of the cheapest dining in town. Some serve safe food, others don't.

Entertainment

Cobán has several places where you can get down and boogie. **Bar Milenio** (3a Av 1-11, Zona 4) has a bar, food, a pool table and mixed-music disco. **Keops** (3a Calle 4-71, Zona 3; US$4.50) is a popular disco; wear your best gear.

Getting There & Away

BUS

The highway connecting Cobán with Guatemala City and the Carretera al Atlántico is the most traveled route between Cobán and the outside world. The road north through Chisec to Sayaxché and Flores has almost all been paved in recent years, providing much easier access than before to El Petén. The off-the-beaten-track routes west to Huehuetenango and northeast to Fray Bartolomé de Las Casas and Poptún remain almost completely unpaved and still a bit of an adventure. Always double-check bus departure times, especially for less frequently served destinations. Tourism staff at the Town Hall try to keep up with the frequent schedule changes and display bus details in the Town Hall foyer.

A few buses depart from a sort of terminal, southeast of the stadium, called Campo 2 or Terminal Nuevo (New Bus Station). Buses to Guatemala City, Salamá, Lanquín and other destinations leave from completely different terminals and stops, most near the Mercado Terminal (stops are shown on the Cobán map). Minibuses, known as *microbuses*, are replacing, or are additional to, chicken buses on many routes. Many buses do a circuit of the plaza before leaving town and stop outside Oficinas Profesionales Fray Bartolomé de Las Casas.

Bus departures from Cobán include:

Biotopo del Quetzal (US$0.65, 1¼hr, 58km) Any bus heading for Guatemala City will drop you at the entrance to the Biotopo.

Cahabón (US$2.60, 4½hr, 85km) Same buses as to Lanquín.

Chisec (US$1.95, 2hr, 66km) Ten buses a day leave from the corner of 1a Av and 2a Calle between 6am and 5pm.

El Estor (US$4, 7hr, 166km) This route via Tactic and Panzós is unsafe and not recommended (see p227). If the situation

changes, you'll find buses departing from outside the Injav football stadium six times daily between 5am and 1pm.

Flores (5-6hr, 224km) Go to Sayaxché and take an onward bus or minibus from there.

Fray Bartolomé de Las Casas (via Chisec US$2.60, 3hr, 121km; via San Pedro Carchá US$2.20, 4hr, 101km) Several buses depart daily from 5am to 3:30pm from the corner of 2a Calle and 3a Av, opposite Inque Renta Autos. Buses might just say 'Las Casas'. Microbuses leave from 2a Calle and 1a Av right by Mercado Terminal.

Guatemala City (US$3.25-4.50, 4-5hr, 213km) Transportes Monja Blanca (☎ 951-3571; 2a Calle 3-77, Zona 4) Has buses leaving for Guatemala City every half hour from 2am to 6am, then hourly until 5pm.

Lanquín (US$1.30-1.95, 2½-3hr, 61km) Buses depart at 5am and 6am from in front of the Dispensa Familiar supermarket just east of the plaza, and at 5:30am, 7am, 8am, 9am, 11am & 1pm from the office of Transportes Gamasa (cnr 3a Calle & 2a Av). Do check these times as they seem to be fluid. There are also assorted micros with no fixed timetable, from the same stop.

Playa Grande, for Laguna Lachuá (US$5.25, 4hr, 141km) Buses depart daily at 5am and 11am from Mercado Terminal; there are also microbuses. Playa Grande is sometimes called Cantabal.

Puerto Barrios (6½hr, 335km) Take any bus headed to Guatemala City and change at El Rancho junction.

Raxrujá (US$2.60, 2½-3hr, 81km) Take a bus or microbus heading to Fray Bartolomé de Las Casas via Chisec; some Sayaxché-bound buses go through Raxrujá too; or go to Chisec and change.

Río Dulce (6½hr, 318km) Take any bus headed to Guatemala City and change at El Rancho junction. You may have to transfer again at La Ruidosa junction, 169km past El Rancho, but there is plenty of transport going through to Río Dulce and on to Flores.

Salamá (US$1.80, 1½hr, 57km) Frequent minivans leave from the corner of 3a Calle and 2a Av, opposite the Transportes Gamasa office, or take any bus to Guatemala City and change at La Cumbre.

San Cristóbal Verapaz (US$0.25, 20min, 19km) Buses run every 15 to 30 minutes, 6am to 6:30pm, from Campo 2 (New Bus Station).

San Pedro Carchá (US$0.25, 20min, 6km) Buses every 10 minutes, 6am to 7pm, from in front of the Injav football stadium.

Sayaxché (US$5.50, 4hr, 184km) Buses at 6am and noon, and microbuses from early until 1pm, from Mercado Terminal.

Tactic (US$0.45, 40min, 32km) Frequent buses from Campo 2 (New Bus Station).

Uspantán (US$3.50, 4½hr, 94km) Buses depart at 10am and noon from the Shell fuel station on 1a Calle near 7a Av. Microbuses go from the corner of 2a Av and 3a Calle with a stop at Oficinas Profesionales Fray Bartolomé de las Casas.

CAR

Cobán has a couple of places that rent cars. Reserve your choice in advance. If you want to go to the Grutas de Lanquín or Semuc Champey, you'll need a vehicle with 4WD. Rental companies include **Inque Renta Autos** (☎ 952-1994, 952-1172; 3a Av 1-18, Zona 4) and **Tabarini** (☎ 952-1504; fax 951-3282; 7a Av 2-27, Zona 1).

AROUND COBÁN

Cobán, and indeed all of Alta Verapaz, has become a magnet for Guatemalan adventure travel, both independent and organized. Not only are there scores of villages where you can experience traditional Mayan culture in some of its purest extant forms, there are also caves running throughout the department, waterfalls, pristine lagoons and many other natural wonders yet to be discovered. Go find them!

San Cristóbal Verapaz is an interesting Poqomchi' Maya village set beside Lake Chicoj, 19km west of Cobán. During Semana Santa (Easter Week), San Cristóbal artists design elaborate *alfombras* (carpets) of colored sawdust and flower petals rivaled only by those in Antigua. In addition, San Cristóbal is home to the **Centro Comunitario Educativo Pokomchi** (Cecep; ☎ 950-4039; www.ajchicho.50g.com), an organization dedicated to preserving traditional and modern ways of Poqomchi' life. To this end, Cecep inaugurated the **Museo Katinamit** (US$0.80) featuring art, tools and textiles still in daily use, and an introduction and orientation on the Poqomchi'. Cecep also offers volunteer and ethnotourism opportunities and runs the **Aj Chi Cho Language Center** (per week including homestay US$120) for teaching Spanish. **El Portón Real** (☎ 950-4604) is a Poqomchi'-owned and operated hostelry.

Tactic is a small town 32km south of Cobán that offers myriad opportunities to experience traditional Mayan culture. On the plaza is the **Cooperativa de Tejadores**, where women demonstrate weaving techniques and sell their wares. On the outskirts of Tactic, atop the hill called Chi Ixhim, is an altar to the God of Maiz; anyone in town can point the direction. There are a few places to stay, but none as nice as **Country Delight** (☎ 709-1149; ecotdms@latinmail.com; Carretera CA-14 Km 166.5) where there are hiking trails, camping facilities, rooms and a restaurant. Staff can supply information on the area

and its attractions. Tactic celebrates the **fiesta of the Virgen de la Asunción** from August 11 to 16.

Balneario Las Islas

At the town of San Pedro Carchá, 6km east of Cobán on the way to Lanquín, is the Balneario Las Islas, with a river coming down past rocks and into a natural pool that's great for swimming. It's a five- to 10-minute walk from the bus stop in Carchá; anyone can point the way. Buses operate frequently between Cobán and Carchá (20 minutes).

San Juan Chamelco

About 8km southeast of Cobán is the village of San Juan Chamelco, where you can swim at the Balneario Chio. The **church** here sits on top of a small rise, providing awesome views of the villages below. The colonial church may have been the first in Alta Verapaz. Paintings inside depict the arrival of the conquistadors. Mass is still held here in both Spanish and Q'eqchi'.

In Aldea Chajaneb, only 12km from Cobán, **Don Jerónimo's** (☎ 308-2255; www.dearbrutus.com/donjeronimo; s/d US$25/45), owned by Jerry Makransky (Don Jerónimo), rents comfortable, simple bungalows. The price includes three ample, delicious vegetarian meals fresh from the garden. He also offers many activities, including tours to caves and the mountains, and inner-tubing on the Río Sotzil. Jerry dotes on his guests, and the atmosphere is friendly. The Rey Marcos Cave is near here.

Buses to San Juan Chamelco leave from 4a Calle, Zona 3, in Cobán. To reach Don Jerónimo's, take a bus or pickup from San Juan Chamelco toward Chamil and ask the driver to let you off at Don Jerónimo's. When you get off, take the footpath to the left for 300m, cross the bridge and it's the first house on the right. Alternatively, hire a taxi from Cobán (US$6.50).

Grutas de Lanquín

One of the best excursions to make from Cobán is to the caves near Lanquín, a pretty village 61km to the east.

The **Grutas de Lanquín** (US$2.60; ☼ 8am-4pm) are about 1km northwest of the town, and extend for several kilometers into the earth. There is now a ticket office here. The first cave has lights but do take a powerful flashlight anyway. You'll also need shoes with good traction, as it's slippery inside with moisture and bat crap.

Though the first few hundred meters of cavern have been equipped with a walkway and are lit by diesel-powered electric lights, most of this subterranean system is untouched. If you are not an experienced spelunker, you shouldn't wander too far into the caves; the entire extent has yet to be explored, let alone mapped.

Aside from funky stalactites, mostly named for animals, these caves are crammed with bats; at sunset, they fly out of the mouth of the cave in formations so dense they obscure the sky. For a dazzling display of navigation skills, sit at the entrance while they exit. The river here gushes from the cave in clean, cool and delicious torrents You can swim in the river, which has some comfortably hot pockets close to shore.

Tours to the Grutas de Lanquín and Semuc Champey, offered in Cobán for US$35 per person (p191), are the easiest way to visit these places. Tours take about two hours to reach Lanquín from Cobán; the price includes a packed lunch.

If you're driving, you'll need a 4WD vehicle. The road from San Pedro Charca to El Pajal, where you turn off for Lanquín, may be paved by the time you read this. The 11km from El Pajal to Lanquín will not be paved, they say. You can head on from Lanquín to Flores in 14 to 15 hours via El Pajal, Sebol, Raxrujá and Sayaxché. The road from El Pajal to Sebol is not paved. Or you can head from Lanquín to Sebol and Fray Bartolomé de Las Casas and on to Poptún.

SLEEPING & EATING
Camping is permitted near the cave entrance, otherwise, there are several places to stay at Lanquín.

La Divina Providencia (s/d US$4/7) In the center of town, it has simple, clean, dark rooms, some with a bit of a terrace and view.

Rabin Itzam (s/d US$4/7) A few doors down the hill, Rabin has big rooms with balconies and good views. The wooden doors are carved with Mayan symbols. This place is quiet and private.

El Recreo (☎ 952-2160; d US$4-7, s/d/tr with bathroom US$19/25/31; P 🔊) Between the town and the caves, this is an attractive place to

stay. It has large gardens, two swimming pools (not overly clean) and a restaurant.

El Retiro (dm US$4-5, d US$9-13) This sublimely located hotel is about 500m along the road beyond Rabin Itzam. *Palapa* buildings look down over the greenest of green fields to a beautiful wide river, the same river that flows out from the Lanquín caves. It's safe to swim, even inner tube if you're a confident swimmer. The place is Guatemalan- and English-owned. Attention to detail in every respect makes this a backpackers' paradise. Dorm rooms have only four beds. Individual decor includes some clever use of tiles, shells, strings of beads and local fabrics. Excellent vegetarian food (three-course dinner US$4.50) is available in the hammock-lined restaurant. Plenty of info is provided for onward journeys and there are organized activities such as jungle walks. New rooms with private bathroom are being built.

Comedor Shalom (meals US$1.55) Near Rabin Itzam, this bright, clean restaurant is good for a plate of chicken, rice and salad.

GETTING THERE & AWAY
Buses operate several times daily between Cobán and Lanquín, continuing to Cahabón. Buses leave Lanquín to return to Cobán at 3am, 4am, 5:30am and 1pm, and there are assorted *microbuses* with no fixed timetable. Since the last reliable return bus departs so early, it's best to stay the night.

Semuc Champey
Nine kilometers south of Lanquín, along a rough, bumpy, slow road, is **Semuc Champey** (US$2.60), famed for its great natural limestone bridge 300m long, on top of which is a stepped series of pools with cool, flowing river water good for swimming. The water is from the Río Cahabón, and much more of it passes underground, beneath the bridge. Though this bit of paradise is difficult to reach, the beauty of its setting and the perfection of the pools, ranging from turquoise to emerald-green, make it worth it. Many people consider this the most beautiful spot in all Guatemala.

If you're visiting on a tour, some guides will take you down a rope-ladder from the lowest pool to the river, which gushes out from the rocks below. Plenty of people do this and love it, though it is a bit risky.

CENTRAL & EASTERN GUATEMALA

It's possible to **camp** at Semuc Champey, but be sure to pitch a tent only in the upper areas, as flash floods are common down below. It's risky to leave anything unattended, as it might get stolen. The place now has 24-hour security, which may reassure potential campers but you should keep your valuables with you. You will also need to bring all supplies, as there's no shop of any kind nearby.

Las Marías (dm US$2, private room per person US$4) is a newish, rustic, laid-back place by the road, 1km short of Semuc Champey. It has a couple of dorm rooms and three private rooms, all in wooden buildings in a verdant setting. Capacity is 22. Cool drinks and vegetarian food are available (full dinner US$2.60). You can swim in the nearby Río Cahabón.

Pickups run from the plaza in Lanquín to Semuc Champey – your chances of catching one are better in the early morning and on market days: Sunday, Monday and Thursday. If there are a lot of local people traveling, expect to pay US$0.65; otherwise, it's US$1.95. The walk is long and hot.

Fray Bartolomé de Las Casas

This town, often referred to simply as Las Casas or Fray, is a way station on the backdoor route between the Cobán/Lanquín area and Poptún on the Río Dulce–Flores highway. This route is nearly all along unpaved roads and is dotted with traditional Mayan villages where only the patriarchs speak Spanish, and then only a little. This is a great opportunity for getting off the 'Gringo Trail' and into the heart of Guatemala.

Las Casas is pretty substantial for being in the middle of nowhere, but don't let its size fool you. This is a place where the weekly soccer game is the biggest deal in town, chickens languish in the streets and siesta is taken seriously.

The town itself is fairly spread out, with the plaza and most tourist facilities at one end and the market and bus terminus at the other. Walking between the two takes about 10 minutes. Coming from Cobán, you'll want to hop off at the central plaza.

The **post office** and **police station** are just off the plaza. Nearby, **Banrural** changes US dollars and traveler's checks. The **Municipalidad** (Town Hall) is on the plaza.

The friendly **Hotel y Restaurante Bartolo** (s/d with bathroom US4/8; 🔊) Behind the plaza,

has the best accommodations in town. The restaurant serves good food for US$2 a plate. Nearby **Hospedaje Ralios** (rooms US$3) has dark, basic rooms around a flower-filled courtyard.

One daily bus departs from the plaza at 3am for Poptún (US$4, five to six hours, 100km). Buses for Cobán leave hourly between 4am and 4pm. Some go via Chisec (US$2, 3½ hours). Others take the slower route via San Pedro Carchá.

LAS CONCHAS

From Las Casas you can visit Las Conchas, a series of limestone pools and waterfalls on the Río Chiyú, which some say are better than those at Semuc Champey. The pools are up to 8m deep and 20m wide and connected by a series of spectacular waterfalls. The ponds are not turquoise like those at Semuc. From Fray you travel east on the gravel road toward Río Dulce and then turn off at the marked sign to Las Conchas, a few kilometers east of Chahal. The pools are 3km north of the main road. You can ask for more information at the Municipalidad in Fray Bartolomé de las Casas.

CHISEC & AROUND

The town of Chisec, 66km north of Cobán, is becoming a center for reaching several exciting destinations. This is thanks to the paving of nearly all the road from Cobán to Sayaxché and Flores, which runs through here, and some admirable community tourism programs aiming to help develop this long-ignored region whose population is almost entirely Q'eqchi' Maya.

From Chisec you can visit the jungle-surrounded **Lagunas de Sepalau** (guided tours US$3.25), 7km east, the **Cuevas de B'omb'il Pek** (US$5) with ancient Mayan drawings, a 3km walk north, and the huge **Cuevas de Candelaria** (guided tours US$3.25) cave system, some 30km northeast near San Antonio. Pickups or vans run to Sepalau every hour from 6am to 3pm; the Candelaria caves are reachable by buses or minibuses bound for Raxrujá or Fray Bartolomé de Las Casas from Cobán via Chisec. Also within reach from Chisec are the Parque Nacional Laguna Lachuá (p199) and the large Classic-Mayan site of **Cancuén** (www.cancuénproject.org) on the Río de la Pasión. About 65km northeast, the journey to Cancuén includes a two-hour river trip from the village of La Isla, which is some 12km north of the town of Raxrujá. Cancuén, which is only now being seriously excavated for the first time, is thought to have been, unusually, a trading rather than religious center.

There's a heap of information on the Chisec area on the website www.puertaal mundomaya.com.

Chisec has a few places to stay.

Hotel La Estancia (☎ 979-7748; s/d/tr US$8/13/18; **P** **⬛**) The best hotel, on the main road at the northern exit from town, it has rooms with private bathroom, fan and TV. It has a restaurant.

Hotel Nopales, (central plaza; s & d US$6.50) This is a cheaper alternative. It too has a restaurant.

Pensión Gutiérrez (rooms per person US$3) In Raxrujá, this two-story wooden house has been recommended for its rooms with mosquito net, fan and shared bathroom.

Buses leave Chisec for Cobán (US$1.95, two hours) eight times daily, 3am to 2pm. Buses or minibuses to San Antonio and Raxrujá (one hour) go hourly, 6am to 4pm. Some of these continue to Fray Bartolomé de Las Casas. There are also two services daily, morning and afternoon, to La Isla (1¼ hours) and two to Playa Grande (two hours), for the Parque Nacional Laguna Lachuá. Some Cobán–Sayaxché minibuses and buses pass through Chisec. There are at least five scheduled departures daily to both Sayaxché and Cobán from Raxrujá.

PARQUE NACIONAL LAGUNA LACHUÁ

This **national park** (US$5.25; camping per tent US$3.25, bunk with mozzie net US$7.75) is renowned for the perfectly round, pristine turquoise lake (220m deep) for which it was named. Until recently, this Guatemalan gem was rarely visited by travelers because it was an active, violent area during the civil war and the road was in pathetic disrepair. Overnight visitors can use the cooking facilities, so come prepared with food and drink. There is only one shower. You can no longer rent canoes for exploring the lake but there are hiking trails. The Cobán tour outfits (p191) offer two-day and one-night trips for US$90 per person. Proyecto EcoQuetzal, also in Cobán, does jungle hikes to the **Río Ikbolay** in the Laguna Lachuá vicinity.

Outside the park, about 7km southwest of the park entrance, is **Finca Chipantún** (www.chipantun.com; camping per person US$1.30, bed per person US$4), 4 sq km of private land bordering the Río Chixoy (Negro). It has teak and cardamom plantations plus virgin tropical rain forest, and some uncovered Mayan ruins. Apart from accommodations, there are horse-riding opportunities, forest trails, river trips, kayaking, and bird- and wildlife watching. The owners can take you by boat on the Río Negro to El Peyan, a magical gorge. Meals cost US$2.50 to US$4.

A new road (though unpaved most of the way from Chisec) means you can get to the park entrance from Cobán in four hours by bus. Take a Playa Grande (Cantabal) bus from Cobán via Chisec and ask the driver to leave you at the park entrance, from which it's about a 4km walk to the lake.

RÍO HONDO

Río Hondo, 50km east of El Rancho junction and 130km from Guatemala City, is where the CA-10 to Chiquimula heads south off the Carretera al Atlántico (CA-9). Beyond Chiquimula are turnoffs to Copán, just across the Honduran border; to Esquipulas and on to Nueva Ocotepeque (Honduras); and a remote border crossing between Guatemala and El Salvador at Anguiatú, 12km north of Metapán (El Salvador).

The actual town of Río Hondo (Deep River) is northeast of the junction. Lodging places hereabouts may list their address as Río Hondo, Santa Cruz Río Hondo or Santa Cruz Teculután. Nine kilometers west of the junction are several attractive motels right on the CA-9, which provide a good base for explorations of this region if you have your own vehicle. By car, it's an hour from here to Quiriguá, half an hour to Chiquimula or 1½ hours to Esquipulas. These motels are treated as weekend resorts by locals and residents of Guatemala City, so they are heavily booked on weekends. They're all modern, pleasant places, with well-equipped bungalows (all have cable TV and bathroom), spacious grounds with large or giant swimming pools, and good restaurants, open 6am to 10pm daily. Note that you can find other eateries along the highway.

The following four motels are all near one another at Km 126 on the Carretera al Atlántico.

Hotel Santa Cruz (☎ 934-7112; fax 934-7075; s/d/tr with air-con US$14/27/39; P X ⊠) The low-key Santa Cruz has rooms in duplex bungalows, with fan or air-con, spread over a large area with plenty of foliage. Its popular **restaurant** (breakfasts US$2-4, 3-course lunches US$4.50) is good value.

Hotel El Atlántico (☎ 934-7160; fax 934-7041; s/d/tr US$18/36/42; P X ⊠) This place has 58 large bungalows set in attractive spacious grounds.

Hotel Nuevo Pasabién (☎ 934-7201; fax 934-8788; pasabien@infovia.com.gt; s/d/tr US$20/39/42; P X ⊠) On the north side of the highway, this establishment has large rooms with big windows. It's a good choice for travelers with children who can enjoy the three pools with all manner of fancy slides.

Hotel Longarone (☎ 934-7126; fax 934-7035; s/d/tr US$31/37/43, with cable TV & fridge US$49/55/61; P X ⊠) Opposite the Hotel Santa Cruz, Hotel Longarone has a long row of rooms, in addition to their super-comfy duplex bungalows. A high toboggan makes for plenty of pool hi-jinks on weekends. You could retreat to the tennis court! The **restaurant** (mains US$6-13) is excellent, the service impeccable, and there's a coffee machine at the bar.

Nine kilometers east of these places, right at the junction with the CA-10, is the beat-up **Hotel Río** (Carretera al Atlántico Km 135).

Valle Dorado

Another attraction of Río Hondo is the Valle Dorado aquatic park and tourist center.

Valle Dorado (☎ 220-8840, 933-1111; Carretera al Atlántico Km 149; d/tr US$58/68, family rooms US$108) This large complex 14km past the Highway CA-10 junction and 23km from the other Río Hondo hotels, includes an **aquatic park** (adult/child Mon-Fri US$5/4, Sat & Sun US$6/5; 8:30am-5:30pm) with giant pools, waterslides, toboggans and other entertainment. Make reservations on weekends.

ESTANZUELA
pop 10,000

Traveling south from Río Hondo along the CA-10, you are in the midst of the Río Motagua valley, a hot expanse of what is known as 'dry tropic,' which once supported a great number and variety of dinosaurs. Three kilometers south of the Carretera al Atlántico you'll see a small monument on the right-hand (west) side of the road commemorating the earthquake disaster of February 4, 1976.

Less than 2km south of the earthquake monument is the small town of Estanzuela, with its **Museo de Paleontología, Arqueología y Geología Ingeniero Roberto Woolfolk Sarvia** (☎ 941-4981; admission free; 9am-5pm), a startling museum filled with dinosaur bones – some reconstructed and rather menacing-looking. Most of the bones of three giant creatures are here, including those of a huge ground sloth some 30,000 years old and a prehistoric whale. Other exhibits include early Mayan artifacts. To find the museum, go west from the highway directly through the town for 1km, following the small blue signs pointing to the *museo*.

ZACAPA
pop 18,000 / elevation 230m

Capital of the department of the same name, Zacapa is just east of Highway CA-10 a few kilometers south of Estanzuela. This town offers little to travelers, though the locals do make cheese, cigars and superb rum. The few hotels in town are basic and will do in an emergency, but better accommodations are available in Río Hondo, Esquipulas and Chiquimula. The bus station is on the road into town from the CA-10.

CHIQUIMULA
pop 24,000 / elevation 370m

Another departmental capital, this one set in a mining and tobacco-growing region, Chiquimula is on CA-10, 32km south of the Carretera al Atlántico. It is a major market town for all of eastern Guatemala, with lots of daily buying and selling activity. For travelers it's not a destination but a transit point. Your goal is probably the fabulous Mayan ruins at Copán in Honduras, just across the border from El Florido. There are also some interesting journeys between Chiquimula and Jalapa, 78km to the east (p203). Among other things, Chiquimula is famous for its sweltering climate and its decent budget hotels (a couple have swimming pools).

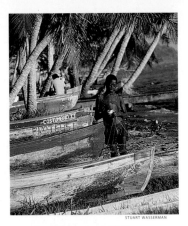
STUART WASSERMAN

Shoreline, **Lívingston** (p232)

LEE FOSTER

Boat tour, **Río Dulce** (p234)

ALFREDO MAIQUEZ

Stela portraying King 18 Rabbit,
Copán (p211)

Semuc Champey (p197)

CHRIS BARTON

Temple, **Tikal** (p257)

ERIC L WHEAT

Flores (p242), El Petén

RICHARD I'ANSON

RALPH LEE HOPKINS

Ocellated turkey (p43), Tikal

RICHARD I'ANSON

Coatis (p43), Tikal

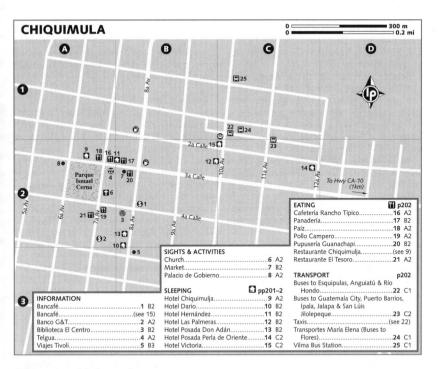

CHIQUIMULA

INFORMATION	
Bancafé......................................1 B2	
Bancafé..................................(see 15)	
Banco G&T................................2 A2	
Biblioteca El Centro...................3 B2	
Telgua.....................................4 A2	
Viajes Tivoli.............................5 B3	

SIGHTS & ACTIVITIES	
Church.......................................6 A2	
Market.......................................7 B2	
Palacio de Gobierno.....................8 A2	

SLEEPING	pp201–2
Hotel Chiquimulja.......................9 A2	
Hotel Dario...............................10 B2	
Hotel Hernández.........................11 B2	
Hotel Las Palmeras......................12 B2	
Hotel Posada Don Adán................13 B2	
Hotel Posada Perla de Oriente........14 C2	
Hotel Victoria............................15 C2	

EATING	p202
Cafetería Rancho Típico................16 A2	
Panadería.................................17 B2	
Paíz..18 A2	
Pollo Campero...........................19 A2	
Pupusería Guanachapi..................20 B2	
Restaurante Chiquimulja.............(see 9)	
Restaurante El Tesoro...................21 A2	

TRANSPORT	p202
Buses to Esquipulas, Anguiatú & Río	
Hondo...................................22 C1	
Buses to Guatemala City, Puerto Barrios,	
Ipala, Jalapa & San Lúis	
Jilolepeque...............................23 C2	
Taxis....................................(see 22)	
Transportes María Elena (Buses to	
Flores)...................................24 C1	
Vilma Bus Station......................25 C1	

Orientation & Information

Though very hot, Chiquimula is easy to get around on foot.

Bancafé (cnr 2a Calle & 10a Av, Zona 1, Comercial Centro El Punto, cnr 4a Calle & 8a Av, Zona 1) Both branches have Visa ATMs.

Banco G&T (7a Av 4-75, Zona 1; 9am-8pm Mon-Fri, 10am-2pm Sat) Half a block south of the plaza. Changes US dollars and traveler's checks, and gives cash advances on Visa and MasterCard.

Biblioteca El Centro (cnr 4a Calle & 8a Av; US$1.30 per hr; 8am-7pm Mon-Fri, 8am-6pm Sat-Sun) For email and Internet.

Post office (10a Av) In a dirt alley between 1a and 2a Calles, around to the side of the building opposite the bus station.

Telgua (3a Calle) Plenty of card-phones, a few doors downhill from Parque Ismael Cerna.

Viajes Tivoli (942-4915, 942-4933; fax 942-2258; 8a Av 4-71, Zona 1) Can help you with travel arrangements.

Sleeping

Hotel Hernández (942-0708; 3a Calle 7-41, Zona 1; s/d US$4/6, s/d with hot-water bathroom US$8/13;) In the block northeast of the plaza, this is the pick of the bunch. It's clean,

pleasant and friendly; the owner speaks English, Spanish and a little French. The sprawling property has a sparkling swimming pool and plenty of greenery. The rooms all have fans and good beds. Overlooking the pool are some singles/doubles with air-con for US$13/20.

Hotel Posada Don Adán (942-3924; 8a Av 4-30, Zona 1; s/d/tr US$16/24/32;) Run by a friendly, efficient *señora* and her polite husband, Adán, this place is spotless. The spacious rooms have hot-water bathroom, cable TV, fan and air-con.

Hotel Chiquimulja (942-0387; 3a Calle 6-51; s/d US$8/16, with air-con US$9/18;) This hotel is on the north side of the plaza. Despite some remodeling and bright bed covers, these rooms with bathroom and TV seem a bit run-down. But don't miss the fantastic *palapa*-style restaurant out back (p202).

Hotel Posada Perla de Oriente (942-0014; fax 942-0534; 12a Av 2-30, Zona 1; s/d/tr/q US$14/25/35/50, s/d with air-con US$33/47;) This hotel is entered through a pleasantly shaded garden, with a small swimming pool, children's play area and a restaurant, on

2a Calle. The simple, old-fashioned rooms have hot-water bathroom, fan and cable TV. There are better, newer rooms with air-con out back.

Hotel Las Palmeras (☎ 942-4647; 10a Av 2-00; s/d US$4/7, with air-con US$7/13; P 🏃) This clean, family-run hotel has 30 rooms with bathroom, cable TV, air-con or fan, and good beds. There's a place to do your laundry, a terrace, and a few splashes of color – pink on one level, blue on another.

Hotel Victoria (☎ 942-2732, 942-2179; cnr 2a Calle & 10a Av; s/d/tr/q US$6/12/18/24) Proximity to the bus station is the main reason to stay here. The small rooms have fan, cable TV and private bath. There is also a telephone service, and a good, cheap restaurant with big breakfasts (US$2 to US$3).

Hotel Dario (☎ 942-0192; 8a Av 4-40, Zona 1; s/d US$3/6, with bathroom US$4/8) Almost next door to the Don Adán, the Dario has 15 rooms of different shapes, sizes and levels of comfort. They cover the gamut from a darkish room with fan and shared bathroom to an airier unit with bathroom and cable TV.

Eating

Restaurante Chiquimulja (3a Calle 6-51; breakfasts US$2-3.25, mains US$4-7) In the Hotel Chiquimulja, this is an impressive palm-roofed building on two levels. Relax with a lovely long *limonada* and choose from the list of pasta dishes, prawns and grilled meats.

Cafetería Rancho Típico (breakfasts US$0.80-4, snacks US$0.65-2) A few doors down the street from Restaurante Chiquimulja, Rancho Típico prepares really good drinks (US$1.20) with lots of ice and serves a variety of light meals – hamburgers, tostadas, enchiladas etc.

Pupusería Guanachapi You can fill up here, in the market area just down from Telgua, for only a few quetzals. A *pupusa* is a dish from El Salvador, consisting of a cornmeal mass stuffed with cheese or refried beans, or a mixture of both.

Restaurante El Tesoro (mains US$3.25-5.80) Just south of the main plaza, El Tesoro serves Chinese food at decent prices. It's cavernous and has lots of overhead fans.

Pollo Campero (cnr 7a Av & 4a Calle) Near the southeast corner of the plaza, Pollo Campero serves up fried chicken, burgers and breakfasts. Open daily, its air-con is a treat.

Paíz (3a Calle) This plaza grocery store is tremendous and sells close to everything

under the sun. Stock up here for a picnic, or stop in to enjoy the air-con.

Panadería Next door to Hotel Hernández, this one opens at 5:30am – perfect for that predawn bus departure.

Getting There & Away

Several companies operate buses to Guatemala City and Puerto Barrios; all of them arrive and depart from the bus station area on 11a Av, between 1a and 2a Calles. Ipala and San Lúis Jilotepeque *microbuses* and the Jalapa bus also go from here. Minibuses to Esquipulas, Río Hondo and Anguiatú and buses to Flores arrive and depart a block away, on 10a Av between 1a and 2a Calles. **Vilma** (☎ 942-2064), which operates buses to El Florido, the border crossing on the way to Copán, has its own bus station a couple of blocks north.

Agua Caliente, Honduras border Take a minibus to Esquipulas and change there.

Anguiatú, El Salvador border (US$1.20, 1hr, 54km) Hourly minibuses, 5am to 5:30 pm.

El Florido, Honduras border (US$1.20, 1½hr, 58km) Chicken buses depart from the Vilma bus station half-hourly, 5:30am to 4:30pm.

Esquipulas (US$1.20, 45min, 52km) Minibuses run every 10min, 4am to 8pm. Sit on the left for the best views of the basilica.

Flores (US$7, 7-8hr, 385km) Transportes María Elena (☎ 942-3420) goes at 6am, 10am and 3pm.

Guatemala City (US$3.25, 3hr,169km) Rutas Orientales and other companies depart at least hourly, 3am to 3:30pm. The 3am bus leaves from the plaza, the rest from the bus station.

Ipala (US$0.65, 1½hr) Microbuses depart half hourly, 5am to 6pm.

Jalapa (US$1.95, 3½hr, 78km) One direct bus at 6am daily. Otherwise take a *microbus* to Ipala or San Lúis Jilotepeque (US$1, 1hr) and change. The road to Ipala and San Lúis is now paved and the last section through to Jalapa is due to be paved soon.

Puerto Barrios (US$3.25, 4½hr, 192km) Buses run every 30 minutes, 4am to 6pm.

Quiriguá (US$2.10, 2 hours, 103km) Take a Puerto Barrios bus.

Río Dulce Take a Flores bus, or a Puerto Barrios bus to La Ruidosa junction (US$3.25, 3hr, 144km) and change there.

Río Hondo (US$1, 35min, 32km) There are minibuses every half hour, 5am to 6pm. Or take any bus heading for Guatemala City, Flores or Puerto Barrios. On Sunday, Guatemala City buses won't let you on for Río Hondo – take a minibus.

AROUND CHIQUIMULA
Volcán de Ipala
Volcán de Ipala is a 1650m volcano, notable for its especially beautiful clear crater lake measuring nearly a kilometer around and nestled below the summit at 1493m. The dramatic hike to the top takes you from 800m to 1650m in about two hours, though you can drive halfway up in a car. There are trails, a visitors center and a campsite on the shores of the lake. To get there, take a bus from Chiquimula (1½ hours) or Jalapa (two hours) to Ipala and transfer to a *microbus* to Agua Blanca (US$0.40, every 15 minutes). The trailhead is at El Sauce just before Agua Blanca; look for the blue Inguat sign. There are several banks and serviceable (but basic) *hospedajes* in Ipala if you want to stay overnight there.

Jalapa
Jalapa is a small, friendly town 78km west of Chiquimula, and the route is a stunning one: verdant gorges choked with banana trees alternate with fog-enveloped valleys. Crossing the rugged mountain passes you'll see waterfalls, rivers and creeks flowing through the undergrowth. Though there isn't much going on in Jalapa proper, it's a good stopover before or after Volcán Ipala. There are plenty of services for travelers. Banks that change US dollars and traveler's checks are clustered around the bus terminal.

SLEEPING & EATING
Posada de Don José Antonio (☎ 922-5751; Av Chipilapa A 0-64, Zona 2; s/d/tr US$13/16/20; P) This place has clean rooms with bathroom and TV around a small courtyard. There's also a restaurant.

Hotel Villa Plaza (☎ 922-4841; 1a Calle 0-70, Zona 2; s/d/tr US$13/20/21) This hotel boasts big rooms with hot-water bathroom and cable TV.

Hotel Villa del Río (☎ 922-4467; Av Chipilapa 2-66, Zona 6; s/d/tr US$11/18/20; P) Run by the same friendly folk as the Villa Plaza, it has much the same facilities but is old-fashioned in style.

Hotel Real del Centro (☎ 922-5383; Av Chipilapa B 1-58, Zona 2; s/d/tr US$16/26/35) This has large, clean rooms with quality beds and hot-water bathroom. Rooms in the back are dark.

Pensión Casa del Viajero (1a Av 0-64; s/d US$4/8, s/d/tr with hot-water bathroom US$8/12/16) Though four long blocks from the bus terminal, this is a safe, clean place to stay. Some rooms and beds are better than others. There's a good restaurant.

Hotel Recinos (☎ 922-2580; s/d US$4/8, with bathroom & cable TV US$8/16) You can't miss this bright pink monster on the west side of the terminal. The clean rooms with fan and shared bathroom are a good deal.

Restaurante Casa Real Next door to the Hotel Villa Plaza, this is an excellent choice for meals.

GETTING THERE & AWAY
Buses leave Jalapa for Chiquimula once daily. This may change when the road through is totally paved. Plenty of *microbuses* head to Ipala where you can change for Chiquimula. For Esquipulas, change in Chiquimula. Buses to Guatemala City leave half-hourly between 2am and 3pm. Transportes Melva travels via Jutiapa and Cuilapa (US$2, 3½ hours, 167km). Other buses take the quicker route via Sanarate and the Carretera al Atlántico.

PADRE MIGUEL JUNCTION & ANGUIATÚ
Between Chiquimula and Esquipulas (35 km from Chiquimula and 14km from Esquipulas), Padre Miguel junction is the turnoff for Anguiatú, the border of El Salvador, which is 19km (30 minutes) away. Minibuses pass by frequently, coming from Chiquimula, Quetzaltepeque and Esquipulas.

The border at Anguiatú is open from 6am to 7pm daily. Plenty of trucks cross here. Across the border there are hourly buses to San Salvador, passing through Metapán and Santa Ana.

ESQUIPULAS
From Chiquimula, the CA-10 goes south into the mountains, where it's a bit cooler. After an hour's ride through pretty country, the highway descends into a valley ringed by mountains, where Esquipulas stands. Halfway down the slope, about a kilometer from the center of town, there is a *mirador* (lookout) from which to get a good view. The reason for a trip to Esquipulas is evident as soon as you catch sight of the place, dominated by the great Basílica de

Esquipulas towering above the town, its whiteness shimmering in the sun. The view has changed little in over 150 years since explorer John L Stephens saw it and described it in his book *Incidents of Travel in Central America, Chiapas and Yucatan* (1841):

> Descending, the clouds were lifted, and I looked down upon an almost boundless plain, running from the foot of the Sierra, and afar off saw, standing alone in the wilderness, the great church of Esquipulas, like the Church of the Holy Sepulchre in Jerusalem, and the Caaba in Mecca, the holiest of temples...I had a long and magnificent descent to the foot of the Sierra.

History

This town may have been a place of pilgrimage before the Spanish conquest. Legend has it that the town takes its name from a noble Mayan lord who ruled this region when the Spanish arrived, and who received them in peace.

With the arrival of the friars, a church was built, and in 1595 an image of Christ carved from black wood was installed behind the altar. The steady flow of pilgrims to Esquipulas became a flood after 1737, when Pedro Pardo de Figueroa, Archbishop of Guatemala, came here on pilgrimage and went away cured of a chronic ailment. Delighted with this development, the prelate commissioned a huge new church to be built on the site. It was finished in 1758, and the pilgrimage trade has been the town's livelihood ever since.

Esquipulas has assured its place in modern history as well: in 1986, President Vinicio Cerezo Arévalo spearheaded a series of meetings here with the other Central American heads of state to negotiate regional agreements on economic cooperation and peaceful conflict resolution. The resulting pact, known as the Esquipulas II Accord, became the seed of the Guatemalan Peace Accords, which were finally signed in 1996.

Orientation & Information

The basilica is the center of everything. Most of the good hotels are within a

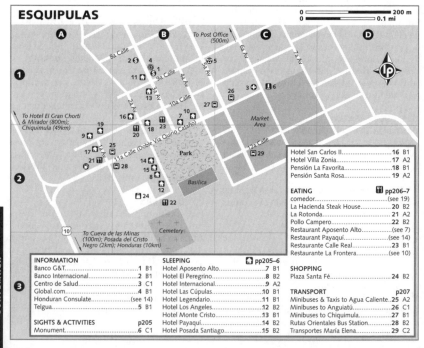

ESQUIPULAS

Hotel San Carlos II	16 B1
Hotel Villa Zonia	17 A2
Pensión La Favorita	18 B1
Pensión Santa Rosa	19 A2

EATING pp206–7
comedor	(see 19)
La Hacienda Steak House	20 B2
La Rotonda	21 A2
Pollo Campero	22 B2
Restaurant Aposento Alto	(see 7)
Restaurant Payaquí	(see 14)
Restaurante Calle Real	23 B1
Restaurante La Frontera	(see 10)

INFORMATION
Banco G&T	1 B1
Banco Internacional	2 B1
Centro de Salud	3 C1
Global.com	4 B1
Honduran Consulate	(see 14)
Telgua	5 B1

SIGHTS & ACTIVITIES p205
Monument	6 C1

SLEEPING pp205–6
Hotel Aposento Alto	7 B1
Hotel El Peregrino	8 B2
Hotel Internacional	9 A2
Hotel Las Cúpulas	10 B1
Hotel Legendario	11 B1
Hotel Los Angeles	12 B2
Hotel Monte Cristo	13 B1
Hotel Payaquí	14 B2
Hotel Posada Santiago	15 B2

SHOPPING
Plaza Santa Fé	24 B2

TRANSPORT p207
Minibuses & Taxis to Agua Caliente	25 A2
Minibuses to Anguiatú	26 C1
Minibuses to Chiquimula	27 B1
Rutas Orientales Bus Station	28 B2
Transportes María Elena	29 C2

block or two of it, as are numerous small restaurants. The town's most luxurious hotel, the Gran Chortí, is on the outskirts, along the road to Chiquimula. The highway does not enter town; 11a Calle, also sometimes called Doble Vía Quirio Cataño, comes in from the highway and is the town's main drag.

Banco Internacional (3a Av 8-87, Zona 1) Changes cash and traveler's checks, gives cash advances on Visa and MasterCard, is the town's American Express agent, and has a Visa ATM.

Global.com (3a Av; per hr US$1.55) Opposite Banco Internacional; check your email here.

Post office (6a Av 2-15) About 10 blocks north of the center.

Telgua (cnr 5a Av & 9a Calle) Plenty of card-phones.

Basilica

A massive pile of stone that has resisted the power of earthquakes for almost 250 years, the Basilica is approached through a pretty park and up a wide flight of steps. The impressive facade and towers are floodlit at night.

Inside, the devout approach the surprisingly small (with all the fuss, you'd think it was life-size) El Cristo Negro with extreme reverence, many on their knees. Incense, murmured prayers and the scuffle of sandaled feet fills the air. When there are throngs of pilgrims, you must enter the church from the side to get a close view of the famous Black Christ. Shuffling along quickly, you may get a good glimpse or two before being shoved onward by the crowd behind you. On Sundays, religious holidays and (especially) during the festival around January 15, the press of devotees is intense. Guatemalan tourist authorities estimate that one million visitors a year come to Esquipulas to see the Black Christ. On weekdays, you may have the place to yourself, which can be very powerful and rewarding. On weekends, you'll probably feel very removed from the intensity of emotion shown by the majority of pilgrims whose faith is very deep.

The annual **Cristo de Esquipulas festival** (January 15) sees mobs of devout pilgrims coming from all over the region to worship at the altar of the Black Christ.

When you leave the church and descend the steps through the park and exit right to the market, notice the vendors selling straw hats that are decorated with artificial flowers and stitched with the name 'Esquipulas,' perfect for pilgrims who want everyone to know they've made the trip. These are very popular rearview mirror accessories for chicken bus drivers countrywide. Cruising the religious kitsch sold by the throngs of vendors around the basilica is an entertaining diversion.

Cueva de las Minas

The **Centro Turístico Cueva de las Minas** (US$0.65; ☉ 6:30am-4pm) has a 50m-deep cave (bring your own light), grassy picnic areas, and the Río El Milagro, where people come for a dip and say it's miraculous. The cave and river are half a kilometer from their entrance gate, which is behind the Basilica's cemetery, 300m south of the turnoff into town on the road heading toward Honduras. Refreshments are available.

Sleeping

Esquipulas has an abundance of places to stay. On holidays and during the annual festival, every hotel in town is filled, whatever the price; weekends are super busy as well, with prices substantially higher. These higher prices are the ones given here. On weekdays when there is no festival, there are *descuentos* (discounts). For cheap rooms, look in the streets immediately north of the towering basilica.

Hotel El Gran Chortí (☎ 943-1148; fax 943-1551; Carretera Internacional a Honduras Km 222; s/d US$46/61, 4-person ste US$92; Ⓟ 🍴 🏊) One kilometer west of the church on the road to Chiquimula, this hotel's lobby floor is composed of a hectare of black marble; behind it a serpentine swimming pool is set amid lawns, gardens and umbrella-shaded café tables. There's a games room and, of course, a good restaurant, bar and cafetería. The rooms have all comforts.

Hotel Posada del Cristo Negro (☎ 943-1482; fax 943-1829; Carretera Internacional a Honduras Km 224; s/d/tr US$17/22/33/39; Ⓟ 🍴 🏊) Perhaps Guatemala's best country-club resort in the 1960s, this hotel is 2km from the church, out of town on the way to Honduras. Broad green lawns, a pretty swimming pool, a large dining room and other services make it elaborate. The comfortable rooms have bathroom, fridge and TV.

Hotel Payaquí (☎ 943-2025; fax 943-1371; 2a Av 11-56; s/d/tr US$23/45/58; 🍴 🏊 Ⓟ) This large, attractive hotel has 55 rooms, all with bathroom, cable TV, phone and fridge. Prices quoted include air-con. Monday to Thursday the same rooms go for US$18/36/54 while rooms without air-con are US$12/24/36. It has a restaurant (p207).

Hotel Legendario (☎ 943-1824/5; www.portahot els.com; cnr 3a Av & 9a Calle, Zona 1; s/d/tr US$38/44/51; P ⊠) You'll find this modern member of the Porta Hotels group appealing. The 40 rooms all have bathroom, fan, cable TV and large windows opening onto a grassy courtyard with an inviting swimming pool. There's also a restaurant

Hotel Villa Zonia (☎ 943-1133; 10a Calle 1-84, Zona 1; s/d from US$16/26; P) This attractive hotel shows less signs of wear and tear than most in Esquipulas. There are 15 bright rooms, all with bathroom and cable TV. Some rooms have one double bed, others have two.

Hotel Aposento Alto (☎ 943-1115, ☎ /fax 943-3325; 3a Av 10-35, Zona 1; s/d US$10/16, with hot-water bathroom US$16/20; P) Try this good-value hotel with ample-sized clean rooms and freshly tiled bathrooms. Some rooms have balconies, albeit over the street. The attached restaurant is excellent (p207).

Hotel Las Cúpulas (☎ /fax 943-1570; cnr 11a Calle & 4a Av; s/d US$26/39) This newish establishment has large pleasant rooms with fan, hot-water bathroom and cable TV; some have balconies. Prices slide down to US$7 per person from Monday to Thursday when there's no religious festival.

Hotel El Peregrino (☎ 943-1054, 943-1859; 2a Av 11-94, Zona 1; s/d US$10/20, with TV US$14/28; P) This hotel on the southwest corner of the plaza has simple rooms with hot-water bathroom opening on to a small courtyard with a few palm trees. There's a new section in the rear with larger, fancier rooms with cable TV. There's also a restaurant.

Hotel Los Ángeles (☎ 943-1254; 2a Av 11-94, Zona 1; s/d/tr US$13/26/39; P) Next door to the Peregrino, this place has 23 rooms arranged around a bright inner courtyard, all with bathroom, fan and cable TV. It also has a restaurant.

Hotel Posada Santiago (☎ 943-2023; s/d US$7/13, with hot-water bathroom & cable TV US$20; P) This hotel has slightly shabby but perfectly acceptable fan-cooled rooms, and a decent restaurant. Guests can use the Hotel Payaqui's pool for US$1.30.

Hotel Internacional (☎ 943-1131, 943-1667; 10a Calle 0-85, Zona 1; s/d/tr US$13/20/29, with air-con US$20/39/45; P ⊠) This establishment is on three levels around a covered courtyard. There are two underground levels, perhaps claustrophobic for some. The 49 clean, pleasant rooms have bathroom, cable TV and phone.

Hotel Monte Cristo (☎ 943-1453; fax 943-1042; 3a Av 9-12, Zona 1; s/d US$9/11, s/d/tr with hot-water bathroom US$20/24/27; P) The 35 rooms are clean and spacious and have carpets and cable TV. They're comfy enough but well used.

Pensión Santa Rosa (☎ 943-2908; cnr 10a Calle & 1a Av, Zona 1; s/d US$4/8, with hot-water bathroom US$5/10) Typical of the small backstreet places, this family-run *pension* has rooms set off a big concrete courtyard. The **Hotel San Carlos II** next door is similar in price, standard and layout, as is the **Pensión La Favorita**, and there are several others on this street.

Eating

Restaurants are slightly more expensive here than in other parts of Guatemala. Budget restaurants are clustered at the north end of the park, where hungry pilgrims can find them readily. Most eateries open from 6:30am until 9pm or 10pm daily.

The street running north opposite the church (3a Av) has several eateries including **Restaurante Calle Real** (breakfasts US$2-4, mains US$4-6), which is large, clean and well priced.

La Rotonda (11a Calle; breakfasts from US$1.55-3.50, large pizza US$10) Opposite Rutas Orientales bus station, this is a round building with chairs arranged around a circular open-air counter under a big awning. It's a welcoming place, clean and fresh. There are plenty of selections to choose from, including pizza, pasta and burgers. Nearby, the **comedor** (cnr 10a Calle & 1a Av, Zona 1; lunch US$3) attached to the Pensión Santa Rosa has good set lunches.

Pollo Campero (11a Calle) The Esquipulas branch of Guatemala's beloved eatery chain, just to the west of the basilica, even has a drive-through.

La Hacienda Steak House (cnr 2a Av & 10a Calle; breakfasts US$3-6, mains US$9-20; ⏰ 8am-10pm) An enjoyable place for grilled steaks, chicken and seafood, it has clean red-and-yellow tablecloths and attractive metal candle holders.

All of the mid-range and top-end hotels have their own dining rooms.

Restaurant Payaquí (breakfasts US$2, mains US$5-7) On the west side of the park in the hotel of the same name, this is a bright and clean cafetería with big windows looking out onto the park. Prices are reasonable, and there's a good selection.

Restaurante La Frontera (breakfasts US$2-4, mains US$4-10) Opposite the park, La Frontera is attached to the Hotel Las Cúpulas. This is a spacious, clean place serving up a good variety of rice, chicken, meat, fish and seafood dishes at good prices.

Restaurante Aposento Alto (breakfasts US$2-3.50, mains US$3-8) Aposento Alto serves up great food in comfy surroundings with some attention to decor. The giant TV might deter some. Fish fans should try the fillet in a cream sauce.

Getting There & Away

Buses to Guatemala City arrive and depart from the bus station of **Rutas Orientales** (☎ 943-1366; cnr 11a Calle & 1a Av), near the entrance to town. Minibuses to Agua Caliente arrive and depart across the street; taxis also wait here, charging the same as the minibuses, once they have five passengers.

Minibuses to Chiquimula and to Anguiatú depart from the east end of 11a Calle; you'll probably see them hawking for passengers along the main street.

Agua Caliente, Honduras border (US$1.30, 30min, 10km) Minibuses run every half hour, 6am to 5pm.

Anguiatú, El Salvador border (US$1, 1hr, 33km) Minibuses run every half hour, 6am to 6pm.

Chiquimula (US$1, 45min, 52km) Minibuses run every 15 minutes, 5am to 6pm.

Flores (US$7.75, 8-10hr, 437km) Transportes María Elena (☎ 943-0448) buses depart at 4am, 8am and 1pm from east of the basilica, amid the market.

Guatemala City (US$4, 4hr, 222km) Rutas Orientales special service buses depart at 6:30am and 7:30am, 1:30pm and 3pm; ordinary buses depart every half hour, 4:30am-6pm.

COPÁN SITE (HONDURAS)

The ancient city of **Copán** (US$10; ⊗ 8am-4pm), 13km from the Guatemalan border in Honduras, is one of the most outstanding Mayan achievements, ranking in splendor with Tikal, Chichén Itzá and Uxmal. To fully appreciate Mayan art and culture, you must visit Copán. This can be done on a long day trip by private car, public bus or organized tour, but it's better to take at least two days, staying the night in the town of Copán Ruinas. This is a sweet town, with good facilities, so unless you're in a huge rush, try to overnight here. Get to the site around opening time to avoid the heat and the crowds.

There are two Copáns: the town and the ruins. The town is about 12km east of the Guatemala-Honduras border. Confusingly, the town is named Copán Ruinas, though the actual ruins are just over 1km further east. Minivans coming from the border may take you on to the ruins after a stop in the town. If not, the *sendero peatonal* (footpath) alongside the road makes for a pretty 20-minute walk, passing several stelae and unexcavated mounds along the way to the Copán ruins and Las Sepulturas archaeological site, a couple of kilometers further.

Crossing the Border

The Guatemalan village of El Florido, which has no services beyond a few soft-drink stands, is 1.2km west of the border. At the border crossing are a branch of **Banrural** (⊗ 7am-6pm Mon-Sat), the Vilma bus office and one or two snack stands. The border crossing is open from 6am to 7pm daily but it closes to vehicles at 6pm.

Money changers will approach you on both sides of the border anxious to change quetzals for Honduran lempiras, or either for US dollars. Usually they're offering a decent rate because there's a Guatemalan bank right there and the current exchange rate is posted in the Honduran immigration office – look for it. There's no bank on the Honduran side of the border. Still, if the money changers give you a hard time, change enough at the border to get you into Copán Ruinas and then hit one of the banks there. Of course, if it's Sunday, you're beholden to the money changers. Though quetzals and US dollars may be accepted at some establishments in Copán Ruinas, it's best to change some money into lempiras.

At the crossing you must present your passport to the Guatemalan immigration and customs authorities, pay fees (some of which are unauthorized) of US$2, then cross the border and do the same thing with the Honduran authorities. You may be offered the possibility of a three-day permit to visit the ruins only and charged

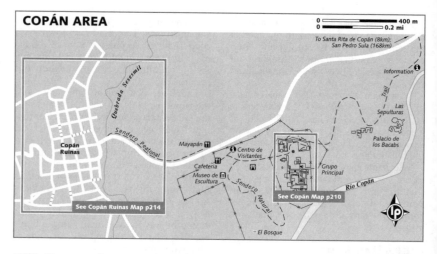

US$2. However, what you want is either a 30-day or 90-day visa, both free. You need to fill out a yellow official paper. It depends on your nationality whether you qualify for 30 or 90 days. Most European nationalities get 90 days. Australians, Canadians and Americans get at least 30 days. The official US$1 fee is payable at customs, though at the passport check they'll ask you for another dollar. This is apparently illegal and a sign between the two borders says so! No one, however, takes action against it. (We don't suggest that you do!)

When you return through this border point, you must again pass through both sets of immigration and customs, but pay no fees. If visiting only Copán from Guatemala, it's fine to return to Guatemala and continue using your original visa or passport stamp.

For information on transport to and from Copán Ruinas, see p218.

History
PRE-COLUMBIAN
People have been living in the Copán valley at least since around 1400 BC; ceramic evidence has been found from around that date. Copán must have had significant commercial activity since early times, as graves showing marked Olmec influence have been dated to around 900 to 600 BC.

In the 5th century AD one royal family came to rule Copán, led by a mysterious king named Mah K'ina Yax K'uk' Mo'

(Great Sun Lord Quetzal Macaw), who ruled from AD 426 to 435. Archaeological evidence indicates that he was a great shaman, and later kings revered him as the semidivine founder of the city. The dynasty ruled throughout Copán's florescence during the Classic period (AD 250 to 900).

Of the subsequent kings who ruled before AD 628 we know little. Only some of their names have been deciphered: Mat Head, the second king (no relation to Bed Head); Cu Ix, the fourth king; Waterlily Jaguar, the seventh; Moon Jaguar, the 10th; and Butz' Chan, the 11th.

Among the greatest of Copán's kings was Smoke Imix (Smoke Jaguar), the 12th king, who ruled from 628 to 695. Smoke Imix built Copán into a major military and commercial power in the region. He may have taken over the nearby princedom of Quiriguá, as one of the famous stelae at that site bears his name and image. By the time he died in 695, Copán's population had grown substantially.

Smoke Imix was succeeded by Uaxaclahun Ubak K'awil (18 Rabbit; 695–738), the 13th king, who willingly took the reins of power and pursued further military conquest. In a war with his neighbor from Quiriguá, King Cauac Sky, 18 Rabbit was captured and beheaded. He was succeeded by Smoke Monkey (738–749), the 14th king, whose short reign left little mark on Copán. Smoke Monkey's son Smoke Shell (749–763) was however one of Copán's greatest builders. He commissioned the city's most famous and important monument, the great Escalinata de los Jeroglíficos (Hieroglyphic Stairway), which immortalizes the achievements of the dynasty from its establishment until 755, when the stairway was dedicated. It is the longest inscription ever discovered in the Mayan lands.

Yax Pac (Sunrise or First Dawn; 763–820), Smoke Shell's successor and the 16th king, continued the beautification of Copán. The final occupant of the throne, U Cit Tok', became ruler in 822, but it is not known when he died.

Until recently, the collapse of the civilization at Copán had been a mystery. Now, archaeologists have begun to surmise that near the end of Copán's heyday the population grew at an unprecedented rate, straining agricultural resources. In the end, Copán was no longer agriculturally self-sufficient and had to import food from other areas. The urban core expanded into the fertile lowlands in the center of the valley, forcing both agricultural and residential areas to spread onto the steep slopes surrounding the valley. Wide areas were deforested, resulting in massive erosion that further decimated food production and brought flooding during rainy seasons. Interestingly, this environmental damage of old is not too different from what is happening today – a disturbing trend, but one that meshes with the Mayan belief that life is cyclical and history repeats itself. Skeletal remains of people who died during Copán's final years show marked evidence of malnutrition and infectious diseases, as well as decreased lifespans.

The Copán valley was not abandoned overnight – agriculturists probably continued to live in the ecologically devastated valley for maybe another one or two hundred years. But by the year 1200 or thereabouts, even the farmers had departed, and the royal city of Copán was reclaimed by the jungle.

EUROPEAN DISCOVERY

The first known European to see the ruins was a representative of Spanish King Felipe II, Diego García de Palacios, who lived in Guatemala and traveled through the region. On March 8, 1576, he wrote to the king about the ruins he found here. Only about five families were living here at the time, and they knew nothing of the history of the ruins. The discovery was not pursued, and almost three centuries went by until another Spaniard, Colonel Juan Galindo, visited the ruins and made the first map of them.

It was Galindo's report that stimulated John L Stephens and Frederick Catherwood to come to Copán on their Central American journey in 1839. When Stephens published the book *Incidents of Travel in Central America, Chiapas and Yucatán* in 1841, illustrated by Catherwood, the ruins first became known to the world at large.

TODAY

The history of Copán continues to unfold today. The remains of 3450 structures have been found in the 24 sq km surrounding the Grupo Principal (Principal Group), most of them within about half a kilometer of it. In a wider zone, 4509 structures have been detected in 1420 sites within 135 sq km of the ruins. These discoveries indicate that at the peak of civilization here, around the end of the 8th century AD, the valley of Copán had over 27,500 inhabitants – a population figure not reached again until the 1980s.

In addition to examining the area surrounding the Grupo Principal, archaeologists continue to make new discoveries in the Grupo Principal itself. Five separate phases of building on this site have been identified; the final phase, dating from AD 650 to 820, is what we see today. But buried underneath the visible ruins are layers of other ruins, which archaeologists are exploring by means of underground tunnels. This is how the Templo Rosalila (Rosalila Temple) was found, a replica of which is now in the Museo de Escultura (p212). Below Rosalila is yet another, earlier temple, Margarita. Two of the excavation tunnels, including Rosalila, are open to the public.

Archaeologists also continue to decipher more of the hieroglyphs, gaining greater understanding of the early Maya in the process. In 1998, a major discovery was made when archaeologists excavated a burial chamber beneath the Acrópolis presumed to be that of the great ruler Mah K'ina Yax K'uk' Mo' (Great Sun Lord Quetzal Macaw). To learn

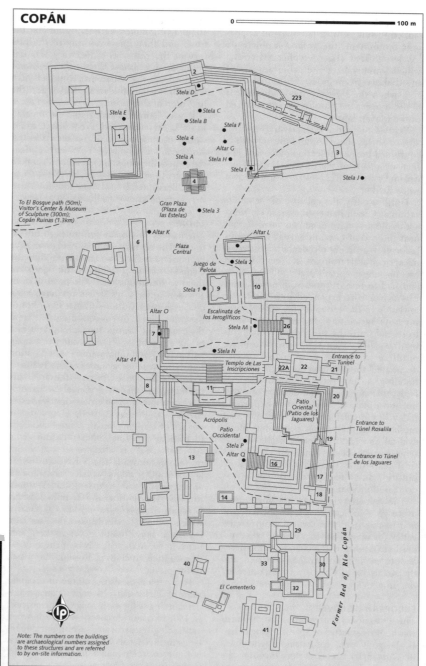

COPÁN

0 ▭▭▭▭▭ 100 m

Stela E

1

2

Stela D

223

Stela C

Stela B

Stela F

Stela 4

Altar G

Stela A

Stela H

Stela I

3

Stela J

4

To El Bosque path (50m);
Visitor's Center & Museum
of Sculpture (300m);
Copán Ruinas (1.3km)

Gran Plaza
(Plaza de
las Estelas)

Stela 3

Altar K

6

Altar L

Plaza
Central

Juego de
Pelota

Stela 2

Stela 1

9

10

Altar O

Escalinata de
los Jeroglíficos

7

Stela M

26

Stela N

Altar 41

Templo de Las
Inscripciones

Entrance to
Tunnel

22A   22   21

8

11

20

Acrópolis

Patio
Occidental

Patio
Oriental
(Patio de los
Jaguares)

Entrance to
Túnel Rosalila

Stela P

19

Entrance to Túnel
de los Jaguares

13

Altar Q

16

17

14

18

29

40   33   30

El Cementerio

32

41

Former Bed of Río Copán

Note: The numbers on the buildings
are archaeological numbers assigned
to these structures and are referred
to by on-site information.

more about this excavation, see the December 1997 *National Geographic* article entitled 'The Royal Crypts of Copán.'

Information

Admission includes entry to **Las Sepulturas** archaeological site but not to the two **excavation tunnels**, for which admission is US$12 (🕐 8am-3:30pm).

Also at the site is the **Museo de Escultura** where many of the original stelae are housed, as well as an awesome replica of the impressive and colorful Rosalila Temple.

The **Centro de Visitantes** (Visitors Center) at the entrance to the ruins houses the ticket office and a small exhibition about the site and its excavation. Nearby are a cafetería, and souvenir and handicrafts shops. There's a picnic area along the path to the Principal Group of ruins. A **Sendero Natural** (Nature Trail) entering the forest several hundred meters from the visitors center passes by a small ball court.

Pick up a copy of the booklet *History Carved in Stone: A guide to the archaeological park of the ruins of Copán* by noted archaeologists William L Fash and Ricardo Agurcia Fasquelle, available at the visitors center for US$4. It will help you to understand and appreciate the ruins. It's also a good idea to go with a guide, who can help to explain the ruins and bring them to life. Guides are US$20 no matter the size of the group; packs of trained guides hang out at the visitors center.

Visitors should not touch any of the stelae or sit on the altars at Copán.

Grupo Principal

The Principal Group of ruins is about 400m beyond the visitors center across well-kept lawns, through a gate in a strong fence and down shady avenues of trees. A group of resident macaws loiter along here. The ruins themselves have been numbered for easy identification and a well-worn path circumscribes the site.

Stelae of the Gran Plaza

The path leads to the **Gran Plaza** (Great Plaza; Plaza de las Estelas) and the huge, intricately carved stelae portraying the rulers of Copán. Most of Copán's best stelae date from AD 613 to 738. All seem to have originally been painted; a few

traces of red paint survive on Stela C. Many stelae had vaults beneath or beside them in which sacrifices and offerings could be placed.

Many of the stelae on the Gran Plaza portray King 18 Rabbit, including stelae A, B, C, D, F, H and 4. Perhaps the most beautiful stela in the Gran Plaza is Stela A (AD 731); the original has been moved inside the Museum of Sculpture, and the one outdoors is a reproduction. Nearby and almost equal in beauty are Stela 4 (731); Stela B (731), depicting 18 Rabbit upon his accession to the throne; and Stela C (782) with a turtle-shaped altar in front. This last stela has figures on both sides. Stela E (614), erected on top of Estructura 1 (Structure 1) on the west side of the Great Plaza, is among the oldest.

At the northern end of the Gran Plaza at the base of Estructura 2, Stela D (736) also portrays King 18 Rabbit. On its back are two columns of hieroglyphs; at its base is an altar with fearsome representations of Chac, the rain god. In front of the altar is the burial place of Dr John Owen, an archaeologist with an expedition from Harvard's Peabody Museum who died during excavation work in 1893.

On the east side of the plaza is Stela F (721), which has a more lyrical design than other stelae here, with the robes of the main figure flowing around to the other side of the stone, where there are glyphs. Altar G (800), showing twin serpent heads, is among the last monuments carved at Copán. Stela H (730) may depict a queen or princess rather than a king. Stela 1 (692), on the structure that runs along the east side of the plaza, is of a person wearing a mask. Stela J, further off to the east, resembles the stelae of Quiriguá in that it is covered in glyphs, not human figures.

Juego de Pelota

South of the Great Plaza, across what is known as the Plaza Central (Central Plaza), is the Juego de Pelota (Ball Court; 731), the second largest in Central America. The one you see is the third one on this site; the other two smaller courts were buried by this construction. Note the macaw heads carved atop the sloping walls. The central marker in the court is the work of King 18 Rabbit.

Escalinata de los Jeroglíficos

South of the ball court is Copán's most famous monument, the Hieroglyphic Stairway (743), the work of King Smoke Shell. Today it's protected from the elements by a roof. The flight of 63 steps bears a history (in several thousand glyphs) of the royal house of Copán; the steps are bordered by ramps inscribed with more reliefs and glyphs. The story told on the inscribed steps is still not completely understood because the stairway was partially ruined and the stones jumbled.

At the base of the Hieroglyphic Stairway is Stela M (756), bearing a figure (probably King Smoke Shell) dressed in a feathered cloak; glyphs tell of the solar eclipse in that year. The altar in front shows a plumed serpent with a human head emerging from its jaws.

Beside the stairway, a tunnel leads to the tomb of a nobleman, a royal scribe who may have been the son of King Smoke Imix. The tomb, discovered in June 1989, held a treasure trove of painted pottery and beautiful carved jade objects that are now in Honduran museums.

Acrópolis

The lofty flight of steps to the south of the Hieroglyphic Stairway mounts the Templo de las Inscripciones (Temple of the Inscriptions). On top of the stairway, the walls are carved with groups of hieroglyphs. On the south side of the Temple of the Inscriptions is the Patio Occidental (West Plaza), with the Patio Oriental (East Plaza), also called the Patio de los Jaguares (Plaza of the Jaguars) to its east. In the West Plaza, be sure to see Altar Q (776), among the most famous sculptures here; the original is inside the Museum of Sculpture. Around its sides, carved in superb relief, are the 16 great kings of Copán, ending with its creator, Yax Pac. Behind the altar is a sacrificial vault in which archeologists discovered the bones of 15 jaguars and several macaws that were probably sacrificed to the glory of Yax Pac and his ancestors.

The East Plaza also contains evidence of Yax Pac – his tomb, beneath Estructura 18. Unfortunately, the tomb was discovered and looted long before archeologists arrived. Both the East and West Plazas hold a variety of fascinating stelae and sculptured heads of humans and animals. To see the most elaborate relief carving, climb Estructura 22 on the northern side of the East Plaza. This was the Templo de Meditación (Temple of Meditation) and has been heavily restored over recent years.

Túnel Rosalila & Túnel de los Jaguares

In 1999, exciting new additions were made to the wonders at Copán when two excavation tunnels were opened to the public. The Túnel Rosalila (Rosalila Tunnel) exposes the Rosalila Temple below Estructura 16, and the Túnel de los Jaguares (Jaguar Tunnel) shows visitors the Tumba Galindo (Galindo Tomb), below Estructura 17 in the southern part of the Patio Oriental.

Descending into these tunnels is interesting but not so exciting as when they were opened in 1999; at the time of writing you could only visit 25m of the Rosalila Tunnel and 95m of the longer Jaguar Tunnel. The Rosalila Tunnel reveals a little of the actual temple over which Estructura 16 was built; the carvings are remarkably crisp and vivid, especially the Sun God mask looming over the doorway. This is considered by some scholars to be the best-preserved stucco edifice in the Mayan world. Everything is behind Plexiglas to protect it from natural and human elements. Under the Rosalila Temple is the Margarita Temple, built 150 years earlier. Beneath that, there are other even earlier platforms and tombs.

The Túnel de los Jaguares is less dramatic, with its burial tombs and niches for offerings. The Galindo Tomb was one of the first tombs discovered at Copán, in 1834. Bones, obsidian knives and beads were found here, and archeologists date the tomb's antebase mask to AD 540. The decorative macaw mask here is incredible. The full extent of this tunnel is 700m.

Though the US$12 price of admission is dear for a short-lived pair of highlights, these tunnels are worth a look if you're into history.

Museo de Escultura

Copán is unique in the Mayan world for its sculpture, and the Museo de Escultura (Museum of Sculpture; US$5; ⏰ 8am-3:40pm) is fittingly magnificent. Just entering the museum is an impressive experience in itself. Walking through the mouth of a serpent, you wind through the entrails of the beast, then suddenly emerge into a fantastic world of sculpture and light.

The highlight of the museum is a true-scale replica (in full color) of the Rosalila Temple, discovered in nearly perfect condition by archaeologists in 1989 by means of a tunnel dug into Estructura 16, the central building of the Acrópolis (p212). Rosalila, dedicated in AD 571 by Copán's 10th ruler, Moon Jaguar, was apparently so sacred that when Estructura 16 was built over it, the temple was not destroyed but was left completely intact. The original Rosalila Temple is still in the core of Estructura 16.

The other displays in the museum are stone carvings, brought here for protection from the elements. All the important stelae may eventually be housed here, with detailed reproductions placed outdoors to show where the stelae originally stood. So far, at least Altar Q and Stelae A, N, P and Estructura 2 have been brought into the museum, and the ones you see outdoors are reproductions.

El Bosque & Las Sepulturas

Excavations at El Bosque and Las Sepulturas have shed light on the daily life of the Maya in Copán during its golden age.

Las Sepulturas, once connected to the Gran Plaza by a causeway, may have been the residential area where rich and powerful nobles lived. One huge, luxurious residential compound seems to have housed some 250 people in 40 or 50 buildings arranged around 11 courtyards. The principal structure, called the **Palacio de los Bacabs** (Palace of the Officials), had outer walls carved with the full-size figures of 10 males in fancy feathered headdresses; inside was a huge hieroglyphic bench.

To get to Las Sepulturas you have to go back to the main road, turn right, then right again at the sign (2km from the Gran Plaza).

The walk to get to El Bosque is the real reason for visiting it, as it is removed from the main ruins. It's a one-hour walk on a well-maintained path through foliage dense with birds, though there isn't much of note

at the site itself save for a small ball court. Still, it's a powerful experience to have an hour-long walk on the thoroughfares of an ancient Mayan city all to yourself. To get to El Bosque, go right at the hut where your ticket is stamped.

COPÁN RUINAS
pop 6000

The town of Copán Ruinas, often simply called Copán, is just over 1km from the famous Mayan ruins of the same name. It's a beautiful place paved with cobblestones and lined with white adobe buildings with red-tile roofs. There's even a lovely colonial church on the recently remodeled plaza. The Maya have inhabited this valley, which has an aura of timeless harmony, for about 2000 years. Copán has become a primary tourist destination, but this hasn't disrupted the town's integrity to the extent one might fear.

Orientation & Information

The Parque Central, with the church on one side, is the heart of town. Copán is very small, and everything is within a few blocks of the plaza. This is fortunate for visitors, since the town doesn't use street signs. The ruins are on the road to La Entrada. Las Sepulturas archaeological site is a few kilometers further along.

Email services cost between US$1.20 and US$1.50 per hour:

Copán Net One block south and one block west of the plaza.

Maya Connections Two locations, one across from Vamos a Ver restaurant, the other in La Casa de Todo, one block east of the plaza. International phone and fax services also available, and both branches offer laundry service (US$0.50 to wash, dry and fold each pound; US$1 per kg), plus book exchange.

For US dollars, the banks give a better rate than the money changers at the border, but slightly less than banks elsewhere in Honduras.

Banco Atlántida (☼ 8:30am-3:30pm Mon-Fri, 8:30am-noon Sat) On the plaza, changes US dollars and traveler's checks and gives cash advances on Visa cards.

Banco Credomatic Also on the plaza, has a Visa and MasterCard ATM.

Banco de Occidente (☼ 8:30am-4:30pm Mon-Fri, 8:30am-noon Sat) on the plaza changes US dollars and traveler's checks, and quetzals, and gives cash advances on Visa and MasterCard.

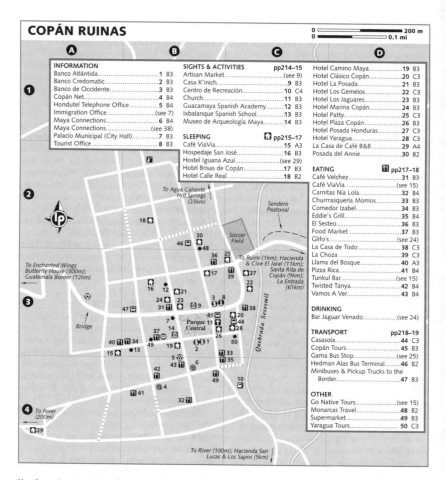

COPÁN RUINAS

0 — 200 m
0 — 0.1 mi

INFORMATION	
Banco Atlántida.............................1	B3
Banco Credomatic........................2	B3
Banco de Occidente.....................3	B3
Copán Net...................................4	B4
Hondutel Telephone Office..........5	B4
Immigration Office................(see 7)	
Maya Connections........................6	B4
Maya Connections.................(see 38)	
Palacio Municipal (City Hall)........7	B3
Tourist Office................................8	B3

SIGHTS & ACTIVITIES	pp214–15
Artisan Market.......................(see 9)	
Casa K'inich.................................9	B3
Centro de Recreación..................10	C4
Church......................................11	B3
Guacamaya Spanish Academy......12	B3
Ixbalanque Spanish School..........13	B3
Museo de Arqueología Maya.......14	B3

SLEEPING	pp215–17
Café ViaVia................................15	A3
Hospedaje San José....................16	B3
Hostel Iguana Azul...............(see 29)	
Hotel Brisas de Copán.................17	B3
Hotel Calle Real.........................18	B2

Hotel Camino Maya...................19	B3
Hotel Clásico Copán...................20	C3
Hotel La Posada.........................21	B3
Hotel Los Gemelos.....................22	C3
Hotel Los Jaguares.....................23	B3
Hotel Marina Copán...................24	B3
Hotel Patty................................25	C3
Hotel Plaza Copán......................26	B3
Hotel Posada Honduras...............27	C3
Hotel Yaragua...........................28	B3
La Casa de Café B&B..................29	A4
Posada del Annie........................30	B2

EATING	pp217–18
Café Velchez.............................31	B3
Café ViaVia........................(see 15)	
Carnitas Nia Lola.......................32	B4
Churrrasquería Momos................33	B3
Comedor Izabel.........................34	B3
Eddie's Grill...............................35	B4
El Sesteo..................................36	B3
Food Market..............................37	B3
Glifo's................................(see 24)	
La Casa de Todo.........................38	C3
La Choza...................................39	C3
Llama del Bosque.......................40	A3
Pizza Rica..................................41	B4
Tunkul Bar..........................(see 15)	
Twisted Tanya...........................42	B4
Vamos A Ver.............................43	B4

DRINKING	
Bar Jaguar Venado...............(see 24)	

TRANSPORT	pp218–19
Casasola....................................44	C3
Copán Tours..............................45	B3
Gama Bus Stop....................(see 25)	
Hedman Alas Bus Terminal..........46	B2
Minibuses & Pickup Trucks to the Border..................................47	B3

OTHER	
Go Native Tours..................(see 15)	
Monarcas Travel.........................48	B2
Supermarket..............................49	B3
Yaragua Tours............................50	C3

Honduran immigration office (Palacio Municipal; 7am-4:30pm Mon-Fri) On the plaza, come here for visa matters.
Hondutel Telephone office around the corner from the post office.
Post office A few doors from the plaza.
Tourist office (www.copanhonduras.org; ☺ 11am-7pm) Run by a chamber of commerce; down the hill half a block east of the plaza.

Sights & Activities

Though the main attraction of the Copán region is the archaeological site, there are other fine places to visit in the area. The **Museo de Arqueología Maya** (US$2; ☺ 8am-4pm Mon-Sat), on the town plaza, is well worth a visit. It contains the original Stela B, portraying King 18 Rabbit. Other exhibits

of painted pottery, carved jade, Mayan glyphs and a calendar round are also interesting and informative, as is the Tumba del Brujo, the tomb of a shaman or priest who died around AD 700 and was buried with many items under the east corner of the Plaza de los Jaguares. **Casa K'inich** (admission free; ☺ 8am-noon & 1-5pm Mon-Sat) on the north side of the plaza, inside the little artisan market, is an interactive museum for kids all about the Maya.

About four blocks north of the plaza is the **Mirador El Cuartel**, the old jail, with a magnificent view over town.

A pleasant, easy walk on the road on the south side of town provides a fine view over the corn and tobacco fields surrounding

Copán. On this same side of town is an agreeable walk to the river.

The **Enchanted Wings Butterfly House** (☎ 651-4133; www.hondurasecotours.com; adult/child US$6/2; ⏰ 8am-5pm) is a nature center about a 10-minute walk west of the plaza on the road back to Guatemala. It has beautiful live and preserved butterflies, and numerous tropical flowers including around 200 species of orchids. With such a pretty name, how could you miss it?

Horse rides can be arranged by any of the town's tour companies and most hotels. You can ride to the ruins or make other, lengthier excursions. Alternatively, you'll likely find a horse for hire by just asking around town and bargaining. The Hotel Hacienda El Jaral (p219) also offers horse riding. Three-hour rides (US$10 to US$15) out of Café ViaVia and the Tunkul Bar (both in the second block west of the plaza) visit a local school sponsored by Spaniards.

A popular horseback excursion is to **Los Sapos** (US$2), 5km from town. The *sapos* (toads) are old Mayan stone carvings in a spot with a beautiful view over the town. This place is connected with Mayan fertility rites. You can get there by horseback in about half an hour or walk in about an hour, all uphill. From Los Sapos you can walk to a stela. Nearby is **Hacienda San Lucas**, a century-old farmhouse that has been converted into a B&B and restaurant (p216). There are walking trails here too.

Language Courses
Ixbalanque Spanish School (☎/fax 651-4432; www.ixbalanque.com), in the same block as the Tunkul Bar, offers 20 hours of one-on-one instruction in Spanish for US$190 per week, including homestay with a local family that provides three meals a day. Instruction only, for 20 hours a week, costs US$130. **Guacamaya Spanish Academy** (☎/fax 651-4360; www.guacamaya.com) uphill from Hotel Marina Copán offers much the same deal to visitors.

Tours
A huge number of tours can be organized from Copán Ruinas. Local companies promote these widely. You can cave, tube a river, visit a Mayan village and make tortillas or manufacture ceramics, plunge into hot springs, visit a coffee plantation or head off into the wilds of Honduras.

Go Native Tours (☎ 651 4410; tunkul2002@yahoo.com), operating out of the Tunkul Bar, offers local trips and ecological tours further afield. It also organizes bird-watching trips to Lago de Yojoa – a mountain lake known for reputedly having some 350 species of birds, in the area known as the Mosquito Coast. Some of the local trips involve and benefit local villagers.

Xukpi Tours (☎ 651-4435, 651-4503), operated by Jorge Barraza, also runs several ecological tours both locally and further afield. His ruins and bird-watching tours are justly famous, and he'll do trips to all parts of Honduras and to Quiriguá (Guatemala). Most days Jorge can be found at the archaeological site.

Yaragua Tours (☎ 651-4147; fax 651-4695) is opposite the Hotel Yaragua. Samuel from Yaragua leads local tours, horseback riding trips and excursions to Lago de Yojoa. Caving trips are another option.

Monarcas Travel (☎ 651-4361; www.mayabus.com), a block north of Banco de Occidente, offers tours to almost anywhere in the Mayan world, including Tikal, Ceibal and Uaxactún. They also operate a shuttle service between Copán and Antigua (p219).

Sleeping
BUDGET
Café ViaVia (☎ 651-4652; www.viaviacafe.com; dm/s/d US$4/10/12) Next door to the Tunkul bar, this small European-style hotel is run by two young, energetic, helpful, travel-loving Belgian couples. (It's part of the Joker group, a Belgian-led organization of cafés with a travel theme around the world including at Louvain, Zanzibar, Kathmandu and Yogyakarta.) Café ViaVia Copán has

five spotless rooms with private hot-water bathroom, tiled floors and great beds (2m long for the tall folks reading this!) One of the rooms functions as a dormitory with six beds. There are hammocks, a small garden and enough space to chill out. English, French, German and Dutch are spoken. Café ViaVia is set to open a new hostel next door to the Hedman Alas Bus Terminal. There'll be 14 dorm beds at around US$4 per person. Facilities will include hot water, a communal kitchen and a big patio area for relaxing.

Hostel Iguana Azul (☎ 651-4620; fax 651-4623; www.todomundo.com/iguanaazul; dm/s/d US$5/7/11) This funky place three blocks west and two blocks south of the plaza is next door to La Casa de Café B&B (p216) and operated by the same friendly people. It has eight comfy bunk beds in two rooms with shared piping hot, terrific bathroom in a colonial-style ranch home. Three private rooms sleep two. There's also a pretty garden. The common area has books, magazines, travel guides and lots of travel information. This is backpacking elegance at its finest.

Hotel Los Gemelos (☎ 651-4077; s/d US$3/6; P) This longtime favorite with budget travelers is a block northeast from the plaza. Operated by a very friendly family (connected with La Casa de Todo), it has a garden patio with flowers and birds, and a place to wash your clothes; coffee is always available. Rooms with shared cold-water bathroom have fans and mosquito screens.

Hotel Posada Honduras (☎ 651-4082; s/d US$4/6, with cold-water bathroom US$7/9; P) In the same block as Los Gemelos, this hotel has 13 simple rooms with fan, encircling a courtyard full of mango, mamey and lemon trees.

Hotel Calle Real (☎ 651-4230; s/d/tr US$9/15/21; P) The three blocks uphill-walk from the plaza is a negative for this hotel but it's worth the effort. The newish clean and quiet rooms with fan, tiled floors and hot-water bathroom make it good value. The grounds are beautifully landscaped and have a little cafetería. Upstairs there is a relaxation area with hammocks under a *palapa*-style roof.

Hotel Yaragua (☎ 651-4464; fax 651-4050; s/d/tr US$15/18/24) Only a half-block east of the plaza, the Yaragua has rooms with hot-water bathroom and cable TV. The dense,

tropical courtyard provides the atmosphere that makes this place.

Hotel Patty (☎ 651-4021; fax 651-4019; s/d/tr US$12/15/20; P) This friendly establishment right by the soccer field has 20 rooms set around a verdant courtyard, all with hot-water bathroom.

Hotel Clásico Copán (☎ 651-4040; s/d/tr US$9/9/15, d/tr with 2 double beds US$18 P) This newly renovated hotel is on the same street as the Gemelos and Honduras, opposite La Casa de Todo. The 20 ample-sized rooms are on two levels around a large treed patio. All have hot-water bathroom and some have cable TV and fans.

Posada del Annie (☎ 942-4020; s/d US$12/15) This place is next door to Monarcas Travel, almost two blocks north of the plaza. The pleasant rooms with bathroom and fan share a terrace overlooking the garden below.

Hospedaje San José (☎ 989-8929; s/d US$3/6, with hot-water bathroom US$6/9) Tucked away on a residential street a block and a half from the plaza is the congenial San José. There are 13 rooms, with fan, some around a patio; the cheaper ones lead off a dark interior passage. The facilities are basic, but you'll feel a part of the family.

MID-RANGE & TOP END

La Casa de Café (☎ 651-4620; fax 651-4623; www.todomundo.com/casadecafe; s/d/tr US$35/45/53) This classy B&B four blocks from the plaza has loads of character in a beautiful setting – the garden area with tables and hammocks has a view over cornfields to the mountains of Guatemala. The 10 rooms with hot-water bathroom have wooden ceilings, antique ceiling fans and other nice touches. They have a good library pertaining to Honduras. All prices include a hearty breakfast.

Hacienda San Lucas (☎ 651-4106; www.haciendasanlucas.com; s/d/tr US$50/60/70) This magical place is 5km south of town. Phone beforehand or head to the Hedman Alas Bus Terminal/Welcome Office two blocks north of the northeast corner of Copán Ruinas' plaza. The recently restored adobe hacienda is solar-powered, but the rooms are candlelit at night, adding to the serene atmosphere. The food here is highly praised. Los Sapos archaeological site (p215) is on the property.

Hotel Marina Copán (☎ 651-4070/1/2; fax 651-4477; www.hotelmarinacopan.com; s/d/tr US$87/99/111;

P ⊠ ⓡ) This is the top place to stay in town. It has all top-end amenities including a spa, sauna and gym. Rooms are spacious and contain one double and one single bed. Two kids stay free with accompanying adults. The restaurant/bar is an attractive wooden jungle-inspired building.

Hotel Plaza Copán (☎ 651-4274; fax 651-4039; www .hotelplazacopan.com; s/d/tr US$46/52/58; P ⊠ ⓡ) Rooms are flash and have all the amenities: hot-water bathroom, fan, good beds, cable TV and phone, plus some extras like private balconies and views of the church. Each room differs, so look at a few before choosing. The hotel has a restaurant and a terrace with views.

Hotel Camino Maya (☎ 651-4518/4646; fax 651-4517; www.caminomayahotel.com; s/d/tr US$48/54/60; P ⊠ ⓡ) This is quite lovely and you won't want for anything in its 23 rooms, but you may not want a room with a balcony overlooking the plaza. The swimming pool area set in large gardens is gorgeous.

Hotel La Posada (☎ 651-4070; laposada@hotel marinacopan.com; s/d/tr US$15/25/30) Good-value, tranquil and comfortable, La Posada is only half a block from the plaza. Its 19 rooms with hot-water bathroom, fan and TV are set around two leafy patios. There's very tasty, free black coffee first thing in the morning.

Hotel Brisas de Copán (☎ 651-4118; s or d US$20-25; P) This attractive place is near the soccer field. All 21 rooms have hot-water bathroom and TV. The best rooms are upstairs with shared terraces and plenty of plants and light. The place is spotless and the bed covers are bright.

Hotel Los Jaguares (☎ 651-4451; fax 651-4075; s/d US$28/32; ⊠) This hotel is right on the plaza and has agreeable rooms set around a pretty courtyard; some of the rooms front the street but it isn't overly noisy here.

Eating

The town's little **food market** is right by the Parque Central.

Tunkul Bar (mains US$2.70-6; ☯ 11am-11pm) Two blocks east of the plaza, this is one of Copán's main gathering spots. It's an attractive covered-patio bar/restaurant that has good food, decent music, gregarious clientele and a book exchange. There is a good variety of meat and vegetarian meals; portions are generous. Happy hour runs

from 7pm to 8pm for beer, 10pm to 11pm for mixed drinks.

Café ViaVia (breakfast US$1.40-2.40, mains US$3-5; ☯ 7am-10pm) This terrific restaurant next door to the Tunkul Bar serves breakfast, lunch and dinner in a convivial atmosphere, with tables overlooking the street and a replica of Altar Q behind the bar. The organically grown coffee they prepare is excellent and their stab at world food with a vegetarian bias works. Bread is homemade.

Carnitas Nia Lola (dishes US$3-6.20; ☯ 7am-10pm) Two blocks south of the plaza, this open-air restaurant has a beautiful view toward the mountains over corn and tobacco fields. It's a relaxing place with simple and economical food; the specialties are charcoal-grilled chicken and beef. Happy hour starts at 6:30pm.

Glifo's (breakfasts US$1.70-4.25, mains US$8-13; ☯ 7am-9:30pm) Some say this restaurant at the Hotel Marina Copán is the best place to eat in town. You'll find fine, international food in comfortable surroundings. The menu includes some fancy dishes with a traditional Mayan twist.

Café Velchez (breakfasts US$0.90-3.50, cakes per slice US$1.80) Next door to the Hotel Marina Copán, this has the only cappuccino machine in town. The coffee and cakes are excellent and you can breakfast here too, fairly cheaply.

Churrasquería Momos (light meals US$2) This little place half a block south of the plaza was a hot favorite when we were last in town. *Pinchos* served with salad and rice are recommended. Next door, **Eddie's Grill** receives accolades for its sizzling steaks.

Vamos A Ver (sandwiches US$1.80-3.25, mains US$4.30; ☯ 7am-10pm) A friendly spot, one block south of the plaza, this is a cozy little covered-patio restaurant with good, inexpensive foods: homemade breads, a variety of international cheeses, tasty soups, fruit or vegetable salads (US$2.65), rich coffee, fruit *licuados*, a wide variety of teas and always something for vegetarians. Happy hour lasts from 5pm to 7pm.

Llama del Bosque (☎ 651-4431; breakfasts US$1.80-3.55, dishes US$4.70; ☯ 6:30am-9pm) This large, popular place opposite Tunkul Bar offers a good selection of Honduran meals and snacks; their *anafre* (fondue cooked in a clay pot, US$3) is especially tasty. In the same block **Comedor Izabel** is a cheap, basic comedor with decent food and similar hours and prices to Llama del Bosque.

La Casa de Todo (meals US$3; ☺ 7am-7pm) This cafetería, one block northeast of the plaza, has a pretty garden, with handcrafted wooden tables and chairs, where light meals and snacks are served.

Pizza Rica ('normal' pizza US$6.50; ☺ 11am-11pm) This place is two blocks south and half a block west of the plaza, on the road to Hostel Iguana Azul. It serves (what else?) pizza, plus pasta dishes for a little variety. A 'normal' pizza should satisfy one hungry person.

Twisted Tanya (☎ 651-4182; 2 courses US$11; ☺ noon-10:30pm) This new restaurant, one block south and one block west of the plaza, is as unusual as its name. Located upstairs in a corner building, it is elegantly decked out with long drapes. Cardboard Moroccan-style lampshades add an artistic flourish. Try the fish fillet with sautéed vegetables. A starter of soup or salad is included in the price. There are only four tables.

Two simple *comedores* serving good and cheap Guatemalan eats, with some concessions (such as pasta) made for international tastes, are **La Choza**, where a plate of fish, salad, *fajita* (grilled meat served on a flour tortilla with condiments) and rice costs only US$3, and **El Sesteo**. They're across the street from each other, near the soccer field. La Choza does sensational long icy drinks.

Entertainment

The **Tunkul Bar** and the bar in **Carnitas Nia Lola** are happening spots in the evening (p217). You might also try the bar in the **Café ViaVia** for after-dark entertainment. **Bar Jaguar Venado**, in the Hotel Marina Copán, has live marimba music on Friday and Saturday nights from 5pm to 8pm. All the other upscale hotels on the plaza have bars in their lobbies as well. The Hotel Camino Maya's **Centro de Recreación** (pool US$2, disco US$1.80; ☺ 6am-10pm Sun-Thu, 6am-2am Fri & Sat) comprises a swimming pool, bar, restaurant and disco beside the Quebrada Sesesmil, two blocks south and one block east of the plaza.

Getting There & Away

If you need a Honduran visa in advance, you can obtain it at the Honduran consulate in Esquipulas or Guatemala City (p62).

Several Antigua travel agencies offer weekend trips to Copán (US$125), which may include stops at other places, including Quiriguá. All-inclusive day trips from Antigua to Copán cost around US$90 and are very rushed. Check with the agencies in Antigua (p79).

BUS

It's 227km (five hours) from Guatemala City to El Florido, the Guatemalan village on the Honduran border. **Hedman Alas** (☎ 651-4106) runs direct first-class services daily in both directions between Copán Ruinas and Guatemala City (US$35), leaving its office in Copán Ruinas at 1pm and 5:30pm and Guatemala City at 5am. Coming from other places, you have to take a bus to Chiquimula, and change there for a connecting service to the border.

If you're coming from Esquipulas, you can get off the bus at Vado Hondo, the junction of CA-10 and the road to El Florido, and wait for a bus there. As the buses to El Florido usually fill up before departing from Chiquimula, it may be just as well to go the extra 8km into Chiquimula and secure your seat before the bus pulls out. Traveling from the border to Esquipulas, there's no need to go into Chiquimula; minibuses ply the route to Esquipulas frequently.

Minivans and some pickups depart for Copán Ruinas from the Honduran side of the border regularly throughout the day. They should charge around US$1.50, payable before you depart, for the 20-minute ride. Drivers may hassle you about the fare but late in the day they have the trump card.

Minibuses and pickups from Copán Ruinas to Guatemala depart from the intersection one block west of the plaza. They leave every 40 minutes (or when full), 6am to 6pm, and charge around US$1.50 – check the price beforehand. On the Guatemala side, buses to Chiquimula (US$1.20, 1½ hours, 58km) leave the border hourly from 5:30am to 11:30am then hourly from noon to 4pm and at 4:30pm.

Buses serving points further afield in Honduras depart from a few different places in Copán Ruinas. Hedman Alas goes to San Pedro Sula (US$8, three hours) and on to Tegucigalpa (US$16, seven hours) at 5:30am daily. **Casasola** (☎ /fax 651-4078) has departures direct to San Pedro Sula

(US$4.20, three hours) at 7am and 2pm from their office next door to the Hotel Clásico Copán, one block east and half a block south of the plaza. Casasola also has buses to La Entrada (US$2.06, two hours) hourly from 4am to 5pm. **Gama** (☎ 651-4421) runs express buses to San Pedro Sula (three hours) at 6am and 3pm from outside the Hotel Patty.

SHUTTLE MINIBUS

Monarcas Travel (p215) in Copán Ruinas and Antigua runs a shuttle between those two towns. In Copán it cooperates with Copán Tours, half a block east of the plaza. Scheduled shuttles leave Copán for Antigua (US$15, minimum four passengers, six hours) at 2pm daily and can drop you in Guatemala City (five hours) en route. Tickets are sold at Monarcas Travel, Maya Connections, hotels and restaurants. Shuttles leave Antigua at 4am and Guatemala City at 5am. Copán Tours also runs shuttles to Río Dulce (US$30, minimum three) and Panajachel (US$25, minimum eight).

CAR

You could conceivably visit the ruins as a day trip from Guatemala City by car, but it's exhausting and far too harried. From Río Hondo, Chiquimula or Esquipulas, it still takes a full day to get to Copán, tour the ruins and return, but it's easier. It's better to spend at least one night in Copán Ruinas if you can.

Drive 10km south from Chiquimula (or 48km north from Esquipulas) and turn eastward at Vado Hondo (Km 178.5 on Highway CA-10). Just opposite the turnoff there is a small motel, which will do if you need a bed. A sign reading 'Vado Hondo Ruinas de Copán' marks the way on the one-hour, 50km drive along the paved road that runs from this junction to El Florido.

Twenty kilometers northeast of Vado Hondo are the Ch'orti' Maya villages of Jocotán and Camotán, set in mountainous tropical countryside dotted with thatched huts in lush green valleys. Jocotán has a small Centro de Salud (medical clinic) and the **Hotel Katú Sukuchuje** (☎ /fax 941-2431; s/d/tr with hot-water bathroom US$4/7/11; P), which also has a restaurant.

If you are driving a rented car, you will have to present the Guatemalan customs authorities at the border with a special letter of permission to enter Honduras, written on the rental company's letterhead and signed and sealed by the appropriate company official. If you do not have such a letter, you'll have to leave your car at El Florido and continue to Copán by minivan or pickup.

AROUND COPÁN RUINAS

Hacienda El Jaral (☎ 552-4457; camping per person US$4, s/d/tr US$55/60/80; [icons] P) This lush ecotourism resort offering many activities is 11km from town on the way to La Entrada. The luxurious rooms with air-con, hot-water bathroom, cable TV and fridge are all in duplex cabins with outdoor terraces. The resort has a shopping mall, cinema, water park, children's play area and a couple of restaurants. The activities offered to guests and nonguests alike include bird-watching in a bird-sanctuary lagoon (thousands of herons reside here from November to May), horseback riding, bicycling, hiking, river swimming, inner-tubing, canoeing and 'soft rafting' on the Río Copán.

Santa Rita de Copán

Nine kilometers from town (20 minutes by bus) on the road toward La Entrada, Santa Rita de Copán is a lovely village at the confluence of two rivers. Just outside Santa Rita – but unfortunately out of bounds due to a sequence of nasty incidents – is **El Rubí** waterfall, with an inviting swimming hole. It's about a half-hour uphill walk on a trail departing from opposite the Esso fuel station beside the bridge on the highway. The protection of tourist police is being sought so that visits can resume.

Agua Caliente

The attractively sited, **Agua Caliente** (hot springs; US$1.20; ⏱ 8am-8pm), not to be confused with Agua Caliente in Honduras, not far from Esquipulas, are 23km north of Copán Ruinas via the road running north out of town. Here hot water flows and mingles with a cold river. If you ford the river and follow the trail on the other side, you will come to the source of the near-scalding spring. Because of the water temperature, soaking is recommended only in places where the hot and cold water mix. There are facilities for changing, a basketball court and bathrooms plus a *tienda* (store) for soft drinks and snacks. To get to the springs, you can drive (45 minutes), hire a pickup (US$25) or catch a ride early with farmers going out there (US$1.20). Fully self-sufficient campers can make an overnighter of it.

QUIRIGUÁ

From Copán it is only some 50km to Quiriguá as the crow flies, but the lay of the land, the international border and the condition of the roads make it a journey of 175km. Quiriguá is famed for its intricately carved stelae – the gigantic brown sandstone monoliths that rise as high as 10.5m, like ancient sentinels, in a quiet well-kept tropical park.

From Río Hondo junction it's 67km along the Carretera al Atlántico to the village of Los Amates, where there are a couple of hotels, a restaurant, food stalls, a bank and a little bus station. The village of Quiriguá is 1.5km east of Los Amates, and the turnoff to the ruins is another 1.5km to the east. The 3.4km access road leads south through banana groves.

History

Quiriguá's history parallels that of Copán, of which it was a dependency during much of the Classic period. Of the three sites in this area, only the present archaeological park is of interest.

Quiriguá's location lent itself to the carving of giant stelae. Beds of brown sandstone in the nearby Río Motagua had cleavage planes suitable for cutting large pieces. Though soft when first cut, the sandstone dried hard in the air. With Copán's expert artisans nearby for guidance, Quiriguá's stonecarvers were ready for greatness. All they needed was a great leader to inspire them – and to pay for the carving of the huge stelae.

That leader was Cauac Sky (725–84), who decided that Quiriguá should no longer be under the control of Copán. In a war with his former suzerain, Cauac Sky took King 18 Rabbit of Copán prisoner in 737 and later had him beheaded. Independent at last, Cauac Sky commissioned his stonecutters to go to work, and for the next 38 years they turned out giant stelae and zoomorphs dedicated to the glory of King Cauac Sky.

Cauac Sky's son Sky Xul (784–800) lost his throne to a usurper, Jade Sky. This last great king of Quiriguá continued the building boom initiated by Cauac Sky, reconstructing Quiriguá's Acrópolis on a grander scale.

Quiriguá remained unknown to Europeans until John L Stephens arrived in 1840. Impressed by its great monuments, Stephens lamented the world's lack of interest in them in his book *Incidents of Travel in Central America, Chiapas and Yucatan* (1841):

> Of one thing there is no doubt: a large city once stood there; its name is lost, its history unknown; and...no account of its existence has ever before been published. For centuries it has lain as completely buried as if covered with the lava of Vesuvius. Every traveler from Yzabal to Guatemala has passed within three hours of it; we ourselves had done the same; and yet there it lay, like the rock-built city of Edom, unvisited, unsought, and utterly unknown.

Stephens tried to buy the ruined city in order to have its stelae shipped to New York, but the owner, Señor Payes, naturally assumed that Stephens (being a diplomat), was negotiating on behalf of the US government and that the government would pay. Payes quoted an extravagant price, and the deal was never made.

Between 1881 and 1894, excavations were carried out by Alfred P Maudslay. In the early 1900s all the land around Quiriguá was sold to the United Fruit Company and turned into banana groves (p223). The company is gone, but the bananas and Quiriguá remain. Restoration of the site was carried out by the University of Pennsylvania in the 1930s. In 1981, Unesco declared the ruins a World Heritage Site, one of only three in Guatemala (the others are Tikal and Antigua).

Ruins

The beautiful park-like **archaeological site** (US$3.25; ☼ 7:30am-5pm) has a small *tienda* near the entrance selling cold drinks and

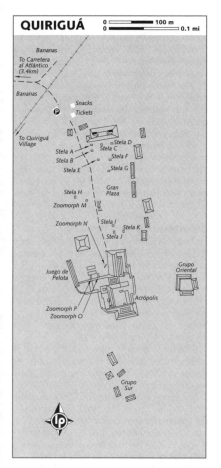

QUIRIGUÁ
0 ————— 100 m
0 ————— 0.1 mi

Bananas
To Carretera
al Atlántico
(3.4km)

Bananas

Snacks
Tickets

To Quiriguá
Village

Stela A
Stela B
Stela E

Stela D
Stela C
Stela F

Stela G

Stela H

Gran
Plaza

Zoomorph M

Zoomorph N
Stela I
Stela K
Stela J

Juego de
Pelota

Grupo
Oriental

Acrópolis
Zoomorph P
Zoomorph O

Grupo
Sur

standing some 8m above ground, with another 3m or so buried in the earth. It weighs almost 60,000kg. Note the exuberant, elaborate headdresses; the beards on some of the figures (an oddity in Mayan art and life); the staffs of office held in the kings' hands; and the glyphs on the sides of the stela.

At the far end of the plaza is the **Acrópolis**, far less impressive than the one at Copán. At its base are several **zoomorphs**, blocks of stone carved to resemble real and mythic creatures. Frogs, tortoises, jaguars and serpents were favorite subjects. The low zoomorphs can't compete with the towering stelae in impressiveness, but as works of art, imagination and mythic significance, the zoomorphs are superb.

Sleeping & Eating

Hotel y Restaurante Royal (☎ 947-3639; rooms per person US$4, s/d with bathroom US$7/13) In the center of the village of Quiriguá, 700m south of the Carretera al Atlántico, is this bright, clean and quiet place. Of the 13 rooms, six have hot-water bathroom. The restaurant serves meat and vegetarian meals. Most guests here are international travelers in town to visit the archaeological site.

Hotel y Restaurante Santa Mónica (☎ 947-3602; Carretera Atlántico Km 200; s/d/tr US$6/13/18) Behind the Texaco station at Los Amates, it has eight reasonable rooms with cold-water bathroom and fan. Lunch and dinner each cost US$4.50.

Parrillada del Atlántico (main meals US$5-8) About 100m east of the Texaco station is the best restaurant in the area, where you can get good, filling meals.

Getting There & Around

The turnoff to Quiriguá village is 205km (four hours) northeast of Guatemala City, 70km northeast of the Río Hondo junction, 41km southwest of La Ruidosa junction (for Río Dulce and Flores) and 90km southwest of Puerto Barrios.

Buses running Guatemala City–Puerto Barrios, Guatemala City–Flores, Esquipulas–Flores or Chiquimula–Flores will drop you off or pick you up here. They'll also drop you at the turnoff to the archaeological site if you ask.

From the highway it's 3.4km to the archaeological site – US$0.25 by bus or

snacks, but you'll be better off bringing your own picnic.

Despite the sticky heat and (sometimes) bothersome mosquitoes, Quiriguá is a wonderful place. The giant stelae on the **Gran Plaza** (Great Plaza) are all much more worn than those at Copán. To impede further deterioration, each has been covered by a thatched roof. The roofs cast shadows that make it difficult to examine the carving closely and almost impossible to get a good photograph, but somehow this does little to inhibit one's sense of awe.

Seven of the stelae, designated A, C, D, E, F, H and J, were built during the reign of Cauac Sky and carved with his image. **Stela E** is the largest Mayan stela known, pickup, but if one doesn't come, don't fret: it's a pleasant walk (without luggage) on a dirt road running through banana plantations to get there. You may have to wait to get from the ruins back to the main highway but eventually some transport will turn up.

If you're staying in the village of Quiriguá or Los Amates and walking to the archaeological site, you can take a shortcut along the railway branch line that goes from the village through the banana fields, crossing the access road very near the entrance to the archaeological site.

To head on to Río Dulce (US$1.95, two hours) if you don't want to wait for a bus to Flores (around 20 daily coming from Guatemala City), you can take any bus or minibus to Morales (the transportation hub for the area) and a bus on from there to Río Dulce. This is a bit of a detour off the main road, but at least you'll get a seat from Morales. Alternatively, take a Puerto Barrios bus and get off at La Ruidosa, where you can wait for a minivan or bus for the 34km to Río Dulce. For Chiquimula, take any bus the 3km from the turnoff to the ruins to Los Amates and wait for the next bus through to Chiquimula (US$1.95, two hours).

LAGO DE IZABAL

Guatemala's largest lake, to the north of the Carretera al Atlántico, is just starting to register on travelers' radar screens. Most visitors checking out the lake stay at Río Dulce town, by the long, tall bridge where Highway CA-13, heading north to Flores and Tikal, crosses the Río Dulce emptying out of the east end of the lake. Downstream, the beautiful river broadens into a lake called El Golfete before meeting the Caribbean at Lívingston. River trips are a highlight of a visit to eastern Guatemala. If you're looking for lakeside ambience minus the Río Dulce congestion and pace, head to Denny's Beach at Mariscos (p228) or, closer, El Castillo de San Felipe (p226), about 3km west of the bridge. The neat town of El Estor near the west end of the lake gives access to the Bocas del Polochic river delta, where there is lots of wildlife (see p227). There are many undiscovered spots in this area waiting to be explored, so don't limit yourself.

Río Dulce

Head northwest from La Ruidosa junction (Km 245 on the Carretera al Atlántico) along the road to Flores in El Petén, and after 34km you'll reach the village of Río Dulce. The part of Río Dulce on the northwest side of the bridge over the river is also called Fronteras; the part on the southeast side is also called El Relleno. Río Dulce has a sizeable transient population of foreign yachties.

The minute you alight from the bus, young men will approach you and try to put you on a motorboat to Lívingston. This may be exactly what you want to do. However, you can spend some relaxing days around the lake if you're so inclined.

ORIENTATION & INFORMATION

Unless you're staying at Hotel Backpacker's (p224) or volunteering at its Casa Guatemala, get off the bus on the north side of the bridge. The Fuente del Norte and Litegua bus offices are both here, opposite each other. Otherwise you'll find yourself trudging over what is believed to be the longest bridge in Central America – it's a very hot 30-minute bummer of a walk.

The main dock is now under the bridge on the opposite side of the main road from Bruno's (p224) – you'll see a side road leading down to it.

You can rent bicycles for US$2 an hour from a *tienda* next door to Tijax Express.

Cap't Nemo's Communications (☎ 930-5174; www.mayaparadise.com; per hr US$3.25; ☯ 7am-8pm Mon-Sat, 9am-2pm Sun) Beside Bruno's on the river, Nemo's offers email and international phone and fax services.

Tijax Express, **Hacienda Tijax** and **Hotel Backpacker's** (p224) are hooked up too, all charging US$3 per hour. The website www.mayaparadise.com has loads of information about Río Dulce.

Tijax Express (☯ daily) In the little lane between the river and the Fuente del Norte bus office, this is Río Dulce's unofficial tourist information center. English is spoken. There are two similar places near the Tijax, **Otitours** and **Atitrans**. You can book *lanchas*, tours, sailing trips and shuttles with all three.

If you need to change cash or traveler's checks, hit one of the banks in town, all on the main road:

Banco Agromercantil Will give cash advances on credit cards if there is a problem with the ATMs.

Banco Industrial (☯ 9am-5pm) Has a Visa ATM.

Banrural Has Visa and MasterCard ATMs.

BANANA REPUBLIC

In 1870, the first year that bananas were imported to the US, few Americans had ever seen a banana, let alone tasted one. By 1898 they were eating 16 million bunches annually.

In 1899 the Boston Fruit Company merged with the interests of the Brooklyn-born Central American railroad baron Minor C Keith to form the United Fruit Company. The aim was to own large areas of Central America and cultivate them by modern methods, providing predictable harvests of bananas that Keith, who controlled virtually all of the railroads in Central America, would then carry to the coast for shipment to the USA.

Central American governments readily granted United Fruit rights at low prices to large tracts of undeveloped jungle. The company created access to the land by road and/or rail, cleared and cultivated it, built extensive port facilities for the export of fruit and offered employment to large numbers of local workers.

By 1930, United Fruit was capitalized at US$215 million and was the largest employer in Central America. The company's Great White Fleet of transport ships was one of the largest private navies in the world. In Guatemala, by controlling Puerto Barrios and the railroads serving it, all of which it had built, United Fruit effectively controlled all the country's international commerce, banana or otherwise.

The company came to be referred to as El Pulpo, 'The Octopus,' by local journalists, who accused it of corrupting government officials, exploiting workers and in general exercising influence far beyond its role as a foreign company in Guatemala.

United Fruit's treatment of its workers was paternalistic. Though they worked long and hard for low wages, these wages were higher than those of other farm workers, and they received housing, medical care and in some cases schooling for their children. Still, indigenous Guatemalans were required to give right of way to whites and remove their hats when talking to them. And the company took out of the country far more in profits than it put in: between 1942 and 1952 the company paid stockholders almost 62 cents (US) in dividends for every dollar invested.

The US government, responding to its rich and powerful constituents, saw its role as one of support for United Fruit and defense of its interests.

On October 20, 1944, a liberal military coup paved the way for Guatemala's first-ever free elections. The winner and new president was Dr Juan José Arévalo, a professor who, inspired by the New Deal policies of Franklin Roosevelt, sought to remake Guatemala into a democratic, liberal nation guided by 'spiritual socialism.' His successor, Jacobo Arbenz, was even more vigorous in undertaking reform. Among Arbenz's many supporters was Guatemala's small communist party.

Free at last from the repression of past military dictators, labor unions clamored for better conditions, with almost constant actions against la Frutera, United Fruit. The Guatemalan government demanded more equitable tax payments from the company and divestiture of large tracts of its unused land.

Alarm bells sounded in the company's Boston headquarters and in Washington, where powerful members of Congress and the Eisenhower administration – including Secretary of State John Foster Dulles – were convinced that Arbenz was intent on turning Guatemala communist. Several high-ranking US officials had close ties to United Fruit, and others were persuaded by the company's expensive and effective lobbying campaign that Arbenz was a threat.

In 1954, the CIA arranged an invasion from Honduras by 'anti-communist' Guatemalan exiles, which resulted in Arbenz's resignation and exile. The CIA's hand-picked 'liberator' was Carlos Castillo Armas, a military man of the old caste, who returned Guatemala to rightist military dictatorship. The tremendous power of the United Fruit Company had set back democratic development in Guatemala by at least half a century.

A few years after the coup, the US Department of Justice brought suit against United Fruit for operating monopolistically in restraint of trade. In 1958 the company was ordered to reduce its size by two-thirds within 12 years. It began by selling some of its Guatemalan holdings to Guatemalan entrepreneurs and its US rival Standard Fruit. It yielded its monopoly on the railroads as well.

Caught up in the 'merger mania' of the 1960s, United Fruit became part of United Brands, which in the early 1970s sold all of its remaining land in Guatemala to the Del Monte corporation. Standard Fruit (now part of the Dole Corporation) and Del Monte are still active in Guatemala.

TOURS

Aventuras Vacacionales (☎ /fax 832-5938; www
.sailing.conexion.com; Centro Comercial María, 4a Calle
Poniente 17, Antigua) runs fun sailing trips on
the sailboat *Las Sirenas* from Río Dulce to
the Belize reefs and islands (US$325-360,
seven days) and Lago Izabal (US$135-165,
four days). The office is in Antigua but you
can also hook up with them in Río Dulce.
They make the Belize and lake trips in alternate weeks.

SLEEPING

Many places in Río Dulce communicate by
radio. Tijax Express, the bar at Bruno's and
Restaurant Río Bravo will radio your choice
of place to stay if necessary.

Hacienda Tijax (☎ 930-5505/7; VHF channel 09;
www.tijax.com; camping per person US$2.60, s/d from
US$8/12; P ☒ ☐) A special place to stay,
this 2-sq-km hacienda/eco-farm is two
minutes by boat across the cove from the
Restaurant Río Bravo or about a kilometer
north of the village by road. Activities
include horseback riding, hiking, bird-
watching, sailboat trips and tours around
the hacienda's rubber plantation, medicinal plant gardens, reforested area and
small jungle. There is a place to swim on
the property and a tall tower that you can
climb up to take in 360-degree views of the
fabulous countryside. The hotel itself has a
beautiful large swimming pool with Jacuzzi.
Tours cost US$10 to US$25 per person.

The cheapest accommodations are the
small, private rooms over the restaurant;
these have partition walls only. There are
also *cabañas* built over the river with fans,
mosquito nets and shared bathroom sleeping up to three people (s/d/tr US$16/21/
27), as well as others here and back from the
river with bathroom (s/d/tr US$25/30/45).
Thai-style thatch-roofed houses have hot-
water bathroom and kitchens. The owner
speaks Spanish, English, French and Italian.
Staff will pick you up from across the river;
ask at the Tijax Express. Arrival and departure boat rides are free but you pay US$0.65
for subsequent rides. The camping area is
reached from the Flores road.

Watch your tab as you eat and drink at
the very good restaurant (p225).

Hotel Catamaran (☎ 930-5494/5; www.hotelcat
amaran.com; s/d/tr from US$52/62/74; ☒ ☒) This
upmarket place occupies a tropical island,
roughly five minutes by *lancha* beyond the
Hacienda Tijax. It has 34 rustic wooden
bungalows (most built over the water), a
fancy restaurant, sports bar, tennis court
and swimming pool.

Casa Perico (☎ 909-0721, VHF channel 68; dm
US$5.25, rooms per person US$6.50) This is a great
riverside jungle hideaway, fine for chilling
out for a couple of days, 10 minutes downstream from Río Dulce by *lancha*. Sleep
beneath the vast *palapa* roof in the dorm
above the restaurant/bar/sitting area, or
in rooms at the rear. It's run by four Swiss
guys who cook up great food (dinner US$4
to US$5). They'll pick you up for free from
Río Dulce when you arrive and drop you
back there for free when you leave; interim
trips are US$1.30 round-trip.

Bruno's (☎ 930-5175; www.mayaparadise.com; dm
US$5, rooms per person US$10, with bathroom per person
US$20-23; P ☒ ☒) A path leads down from
the northwest end of the bridge to this
riverside hangout for yachties needing to
get some land under their feet. All rooms
are clean and comfortable and look out to
the river. The cheapest have a sink, fan and
shared bathroom. There are four rooms with
hot-water bathroom and air-con. There
are also bungalows, and an air-con apartment with two bedrooms (sleeps eight),
costing US$24 per person. There's plenty of
space to kick back here – poolside is highly
recommended.

Hotel Backpacker's (☎ 930-5169; casaguatemal@
guate.net; dm US$4, s/d US$8/16, with bathroom
US$10/20; ☐) Across on the south side of
the bridge is this business run by Casa
Guatemala, a nonprofit organization with
a center for abandoned and malnourished
children on El Golfete. The beautiful
location over the river makes it popular,
though some guests find the place too
noisy. A 30-bed dormitory overlooking
the river has lockers for luggage-storage
and cubicle bathroom facilities. There are
no nets or fans but the location should
guarantee some sort of a breeze. Some of
the basic private rooms with and without
bathroom are a bit more enclosed. Paint-
work is cheerful throughout. There's a
restaurant and bar, and services include
lancha, laundry, phone, fax and email. If
you're coming by *lancha*, ask the driver to
let you off here to spare yourself that walk
across the bridge. There are opportunities

for volunteer work with Casa Guatemala either in the children's home or here in the hotel.

Las Brisas Hotel (☎ 930-5124; s/d per person US$6, s/d/tr with bathroom US$10/13/20; 🏊) This hotel is opposite Tijax Express. All rooms are clean enough and have three beds and fans. Three rooms have bathroom and air-con (US$45). It's a bit exposed to pedestrian traffic.

Hospedaje Marilu (☎ 930-5403; s/d US$4/7, with bathroom US$4/8) is a clean, cheap option on the main drag, opposite Las Brisas. Rooms have a double bed, fan and mosquito screen.

Hospedaje Golding (☎ 930-5123; Carretera a San Felipe; rooms per person US$4, with bathroom US$7) A yellow building with no sign, just off the main road, Golding is a simple place. It has some pretty trees and its brightly colored upstairs rooms have a bit of a view.

Hotel Portal del Río (☎ 391-3034; s/d US$7/12, with bathroom US$11/16; 🅿 🏊) In spacious grounds, this is a fine choice.

Also recommended:

Hotel Río Dulce (s/d/tr US$12/12/16) Near the foot of the bridge.

Hotel Posada del Río (s/d/tr US$6/11/21) In the vicinity of the foot of the bridge and the dock.

Riverside Motel (☎ 514-3586; s/d US$4/8, with bathroom & TV US$8/16) On the highway, basic ground-floor rooms have shared bathroom and fan while four upstairs rooms have fan, mosquito screen and bathroom. The rooms are clean but the grounds are littered with rubbish.

Hotel Café Sol (d US$8, with TV US$12) Along and across the street from Riverside Motel; has very basic rooms with bathroom, fan and mosquito screen but no shade.

EATING

Restaurant Río Bravo (breakfasts US$1.70-3, pizzas US$4-50-9.25) The best place in town is the Río Bravo with its open-air deck over the lake, just at the northwest end of the bridge. It has a good variety of seafood and pasta dishes, and a full bar.

Bruno's (breakfasts US$2.60-4, mains US$8) Nearby, this is an open-air place right beside the water. It's a restaurant/sports bar with satellite TV and video; its floating dock makes it popular with yachties.

Cafetería La Carreta, (breakfasts US$1.55, mains US$10) A bright and clean *palapa*-style restaurant off the highway on the road toward San Felipe, it is recommended by locals.

Hacienda Tijax (mains US$4.25-13) This place has a fine restaurant with a wide range of dishes, a full bar and good coffee.

Several (more expensive) places to stay with restaurants are on the waterfront further from town and are accessible only by boat. Beyond the Hotel Catamaran on the lakeshore, **Mario's Marina** has good food and is a popular hangout for the sailing set, with popular nacho nights (US$3.25 for all you can eat).

GETTING THERE & AWAY

Beginning at 7am, 14 Fuente del Norte buses a day head north along a paved road to Poptún (US$3.90, two hours, 99km), and Flores (US$6.50, four hours, 208km). The 12:30pm, 7:30pm, 9:30pm and 11:30pm buses continue all the way to Melchor de Mencos (US$10) on the Belize border. With good connections you can get to Tikal (279km) in a snappy six hours. In the other direction, at least 17 buses daily go to Guatemala City (US$5.25, six hours, 280km) with Fuente del Norte and Litegua. Línea Dorada/Fuente del Norte has first-class buses departing at 1:30pm for Guatemala City and at 2:30pm for Flores (both US$15.60). This shaves up to an hour off the journey times.

To get to Puerto Barrios, take any bus heading for Guatemala City and change at La Ruidosa.

Atitrans' shuttle minibus operates from their office on the highway. Shuttles to Antigua cost US$37, to Copán Ruinas US$30 and Guatemala City US$30 with a minimum of four passengers in each case. Otitours and Tijax Express offer much the same service.

Dilapidated Fuente del Norte buses leave for El Estor (US$1.30, 1½ hours, 43km) from the Pollolandia restaurant at the San Felipe and El Estor turnoff in the middle of town, hourly from 7am to 4pm. The road is only paved for 15km.

Colectivo lanchas go down the Río Dulce (from the new dock) to Lívingston, usually requiring eight to 10 people, charging US$10 per person. The trip is a beautiful one and they usually make a 'tour' of it, with several halts along the way (p234). If everyone wants to get there as fast as possible, it takes one hour without stops. Boats usually leave from 9am to about 2pm. The three tour offices offer *lancha* service to Lívingston and most other places you'd care to go but charge more.

El Castillo de San Felipe

The fortress and castle of San Felipe de Lara, **El Castillo de San Felipe** (US$1.30; ☯ 8am-5pm), about 3km west of the bridge, was built in 1652 to keep pirates from looting the villages and commercial caravans of Izabal. Though the fortress deterred the buccaneers a bit, a pirate force captured and burned it in 1686. By the end of the next century, pirates had disappeared from the Caribbean, and the fort's sturdy walls served as a prison. Eventually, though, the fortress was abandoned and became a ruin. The present fort was reconstructed in 1956.

Today the castle is protected as a park and is one of the Lago de Izabal's principal tourist attractions. In addition to the fort itself, there are grassy grounds, barbeque and picnic areas, and the opportunity to swim in the lake. The place rocks from April 30 to May 4 during the **Feria de San Felipe**.

SLEEPING & EATING

Hotel Don Humberto (☎ /fax 930-5051; s/d/tr US$5/ 10/15; ℗) Near the Castillo, Don Humberto has simple but clean rooms of varying sizes, with bathroom. If the restaurant here is not up and running, try **Cafetería Don Miguel**, next to the Castillo entrance.

Viñas del Lago (☎ 930-5053; fax 476-0707; www .infovia.com.gt/hotelvinasdellago; s/d/tr from US$21/31/ 40; ℗ ☒ ☒) The much fancier del Lago, nearby, has 18 clean, spacious rooms, all with hot-water bathroom, air-con and TV. The grounds are large and there's a **restaurant** (mains US$7.75-10.50) with views of Lago de Izabal. Between here and the castle are a couple of good medium-priced places with fresh, bright, homely decor and little restaurants: **Hotel Changri-la** (☎ 930-5467; hotelchangrila@yahoo.com; s/d US$19/32; 6-person bungalow US$152; ℗ ☒ ☒) and the more rustic **La Cabaña del Viajero** (☎ 930-5062; s/d US$5/9, with bathroom & fan US$7/13, with bathroom, air-con & TV US$10/20; ℗ ☒ ☒).

GETTING THERE & AWAY

San Felipe is on the lakeshore, 3km west of Río Dulce. It's a beautiful 45-minute walk between the two towns, or take a minivan (US$0.50, every 30 minutes). In Río Dulce it stops on the corner of the highway and road to El Estor, across from the Pollolandia restaurant; in San Felipe it stops in front of the Hotel Don Humberto, at the entrance to El Castillo.

Boats coming from Lívingston will drop you in San Felipe if you ask. The Río Dulce river tours usually come to El Castillo, allowing you to get out and visit the castle if you like. Or you can come over from Río Dulce by private *lancha* for US$5.

Finca El Paraíso

On the north side of the lake, between Río Dulce and El Estor, **Finca El Paraíso** (☎ 949- 7122, 230-3028; US$1.30) makes a great day trip from either place. This working ranch's territory includes an incredibly beautiful spot in the jungle where a wide, hot waterfall drops about 12m into a clear, deep pool. You can bathe in the hot water, swim in the cool pool or duck under an overhanging promontory and enjoy a jungle-style sauna. Also on the *finca* are a number of interesting caves and a restaurant by a sandy lake beach. If you like you can stay on in comfortable bungalows for around US$25 for two people.

The *finca* is on the Río Dulce–El Estor bus route, about one hour (US$0.90) from Río Dulce and 30 minutes (US$0.60) from El Estor. The last bus in either direction passes at around 4:30pm to 5pm.

El Estor

The major settlement on the northern shore of Lago de Izabal is El Estor. The nickel mines a few kilometers to the northwest (for which the town grew up) closed in 1980 but are set to be reopened by Canadian companies as world nickel stocks run low. A friendly, somnolent little town with a lovely setting, El Estor is the jumping-off point for the Bocas del Polochic, a highly biodiverse wildlife reserve at the west end of the lake. The town is also a staging post on a possible route between Río Dulce and Lanquín.

ORIENTATION & INFORMATION

The main street, running parallel to the lakeshore two blocks back from the water, is 3a Calle. Buses from Río Dulce terminate at Tienda Cobanerita on the corner of 3a Calle and 4a Av. Walk one block west from here along 3a Calle to find the Parque Central.

Asociación Feminina Q'eqchi' sells clothes, blankets and accessories that are made from traditional cloth woven by the association's members. To find it go two blocks north along 5a Av from the Parque Central, then two blocks west. All profits benefit the women involved in the program.

Local tourism businesses have put together a fine website (www.ecoturismoel estor.com) about the area.

Banrural (cnr 3a Calle & 6a Av; ⏱ 8:30am-5pm Mon-Fri, 9am-1pm Sat) Changes US dollars and Amex traveler's checks.

Café Portal (☎ 818-0843; eloydam@hotmail.com; 5a Av 2-65; ⏱ 6:30am-10pm) On the east side of Parque Central, this place provides information, tours and transport.

Municipal police (cnr 1a Calle & 5a Av) Near the lakeshore.

SLEEPING & EATING

Hotel Vista al Lago (☎ 949-7205; vistalago@int elnett.com; 6a Av 1-13; s/d/tr US$10/18/23) Overlooking the lake as its name implies, this hotel is inviting and clean. Built between 1815 and 1825, the wooden building was once a general store owned by an Englishman and a Dutchman; 'the store' gave the town of El Estor its name. The 21 rooms are small and clean, with fans. Get one upstairs at the front if you can. The friendly owners can arrange tours and guides.

Restaurante Típico Chaabil (☎ 949-7272; west end 3a Calle; rooms per person US$7; Ⓟ) The four sizeable rooms behind this excellent restaurant are attractive, wooden and almost brand-new. Two, with bunks, hold up to five people each. The upper two have beds, and all have bathroom. The restaurant itself, on a lovely lakeside terrace, does great food ranging from large breakfasts for US$2 to *tapado* (seafood casserole) for US$9. You can have *mojarra* (perch) from the lake fried, grilled, steamed, in garlic, *escabeche* (pickle) or salsa, for US$4 to US$7.

Hotel Villela (☎ 949-7214; 6a Av 2-06; s/d US$5/9) The rooms are less attractive than the neat lawn and trees they're set around, but some are airier and brighter than others. All have fan and bathroom.

Hotel Central (☎ 949-7497; 5a Av; s/d US$7/10; Ⓟ) This hotel provides rooms with fan and bathroom, at the northeast corner of the Parque Central.

Hotel Santa Clara (☎ 949-7244; 5a Av 2-11; s/d/tr US$3/4/6, with bathroom US$5/7/8) Upstairs rooms are clean, with bathroom and fan. Downstairs rooms are dark and box-like, with shared bathrooms.

The Chaabil apart, the best place to look for food is around the Parque Central, where **Café Portal** and **Restaurante Hugo's** both serve a broad range of fare with some vegetarian options. Main dishes are around US$3 to US$4 at either.

GETTING THERE & AWAY

See Río Dulce (p195) for information on buses from there. The schedule from El Estor to Río Dulce is hourly, 6am to 4pm.

The road west from El Estor via Panzós and Tucurú to Tactic, south of Cobán, has a bad reputation for highway holdups and robberies, especially around Tucurú, and we do not recommend it. You can get to Lanquín by taking the truck that leaves El Estor's Parque Central at 9am for Cahabón (US$2, four to five hours), and then a bus or pickup straight on from Cahabón to Lanquín the same day. This route is not recommended in the reverse direction because the truck leaves Cahabón about 4am, meaning that you have to spend the preceding night in impoverished Cahabón, where things can get pretty rough after dark.

There are no public boat services between El Estor and other lake destinations. Private *lanchas* can be contracted, though this can be pricey. Ask at your hotel.

Around El Estor

REFUGIO BOCAS DEL POLOCHIC & RESERVA DE BIOSFERA SIERRA DE LAS MINAS

The Bocas del Polochic Wildlife Reserve covers the delta of the Río Polochic, which provides most of Lago de Izabal's water. A visit here provides great bird-watching and howler-monkey observation. The reserve supports more than 300 species of birds – the migration seasons, September to October and April to May, are reportedly fantastic – and many varieties of butterflies and fish. You may well see alligators and, if you're very lucky, glimpse a manatee. **Café Portal** (p226) can set up early-morning trips with local boatman **Benjamín Castillo** costing US$32 for two people plus US$13 for each extra person for 3½ hours. The reserve is managed by the **Fundación Defensores de la Naturaleza** (☎ 815-1736; www.defensores.org.gt in Spanish; cnr 5a Av & 2a Calle, El Estor) whose research station, the **Estación Científica Selempim**, just south of the Bocas del Polochic reserve, in the Reserva de la Biosfera Sierra de las Minas, is open for ecotouristic visits. Contact Defensors' El Estor office for bookings and further information: ask for Luis Pérez, who speaks English. You can get to the station on a local *lancha* service leaving El Estor at 11am Monday, Wednesday and Saturday (US$6.50 round-trip, 1¼ hours each way) or by special hire (US$65-US$90 for a boatload of up to 12), and stay in attractive wood-and-thatch *cabañas* (per person US$6.50) or camp (for two people US$4). Meals are available for US$2 each or you can use the Estación Científica's kitchen (for campers US$2.50). To explore the reserves you can rent canoes (US$2 an hour) or bicycles (US$3.25 a day), take boat trips (US$20 to US$32) or walk trails.

El Boquerón

This beautiful, lushly vegetated canyon abutting the tiny Mayan settlement of the same name is about 6km east of El Estor. For around US$2, villagers will paddle you up the Río Sauce through the canyon, drop you at a small beach, where you can swim and if you like scramble up the rocks, and return for you at an agreed time. Río Dulce–bound buses from El Estor will drop you at El Boquerón (US$0.30, 15 minutes), as will El Estor–bound buses from Río Dulce.

Mariscos

Mariscos is the principal town on the lake's south side. Ferries from here used to be the main access to El Estor and the north side of the lake, but since a road was built from Río Dulce to El Estor, Mariscos has taken a back seat. As a result, **Denny's Beach** (☎ 302-8121; www.mayaparadise.com; camping per tent US$4, hammocks US$2, cabañas per person US$5-10), 10 minutes by boat from Mariscos, is a good place to get away from it all. Dennis Gulck and his wife, Lupe, offer tours, hiking and swimming, and host full-moon parties. When you arrive in Mariscos, you can radio them on VHF channel 63 – many people and businesses in Mariscos use radios – and they'll come to pick you up. Otherwise, you can hitch a ride with a *cayuco* (dugout canoe) at the market for US$1.30 or go to Shop-n-Go and hire a speedboat for US$13, fine if you're a group. In Río Dulce, you can radio from Cap't Nemo's Communications or Atitrans (p222) and they'll send someone to pick you up.

Karlinda's has a restaurant and also offers lake tours.

PUERTO BARRIOS

pop 35,000

Heading east from La Ruidosa junction, the country becomes even more lush, tropical and humid until you arrive at Puerto Barrios, Guatemala's broiling hot Caribbean port.

The powerful United Fruit Company once owned vast plantations in the Motagua valley and many other parts of Guatemala. The company built railways to ship its produce to the coast, and it built Puerto Barrios early in the 20th century to put that produce onto ships sailing for New Orleans and New York (p223). Laid out as a company town, Puerto Barrios has long, wide streets arranged neatly on a grid plan and lots of Caribbean-style wood-frame houses, many of which have seen better days.

When United Fruit's power and influence declined in the 1960s, the Del Monte company became successor to its interests. But the heyday of the imperial foreign firms was past, as was that of Puerto Barrios. A more modern and efficient port was built a few kilometers to the southwest at Santo Tomás de Castilla, and Puerto Barrios sank into tropical torpor. In the last few years however things have started to look up again with the construction of a huge new truck container depot where the old railway yards were. The amount of sleaze and lowlife around the town center has decreased markedly, though there are still a few noisy bars along 9a Calle.

For foreign visitors, Puerto Barrios remains little more than a place to get a boat across the Bahía de Amatique to Punta Gorda (Belize) or the Garífuna enclave Lívingston or the Punta de Manabique wetland reserve.

Orientation & Information

Because of its spacious layout, you must walk or ride further in Puerto Barrios to get from place to place. For instance, it's 800m from the bus terminals by the market in the town center to the Muelle Municipal (Municipal Boat Dock) at the end of 12a Calle, from which passenger boats depart.

Bancafé (cnr 13a Calle & 7a Av; ☼ 9am-7pm Mon-Fri, 9am-1pm Sat) Changes US-dollars cash and traveler's checks, and has Visa ATMs.

Banco Industrial (7a Av; ☼ 9am-5pm Mon-Fri, 9am-1pm Sat) Changes US-dollars cash and traveler's checks, and has Visa ATMs.

PUERTO BARRIOS

0 |_____| 300 m
0 |_____| 0.2 mi

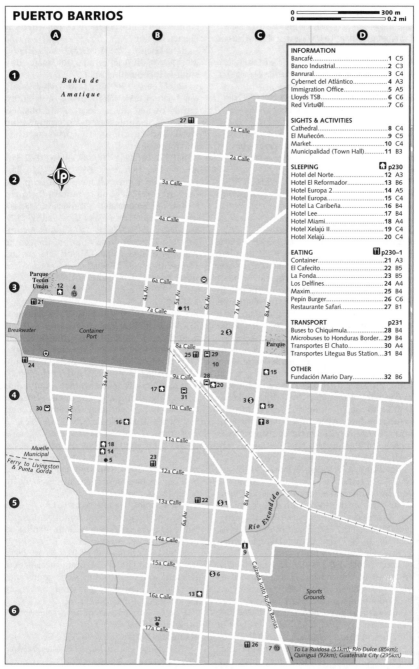

INFORMATION
Bancafé..................................1 C5
Banco Industrial.......................2 C3
Banrural...............................3 C4
Cybernet del Atlántico.................4 A3
Immigration Office.....................5 A5
Lloyds TSB............................6 C6
Red Virtu@l...........................7 C6

SIGHTS & ACTIVITIES
Cathedral.............................8 C4
El Muñecón............................9 C5
Market...............................10 C4
Municipalidad (Town Hall).........11 B3

SLEEPING   ⌂ p230
Hotel del Norte.....................12 A3
Hotel El Reformador.................13 B6
Hotel Europa 2......................14 A5
Hotel Europa........................15 C4
Hotel La Caribeña...................16 B4
Hotel Lee...........................17 B4
Hotel Miami.........................18 A4
Hotel Xelajú II.....................19 C4
Hotel Xelajú........................20 C4

EATING   🍴 p230–1
Container............................21 A3
El Cafecito..........................22 B5
La Fonda.............................23 B5
Los Delfines.........................24 A4
Maxim................................25 B4
Pepín Burger.........................26 C6
Restaurante Safari..................27 B1

TRANSPORT   p231
Buses to Chiquimula.................28 B4
Microbuses to Honduras Border....29 B4
Transportes El Chato................30 A4
Transportes Litegua Bus Station...31 B4

OTHER
Fundación Mario Dary................32 B6

Banrural (8a Av; ☺ 8:30am-5pm Mon-Fri, 9am-1pm Sat) Changes cash dollars only and has a MasterCard ATM.

Cybernet del Atlántico (7a Calle west of 2a Av) Internet access US$1.30 per hour.

El Muñecón (intersection 8a Av, 14a Calle & Calzada Justo Rufino Barrios) A statue of a dock worker; it's a favorite landmark and monument in the town.

Immigration office (cnr 12a Calle & 3a Av; ☺ 24hr) A block from the Muelle Municipal. Come here for your entry or exit stamp if you're arriving from or leaving for Belize: if you're leaving, there is a US$10 departure tax to pay. If you are heading to Honduras, you get your exit stamp at another immigration office on the road to the border.

Red Virtu@l (cnr 17a Calle & Calzada Justo Rufino Barrios; ☺ 8am-9:30pm daily) Internet access US$1.30 per hour.

Sleeping

Hotel del Norte (☎ 948-2116; fax 948-0087; 7a Calle; s/d US$11/16, with air-con US$16/26; P ✖ ✖) The century-old Hotel del Norte is in a class by itself. A large, classically tropical wooden construction with corridors wide enough to run a banana train through, its weathered and warped frame is redolent of history. In the airy dining room overlooking the Bahía de Amatique you can almost hear the echoing conversation of bygone banana moguls and smell their pungent cigars. Spare, simple and agreeably dilapidated, this is a real museum piece. Meals are served with old-fashioned refinement by white-jacketed waiters, though the food isn't always up to the same standard. All rooms have bathroom, and are kept very clean, though some floors have an interesting tilt. There's a swimming pool beside the sea.

Hotel Europa 2 (☎ 948-1292; 3a Av; s/d US$7/11; P) This hotel just 1½ blocks from the Muelle Municipal is run by a friendly family and has clean rooms with bathroom and fan arranged around a parking courtyard.

Hotel Miami (☎ 948-0537; s/d US$6/12, with air-con US$10/20; P ✖) Next door to Hotel Europa 2, this is a friendly family-run place.

Hotel Europa (☎ 948-0127; 8a Av; s/d US$6/12; P) East of the market, Europa also provides plain, clean rooms with bathroom, set around a parking courtyard.

Hotel Xelajú (☎ 948-0482; 9a Calle; s/d/tr US$5/7/9, with bathroom US$7/11/16) The Xelajú is right in the thick of the town center, facing the market, but it's secure: no rooms are let after 10pm and 'señoritas de clubes nocturnos'

are not allowed. It has clean fan-cooled rooms and its own generator for when the electricity fails.

Hotel Xelajú II (☎ 948-1117; 8a Av; s/d/tr US$5/7/9, with bathroom US$11-16) Similar to Xelajú, in a slightly less bustling area.

Hotel Lee (☎ 948-0685; 5a Av; s/d/tr US$5/9/13, with bathroom US$8/14/16) This is a friendly, family-owned place close to the bus terminals. The rooms are a bit cramped but clean, and have fans, TV, drinking water and Chinese art.

Hotel La Caribeña (☎ 948-0384; fax 948-2216; 4a Av; s/d US$7/9, with air-con US$16/20; P ✖) The plain, clean rooms all have bathroom and fan and there's a good restaurant (below).

Hotel El Reformador (☎ 948-0533, 948-5489; reformador@intelnet.net.gt; 7a Av 159; s/d/tr US$9/18/27, with air-con US$15/20/29; P ✖) This is a comfortable 52-room hotel south of the center. All rooms have cable TV and fan; air-con rooms also have hot water and phone. The hotel has its own restaurant.

Eating

Restaurante Safari (☎ 948-0563; 5a Av; seafood US$6.50-10; ☺ 10am-9pm) The town's most enjoyable restaurant is on a thatch-roofed, open-air platform right over the water about 1km north of the town center. Locals and visitors alike love to eat and catch the sea breezes here. Excellent seafood of all kinds (including that great Garífuna casserole, *tapado*) is the specialty; chicken and meat dishes are also available (US$3 to US$6).

Maxim (☎ 948-2258; cnr 6a Av & 8a Calle; mains US$4-6) Whirring fans provide the breezes at this busy and enjoyable Chinese place opposite the market. The food is well prepared and comes in generous quantities, beneath a big Taiwanese flag.

Pepín Burger (17a Calle; fajitas US$1.80; ☺ closed Tue) Come here for great *fajitas* and good-value burgers, chicken and flour tortillas on an open-air upstairs terrace.

Hotel La Caribeña (☎ 948-0860; 4a Av; seafood US$9) This good hotel restaurant specializes in fish and seafood including some good soups and *tapado*. Plain rice, beans and chicken are also available for US$3.25.

Puerto Barrios has quite a selection of other appealing eateries:

El Cafecito (13a Calle; light meals US$2-2.50; ☺ 7:30am-11pm Mon-Sat) Neat, air-conditioned haven; serves seafood too.

Los Delfines (☎ 948-2301; 9a Calle; mains US$4.50-9; ⏱ 11am-10pm) Breezy waterside terrace, with a broad range of seafood and meat dishes.
La Fonda (cnr 5a Av & 12a Calle; mains US$9) Air-con restaurant with dishes of the day for around US$5.
Container (7a Calle) The oddest café in town, made of two steel shipping containers – with good bay views.

Getting There & Around
BUS & MINIBUS
Transportes Litegua (☎ 948-1172; cnr 6a Av & 9a Calle) leaves for Guatemala City (US$5.25, five to six hours, 295km), via Quiriguá and Río Hondo, 15 times between 1am and noon, and also at 4pm. *Directo* services avoid a half-hour detour into Morales.

Buses for Chiquimula (US$2.50, 4½ hours, 192km), also via Quiriguá, leave every half hour, 4am to 4pm, from the corner of 6a Av and 9a Calle.

For Río Dulce, take a Chiquimula bus to La Ruidosa junction (US$0.65, 50 minutes) and change to a bus or minibus (US$0.65, 35 minutes) there.

Minibuses leave for the Honduras frontier (US$1.30, 1¼ hours) every 20 minutes, 5:30am to 6pm, from 6a Av outside the market. The paved road to the border turns off the CA-9 at Entre Ríos, 13km south of Puerto Barrios. Buses and minibuses going in all directions wait for passengers at Entre Ríos, meaning that you can get to or from the border fairly easily, whichever direction you are traveling in. The minibuses from Puerto Barrios stop en route to the border at Guatemalan immigration, where you may be required to pay US$1.30 for an exit stamp. Honduran entry formalities may leave you US$1 or so lighter. Pickups shuttle between the border and the small Honduran town of Corinto, nearby, for about US$1 (or you can walk, about 15 minutes). From Corinto buses leave for Omoa and Puerto Cortés (US$2, two hours) about every two hours. You can continue by bus from Puerto Cortés to San Pedro Sula and from there to La Ceiba, but it's touch and go whether you would make the 3pm ferry from La Ceiba to Roatán island in one day from Puerto Barrios, even if you took the first vehicle out in the morning.

BOAT
Boats depart from the Muelle Municipal at the end of 12a Calle.

A ferry departs for Lívingston (US$1.30, 1½ hours) every day at 10am and 5pm. From Lívingston, it leaves for Puerto Barrios at 5am and 2pm. Get to the dock from 30 to 45 minutes before departure for a seat, otherwise you could end up standing.

Smaller, faster *lanchas* depart from both sides whenever they have about a dozen people ready to go; they cost US$3.25 and take 30 minutes.

Most of the movement from Lívingston to Puerto Barrios is in the morning, returning in the afternoon. From Lívingston, your last chance of the day may be the 2pm ferry, especially during the low season when fewer travelers are shuttling back and forth.

A *lancha* service of **Transportes El Chato** (☎ 948-5525; 1a Av) departs from the Muelle Municipal at 10am daily for Punta Gorda, Belize (US$15.50, one hour), arriving in time for the noon bus from Punta Gorda to Belize City. Tickets are sold at El Chato's office. Before boarding you also need to get your exit stamp at the nearby immigration office (p230). The return boat leaves Punta Gorda at 4pm.

If you want to leave a car in Puerto Barrios while you visit Lívingston for a day or two, hotels such as the Europa 2 and Miami (p230) provide off-street parking for US$2.50 to US$3 a day.

TAXI
A cab between the market area and the Muelle Municipal, Hotel del Norte or Restaurante Safari costs around US$2.50.

PUNTA DE MANABIQUE
The Punta de Manabique promontory, which separates the Bahía de Manabique from the open sea, along with the coast and hinterland all the way southeast to the Honduran frontier, comprise a large, ecologically fascinating, sparsely populated wetland area. Access to the area, which is under environmental protection as the Área de Protección Especial Punta de Manabique, is not cheap, but the attractions for those who make it there include pristine Caribbean beaches, boat trips through the mangrove forests, lagoons and waterways, bird-watching, fishing with locals, and crocodile and possible manatee sightings. To visit, get in touch – a week in advance, if possible – with the nongovernment organization involved

in the reserve's management, **Fundary** (Fundación Mario Dary; ☎ 948-0435; manabique@intelnet.net .gt; 17a Calle, Puerto Barrios; Guatemala City ☎ 232-3230; fundary@intelnet.net.gt).

Fundary is helping to develop several ecotouristic possibilities in the reserve. It offers accommodation for groups of two to four people at the **Estación Biológica Julio Obiols** (1/2/3 nights per person US$65/90/115) at the small community of Cabo Tres Puntas on the north side of the promontory, near a lovely beach. The price includes round-trip transport from Puerto Barrios or Lívingston (one hour each way from either place by *lancha*) and meals. Rooms have two to four beds and mosquito nets. If you want a program of trips around the reserve, you're looking at a total of about US$100 per person per day. Another option is **camping** (per person US$3), at the Estación Biológica or at the small community of Estero Lagarto on the south side of the promontory, or at El Quetzalito near the mouth of the Río Motagua at the eastern end of the reserve. At **Estero Lagarto**, villagers will provide a fresh fish lunch (US$3.25) or take you on a boat trip through the lagoons and mangroves (per person US$6.50). Ask for Ingris, who lives by the school. Accommodations in local homes may become available here for about US$6.50 per person. A visitors center offering information and meals is under construction at **Santa Isabel** on the Canal de los Ingleses, a waterway connecting the Bahía de Manabique with the open sea, with canoe trips along the canal available – also fishing with locals and demonstrations of the local charcoal-making process. **El Quetzalito** – about one hour by pickup from Puerto Barrios then half an hour by boat down the Río Motagua – is a good area for bird-watching and crocodile spotting, and for fishing with locals.

If you want to organize your own transport, a *lancha* from Puerto Barrios or Lívingston will cost between US$65 and US$125 round-trip depending on the deal you strike. A small boat (four passengers) to Estero Lagarto might be US$50.

LÍVINGSTON

pop 6000

As you come ashore in Lívingston, which is only reachable by boat, you will be surprised to meet black Guatemalans who speak Spanish as well as their own Garífuna language; some also speak the musical English of Belize and the islands. The town of Lívingston is an interesting anomaly, with a laid-back, very Belizean way of life (including a bit of reefer madness), groves of coconut palms, gaily painted wooden buildings, and an economy based on fishing and tourism.

The Garífuna (Garinagu, or Black Carib) people of Caribbean Guatemala, Honduras, Nicaragua and southern Belize trace their roots to the Caribbean island of St Vincent, where shipwrecked African slaves mixed with the indigenous Carib in the 17th century. It took the British a long time, and a lot of fighting, to establish colonial control over St Vincent, and when they finally succeeded in 1796 they decided to deport its surviving Garífuna inhabitants. Most of the survivors wound up, after many had starved on Roatán island off Honduras, in the Honduran coastal town of Trujillo. From there, they have spread along the Caribbean coast. Their main concentration in Guatemala is in Lívingston but there are also a few thousand in Puerto Barrios and elsewhere. The Garífuna language is a unique mélange of Caribbean and African languages with a bit of French. Other people in Lívingston include the indigenous Q'eqchi' Maya – who have their own community a kilometer or so upriver from the main dock – ladinos and a smattering of international travelers.

Orientation & Information

Lívingston stands where the Río Dulce opens out into the Bahía de Amatique. After being here half an hour, you'll know where everything is. The main street, Calle Principal, heads straight ahead, uphill, from the main dock, curving round to the right at Hotel Río Dulce. The other most important streets head off to the left of this: Calle Marcos Sánchez Díaz heading southwest, parallel to the river, to the Q'eqchi' Maya community, and another street leading northwest from the town center to several places to stay, eat and drink. Though we use such street names here for ease of orientation, in reality no one uses them.

Several private businesses around the town will change US-dollar cash and traveler's checks.

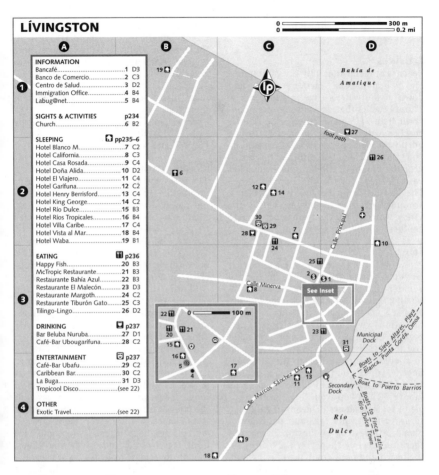

LÍVINGSTON

INFORMATION	
Bancafé	1 D3
Banco de Comercio	2 C3
Centro de Salud	3 D2
Immigration Office	4 B4
Labug@net	5 B4

SIGHTS & ACTIVITIES	p234
Church	6 B2

SLEEPING	pp235–6
Hotel Blanco M	7 C2
Hotel California	8 C3
Hotel Casa Rosada	9 C4
Hotel Doña Alida	10 D2
Hotel El Viajero	11 C4
Hotel Garifuna	12 C2
Hotel Henry Berrisford	13 C4
Hotel King George	14 C2
Hotel Río Dulce	15 B3
Hotel Rios Tropicales	16 B4
Hotel Villa Caribe	17 C4
Hotel Vista al Mar	18 B4
Hotel Waba	19 B1

EATING	p236
Happy Fish	20 B3
McTropic Restaurante	21 B3
Restaurante Bahía Azul	22 B3
Restaurante El Malecón	23 D3
Restaurante Margoth	24 C2
Restaurante Tiburón Gato	25 C3
Tilingo-Lingo	26 D2

DRINKING	p237
Bar Beluba Nuruba	27 D1
Café-Bar Ubougarifuna	28 C2

ENTERTAINMENT	p237
Café-Bar Ubafu	29 C2
Caribbean Bar	30 C2
La Buga	31 D3
Tropicool Disco	(see 22)

OTHER	
Exotic Travel	(see 22)

Bancafé (Calle Principal; ☺ 9am-5pm Mon-Fri, 9am-1pm Sat) This bank changes US-dollars cash and traveler's checks.

Banco de Comercio (Calle Principal; ☺ 9am-5pm Mon-Fri, 9am-1pm Sat) Changes US-dollars cash and traveler's checks.

Happy Fish (Calle Principal; per half hr/hr US$1.30/2.60) Internet access available.

Immigration office (Calle Principal; ☺ 6am-7pm) Issues entry and exit stamps for travelers arriving direct from or going direct to Belize or Honduras, charging US$10 for exit stamps. Outside business hours, you can knock for attention at any time.

Labug@net (Calle Principal; per half hr/hr US$2/3.25) Internet access.

Laundry (Hotel Casa Rosada) It can be difficult to get laundry properly dry in the rainy season.

Dangers & Annoyances

Lívingston has its edgy aspects and a few hustlers operate here, trying to sweet-talk tourists into 'lending' money, paying up front for tours that don't happen etc. Take care with anyone who strikes up conversation for no obvious reason on the street or elsewhere.

Several robberies, often armed, have happened along the beach between Lívingston and the Río Quehueche, and at Siete Altares. A police-escorted tour is the best way to go to these places.

Use mosquito repellent and other sensible precautions, especially if you go out into the jungle; remember that the mosquitoes here on the coast carry both malaria and dengue fever.

Don't sleep on the beach in Lívingston – it isn't safe.

Activities

Beaches in Lívingston itself are disappointing, as buildings or vegetation come right down to the water's edge in most places. Those beaches that do exist are often contaminated. However there are better beaches within a few kilometers to the northwest. You can reach **Playa Quehueche** by taxi (US$2) in about 10 minutes: this beach near the mouth of the Río Quehueche has been cleaned up by Exotic Travel (below). The best beach in the area is **Playa Blanca**, around 12km from Lívingston. This is privately owned (US$2) and you need a boat to get there: it's best to go by tour (below).

Tours

A few outfits in Lívingston offer tours that let you get out and experience the natural wonders of the area. **Exotic Travel** (☎ 947-0049, 947-0151; exotictravelagency@hotmail.com; Restaurante Bahía Azul, Calle Principal) is a well-organized operation with several good trips. Their popular Ecological Tour/Jungle Trip takes you for a walk through town, out west up to a lookout spot and on to the Río Quehueche, where you take a half-hour canoe trip down the river to Playa Quehueche (above). Then you walk through the jungle to **Los Siete Altares** (The Seven Altars), a series of freshwater falls and pools about 5km northwest of Lívingston. Hang out there for a while then you walk down to the beach and back along it to Lívingston. The trip leaves the Restaurant Bahía Azul every day at 9am and arrives back around 4:30pm; it costs US$6.50 including lunch. This is a great way to see the area, and the friendly local guides can also give you a good introduction to the Garífuna people who live here. Since robberies have happened at Siete Altares and on the beach between Lívingston and the Río Quehueche, this tour was going with a police escort at the time of writing.

Exotic Travel's Playa Blanca tour goes by boat first to the Seven Altars, then on to the Río Cocolí where you can swim, and then on to Playa Blanca for two or three hours at the best beach in the area. This trip goes with a minimum of six people and costs US$13.

Exotic Travel also offers day trips to the Cayos Sapodillas (or Zapotillas), well off the coast of southern Belize, where there is great snorkeling (US$40 plus US$10 to enter the islands) and to Punta de Manabique (p231) for US$13 per person. A minimum of six people is needed for each of these trips.

Hotel Casa Rosada (p235) and the Happy Fish (p236) also offer Siete Altares and Playa Blanca tours.

RÍO DULCE TOURS

The above three agencies all offer day trips up the Río Dulce to Río Dulce town, as do most local boatmen at the Lívingston dock. Many travelers use these tours as one-way transport to Río Dulce (see p222), paying around US$10. If you want to return to Lívingston the cost is US$15 to US$18. It's a beautiful ride through tropical jungle scenery, with several places to stop on the way.

Shortly after you leave Lívingston, you pass the tributary Río Tatín on the right, then will probably stop at an indigenous arts museum set up by Asociación Ak' Tenamit, a nongovernment organization (NGO) working to improve conditions for the Q'eqchi' Maya population of the area. The river enters a gorge called **La Cueva de la Vaca**, its walls hung with great tangles of jungle foliage and the humid air noisy with the cries of tropical birds. Just beyond that is **La Pintada**, a rock escarpment covered with graffiti. Local legend says people have been tagging this spot since the 1700s, though the oldest in evidence is from the 1950s. If you're lucky, you might spot a freshwater dolphin in these parts. Further on, a **thermal spring** forces sulfurous water out of the base of the cliff, providing a chance for a warm swim. The river widens into **El Golfete**, a lake-like body of water that presages the even vaster expanse of Lago de Izabal further upstream.

On the northern shore of El Golfete is the **Biotopo Chocón Machacas**, a 72-sq-km reserve established within the Parque Nacional Río Dulce to protect the beautiful river landscape, the valuable forests and mangrove swamps and their wildlife, which includes such rare creatures as the tapir and above all the manatee. The huge, walrus-like manatees are aquatic mammals weighing up to a ton, yet they glide effortlessly beneath the calm surface of the river. They are very elusive, however, and the chances of seeing one are very slim. A network of 'water trails' (boat routes around several jungle lagoons) provide ways to see other bird, animal and plant life of the reserve. A nature trail begins at the visitors center (US$2.50) and winds its way through forests of mahogany, palms and rich tropical foliage.

Boats will probably visit the **Islas de Pájaros**, a pair of islands where thousands of waterbirds live, in the middle of El Golfete. From El Golfete you continue upriver, passing increasing numbers of expensive villas and boathouses, to the town of Río Dulce, where the soaring Highway CA-13 road bridge crosses the river, and on to El Castillo de San Felipe on Lago de Izabal (p226).

You can also do this trip starting from Río Dulce with *colectivo lanchas* (p252).

Festivals & Events

Lívingston is packed with merrymakers during **Semana Santa**. Garífuna national day is celebrated on November 26 with a variety of cultural events.

Sleeping

BUDGET

Hotel Casa Rosada (☎ 947-0303; info@hotelcasarosada.com; Calle Marcos Sánchez Díaz; s & d US$20) The Casa Rosada (Pink House) is an attractive place to stay right on the river, 500m upstream from the main dock; it has its own pier where boats will drop you if you ask. Neat little riverside gardens, a gazebo on the dock, and one of the best restaurants in town (p236) all contribute to a relaxed, friendly ambience. The rooms are well kept in thatch-roofed, wooden bungalows with fans, screens, mosquito nets and folksy, hand-painted furniture. The shared bathrooms are very clean. Also available are a laundry service and tours.

Hotel Ríos Tropicales (☎ 947-0158, 494-7093; rios-tropico@hotmail.com; Calle Principal; s&d US$9-12, with bathroom US$14-16) The Ríos Tropicales has a variety of quite big rooms accommodating up to three people, with bits of homey decoration including murals by some past guests. There's a central patio, hammocks for chilling out and a restaurant, and you can hand-wash clothes.

Hotel Doña Alida (☎ /fax 947-0027; d US$11-24, tr US$40-45; 🖳) In a great position just above the sea a few blocks from the center of town, the Doña Alida has a variety of good, clean, mostly breezy rooms and bungalows. It's one of Lívingston's best places and has its own restaurant.

Hotel California (☎ 947-0178/6; Calle Minerva; s/d/tr US$7/8/12) This is a fine, clean place with 10 simple rooms with bathroom and fan. The friendly Garífuna owner, Ruben, lived in Los Angeles for 17 years.

Hotel Río Dulce (☎ 947-0764; Calle Principal; rooms per person US$4, with bathroom US$6) This authentic Caribbean two-story wood-frame building has bare but clean wooden rooms, in various colors, with fans. The wide verandas are great for watching the street life and catching a breeze, and the food in the restaurant below (p236) is superb. The three rooms with bathroom are in a separate little block behind.

Finca Tatin (☎ 902-0831; www.fincatatin.centramerica.com; rooms per person US$8-11.50) This is a wonderful jungle B&B on the Río Tatín, 400m up from its confluence with the Río Dulce and about 10km from Lívingston. Finca Tatín is right by the river and right in the rain forest, abounding with exotic tropical birds. It's a great place for experiencing the forest, and four-hour guided walks and kayak trips through the jungle – some visiting local Q'eqchi' villages – are offered. The wood-and-thatch accommodations range from dormitories to bungalows with private bathroom. Room rates include breakfast; other good meals, with vegetarian options, are served (lunch US$3.50, dinner US$4.50). You can even take Spanish classes here. *Lanchas* traveling between Río Dulce and Lívingston (or vice versa) will drop you here. It costs around US$5 from Lívingston, 20 minutes away. Or the *finca* may be able to send its own *lancha* to pick you up at Lívingston (per person US$5, minimum two people).

Hotel El Viajero (Calle Marcos Sánchez Díaz; d US$4, s/d with bathroom US$3/6) Two minutes' walk from the main dock, the Viajero has basic rooms kept reasonably clean. Those out toward its waterfront café tend to be brighter and airier.

Hotel Blanco M (snoweblanco@hotmail.com; per person US$6) This place is quite popular with long-term budget travelers: five large, bare upstairs rooms with fan and bathroom hold up to four people each. There are also two marginally cheaper downstairs rooms with shared bathroom. English-speaking owner Marcos, a Garífuna who has lived in New York, is improving the place and has ideas of opening a language school here.

Hotel Vista al Mar (☎ 947-0131; fax 947-0134; Calle Marcos Sánchez Díaz; s/d/tr US$8/12/18, with bathroom US$13/20/26) The Vista al Mar has six quite spacious wooden bungalows, three with bathroom. They rent bicycles and canoes, offer laundry service and accept credit cards. They'll install mosquito nets if you ask, which may be a good thing as the stream at the back is pretty slow-moving.

Hotel King George (☎ 947-0326; Barrio San José; s US$5, d US$5-10) The King George is simple and clean, if a little rough around the edges. Rooms have fan and private bathroom.

Hotel Garífuna (☎ 947-0183; fax 947-0184; Barrio San José; s/d/tr US$6/9/11) The Garífuna, a solid brick building, is very presentable, with large rooms boasting bedside tables, and a sink where you can wash clothes.

Hotel Waba (☎ 947-0193; s US$4, s & d with bathroom US$8) The Waba, down a lane about 500m from the center, has upstairs rooms with bathroom, fan and a few sticks of furniture and two downstairs singles with shared bathroom. The balcony has a sea view, and there's an open-air *palapa* restaurant in the yard.

Hotel Henry Berrisford (☎ 947-0471; fax 947-0472; Calle Marcos Sánchez Díaz; s/d US$6/11, with air-con US$8/16; 🌣) This large place has decent, clean rooms all with bathroom and fan. Beware, though: it often runs out of water and/or electricity.

TOP END

Hotel Villa Caribe (☎ 334-1818; www.villasdegua temala.com; Calle Principal; s/d/tr US$63/75/88; 🌣) The 45-room Villa Caribe is a luxurious anomaly among Lívingston's laid-back, low-priced Caribbean lodgings. Modern but still Caribbean in style, it has many conveniences and comforts, including extensive tropical gardens, a big swimming pool and a large poolside bar. Rooms are fairly large, with modern bathrooms, ceiling fans and little balconies overlooking the gardens and river mouth.

Eating

Food in Lívingston is relatively expensive because most of it (except fish and coconuts) must be brought in by boat. There's fine seafood here and some unusual flavors for Guatemala, including coconut and curry. *Tapado*, a rich stew made from fish, shrimp, shellfish and coconut milk, spiced with coriander, is the delicious local specialty. A potent potable is made by slicing off the top of a green coconut and mixing in a healthy dose of rum. These *coco locos* hit the spot.

Calle Principal is dotted with many open-air eateries.

Happy Fish (☎ 947-0661; www.happyfishresort.com; Calle Principal; mains US$3.50-7; 🖳) This is a consistently popular place right in the center of town, with reliably good fish, seafood and salads.

Tilingo-Lingo (Calle Principal; mains US$3.25-6.50) Down at the seaward end of the main street, this great little place serves up a fine array of well-concocted international flavors, among them curries, pasta, fish, *tapado* and Spanish omelette.

Hotel Río Dulce (Calle Principal; mains US$3.50-9) The owner here has been a chef at Antigua's famed Panza Verde and produces superb Italian and international food. Try the Bombay prawns (curried with bananas, peanuts and cream) or *pasta alle vongole* (in a sauce of white wine, clams, garlic and parsley). There are burgers, sandwiches and Garífuna-style rice and beans as well.

Hotel Casa Rosada (Calle Marcos Sánchez Díaz; mains US$5.75-9.75) This open-air restaurant serves carefully prepared food in neat, breezy surroundings. All three meals are available. Dinner is served between 7pm and 7:30pm: you need to order it by 6pm. We recommend the tapado and the garlic shrimps.

Also recommended:

Restaurante Bahía Azul (Calle Principal; mains US$5-7) This central place has good food, including chicken, fish and curries.

McTropic Restaurante (seafood mains US$4.50-6)

Restaurante El Malecón (meals US$4-7) Caribbean-inspired fare.

Restaurante Tiburón Gato (pasta US$2-3.50, seafood US$3-4.50).

Restaurante Margoth (mains US$4-7) Serves filling fish, chicken, Chinese and *ceviche* dishes. They're well prepared and there's a full bar, but service is haphazard.

Hotel Villa Caribe (Calle Principal; dinner US$15) The price brings you a good, complete dinner with drinks.

Drinking & Entertainment

A handful of bars down on the sea beach to the left of the end of Calle Principal pull in travelers and locals at night (after about 10pm or 11pm). It's very dark down here, so take care. In vogue at the time of writing was **Bar Beluba Nuruba**, which has a small dance floor and a few tables on the sand. Just sitting on the beach and enjoying the cool breezes is as much an attraction as anything.

The traditional Garífuna band is composed of three large drums, a turtle shell, some maracas and a big conch shell, producing throbbing, haunting rhythms and melodies. The chanted words are like a litany, with responses often taken up by the audience. Punta is the Garífuna dance; it's got a lot of gyrating hip movements. Several places around town have live Garífuna music though schedules are unpredictable. Probably most dependable is **Café-Bar Ubafu**, supposedly with music and dancing nightly, but liveliest on weekends. Across the street, **Café-Bar Ubougarífuna** is a popular gathering spot. Next door, the **Caribbean Bar** is more of a mainstream disco.

Diners at the **Hotel Villa Caribe** can enjoy a Garífuna show nightly at 7pm. **Restaurante Bahía Azul** has live Garífuna music on weekends and sometimes on other evenings. **Tropicool Disco** next door has more mainstream pop to dance to. On weekend nights it's also worth checking out **Hotel Henry Berrisford** and **La Buga** bar, by the main dock, for Garífuna music and dance.

Getting There & Away

Frequent boats come downriver from Río Dulce (p222) and across the bay from Puerto Barrios (p228). There are also international boats from Honduras and Belize.

Exotic Travel (p234) operates international boat routes to Omoa, Honduras (US$35, 2½ hours) and Punta Gorda, Belize (US$16, 1¼ hours), both leaving at 7am on Tuesday and Friday. For both trips you must book by 5pm the day before, and get your exit stamp from immigration in Lívingston (p234) the day before, too. In Punta Gorda, the boat connects with a bus to Placencia and Belize City. The boat waits for this bus to arrive from Placencia before it sets off back for Lívingston from Punta Gorda at about 10:30am. In Omoa, the boat docks near the bus stop where you can catch a bus to Puerto Cortés. Change there and again at San Pedro Sula to reach La Ceiba (the cheapest gateway to Honduras' Bay Islands) – but you might not make the 3pm boat from La Ceiba to Roatán island the same day. You can also reach Omoa by taking a ferry or *lancha* to Puerto Barrios then continuing overland (p231), but you're unlikely to get there any earlier. The boat from Omoa to Lívingston leaves about 10:30am, Tuesday and Friday.

The travel agency at the Happy Fish (p236) offers private trips to Punta Gorda for US$100 per boat, and shuttle services to Omoa, La Ceiba, Copán and San Pedro Sula, all in Honduras.

EL PETÉN

El Petén

CONTENTS

In the dense jungle cover of Guatemala's vast, hot and humid northern department of El Petén, you may hear the squawk of parrots, the chatter of monkeys and the rustlings of strange animals moving through the bush. Your usual means of perception will prove inadequate for your Petén adventures, which may seem supernatural at times – and in the wet season (May to November) you should have plenty of bug repellent at the ready!

The monumental ceremonial center at Tikal is, for many, the most impressive of all Mayan archaeological sites. The ruins of Yaxhá, Ceibal and Aguateca, though less easily accessible, can be just as exciting to visit for that very reason. The remains of several dozen other great centers previously locked away in El Petén's jungles are now open to determined travelers with guides from local forest communities – but everyone needs to remember some simple rules of ecotourism, such as carrying out garbage, to avoid impacting negatively on these areas.

In 1990, Guatemala established the 21,000 sq km Reserva de Biosfera Maya (Maya Biosphere Reserve), occupying approximately the whole northern third of El Petén. This Guatemalan reserve adjoins the vast Calakmul biosphere reserve in Mexico and the Río Bravo Conservation Area in Belize, forming a huge multinational reserve totaling more than 30,000 sq km. The great abundance and variety of animal, bird and plant life are as exciting as the mysteries of the ancient Mayan cities – and many sites in El Petén combine both.

TOP FIVE

- Exploring the imperial, awe-inspiring ruins set deep in lush jungle at **Tikal** (p257)

- Trekking deep into the jungle to little-excavated ruins such as **El Mirador** (p273)

- Encountering **rain forest wildlife** (p257) at close quarters at Tikal and other sites

- Chilling out at travelers' hideaway **Finca Ixobel** (p240) or the tranquil island town of **Flores** (p240)

- Taking the tropical river route to ancient Mayan ruins around **Sayaxché** (p269)

EL PETÉN

CLIMATE

If you visit from December to February, expect some cool nights and mornings. Weather-wise this can be the best time to visit El Petén. March and April are the hottest and driest months. The rains begin in May or June, and with them come the mosquitoes – bring rain gear, repellent and, if you plan on slinging a hammock, a mosquito net. July to September is muggy and buggy. October and November see the end of the occasional rains and a return to cooler temperatures.

GETTING THERE & AROUND

El Petén's main tourism node is the twin towns of Flores and Santa Elena, about 60km southwest of Tikal. The main roads to Flores from Río Dulce to the southeast, from Cobán and Chisec to the southwest, from Melchor de Mencos on the Belize border to the east, and from El Naranjo to the northwest are now all paved and in good condition, except for a few short stretches. Frequent buses and minibuses ferry travelers along these routes. Flores also has the only functioning civil airport in the country except for Guatemala City.

POPTÚN

pop 8000 / elevation 540m

The small town of Poptún is about halfway between Río Dulce and Flores. The reason most travelers come here is to visit Finca Ixobel (below).

On the corner of 5a Calle, just south of the Flores minibus stop, **Bancafé** (5a Calle 7-98; 9am-5pm Mon-Fri, 9am-1pm Sat) has a Visa ATM and changes cash US dollars and Visa and American Express traveler's checks. One block along 5a Calle, **Banrural** (8:30am-5pm Mon-Fri, 9am-1pm Sat) has a MasterCard ATM and changes cash US dollars and American Express traveler's checks.

Sleeping & Eating

Finca Ixobel (☎ 410-4307, 892-3188; www.fincaixobel .com; camping per person US$3, dm US$4, s US$7-20, d US$10-29; P 🖳 🕿) With by far the best facilities, this 2 sq km venue is 5km south of Poptún. For several decades Carole De-Vine has offered travelers tent sites, *palapas* (thatched palm-leaf shelters) for hanging hammocks, beds and lip-smacking home-made meals, with veggie options galore. Carole founded this bohemian hideaway in the

1970s with her husband Michael, who was tragically murdered in 1990 during the civil war, when Poptún was a training ground for the vicious anti-guerrilla forces called Kaibiles. Finca Ixobel is a special place, with large and beautiful grounds and famous for its friendly, relaxed atmosphere, a great place for meeting other travelers from all parts of the globe. It's also renowned for its food and its activities. The grounds contain a lovely natural pool for swimming, and horseback riding (from two hours to four days), treks, cave trips and inner-tubing on the Río Machaquilá (in the rainy season) are all organized on a daily basis, at reasonable prices. The six-hour Cueva del Río outing, to an underground river complete with rapids and waterfalls, costs US$9. Internet use is US$2.50 an hour, and you can rent bicycles for US$4 a day.

The camping area is large and grassy, with good bathrooms and plenty of shade. Dotted around it are several treehouses (actually mostly cabins on stilts), which are fun places to sleep. The assorted other accommodations range from a couple of dormitories to rooms with shared and private bathroom and a bungalow with hot shower. The rooms and bungalow all have fan, mosquito nets and mosquito-screened windows. Meals here are excellent, including the eat-all-you-like buffet dinner for US$3.25 (salads, garlic bread, drinks) or US$6.50 (with a main dish too). Finca Ixobel has its own bakery, grows its own salads and produces its own eggs. You can cook in the campground if you bring your own supplies. After 9pm many people move on to the pool bar, where reasonably priced cocktails and other drinks are served.

Everything here is on the honor system: guests keep an account of what they eat and drink and the services they use. Watch your budget and don't neglect the tip box for the staff when you settle up! There are often volunteer opportunities for fluent English and Spanish speakers in exchange for room and board. If the *finca* (ranch) suits your style and you want to help/hang out for six weeks minimum, ask about volunteering.

The turnoff for the *finca* is marked on highway 13. In the daytime, you can ask the bus or minibus driver to let you off there; it's a 15-minute walk to the *finca*. If you're coming from Poptún, the best bet is a

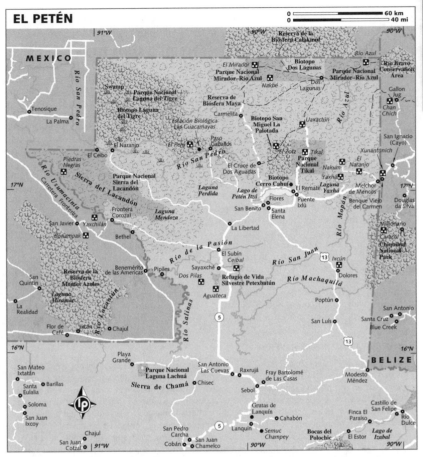

EL PETÉN

San Luís–bound minibus: these leave when full from the corner of 4a Calle and the main road in town and charge US$0.50 for the 10-minute trip. At night, or if you don't feel like making the walk, get off the bus in Poptún and take a taxi for US$2.50. It's not advisable to walk to the *finca* at night, as it's an isolated spot and robberies have been known to occur on the way. When you leave Finca Ixobel, most buses will stop on the highway to pick you up, but not after dark.

Other recommendations in Poptún town:
Hotel Posada de los Castellanos (☎ 927-7222; cnr 4a Calle & 7a Av; s/d/tr US$5/6/8) Has clean rooms with fan and a bathroom, arranged around a courtyard.
Pensión Isabelita (s & d US$4) Around the corner on 4a Calle; has fanless rooms sharing bathrooms.

Hotel Izalco (☎ 927-7372; 4a Calle 7-11; s/d US$4/5, upstairs US$4/6) Also around the corner on 4a Calle, this slightly better place offers rooms with shared bathroom and fan. Splurge for the fan!

Getting There & Away

Most buses and minibuses stop on the main road through town: Fuente del Norte buses stop by the Shell station; minibuses to San Luís, 16km south, go from the next corner south, and minibuses to Flores start half a block further along.

Bus departures from Poptún include the following:
Flores/Santa Elena (2hr, 113km) Fuente del Norte (US$2, every 1-2hr); minibuses (US$2.60, every 30 min 6am-6pm)
Fray Bartolomé de Las Casas (US$4, 5hr, 100km) One

bus departs at 10am from the market area. If you want to push on from Las Casas to Lanquín the same day, try getting a Guatemala City-bound bus as far as Modesto Méndez (also called Cadenas), 60km south on Hwy 13, and changing there to a westbound bus or minibus to Las Casas.

Guatemala City (US$7-10.50, 6-7hr, 387km, every 30min 5:30am-midnight) Covered by Fuente del Norte.

Río Dulce (US$3.25-4, 2hr, 99km, every 30min 5:30am-midnight) Covered by Fuente del Norte.

MACHAQUILÁ

This unremarkable little town 7km north of Poptún is worth considering as a halt because of the **Hotel Ecológico Villa de los Castellanos** (☎ 927-7541/2; ecovilla@intelnet.net.gt; s/d/tr US$20/25/30, for students US$8/16/20; **P**), by the highway at the north end of town. The hotel is right by the Río Machaquilá, which is good for swimming, and its large grounds – through which you can take a 3km circuit tour or walk – are dedicated to cultivating over 60 medicinal plants. Accommodations are in wooden, thatch-roofed bungalows each with two four-poster beds, mosquito nets, hot-water bathroom and TV, and there's a good, medium-priced restaurant.

Machaquilá is served by the same buses and minibuses as Poptún.

FLORES & SANTA ELENA

pop Flores 2000, Santa Elena 25,000 / elevation 110m

The town of Flores is built on an island in Lago de Petén Itzá. A 500m causeway connects Flores to its sister town of Santa Elena on the lakeshore. Adjoining Santa Elena to the west is the town of San Benito (population 25,000). The three towns actually form one large settlement, often referred to simply as Flores.

Flores, the departmental capital, is much the most dignified and tranquil town, with its church, small government building and municipal basketball court arranged around the hilltop plaza in the center of the island. The narrow streets are paved in cement blocks and flanked by charming, red-roofed houses, many of which are small hotels or restaurants. Breezes off the lake keep temperatures a degree or two lower than on the mainland, and altogether Flores is easily the most pleasant of the three towns to base yourself in, though also the most expensive.

THE MAYA BIOSPHERE RESERVE

The Reserva de Biosfera Maya, occupying 21,000 sq km stretched right across the north of El Petén, is part of the Unesco world biosphere reserve network, which recognizes that the many human demands on this planet's land require innovative strategies if nature is to be conserved. In this vein, the Maya reserve is split into three spheres. Along its southern fringe is a buffer zone where economic activities are permitted, supposedly within a framework of environmental protection. The main part of the reserve is divided into a multiple use zone, composed of tropical forest and supposedly dedicated to the sustainable harvest of *xate* ferns, *chicle* gum and timber, and eight core areas (the Sierra del Lacandón, Tikal, Laguna del Tigre and Mirador–Río Azul national parks, and the Cerro Cahuí, San Miguel La Palotada, Laguna del Tigre and Dos Lagunas biotopes) for scientific research, conservation of the natural environment and/or archaeological sites, and tightly controlled ecological and cultural tourism. Unfortunately, the theory is prettier than the reality: the forest is still being ravaged by people illegally harvesting timber on a massive scale, looters desecrating Mayan tombs and tourists (no matter how conscientious) negatively impacting on the fragile ecosystem. Even some core areas have been subject to illegal settlements by land-hungry peasants from further south. In 1998 the environmental organization Conservation International had a camp in the reserve burned down by angry settlers. At least two conservationists who have spoken out about abuses in the reserve have been shot dead. The buffer zone is rapidly changing from a forested landscape with scattered agricultural patches to an agricultural landscape with scattered forest patches.

Meanwhile the remaining forests of southern Petén are falling at an alarming rate to the machetes of subsistence farmers. Sections of forest are felled and burned off, crops are grown for a few seasons until the fragile jungle soil is exhausted, and then the farmer moves deeper into the forest to slash and burn new fields. Cattle ranchers, also slashing and burning the forest in order to make pasture, have also contributed to the damage, as have resettled refugees and urban Guatemalans moving from the cities to El Petén in their endless struggle to make a living.

Santa Elena is a rumpled place of dusty streets, with a hot, crowded market and a main street strung with bus stops, banks and some hotels and restaurants. San Benito is even less attractive, but its honky-tonk bars keep it lively.

History

Flores was founded on an island (petén) by a people called the Itzáes who wound up here after being expelled from the city of Chichén Itzá on Mexico's Yucatán Peninsula, maybe in 13th century AD, maybe in the 15th. Flores was originally named Tayasal. Hernán Cortés dropped in on King Canek of Tayasal in 1525 while on his way to Honduras, but the meeting was, amazingly,

peaceable. Cortés left behind a lame horse, which the Itzáes fed on flowers and turkey stew. When it died, the Itzáes made a statue of it which, by the time a couple of Spanish friars visited in 1618, was being worshiped as a manifestation of the rain god Chac. It was not until 1697 that the Spaniards brought the Itzáes of Tayasal – by some distance the last surviving independent Mayan kingdom – forcibly under their control. The God-fearing Spanish soldiers destroyed its many pyramids, temples and statues, and today you won't see a trace of them, although the modern town is doubtless built on the ruins and foundations of Mayan Tayasal. Confusingly, the overgrown ruins named Tayazal, on the mainland

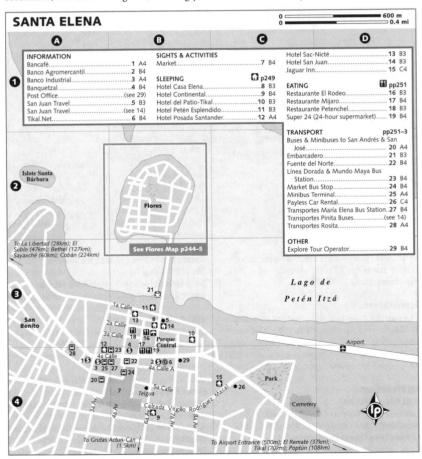

SANTA ELENA

0 — 600 m
0 — 0.4 mi

INFORMATION	
Bancafé	1 A4
Banco Agromercantil	2 B4
Banco Industrial	3 A4
Banquetzal	4 B4
Post Office	(see 29)
San Juan Travel	5 B3
San Juan Travel	(see 14)
Tikal.Net	6 B4

SIGHTS & ACTIVITIES	
Market	7 B4

SLEEPING	p249
Hotel Casa Elena	8 B3
Hotel Continental	9 B4
Hotel del Patio-Tikal	10 B3
Hotel Petén Esplendido	11 B3
Hotel Posada Santander	12 A4

Hotel Sac-Nicté	13 B3
Hotel San Juan	14 B3
Jaguar Inn	15 C4

EATING	pp251
Restaurante El Rodeo	16 B3
Restaurante Mijaro	17 B4
Restaurante Petenchel	18 B3
Super 24 (24-hour supermarket)	19 B4

TRANSPORT	pp251–3
Buses & Minibuses to San Andrés & San José	20 A4
Embarcadero	21 B3
Fuente del Norte	22 B4
Línea Dorada & Mundo Maya Bus Station	23 B4
Market Bus Stop	24 B4
Minibus Terminal	25 A4
Payless Car Rental	26 C4
Transportes María Elena Bus Station	27 B4
Transportes Pinita Buses	(see 14)
Transportes Rosita	28 A4

OTHER	
Explore Tour Operator	29 B4

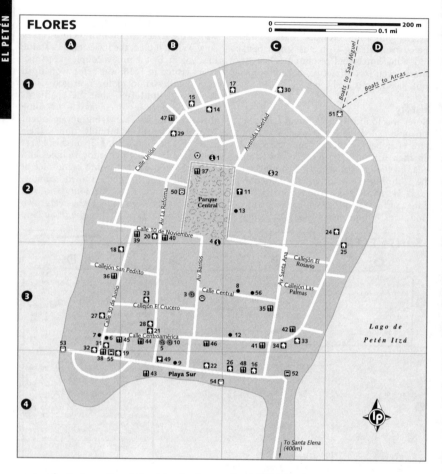

peninsula just north of the island, date mostly from the Classic period, well before the Itzáes came to Flores.

Orientation

The airport is on the eastern outskirts of Santa Elena, 2km from the causeway connecting Santa Elena and Flores. Long-distance buses drop passengers on or just off Santa Elena's main drag, 4a Calle.

Information

AIRLINE OFFICES

Contact numbers at Flores airport:

Inter/Grupo TACA (☎ 926-1238, 926-0295, 926-0650)
Jungle Flying Tours (☎ 926-0292)
Maya Island Air (☎ 926-3386)

Racsa (☎ 926-0596, 332-1831, 926-1477)
TAG (☎ 926-0653)
Tikal Airlines (Tikal Jets; ☎ 926-0386, 926-3823)
Tropic Air (☎ 926-0348)

EMERGENCY

Hospital San Benito (☎ 926-1459)
Policía Nacional (national police; ☎ 926-1365)

INTERNET ACCESS

You can access the web at the following:
Flores.Net (Av Barrios, Flores) US$1.30 an hour.
Internet Petén (Calle Centroamérica, Flores; ✆ 8am-10pm) US$1.60 an hour.
Naomi's Café (Calle Centroamérica, Flores) US$1.80 an hour.
TikalNet (Calle Centroamérica, Flores)
Tikal.Net (4a Calle 6-76, Santa Elena)

LAUNDRY

In Flores, take your clothes to the **Mayan Princess Travel Agency** (Calle 30 de Junio; ☯ 8am-8pm), which will wash and dry a load for US$3.25.

MONEY

At the airport, **Banquetzal** (☯ 7am-noon & 2-5pm) changes US-dollar cash and traveler's checks. **Banrural**, just off the Parque Central in Flores, changes US-dollar cash and traveler's checks.

Other banks are on 4a Calle in Santa Elena. The following all change cash US dollars and at least American Express US-dollar traveler's checks:

Banco Agromercantil (☯ 9am-6pm Mon-Fri, 9am-1pm Sat) Has MasterCard ATM.

Banco Industrial (☯ 9am-7pm Mon-Fri, 10am-2pm Sat) Has Visa ATM.

Banquetzal (☯ 9am-1pm & 2-5:30pm Mon-Fri, 9am-1pm Sat)

Bancafé (☯ 9am-7pm Mon-Fri, 9am-1pm Sat) Has Visa ATM.

Many travel agencies and places to stay will change cash US dollars, and sometimes traveler's checks, at poor rates. **San Juan Travel** (p246) will also change Belize dollars and Mexican pesos, and give Visa,

MasterCard, Diner's Club and American Express cash advances.

POST

Post office Flores (Av Barrios); Santa Elena (4a Calle east of 7a Av).

TELEPHONE & FAX

Martsam Travel (p246) Offers domestic and international telephone and fax services.

TOURIST OFFICES

Inguat tourist offices (airport ☎ 926-0533; ☯ 7am-noon & 3-6pm Flores ☎ 926-0669; Parque Central; ☯ 8am-12:30pm & 1:30-4pm) have helpful tourist information.

Cincap (Centro de Información sobre la Naturaleza, Cultura y Artesanía de Petén; Petén Nature, Culture & Handicrafts Information Center; ☎ 926-0718; mercadeo@peten.net; Parque Central, Flores; ☯ 9am-noon & 2-9pm) has interesting displays on the archaeological sites, nature conservation areas and local way of life of Petén. It also sells handicrafts of the region and has an information desk where you can ask about, among other things, El Petén's community tourism committees and visits to some of the region's remoter natural and archaeological sites. Cincap is run by the **Asociación Alianza**

Verde (☎ /fax 926-0718; www.alianzaverde.org), an association dedicated to sustainable, responsible, low-impact tourism in the Maya Biosphere Reserve. Alianza Verde is responsible for *Destination Petén* magazine and the website www.peten.net, and its Green Deal program awards a seal of excellence to tourism businesses that meet stringent environmental and social standards.

TRAVEL AGENCIES

Several travel agencies in Flores and Santa Elena offer trips to archaeological sites, shuttle minibuses and other services. **Martsam Travel** (☎ /fax 926-3225; www.martsam.com; Calle Centroamérica, Flores) is a well-established, well-organized agency with a particularly wide range of services, as you'll see from the frequency with which its name crops up in this chapter. **San Juan Travel** (☎ 926-0041/2, 926-2146; sanjuant@internetdetelgua.com.gt; 2a Calle, Santa Elena & Playa Sur, Flores) provides various shuttles and tours and offers the most regular service to Tikal and Palenque.

Several hotels can book you on tours, shuttles, buses and flights. **Hotel Posada Tayazal** (p241) has some good prices.

Volunteer Work

The **Estación Biológica Las Guacamayas** (p272), in the Parque Nacional Laguna del Tigre, and the rehabilitation center at **Arcas** (p253) both offer the chance of volunteer work with wildlife. At Las Guacamayas you pay US$7.75 a day for the first two weeks, US$7 a day the third week and US$6.50 a day the fourth week, and provide your own food. If you're interested, contact **ProPetén** (Proyecto Petenero para un Bosque Sostenible; ☎ 926-1370, 926-1141; www.propeten.org; Calle Central, Flores; ☿ 9am-5pm Mon-Fri), the Guatemalan nongovernment organization (NGO) that owns the station. At Arcas you pay US$100 a week including food. The language schools in San Andrés and San José (p253) provide the chance to get involved in community and environmental projects.

Language Courses

Ixchel Spanish Academy (☎ 926-0346, ☎ /fax 926-3225; info@martsam.com; Calle Central) offers four hours of one-on-one tuition five days a week for US$110, or US$175 including a week's lodging and meals in a local home. There are further language schools in the lakeside villages San Andrés and San José (p254).

Tours

Many travel agencies in Flores offer day tours to the more accessible archaeological sites such as Tikal, Uaxactún, Yaxhá and Ceibal. Day trips to these places with guide and lunch cost US$40 to US$60 with agencies such as **Martsam Travel**, **Hotel Posada Tayazal** and **San Juan Travel** (p246). They're cheaper (US$25 to US$40) with **Ecomaya** (☎ 926-3202; www.ecomaya.com; Calle Centroamérica, Flores) and **Explore Tour Operator** (☎ 926-2375; www.exploreguate.com; cnr 4a Calle & 7a Av, Santa Elena).

Ecomaya, which is a joint venture of several community-based businesses, and Martsam also offer more demanding hiking-and-camping eco-trails and eco-tours to exciting remoter archaeological sites such as Nakum, El Perú, El Zotz, El Mirador, Nakbé, Waxná and La Muralla, working with local Comités Comunitarios de Ecoturismo (Community Ecotourism Committees) which provide guides to these sites deep in the Petén jungles. The three ecotourism committees, in the villages of El Cruce de Dos Aguadas (about 45km north of Flores by dirt road), Carmelita (some 35km beyond El Cruce de Dos Aguadas) and Paso Caballos (west of El Cruce de Dos Aguadas), were set up with the help of Conservation International and ProPetén, with the aim of fostering low-impact tourism benefiting local jungle communities. Comité guides are usually *xateros* (collectors of *xate*, a palm used in flower bouquets) or *chicleros* (collectors of *chicle*, used to make chewing gum) who know the forest very well, but may be light on the archaeological significance of the sites. There's no luxury on these trips: participants should be in good shape mentally and physically, as they'll sleep in hammocks, hike for long stretches through thick jungle, eat what's fed them and be munched by whatever ants, mosquitoes and ticks they're sharing the forest with.

The sample prices following are per person for two-/four-/five-plus people, normally including food, water, sleeping gear and Spanish-speaking guide:

EL PETÉN

ECOMAYA

Location	Duration	Cost
El Zotz and Tikal	3 days	US$192/147/133
	2 days	US$148/125/116
El Perú	3 days	US$247/146/133
	2 days	US$213/120/108
El Mirador	5 days	US$391/343/322
El Mirador–Nakbé–		
La Muralla	7 days	US$494/444/405
Estación Biológica		
Las Guacamayas	3 days	US$574/371/330

MARTSAM TRAVEL

Location	Duration	Cost
El Zotz and Tikal	3 days	US$159/118/113
El Perú	3 days	US$198/122/109
	2 days	US$180/100/93
El Mirador–Nakbé–Wakná	7 days	US$390/330/311
Yaxhá–Nakum–Tikal	3 days	US$163/125/120
Yaxhá and Nakum	2 days	US$115/85/80

Ecomaya also goes to Uaxactún, Dos Lagunas and Río Azul and both firms offer three-day trips covering Dos Pilas and Aguateca along with Ceibal (US$206/150/122 with Martsam; US$115 per person, minimum two and excluding meals and drinks, with Ecomaya).

Another outfit going to some adventurous destinations is **Monkey Eco Tours** (p254).

LAKE TOURS
Boats at the *embarcaderos* (docks) opposite Hotel Petenchel and beside Hotel Santana in Flores, and beside the Hotel Petén Espléndido in Santa Elena, can be hired for lake tours. Prices are very negotiable. You might pay US$25 for an hour on board, with stops and waiting time at no extra charge.

Carlos, the owner of Café-Bar Las Puertas in Flores, offers boat trips around the lake and along to the far end, where he has a house in the form of a Mayan pyramid, with a private beach for swimming and sunning. He's a former guide at Tikal and very knowledgeable about the area.

Sleeping
FLORES
Hotel Casona de la Isla (☎ 926-0593; www.corpetur.com; Calle 30 de Junio; s US$30-33, d US$36-41; ☒ ⓡ) This is a romantic place with a pool with waterfall and an open-air bar/restaurant overlooking the lake. All 27 rooms have a

bathroom, cable TV, phone, air-con, fan and cane furniture. Rooms 31, 303 and 304 have windows facing right out to the lake and gorgeous sunsets.

Hotel La Mesa de los Mayas (☎ /fax 926-1240; mesamayas@hotmail.com; Av La Reforma; s/d/tr US$10/17/25, with air-con US$15/25/35; ☒) This is a lovely place, very clean and well kept. All 20 rooms have TV, cerise walls, colorful bedspreads, reading lamp, hot-water bathroom and fan.

Hotel Villa del Lago (☎ /fax 926-0629; hotelvilladelago@itelgua.com; s & d US$20-33; ☒) Beside the lake on the east side of the island, this is a fine, clean place to stay. Its once drab exterior now sports a classical facade more in keeping with the quality of the 18 rooms. Prices depend on whether they have air-conditioning (most do) and a lake view (four do). All have a hot-water bathroom, fan, cable TV and tiled floors. Breakfast is available, there's a breezy upstairs terrace, and the staff can do your laundry, exchange books and book flights.

Hotel Santana (☎ /fax 926-0491/2, 926-0662; www.santanapeten.com; Calle 30 de Junio; s/d/tr US$31/38/50; ☒ ⓛ ⓡ) Twenty of the 34 good-sized rooms have great lake views, with private balconies with chairs. All have hot-water bathroom, cable TV, telephone, safe, air-con and fan. There's a restaurant with a lakeside terrace.

Hospedaje Doña Goya (☎ 926-3538; Calle Unión; s/d/tr US$7/11/13, with bathroom US$8/13/16) This family-room guesthouse is one of the best budget choices in town and often full as a result. Three of the six secure, spotless rooms have bathroom. All six have fans. The beds are comfortable, the water's hot and there's a roof terrace with a palm-thatched shelter from which to enjoy lake views. There's a safe for valuables too.

Hotel Mirador del Lago (☎ 926-3276; s/d/tr US$7/11/16) With a waterside position on the east side of the island, this is a good value. The clean, blue-painted rooms have a fan, good beds, hot-water bathroom and mosquito-netted windows. There are 18 of them on three floors, with a roof terrace above. As usual, the higher the better. Hotel Mirador del Lago II, opposite, has 13 more rooms of the same type.

Hotel Isla de Flores (☎ 926-0614; www.junglelodge.guate.com; Av La Reforma; s/d US$36/41; ☒) This clean and attractive hotel has large

EL PETÉN

CHICLE & CHEWING GUM

Chicle, a pinkish to reddish-brown gum, is actually the coagulated milky sap, or latex, of the sapo-dilla tree *(Achras zapota)*, a tropical evergreen native to the Yucatán Peninsula and Central America. *Chicleros* (*chicle* workers) cut large gashes in the sapodillas' trunks, making a pattern of V-shaped cuts as high up as 9m. The sap runs from the wounds and down the trunk to be collected in a container at the base. After being boiled, it is shaped into blocks for shipping. The cuts can kill the tree, and thus *chicle* harvesting tends to result in the serious depletion of sapodilla forests. Even if the tree survives the first round of cuts, a typical tree used for harvesting *chicle* has a life span of just 10 years.

First used as a substitute for natural rubber (to which the sapodilla is related), by about 1890 *chicle* was best known as the main ingredient in chewing gum.

As a result of war research for a rubber substitute during the 1940s, synthetic substitutes were developed for *chicle*. Now chewing gum is made mostly from these synthetic substitutes. However, in the northern reaches of El Petén, *chicleros* still live in the forest for months at a time harvesting the sap for gum.

---

rooms well equipped with cable TV, air-con, ceiling fan, telephone and a hot-water bathroom with tub. Many rooms have little balconies with a view of the lake. Breakfast is available.

Hotel Petén (☎ 926-0692; www.corpetur.com; Calle 30 de Junio; s/d/tr US$33/40/50; ✖ 💻 💸) This hotel, another on the western shore of the island, has a small courtyard with tropical plants, a pleasant lakeside terrace and restaurant, and a small indoor swimming pool. The 19 comfy-if-plain rooms all have a bathroom, air-con and fan: try to get one on the top floor with a lake view: the interior rooms can be a little gloomy.

Hotel El Itzá 1 (☎ 926-3666; inverglob@guate.net; Playa Sur; s/d/tr US$20/25/35; ✖) This is a solid choice with 14 clean, tiled, good-sized rooms equipped with fan, hot-water bathroom and cable TV. Four are air-conditioned.

Hotel Posada del Peregrino (☎ 926-0477, ☎ /fax 926-0972; peregrino@itelgua.com; Av La Reforma 3; d US$8, s/d/tr with bathroom US$6/11/16) This is a friendly, family-run place with fairly well-kept, fan-cooled rooms on two levels around a central patio. The top floor is generally brighter; all bathrooms have hot water. There's a good restaurant here (p250).

Hotel Casazul (☎ 926-1138; www.corpetur.com; s/d/tr US$21/36/45; ✖) On the northern shore, the Casazul is a comfortable and quiet place with nine quirky, all-different rooms. All are clean, though, with hot-water bathroom, cable TV, refrigerator, telephone, air-con, reading lamps and white-tile floors. The ones facing the water are the most desirable. A couple

have balconies and everyone can enjoy the 3rd-floor terrace.

Hotel Sabana (☎ /fax 926-1248; hotelsabana@ yahoo.com; s/d/tr US$25/29/39; ✖ 💸) On the north side of the island, this is a larger, 28-room, less personal place with a small pool and a terrace overlooking the lake. Rooms have bathroom, air-con and cable TV. Rates rise to US$30/36/49 for Semana Santa, Christmas/New Year's, July and August.

Hotel Casablanca (☎ 926-3464; Playa Sur; s & d US$16) Just off the causeway, the Casablanca provides a dozen acceptable yellow rooms with fan and bathroom. Those on the top floor have most air and the best views.

Hotel La Canoa (☎ 926-0852/53; s/d/tr US$8/11/16) This dependable budget place has bare but clean and decent-sized fan-cooled rooms with hot-water bathroom tucked into the corner. Upstairs rooms are airier, and downstairs triples can be crowded. Two rooms with shared bathroom cost US$4 per person.

Hotel Petenchel (☎ 926-3359; s/d/tr US$8/11/13) This is a solid value, with clean rooms with hot-water bathroom, ceiling fan and comfortable beds. A small courtyard jammed with plants provides a little character; some rooms are dark, however.

Hotel Santa Rita (☎ 926-3224; Calle 30 de Junio; s/d/tr US$7/10/13) The 11 rooms on three floors here are clean, with fan and hot-water bath-room, and that's all there is to say about the place.

Hotel Posada Tayazal (☎ 926-0568; Calle Unión; s/d US$4/8, s/d/tr/q with bathroom US$6/9/12/16) The 26 rooms here vary from dark and airless ground-floor cells with shared bathroom to bright and breezy top-floor rooms with lake view, big windows and balcony. There's a useful in-house travel agency here, and a roof terrace for all to enjoy.

Posada El Tucán (☎ 926-0536; s/d/tr US$6/7/8) El Tucán has a friendly proprietor but the four rooms are airless and bare, off to one side of the restaurant. The shared bathroom is clean, with hot water.

Two further budget hotels with respectable, fan-cooled rooms are **Hotel Casa del Lacandón** (☎ 926-4359; Calle Unión; s/d US$8/9) and **Hotel Itzá 2** (☎ 926-3654; Av La Reforma; s/d/tr with bathroom US$9/9/12).

SANTA ELENA

Hotel Casa Elena (☎ 926-2235/6/8/9; caselena@amigo.net.gt; 6a Av; s/d US$43/55; P ⊠ ⊠) Just south of the causeway, Casa Elena has nice, clean, air-conditioned rooms that are short on character but long on comfort. Each is equipped with hot-water bathroom, cable TV and telephone. Some rooms overlook Santa Elena's plaza, others overlook the hotel pool. There's a bar, restaurant and roof terrace.

Hotel Posada Santander (☎ 926-0574; 4a Calle; s/d/tr with TV & shared bathroom US$7/7/9, s/d with bathroom & no TV US$7/8) This is a simple, spotless and friendly family-run hostelry in a convenient but loud location. The rooms with a cold-water bathroom are large and bare except for garish bedspreads and fans. The hotel has a good, clean restaurant (p251) and the family also operates Transportes Inter Petén, with economical minibus service to Tikal and other places.

Jaguar Inn (☎ 926-0002; fax 926-2413; Calzada Virgilio Rodríguez Macal 8-79; s/d with fan US$12/16/21, with air-con US$17/21/26; P) Comfortable without being fancy, the Jaguar Inn has rooms with cable TV, bright bedspreads and hot-water bathrooms set along a garden patio. It's slightly inconveniently located 150m off the main road near the airport – good if you have a vehicle.

Hotel Petén Espléndido (☎ 926-0880; www.peten esplendido.com; 1a Calle 5-01; s/d US$98/122; P ⊠ ⊠) This glitzy waterside fun palace may have the only elevator in all of El Petén. Its amenities include a lakeside pool, poolside bar, a restaurant that is lakeside, poolside and barside all at once, and a free airport shuttle. The 62 spotless rooms have air-con, fan, cable TV, safe, phone, computer jacks

and little balconies, and are wheelchair accessible. Staff sport garish tropical shirts and some of them speak English, Italian or German.

Hotel Continental (☎ 926-0095; 6a Av south of Calzada Virgilio Rodríguez Macal; s/d US$4/8, with fan, bathroom & TV US$7/12, with air-con, bathroom & TV US$13/18; P ⊠) A 51-room hotel with friendly reception staff, the Continental provides a range of rooms on three floors along a courtyard painted in vaguely refreshing shades of blue and green. The private bathrooms are good and clean, but there's no hot water.

Hotel del Patio-Tikal (☎ 926-0104; www.hotel delpatio.com.gt; cnr 8a Av & 2a Calle; s/d/tr US$61/61/70; ⊠ ⊠) This looks severe from the outside but is actually a colonial-style hotel with a pretty courtyard. Its 21 rooms all have air-con and ceiling fan, cable TV, telephone and bathroom, and there's a restaurant and pool.

Hotel Sac-Nicté (☎ 926-0092, 926-1731; 1a Calle; s/d/tr US$7/8/10, upstairs US$7/11/13) The rooms here are tolerably clean and will do in a pinch. They all have bathroom and fan, and those upstairs have small balconies from which you might just glimpse the lake. They will pick you up from the airport for free, where they have a desk.

Santa Elena has other cheap but less attractive hotels, including **Hotel San Juan** (☎ 926-2146, 926-0042; 2a Calle; s/d US$5/7, with bathroom US$8/10, with bathroom & air-con US$16/19; ⊠).

Eating

On the menu at many places are a variety of local game, including *tepescuintle* (agouti, a rabbit-sized jungle rodent), *venado* (venison), armadillo, *pavo silvestre* (wild turkey) and *pescado blanco* (white fish). You may want to avoid dishes that may soon jump from the menu to the endangered species list.

FLORES

La Luna (☎ 926-3346; cnr Calle 30 de Junio & Calle 10 de Noviembre; mains US$6.50-10; ☽ lunch & dinner Mon-Sat) In a class by itself, this very popular restaurant cultivates a classic tropical ambience, with potted palms to catch the breeze from the whirling overhead fans. The food is continental and delectable, with innovative chicken, fish and beef dishes the likes of which you'll be hard-pressed to find anywhere else in Guatemala. There are also good pasta and vegetarian options, such as falafel, salad and rice, for US$4 to US$5.

Café-Bar Las Puertas (☎ 926-1061; cnr Calle Central & Av Santa Ana; mains US$8-9; ⏰ 8am-late Mon-Sat) This is a very popular restaurant and bar with good, if pricey, food. It's an arty sort of place with walls painted Jackson Pollock–style, and a hangout for an interesting mix of people. There's live music some nights (mainly weekends). The *camarones a la orientall,* prawns served with vegetables and rice, are a treat. For something cheaper it has 10 ways of doing spaghetti and nine types of salad. Round it off with a crepe (US$2). This is a good place for breakfast (US$2.50) too.

Capitán Tortuga (Captain Turtle; Calle 30 de Junio; mains US$3.50-7) A long, barn-like place stretching down to a small lakeside terrace, Captain Turtle serves large plates of a wide variety of tasty food, such as pizzas, steaks, chicken, pasta, salads, sandwiches and tacos, at medium prices. Big tour groups turn up here from time to time.

Restaurante La Unión (Calle Unión; mains US$3-5) La Unión serves decent-value chicken, pasta and meat dishes. What's special is the location, right on the water with terrific views.

Restaurant El Barco (☎ 926-0346; Playa Sur; light meals US$2.25-2.75, meals US$4.50-7) On a boat moored on the island's southern shore, El Barco does good food in a Tex-Mex vein. The *tacos hawaianas* are yummy.

Isla Bonita (Hotel Casona de la Isla, Calle 30 de Junio; mains US$5.50-7) This hotel restaurant has fairly good food and a great position on a deck right by the lake. **Hotel Santana** and **Hotel Petén**, along the same street, have further lakeside eateries of similar standards.

La Hacienda del Rey (south end Calle 30 de Junio; meals US$6.50-13; ⏰ 4am-evening) This spacious two-story wooden affair, open to the air and invitingly strung with white lights, specializes in meat. It isn't cheap (US$13 for a 16oz T-bone); but has a pleasant atmosphere and is open early for breakfast (US$2.70 to US$4) before that pre-dawn shuttle to Tikal.

La Mesa de los Mayas (Hotel La Mesa de los Mayas, Av La Reforma; breakfast mains US$2.50-3.25, mains US$6.50-10; ⏰ 7am-11pm) This popular restaurant serves good, varied food amid a large amount of fake vegetation and striking dart-board-pattern cane walls.

Restaurante El Gran Jacal (Calle Centroamérica; mains US$4.50-7.75) This large restaurant has a central fountain (for decoration only) and plenty of ceiling fans (don't hesitate to ask the staff to turn on the one nearest you). It serves fairly good tourist-type food. It does a decent rice, beans and vegetables (US$2.25) for tight budgets.

Restaurante El Club del Cocodrilo (Calle Centroamérica; mains US$4.50-6, light meals US$2.50-3.25) This is another standard decent tourist restaurant. It's quite cheerful, with blue tablecloths and cable TV.

Mayan Princess Café (cnr Calle 10 de Noviembre & Av La Reforma; mains US$3.50-5) This inexpensive traveler's haunt serves OK Western food along the lines of chicken Florentine and vegetarian fettuccini. It does it reasonably well, with friendly service

Hotel Posada del Peregrino (Av La Reforma 3; mains US$3.25-4.50) The restaurant here serves great food at good prices. The US$2.20 *plato del día* is usually meat or chicken with rice, salad, tortillas and a soft drink. A liter jug of beer is just US$2.40.

Restaurante Peche's (Playa Sur; mains US$2.50-3.25; ⏰ 4am-10pm) Busy Peche's serves inexpensive plates of meat, rice, tortillas and salad – and it's open for early breakfast.

Pizzería Picasso (pizza US$4-5; ⏰ 10:30am-10:30pm Tue-Sun) Opposite Hotel Villa del Lago, the Picasso serves reasonable pizzas and pasta at fair prices.

Naomi's Café (☎ /fax 926-3225; Calle Centroamérica; light meals & breakfast mains US$2-2.75; ⏰ 4:30am-evening) You can get breakfast here before that early departure, and inexpensive snacks at any time of day. It has Internet access and sells guidebooks too.

Restaurante La Canoa (☎ 926-0852/3; meals US$2.50) This dark, high-ceilinged dining room will appeal to budget travelers with its decent food at low prices. Breakfasts, sandwiches and *quesadillas* (flour tortillas topped or filled with cheese) are US$1.50 to US$2. Make sure you don't miss the killer tortillas.

Posada El Tucán (breakfast mains US$2-3, lunch & dinner mains US$4.50-6.50) This lakeside place has a thatched roof and a terrace that catches any breezes.

The **food stalls** (Parque Central; tacos & burritos US$0.70) at the breezy northwest corner of the plaza are good places to dine cheap on *antojitos* (snacks).

SANTA ELENA

Restaurante Mijaro (4a Calle; mains US$3.50-4.25) Cool off at this friendly *comedor* (cheap eatery) on the main street, which has fans not only inside but also in its little thatch-roofed garden area. It does good long *limonadas* (lime drink) and light eats like sandwiches and burgers (US$1.30 to US$2) as well as weightier food.

Hotel Posada Santander (4a Calle; breakfast mains US$1.50, lunch mains US$2.50) This budget hotel has a clean upstairs restaurant serving good-value set meals.

Restaurante El Rodeo (cnr 2a Calle & 5a Av) is often recommended by locals. In the next block of 2a Calle, **Restaurante Petenchel** is also popular. **Super 24** (4a Calle) is a 24-hour supermarket where you can load up for a multiday jungle trek: get enough goodies to share with your guides and any people living in the forest you may encounter.

For a splurge, try one of the two fancy restaurants overlooking the water at the **Hotel Petén Espléndido**.

Drinking & Entertainment

Flores doesn't exactly jive at night but there are a couple of places to hang out.

Restaurante La Unión (Calle Unión) The terrace overlooking the lake at this restaurant is a magnificent spot to watch the sun go down over a Cuba libre (US$1) or a margarita or pina colada (US$2).

If you're hankering to hear reggae, try the little patio-bar **El Trópico** (Playa Sur). Restaurants such as **La Luna**, **Las Puertas** and **El Barco** are all places you can go just for a drink if you like, and Las Puertas has live music, often jazz, some nights (most often weekends).

Mayan Princess Café (cnr Calle 10 de Noviembre & Av La Reforma) This café shows free movies in the evening if the customers want them.

There are also nightly **films** in a house on Calle Central opposite Las Puertas.

Locals gather in the cool of the evening for long drinks, snacks and relaxation in the **Parque Central**, where a *marimba* (xylophone-like instrument) ensemble plays some nights. Teenage boys play pool at **Restaurante Bellos Horizontes**.

Getting There & Away

AIR

The airport at Santa Elena is usually called Flores airport and sometimes Tikal airport.

Five airlines fly daily from and back to Guatemala City. Tikal Airlines (Tikal Jets), Jungle Flying Tours, Racsa and TAG all make this one-hour flight in the morning, arriving between 7am and 8am, and starting back at 4:30pm or 5pm. Inter of Grupo TACA makes two return flights daily, arriving at Flores at 7am and 5:30pm and starting back half an hour later in each case. One-way/roundtrip tickets from the airlines cost US$56/100 with Racsa, US$65/90 with Jungle Flying Tours, US$70/100 with TAG, US$89/112 with Tikal Airlines and US$90/124 with Inter, but you may get discounts at travel agencies. Four days a week, Inter of Grupo TACA makes an extra morning flight from Guatemala City to Flores and on to Cancún, Mexico, returning in the afternoon. The one-way/roundtrip fare from Flores to Cancún is US$207/316. Two Belizean airlines, Tropic Air and Maya Island Air, fly twice a day each from and to Belize City, both charging US$88 each way for the one-hour trip.

BUS & MINIBUS

In Santa Elena, buses of **Fuente del Norte** (☎ 926-0517), **Transportes María Elena**, **Línea Dorada/Mundo Maya** (☎ 926-1788, 926-0528) and **Transportes Rosita** (☎ 926-1245) all stop at their own ticket offices on 4a Calle. Línea Dorada/Mundo Maya has a second office in Flores (☎ 926-3649; Playa Sur), where its buses also pick up passengers.

The bus stop in Santa Elena's crowded market area off the south side of 4a Calle is used by the chicken buses of Transportes Pinita and Transportes Rosío. Minibuses *(microbuses)* to El Remate, Melchor de Mencos, Poptún, El Naranjo and Sayaxché have their own yard on 4a Calle just west of the market entrance. Buses and minibuses to San Andrés and San José go from 5a Calle just west of the market. **San Juan Travel** (☎ 926-0041/2, 926-2146) buses leave from its office on 2a Calle, Santa Elena.

Bus and minibus departures include the following:

Belize City (4-5hr, 220km); Línea Dorada/Mundo Maya (US$15.50, 2 daily 5am & 7am, returns 2pm & 5pm); San Juan Travel (US$20, 1 daily 5am, returns 9:30am & 4:30pm) These buses to Belize City all connect with boats to Caye Caulker and Ambergris Caye. It's cheaper but slower from Flores to take local buses to the border and on from it.
Bethel, Mexico border (US$3.25, 4hr, 127km) Fuente del

Norte (1 daily 5am, returns 4pm); Pinita (4 daily 5am, 8am, noon & 1pm, returns 5am, noon & 2pm)

Carmelita (US$3.25, 3hr, 80km) Pinita (1 daily 1pm, returns 5am)

Chetumal, Mexico (7-8hr, 350km) Línea Dorada/Mundo Maya (US$22, 2 daily 5am & 7am, returns 6:30am & 2pm); San Juan Travel (contact Posada Chaktemal, ☎ 832-0727, 832-6348; US$25, 1 daily 5am, returns 9:30am & 4:30pm) Check Belize visa regulations before you set off.

Cobán (US$6.50, 6hr, 245km, 1 daily 10:30am) A Rosío bus leaves the market bus stop – or take a bus or minibus to Sayaxché, from where a bus leaves for Cobán at 10am. See also the Shuttle Minibus section (right).

El Naranjo (Río San Pedro) (US$3.25, 4hr, 151km, minibuses every hour 5am-6pm, buses 5 daily 5am, 7am, 11am, 2pm & 3pm) Buses leave from the market.

El Remate (US$2, 40min, 29km, minibuses hourly 6am-1pm) Alternatively, buses and minibuses to/from Melchor de Mencos will drop you at Puente Ixlú junction, 2km south of El Remate.

Esquipulas (US$10.50, 10hr, 440km) Transportes María Elena (US$7.75, 9hr, 3 daily 6am, 10am & 2pm) Goes via Chiquimula.

Fray Bartolomé de Las Casas (US$4.50, 5hr, 178km) Transportes Rosío (10:30am) Leaves from the market.

Guatemala City (8-10hr, 500km); Línea Dorada/Mundo Maya (deluxe US$28, 2 daily 10am & 9pm; economy US$14.50, 1 daily 10pm); Transportes Rosita (US$6.50-9.75, 2 daily 7pm & 8pm); Fuente del Norte (US$9-10.50, 29 daily 3:30am-11pm) Fuente price exceptions are: the 10am and 9pm buses cost US$17, and the 2pm, 8pm and 10pm departures cost US$13.

La Técnica, Mexico border Pinita (US$4, 5hr, 140km, 2 daily 5am & 1pm, returns 4am & 11am)

Melchor de Mencos, Belize border (2hr, 100km) minibuses (US$2.60, hourly 5am-6pm); Transportes Rosita (US$1.30, 5 daily 5am, 11am, 2pm, 4pm & 6pm); Pinita (US$2, 1 daily 8am)

Poptún (2hr, 113km, every 30min 5am-6pm) Fuente del Norte (US$2); minibus (US$2.60) The buses are Guatemala City–bound.

Puerto Barrios Take a Guatemala City–bound Fuente del Norte bus and change at La Ruidosa junction, south of Río Dulce.

Río Dulce (4½hr, 212km); Fuente del Norte (US$6.50); Línea Dorada (US$10.50/19.50 economy/deluxe) Take a Guatemala City–bound bus.

San Andrés (US$0.50, 30min, 20km, hourly 5am-5pm)

San José (US$0.50, 45 minutes, 25km, hourly 5am-5pm)

Sayaxché (US$1.30, 1½hr, 60km); minibuses (every 30min 5am-6pm); Pinita (3 daily 11am, 2pm & 2:30pm)

CAR & MOTORCYCLE

Several car rental companies have desks at the airport, including the following:

Garrido (☎ 926-0092)
Hertz (☎ 926-0332)
Koka (☎ 926-0526, 926-1233)
Nesa (☎ 926-0082)
Payless (☎ 926-0455)
Tabarini (☎ 926-0277, in Santa Elena ☎ 926-0253)

San Juan Travel rents 4WD vehicles, the cheapest being a Suzuki Jeep (US$70 a day). Martsam Travel rents 125cc motorcycles at US$14.25/32.50/36.50 for two/eight/24 hours.

SHUTTLE MINIBUS

Mundo Maya (p251) and San Juan Travel (p246) operate shuttle minibuses to **Tikal** (US$2.50/5 one-way/roundtrip, 1¼ hours each way). San Juan leaves hourly from 5am to 10am and usually at 2pm. Mundo Maya goes at 5am and 8:30am and some days at 3:30pm. Most accommodations and travel agencies can book these shuttles for you and the vehicles will pick you up where you're staying or at any other agreed spot. Return trips leave Tikal at 12:30pm, 2pm, 3pm, 4pm, 5pm and 6pm with San Juan and at 2pm and 5pm with Mundo Maya. If you know which return trip you plan to be on, ask your driver to hold a seat for you or arrange a seat in a colleague's minibus. If you stay overnight in Tikal and want to return to Flores by minibus, it's a good idea to reserve a seat with one of the drivers when they arrive in the morning. Don't wait until departure time and expect to find a seat. Outside the normal timetable, you can rent a whole minibus for US$30.

Martsam Travel (p246) runs shuttles to Cobán (US$25 per person, five to six hours) for a minimum of four people. It also does a US$90 trip to Palenque, Mexico, visiting the outstanding Maya ruins at Yaxchilán and Bonampak en route. San Juan Travel does a more basic Palenque minibus-boat-minibus shuttle leaving at 5am (US$30, eight hours). On the Palenque run (in either direction) make sure you get a ticket, receipt or other documentation that proves you have paid for the whole trip from Flores to Palenque or vice-versa. Occasionally travelers find that the driver waiting on the far side of the Río Usumacinta to take them on to their destination attempts to extract an extra payment.

Getting Around

A taxi from the airport to Santa Elena or Flores costs US$1.30. Yellow local buses (US$0.15) shuttle between 6a Av in Santa Elena and the north end of the causeway in Flores. Martsam Travel rents mountain bikes with helmets for US$2.60 an hour.

AROUND FLORES
El Mirador & Tayazal

Boats (US$0.15 per person) make the five-minute crossing to San Miguel village from beside Restaurante La Guacamaya on the northeast side of Flores whenever they have a boatload. San Miguel itself is a quiet, slow-moving place. To reach the lookout point called El Mirador (1.75km west), walk 250m to the left along the shore from where the boat drops you, then turn up the street to the right, which passes the Iglesia Evangélica Príncipe de Paz. After 200m turn left, passing a football field on your right to reach a sign telling you that you are entering the Tayazal archaeological site, which is a set of chiefly Classic-era mounds scattered around this western end of the peninsula and largely overgrown by vegetation. Some 180m downhill beyond this sign, fork left following a 'Mirador' sign (the straight-on road leads to the **Playita**, a small lake beach). After 200m the track enters a clearing surrounded by low mounds with an upright rock carved with a skull in the middle. Fork right onto a single-track path passing the left side of the **skull rock** and winding on through the trees. After some 450m the track bends sharp left then forks: choose the right-hand path here and continue for some 230m, mainly downhill, till you see steps mounting the hillside on your right. The hillside is actually one of the **pyramids** of ancient Tayazal and on its summit wooden steps have been built up to a platform around a tree: this is **El Mirador**, with fine views of Flores and around Lago de Petén Itzá. The walk is best done in the morning, to avoid afternoon heat and the danger of being overtaken by dusk.

Arcas

The **Asociación de Rescate y Conservación de Vida Silvestre** (Wildlife Rescue & Conservation Association; ☎ 926-0946; www.arcasguatemala.com; Biblioteca Arcas, Barrio La Ermita, San Benito), a Guatemalan NGO, has a rescue and rehabilitation center on the mainland northeast of Flores for wildlife such as macaws, parrots, jaguars, monkeys, kinkajous and coatis that have been rescued from smugglers and the illegal pet trade. The rehabilitation center itself is closed to visitors but a Centro de Educación e Interpretación Ambiental (CEIA, Environmental Education & Interpretation Center) has been set up for visitors, with a 1.5km interpretative trail featuring medicinal plants and animal tracks, an area for viewing animals that cannot be returned to the wild, a beach and a bird observation deck. A boat leaves from beside Restaurante La Guacamaya on the northeast side of Flores at 4pm daily for tours of the CEIA costing US$6.50 per person for one or two people, US$5.25 for three to five people and US$4 for six or more. It's best to call the Arcas office in San Benito beforehand to confirm that the boat is going. You can also reach Arcas by walking about 45 minutes east from San Miguel; tours for people who arrive independently between 9am and 3pm cost US$1.30 each.

Grutas Actun-Can

The **Actun-Can caves** (La Cueva de la Serpiente, Cave of the Serpent; admission US$1.30; ☟ 8am-5pm) are of standard limestone. No serpents are in evidence, but the cave-keeper will turn on the lights for you (if the electricity's not working, they rent flashlights for US$0.50) and may give you the rundown on the cave formations, which suggest animals, humans and various scenes. Bring your own flashlight if you have one and adequate shoes – it can be slippery. Explorations take about 30 to 45 minutes.

At the cave entrance is a shady picnic area. Actun-Can makes a good goal for a long walk from Santa Elena. To find it, walk south on 6a Av past the Telgua office. About 1km from the center of Santa Elena, turn left, go 300m and turn right at the electricity generating plant. Go another 1km to the site. A taxi from Santa Elena costs US$2.

Laguna Petenchel

Hotel Villa Maya (☎ 410-1592; www.villasdegua temala.com; s/d/tr US$77/85/93; Ⓟ ⓐ), on Laguna Petenchel, a small lake east of Santa Elena, is one of the best hotels in the area, with 36 double rooms in bungalows with bathroom, ceiling fan, hot water, beautiful views of the lake and blissful quiet. There's a patio restaurant, tennis, two swimming pools, two lagoons and a wildlife refuge. It's 4km north of the crossroads where the Guatemala City road diverges from the Tikal road 8km east of Flores.

San Andrés

This small town on the northwest side of the lake is home to two Spanish-language schools:

Eco-Escuela de Español (☎ 926-3202; www.ecom aya.com) This community-owned school emphasizes ecological and cultural issues and organizes environmentally related trips and volunteer opportunities; cost is US$100 a week plus US$75 for room and board with a local family. Ecomaya in Flores (246) can provide information on this school.

Nueva Juventud Spanish School (☎ 711-0040, 496-2276; www.volunteerpeten.com; Restaurant La Troja, San Andrés) Also environmentally oriented, this school is closely tied to a volunteer program that cares for the ecological park where the school is sited, and encourages volunteers to develop community projects. Classes cost US$120 a week, with accommodation options from US$30 to US$50.

A few kilometers west of San Andrés, **Ni'tun Ecolodge** (☎ 201-0759; fax 331-7829; www.nitun.com; s/d/tr US$45/70/100) is a beautiful place on the lakeshore with 350,000 sq meters of grounds where six species of hummingbird nest year-round. Each of the four spacious, attractive houses has three double beds, thatched roof, stone walls and patio. The restaurant here is also very beautiful. The room rates include airport transfers and breakfast. A package of airport transfers, accommodations and three meals a day is US$65 per person. Bernie and Lore, who built and operate the lodge, are adventurers and conservationists who also operate Monkey Eco Tours which offers adventure trips with transport in Land Cruisers. Portable showers, inflatable mattresses and crystalware are provided, and they employ specialized guides such as birders, archaeologists and biologists. Tours go to El Mirador, Río Azul, Ceibal, Dos Pilas and Tikal, among other sites, with prices ranging from US$90 to US$200 a day.

For information on minibuses and buses to San Andrés, see p251.

San José

San José, a town of about 3000 a few kilometers along the lake from San Andrés, is peopled by Itzá Maya, descendants of the Flores area's pre-Hispanic inhabitants. It has one of the best beaches on the lake. One of its two Spanish-language schools, the community-owned **Escuela Bio-Itzá** (☎ /fax 926-1363; www.conservation.org/guatemala, www.ecomaya.com), is part of an association working to keep Itzá traditions and language alive. Cost for the usual 20 hours of one-on-one classes per week is US$200 if you live with a local family, or US$125 if you camp and organize your own meals. Students can participate with the Itzá community on projects such as their medicinal plant garden and Itzá language academy. Ecomaya in Flores (p246) can provide information on this school. The other Spanish-language school in San José is **Mundo Maya Ecological Spanish School** (☎ 928-8321, 514-8889; www.mundomayaguatemala.com; Barrio La Trinidad), which offers a whole host of free-time activities and charges US$95 for classes plus US$65 in family accommodations or US$40 a week (plus meals) in its student guesthouse.

San José is a special place to be on the night of October 31/November 1, when perfectly preserved human skulls that are housed in the church are paraded around town on a velvet pillow. Throughout the night, the skulls make visits to predetermined houses, where blessings are sought, offerings made and a huge feast eaten.

For information on minibuses and buses to San José, see p251. There is no regular boat service. Renting a boat from beside the Hotel Santana in Flores or Hotel Petén Espléndido in Santa Elena costs around US$13 for the 30-minute crossing.

Parque Natural Ixpanpajul

At **Parque Natural Ixpanpajul** (☎ 926-4220, 336-0576; admission US$13; ☼ 7:30am-6:30pm) you can ride horses, mountain bikes or tractors, but the big attraction is the Sky Way, a series of six linked suspension bridges through the upper levels of the forest. Its 2km south down the Guatemala City road from its junction with the Tikal road, 8km east of Flores.

EL REMATE

Once little more than a few thatched huts 29km northeast of Santa Elena on the Tikal road, the lakeside village of El Remate keeps

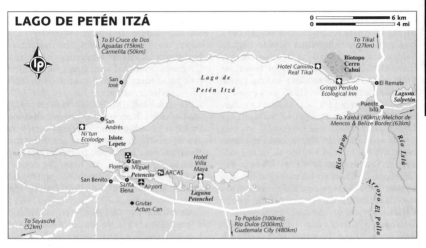

LAGO DE PETÉN ITZÁ

on growing, thanks to its location which makes it a convenient alternative to Flores as a base for visiting Tikal. It now offers plenty of economical accommodations and a couple of decent places to eat.

El Remate begins 1km beyond Puente Ixlú (also called El Cruce), the village where the road to Melchor de Mencos on the Belize border diverges from the Tikal road. El Remate is strung along the Tikal road for 1km to another junction, where an unpaved road branches west along the north shore of the Lago de Petén Itzá to the Biotopo Cerro Cahuí and beyond. Several more places to stay and eat are dotted along this road, which continues all the way to the villages of San José and San Andrés near the west end of the lake, making it possible to go all the way around the lake by road.

If you're stuck for cash, you can change US-dollar cash and traveler's checks and Belize dollars, at low rates, at La Casa de Don David (p256). El Remate is known for its wood carving. Several small shops on the lakeshore opposite La Mansión del Pájaro Serpiente sell local handicrafts.

Sights & Activities
BIOTOPO CERRO CAHUÍ
The entrance to the 6.5 sq km subtropical forest reserve, **Biotopo Cerro Cahuí** (admission US$2.50; 6:30am-dusk), is 1.75km west along the north-shore road from El Remate. The vegetation here ranges from *guamil* (regenerating slash-and-burn land) to rain

forest. Trees here include mahogany, cedar, ramón, broom, sapodilla and cohune palm, and you'll also see many species of liana and epiphyte, these last including bromeliads, ferns and orchids. The hard wood of the sapodilla was used in Mayan temple door lintels, some of which have survived from the Classic period to our own time. This is also the tree from which *chicle* is sapped.

More than 20 mammal species roam the reserve including spider and howler monkeys, ocelots, white-tailed deer, raccoons and armadillos. The bird life, of course, is rich and varied. Some 179 species have been identified. Depending upon the season and migration patterns, you might see kingfishers, ducks, herons, hawks, parrots, toucans, woodpeckers and the famous ocellated (or Petén) turkey, a beautiful big bird resembling a peacock.

A network of loop trails starts at the road and goes up the hill, affording a view of the whole lake and of Laguna Salpetén to the east and Laguna Petenchel to the south. The one called Los Escobos (6km long – it takes about 2¼ hours) is good if you want to see monkeys. The guards at the entrance can give you directions.

The admission fee includes the right to camp or sling your hammock under small thatch shelters inside the entrance. There are toilets and showers.

The dock opposite the entrance is one of the best places to swim along the generally rather muddy shore of the lake.

OTHER ACTIVITIES

Most El Remate accommodations can book you on five-hour **horseback rides** to Laguna Salpetén and a small archaeological site there (US$16.50 per person) or two-hour boat trips for **bird-watching** or nocturnal **crocodile spotting** (each US$8 per person). Casa Mobego and Casa Yaikán do five-hour **walking tours** to Laguna Salpetén for US$10 per person.

Ask around about **bicycle, kayak and canoe rental**. At the time of writing all were available at **Casa de Dona Tonita** for US$4 a day for bikes, US$1.30 an hour for canoes and kayaks. **Casa Mobego** rents double kayaks for US$3.25/4/8 for one/two/four hours. **Hotel Las Sirenas**, on the main road south of Posada Ixchel, rents bicycles at US$2/3.25/4.50 for two/four/24 hours, with a deposit of US$39.

At the **Mirador del Duende** (p256) you can **rent horses** (US$10 a day).

Tours

The **Mirador del Duende** (p256) offers very reasonably priced jungle treks (a six-day El Mirador trip is US$180 per person; a two-day Yaxhá and Nakum venture is US$70).

La Casa de Don David (p256) offers tours to Yaxhá (US$15 to US$20 per person), Uaxactún (US$20 per person) and Ceibal (US$35 to US$40 per person). Prices do not include guides.

Sleeping

ALONG THE MAIN ROAD

These establishments are listed in south-to-north order.

Mirador del Duende (☎ 707-1093, 806-2231; camping per person US$3, bungalows US$5) One of the first places you encounter as you enter El Remate, this has great lake views and quirky bungalows that are almost completely open to the air. You can sling your hammock here for US$3 too. Healthy, economical vegetarian food is served and the owner boasts that this is a 'mosquito-free zone,' thanks to breezes off the lake.

Hotel La Mansión del Pájaro Serpiente (☎ 702-9434, Flores airport office ☎ /fax 926-4264; s/d/tr US$20/40/60; ☒) Just north of the Mirador del Duende, this American-owned establishment has the loveliest rooms and grounds in El Remate. The 11 rooms, in bungalows dotted about beautiful hillside gardens and

all with lake views, sport colorful textiles, tile floors, fans and netted windows, and each has a sitting room and hot-water bathroom as well as a bedroom. There's a gorgeous pool too, with hammocks under *palapa* shelters nearby, and a reasonably priced restaurant/bar.

Hotel Sak-Luk (☎ 494-5925, in Guatemala City ☎ 473-5231; s/d per person without/with bathroom US$4/7) The white stucco bungalows here are up on the hillside above the road and there's a nice lake view from the upstairs terrace. The bungalows have big round, mosquito-netted windows, hot water and fans. It's 200m north of the Mansión del Pájaro Serpiente.

Casa Yaikán (☎ 809-6187; r per person US$3) Up a lane 200m north of the Sak-Luk, Yaikán has a friendly young owner and simple, airy rooms with three double beds and mosquito nets. Meals are available.

Posada Ixchel (☎ 928-8475, 928-8396; s/d/tr US$5/8/11) This friendly, family-owned place another 200m north has just a couple of rooms but they're spotless, with curtains, mosquito nets, fan and attractive wicker furniture.

Hotel Sun Breeze (☎ 807-1487; s/d US$4/7) This is a pleasant little place down the lane toward the lake. The clean, bare rooms sport mosquito nets and share cold-water bathrooms.

Hotel Don Juan (☎ 204-2555; r per person US$3) Just south of the junction where the north-shore road branches west off the main Tikal road, the Don Juan has three super-basic rooms, with walls reaching only partway to the ceiling, holding three people each. It does have fans and nets.

ALONG THE NORTH-SHORE ROAD

La Casa de Don David (☎ 928-8469, 306-2190; www.la casadedondavid.com; s/d with cold shower US$16/20, with hot shower US$26/30; ☒) Just 50m along the north-shore road from the main road at the north end of the village, this popular place is operated by American-born David Kuhn, a Petén resident for three decades, and his Guatemalan wife Rosita. The clean, simple, nonsmoking rooms are equipped with fan and terrace, overlooking large gardens stretching towards the lake. The restaurant (open 6:30am to 8pm) serves reliable meals at reasonable prices (lunch and dinner mains are around US$4), and has a rack of good local-interest reading material. Try the excellent toasted German bread at breakfast. Don David's is popular with groups but is big enough to accommodate independent travelers too.

Casa Mobego (Casa Roja; ☎ 909-6999; camping per own/rented tent US$3/4; s/d/tr with breakfast US$9/18/27) Five airy rooms in thatched bungalows, sharing spotless toilets and showers, comprise the rustic but attractive accommodations here, 750m west from La Casa de Don David along the north-shore road. Breakfast, snacks and sandwiches are served in a pleasant restaurant area dotted with curious sculptures and paintings. The friendly owner, Gonzalo, is an artist and sculptor who worked for 10 years restoring monuments at Tikal and other sites. There's a swimming dock across the road.

Casa de Doña Tonita (☎ 701-7114; s/d US$4/8) Just past Casa Mobego, Doña Tonita's has four simple rooms with two single beds each, in a two-story wood-and-thatch *rancho*. There's an inexpensive restaurant with vegetarian food available.

Mon Ami (☎ 928-8413, 928-8480; demonsb@hotmail .com; s/d/f US$5/7/11, d with bathroom US$13) Some 350m beyond Doña Tonita, Mon Ami has a handful of simple thatch-roofed, stucco bungalows with the odd touch of colorful mural or textile. They're clean.

Gringo Perdido Ecological Inn (in Guatemala City ☎ 334-2305, 334-1967; gringo_perdido@hotmail.com; camping per person US$3, bed per person in open-air shelter US$6, r per person with bathroom US$14; Ⓟ) Waking up here is like waking up in paradise, with no sound but the lake lapping at the shore a few steps from your door. The rooms have one double and one single bed, stone walls and floors, mosquito nets and full-wall canvas roll-up blinds that can almost give you the sensation of sleeping in the open air. Mostly vegetarian food is served, with breakfast costing US$3 to US$6 and dinner US$6 to US$10. When there are only a few guests in, it doesn't switch on the generator, meaning no hot water and no cold drinks but plenty of soothing, romantic candlelight. The Gringo Perdido is 3km along the north shore road from the main Tikal road.

Hotel Camino Real Tikal (☎ 926-0204/09, 333-3000; www.caminorealtikal.com.gt; s & d US$134; Ⓟ ⊠ ⓢ) Two kilometers further along the lake is the luxury Camino Real, the fanciest hotel in El Petén, with 72 air-con rooms with balconies,

lake views and all the comforts. Two restaurants, a bar and a coffee shop keep guests happy, as do the Tikal and Cerro Cahuí tours, swimming pool, kayaking, sailing, windsurfing and beach sports. This hotel is rather remote: check out its special packages, which include airport transfers.

Eating

Las Orquideas (pasta US$3.25-5, mains US$7-9.50) Almost next door to Casa de Doña Tonita, Las Orquideas has a genial Italian owner-chef cooking up genuine Italian fare, with tempting desserts too.

Mon Ami (mains US$3.25-4.25, crepes US$2) Further along the north shore road (1200m from the main Tikal road), Mon Ami serves good French and Guatemalan food in a peaceful palm-thatched, open-walled area. Try the *carne al vino* with rice and tomato salad, or the big *ensalada francesa*.

Among the simple *comedors* along the main road, **Restaurante Cahuí** (mains US$3.25), 60m south of Posada Ixchel, stands out for its rustic wooden terrace overlooking the lake. The food is straightforward and inexpensive: meat or chicken main dishes include rice, salad and tortillas. Spaghetti and salads cost a little less.

Several accommodations including **La Casa de Don David** have restaurants too.

Getting There & Around

El Remate is linked to Flores by a public minibus service (p251).

A minibus leaves El Remate at 5:30am for Tikal, starting back from Tikal at 2pm (US$4 roundtrip). Any El Remate accommodations can book you on this. Or you can catch one of the shuttles passing through from Flores to get to Tikal. They normally charge US$2.50 per person.

For taxis, ask at Hotel Sun Breeze, Hotel Don Juan or Hotel Bruno's Place, next door to Don Juan. A one-way ride to Tikal or Flores costs about US$15.

For Melchor de Mencos on the Belize border, get a minibus or bus from Puente Ixlú, 2km south of El Remate.

TIKAL

Towering pyramids poke above the jungle's green canopy to catch the sun. Howler monkeys swing noisily through the branches of ancient trees as brightly colored parrots and toucans dart from perch to perch in a cacophony of squawks. When the complex warbling song of some mysterious jungle bird tapers off, the buzz of tree frogs fills the background and it will dawn on you that this is indeed hallowed ground.

Certainly the most striking feature of **Tikal** (☎ 361-1399; admission US$6.50; 6am-6pm) is its steep-sided temples, rising to heights of more than 44m. But Tikal is different from Copán, Chichén Itzá, Uxmal, and most other great Mayan sites because it is fairly deep in the jungle. Its many plazas have been cleared of trees and vines, its temples uncovered and partially restored, but as you walk from one building to another you pass beneath the dense canopy of rain forest. Rich, loamy smells of earth and vegetation, a peaceful air and animal noises all contribute to an experience not offered by other Mayan sites.

You can, if you wish, visit Tikal on a day trip from Flores or El Remate. You can even make a literally flying visit from Guatemala City in one day, using the daily flights between there and Flores airport. But you'll get more out of Tikal if you spend a night here, enabling you to visit the ruins twice and to be here in the late afternoon and early morning, when other tourists are fewest and the wildlife is more active.

History

Tikal is set on a low hill, which becomes evident as you walk up to the Gran Plaza from the entry road. The hill, affording relief from the surrounding low-lying swampy ground, may be why the Maya settled here around 700 BC. Another reason was the abundance of flint, the valuable stone used by the ancients to make clubs, spear points, arrowheads and knives. The wealth of flint meant good tools could be made, and flint could be traded for other goods. Within 200 years the Maya of Tikal had begun to build stone ceremonial structures, and by 200 BC there was a complex of buildings on the site of the Acrópolis del Norte.

CLASSIC PERIOD

The Gran Plaza was beginning to assume its present shape and extent by the time of Christ. By the dawn of the Early Classic period, around AD 250, Tikal had become an important religious, cultural and commercial city with a large population. King Yax Moch Xoc, in power about AD 230, is looked upon as the founder of the dynasty that ruled Tikal thereafter.

Under King Great Jaguar Paw, who ruled in the mid-4th century, Tikal adopted a new and brutal method of warfare used by the rulers of Teotihuacán in central Mexico. Rather than meeting their adversaries on the plain of battle in hand-to-hand combat, the army of Tikal used auxiliary units to encircle the enemy and throw spears to kill them from a distance. This first use of 'air power' among the Maya of Petén enabled Smoking Frog, the Tikal general, to conquer the army of Uaxactún; thus Tikal became the dominant kingdom in El Petén.

By the middle of the Classic period, in the mid-6th century, Tikal's military prowess and its association with Teotihuacán allowed it to grow until it sprawled over 30 sq km and had a population of perhaps 100,000. But in 553, Lord Water came to the throne of Caracol (in southwestern Belize), and by 562, using warfare methods learned from Tikal, he had conquered Tikal and sacrificed its king. Tikal and other Petén kingdoms suffered under Caracol's rule until the late 7th century.

TIKAL'S RENAISSANCE

A powerful king named Moon Double Comb (682–734), also called Ah Cacau (Lord Chocolate), 26th successor of Yax Moch Xoc, restored not only Tikal's military strength but also its primacy in the Mayan world. He conquered the greatest rival Mayan state, Calakmul in Mexico, in 695, and his successors were responsible for building most of the great temples around the Gran Plaza that survive today. King Moon Double Comb was buried beneath the staggering height of Templo I.

Tikal's greatness waned around 900, but it was not alone in its downfall, which was part of the mysterious general collapse of lowland Mayan civilization.

REDISCOVERY

No doubt the Itzáes, who occupied Tayasal (now Flores), knew of Tikal in the Late Postclassic period (1200–1530). Perhaps they even came here to worship at the shrines of old gods. Spanish missionary friars who moved through El Petén after the conquest left brief references to these junglebound structures, but their writings moldered in libraries for centuries.

It wasn't until 1848 that the Guatemalan government sent out an expedition, under the leadership of Modesto Méndez and Ambrosio Tut, to visit the site. This may have been inspired by John L Stephens' bestselling accounts of fabulous Mayan ruins, published in 1841 and 1843 (though Stephens never visited Tikal). Like Stephens, Méndez and Tut took an artist, Eusebio Lara, to record their archaeological discoveries. An account of their findings was published by the Berlin Academy of Science.

In 1877, the Swiss Dr Gustav Bernoulli visited Tikal. His explorations resulted in the removal of carved wooden lintels from Templos I and IV and their shipment to Basel, where they are still on view in the Museum für Völkerkunde.

Scientific exploration of Tikal began with the arrival of English archaeologist Alfred P Maudslay in 1881. Others continued his work, Teobert Maler, Alfred M Tozzer and RE Merwin among them. Tozzer worked tirelessly at Tikal on and off from the beginning of the 20th century until his death in 1954. The inscriptions at Tikal were studied and deciphered by Sylvanus G Morley.

Since 1956 archaeological research and restoration have been carried out by the University Museum of the University of Pennsylvania (until 1969) and the Guatemalan Instituto de Antropología y Historia. Since 1991, a joint Guatemalan–Spanish project has worked on conserving and restoring Templos I and V.

In the mid-1950s, an airstrip was built at Tikal. In the early 1980s, the road between Tikal and Flores was improved and paved, and direct flights to Tikal were abandoned. The Parque Nacional Tikal (Tikal National Park) was declared a Unesco World Heritage Site in 1979.

Orientation & Information

The 550 sq km Parque Nacional Tikal contains thousands of separate ruined structures. The central area of the city occupied about 16 sq km, with more than 4000 structures.

The road from Flores enters the national park 17km south of the ruins. The gate opens at 6am. Here you must pay a fee of US$6.50 for the day; if you enter after about 3pm, your ticket should be stamped with the following day's date, meaning that it will be valid for the next day too. Multilingual guides are available at the visitors center (US$40 for a half-day tour for up to four people, plus US$5 for each extra person). These authorized guides always display their accreditation carnet, listing the languages they speak. The visitors center sells books, souvenirs, print film, hats, insect repellent, sun block and other necessities.

Near the visitors center are Tikal's three hotels, a camping area, a few small *comedors,* a tiny post office, a police post, two museums and a disused airstrip. From the visitors center it's a 1.5km walk (20 to 30 minutes) southwest to the Gran Plaza.

The walk from the Gran Plaza southeast to the Templo de las Inscripciones is over 1km; from the Gran Plaza north to Complejo P, it's 800m; from the Gran Plaza west to Templo IV it's over 600m. To visit all the major building complexes, you must walk at least 10km, probably more, so wear comfortable shoes.

For more complete information on the monuments at Tikal, pick up a copy of *Tikal – A Handbook of the Ancient Maya Ruins,* by William R Coe, which is available in Flores and at Tikal for around US$14. A book you're best off finding before you come is *The Lords of Tikal,* by Peter D Harrison, a vivid, cogent summary of the city's history. *The Birds of Tikal: An Annotated Checklist,* by Randell A Beavers, and *The Birds of Tikal,* by Frank B Smythe, also available at Tikal, are good resources for bird-watchers.

The ruins are open from 6am to 6pm daily. Tickets are checked at a booth on the approach track between the visitors center and the ruins. Seeing sunrise from Templo IV at the west end of the main site is possible from about October to March, but you need to leg it from this ticket booth!

It's a good idea to wear shoes with good rubber treads that grip well. The ruins here can be very slick from rain and organic material, especially during the wet season. Bring plenty of water, as dehydration is a real danger if you're walking around all day

TIKAL

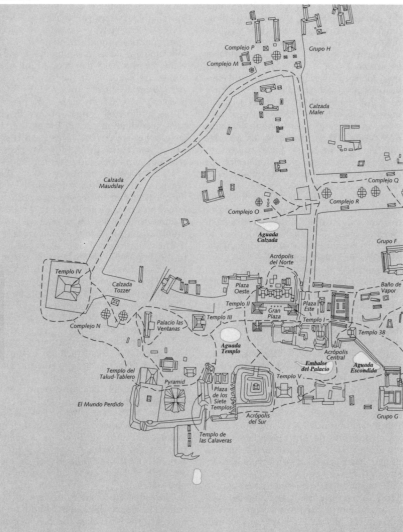

in this heat. Please don't feed the coatis (*pisotes*) that wander about the site.

The Jaguar Inn will exchange US-dollar cash and traveler's checks at a poor rate.

Dangers & Annoyances

The number of guards and rangers at Tikal has been stepped up since several robber-ies and, apparently, rapes happened there a few years ago. On our visit it seemed safe and secure enough, but when visiting the more isolated parts of the site, such as the Templo de las Inscripciones, it still pays to be in your guard and not to go alone. If in doubt, you can always ask a guard whether it is safe to go there.

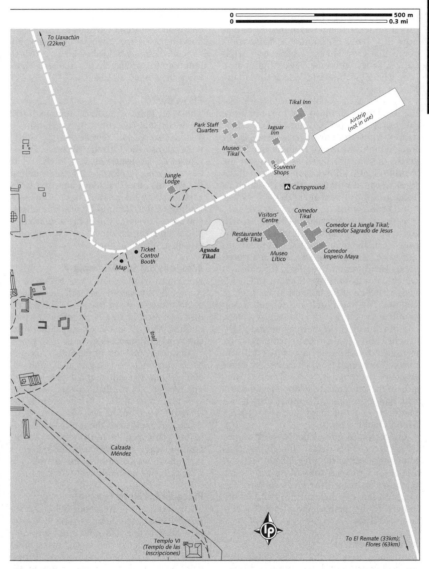

0 [=========] 500 m
0 [=========] 0.3 mi

To Uaxactún
(22km)

Tikal Inn

Airstrip
(not in use)

Park Staff
Quarters

Jaguar
Inn

Museo
Tikal

Souvenir
Shops

Jungle
Lodge

Campground

Comedor
Tikal

Visitors'
Centre

Comedor La Jungla Tikal;
Comedor Sagrado de Jesus

Restaurante
Café Tikal

Águada
Tikal

Museo
Lítico

Comedor
Imperio Maya

Ticket
Control
Booth

Map

trail

Calzada
Méndez

Templo VI
(Templo de las
Inscripciones)

To El Remate (33km);
Flores (63km)

Gran Plaza

The path comes into the Gran Plaza around the awesome **Templo I**, the Templo del Gran Jaguar (Temple of the Grand Jaguar). This was built to honor – and bury – King Moon Double Comb. The king may have worked out the plans for the building himself, but it was actually erected above his tomb by his son, who succeeded to the throne in 734. The king's rich burial goods included stingray spines, which were used for ritual bloodletting, 180 beautiful jade objects, pearls and 90 pieces of bone carved with hieroglyphs. At the top of the 44m-high temple is a small enclosure of three rooms covered by a corbeled arch. The sapodilla-wood lintels over the doors were richly carved; one of them was removed and is now in a Basel museum. The lofty roofcomb that crowned the temple was originally adorned with reliefs and bright paint. It may have symbolized the 13 realms of the Mayan heavens.

Visitors used to be allowed to make the dangerous climb to the top, but since (at least) two people tumbled to their deaths, the stairs have been closed. Don't fret, though, the views from **Templo II** just across the way are nearly as awe-inspiring. Templo II, also known as the Temple of the Masks, was at one time almost as high as Templo I, but it now measures 38m without its roofcomb.

Nearby, the **Acrópolis del Norte** (North Acropolis), while not as immediately impressive as the twin temples, is of great significance. Archaeologists have uncovered about 100 different structures, the oldest of which dates from before the time of Christ, with evidence of occupation as far back as 400 BC. The Maya built and rebuilt on top of older structures, and the many layers, combined with the elaborate burials, added sanctity and power to their temples. Look especially for the two huge, powerful wall masks, uncovered from an earlier structure and now protected by roofs. The final version of the acropolis, as it stood around AD 800, had more than 12 temples atop a vast platform, many of them the work of King Moon Double Comb.

On the plaza side of the North Acropolis are two rows of stelae. Though hardly as bowl-you-over as the magnificent stelae at Copán or Quiriguá, these served the same purposes: to record the great deeds of the kings, to sanctify their memory and to add 'power' to the temples and plazas that surrounded them.

Acrópolis Central

South and east of the Gran Plaza, this maze of courtyards, little rooms and small temples is thought by many to have been a palace where Tikal's nobles lived. Others think the tiny rooms may have been used for sacred rites and ceremonies, as graffiti found within them suggest. Over the centuries the configuration of the rooms was repeatedly changed, suggesting that perhaps this 'palace' was in fact a noble

or royal family's residence changed to accommodate different groups of relatives. A hundred years ago, one part of the acropolis, called the Palacio de Maler, provided lodgings for archaeologist Teobert Maler when he worked at Tikal.

Plaza Oeste

The West Plaza is north of Templo II. On its north side (obscured by vegetation) is a large Late Classic temple. To the southwest, across the Calzada Tozzer (Tozzer Causeway), is **Templo III**, 55m high. Yet to be uncovered, it allows you to see a temple the way the last Tikal Maya and first white explorers saw them. The Tozzer Causeway leading west to Templo IV was one of several sacred byways built in the temple complexes of Tikal, no doubt for astronomical as well as aesthetic purposes.

Acrópolis del Sur & Templo V

Due south of the Gran Plaza is the South Acropolis. Excavation has hardly even begun on this huge mass of masonry. The palaces on top are from Late Classic times (the time of King Moon Double Comb), but earlier constructions probably go back 1000 years.

Templo V, just east of the South Acropolis, is 58m high and was built around AD 600. Unlike the other great temples, this one has slightly rounded corners, and one very tiny room at the top. The room is less than 1m deep, but its walls are up to 4.5m thick. The view from the top is wonderful, giving you a 'profile' of the temples on the Gran Plaza – but with restoration work still under way, climbing the temple was not permitted at the time of writing.

Plaza de los Siete Templos

To the west of the Acrópolis del Sur is the Plaza of the Seven Temples. The little temples, all in a line and now most sprouting trees, were built in Late Classic times. On the north side of the plaza is an unusual triple ball court; another, larger version in the same design stands just south of Templo I.

El Mundo Perdido

About 400m southwest of the Gran Plaza is El Mundo Perdido (Lost World), a large complex of 38 structures with a huge pyramid in its midst. Unlike the rest of Tikal, where Late Classic construction overlays work of earlier periods, El Mundo Perdido exhibits buildings of many different periods: the large pyramid is thought to be essentially Preclassic (with some later repairs and renovations); the Templo del Talud-Tablero, Early Classic; and the Templo de las Calaveras (Temple of the Skulls), Late Classic.

The pyramid, 32m high and 80m along the base, has a stairway on each side, and had huge masks flanking each stairway, but no temple structure at its top. Each side of the pyramid displays a slightly different architectural style. Tunnels dug into the pyramid by archaeologists reveal four similar pyramids beneath the outer face; the earliest (Structure 5C-54 Sub 2B) dates from 700 BC, making this pyramid the oldest Mayan structure at Tikal.

Templo IV & Complejo N

Complex N, near Templo IV, is an example of the 'twin-temple' complexes popular with Tikal's rulers during the Late Classic period. These complexes are thought to have commemorated the completion of a *katun*, or 20-year cycle in the Mayan calendar. This one was built in 711 by King Moon Double Comb to mark the 14th *katun* of baktun 9. (A baktun equals 400 years.) The king himself is portrayed on Stela 16, one of the finest stelae at Tikal.

Templo IV, at 64m, is the highest building at Tikal and the second highest pre-Columbian building known in the Western Hemisphere, after El Tigre at El Mirador. It was completed about 741, in the reign of King Moon Double Comb's son. From the base it looks like a precipitous little hill. Steep wooden steps will take you to the top. The view is almost as good as from a helicopter – a panorama across the jungle canopy. If you stay up here for the sunset, climb down immediately thereafter, as it gets dark on the path very quickly.

Templo de las Inscripciones (Templo VI)

Compared to Copán or Quiriguá, there are relatively few inscriptions on buildings at Tikal. The exception is this temple, 1.2km southeast of the Gran Plaza. On the rear of the 12m-high roofcomb is a long inscription; the sides and cornice of the roofcomb bear glyphs as well. The inscriptions give us the date AD 766. Stela 21 and Altar 9, standing before the temple, date from 736.

The stela had been badly damaged (part of it was converted into a *metate* for grinding corn!) but has now been repaired.

Northern Complexes

About 1km north of the Gran Plaza is **Complejo P**. Like Complejo N, it's a Late Classic twin-temple complex that probably commemorated the end of a *katun*. **Complejo M**, next to it, was partially torn down by the Late Classic Maya to provide building materials for a causeway, now named after Alfred Maudslay, which runs southwest to Templo IV. **Grupo H**, northeast of Complexes P and M, with one tall, cleared temple, had some interesting graffiti within its temples (we're not talking about the moronic modern scrawls now disfiguring them).

Complejo Q and **Complejo R**, about 300m due north of the Gran Plaza, are very Late Classic twin-pyramid complexes with stelae and altars standing before the temples. Complex Q is perhaps the best example of the twin-temple type, as it has been partly restored. Stela 22 and Altar 10 are excellent examples of Late Classic Tikal relief carving, dated 771.

Museums

Tikal has two museums. The **Museo Lítico** (Museum of Stone; admission free; ✆ 9am-noon & 1-4:30pm Mon-Fri, 9am-4pm Sat & Sun), the larger of the two, is in the visitors center. It houses a number of stelae and carved stones from the ruins. Outside is a large model showing how Tikal would have looked around AD 800. The photographs taken by Alfred P Maudslay and Teobert Maler of the jungle-covered temples in various stages of discovery in the late 19th century are particularly striking.

The **Museo Tikal** (Museo Cerámico, Museum of Ceramics; admission US$1.30; ✆ 9am-5pm Mon-Fri, 9am-4pm Sat & Sun) is near the Jaguar Inn. It has some fascinating exhibits, including the burial goods of King Moon Double Comb, carved jade, inscribed bones, shells, stelae, ceramics and other items recovered from the excavations.

Birding

As well as howler and spider monkeys romping through the trees of Tikal, the plethora of birds flitting through the canopy and across the green expanses of the plazas is sure to impress you. Around 300 bird species (migratory and resident) have been recorded at Tikal. Early morning is the best time to go birding, and even amateur bird-watchers will have their share of sightings here. Bring binoculars if you have them, tread quietly and be patient, and you will probably see some of the following birds in the areas specified:

- tody motmots, four trogon species and royal flycatchers around the Templo de las Inscripciones
- two oriole species, keel-billed toucans and collared aracaris in El Mundo Perdido
- great curassows, three species of woodpecker, crested guans, plain chachalacas and three tanager species around Complejo P
- three kingfisher species, jacanas, blue herons, two species of sandpiper and great kiskadees at the Aguada Tikal (Tikal Reservoir) near the entrance. Tiger herons sometimes nest in the huge ceiba tree along the entrance path
- red capped and white collared manakins near Complejo Q; emerald toucanets near Complejo R

In addition, look for several hawk species near the reservoirs, hummingbirds and ocellated turkeys (resembling a cross between a turkey and peacock) throughout the park, and several parrot species and Aztec parakeets while exploring the ruins.

Tikal Canopy Tour

At the national park entrance, you can take a fairly expensive one-hour treetop tour through the forest by harness attached to a series of cables linking trees up to 300m apart, with **Tikal Canopy Tour** (☎ 412-7252; admission US$25; ☼ 7am-5pm).

Sleeping & Eating

The days when intrepid visitors could convince park guards (with a US$5 'tip') to let them sleep atop Templo IV are over. If you are caught in the ruins after hours, you're likely to be escorted out for your own safety. Your best bet to catch some solitude at the ruins and get an early glimpse of the wildlife is to stay overnight and be at the ticket control booth at opening time.

Other than camping, there are only three places to stay at Tikal, all overpriced, and tour groups often have many of the rooms reserved, but staying here does enable you to relax and savor the dawn and dusk, when most of the jungle birds and animals can be seen and heard (especially the howler monkeys). The chances of getting a room depend a lot on the season. In the low season (from after Easter to late June, and from early September to Christmas), you will probably secure a room without reservation. At other times it's advisable to book. It's always advisable to arrive by early afternoon so that you have time to sort out any difficulties – and to get back to El Remate if everything fails. One way of ensuring a room is to become a group tourist yourself. Almost any travel agency in Guatemala offers Tikal tours, including lodging, a meal or two, a guided tour and transportation, and they needn't be prohibitively expensive.

There's no need to make reservations if you want to stay at Tikal's **campground** (camping per person US$4, cabañas per person US$6.50) opposite the visitors' center. This is a large, grassy area with a clean bathroom block, plenty of space for tents, *palapa* shelters for hanging hammocks, and tiny *cabañas* with just enough room for two people to stretch out on foam mattresses.

Jungle Lodge (☎ 926-0519, 361-4098; www.junglelodge.guate.com; s/d US$26/31, with bathroom US$54/72; P ☒) This largest and most attractive of the three hotels was built originally to house archaeologists excavating and restoring Tikal. It has 34 decent rooms in duplex bungalows, each room with a hot-water bathroom, ceiling fan and two double beds. In an older section are 12 much less attractive rooms with shared bathroom. There's a swimming pool, large garden grounds, and a restaurant/bar with breakfast for US$5 and lunch or dinner for US$10.

Tikal Inn (☎ 926-1917/50/53, ☎ /fax 926-0065; hoteltikalinn@itelgua.com; s/d with dinner & breakfast US$57/81; P ☒) This is the second most attractive. It has 17 rooms in the main building, as well as bungalows, which are slightly nicer, plus gardens, a swimming pool and restaurant. The accommodations are simple but clean and quite large, all with a hot-water bathroom and ceiling fan. The rooms in the main building go down to US$37/54 when the hotel decides it isn't high season. The electricity only operates from 6pm to 10pm, and checkout time is 11am (but you can leave baggage in the lobby if you want to depart later).

Jaguar Inn (☎ 926-0002; www.jaguartikal.com; camping per person US$3.25, hammocks per person US$5, dm US$10, s/d/tr/q US$30/48/66/78, May–mid-July US$20/32/44/52; P) Here you can rent a hammock with mosquito net and locker, or sleep in the dorm, or take one of nine bungalow rooms with fan, a hot-water bathroom, fan, reading lamp and terrace with hammock. The restaurant serves breakfasts for around US$3, and a three-course lunch or dinner with coffee for US$7 to US$8. The electricity goes off at 9pm. Unfortunately we have to report that we received a complaint of unauthorized transactions being made on a credit card that was left for safe-keeping at the reception here.

As you arrive in Tikal, look on the right-hand side of the road to find the little *comedors*: **Comedor Imperio Maya**, **Comedor La Jungla Tikal**, **Comedor Tikal**, **Comedor Sagrado de Jesús** and **Tienda Angelita**. Comedor Tikal seems to be the most favored one. These *comedors* offer rustic and agreeable surroundings and are run by local people serving huge plates of fairly tasty food at low prices. Chicken or meat dishes cost around US4.50, pasta and burgers a little less. All these places are open 5am to 9pm daily.

Picnic tables beneath shelters are located just off Tikal's Gran Plaza, with soft-drink and water peddlers standing by, but no food is sold. If you want to spend all day at the ruins without having to make the 20- to 30-minute walk back to the *comedors*, carry food and water with you.

Restaurant Café Tikal (mains US$6.50-10) In the visitors center, this eatery serves fancier food at fancier prices. *Lomito* (tenderloin of beef) and steaks are featured. Plates of fruit cost less. All the hotels also have restaurants.

Getting There & Away
For details of transport to and from Flores and Santa Elena, see p251. Coming from Belize, you could consider taking a taxi from the border to Tikal for around US$40. Otherwise get a bus to Puente Ixlú, sometimes called El Cruce, and switch there to a northbound minibus or bus for the remaining 36km to Tikal. Note that there is little northbound traffic after lunch. Heading from Tikal to Belize, start early in the morning and get off at Puente Ixlú to catch a bus or minibus eastward. Be wary of shuttles to Belize advertised at Tikal: these have been known to detour to Flores to pick up passengers!

UAXACTÚN
Uaxactún (wah-shahk-*toon*), 23km north of Tikal along an unpaved road through the jungle, was Tikal's political and military rival in Late Preclassic times. It was conquered by Tikal's King Great Jaguar Paw in the 4th century, and was subservient to its great sister to the south for centuries thereafter.

Uaxactún village lies either side of a disused airstrip, which now serves as pasture and a football field. Villagers make an income from collecting *chicle*, *pimienta* (allspice) and *xate* in the surrounding forest. A recently started timber extraction operation is supposedly employing sustainable methods but critics have their doubts about this.

About halfway along the airstrip, roads go off to the left and right to the ruins. Village boys will want to guide you: you don't need a guide to find the ruins, but you might want to let one or two of them earn a small tip.

Ruins
The pyramids at Uaxactún were uncovered and stabilized so that no further deterioration would result, but they were not restored. White mortar is the mark of the repair crews, who patched cracks in the stone to prevent water and roots from entering.

Head south from the airstrip to reach Grupo E, a 10- to 15-minute walk. Perhaps the most significant temple here is E-VII-Sub, among the earliest intact temples excavated, with foundations going back perhaps to 2000 BC. It lay beneath much larger structures, which have been stripped away. On its flat top are holes, or sockets, for the poles that would have supported a wood-and-thatch temple. The pyramid is part of a group with astronomical significance: seen from it, the sun rises behind Templo E-I on the longest day of

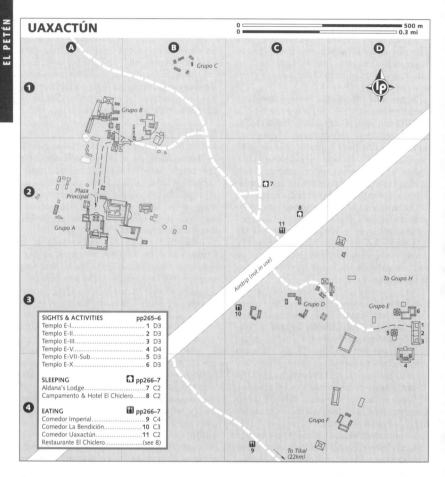

UAXACTÚN

0 ——— 500 m
0 ——— 0.3 mi

Grupo C

Grupo B

Plaza Principal

Grupo A

Airstrip (not in use)

Grupo D

Grupo E

Grupo F

Grupo H

To Grupo H

To Tikal (22km)

SIGHTS & ACTIVITIES	pp265–6
Templo E-I..1	D3
Templo E-II...2	D3
Templo E-III..3	D3
Templo E-V...4	D4
Templo E-VII-Sub................................5	D3
Templo E-X...6	D3

SLEEPING	pp266–7
Aldana's Lodge...................................7	C2
Campamento & Hotel El Chiclero......8	C2

EATING	pp266–7
Comedor Imperial................................9	C4
Comedor La Bendición.......................10	C3
Comedor Uaxactún.............................11	C2
Restaurante El Chiclero..................(see 8)	

the year and behind Templo E-III on the shortest day. Also look for the somewhat deteriorated jaguar and serpent masks on this pyramid's sides.

About a 20-minute walk to the northwest of the runway are Grupo B and Grupo A. At Group A, early excavators sponsored by Andrew Carnegie simply cut into the sides of the temples indiscriminately, looking for graves. Sometimes they used dynamite. This unfortunate work destroyed many of the temples, which are now in the process of being reconstructed.

If you are visiting Uaxactún from Tikal, no fee is charged. But if you are going to Uaxactún without stopping to visit Tikal, you still have to pass through the Parque Nacional Tikal and will have to pay a US$2 Uaxactún-only fee at the park entrance.

Tours
Tours to Uaxactún can be arranged in Flores or at the hotels in Tikal. The Jungle Lodge has a trip departing daily at 8am and returning at 1pm, costing US$60 for one to four people.

Sleeping & Eating
Campamento, Hotel & Restaurante El Chiclero (in San Benito ☎ /fax 926-1095; camping US$5, s/d US$12/15) On the north side of the airstrip, El Chiclero has 10 small and very basic rooms, but with good mattresses and mosquito-netted ceilings and windows, and does the best food

in town (US$6 for soup and a main course with rice). Accommodation prices are very negotiable. Also here is a small museum with shelves full of Mayan pottery from Uaxactún and around. Neria, the owner, can organize trips to more remote sites such as El Mirador, Xultún, Río Azul, Nakbe and La Muralla.

Aldana's Lodge (camping per person US$2, r per person US$3.25) To the right off the street leading to Grupos B and A, Aldana's has alternative, cheaper accommodations, and also offers tours to other sites, but has erratic water supplies. Camping using Aldana's equipment costs US$2.50 per person.

A few basic *comedores* also provide food: **Comedor Uaxactún**, **Comedor La Bendición** and **Comedor Imperial**.

You can contact any of these establishments by leaving a message at Uaxactún's **teléfono comunitario** (community telephone; ☎ 8061-2558/9).

Getting There & Away

A Pinita bus supposedly leaves Santa Elena for Uaxactún (US$2.50) at 1pm, passing through Tikal about 3pm to 3:30pm, and starting back for Santa Elena from Uaxactún at 6am. But its schedule is rubbery and it can arrive in Tikal any time up to about 5pm and in Uaxactún up to about 6:30pm. During the rainy season (from May to October, sometimes extending into November), the road from Tikal to Uaxactún can become pretty muddy: locals say it is always passable but a 4WD vehicle might be needed during the wet.

If you're driving, the last chance to fill your fuel tank as you come from the south is at Puente Ixlú, just south of El Remate. A taxi from El Remate to Uaxactún and back, including waiting time, should cost about US$40; bargain hard.

From Uaxactún, unpaved roads lead to other ruins at El Zotz (about 30km southwest), Xultún (35km northeast) and Río Azul (100km northeast).

YAXHÁ

A beautiful and quite large Classic Mayan ceremonial site, **Yaxhá** (admission US$1.30; 🕑 6am-5pm), is 11km north of the Puente Ixlú–Melchor de Mencos road, from a turning 32km from Puente Ixlú and 33km from Melchor de Mencos. The access road is unpaved.

Yaxhá's setting, on a hill overlooking two sizable lakes, Laguna Yaxhá and Laguna Sacnab, makes it particularly worth visiting. It takes about 1½ hours to wander round the main groups of ruins, which are gradually being cleared and restored, though many mounds are still under vegetation. The high point (literally), towering above all else, is **Templo 216** in the Acrópolis Este (Eastern Acropolis), which affords magnificent views in every direction. On an island near the far (south) shore of Laguna Yaxhá is a separate, late Postclassic archaeological site, Topoxté, whose dense covering of ruined temples and dwellings may date back to the Itzá culture that occupied Flores island at the time the Spanish came. On the northern lake shore below the Yaxhá ruins is **Campamento Yaxhá**, where you can camp for free on raised platforms with thatched roofs and where you might be able to find a boatman to take you over to Topoxté.

Campamento Ecológico El Sombrero (☎ 800-0179; sombrero@guate.net; s/d/tr US$18/29/44, with bathroom US$29/40/55; Ⓟ) On the southern shore, 250m off the approach road, is this excellent place to stay which has good-sized, neat and clean rooms in mosquito-netted bungalows overlooking the lake. There's a good restaurant here, with a small library on local archaeology, and *lancha* (motor boat) tours to Topoxté are offered (US$20 for up to three people, US$26 for four to nine people) as well as horseback riding and day trips to Nakum and El Naranjo, other Classic period sites to the north and northeast of Yaxhá.

Don't swim in the lakes by the way – there are crocodiles!

Agencies in Flores (p246) and El Remate (p256) offer organized trips to Yaxhá, some combined with Nakum and/or Tikal. To get there independently you could get a Melchor de Mencos-bound bus or minibus as far as the Yaxhá turnoff (and be prepared to walk the 11km to the site) – or find a taxi in El Remate, Puente Ixlú (about US$30 roundtrip) or elsewhere.

BELIZE BORDER

It's 100km from Flores to Melchor de Mencos, the Guatemalan town on the border with Belize. For information on bus services to the border and also on more expensive services going right through to Belize City and Chetumal, Mexico, see p251.

The road to the border diverges from the Flores–Tikal road at Puente Ixlú (also called El Cruce), 27km from Flores. It continues paved until about 25km short of the border. The stretch between Puente Ixlú and the border has been the scene of a few highway robberies.

There should be no fees at the border for entering or leaving Guatemala, and none for entering Belize. But travelers leaving Belize usually have to pay a US$10 departure tax and a US$3.75 protected areas conservation fee.

There are money changers at the border with whom you can change sufficient funds for immediate needs. Taxis run between the border and the nearest town in Belize, Benque Viejo del Carmen, 3km away, for around U$0.50 per person. Buses run from Benque to Belize City (US$3, three hours) about every half-hour from 11am to 4pm. You might want to stop over at San Ignacio, 13km beyond Benque: there are many serviceable hotels and interesting things to do around San Ignacio. If you arrive in Benque early enough in the day, you may have sufficient time to visit the Mayan ruins of Xunantunich on your way to San Ignacio.

TO/FROM CHIAPAS & TABASCO (MEXICO)
Via Bethel/La Técnica & Frontera Corozal

The only route with regular transport connections is via Bethel or La Técnica on the eastern (Guatemalan) bank of the Río Usumacinta and Frontera Corozal on the Mexican bank. For details of bus services to and from Bethel and La Técnica and shuttle minibus services all the way through to Palenque, see p251. Guatemalan immigration is in Bethel: bus drivers to La Técnica will normally stop and wait for you to do the formalities in Bethel.

See p289 for information on river crossings: it's cheaper and quicker from La Técnica than from Bethel, but crossing at La Técnica means a longer bus journey on the Guatemalan side. Minibuses leave Frontera Corozal for Palenque at about 5am, 10am, noon and 3pm (US$5, three hours).

If you should want to stay in the Usumacinta area, perhaps to visit the Mayan

ruins at Yaxchilán on the Mexican side of the river, the riverside **Posada Maya** (☎ 801-1799, 801-1800; s/d/tr US$9/18/28), 1km outside Bethel, has a great location and comfortable thatched bungalows, plus tent and hammock shelters. Boats from Bethel to Yaxchilán cost from US$11 to US$22 per person for four to 12 people, roundtrip.

Other Routes

You can also cross into Mexico by boat down the Río de la Pasión from Sayaxché to Benemérito de las Américas or down the Río San Pedro from El Naranjo to La Palma. But there are no regular passenger services on either river and you will probably have to rent a boat privately for around US$80 on the Río San Pedro or US$100-plus on the Río de la Pasión. Both trips take around four hours. La Palma has transport connections with Tenosique, Tabasco, from where minibuses leave for Palenque up to 5:30pm. Benemérito has good bus and minibus connections with Palenque. Both Sayaxché and El Naranjo have bus and minibus connections with Flores (p251).

A possible alternative on the Río San Pedro route is to get a boat from El Naranjo only as far as El Ceibo, on the border, for around US$30. From El Ceibo there are a few buses on to Tenosique (US$2.50, 1½ hours), the last one leaving about 5:30pm. Mexico has no immigration facilities at Benemérito or El Ceibo: you have to get your passport stamped at Frontera Corozal or Tenosique, or failing that Palenque.

El Naranjo, Tenosique and Benemérito all have a few basic accommodations.

SAYAXCHÉ

Sayaxché, on the south bank of the Río de la Pasión, 61km southwest of Flores, is the closest town to nine or 10 scattered Mayan archaeological sites, including Ceibal, Aguateca, Dos Pilas, Tamarindito and Altar de Sacrificios (p269). Otherwise, for travelers it's little more than a transportation halt between Flores and the Cobán area.

Minibuses and buses from Santa Elena drop you on the north bank of the Río de la Pasión. Frequent ferries (US$0.15 for pedestrians, US$2 for cars) carry you across to the town.

Banoro (🕒 9am-4pm Mon-Fri, 10am-1pm Sat), just up the main street from Hotel

Guayacán, changes US-dollar cash and traveler's checks.

Sleeping & Eating

Hotel Guayacán (☎ 926-6111; s & d downstairs with fan US$17, upstairs with air-con US$20; P ☺) Right on the south bank of the river in Sayaxché, the Guayacán is the best place in town, with good rooms equipped with solid wooden beds and tile floors. It also has the best restaurant, on a terrace overlooking the river. Chicken, fish or meat with salad and fries costs US$4 to US$6.

Hotel Petexbatún (☎ 928-6166; s US$8, d with bathroom US$15) This is the second-best place. All rooms have fan and TV. Go one block up the street past the Hotel Guayacán, then three blocks to the right. It overlooks the Río Petexbatún.

Hotel Mayapán (no ☎ ; s & d without/with bathroom US$5/8) Half a block to the left from the Guayacán's door, this is a serviceable cheapie. The rooms have a fan: those upstairs are cleaner and have better beds.

El Botanero (mains around US$3.50) Directly behind Hotel Mayapán on the next street up the hill, this is a dark, funky place full of atmosphere, with stools and tables hewn from tree trunks. It serves a variety of beef, chicken and seafood dishes and it's a good place to kick back and have a beer. **Restaurant Yaxkin**, a couple of doors from Hotel Mayapán, is typical of the few other eateries in town: basic, family-run and inexpensive.

Getting There & Away

Highway 5 from Flores to Sayaxché is now all paved except for the first 20km or so out of Flores. The road south from Sayaxché to Cobán is now also all paved except for one stretch of about 20km. For details of minibuses and buses from Flores, see p251. The return schedule is similar.

Southbound from Sayaxché, buses and minibuses leave at 5am, 6am, 10am and 3pm for Cobán (US$5.25, five hours). Most if not all of these go via Raxrujá and Sebol, not via Chisec. Other minibuses and buses go just to Raxrujá (US$2.60), about hourly from 7am to 3pm. For Chisec, you can change in Raxrujá or at San Antonio Las Cuevas. Vehicles may start from the southern riverbank or may start from the Texaco station opposite Hotel Guayacán.

For river transport, talk to any of the boatmen on the riverbank, or to **Servicio de Lanchas Don Pedro** (☎ /fax 928-6109), run by the experienced and affable Pedro Mendéz, with an office on the riverbank where you can arrange transportation and guides to any of the area sites, for slightly higher prices than in most other boats. For further information on boats to these sites, see p269.

A trip all the way down the Río de la Pasión to Benemérito de las Américas (Mexico), with stops at the ruins of Altar de Sacrificios and Guatemalan immigration at Pipiles, should cost from US$100 to US$150.

AROUND SAYAXCHÉ

Of the archaeological sites reached from Sayaxché, Ceibal and Aguateca are the most interesting to the amateur visitor. Ceibal is fairly well restored, Aguateca has an impressive location, and both are reached by boat trips along jungle-fringed rivers and/ or lakes followed by forest walks.

Ceibal

Unimportant during most of the Classic period, Ceibal (sometimes spelt Seibal) grew rapidly in the 9th century AD under the rule of the Putun Maya merchant-warrior culture from the Tabasco area of Mexico. It attained a population of perhaps 10,000 by AD 900, then was abandoned shortly afterwards. Its low, ruined temples were quickly covered by a thick carpet of jungle.

Ceibal is not one of the most impressive Mayan sites, but the river journey to it is among the most memorable. A one-hour ride up the Río de la Pasión from Sayaxché brings you to a primitive dock. After landing, you clamber up a narrow, rocky path beneath gigantic ceiba trees and ganglions of jungle vines to reach the archaeological zone.

Smallish temples, many of them still (or again) covered with jungle, surround two principal plazas. In front of a few temples, and standing seemingly alone on paths deeply shaded by the jungle canopy, are magnificent stelae, their intricate carvings still in excellent condition. It takes about two hours to explore the site.

For information on tours to Ceibal, see p246. Otherwise, talk to any of the boatmen by the river at Sayaxché. For a round trip including waiting time, they charge around US$30 for one person plus US$3 for each extra person. You should hire a guide to see the site, as some of the finest stelae are off the plazas in the jungle. Most *lancheros* (motorboat drivers), conveniently, also serve as guides.

If you wish, you can get to Ceibal cheaper by land: get any bus, minibus or pickup heading south from Sayaxché on Highway 5 (toward Raxrujá and Chisec) and get off after 9km at Paraíso (US$0.25), from which a dirt track leads 8km east to Ceibal. You may have to walk the last 8km. In the rainy season check first that this stretch is passable.

LAGUNA PETEXBATÚN

Laguna Petexbatún is a 6km-long lake southwest of Sayaxché approached by an hour's *lancha* ride up the Río Petexbatún, a tributary of the Río de la Pasión, from Sayaxché. The lake, river and surrounding forests harbor many birds, including kingfishers, egrets, vultures, eagles, cormorants and herons. Within reach of the waterways are five archaeological sites (Dos Pilas, Tamarindito, Arroyo de Piedra, Punta de Chiminos and Aguateca), and three jungle-hideaway accommodations close to the waters' edge. What we know of the history of these archaeological sites has mostly been unraveled by archaeologists since the late 1980s. Dos Pilas was founded about AD 640 by a prince

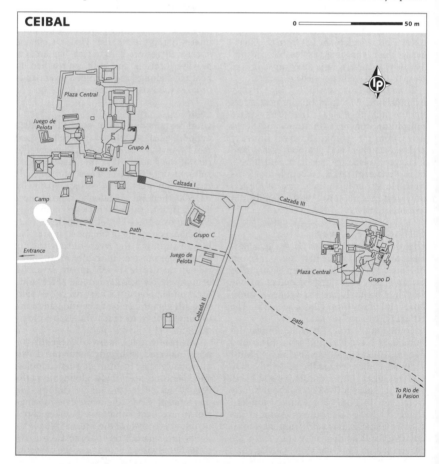

who had left Tikal and later defeated Tikal in two wars, capturing its ruler Shield Skull in 679, according to inscriptions at Dos Pilas. Dos Pilas' second and third rulers carried out monumental building programs, waged wars of conquest and came to dominate most of the territory between the Pasión and Chixoy rivers, but in AD 761 their vassal Tamarindito rebelled and killed the fourth ruler, causing the Dos Pilas nobility to relocate to the naturally fortified site of Aguateca, which was already functioning as a twin capital. Aguateca in turn was abandoned in the early 9th century, at around the same time as three defensive moats were cut across the neck of the Chiminos peninsula on the edge of Laguna Petexbatún. Archaeologists surmise that Punta de Chiminos was the last refuge of the Petexbatún dynasty founded at Dos Pilas.

The first landmark you reach, on the river a few kilometers before the lake, is **Posada Caribe** (☎ 928-6334; posadacaribe@peten.net; s/d US$50/60) with thatched bungalows. From here you can walk to the **Dos Pilas** ruins in about three hours, including stops at the lesser ruins of **Tamarindito** and **Arroyo de Piedra** en route. You can organize horses for this trip at Posada Caribe for around US$8 each. The archaeological highlight of the partly excavated and cleared Dos Pilas site is a hieroglyphic stairway with five 6m-wide steps, each with two rows of superbly preserved glyphs, climbing to the base of the royal palace near the main plaza.

Just up from the western shore of the lake itself is the fairly comfortable **Petexbatún Lodge** (☎ 331-7561, 331-7646, 910-6963, 926-0501; philippe_petex@yahoo.fr; rooms per person with bunks US$10, bungalows with bathroom US$40), with mosquito-netted rooms and meals available if you ask in advance. Two minutes further south by *lancha* is the choicest of the three places to stay, **Chiminos Island Lodge** (☎ 335-3506; www.chiminosisland.com; rooms per person US$75 incl 3 meals). This has just five lovely, large, comfortable, thatched bungalows set along forest paths, each with one double and two single beds, hot-water bathroom, fan, electric light, mosquito screens, balcony and lake view. Good food is served in an open-air restaurant and the lodge shares its promontory with the Punta de Chiminos ruins where you can make out a ball court, stela and several mounds. Fat folders full

of absorbing archaeological information and articles about the area are available to peruse as you chill out here.

If you have limited time and funds, **Aguateca**, just off the far south end of the lake, is both the easiest reached of the sites and the most immediately impressive. It's a 1¼-hour *lancha* trip direct from Sayaxché. It's a five-minute walk up from the dock to the office of the rangers, who will guide you round the site in about 1½ hours (a tip of a few dollars is in order). The ruins are on a hilltop, defended by cliffs facing the lake and by a ravine. There are two main groups, both in process of restoration: the Grupo del Palacio where the ruler lived, and the Plaza Mayor (Main Plaza) to its south, where glass fiber copies of several stelae showing finely attired rulers stand beside the fallen originals. The two groups are connected by a causeway. The rangers are usually happy to let people camp at Aguateca (bring supplies with you). They might even be willing to show you the way overland to Dos Pilas (11km northwest). Howler monkeys are much in evidence early and late in the day.

Getting to all these places involves making your own arrangements with boatmen at Sayaxché, or taking a tour. A straightforward half-day return trip from Sayaxché to Aguateca costs around US$35 for one person plus US$3 for each extra person. You could, for example, arrange to be dropped at one of the lodges afterwards and to be picked up the next afternoon after making a trip to Dos Pilas. Martsam Travel (p246) and Ecomaya (p246) both offer tours to these sites: Martsam camps at Aguateca.

REMOTE MAYAN SITES

Several Mayan sites buried in the Petén forest of interest to archaeology buffs and adventurous travelers are open for limited tourism. They're exciting not just because of the ruins but because of the jungle and its wildlife that you encounter en route. Few of these sites can be visited without a guide because of their remote location, the difficult jungle terrain you must brave to get there and the lack of water (potable or otherwise), but several businesses in Flores (p246) and Santa Elena (p246) and others in El Remate (p256) and San Andrés (p254) offer trips to these sites. Few of these tours offer anything approaching comfort, and you should be prepared for buggy, basic conditions. People reluctant to use a mosquito repellent containing DEET may want to reconsider taking one of these trips.

If you take a trip with an outfit that works with the local Comités Comunitarios de Ecoturismo (Community Ecotourism Committees) in the remote villages that serve as starting points for these treks, you will be participating in a considered program of low-impact, sustainable tourism and you will have a guide who is highly knowledgeable about local conditions. Freelance guides can lead tourists to some of these sites, which may save you some money, but they may have little concept of responsible tourism and little knowledge of what you are seeing. Nor is there any assurance, given the difficulty of these treks, that your freelance trip will come off successfully, and in case of failure, you'll have no claim to any money you may have paid up front.

El Perú & Around

Trips to this site 62km northwest of Flores in the Parque Nacional Laguna del Tigre are termed La Ruta Guacamaya (the Scarlet Macaw Trail), because the chances of seeing these magnificent birds are high, chiefly during their February-to-June nesting season. You normally journey by road to Paso Caballos (2½ hours from Flores) then travel by boat an hour down the Río San Pedro to El Perú, making various trips out from a camp in the area including nighttime observation of El Petén's endangered endemic crocodile, *Cocodrilo moreletti*. There are several important Classic-period structures at El Perú, including the Mirador de los Monos (Monkey Lookout). Despite its proximity to Tikal, archaeologists believe El Perú may have allied with Tikal's great rival Calakmul in Mexico.

Another destination in Parque Nacional Laguna del Tigre that is sometimes combined with El Perú trips is the **Estación Biológica Las Guacamayas** (Scarlet Macaw Biological Station) on the Río San Juan. This is a scientific station surrounded by rainforest, where among other things scarlet macaws and white tortoises are observed.

A further site that may start to be combined with El Perú trips is **La Joyanca**, 20km west of El Perú, a Classic-period site where several structures have recently been restored and walking trails and information panels installed.

El Zotz

Zotz means bat in many Mayan languages, and you'll interact with plenty of them on

---

RESPONSIBLE TOURISM

Visitors to sites deep in the Petén forest need to be very conscious of their impact on the ecological balance. Observing a few basic guidelines and insisting your guides do the same will help protect this area. All nonorganic garbage should be carried out, human waste and toilet paper should be buried in a pit at least 15cm deep and 100m from a water source, and only dead wood should be used to build fires.

One issue of particular concern is the use of pack animals on these trips. Generally, a four-person expedition (two tourists, a guide and a cook) requires four mules or horses. Mules eat copious amounts of sapodilla tree leaves; nearly an entire mature tree will be stripped of its branches to feed four mules for one day. Multiply this over a three-day trip with four paying participants, and you begin to see the scope of the problem. If you can avoid using mules on your trip, do so. Otherwise, inquire about alternative food sources for the animals.

Another nagging problem is mud. There's lots of it between May and November (halfway up a mule's leg is the norm), and machete-wielding guides hacking trails around mud patches kills new forest growth. Walking around a mud patch also makes it bigger. Hiking in these muddy conditions is no treat anyway, so try to arrange your trip for the dry season.

Trekking in El Petén in a responsible way gets really tricky when tourists contract freelance guides. Whereas the Comité guides are required to do courses pertaining to responsible tourism, independent guides won't necessarily adhere to ecotouristic ideals. Indeed, they're often unaware of rudimentary concepts of low-impact travel. In this case, it is up to you, the traveler, to ensure that basic tenets of responsible tourism are respected.

a trek to this archaeological site in the Biotopo San Miguel La Palotada, 24km northeast from El Cruce de Dos Aguadas. So many bats pour from the caves near the ruins at dusk that they blacken the sky. Among the many unexcavated mounds and ruins at El Zotz is the Diablo (Devil) pyramid, which is so tall you can see clear over the canopy to the temples of Tikal. Trips to El Zotz can be extended to include a 36km backdoor trek to Tikal through dense forest.

Río Azul

These small, important ruins are just over 80km northeast of Tikal, very near the tripartite border of Guatemala, Belize and Mexico, and within the Parque Nacional Mirador–Río Azul. Scholars surmise Río Azul was a military base abandoned around AD 535. There are some 350 buildings and several temples here, but the biggest attractions are the vibrant cave paintings that adorn tombs sprinkled throughout the site. Unfortunately, widespread looting has severely compromised the integrity of Río Azul, facilitated by the airstrip that services the *campamento chiclero* (*chicle*-gatherers' camp) very close to this site. Treaties banning the trafficking in Mayan artifacts were precipitated, in part, by the volume of ceramics being flown out of Río Azul. A trip here can be combined with visits to Tikal and Uaxactún. It's accessible by vehicle.

El Mirador

This archaeological site is buried within the furthest reaches of the Petén jungle, just 7km south of the Mexican border. A visit here involves an arduous jungle trek of at least five days and four nights (it's about 60km each way), with no facilities or amenities aside from what you carry in and what can be rustled from the forest. The trip departs from a cluster of houses called Carmelita – the end of the line.

The metropolis at El Mirador, dated to 150 BC to AD 150, contains the largest cluster of buildings in any single Mayan site, among which is the biggest pyramid ever built in the Mayan world: El Tigre. This pyramid measures 18 stories high (more than 60m) and its base covers 18,000 sq meters – six times the area of Tikal's biggest structure, Templo IV. El Tigre's twin, La Danta (The Tapir), though technically smaller, soars higher because it's built on a rise. From atop La Danta, some 105m above the forest floor, virgin canopy stretches into the distance as far as your eye can see. The green bumps hovering on the horizon are other pyramids still buried under dense jungle. There are hundreds of buildings at El Mirador, but a major ongoing excavation has never been tackled, so almost everything is still hidden beneath the jungle. You'll have to use your imagination to picture this city that at its height spread over 16 sq km and supported tens of thousands of citizens.

Scholars are still figuring out why and how El Mirador thrived (there are few natural resources and no water sources save for the reservoirs built by ingenious, ancient engineers) and what led to its abandonment. It was certainly the greatest Mayan city of the Preclassic era.

Trips to El Mirador can include a couple of extra days to see Nakbé, another Preclassic site 13km southeast of El Mirador (and joined to it by an ancient causeway) and other sites. Trekking to El Mirador is not for the faint of heart. Conditions are rudimentary: There are no toilets, beds, cold beverages or bathrooms. The ants, ticks and mosquitoes never relent, the mud is knee-deep and the hiking is strenuous and dirty. That said, folks who make this journey will never forget it.

For more on this incredible site, see the September 1987 *National Geographic* article 'An Early Maya Metropolis Uncovered: El Mirador.' This is the most thorough mainstream report on the site and sheds lots of light on the mystery of this great city.

Directory

CONTENTS

ACCOMMODATIONS

Guatemalan accommodations range from luxury hotels to budget hotels to ultra-budget guesthouses called *hospedajes*, *casas de huéspedes* or *pensiones*.

This book's budget category covers places where a typical double costs US$25 or less. Doubles under US$10 are generally small, dark and not particularly clean. Nor may security be the best in such places. An exception is the low-priced dormitories that exist alongside other rooms in generally better establishments. A US$20 double should be clean, sizable and airy, with a bathroom, TV and, in hot parts of the country, a fan.

Mid-range covers establishments with doubles between US$25 and US$70. These rooms are always comfortable: private hot-water bathroom, TV, decent beds, fan and/or air-con are standard. Good mid-range hotels have attractive public areas such as dining rooms, bars and swimming pools. In hot regions, the rooms may be attractive wooden bungalows, with thatch roofs, verandas and hammocks; in cooler areas they may be in beautiful old colonial-style houses with antique furnishings and lovely patios. The smaller the establishment, the better the attention to guests is likely to be. Many B&Bs in Guatemala fit this description.

Anything more expensive than US$70 is top end. Guatemala City's international-class business-oriented hotels, Antigua's very finest hostelries, and a few resort hotels elsewhere constitute nearly the whole of the top end options.

Room rates often go up in places tourists go during Semana Santa (the week leading up to Easter Sunday), Christmas–New Year and July and August. Semana Santa is the major Guatemalan holiday week of the year, and prices can rise by anything from 30% to 100% on the coast and in the countryside – anywhere Guatemalans go to relax – as well as in international-tourism destinations such as Antigua. At this time advance reservations are a very good idea. We indicate throughout this book where and when you should expect seasonal price hikes.

Be aware that room rates are subject to two large taxes – 12% IVA (value-added tax) and 10% to pay for the activities of the Guatemalan Tourism Institute (Inguat). All prices in this book include both taxes, though some of the more expensive hotels forget to include them when they quote their prices.

Camping

In Guatemala, camping can be a hit-or-miss affair, as there are few designated campgrounds and safety is rarely guaranteed. Where campsites are available, expect to pay from US$3 to US$5 per night.

Homestays

Travelers attending Spanish school have the option of living with a Guatemalan family. This is usually a pretty good bargain – expect to pay between US$35 and US$60 a week for your own room, shared bathrooms, and three meals a day except Sunday. It's important to find a homestay that gels with your goals. For example, some families host several students at a time, creating more of an international hostel atmosphere than a family environment.

ACTIVITIES
Climbing, Trekking & Hiking

The many volcanoes are irresistible challenges, and many of them can be done in one day from Antigua (p85) or Quetzaltenango (p143). There's further great hill country in the Ixil Triangle and the Cuchumatanes mountains to the north of Huehuetenango, especially around Todos Santos Cuchumatán (161). The Lago de Atitlán (p103) is surrounded by spectacular trails though robberies here have made some routes inadvisable. Treks of several days are perfectly feasible, and agencies in Antigua, Quetzaltenango and Nebaj (p137) can guide you. In the Petén jungles, treks to remote archaeological sites such as El Mirador and El Perú (p271) offer an exciting challenge.

Cycling

There's probably no better way to experience the Guatemalan highlands than by bicycle. Panajachel (p107), Quetzaltenango (p151) and Antigua in particular (p86) are the best launch points, with agencies offering trips and equipment.

Horse Riding

Opportunities for a gallop, a trot or even a horse trek are on the increase in Guatemala. There are stables in Antigua (p85), Santiago Atitlán (p120), Quetzaltenango (p143), El Remate, Salamá (p185) and Río to the Dulce (p224). Unicornio Azul (p161), north of Huehuetenango, offers treks of up to nine days in the Cuchumatanes.

Spelunking

Guatemala attracts cavers from the world over. The limestone area around Cobán is particularly riddled with cave systems whose full extents are unknown. The caves of Lanquín (p196), B'omb'il Pek, Candelaria (p198) and Rey Marcos (p191) are all open for tourist visits. There are also exciting caves to visit from Finca Ixobel (p240), near Poptún.

Water Sports

You can dive inside a volcanic caldera at Lago de Atitlán (p103), raft the white waters of the Río Cahabón (p197) near Lanquín, sail from the yachtie haven of Río Dulce (p222), and canoe or kayak the waterways of Monterrico (p177), Lívingston (p234), the Bocas del Polochic (p227) or Punta de Manabique (p231).

Wildlife Viewing & Bird-Watching

National parks and reserves generally have few tourist facilities, but they do have lots of wildlife and bird-watching. Fine locales in the Petén jungles for bird-watching include Tikal (p257), El Mirador (p253), Cerro Cahuí (p255), Laguna Petexbatún (p270) and (for scarlet macaws) Las Guacamayas biological station (pp271-2). Elsewhere, the wetlands of Bocas del Polochic, Punta de Manabique (p231) and Monterrico (p177), the Río Dulce (p224) and Laguna Lachuá (p199) national parks and the Biotopo del Quetzal (p188) also provide lots of avian variety. Mammals are more elusive but you should see several species at Tikal. Monkey fans will also be happy at the Reserva Natural Atitlán (p107), the Bocas del Polochic and Cerro Cahuí.

BUSINESS HOURS

Guatemalan shops and businesses are generally open from 8am to noon and 2pm to 6pm, Monday to Saturday, but there are many variations. Banks typically open 9am to 5pm Monday to Friday (again with variations), and 9am to 1pm Saturday. Government offices usually open 8am to 4pm, Monday to Friday. Official business is always better conducted in the morning.

Restaurant hours are typically 7am to 9pm, but can vary by up to two hours either way. Most bars open from 10am or 11am to 10pm or 11pm. If restaurants or bars have a closing day, it's usually Sunday. Typical shopping hours are 8am to noon and 2pm to 6pm, Monday to Saturday.

CHILDREN

Young children are highly regarded in Guatemala and can often break down barriers and open the doors to local hospitality. However, Guatemala is so culturally dense, with such an emphasis on history and archaeology, that children can get easily bored. Parents need to make a point of visiting some of the more kid-friendly sites like Guatemala City's Museo de los Niños (p64) and La Aurora Zoo (p64), Auto Safari Chapín (p176) south of the capital, and Retalhuleu's Xocomil water park (p171) and Xetulul theme park (p171). Most Spanish courses are open to kids, too. Many older kids will enjoy activities such as kayaking and horseback riding.

Facilities such as safety seats in hired cars and high chairs in restaurants are rare. If you need supplies such as diapers (nappies) and creams, bring what you can with you and stock up in Guatemala City or, failing that, Antigua or Quetzaltenango. Fresh milk is rare and may not be pasteurized. Packet UHT milk and, even more so, milk powder

to which you must add purified water are much more common. If your child has to have some particular tinned or packaged food, bring supplies with you. Public breast-feeding is not common and, when done, is done discreetly.

For a wealth of good ideas, get hold of Lonely Planet's *Travel with Children*.

CLIMATE CHARTS

For climatic considerations concerning your trip, see When to Go (p9).

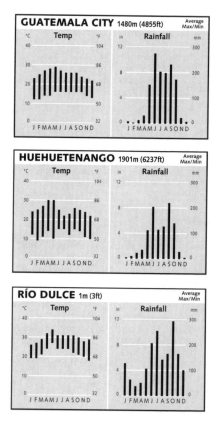

CUSTOMS

Customs officers only get angry and excited about a few things: weapons, drugs and paraphernalia, large amounts of currency, and automobiles and other expensive items that might be sold while you're in the country. It is also illegal to bring fruit, vegetables or plants through the international airports at Guatemala City and Flores.

Normally customs officers won't look seriously in your luggage and may not look at all. At some border points the amount of search is inversely proportional to the amount of 'tip' you have provided: big tip no search, no tip big search.

Whatever you do, keep it formal. Anger, hostility or impoliteness can get you thrown out of the country or into jail, or worse.

DANGERS & ANNOYANCES

No one could pretend that Guatemala is a very safe country. There are just too many stories of robbery, often armed robbery, for that. Rapes and murders of tourists have also happened. The two most frequently reported types of nasty incident involving tourists are highway robbery, when a vehicle is stopped and its occupants relieved of their belongings, and robberies on walking trails. For a scary litany of recent incidents, visit the website of Guatemala City's **US embassy** (usembassy.state.gov/guatemala) and click on 'Recent Crime Incidents Involving Foreigners.' Further, marginally less alarming, information is on the website of the **US Department of State** (travel.state.gov/travel_warnings.html) and the website of the **UK Foreign and Commonwealth Office** (www.fco.gov.uk).

Vehicles carrying tourists, such as shuttle minibuses and buses, along heavily touristed routes seem to be a prime target for highway robbery. On this basis, some people argue that chicken buses are the most risk-free way to travel, but chicken buses are certainly not exempt from hold-ups. No road in the country is exempt from this risk, but those that are most frequently mentioned include the Interamericana (Highway CA-1) between the Antigua and Panajachel turnoffs and near the Salvadoran border, Highway CA-2 near the Salvadoran and Mexican borders, and Highway CA-13 between the Belizean border and the Puente Ixlú (El Cruce) junction.

Robberies against tourists on walking trails tend to occur in isolated spots on well-known walks. Some trails around the Lago de Atitlán (p103) and near Lívingston (p233) and on Volcán Agua outside Antigua are particularly notorious. The Tikal archaeological site, Volcán Pacaya and Cerro de la Cruz (Antigua), all the scenes of several incidents not so long ago, have become, for now, safer because of increased police and ranger presence designed to protect tourism.

Other potential dangers are pickpocketing, bag-snatching, bag-slitting and the like in crowded bus stations, buses, streets and markets, but also in empty, dark city streets.

It is impossible to remove the element of risk from traveling in Guatemala, but it is possible to reduce that risk by always staying alert to the behavior of other people around you (watch out for people who get unwarrantedly close to you in any situation) and by following a few simple precautions:

- Only carry on your person the money, cards, checks and valuables that you have immediate need of. Leave the rest in a sealed, signed envelope in your hotel's safe, and obtain a receipt for the envelope. If your hotel doesn't have a safe, it is usually safer to secrete your money and valuables in three or four different stashes among your locked luggage in your room than to carry them with you.
- Be aware that any purse or bag in plain sight may be slashed or grabbed. At ticket counters in bus stations, keep your bag between your feet.
- Don't flaunt jewelry, cameras or valuable-looking watches. Keep your wallet or purse out of view.
- On buses keep your important valuables with you, and keep a close hold on them.
- Don't wander alone in empty city streets or isolated areas, particularly at night.
- When using ATMs (cash machines), keep alert to people nearby. Don't accept help from strangers when using ATMs.
- Keep informed by talking to travelers, hotel staff and others, and consulting official information sources such as the US and UK government websites mentioned on this page, your country's embassy in Guatemala City, and Inguat (see Tourist Information, p284).
- Hiking in large groups and/or with a police escort reduces the risk of robbery.
- Resisting or trying to flee from robbers usually makes the situation worse.

Hiking on active volcanoes obviously has an element of risk. Get the latest story before you head out. In the wet season, go up volcanoes in the morning before rain and possible thunderstorms set in. A Canadian tourist was killed by lightning on Pacaya volcano in 2002.

There have been a few bizarre incidents in which foreign visitors have been unjustly suspected of malicious designs against Guatemalan children; see p33. Be careful not to put yourself in any situation that might be misinterpreted.

Any crowd can be volatile, especially when drunk or at times of political tension.

Reporting a Robbery or Theft

After a theft you may need a statement from the police for your insurance company. Tell them: '*Yo quisiera poner una acta de un robo*' ('I'd like to report a robbery'). This should make it clear that you merely want a piece of paper and aren't going to ask the police to do anything active.

Scams

One common scenario is for someone to spray ketchup or some other sticky liquid on your clothes. An accomplice then appears to help you clean up the mess and robs you in the process. Other methods of distraction, such as dropping a purse or coins, or someone appearing to faint, are also used by pickpockets and bag snatchers.

DISABLED TRAVELERS

Guatemala is not the easiest country to negotiate with a disability.

Although many sidewalks in Antigua have ramps and cute little inlaid tiles depicting a wheelchair, the streets are cobblestone, so the ramps are anything but smooth and the streets are worse!

Many hotels in Guatemala are old converted houses with rooms around a courtyard; such rooms are wheelchair accessible. The most expensive hotels have facilities such as ramps, elevators and accessible toilets. Transportation is the biggest hurdle for travelers with limited mobility: travelers in a wheelchair may consider renting a car and driver as the buses will prove especially challenging due to lack of space.

Mobility International USA (www.miusa.org) advises disabled travelers on mobility issues, runs exchange programs (including in Guatemala) and publishes some useful

books. Also worth consulting are **Access-Able Travel Source** (www.access-able.com) and **Accessible Journeys** (www.disabilitytravel.com).

Transitions (☎ 832-4261; transitions@guate.net; Colonia Candelaría 80, Antigua) is an organization aiming to increase awareness and access for disabled persons in Guatemala.

EMBASSIES & CONSULATES
Guatemalan Embassies & Consulates

You'll find a full listing of Guatemala's embassies and consulates at www.minex.gob.gt /sistemaprotocolo/protocolos/cmisiones.asp. The following listings are for embassies unless noted:

Australia Contact the Guatemalan embassy in Tokyo.
Belize Belize City (☎ 2-33314, 2-33150; embbelice1@ minex.gob.gt; 8 A Street, PO Box 1771); consulate in Benque Viejo del Carmen (☎ 9-32531; fax 9-32532; No 4 Calle Church)
Canada Ottawa (☎ 613-233-7237; embassy1@ embaguate.canada.com; 130 Albert St, Suite 1010, Ontario K1P 5G4); consulate in Vancouver.
El Salvador San Salvador (☎ 271-2225; embelsalvador@ minex.gob.gt; 15 Av Norte 135)
France Paris (☎ 01-42-27-78-63; embfrancia@minex .gob.gt; 73 rue de Courcelles, 75008)
Germany Berlin (☎ 030-206-43-63; embalemania@ minex.gob.gt; Joachim-Karnatz-Allee 45-47 Ecke Paulstrasse, 10557 Berlin Tiergarten)
Honduras Tegucigalpa (fax 232-1580; embhonduras@ minex.gob.gt; Calle Arturo López Rodezno 2421, Colonia Las Minitas); consulate in San Pedro Sula (☎ 556-9550; fax 556-9551; 12 Calle & 24 Av, SO Colonia Trejo, a la par de telered 21)
Ireland Contact the Guatemalan embassy in London.
Japan Tokyo (☎ 3-3800-1830; fax 3-3400-1820; 38 Kowa Bldg, Room 905, 4-12-24 Nishi-Azabu, 106-0031)
Mexico Mexico City (☎ 55-5540-7520; embmexico@ minex.gob.gt; Av Explanada 1025, Lomas de Chapultepec, 11000); consulate in Chetumal (☎ 983-832-30-45; Av Independencia 326); consulate in Ciudad Hidalgo, Chiapas (☎ 962-628-02-84; 5a Calle Oriente s/n entre 1a & 3a Norte); consulate in Comitán, Chiapas (☎ 963-632-04-91; fax 963-22669; 1a Calle Sur Poniente 26); consulate in Tapachula, Chiapas (☎ 962-625-63-80; 3a Av Norte 85); also consulates in Puebla and Tijuana.
Netherlands The Hague (☎ 070-302-0253; embpaises bajos@minex.gob.gt; Java Straat 44, 2585AP)
New Zealand Contact the Guatemalan embassy in Tokyo.
Spain Madrid (☎ 91-344-1417;embespaña@minex.gob.gt; Calle Rafael Salgado 3, 100 derecha, 28036)
UK London (☎ 020-7351-3042; www.embaguatelondon .btinternet.co.uk; 13 Fawcett St, SW10 9HN)
USA Washington DC (☎ 202-745-4952/53/54; www.gua

temala-embassy.org; 2220 R St NW, 20008); consulates in Los Angeles (www.guatemala-consulate.org), San Francisco (www.sfconsulguate.org), Chicago, Houston, Miami, New York.

Embassies & Consulates in Guatemala

All the following are embassies in Guatemala City unless otherwise noted:

Belize (☎ 334-5531; embelguate@guate.net; Av La Reforma 1-50, Zona 9, Edificio El Reformador, Office 803)

Canada (☎ 333-4348; www.dfait-maeci.gc.ca/guatemala; 8th fl, Edificio Edyma Plaza, 13a Calle 8-44, Zona 10)

El Salvador (☎ 360-7660; emsalva@pronet.net.gt; 5a Av 8-15, Zona 9)

France (☎ 337-3639; ambfrguate@intelnet.net.gt; 11th fl, Edificio Marbella, 16a Calle 4-53, Zona 10)

Germany (☎ 364-6700; embalemana@intelnet.net.gt; Edificio Plaza Marítima, 20a Calle 6-20, Zona 10)

Honduras (☎ 366-5640; embhond@intelnet.net.gt; 19a Av A 20-19, Zona 10); consulate in Esquipulas (☎ 943-2027; fax 943-1371; Hotel Payaquí)

Mexico (☎ 333-7254; 7th fl, Edificio Centro Ejecutivo, 15a Calle 3-20, Zona 10); consulate in Guatemala City (☎ 339-1007/08/09; consulmex@guate.net; Oficina J-300, Edificio Plaza Corporativa Reforma Torre Jardín, Av La Reforma 6-64, Zona 9); consulate in Huehuetenango (5a Av 4-11, Zona 1); consulate in Quetzaltenango (21a Av 8-64, Zona 3)

Netherlands (☎ 367-4761; nigovgua@intelnet.net.gt; 13th fl, Torre Internacional, 16a Calle 0-55, Zona 10)

New Zealand Honorary Consulate (☎ 593-2405; 13a Calle 7-85, Zona 10)

Spain (☎ 379 -3530; embespgt@correo.mae.es; 6a Calle 6-48, Zona 9)

UK (☎ 367-5425/6/7/8/9; embassy@intelnett.com; 11th fl, Torre Internacional, 16a Calle 00-55, Zona 10)

USA (☎ 331-1541 to 331-1555; usembassy.state.gov /guatemala; Av La Reforma 7-01, Zona 10)

FESTIVALS & EVENTS

The following events are of national significance in Guatemala:

JANUARY

El Cristo de Esquipulas On January 15 this super-devout festival in Esquipulas brings pilgrims from all over Central America to catch a glimpse of the Black Jesus housed in the Basilica.

MARCH/APRIL

Semana Santa Easter week – the week leading up to Easter Sunday – sees statues of Jesus and Mary carried around the streets of towns all round the country, followed by devout, sometimes fervent crowds, to mark Christ's crucifixion. The processions walk over and destroy *alfombras*,

elaborate carpets of colored sawdust and flower petals. The week peaks on Good Friday.

AUGUST

Fiesta de la Virgen de la Asunción Peaking on August 15, this is celebrated with folk dances and parades in Tactic, Sololá, Guatemala City and Jocotenango.

NOVEMBER

Día de Todos los Santos All Saints' Day, November 1, sees giant kite festivals in Santiago Sacatepéquez and Sumpango, near Antigua, and the renowned drunken horse races in Todos Santos Cuchumatán.

DECEMBER

Quema del Diablo On December 7 the Burning of the Devil starts at around 6pm throughout the country when everyone takes to the streets with their old garbage, physical and psychic, to stoke huge bonfires of trash. This is followed by impressive fireworks displays.

FOOD

See the Food & Drink chapter (p48) for the lowdown on what you can eat where and when and what it will cost. Where we have divided city eating sections into different price ranges, you can expect a main dish to cost under US$5 in a budget eatery, US$5 to US$9 in the mid-range and more than US$9 in the top end.

GAY & LESBIAN TRAVELERS

Few places in Latin America are outwardly gay-friendly, and Guatemala is no different. Technically, homosexuality is legal for persons 18 years and older, but the reality can be another story, with harassment and violence against gays too often poisoning the plot. Don't even consider testing the tolerance for homosexual public displays of affection here.

Though Antigua has a palatable – if subdued – scene, affection and action are still kept behind closed doors; the chief exception is the gay-friendly club La Casbah (p95). In Guatemala City, Pandora's Box and Ephebus are the current faves. In large part though, gays traveling in Guatemala will find themselves keeping it low key and pushing the twin beds together.

The websites of the **Gully** (www.thegully.com) and **Gay.com** (www.gay.com) have some articles and information relevant to Guatemala. The best site, **Gay Guatemala** (www.gayguatemala.com), is in Spanish.

HOLIDAYS

The main Guatemalan holiday periods are Semana Santa, Christmas–New Year and July and August. During Semana Santa room prices rise in many places and it's advisable to book all accommodation and transport in advance.

Guatemalan public holidays include:

New Year's Day January 1
Easter (Holy Thursday to Easter Sunday inclusive) March/April
Labor Day May 1
Army Day June 30
Assumption Day (Dia de la Asunción) August 15
Independence Day September 15
Revolution Day October 20
All Saints' Day November 1
Christmas Eve afternoon December 24
Christmas Day December 25
New Year's Eve afternoon December 31

INSURANCE

Signing up for a travel insurance policy to cover theft, loss and medical problems is a good idea. Some policies specifically exclude dangerous activities, which can include scuba diving, motorcycling, even trekking.

You may prefer a policy that pays doctors or hospitals directly, rather than you having to pay on the spot and claim later. If you have to claim later ensure you keep all documentation.

Check that the policy covers ambulances or an emergency flight home.

For more information on insurance, see p292 and p288.

INTERNET ACCESS

Most travelers make constant use of internet cafes and free web-based email such as **Yahoo** (www.yahoo.com) or **Hotmail** (www.hotmail.com). Another option for collecting mail through cybercafés is to open a free ekno web-based email account online at www.ekno.lonely planet.com. Most medium-size towns have cybercafés with fairly reliable connections. Internet cafés typically charge between US$1 and US$1.50 an hour.

To access a specific account of your own, you'll need to know your incoming (POP or IMAP) mail server name, your account name and your password. Get these from your Internet service provider (ISP) or network supervisor.

If you're traveling with a notebook or handheld computer, first be aware that your modem may not work once you leave your home country. The safest option is to buy a reputable 'global' modem before you leave home, or buy a local PC-card modem if you're spending an extended time in any one country. A second issue is the plug: Guatemala uses 110V, two-pronged, flat plugs like those found in the US. A third issue is that unless you're sporting a completely wireless system, you'll have to hunt down a hotel room with a phone jack to plug into – or find a jack you can use somewhere else.

If you really want to travel with a laptop, consider using a local ISP, unless you use an international server with access numbers in Guatemala such as AOL or Compu-Serve. A good bet for a Guatemalan ISP is Conexion in Antigua (p78), which charges US$7.75/18/36/62 for five/24/72/unlimited hours online a month, plus a US$3.25 set-up fee.

For more information on traveling with a portable computer, see www.teleadapt.com or www.warrior.com/default.asp?hp=1. See p10 for a few Guatemala-related websites to start on.

LANGUAGE COURSES

Guatemala is celebrated for its many language schools. A spot of study here is a great way not only to learn Spanish but also to meet locals and get an inside angle on the culture. Many travelers heading down through Central America to South America make Guatemala an early stop so that they can pick up the Spanish skills they need for their trip.

Guatemalan language schools are a lot cheaper than those in Mexico, but few people go away disappointed. There are so many schools to choose from that it's essential to check out a few before choosing. It's not hard to see whether a school is professional and well organized, or whether its teachers are qualified and experienced.

Antigua is the most popular place to study, with about 75 schools (p86). Quet-zaltenango (p143), the second most popular, perhaps attracts a more serious type of student; Antigua has a livelier students' and travelers' social scene. San Pedro La Laguna (p122) and Panajachel (p108) on the Lago de Atitlán both have a handful of language schools, and if you'd like to learn Spanish while hanging out in a remote mountain town, there are schools in Todos Santos Cuchumatán (p162) and Nebaj (p138). On average, schools charge US$110 to US$120 for four hours of one-on-one classes five days a week and accommodation with a local family.

You can start any day at many schools, any week at all of them, and study for as long as you like. All decent schools offer a variety of elective activities from salsa classes to movies to volcano hikes. Many schools offer classes in Mayan languages as well as Spanish. See p86 for more tips on language schools.

LEGAL MATTERS

Police officers in Guatemala are sometimes part of the problem rather than the solution. The less you have to do with the law, the better.

Whatever you do, don't get involved in any way with illegal drugs: don't buy or sell, use or carry, or associate with people who do – even if the locals seem to do so freely. As a foreigner, you are at a distinct disadvantage, and you may be set up by others. Drug laws in Guatemala are strict, and though enforcement may be uneven, penalties are severe. If you do get caught buying, selling, holding or using drugs, your best first defense might be to suggest that you and the officer 'work things out.'

MAPS

International Travel Maps' *Guatemala* (1: 500,000) is overall the best country map for travelers, costing around US$10 in Guatemala. The cheaper *Mapa Turístico Guatemala*, produced locally by Intelimapas, tends to be the most up to date on the state of Guatemala's roads, many of which have been newly paved in recent years. It also includes plans of many cities. Inguat's *Mapa Vial Turístico* is another worthwhile map. Bookstores that sell these maps can be found in Guatemala City (p61), Antigua (p77), Panajachel (p106) and Quetzaltenango (p140). For 1:50,000 and 1:250,000 topographical sheets of all parts of Guatemala, head to the Instituto Geográfico Nacional (p57).

MONEY

Guatemala's currency, the quetzal (ket-*sahl*, abbreviated to Q), has been fairly stable at about Q8 = US$1 for several years. The quetzal is divided into 100 centavos. For exchange rates, see inside the front cover; for information on costs in Guatemala; see p9.

You'll find ATMs (cash machines, *cajeros automáticos*) for Visa/Plus System cards in all but the smallest towns, and there are MasterCard/Cirrus ATMs in many places too, so one of these cards is the best basis for your supplies of cash in Guatemala. In addition, many banks give cash advances on Visa cards, and some on MasterCard. And you can pay for many purchases with these cards or with American Express (Amex) cards.

If you don't have one of these cards, a combination of Amex US-dollar traveler's checks and a limited amount of cash US dollars is the way to go. Take some of these as a backup even if you do have a card. Banks all over the country change cash US dollars, and many of them also change US-dollar traveler's checks too. Amex is easily the most recognized traveler's check brand.

In many places you can make payments with cash dollars, and a few places will accept traveler's checks. Currencies other than the US dollar are virtually useless in any form, although a small handful of places will now change cash euros.

Banks generally give the best exchange rates on both cash and traveler's checks. If you can't find an open bank you can often change cash (and occasionally checks) in travel agencies, hotels or shops.

Some towns suffer from change shortages: always try to carry a stash of small bills.

See Dangers & Annoyances (p277) for security tips about your money.

Tipping

A 10% tip is expected at restaurants. In small *comedors* (basic, cheap eateries) tipping is optional, but follow the local practise of leaving some spare change. Tour guides are generally tipped, around 10%, especially on longer trips.

PHOTOGRAPHY & VIDEO

Ubiquitous film stores and pharmacies sell film, though you may not find the brand you like without a hunt. A 36-exposure, 100-ASA print film normally costs around US$4. There are quick processing labs in the main cities.

Photographing People

Photography is a sensitive subject in Guatemala. Always ask permission before taking portraits, especially of Mayan women and children. Don't be surprised if your request is denied. Indigenous children often request payment (usually Q1) in return for posing. In certain places, such as the church of Santo Tomás in Chichicastenango, photography is forbidden. Mayan ceremonies (should you be so lucky to witness one) are off limits for photography unless you are given explicit permission to take pictures. If local people make any sign of being offended, you should put your camera away and apologize immediately, both out of decency and for your own safety. Never take photos of army installations, men with guns or other sensitive military subjects.

POST

The Guatemalan postal service was privatized in 1999. Generally, letters take eight to 10 days to travel to the US and Canada and 10 to 12 days to reach Europe. Almost all cities and towns (but not villages) have a post office where you can buy stamps and send mail. A letter sent to North America costs around US$0.40 and to anywhere else around US$0.50.

The Guatemalan mail system no longer holds poste restante or general delivery mail. The easiest and most reliable way to receive mail is through a private address. Amex offices will hold mail for card members and people using their traveler's checks. It is important to address mail clearly: the last lines should read 'Guatemala, Centro América.'

SHOPPING
Textiles

Guatemala's intricate and brilliantly colored textiles are world-famous. Weaving is a traditional and thriving art of the Mayan people here. Clothing – especially the beautiful embroidered *huipiles* (tunics), *cortes* (skirts) and *fajas* (belts) of the Mayan women – as well as purses, tablecloths, blankets, hackysacks and many other woven items are ubiquitous and good value, some for practical use, some more for souvenirs.

The largest crafts markets are the Thursday and Sunday markets in Chichicastenango, the permanent stalls lining Calle Santander in Panajachel, Mercado Central and Mercado de Artesanías in Guatemala City, and the Mercado de Artesanías in Antigua. Fine textiles of an infinite variety are also available in Antigua's shops. Elsewhere, in places such as Nebaj, Sololá, Santa Catarina Palopó, Santiago Atitlán and Todos Santos Cuchumatán, you can obtain local textiles at weekly markets or a few permanent stalls.

Leather Goods

Guatemala has some terrific leather goods. Fine briefcases, duffel bags, backpacks and belts are sold in most handicrafts markets. Cowboy boots and hats are a specialty in some areas, and custom work is welcome. The prices and craftsmanship of these items are usually phenomenal.

Wooden Masks

Ceremonial masks are fascinating, eye-catching and still in regular use. In Chichicastenango you can visit the artists in their *morerías* (workshops).

Coffee

Although most of Guatemala's finest beans are exported, some are (thankfully) held back for the tourist trade. To ensure you're getting the finest, freshest coffee beans available, visit a coffee farm and/or roaster and buy from them directly. Cobán and Antigua produce some of the world's greatest coffee and both towns support growers and roasters.

Jade

Beloved of the ancient Maya, jade is mined in Guatemala today and you'll find it both as jewelry and as miniature sculpture. For more on jade, see p95.

Bargaining

Be aware that bargaining is essential in some situations and not done in others. It's standard practise when buying handicrafts: the first price you're told may be double or triple what the seller really expects. Remember that bargaining is not a fight to the death. The object is to arrive at a price agreeable to both you and the seller, thereby creating a win-win situation.

Shipping

It's best to use an international shipping service if you want to ensure the relatively safe, timely arrival of your goods. You'll find information on such courier services in this book's city sections, under Post. A 1kg package sent from Antigua to California by UPS, for example, will cost you from US$16.80 for a two-week service (using terrestrial transport once inside the USA) up to US$48.90 for express (two-day) service.

SOLO TRAVELERS

On your own, you need to be even more alert to what's going on around you than other travelers, and you need to be more cautious about where you go.

Guatemala is a pretty good place for meeting people, both locals and other travelers. Language schools, group tours, volunteer work, dormitory accommodations and sociable lodgings where everyone eats together are just a few of the situations where travelers are thrown together with other people.

Since single rooms cost more per person than doubles and triples, solo travelers face higher accommodation costs than others unless they sleep in dormitories (available in a number of places) or find others to share with.

TELEPHONE & FAX

Guatemala has no area or city codes. Calling from other countries, you just dial the international access code (☎ 00 in most countries), then the Guatemala country code (☎ 502), then the seven-digit local number. Calling within Guatemala, just dial the seven-digit local number. The international access code from Guatemala is ☎ 00.

Many towns and cities frequented by tourists have privately run call offices where you can make local and international calls for reasonable rates. If the telephone connection is by Internet, the rates can be very cheap (eg US$0.15 a minute to the USA, US$0.30 to Europe), but line quality is unpredictable. Calling from a hotel is the most expensive way of telephoning, but you *can*

just make a quick call to get your party to call you back there.

A number of companies provide public-phone services. The most common street phones, found all over Guatemala, are those of Telgua, for which you need to buy a Telgua phone card *(tarjeta telefónica de Telgua)* from shops, kiosks and the like. Card sales points may advertise the fact with red signs saying *'Ladatel de Venta Aquí.'* The cards come in denominations of Q20, Q30 and Q50: you slot them into a Telgua phone, dial your number, and the display will tell you how much time you have left. The second most common street phones are those of Telefónica, which require a Telefónica card, also sold by shops and kiosks. Telefónica cards are not meant to be inserted into the phone, but simply bear codes to be keyed in and instructions to be followed. In our experience Telgua is cheaper than Telefónica for local calls (about US$0.01 per minute against US$0.05) and for calls to Europe (about US$1 a minute against US$1.60), but Telefónica is cheaper for calls to the USA (about US$0.20 a minute against US$0.50 with Telgua).

Unless it's an emergency, don't use the black phones placed strategically in tourist towns that say 'Press 2 to call the United States free!' This is a bait and switch scam; you put the call on your credit card and return home to find you have paid between US$8 and US$20 per minute.

Telgua street phones bear instructions to dial ☎ 147110 for domestic collect calls and ☎ 147120 for international collect calls. The latter number is usually successful for the USA and Canada, less so for the rest of the world. International collect calls using País Directo (Home Country Direct) services and North American calling cards are usually impossible from street phones but can usually be made from hotel or private phones. País Directo numbers include the following:

USA (MCI)	☎ 9999189
USA (AT&T)	☎ 9999190
USA (Sprint)	☎ 9999195
Canada	☎ 9999198
UK	☎ 9999044

Cell phones are widely used in Guatemala. If you want to rent one during your stay, try

Guatemala Ventures (☎ /fax 832-3383; 1a Av Sur 15) in Antigua (pp80-1) or **Digital Mundo Celular** (☎ 614-2731; 13a Calle 8-16, Zona 1, Guatemala City) in Guatemala City (pp58-9). Public fax services are available in most sizable towns: look for 'Fax' signs outside shops and offices.

TIME
North American Central Standard Time (GMT/UTC minus six hours) is the basis of time in Guatemala. Daylight saving time is *not* used in Guatemala. The 24-hour clock is often used, so 1pm may be written as 13 or 1300. When it's noon in Guatemala, it's 1pm in New York, 6pm in London, 10am in San Francisco and 4am next day in Sydney (add one hour to those times during daylight saving).

TOILETS
You cannot throw anything into Guatemalan toilets, including toilet paper. For this reason, bathrooms are equipped with some sort of receptacle (usually a small wastebasket) for soiled paper. Toilet paper is not always provided, so always carry some.

Public toilets are few and far between. Use the ones at cafés, restaurants, your hotel and the archaeological sites. At bus stations, you can pay US$0.15 to use the toilets in bus company offices. Buses rarely have toilets on board.

TOURIST INFORMATION
Guatemala's national tourism institute, **Inguat** (www.mayaspirit.com.gt), has information offices in Guatemala City, Antigua, Panajachel, Quetzaltenango and Flores; a few other towns have departmental, municipal or private-enterprise tourist information offices. See city sections for details. Inguat operates a free 24-hour tourist information and assistance line, ☎ 1-801-464-8281.

The Guatemalan embassies in the US, Germany, France, Italy, Spain and the UK can provide some tourist information. From the US you can call Inguat toll-free at ☎ 800-464-8281.

VISAS
Citizens of the US, Canada, EU countries, Norway, Switzerland, Australia, New Zealand, Israel and Japan are among those who do not need visas for tourist visits to Guatemala. On entry into Guatemala you will normally be given a 90-day stay. (The number 90 will be written in the stamp in your passport.) This can normally be extended for a further 90 days at the **Departamento de Extranjería** (Foreigners' Office; ☎ 361-8476/9, 331-1333; 7a Av 1-17, Zona 4, Guatemala City; ☺ 8am-2:30pm Mon-Fri), on the second floor of the Inguat headquarters (pp58-9). For an extension take with you *one* of the following:

- a credit card with a photocopy of both of its sides
- an airline ticket out of Guatemala with a photocopy
- US$500 worth of traveler's checks

The extension will normally be issued in the afternoon of the working day after the day you apply.

Citizens of Iceland, South Africa and Eastern European countries are among those who do need visas to visit Guatemala. Inquire at a Guatemalan embassy well in advance of travel.

Visa regulations are subject to change and it's always worth checking them with a Guatemalan embassy before you go.

If you have been in Guatemala for your original 90 days and a 90-day extension, you must leave the country for 72 hours, after which you can return to Guatemala to start the process all over again. Some foreigners have been repeating this cycle for years.

WOMEN TRAVELERS
Women should encounter no special problems traveling in Guatemala. In fact, solo women will be pleasantly surprised by how gracious and helpful most locals are. The primary thing you can do to make it easy for yourself while traveling here is to dress modestly. Modesty in dress is highly regarded, and if you practice it, you will usually be treated with respect.

Specifically, shorts should be worn only at the beach, not in town, and especially not in the Highlands. Skirts should be at or below the knee. Wear a bra, as going braless is considered provocative. Many local women swim with T-shirts over their swimsuits; in places where they do this, you may want to follow suit to avoid stares.

Women traveling alone can expect plenty of attempts by men to talk to them. Often they are just curious and not out for a foreign conquest. It's up to you how to respond, but there's no need to be intimidated. Consider the situation and circumstances (on a bus is one thing, on a barstool another) and stay confident. Try to sit next to women or children on the bus if that makes you more comfortable. Local women rarely initiate conversations, but usually have lots of interesting things to say once the ball is rolling.

Nasty rumors about Western women kidnapping Guatemalan children for a variety of sordid ends have all but died down. Still, women travelers should be cautious around children, especially indigenous kids, lest misunderstandings occur.

While there's no need to be paranoid, the possibility of rape and assault does exist. Use your normal traveler's caution – avoid walking alone in isolated places or through city streets late at night, and skip hitchhiking.

WORK

Some travelers find work in bars, restaurants and places to stay in Antigua, Panajachel or Quetzaltenango, but the wages are just survival pay.

Voluntary Work

If you really want to get to the heart of Guatemalan matters and you've altruistic leanings, consider volunteer work. Volunteering is rewarding and exposes foreigners to the rich and varied local culture typically out of reach for the average traveler. Opportunities abound, from caring for abandoned animals and kids to tending fields. Travelers with specific skills such as nurses, doctors or teachers are particularly encouraged to investigate volunteering in Guatemala.

Most volunteer posts require basic or better Spanish skills and a minimum time commitment. Depending on the position and the organization, you may have to pay for room and board for the duration of your stay. Before making a commitment, you may want to talk to past volunteers and read the fine print associated with the position.

Four excellent sources of information on volunteer opportunities are Proyecto Mosaico Guatemala and AmeriSpan Guatemala, both in Antigua (p79), and EntreMundos and Guatemaya Intercultural, both based in Quetzaltenango (p144). You only have to visit the websites of Entremundos or Proyecto Mosaico to realize what a huge range of volunteer action is happening in Guatemala. Many language schools have close links to volunteer projects and can introduce you to the world of volunteering. Well-established volunteer organizations include Quetzaltrekkers, Tortugario Monterrico and Reserva Natural Hawaii, Casa Guatemala, Arcas and Estación Biológica Las Guacamayas.

Transport

To enter Guatemala, you need a valid passport. For information on visas, see p284.

THINGS CHANGE...

The information in this chapter is particularly vulnerable to change. Check directly with the airline or a travel agent to make sure you understand how a fare (and ticket you may buy) works and be aware of the security requirements for international travel. Shop carefully. The details given in this chapter should be regarded as pointers and are not a substitute for your own careful, up-to-date research.

GETTING THERE & AWAY

ENTERING THE COUNTRY

When you enter Guatemala, by land, air, sea or river, you should simply have to fill out straightforward immigration and customs forms. In the normal course of things you should not have to pay a cent.

However, immigration officials sometimes request unofficial fees from travelers. To determine whether these are legitimate, you can ask for *un recibo* (a receipt). You may find that the fee is dropped. When in doubt, try to observe what, if anything, other travelers are paying before it's your turn.

AIR
Airports & Airlines

Guatemala City's Aeropuerto La Aurora (GUA) is the country's major international airport. The only other airport with international flights (from Cancún, Mexico, and Belize City) is Flores (FRS). The Guatemalan national airline, Aviateca, is part of the regional Grupo TACA, along with El Salvador's TACA, Costa Rica's Lacsa and Nicaragua's Nica. The US Federal Aviation Administration has assessed Guatemala's and El Salvador's civil aviation authorities as Category 2, which means they are not in compliance with international aviation safety standards.

Airlines flying to and from Guatemala:
American Airlines (☎ 337-1177; www.aa.com; airline code AA; hub Dallas & Miami)
Aviateca see Grupo TACA
Continental Airlines(☎ 366-9985; www.continental.com; airline code CO; hub Houston)
Copa Airlines (☎ 385-5500; www.copaair.com; airline code CM; hub Panama City)
Cubana (☎ 367-2288/89/90; www.cubana.cu; airline code CU; hub Havana)
Delta Airlines (☎ 1-800-300-0005; www.delta.com; airline code DL; hub Atlanta)
Grupo TACA (☎ 470-8222; www.taca.com; airline code TA; hub San Salvador)
Iberia (☎ 331-1012; www.iberia.com; airline code IB; hub Madrid)
Inter see Grupo TACA
Lacsa see Grupo TACA
Maya Island Air (☎ 926-3386; www.mayaairways.com; airline code MW; hub Belize City)
Mexicana (☎ 333-6001; www.mexicana.com; airline code MX; hub Mexico City)
TACA see Grupo TACA
Tropic Air (☎ 926-0348; www.tropicair.com; airline code PM; hub Belize City)
United Airlines (☎ 336-9923/4/5/6; www.united.com; airline code UA; hub Los Angeles)

From Guatemala
The best place to buy flight tickets out of Guatemala is Antigua, which has many agencies offering good fares (p79). Some agencies

DEPARTURE TAX

Guatemala levies a departure tax of US$30 on outbound air passengers. This has to be paid in cash US dollars or quetzals at the airline check-in desk.

also issue the student, youth and teacher cards needed to obtain the best fares.

From Australia & New Zealand

The cheapest routings usually go via the USA (often Los Angeles). Many Australasians visiting Guatemala are doing so as part of a longer trip through Latin America, so the most suitable ticket might be an open-jaw (into one city, out of another) or even a round-the-world ticket. From Sydney, you'll pay approximately A$2700 return to Guatemala City via LA or San Francisco.

The following are well-known agents for cheap fares, with branches throughout Australia and New Zealand:

STA Travel Australia (☎ 1300-733-035; www.statravel .com.au); New Zealand (☎ 0508-782-872; www.statravel .co.nz).

Flight Centre Australia (☎ 133-133; www.flightcentre .com.au); New Zealand (☎ 0800-243-544; www.flight centre.co.nz).

From Canada

There are no direct flights. Routings are usually via the USA. Montreal to Guatemala City costs in the region of C$1100 return.

Travel Cuts (☎ 800-667-2887; www.travelcuts.com) is Canada's national student travel agency. For online bookings try www.expedia.ca and www.travelocity.ca.

From Central America & Cuba

Grupo TACA flies from San Salvador (economy return fare US$100 to US$140); Tegucigalpa, Honduras (US$150 to US$200) via San Pedro Sula; Managua, Nicaragua (US$260); and San José, Costa Rica (US$200 to US$220). Copa flies direct from Panama City (US$600), and from San José (US$270) via Managua (US$360). United Airlines also flies from San José to Guatemala City. Tropic Air and Maya Island Air both fly daily from Belize City to Flores and back for around US$90 each way. Cubana flies twice weekly to/from Havana. Return fares cost around US$350.

From Europe

Iberia is the only airline flying direct from Europe to Guatemala at the time of writing (with a stop in Miami), and the cheapest fares from many European cities are usually with Iberia via Madrid. Depending on season, you can expect to pay from £450 to £750 round-trip from London and from €850 to €1000 from Frankfurt.

Recommended UK ticket agencies include the following:

Journey Latin America (☎ 020-8747-3108; www .journeylatinamerica.co.uk)

STA Travel (☎ 0870-160-0599; www.statravel.co.uk) For travelers under the age of 26.

Trailfinders (☎ 020-7937-1234; www.trailfinders.co.uk)

For online bookings try www.dialaflight .com or www.lastminute.com.

From Mexico

Grupo TACA and Mexicana both fly daily direct between Mexico City and Guatemala City, with round-trip fares starting around US$430. Inter, part of Grupo TACA, flies most days from Guatemala City to Flores to Cancún and back. Round-trip fares from Cancún to Flores/Guatemala City are US$350/430.

From South America

Lacsa (with transfers in San José, Costa Rica) and Copa (with transfers in Panama City) both fly to Guatemala City from Bogotá, Caracas, Quito and Lima.

From the USA

Nonstop flights to Guatemala City arrive from Atlanta (October-November/April-May US$500/560) with Delta; from Dallas with American; from Houston (US$500/750) with Continental; from Los Angeles (US$600/650) with United and Grupo TACA; from Miami (US$350/580) with American, Grupo TACA and Iberia; and from New York (US$550/650) with American and Grupo TACA.

The following websites are recommended for online bookings:

- www.cheaptickets.com
- www.expedia.com
- www.itn.net
- www.lowestfare.com
- www.orbitz.com
- www.sta.com

TRANSPORT

LAND

Bus is the commonest way to enter Guatemala, though you can also do so by car, river or sea. It's advisable to get through all borders as early in the day as possible. Onward transportation tends to wind down in the afternoon and border areas are not always the safest places to hang around late. You'll find more detail on the services mentioned here in the destination sections of this book. There is no departure tax when you leave Guatemala by land.

Car & Motorcycle

The mountain of paperwork and liability involved in driving into Guatemala deters most travelers. You will need the following documents, all clear and consistent, to enter Guatemala with a car:

- current and valid registration
- proof of ownership (if you don't own the car, you'll need a notarized letter of authorization from the owner that you are allowed to take it)
- your current and valid driver's license or an International Driving Permit (IDP), issued by the automobile association in your home country
- temporary import permit available free at the border and good for a maximum 30 days

Insurance from foreign countries is not recognized by Guatemala, forcing you to purchase a policy locally. Most border posts and nearby towns have offices selling liability policies. To deter foreigners from selling cars in Guatemala, the authorities make you exit the country with the vehicle you used to enter it. Do not be the designated driver when crossing borders if you don't own the car, because you and it will not be allowed to leave Guatemala without each other.

From Belize

The border is at Benque Viejo del Carmen/ Melchor Mencos. **Línea Dorada** (☎ 926-1788; Flores) runs two direct daily buses from Belize City to Flores (US$15, four to five hours) and back. **San Juan Travel** (☎ 926-0041/ 2; Flores) also covers this route daily. Otherwise, Novelo's buses depart Belize City for Benque (US$3, three hours) and vice versa about every half hour from 11am to 4pm. Buses and minibuses run between Melchor

Mencos and Flores (US$1.50 to US$2, two hours). There are also a few buses daily between Melchor Mencos and Guatemala City via Poptún and Río Dulce.

From El Salvador

There are road borders at La Hachadura/ Ciudad Pedro de Alvarado on coastal highway CA-2, Las Chinamas/Valle Nuevo (Highway CA-8), San Cristóbal/San Cristóbal (Highway CA-1, the Interamericana) and Anguiatú/Anguiatú (Highway CA-10). Several companies run buses between San Salvador and Guatemala City, taking five to six hours and costing from US$8 to US$45 depending on the service. One of them, Tica Bus, has buses between San Salvador and all other Central American capitals except Belize City. Crossing at the other border points is usually a matter of taking one bus to the border and another onward from it.

From Honduras

The main road crossings are at Agua Caliente (between Nueva Ocotepeque, Honduras, and Esquipulas, Guatemala), El Florido (between Copán Ruinas, Honduras, and Chiquimula, Guatemala) and Corinto (between Omoa, Honduras, and Puerto Barrios, Guatemala). **Hedman Alas** (☎ 237-7143 Tegucigalpa; ☎ 441-5347 La Ceiba; ☎ 553-1361 San Pedro Sula; ☎ 651-4037 Copán Ruinas) runs daily 1st-class buses via El Florido to Guatemala City from Tegucigalpa (US$52 one way, 11½ hours), La Ceiba (US$52, 12 hours), San Pedro Sula (US$45, eight hours) and Copán Ruinas (US$35, 4½ hours). Cheaper local transportation serves all three border points. Shuttle minibus services run between Copán Ruinas, Guatemala City and Antigua.

From Mexico

The main border points are at Ciudad Hidalgo/Ciudad Tecún Umán and Talismán/ El Carmen, both near Tapachula, Mexico, and Ciudad Cuauhtémoc/La Mesilla, on the Interamericana between Comitán, Mexico, and Huehuetenango, Guatemala. All these borders are linked by plentiful buses to nearby cities within Guatemala and Mexico, and a few buses run all the way between Tapachula and Guatemala City by the Pacific Slope route through Mazatenango and

Escuintla. There are also direct buses between Guatemala City and all three border points. **Línea Dorada** (☎ 926-1788 Flores) runs two direct daily buses from Chetumal, Mexico, to Flores (US$22, seven to eight hours) and back, via Belize City. **San Juan Travel** (☎ 926-0041/2 Flores; ☎ 837-0727 Chetumal) also covers this route daily for US$25.

See River, below, for information on routes between Mexico and Guatemala's Petén department.

RIVER

Autotransportes Río Chancalá (5 de Mayo 120, Palenque) and **Transportes Montebello** (Calle Velasco Suárez, Palenque) run from Palenque, Mexico, to Frontera Corozal (US$5, three to four hours) on the Río Usumacinta, which divides Mexico from Guatemala. Boats across the river to Guatemala cost US$0.60 per person to La Técnica (five minutes) and US$4 to US$6 per person to Bethel (40 minutes). From La Técnica buses leave for Flores at 4am and 11am (US$4, five to six hours); from Bethel, buses leave for Flores at 5am, noon, 2pm and 4pm (US$3.50, four hours). Travel agencies in Palenque and Flores offer bus-boat-bus packages between the two places for US$30 to US$35. If you're making this trip it's well worth the time and expense of detouring to the outstanding Mayan ruins at Yaxchilán, near Frontera Corozal: packages incorporating this are available too.

There are other river routes from Mexico into Guatemala's Petén department: up the Río de la Pasión from Benemérito de las Américas, south of Frontera Corozal, to Sayaxché; and up the Río San Pedro from La Palma, Tabasco, to El Naranjo. There are no reliable passenger services along either river, however: you may have to hire your own boat, which can be expensive. Both Sayaxché and El Naranjo have bus and minibus connections with Flores. La Palma has transport from Tenosique, and Benemérito has good bus and minibus connections with Palenque.

SEA

Exotic Travel (☎ 947-0049 Lívingston) operates boats to and from Omoa in Honduras (US$35, 2½ hours) and Punta Gorda in Belize (US$16, 1¼ hours) every Tuesday and Friday. **Transportes El Chato** (☎ 948-5525

Puerto Barrios) operates a daily boat to and from Punta Gorda in Belize (US$15.50, one hour). The Punta Gorda services connect with bus services to/from Belize City.

There is a US$10 departure tax when leaving Guatemala by sea.

GETTING AROUND

AIR

At the time of writing the only scheduled internal flights are between Guatemala City and Flores, a route operated daily by five companies with one-way/return fares ranging from US$70/100 to US$90/125. For further details, see p71. A departure tax of five quetzals (about US$0.65) has to be paid in cash at check-in for these flights.

BICYCLE

Bike rentals are available in a few places: the most professional outfits include Old Town Outfitters and Guatemala Ventures/Mayan Bike Tours in Antigua (p85), and Vrisa Bookshop in Quetzaltenango (p151).

BOAT

The Caribbean town of Lívingston is only reachable by boat, across the Bahía de Amatique from Puerto Barrios or down the Río Dulce from the town of Río Dulce – great trips both. In Lago de Atitlán fast fiberglass launches zip across the waters between villages.

BUS, MINIBUS & PICKUP

Buses go almost everywhere in Guatemala. Guatemala's buses will leave you with some of your most vivid memories of the country. Most of them are ancient school buses from the US and Canada. It is not unusual for a local family of five to squeeze into seats that were originally designed for two child-sized bottoms. Many travelers know these vehicles as chicken buses after the live cargo accompanying many passengers. They are frequent, crowded and cheap. Expect to pay US$1 (or less!) for an hour of travel.

Chicken buses will stop anywhere, for anyone. Helpers will yell '*hay lugares!*' (eye loo-*gar*-ays), which literally means 'there are places.' Never mind that the space they refer to may be no more than a sliver of air between hundreds of locals mashed against one another. These same helpers will also yell their bus's destination in voices of varying hilarity and cadence; just listen for the song of your town. Tall travelers will be especially challenged on these buses. To catch a chicken bus, simply stand beside the road with your arm out parallel to the ground.

Some routes, especially between big cities, are served by more comfortable buses with the luxury of one seat per person. The best buses are labeled *pullman*, *especial* or *primera clase*. Occasionally, these may have bathrooms, televisions and even food service.

In general, more buses leave in the morning (some leave as early as 3am) than the afternoon. Bus traffic drops off precipitously after about 4pm; night buses are rare and not generally recommended. An exception is Línea Dorada's overnight *de lujo* from Guatemala City to Flores, which has not experienced (to our knowledge) any trouble of note in several years (we hope we're not tempting fate here).

Distances in Guatemala are not huge and you won't often ride for more than four hours at a time. On a typical four-hour bus trip you'll cover 175km to 200km for US$3.50 to US$4.

For a few of the better services you can buy tickets in advance, and this is generally worth doing as it ensures that you get a place.

On some shorter routes minibuses, usually called *microbuses,* are replacing chicken buses. These are operated on the same cram-'em-all-in principles and can be even more uncomfortable because they have less leg room. Where neither buses nor minibuses roam, pickup *(picop)* trucks serve as de facto buses; you hail them and pay for them as if they were the genuine article.

At least a couple of times a month, a bus plunges over a cliff or rounds a blind bend into a head-on collision. Newspapers are full of gory details and diagrams of the latest wreck, which doesn't foster affectionate feelings toward Guatemalan public transportation. Equally if not more often, buses are held up by armed robbers and the passengers are relieved of their money and valuables. If this happens to you, do not try to resist or get away. You could end up losing more than your valuables.

For more information on this unpleasant subject, see p277.

CAR & MOTORCYCLE

You can drive in Guatemala with your home-country driver's license or with an International Driving Permit (IDP). Gasoline (petrol) and diesel are widely available. Motor parts may be hard to find, especially for modern vehicles with sophisticated electronics and emissions-control systems. Old Toyota pickups are ubiquitous, though, so parts and mechanics will be more widely available.

Guatemalan driving etiquette will probably be very different from what you're used to back home: passing on blind curves, ceding the right of way to vehicles coming uphill on narrow passes and deafening honking for no apparent reason are just the start. Expect few road signs and no indication from other drivers of what they are about to do. A vehicle coming uphill always has the right of way. *Tumulos* are speed bumps that are generously (sometimes oddly) placed throughout the country, usually on the main drag through a town. Use of seat belts is obligatory, but generally not practiced.

In Guatemala driving at night is a bad idea for many reasons, not the least of which are armed bandits, drunk drivers and decreased visibility.

Every driver involved in an accident that results in injury or death is taken into custody until a judge determines responsibility.

Rental

You can rent cars in Guatemala City (p73), Antigua (p97), Panajachel (p116), Quetzaltenango (p151), Huehuetenango (p161), Cobán (p196) and Flores (p252). A four-door, five-seat, five-gear vehicle with air-con such as a Mitsubishi Lancer will normally cost around US$50 a day including insurance and unlimited kilometers. The smallest cars start at around US$40 a day. Discounts may apply if you rent for three days or more.

To rent a car or motorcycle you need to show your passport, driver's license and a major credit card. Usually, the person renting the vehicle must be 25 years or older. Insurance policies accompanying rental cars may not protect you from loss or theft, in which case you could be liable for hundreds or even thousands of dollars in damages. Be careful where you park, especially in Guatemala City and at night.

Motorcycles are available for rent in Antigua (p97), Panajachel (p116), Quetzaltenango (p151) and Flores (p252). Bringing safety gear is highly recommended.

HITCHING

Hitchhiking in the strict sense of the word is not practiced in Guatemala because it is not safe. However, where the bus service is sporadic or nonexistent, pickup trucks and other vehicles serve as public transport. If you stand beside the road with your arm out, someone will stop. You are expected to pay the driver as if it were a bus and the fare will be similar. This is a safe and reliable system used by locals and travelers, and the only inconvenience you're likely to encounter is full to overflowing vehicles – get used to it.

LOCAL TRANSPORT

Bus

Public transportation within towns and cities and to nearby villages is chiefly provided by aged, polluting, crowded and loud buses. They're useful to travelers chiefly in the more spread-out cities such as Guatemala City, Quetzaltenango and Huehuetenango. Quetzaltenango has a lovely fleet of quiet, smooth, comfortable, modern minibuses (operating alongside the usual city buses).

Taxi

Taxis are fairly plentiful in most significant towns. A 10-minute ride normally costs about US$3. They don't use meters: you must agree upon the fare before you set off – best before you get in, in fact. Taxis will also often take you to out-of-town archaeological sites and other places for reasonable round-trip fares, including waiting time while you look around.

SHUTTLE MINIBUS

Shuttle minibuses run by travel agencies provide comfortable and quick transport along the main routes plied by tourists. You'll find these heavily advertised wherever they are offered. They're much more expensive than buses (anywhere between five and 15 times as expensive), but more convenient: they usually offer a door-to-door service. The most popular shuttle routes include Guatemala City airport–Antigua, Antigua–Panajachel, Panajachel–Chichicastenango and Flores–Tikal.

TRANSPORT

Health By Dr David Goldberg

Travelers to Central America need to be concerned about food- and water-borne, as well as mosquito-borne, infections. Most of these illnesses are not life-threatening, but they can certainly ruin your trip. Besides getting the proper vaccinations, it's important that you bring along a good insect repellent and exercise great care in what you eat and drink.

BEFORE YOU GO

Since most vaccines don't produce immunity until at least two weeks after they're given, visit a physician four to eight weeks before departure. Ask your doctor for an international certificate of vaccination (otherwise known as the yellow booklet), which will list all the vaccinations you've received. This is mandatory for countries that require proof of yellow fever vaccination upon entry, but it's a good idea to carry it wherever you travel.

INSURANCE

If your health insurance does not cover you for medical expenses abroad, strongly consider getting supplemental insurance. Check the Subway section of the **Lonely Planet website** (www.lonelyplanet.com/subwwway) for more information. See also the **US State Department website** (www.travel.state.gov/medical.html) for a list of medical evacuation and travel insurance companies. Find out in advance if your insurance plan will make payments directly to providers or reimburse you later for overseas health expenditures.

MEDICAL CHECKLIST

- antibiotics
- antidiarrheal drugs (eg loperamide)
- acetaminophen/paracetamol (Tylenol) or aspirin
- anti-inflammatory drugs (eg ibuprofen)
- antihistamines (for hay fever and allergic reactions)
- antibacterial ointment (eg Bactroban) for cuts and abrasions
- steroid cream or cortisone (for poison ivy and other allergic rashes)
- bandages, gauze, gauze rolls
- adhesive or paper tape
- scissors, safety pins, tweezers
- thermometer
- pocket knife
- DEET-containing insect repellent for the skin
- permethrin-containing insect spray for clothing, tents and bed nets
- sunblock
- oral-rehydration salts
- iodine tablets (for water purification)
- syringes and sterile needles

INTERNET RESOURCES

There is a wealth of travel health advice available on the Internet. For further information, the **Lonely Planet website** (www.lonelyplanet.com) is a good place to start. A superb book called *International Travel and Health*, which is revised annually and is available online at no cost is published by the **World Health Organization** (www.who.int/ith/). Another website of general interest is **MD Travel Health** (www.mdtravelhealth.com), which provides complete travel health recommendations for every country, updated daily, also at no cost.

It's usually a good idea to consult your government's travel health website before departure, if one is available.

RECOMMENDED VACCINATIONS

The only required vaccine is yellow fever, and that's only if you're arriving in Guatemala from a yellow-fever-infected country in Africa or South America. However, a number of vaccines are recommended. Note that some of these are not approved for use by children and pregnant women – check with your physician.

Vaccine	Recommended for	Dosage	Side Effects
hepatitis A	all travelers	1 dose before trip; booster 6-12 months later	soreness at injection site; headaches; body aches
typhoid	all travelers	4 capsules, 1 taken every other day	abdominal pain; nausea; rash
yellow fever	required for travelers arriving from a yellow-fever-infected area in Africa or the Americas	1 dose lasts 10 years	headaches; body aches; severe reactions are rare
hepatitis B	long-term travelers in close contact with the local population	3 doses over 6 months	soreness at injection site; low-grade fever
rabies	travelers who may have contact with animals and may not have access to medical care	3 doses over 3-4 weeks	soreness at injection site; headaches; body aches
tetanus-diphtheria	all travelers who haven't had booster within 10 years	1 dose lasts 10 years	soreness at injection site
measles	travelers born after 1956 who've had only 1 measles vaccination	1 dose	fever; rash; joint pains; allergic reactions
chickenpox	travelers who've never had chickenpox	2 doses 1 month apart	fever; mild case of chickenpox

Bring medications in their original containers, clearly labeled. A signed, dated letter from your physician describing all medical conditions and medications, including generic names, is also a good idea. If carrying syringes or needles, be sure to have a physician's letter documenting their medical necessity.

United States (www.cdc.gov/travel/)
Canada (www.hc-sc.gc.ca/pphb-dgspsp/tmp-pmv/pub_e.html)
United Kingdom (www.doh.gov.uk/traveladvice/index.htm)
Australia (www.dfat.gov.au/travel/)

FURTHER READING

For further information, see *Healthy Travel Central & South America,* also from Lonely Planet. If traveling with children, Lonely Planet's *Travel with Children* may be useful. The *ABC of Healthy Travel,* by E Walker et al, and *Medicine for the Outdoors,* by Paul S Auerbach, are other valuable resources.

IN TRANSIT

DEEP VEIN THROMBOSIS (DVT)

Blood clots may form in the legs during plane flights, chiefly because of prolonged immobility. The longer the flight, the greater the risk. Though most blood clots are reabsorbed uneventfully, some may break off and travel through the blood vessels to the lungs, where they could cause life-threatening complications.

The chief symptom of deep vein thrombosis is swelling or pain of the foot, ankle or calf, usually but not always on just one side. When a blood clot travels to the lungs, it may cause chest pain and difficulty breathing. Travelers with any of these symptoms should immediately seek medical attention.

To prevent the development of deep vein thrombosis on long flights you should walk about the cabin, perform isometric compressions of the leg muscles (ie contract the leg muscles while sitting), drink plenty of fluids, and avoid alcohol and tobacco.

JET LAG & MOTION SICKNESS

Jet lag is common when crossing more than five time zones, and can result in insomnia, fatigue, malaise or nausea. To avoid jet lag try drinking plenty of fluids (nonalcoholic) and eating light meals. Upon arrival, get exposure to natural sunlight and readjust your schedule (for meals, sleep etc) as soon as possible.

Antihistamines such as dimenhydrinate (Dramamine) and meclizine (Antivert or Bonine) are usually the first choice for treating motion sickness. Their main side-effect is drowsiness. An herbal alternative is ginger, which works like a charm for some people.

IN GUATEMALA

AVAILABILITY & COST OF HEALTH CARE

Good medical care is available in Guatemala City, but options are limited elsewhere. In general, private hospitals are more reliable than public facilities, which may experience significant shortages of equipment and supplies. Many travelers use **Hospital Herrera Llerandi** (☎ 334-5959; 6a Av 8-71, Zona 10; www.herrerallerandi.com). For an online list of hospitals and physicians in Guatemala, go to the **US embassy website** (http://usembassy.state.gov /guatemala/wwwhacsemedass.html).

Many doctors and hospitals expect payment in cash, regardless of whether you have travel health insurance. If you develop a life-threatening medical problem, you'll probably want to be evacuated to a country with state-of-the-art medical care. Since this may cost tens of thousands of dollars, be sure you have insurance to cover this before you depart.

Many pharmacies are well-supplied, but important medications may not be consist-

ently available. Be sure to bring along adequate supplies of all prescription drugs.

INFECTIOUS DISEASES
Cholera

Cholera is an intestinal infection acquired through ingestion of contaminated food or water. The main symptom is profuse, watery diarrhea, which may be so severe that it causes life-threatening dehydration. The key treatment is drinking oral rehydration solution. Antibiotics are also given, usually tetracycline or doxycycline, though quinolone antibiotics such as ciprofloxacin and levofloxacin are also effective.

Cholera outbreaks occur periodically in Guatemala, but the disease is rare among travelers. Cholera vaccine is no longer required, and is in fact no longer available in some countries, including the US, because the old vaccine was relatively ineffective and caused side effects. There are new vaccines that are safer and more effective, but they're not available in many countries and are only recommended for those at particularly high risk.

Dengue Fever (Breakbone Fever)

Dengue fever is a viral infection found throughout Central America. Thousands of cases occur each year in Guatemala. Dengue is transmitted by aedes mosquitoes, which bite predominantly during the daytime and are usually found close to human habitations, often indoors. They breed primarily in artificial water containers, such as jars, barrels, cans, cisterns, metal drums, plastic containers, and discarded tires. As a result, dengue is especially common in densely populated, urban environments.

Dengue usually causes flu-like symptoms, including fever, muscle aches, joint pains, headaches, nausea and vomiting, often followed by a rash. The body aches may be quite uncomfortable, but most cases resolve uneventfully in a few days. Severe cases usually occur in children under the age of 15 who are experiencing their second dengue infection.

There is no treatment for dengue fever except to take analgesics such as acetaminophen/paracetamol (Tylenol) and drink plenty of fluids. Severe cases may require hospitalization for intravenous fluids and supportive care. There is no vaccine. The cornerstone of prevention is protecting against insect bites; see p297.

Hepatitis A

Hepatitis A occurs throughout Central America. It's a viral infection of the liver that is usually acquired by ingestion of contaminated water, food or ice, though it may also be acquired by direct contact with infected persons. The illness occurs all over the world, but the incidence is higher in developing nations. Symptoms may include fever, malaise, jaundice, nausea, vomiting and abdominal pain. Most cases resolve uneventfully, though hepatitis A occasionally causes severe liver damage. There is no treatment.

The vaccine for hepatitis A is extremely safe and highly effective. If you get a booster six to 12 months later, it lasts for at least 10 years. You really should get it before you go to Guatemala or any other developing nation. Because the safety of hepatitis A vaccine has not been established for pregnant women or children under the age of two, they should instead be given a gammaglobulin injection.

Hepatitis B

Like hepatitis A, hepatitis B is a liver infection that occurs worldwide but is more common in developing nations. Unlike hepatitis A, the disease is usually acquired by sexual contact or by exposure to infected blood, generally through blood transfusions or contaminated needles. The vaccine is recommended only for long-term travelers (on the road more than six months) who expect to live in rural areas or have close physical contact with the local population. Additionally, the vaccine is recommended for anyone who anticipates sexual contact with the local inhabitants or a possible need for medical, dental or other treatments while abroad, especially if a need for transfusions or injections is expected.

Hepatitis B vaccine is safe and highly effective. However, a total of three injections are necessary to establish full immunity. Several countries added hepatitis B vaccine to the list of routine childhood immunizations in the 1980s, so many young adults are already protected.

Malaria

Malaria occurs in every country in Central America. It's transmitted by mosquito bites, usually between dusk and dawn. The main symptom is high spiking fevers, which may be accompanied by chills, sweats, headache, body aches, weakness, vomiting, or diarrhea. Severe cases may involve the central nervous system and lead to seizures, confusion, coma and death.

Taking malaria pills is strongly recommended for all rural areas in Guatemala except at altitudes greater than 1500m. The risk is high in the departments of Alta Verapaz, Baja Verapaz, Petén and San Marcos, and moderate in the departments of Escuintla, Huehuetenango, Izabal, Quiché, Retalhuleu, Suchitepéquez and Zacapa. Transmission is greatest during the rainy season (June through November). There is no risk in Antigua or Lago de Atitlán.

For Guatemala, the first choice malaria pill is chloroquine, taken once weekly in a dosage of 500mg, starting one to two weeks before arrival and continuing through the trip and for four weeks after departure. Chloroquine is safe, inexpensive and highly effective. Side effects are typically mild and may include nausea, abdominal discomfort, headache, dizziness, blurred vision and itching. Severe reactions are uncommon.

Protecting yourself against mosquito bites is just as important as taking malaria pills (see the recommendations on p297), since no pills are 100% effective.

If you may not have access to medical care while traveling, you should bring along additional pills for emergency self-treatment, which you should undergo if you can't reach a doctor and you develop symptoms that suggest malaria, such as high spiking fevers. One option is to take four tablets of Malarone once daily for three days. If you start self-medication, you should try to see a doctor at the earliest possible opportunity.

If you develop a fever after returning home, see a physician, as malaria symptoms may not occur for months.

Rabies

Rabies is a viral infection of the brain and spinal cord that is almost always fatal if not treated. The rabies virus is carried in the saliva of infected animals and is typically

HEALTH

transmitted through an animal bite, though contamination of any break in the skin with infected saliva may result in rabies. Rabies occurs in all Central American countries. In Guatemala, the risk is greatest in the northern provinces along the Mexican border. Most cases are related to dog bites.

Rabies vaccine is safe, but a full series requires three injections and is quite expensive. Those at high risk for rabies, such as animal handlers and spelunkers (cave explorers), should certainly get the vaccine. In addition, you should consider asking for the vaccine if you might be traveling to remote areas and might not have access to appropriate medical care if needed. The treatment for a possibly rabid bite consists of rabies vaccine with rabies immune globulin. It's effective, but must be given promptly. Most travelers don't need rabies vaccine.

All animal bites and scratches must be promptly and thoroughly cleansed with large amounts of soap and water and local health authorities contacted to determine whether or not further treatment is necessary (see p297).

Typhoid

This fever is caused by ingestion of food or water contaminated by a species of salmonella known as *Salmonella typhi*. Fever occurs in virtually all cases. Other symptoms may include headache, malaise, muscle aches, dizziness, loss of appetite, nausea, and abdominal pain. Either diarrhea or constipation may occur. Possible complications include intestinal perforation, intestinal bleeding, confusion, delirium or (rarely) coma.

Unless you expect to take all your meals in major hotels and restaurants, typhoid vaccine is a good idea. It's usually given orally, but is also available as an injection. Neither vaccine is approved for use in children under the age of two.

The drug of choice for typhoid fever is usually a quinolone antibiotic such as ciprofloxacin (Cipro) or levofloxacin (Levaquin), which many travelers carry for treatment of travelers' diarrhea. However, if you self-treat for typhoid fever, you may also need to self-treat for malaria, since the symptoms of the two diseases may be indistinguishable.

Yellow Fever

Yellow fever no longer occurs in Central America, but many countries in this region, including Guatemala, require yellow fever vaccine before entry if you're arriving from a country in Africa or South America where yellow fever is known to occur. If you're not arriving from a country with yellow fever, the vaccine is neither required nor recommended. Yellow fever vaccine is given only in approved yellow fever vaccination centers, which provide validated international certificates of vaccination (also known as yellow booklets). The vaccine should be given at least 10 days before departure and remains effective for approximately 10 years. Reactions to the vaccine are generally mild and may include headaches, muscle aches, low-grade fevers, or discomfort at the injection site. Severe, life-threatening reactions have been described but are extremely rare.

Other Infections

CHAGAS' DISEASE

This is a parasitic infection that is transmitted by triatomine insects (reduviid bugs), which inhabit crevices in the walls and roofs of substandard housing in South and Central America. The triatomine insect lays its feces on human skin as it bites, usually at night. A person becomes infected when he or she unknowingly rubs the feces into the bite wound or any other open sore. Chagas' disease is extremely rare in travelers. However, if you sleep in a poorly constructed house, especially one made of mud, adobe or thatch, you should be sure to protect yourself with a bed net and a good insecticide.

HISTOPLASMOSIS

Caused by a soil-based fungus, histoplasmosis is acquired by inhalation, often when the soil has been disrupted. Initial symptoms may include fever, chills, dry cough, chest pain and headache, sometimes leading to pneumonia. Histoplasmosis has been reported in European travelers returning from Mazatenango.

HIV/AIDS

This has been reported in all Central American countries. Be sure to use condoms for all sexual encounters.

LEISHMANIASIS

This occurs in the mountains and jungles of all Central American countries. The infection is transmitted by sandflies, which are about one-third the size of mosquitoes. Leishmaniasis may be limited to the skin, causing slowly growing ulcers over exposed parts of the body, or (less commonly) disseminate to the bone marrow, liver and spleen. The disease may be particularly severe in those with HIV. In Guatemala, most cases of cutaneous leishmaniasis are reported from the northern parts of the country at elevations less than 1000m. The greatest risk occurs in the forested areas of El Petén. The disseminated form may occur in the semiarid valleys and foothills in the east central part of the country. There is no vaccine for leishmaniasis. To protect yourself from sandflies, follow the same precautions as for mosquitoes (p297), except that netting must be finer-mesh (at least 18 holes to the linear inch).

LEPTOSPIROSIS

This is acquired by exposure to water contaminated by the urine of infected animals. Outbreaks often occur at times of flooding, when sewage overflow may contaminate the water sources. The initial symptoms, which resemble a mild flu, usually subside uneventfully in a few days, with or without treatment, but a minority of cases are complicated by jaundice or meningitis. There is no vaccine. You can minimize your risk by staying out of bodies of fresh water that may be contaminated by animal urine. If you're visiting an area where an outbreak is in progress, as occurred in Guatemala after flooding in 1998, you can take 200mg of doxycycline once weekly as a preventative measure. If you actually develop leptospirosis, the treatment is 100mg of doxycycline twice daily.

ONCHOCERCIASIS (RIVER BLINDNESS)

Onchocerciasis is caused by a roundworm that may invade the eye, leading to blindness. The infection is transmitted by black flies, which breed along the banks of rapidly flowing rivers and streams. In Guatemala, the disease occurs in heavily forested areas between 500m and 1500m, chiefly the Pacific slope of the Sierra Madre and in Escuintla along the Verde and Guachipilín rivers.

TYPHUS

This may be transmitted by lice in scattered pockets of the country.

TRAVELERS' DIARRHEA

To prevent diarrhea, avoid tap water unless it has been boiled, filtered or chemically disinfected (see p298); only eat fresh fruits or vegetables if cooked or peeled; be wary of dairy products that might contain unpasteurized milk; and be highly selective when eating food from street vendors.

If you develop diarrhea, be sure to drink plenty of fluids, preferably an oral rehydration solution containing lots of salt and sugar. A few loose stools don't require treatment, but if you start having more than four or five stools a day, you should start taking an antibiotic (usually a quinolone drug) and an antidiarrheal agent (such as loperamide). If diarrhea is bloody or persists for more than 72 hours or is accompanied by fever, shaking chills or severe abdominal pain, you should seek medical attention.

ENVIRONMENTAL HAZARDS
Animal Bites

Do not attempt to pet, handle or feed any animal, with the exception of domestic animals known to be free of any infectious disease. Most animal injuries are directly related to a person's attempt to touch or feed the animal.

Any bite or scratch by a mammal, including bats, should be promptly and thoroughly cleansed with large amounts of soap and water, followed by application of an antiseptic such as iodine or alcohol. The local health authorities should be contacted immediately for possible postexposure rabies treatment, whether or not you've been immunized against rabies. It may also be advisable to start an antibiotic, since wounds caused by animal bites and scratches frequently become infected. One of the newer quinolones, such as levofloxacin (Levaquin), which many travelers carry in case of diarrhea, would be an appropriate choice.

Mosquito Bites

To prevent mosquito bites, wear long sleeves, long pants, hats and shoes (rather than sandals). Bring along a good insect

TRADITIONAL MEDICINE

The following are some traditional remedies for common travel-related conditions.

Problem	Treatment
jet lag	melatonin
motion sickness	ginger
mosquito bite prevention	oil of eucalyptus or soybean oil

repellent, preferably one that contains DEET, which should be applied to exposed skin and clothing, but not to eyes, mouth, cuts, wounds or irritated skin. Products containing lower concentrations of DEET are as effective, but for shorter periods of time. In general, adults and children over 12 should use preparations containing 25% to 35% DEET, which usually lasts about six hours. Children between two and 12 years of age should use preparations containing no more than 10% DEET, applied sparingly, which will usually last about three hours. Neurologic toxicity has been reported from DEET, especially in children, but appears to be extremely uncommon and generally related to overuse. Compounds containing DEET should not be used on children under the age of two.

Insect repellents containing certain botanical products, including oil of eucalyptus and soybean oil, are effective but last only 1½ to two hours. Repellents containing DEET are preferable for areas where there is a high risk of malaria or yellow fever. Products based on citronella are not effective.

For additional protection, you can apply permethrin to clothing, shoes, tents and bed nets. Permethrin treatments are safe and remain effective for at least two weeks, even when items are laundered. Permethrin should not be applied directly to skin.

Don't sleep with the window open unless there is a screen. If sleeping outdoors or in an accommodation that allows entry of mosquitoes, use a bed net, preferably treated with permethrin, with edges tucked in under the mattress. The mesh size should be less than 1.5mm. If the sleeping area is not otherwise protected, use a mosquito coil, which will fill the room with insecticide through the night. Repellent-impregnated wristbands are not effective.

Snake Bites

Snakes are a hazard in some areas of Central America. In Guatemala, the chief concern is *Bothrops asper*, the Central American or common lancehead, also called the fer-de-lance and known locally as *barba amarilla* (yellow beard) or *terciopelo* (velvet skin). This heavy-bodied snake reaches up to 2m in length and is commonly found along fallen logs and other small animal runs, especially in the northern provinces.

In the event of a venomous snake bite, place the victim at rest, keep the bitten area immobilized and move the victim immediately to the nearest medical facility. Avoid tourniquets, which are no longer recommended.

Sun

To protect yourself from excessive sun exposure, you should stay out of the midday sun, wear sunglasses and a wide-brimmed sun hat, and apply sunscreen with SPF 15 or higher, with both UVA and UVB protection. Sunscreen should be generously applied to all exposed parts of the body approximately 30 minutes before sun exposure and should be reapplied after swimming or vigorous activity. Travelers should also drink plenty of fluids and avoid strenuous exercise when the temperature is high.

Water

Tap water in Guatemala is not safe to drink. Vigorous boiling for one minute is the most effective means of water purification. At altitudes greater than 2000m, boil for three minutes.

Another option is to disinfect water with iodine pills. Instructions are usually enclosed and should be carefully followed. Or you can add 2% tincture of iodine to one quart or liter of water (five drops to clear water, 10 drops to cloudy water) and let stand for 30 minutes. If the water is cold, longer times may be required. The taste of iodinated water may be improved by adding vitamin C (ascorbic acid). Iodinated water should not be consumed for more than a few weeks. Pregnant women, those with a history of thyroid disease and those allergic to iodine should not drink iodinated water.

A number of water filters are on the market. Those with smaller pores (reverse osmosis filters) provide the broadest protection, but they are relatively large and are readily plugged by debris. Those with somewhat larger pores (microstrainer filters) are ineffective against viruses, although they remove other organisms. Manufacturers' instructions must be carefully followed.

Safe-to-drink, inexpensive purified water *(agua pura)* is widely available in hotels, shops and restaurants. Salvavida is a universally trusted brand.

CHILDREN & PREGNANT WOMEN

In general, it's safe for children and pregnant women to go to Guatemala. However, because some of the vaccines listed on p293 are not approved for use in children and pregnant women, these travelers should be particularly careful not to drink tap water or consume any questionable food or beverage. Also, when traveling with children, make sure they're up-to-date on all routine immunizations. It's sometimes appropriate to give children some of their vaccines a little early before visiting a developing nation. You should discuss this with your pediatrician. Lastly, if pregnant, you should bear in mind that should a complication such as premature labor develop while abroad, the quality of medical care may not be comparable to that in your home country.

Since yellow fever vaccine is not recommended for pregnant women or children less than nine months old, these travelers, if arriving from a country with yellow fever, should obtain a waiver letter, preferably written on letterhead stationery and bearing the stamp used by official immunization centers to validate the international certificate of vaccination.

HEALTH

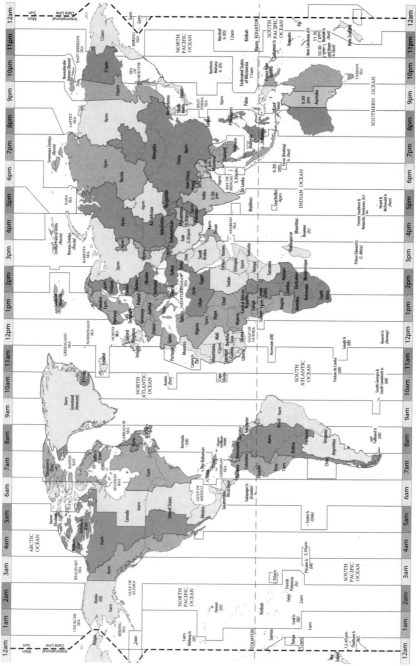

Language

CONTENTS

There are 21 Mayan indigenous languages used in and around Guatemala, but Spanish is still the most commonly spoken language, and what visitors will encounter on a daily basis. If you're keen to try out some Mayan languages, see the short and sweet Mam and K'iche' sections at the end of this chapter.

It's easy enough to pick up some basic Spanish, and for those who want to learn the language in greater depth, courses are available in Antigua (p86), Panajachel (p108), San Pedro La Laguna (p121), Nebaj (p138), Quetzaltenango (p143), Todos Santos Cuchumatán (p162), Monterrico (p179), Cobán (p191) and Flores (p246). Alternatively, you can study books, records and tapes before you leave home. These resources are often available free at public libraries. Evening or college courses are also an excellent way to get started. For words and phrases for use when ordering at a restaurant, see Eat Your Words on p51.

For a more comprehensive guide to the Spanish of Guatemala, get a copy of Lonely Planet's *Latin American Spanish phrasebook*.

PRONUNCIATION

Spanish spelling is phonetically consistent, meaning that there's a clear and consistent relationship between what you see in writing and how it's pronounced. In addition, most Spanish sounds have English equivalents, so English speakers shouldn't have too much trouble being understood.

Vowels

a	as in 'father'
e	as in 'met'
i	as in 'marine'
o	as in 'or' (without the 'r' sound)
u	as in 'rule'; the 'u' is not pronounced after **q** and in the letter combinations **gue** and **gui**, unless it's marked with a diaeresis (eg *argüir*), in which case it's pronounced as English 'w'
y	at the end of a word or when it stands alone, it's pronounced as the Spanish **i** (eg *ley*); between vowels within a word it's as the 'y' in 'yonder'

Consonants

As a rule, Spanish consonants resemble their English counterparts. The exceptions are listed below.

While the consonants **ch**, **ll** and **ñ** are generally considered distinct letters, **ch** and **ll** are now often listed alphabetically under **c** and **l** respectively. The letter **ñ** is still treated as a separate letter and comes after **n** in dictionaries.

b	similar to English 'b,' but softer; referred to as 'b larga'
c	as in 'celery' before **e** and **i**; otherwise as English 'k'
ch	as in 'church'
d	as in 'dog,' but between vowels and after **l** or **n**, the sound is closer to the 'th' in 'this'
g	as the 'ch' in the Scottish *loch* before **e** and **i** ('kh' in our guides to pronunciation); elsewhere, as in 'go'
h	invariably silent. If your name begins with this letter, listen carefully if you're waiting for public officials to call you.
j	as the 'ch' in the Scottish *loch* (written as 'kh' in our guides to pronunciation)
ll	as the 'y' in 'yellow'

LANGUAGE

ñ	as the 'ni' in 'onion'
r	a short **r** except at the beginning of a word, and after **l**, **n** or **s**, when it's often rolled
rr	very strongly rolled
v	similar to English 'b,' but softer; referred to as 'b corta'
x	usually pronounced as **j** above; in some indigenous place names it's pronounced as an 's'; as in 'taxi' in other instances
z	as the 's' in 'sun'

Word Stress

In general, words ending in vowels or the letters **n** or **s** have stress on the next-to-last syllable, while those with other endings have stress on the last syllable. Thus *vaca* (cow) and *caballos* (horses) both carry stress on the next-to-last syllable, while *ciudad* (city) and *infeliz* (unhappy) are both stressed on the last syllable.

Written accents will almost always appear in words that don't follow the rules above, eg *sótano* (basement), *América* and *porción* (portion).

GENDER & PLURALS

In Spanish, nouns are either masculine or feminine, and there are rules to help determine gender (there are of course some exceptions). Feminine nouns generally end with -**a** or with the groups -**ción**, -**sión** or -**dad**. Other endings typically signify a masculine noun. Endings for adjectives also change to agree with the gender of the noun they modify (masculine/feminine -**o**/-**a**). Where both masculine and feminine forms are included in this language guide, they are separated by a slash, with the masculine form first, eg *perdido/a*.

If a noun or adjective ends in a vowel, the plural is formed by adding **s** to the end. If it ends in a consonant, the plural is formed by adding **es** to the end.

ACCOMMODATIONS

I'm looking for ...	*Estoy buscando ...*	e·*stoy* boos·*kan*·do ...
Where is ...?	*¿Dónde hay ...?*	*don*·de ai ...
a hotel	*un hotel*	oon o·*tel*
a boarding house	*una pensión/ residencial/ un hospedaje*	*oo*·na pen·*syon*/ re·see·den·*syal*/ oon os·pe·*da*·khe
a youth hostel	*un albergue juvenil*	oon al·*ber*·ge khoo·ve·*neel*

Are there any rooms available?

¿Hay habitaciones libres?	ay a·bee·ta·*syon*·es *lee*·bres

I'd like a ... room.	*Quisiera una habitación ...*	kee·*sye*·ra oo·na a·bee·ta·*syon* ...
double	*doble*	*do*·ble
single	*individual*	een·dee·vee·*dwal*
twin	*con dos camas*	kon dos *ka*·mas

How much is it per ...?	*¿Cuánto cuesta por ...?*	*kwan*·to *kwes*·ta por ...
night	*noche*	*no*·che
person	*persona*	per·*so*·na
week	*semana*	se·*ma*·na

full board	*pensión completa*	pen·*syon* kom·*ple*·ta
private/shared bathroom	*baño privado/ compartido*	*ba*·nyo pree·*va*·do/ kom·par·*tee*·do
too expensive	*demasiado caro*	de·ma·*sya*·do *ka*·ro
cheaper	*más económico*	mas e·ko·*no*·mee·ko
discount	*descuento*	des·*kwen*·to

Does it include breakfast?

¿Incluye el desayuno?	een·*kloo*·ye el de·sa·*yoo*·no

MAKING A RESERVATION

(for phone or written requests)

To ...	*A ...*
From ...	*De ...*
Date	*Fecha*
I'd like to book ...	*Quisiera reservar ...* (see the list under 'Accommodations' for bed and room options)
in the name of ...	*en nombre de ...*
for the nights of ...	*para las noches del ...*
credit card ...	*tarjeta de crédito ...*
number	*número*
expiry date	*fecha de vencimiento*
Please confirm ...	*Puede confirmar ...*
availability	*la disponibilidad*
price	*el precio*

May I see the room?

¿Puedo ver la habitación?	*pwe*·do ver la a·bee·ta·*syon*

I don't like it.

No me gusta.	no me *goos*·ta

It's fine. I'll take it.
OK. La alquilo.   o·*kay* la al·*kee*·lo
I'm leaving now.
Me voy ahora.   me *voy* a·o·ra

CONVERSATION & ESSENTIALS

In their public behavior, South Americans are very conscious of civilities, sometimes to the point of ceremoniousness. Never approach a stranger for information without extending a greeting, and use only the polite form of address, especially with the police and public officials. Young people may be less likely to expect this, but it's best to stick to the polite form unless you're quite sure you won't offend by using the informal mode. The polite form is used in all cases in this guide; where options are given, the form is indicated by the abbreviations 'pol' and 'inf.'

Saying *por favor* (please) and *gracias* (thank you) are second nature to most Guatemalans and a recommended tool in your travel kit. The three most common Spanish greetings are often shortened to simply *buenos* (for *buenos días*) and *buenas* (for *buenas tardes* and *buenas noches*).

Hello.	*Hola.*	o·la
Good morning.	*Buenos días.*	bwe·nos *dee*·as
Good afternoon.	*Buenas tardes.*	bwe·nas *tar*·des
Good evening/	*Buenas noches.*	bwe·nas *no*·ches
night.		
Goodbye.	*Adiós.*	a·*dyos* (rarely used)
Bye/See you soon.	*Hasta luego.*	as·ta *lwe*·go
Yes.	*Sí.*	see
No.	*No.*	no
Please.	*Por favor.*	por fa·*vor*
Thank you.	*Gracias.*	gra·syas
Many thanks.	*Muchas gracias.*	moo·chas gra·syas
You're welcome.	*De nada.*	de na·da
Pardon me.	*Perdón.*	per·*don*
Excuse me.	*Permiso.*	per·*mee*·so
(used when asking permission)		
Forgive me.	*Disculpe.*	dees·*kool*·pe
(used when apologizing)		

How are things?
¿Qué tal?   ke tal
What's your name?
¿Cómo se llama?   ko·mo se *ya*·ma (pol)
¿Cómo te llamas?   ko·mo te *ya*·mas (inf)
My name is ...
Me llamo ...   me *ya*·mo ...

It's a pleasure to meet you.
Mucho gusto.   moo·cho goos·to
The pleasure is mine.
El gusto es mío.   el goos·to es *mee*·o
Where are you from?
¿De dónde es/eres?   de don·de es/er·es (pol/inf)
I'm from ...
Soy de ...   soy de ...
Where are you staying?
¿Dónde está alojado?   don·de es·ta a·lo·*kha*·do (pol)
¿Dónde estás alojado?   don·de es·tas a·lo·*kha*·do (inf)
May I take a photo?
¿Puedo sacar una foto?   pwe·do sa·*kar* oo·na *fo*·to

DIRECTIONS
How do I get to ...?
¿Cómo puedo llegar a ...?   ko·mo pwe·do ye·*gar* a ...
Is it far?
¿Está lejos?   es·ta le·khos
Go straight ahead.
Siga/Vaya derecho.   see·ga/va·ya de·re·cho
Turn left.
Voltée a la izquierda.   vol·te·e a la ees·*kyer*·da
Turn right.
Voltée a la derecha.   vol·te·e a la de·*re*·cha
I'm lost.
Estoy perdido/a.   es·toy per·*dee*·do/a
Can you show me (on the map)?
¿Me lo podría indicar   me lo po·*dree*·a een·dee·*kar*
(en el mapa)?   (en el *ma*·pa)

north	*norte*	nor·te
south	*sur*	soor
east	*este/oriente*	es·te/o·*ryen*·te
west	*oeste/occidente*	o·es·te/ok·see·*den*·te
here	*aquí*	a·*kee*
there	*allí*	a·*yee*
avenue	*avenida*	a·ve·*nee*·da
block	*cuadra*	kwa·dra
street	*calle/paseo*	ka·lye/pa·*se*·o

SIGNS	
Entrada	Entrance
Salida	Exit
Información	Information
Abierto	Open
Cerrado	Closed
Prohibido	Prohibited
Comisaria	Police Station
Servicios/Baños	Toilets
Hombres/Varones	Men
Mujeres/Damas	Women

LANGUAGE

EMERGENCIES

Help!	¡Socorro!	so·ko·ro
Fire!	¡Incendio!	een·sen·dyo
I've been robbed.	Me robaron.	me ro·ba·ron
Go away!	¡Déjeme!	de·khe·me
Get lost!	¡Váyase!	va·ya·se

Call ...!	¡Llame a ...!	ya·me a
the police	la policía	la po·lee·see·a
a doctor	un médico	oon me·dee·ko
an ambulance	una ambulancia	oo·na am·boo·lan·sya

It's an emergency.
Es una emergencia.   es oo·na e·mer·khen·sya
Could you help me, please?
¿Me puede ayudar, por favor?   me pwe·de a·yoo·dar por fa·vor
I'm lost.
Estoy perdido/a.   es·toy per·dee·do/a
Where are the toilets?
¿Dónde están los baños?   don·de es·tan los ba·nyos

HEALTH

I'm sick.
Estoy enfermo/a.   es·toy en·fer·mo/a
I need a doctor.
Necesito un médico.   ne·se·see·to oon me·dee·ko
Where's the hospital?
¿Dónde está el hospital?   don·de es·ta el os·pee·tal
I'm pregnant.
Estoy embarazada.   es·toy em·ba·ra·sa·da
I've been vaccinated.
Estoy vacunado/a.   es·toy va·koo·na·do/a

I'm allergic to ...	Soy alérgico/a a ...	soy a·ler·khee·ko/a a ...
antibiotics	los antibióticos	los an·tee·byo·tee·kos
penicillin	la penicilina	la pe·nee·see·lee·na
nuts	las fruta secas	las froo·tas se·kas

I'm ...	Soy ...	soy ...
asthmatic	asmático/a	as·ma·tee·ko/a
diabetic	diabético/a	dya·be·tee·ko/a
epileptic	epiléptico/a	e·pee·lep·tee·ko/a

I have ...	Tengo ...	ten·go ...
altitude sickness	soroche	so·ro·che
diarrhea	diarrea	dya·re·a
nausea	náusea	now·se·a

a headache	un dolor de cabeza	oon do·lor de ka·be·sa
a cough	tos	tos

LANGUAGE DIFFICULTIES

Do you speak (English)?
¿Habla/Hablas (inglés)?   a·bla/a·blas (een·gles) (pol/inf)
Does anyone here speak English?
¿Hay alguien que hable inglés?   ai al·gyen ke a·ble een·gles
I (don't) understand.
Yo (no) entiendo.   yo (no) en·tyen·do
How do you say ...?
¿Cómo se dice ...?   ko·mo se dee·se ...
What does ...mean?
¿Qué quiere decir ...?   ke kye·re de·seer ...

Could you please ...?	¿Puede ..., por favor?	pwe·de ... por fa·vor
repeat that	repetirlo	re·pe·teer·lo
speak more slowly	hablar más despacio	a·blar mas des·pa·syo
write it down	escribirlo	es·kree·beer·lo

NUMBERS

1	uno	oo·no
2	dos	dos
3	tres	tres
4	cuatro	kwa·tro
5	cinco	seen·ko
6	seis	says
7	siete	sye·te
8	ocho	o·cho
9	nueve	nwe·ve
10	diez	dyes
11	once	on·se
12	doce	do·se
13	trece	tre·se
14	catorce	ka·tor·se
15	quince	keen·se
16	dieciséis	dye·see·says
17	diecisiete	dye·see·sye·te
18	dieciocho	dye·see·o·cho
19	diecinueve	dye·see·nwe·ve
20	veinte	vayn·te
21	veintiuno	vayn·tee·oo·no
30	treinta	trayn·ta
31	treinta y uno	trayn·ta ee oo·no
40	cuarenta	kwa·ren·ta
50	cincuenta	seen·kwen·ta
60	sesenta	se·sen·ta
70	setenta	se·ten·ta
80	ochenta	o·chen·ta
90	noventa	no·ven·ta
100	cien	syen

LANGUAGE

101	*ciento uno*	syen·to *oo*·no
200	*doscientos*	do·*syen*·tos
1000	*mil*	meel
5000	*cinco mil*	*seen*·ko meel
10,000	*diez mil*	*dyes* meel
50,000	*cincuenta mil*	seen·*kwen*·ta meel

SHOPPING & SERVICES

I'd like to buy ...
Quisiera comprar ... kee·*sye*·ra kom·*prar* ...
I'm just looking.
Sólo estoy mirando. so·lo es·*toy* mee·*ran*·do
May I look at it?
¿Puedo mirarlo/la? pwe·do mee·*rar*·lo/la
How much is it?
¿Cuánto cuesta? kwan·to *kwes*·ta
That's too expensive for me.
Es demasiado caro es de·ma·*sya*·do *ka*·ro
para mí. pa·ra mee
Could you lower the price?
¿Podría bajar un poco po·*dree*·a ba·*khar* oon *po*·ko
el precio? el *pre*·syo
I don't like it.
No me gusta. no me *goos*·ta
I'll take it.
Lo llevo. lo *ye*·vo

Do you accept ...?	*¿Aceptan ...?*	a·sep·*tan* ...
American dollars	*dólares americanos*	do·la·res a·me·ree·*ka*·nos
credit cards	*tarjetas de crédito*	tar·*khe*·tas de *kre*·dee·to
traveler's checks	*cheques de viajero*	che·kes de vya·*khe*·ro
less	*menos*	*me*·nos
more	*más*	mas
large	*grande*	*gran*·de
small	*pequeño/a*	pe·*ke*·nyo/a

I'm looking for (the) ...	*Estoy buscando ...*	es·*toy* boos·*kan*·do
ATM	*el cajero automático*	el ka·*khe*·ro ow·to·*ma*·tee·ko
bank	*el banco*	el *ban*·ko
bookstore	*la librería*	la lee·bre·*ree*·a
embassy	*la embajada*	la em·ba·*kha*·da
exchange house	*la casa de cambio*	la *ka*·sa de *kam*·byo
general store	*la tienda*	la *tyen*·da
laundry	*la lavandería*	la la·van·de·*ree*·a
market	*el mercado*	el mer·*ka*·do
pharmacy/ chemist	*la farmacia/ la droguería*	la far·*ma*·sya/ la dro·ge·*ree*·a
post office	*los correos*	los ko·*re*·os

supermarket	*el supermercado*	el soo·per· mer·*ka*·do
tourist office	*la oficina de turismo*	la o·fee·*see*·na de too·*rees*·mo

What time does it open/close?
¿A qué hora abre/cierra? a ke *o*·ra a·bre/*sye*·ra
I want to change some money/traveler's checks.
Quiero cambiar dinero/ *kye*·ro kam·*byar* dee·*ne*·ro/
cheques de viajero. che·kes de vya·*khe*·ro
What is the exchange rate?
¿Cuál es el tipo de kwal es el *tee*·po de
cambio? *kam*·byo
How many quetzals per dollar?
¿Cuántos quetzales *kwan*·tos ket·*za*·les
por dólar? por *do*·lar
I want to call ...
Quiero llamar a ... *kye*·ro lya·*mar* a ...

airmail	*correo aéreo*	ko·*re*·o a·*e*·re·o
letter	*carta*	*kar*·ta
registered mail	*certificado*	ser·tee·fee·*ka*·do
stamps	*estampillas*	es·tam·*pee*·lyas

TIME & DATES

What time is it?	*¿Qué hora es?*	ke *o*·ra es
It's one o'clock.	*Es la una.*	es la *oo*·na
It's seven o'clock.	*Son las siete.*	son las *sye*·te
midnight	*medianoche*	me·dya·*no*·che
noon	*mediodía*	me·dyo·*dee*·a
half past two	*dos y media*	dos ee *me*·dya
now	*ahora*	a·*o*·ra
today	*hoy*	oy
tonight	*esta noche*	es·ta *no*·che
tomorrow	*mañana*	ma·*nya*·na
yesterday	*ayer*	a·*yer*
Monday	*lunes*	*loo*·nes
Tuesday	*martes*	*mar*·tes
Wednesday	*miércoles*	*myer*·ko·les
Thursday	*jueves*	*khwe*·ves
Friday	*viernes*	*vyer*·nes
Saturday	*sábado*	*sa*·ba·do
Sunday	*domingo*	do·*meen*·go
January	*enero*	e·*ne*·ro
February	*febrero*	fe·*bre*·ro
March	*marzo*	*mar*·so
April	*abril*	a·*breel*
May	*mayo*	*ma*·yo
June	*junio*	*khoo*·nyo
July	*julio*	*khoo*·lyo
August	*agosto*	a·*gos*·to
September	*septiembre*	sep·*tyem*·bre

October	octubre	ok·*too*·bre
November	noviembre	no·*vyem*·bre
December	diciembre	dee·*syem*·bre

TRANSPORT
Public Transport

What time does	¿A qué hora ...	a ke *o*·ra ...
... leave/arrive?	sale/llega?	sa·le/ye·ga
the bus	el autobus/	el ow·to·*boos*/
	la camioneta	la ka·mee·o·*ne*·ta
the pickup	el picop/	el a·*vyon*/
	la camioneta	la ka·mee·o·*ne*·ta
the bus (long	el autobus/	el ow·to·*boos*/
distance)	la flota	la *flo* ta
the plane	el avión	el a·*vyon*
the ship	el barco/buque	el *bar*·ko/boo·*ke*

airport	el aeropuerto	el a·e·ro·*pwer*·to
bus station	la estación de	la es·ta·*syon* de
	autobuses	ow·to·*boo*·ses
bus stop	la parada de	la pa·*ra*·da de
	autobuses	ow·to·*boo*·ses
luggage check	guardería/	gwar·de·*ree*·a/
room	equipaje	e·kee·*pa*·khe
ticket office	la boletería	la bo·le·te·*ree*·a

I'd like a ticket to ...
Quiero un boleto a ... kye·ro oon bo·*le*·to a ...
What's the fare to ...?
¿Cuánto cuesta hasta ...? kwan·to *kwes*·ta *a*·sta ...

student's	de estudiante	de es·too·*dyan*·te
1st class	primera clase	pree·me·ra *kla*·se
2nd class	segunda clase	se·*goon*·da *kla*·se
single/one-way	ida	ee·da
return/round trip	ida y vuelta	ee·da ee *vwel*·ta
taxi	taxi	*tak*·see

Private Transport

I'd like to	Quisiera	kee·*sye*·ra
hire a/an ...	alquilar ...	al·kee·*lar* ...
4WD	un todo terreno	oon *to*·do te·*re*·no
car	un auto	oon *ow*·to
motorbike	una moto	*oo*·na mo·to
bicycle	una bicicleta	*oo*·na bee·see·*kle*·ta

pickup (truck)	camioneta	ka·myo·*ne*·ta
truck	camión	ka·*myon*
hitchhike	hacer dedo	a·ser *de*·do

Is this the road to (...)?
¿Se va a (...) por se va a (...) por
esta carretera? es·ta ka·re·*te*·ra

ROAD SIGNS

Acceso	Entrance
Aparcamiento	Parking
Ceda el Paso	Give way
Despacio	Slow
Dirección Única	One-way
Mantenga Su Derecha	Keep to the Right
No Adelantar/	No Passing
No Rebase	
Peaje	Toll
Peligro	Danger
Prohibido Aparcar/	No Parking
No Estacionar	
Prohibido el Paso	No Entry
Pare/Stop	Stop
Salida de Autopista	Exit Freeway

Where's a petrol station?
¿Dónde hay una don·de ai oo·na
gasolinera/un grifo? ga·so·lee·ne·ra/oon gree·fo
Please fill it up.
Lleno, por favor. ye·no por fa·*vor*
I'd like (20) liters.
Quiero (veinte) litros. kye·ro (vayn·te) lee·tros

diesel	diesel	dee·sel
leaded (regular)	gasolina con	ga·so·lee·na kon
	plomo	plo·mo
petrol (gas)	gasolina	ga·so·lee·na
unleaded	gasolina sin	ga·so·lee·na seen
	plomo	plo·mo

(How long) Can I park here?
¿(Por cuánto tiempo) (por kwan·to tyem·po)
Puedo aparcar aquí? pwe·do a·par·*kar* a·kee
Where do I pay?
¿Dónde se paga? don·de se *pa*·ga
I need a mechanic.
Necesito un ne·se·*see*·to oon
mecánico. me·*ka*·nee·ko
The car has broken down (in ...).
El carro se ha averiado el *ka*·ro se a a·ve·*rya*·do
(en ...). (en ...)
The motorbike won't start.
No arranca la moto. no a·*ran*·ka la *mo*·to
I have a flat tyre.
Tengo un pinchazo. ten·go oon peen·*cha*·so
I've run out of petrol.
Me quedé sin gasolina. me ke·*de* seen ga·so·*lee*·na
I've had an accident.
Tuve un accidente. *too*·ve oon ak·see·*den*·te

TRAVEL WITH CHILDREN

I need ...	Necesito ...	ne·se·see·to ...
Do you have ...?	¿Hay ...?	ai ...
a car baby seat	un asiento de seguridad para bebés	oon a·syen·to de se·goo·ree·da pa·ra be·bes
a child-minding service	un servicio de cuidado de niños	oon ser·vee·syo de kwee·da·do de nee·nyos
a children's menu	una carta infantil	oona kar·ta een·fan·teel
a creche	una guardería	oo·na gwar·de·ree·a
(disposable) diapers/nappies	pañoles (de usar y tirar)	pa·nyo·les de oo·sar ee tee·rar
an (English-speaking) babysitter	una niñera (de habla inglesa)	oo·na nee·nye·ra (de a·bla een·gle·sa)
formula (milk)	leche en polvo	le·che en pol·vo
a highchair	una trona	oo·na tro·na
a potty	una pelela	oo·na pe·le·la
a stroller	un cochecito	oon ko·che·see·to

Do you mind if I breast-feed here?

¿Le molesta que dé de pecho aquí?	le mo·les·ta ke de de pe·cho a·kee

Are children allowed?

¿Se admiten niños?	se ad·mee·ten nee·nyos

MODERN MAYAN

Since the Classic period, the two ancient Mayan languages, Yucatecan and Cholan, have subdivided into 35 separate Mayan languages (such as Yucatec, Chol, Chortí, Tzeltal, Tzotzil, Lacandón, Mam, K'iche' and Kaqchiquel), some of them unintelligible to speakers of others, some not. Indigenous languages are seldom written, but when they are, the Roman alphabet is used. Most literate Maya will only be able to read and write Spanish, the language of government, schools, the church and the media – they may not be literate in Mayan.

Pronunciation

There are several rules to remember when pronouncing Mayan words and place names. Mayan vowels are pretty straightforward, but consonants can be tricky.

c	always hard, as in 'cat'
j	an aspirated 'h' sound, eg *jipijapa* is pronounced 'hee-pee-haa-pah' and *abaj* is pronounced 'ah-bahh'; to get

the 'ah' sound, imagine the 'h' sound from 'half' at the end of a word

u	as in 'prune', except when it occurs at the beginning or end of a word, in which case it is like English 'w'; thus *baktun* is 'bahk-toon,' but *Uaxactún* is 'wah-shahk-toon' and *ahau* is 'ah-haw'
x	as English 'sh'

Mayan glottalized consonants (indicated by an apostrophe: **b', ch', k', p', t'**) are similar to normal consonants, but are pronounced more forcefully and 'explosively.' An apostrophe following a vowel signifies a glottal stop (like the momentary stop between the syllables in 'oh-oh'), not a more forceful vowel.

Another rule to remember is that in most Mayan words the stress falls on the last syllable. Sometimes this is indicated by an acute accent, sometimes not. The following place names are useful guides to pronunciation:

Abaj Takalik	a·*bah* ta·ka·leek
Acanceh	a·kan·*keh*
Ahau	a·*haw*
Kaminaljuyú	ka·mee·nal·hoo·*yoo*
Pop	pope
Tikal	tee·*kal*
Uaxactún	wa·shak·*toon*

K'ICHE'

K'iche' is widely spoken throughout the Guatemalan Highlands, from around Santa Cruz del Quiché to the area adjacent to Lake Atitlán and around Quetzaltenango. There are estimated to be around 2 million K'iche' Maya living in Guatemala, giving you plenty of opportunity to practice some of the common terms and phrases listed below.

Greetings & Civilities

These are great icebreakers, and even if you're not completely and accurately understood, there'll be goodwill and smiles all around just for making the effort.

Good morning.	Saqarik.
Good afternoon.	Xb'eqij.
Good evening/night.	Xokaq'ab'.
Goodbye.	Chab'ej.
Bye. See you soon.	Kimpetik ri.

Thank you.	Uts awech?
Excuse me.	Kyunala.
What's your name?	Su ra'b'i?
My name is ...	Nu b'i ...
Where are you from?	Ja kat pewi?
I'm from ...	Ch'qap ja'kin pewi ...

Useful Words & Phrases

Where is (a/the) ...?	Ja k'uichi' ri ...?
bathroom	b'anb'al chulu
hotel	jun worib'al
police station	ajchajil re tinamit
doctor	ajkun
bus stop	tek'lib'al

Do you have ...?	K'olik ...?
coffee	kab'e
boiled water	saq'li
copal	kach'
a machete	choyib'al
rooms	k'plib'al

We have it.	K'olik.
We don't have it.	K'otaj.

vegetables	ichaj
blanket	k'ul
soap	ch'ipaq
good	utz
bad	itzel
open	teb'am
closed	tzapilik
hard	ko
soft	ch'uch'uj
hot	miq'in
cold	joron
sick	yiwab'
north (white)	saq
south (yellow)	k'an
east (red)	kaq
west (black)	k'eq

Numbers

1	jun
2	keb'
3	oxib'
4	kijeb'
5	job'
6	waq'ib'
7	wuqub'
8	wajxakib'
9	b'elejeb'
10	lajuj
11	julajuj
12	kab'lajuj
13	oxlajuj
14	kajlajuj
15	o'lajuj
16	waklajuj
17	wuklajuj
18	wajxaklajuj
19	b'elejlajuj
20	juwinak
30	lajuj re kawinak
40	kawinak
50	lajuj re oxk'al
60	oxk'al
70	lajuj re waqk'al
80	waqk'al
90	lajuj re o'k'al
100	o'k'al
200	lajuj k'al
400	omuch'

MAM

Mam is spoken in the department of Huehuetenango, in the western portion of the country. This is the indigenous language you'll hear in Todos Santos Cuchumatán, which is nestled among the Cuchumatanes mountains.

Greetings & Civilities

Luckily, in Mam you only need two phrases for greeting folks, no matter what time of day it is.

Good morning/ afternoon/evening.	Chin q'olb'el teya. (informal singular) Chin q'olb'el kyeyea. (informal plural)
Goodbye.	Chi nej.
Bye. See you soon.	Chi nej. Ak qli qib'.
Thank you.	Chonte teya.
How are you?	Tzen ta'ya?
Excuse me.	Naq samy.
What's your name?	Tit biya?
My name is ...	Luan bi ...
Where are you from?	Jaa'tzajnia?
I'm from ...	Ac tzajni ...

Useful Words & Phrases

Where is (a/the) ...?	Ja at ...?
bathroom	bano
hotel	hospedaje
doctor	medico/doctor

Many words in Mam have been in disuse for so long that the Spanish equivalent is now used almost exclusively.

Where is the bus stop?	*Ja nue camioneta?* (literally, where does the bus stop?)
How much is the fruits & vegetables?	*Je te ti lobj?*
Do you have ...?	*At ...?*
coffee	*café*
boiled water	*kqa'*
rooms	*cuartos*
Is there somewhere we can sleep?	*Ja tun kqta'n?*
We have it.	*At.*
We don't have it.	*Nti'.*
I'm cold.	*At xb'a'j/choj.*
I'm sick.	*At yab'*

good	*banex/g'lan*
bad	*k'ab'ex/nia g'lan*
open	*jqo'n*
closed	*jpu'n*
hard	*kuj*
soft	*xb'une*
hot	*kyaq*
north (white)	*okan*
south (yellow)	*eln*
east (red)	*jawl*
west (black)	*kub'el*

Numbers

The numbers from one to 10 are the same as in K'iche' (p308). For numbers higher than 10, Mam speakers use the Spanish equivalents.

Also available from Lonely Planet:
Latin American Spanish phrasebook

Glossary

abrazo – embrace, hug; in particular, the formal, ceremonial hug between political leaders

alux, aluxes – Mayan for gremlin, leprechaun, benevolent 'little people'

Apartado Postal – post-office box; abbreviated Apdo Postal

Ayuntamiento – often seen as H Ayuntamiento (Honorable Ayuntamiento) on the front of town hall buildings; translates as 'Municipal Government'

barrio – district, neighborhood

billete – bank note (unlike in Spain, where it's a ticket)

boleto – ticket (bus, train, museum etc)

bolo – colloquial term for drunk (noun)

cabañas – cabins

cacique – Mayan chief; also used to describe provincial warlord or strongman

cafetería – literally 'coffee-shop,' but refers to any informal restaurant with waiter service; not usually a cafeteria in the North American sense of a self-service restaurant

cajero automático – automated teller machine (ATM)

callejón – alley or narrow or very short street

camión – truck or bus

camioneta – bus or pickup truck

cardamomo – cardamom; a spice grown extensively in the Verapaces and used as a flavor enhancer for coffee and tea, particularly in the Middle East

casa de cambio – currency exchange office; offers exchange rates comparable to those of banks and is much faster to use (uncommon in Guatemala)

cazuela – clay cooking pot; usually sold in a nested set

cenote – large, natural limestone cave used for water storage (or ceremonial purposes)

cerveza – beer

Chac – Mayan god of rain

chac-mool – Mayan sacrificial stone sculpture

chapín – citizen of Guatemala

charro – cowboy

chicle – sap of the sapodilla tree; used to manufacture chewing gum

chicleros – men who collect *chicle*

chingar – literally 'to rape' but in practice a word with a wide range of colloquial meanings similar to the use of 'to screw' in English

Chinka' – small, non-Mayan indigenous group living on the Pacific Slope

chuchkajau – Mayan prayer leader

chuj – traditional Mayan sauna; see also *tuj*

chultún – artificial Mayan cistern

cigarro – cigarette

cocina – kitchen; also used for a small, basic one-woman place to eat, often located in or near a municipal market, and in the phrases cocina económica (economical kitchen) or a cocina familiar (family kitchen)

cofradía – religious brotherhood, most often found in the Highlands

colectivo – jitney taxi or minibus (usually a combi or minibus) that picks up and drops off passengers along its route

comal – hot griddle or surface used to cook tortillas

comedor – basic and cheap eatery, usually with a limited menu

completo – full; a sign you may see on hotel desks in crowded cities

conquistador – explorer-conqueror of Latin America from Spain

copal – tree resin used as incense in Mayan ceremonies

correos – post office

corte – Mayan wraparound skirt

costumbre – traditional Mayan rites

criollos – people born in Guatemala of Spanish blood

cruce – crossroads, usually where you make bus connections; also known as *entronque*

curandero – traditional indigenous healer

damas – ladies; the usual sign on toilet doors

dzul, dzules – Mayan for foreigners or 'townsfolk'

encomienda – Spanish colonial practice of putting indigenous people under the 'guardianship' of landowners; practically akin to medieval serfdom

entronque – see *cruce*

faja – Mayan waist sash or belt

ferrocarril – railroad

finca – plantation, farm

galón, galones – US gallons; fluid measure of 3.79L

glyph – symbolic character or figure; usually engraved or carved in relief

gringo/a – a mildly pejorative term applied to a male/female North American visitor; sometimes applied to any visitor of European heritage

gruta – cave

guayabera – man's thin fabric shirt with pockets and appliquéd designs on the front, over the shoulders and down the back; often worn in place of a jacket and tie on formal occasions

hacienda – estate; also 'treasury,' as in Departamento de Hacienda, Treasury Department

hay – pronounced like 'eye,' meaning 'there is' or 'there are'; you're equally likely to hear *no hay*, meaning 'there isn't' or 'there aren't'
hombre/s – man/men
huipil – Mayan woman's woven tunic; often very colorful and elaborately embroidered

IVA – impuesto al valor agregado or value-added tax; on hotel rooms it is 12%

juego de pelota – ball game

kaperraj – Mayan woman's all-purpose cloth; used as a head covering, baby sling, produce sack, shawl and more
Kukulcán – Mayan name for the Aztec-Toltec plumed serpent Quetzalcóatl

ladino – person of mixed indigenous and European race; a more common term in Guatemala than *mestizo*
lancha – motorboat used to transport passengers; driven by a lanchero
larga distancia – long-distance telephone
lavandería – laundry; a lavandería automática is a coin-operated laundry
leng – in the highlands, a colloquial Mayan term for coins
libra – pound; weight measurement of 0.45kg
lleno – full (fuel tank)

machismo – maleness, masculine virility
malecón – waterfront boulevard
manglar – mangrove
manzana – apple; also a city block; see also *supermanzana*
mariachi – small group of street musicians featuring stringed instruments, trumpets and often an accordion; sometimes plays in restaurants
marimba – Guatemala's xylophone-like national instrument
mestizo – person of mixed indigenous and European blood; the word *ladino* is more common in Guatemala
metate – flattish stone on which corn is ground with a cylindrical stone roller
milla – mile; distance of 1.6km
milpa – maize field
mirador – lookout, vista point
mochilero – backpacker
mordida – 'bite'; small bribe paid to keep the wheels of bureaucracy turning
mudéjar – Moorish architectural style
mujer/es – woman/women

na – thatched Mayan hut

onza – ounce; weight of 28g

pachete – a squash-type vegetable; can be eaten or used as a loofah
palacio de gobierno – building housing the executive offices of a state or regional government
palacio municipal – city hall; seat of the corporation or municipal government
palapa – thatched shelter with a palm-leaf roof and open sides
panza verde – literally 'green belly,' a nickname given to Antigua residents who are said to eat lots of avocados.
parada – bus stop; usually for city buses
picop – pickup truck
pie – foot; measure of 0.30m
pisto – colloquial Mayan term for money, quetzals
posada – guesthouse
propino, propina – a tip, different from a *mordida*, which is really a bribe
punta – sexually suggestive dance enjoyed by the Garífuna of the Caribbean coast
puro – cigar

Quetzalcóatl – plumed serpent god of the Aztecs and Toltecs; see also *Kukulcán*

rebozo – long woolen or linen scarf covering the head or shoulders
refago – Mayan wraparound skirt
retablo – ornate, often gilded altarpiece
retorno – 'return'; used on traffic signs to signify a U-turn or turnaround
roofcomb – a decorative stonework lattice atop a Mayan pyramid or temple
rutelero – jitney

sacbé, sacbeob – ceremonial limestone avenue or path between great Mayan cities
sacerdote – priest
sanatorio – hospital, particularly a small private one
sanitario – literally 'sanitary'; usually means toilet
secadora – clothes dryer
Semana Santa – Holy Week preceding Easter
stela, stelae – standing stone monument(s); usually carved
supermanzana – large group of city blocks bounded by major avenues; see also *manzana*
supermercado – supermarket; anything from a corner store to a large, US-style supermarket

taller – shop or workshop
taller mecánico – mechanic's shop, usually for cars
teléfono comunitario – community telephone; found in the smallest towns
tepezcuintle – edible jungle rodent the size of a rabbit
tequila – clear, distilled liquor produced, like pulque and mezcal, from the maguey cactus

tienda – small store that may sell anything from candles and chickens to aspirin and bread
típico – typical or characteristic of a region; particularly used to describe food
tocoyal – Mayan head covering
traje – traditional clothing worn by the Maya
tuj – traditional Mayan sauna; see also *chuj*
túmulos – speed bumps found in many towns; sometimes indicated by a highway sign bearing a row of little bumps
tzut – Mayan man's equivalent of a *kaperraj*

viajero – traveler
vulcanizadora – automobile tire repair shop

xate – low-growing fern native to the Petén region and exported for use in floral arrangements, particularly in the US
xateros – men who collect *xate*

zonas – zones
zotz – bat (the mammal) in many Mayan languages

Behind the Scenes

THIS BOOK

This 2nd edition of *Guatemala* was written by John Noble and Susan Forsyth. Susan wrote most of the Central & Eastern Guatemala chapter, parts of the Antigua and Transport chapters, and the Quetzaltenango & Around section of the Highlands chapter. John, the coordinating author, wrote the rest of the book. The Health chapter was written by Dr David Goldberg. The 1st edition was researched and written by Conner Gorry. For the 1st edition, Conner drew on information written by Nancy Keller and Tom Brosnahan for the 3rd edition of *Guatemala, Belize & Yucatán*.

THANKS FROM THE AUTHORS

We met and were helped by so many wonderful people while researching this book that it is impossible to even begin to name them all. But special thanks to Andrew and Bismark in Huehue. Conner, Heather and Dan, Patrick and staff in Xela, and Nicole in Todos Santos. Thanks also to Oliver Ordoñez at Inguat in Guatemala City, Annemie, Cindy, Dirk and Geert in Copán Ruinas, and Thomas and Flor de María Stutzer-Pódriguez, Helena Helde and Mercedes in Monterrico. Also special thanks to David Zingarelli in Oakland and Simon Williamson and Alison Lyall in Melbourne for skilfully steering this book through its preparatory and production phases amid all the challenges of the 'New Look.'

CREDITS

Guatemala 2 was commissioned and developed in Lonely Planet's Oakland office by David Zingarelli. Cartography for this title was developed by Graham Neale. The book was coordinated by

Simon Williamson (editorial) and Herman So (cartography). Simone Egger, Lara Morcombe, Michelle Coxall, Cherry Prior, Anne Mulvaney and Melanie Dankel assisted with editing and proofing. Anneka Imkamp and Tony Fankhauser assisted with cartography. Andrew Ostroff laid the book out, and Maria Vallianos designed the cover. Victoria Harrison and Hilary Ericksen assisted with layout checking, while Evan Jones and Steven Cann assisted with layout. Quentin Frayne prepared the Language chapter, and Anne Mulvaney and Simon Williamson prepared the index. Overseeing production were Eoin Dunlevy (Project Manager), Kerryn Burgess (Managing Editor) and Alison Lyall (Managing Cartographer), who was assisted by Anthony Phelan. Series Publishing Manager Virginia Maxwell oversaw the redevelopment of the country guides series with help from Maria Donohoe, who was also the Regional Publishing Manager and steered the development of this title. The series was designed by James Hardy, with mapping development by Paul Piaia. The series development team included Shahara Ahmed, Susie Ashworth, Gerilyn Attebery, Jenny Blake, Anna Bolger, Verity Campbell, Erin Corrigan, Nadine Fogale, Dave McClymont, Leonie Mugavin, Lynne Preston, Rachel Peart and Howard Ralley.

THANKS FROM LONELY PLANET

Many thanks to the hundreds of travelers who used the last edition and wrote to us with helpful hints, useful advice and interesting anecdotes:

A Hamish Abbie, Johannes Abeling, Harm Aben, Bruce Aisthorpe, Natasha Aisthorpe, Nick Ambridge, Mark Anderson, Ervin Andrino,

---

THE LONELY PLANET STORY

The story begins with a classic travel adventure: Tony and Maureen Wheeler's 1972 journey across Europe and Asia to Australia. There was no useful information about the overland trail then, so Tony and Maureen published the first Lonely Planet guidebook to meet a growing need.

From a kitchen table, Lonely Planet has grown to become the largest independent travel publisher in the world, with offices in Melbourne (Australia), Oakland (USA), London (UK) and Paris (France).

Today Lonely Planet guidebooks cover the globe. There is an ever-growing list of books and information in a variety of media. Some things haven't changed. The main aim is still to make it possible for adventurous travelers to get out there – to explore and better understand the world.

At Lonely Planet we believe travelers can make a positive contribution to the countries they visit – if they respect their host communities and spend their money wisely.

Beata Antal, Enrique Araoz, Eve Astrid Andersson, Jörg Ausfelt, Christie Ayral, Arturo Azcarraga **B** E Baltus, Marco Balzarini, Fabio Barbieri, Jenny Barnes, Pennan Barry, Ullvi Båve, Alec Beardsell, Laresa Beck, Bettina Berch, Michal Beressi, Andrew Bergmann, Harald Berninger, Christophe Bevilacqua, Hilmar Bijma, Vashti Blacker, Tracy Blahy, Norbert Bolis, Maaike Bosschart, Tony Bourke, George Boutilier, Richard Bovenschen, Sue Bowling, Henri et Nathalie Boyer, Hank Bragg, Jan Brascamp, Liesbeth Breesch, Dannie Brooke, Graeme Brooks, Corina Browne, Simon Burchell, Alexandra Burke, Craig Burton, Mark Burton, Ute Buscher, Janey Byrne **C** Alan & Clare Cannon, Giovanni Capellini, Michael Carbone, Denny Carhart, Kimber Carhart, Luis Carreras, Olivia Carrescia, Gaetano Carubia, Eva Casas, Nelita Castillo, Sophia Castillo, Daniela Cellino, Marco Ceschi, Steve Chaplain, Julia Chen, fred chevre, Jinsook Choi, Chungwah Chow, Mike and Trena Christensen, Peter Cogo, Jeff Collard, Gerald Conrad, Monica Contini, Diane Cooke, Richard Cooper, Karen Copsey, Paolo Cotta-Ramusino, Andrew Cox, Olivia Cozzolino, Mick Creedon, Jai Cross, Martin Crossland, Lucy Curry **D** Gail D'Alessio, Emma Darley, Hannah Dawson, Dennis de Graaf, Stefan De Hert, Edwin de Lange, Jose De Leon Guzman, Emily Dean, Neil Dickinson, Irene Dijkstra, Jennifer Ditchburn, Andrew Dix, Andrew Doak, Kate Dodson, Kate Donaldson-Fletcher, Thomas Donegan, Danielle Douglas, Alejandra Duarte, Catherine Duclos, Stephanie Dula, Jean-Marc Dumont **E** Emery Edwards, Jay Edwards, Simone Egger, Peter Ehrenkranz, Demetre Eliopoulos, Litza Escobar, Robert Ettinger, Will Everett **F** Roi Faust, Greg Feather, Stacy Fehlenberg, Chuck Fields, Roy Fitzroy, Dorothee Flaig, Annelies Florquin, Ben Flynn, Kathy Fournier, Shana Frank, Heather frankel, Jacob Frederiksen, Robin Freedman, Karen Fu, **G** Joan Gaffiney, Simon Cloutier Gagne, Katerina Gaita, Christian Gandara, Dario Garcia, Jennifer Garcia, Richard Garcia, Marcelo Garza, Robert Gehrung, Martina Gempp, Sandra Gennai, Rose George, Roger Gerritzen, Monique Giammatei, Rachel Gibbs, Paula Gijsman, Andrew Gill, WJ Glass, Jackie and Steven Gloor, Nicolas Gonze, Lisa Goodlin, Amanda Graves, Lisa Graybill, David Green, Stacey Grove, Oliver Guba, Shamir Gurfinkel, Peder Gustafsson, Jacquelline Gygax **H** Wolfgang Haertel, Marita Hagen, Chrystal Hagerty, Peter Hahn, Aaron Hall, Evan Hall, Tom Hall, Richard Hamerton-Stone, Lisa Hamilton, Kelly Hammond, Kim Haney, Kim Hannah, Jill Harmer, Susan Hart, brooke hauser, Liselotte Hedegaard, Rainard Heerde, Rita Heerde, Carl Heffington, Pat Heron, Greg Hill, Rachel Hill, Michiel Hillenius, Justin Hines, Ana María Hintermann-Villamil, Krista Hoffs, Mary Ann Hollebeck, Olivia Horgan, Celina & Mirek Hrabanek, Fer Hurk, Tomi Hurtado **I** Eran Inbar, Dave Ingram, Nadler Ishay, Shamim Islam **J** Eric Jansson, Marjolaine Janvier-Houde, Jan Jasiewicz, Magali Jean, Alice Jelinek, Marije Jeltes, Alex Jensen, Irfaan Jogee, Carlisle Johnson, Helen Johnson, Jennifer Jones, Paul Jones, Margreet Joosen, Tammy Jorgensen, Vince Jorgensen **K** Thomas Kaeslin, Vanessa Kallaway, Stanley F Kapica, Ofer Kashtan, Christian Kasprzyk, Gerd Kattnig, Rupert Kaufmann, Klaus Kemnitzer, Noa Kfir, Judy king, Trevor King, Gregory Kipling, vincent kleinekorte, Linda Knight, Will Koch, Meike Kolb, Leo Kooi, Mil Kooyman, Rastko Kozlevcar, Julie Kramer, Katrin Krueger, Katarzyna Kubacha, Astrid Kueffer, David Kuhn **L** L Ladouceur, Bonnet Laetitia, Tab Lamoureux, José

Larios, Shirley Larsen, Harriet Lavender, Annette Lavers, Eve Lavigne, Khiem Lé, Viviane Le Courtois, Danisa Lederer, Michelle Legere, Ruben Lehnert, Andre Lehovich, Vikki Leone Milton Lever, Lluis Lopez Bayona, Stephen Lowe, Sita Luca, Bob Luckey, **M** Campbell Macdonald, Renee MacDonald, Zoe Macfarlane, Ken Macgregor, Leslie MacKay, David Madden, Jan Maes-Petra Waeckens, Jane Majken Hove Roehl, Charles Maliszewski, Uwe Mall, Casper Maltha, Boris Marie, Mercedes Marin, Birgit Maris, Montserrat Marli, Kathy Martens, Dave Martin, Itziar Martin, Luis Martinez, Andrea Masnata, Francois Maurice, Beth McCall, Rory McCall, Bruce McCartney, Tristan McCoy, Sarah McKinnon, Kimberly McLaughlin, Sean McNulty, Michael Meallem, Toni Meier, Yurinia Mejia, Guadalupe Mendoza, Joseph Mendoza, Nick Menzies, Bruce Meyer, Heidi Meyer, Stephanie Mignacca, Virginia Milliner, Alejandro Salvador Morales, Steffi Morgner, Susanne & Christian Moskob, Connie Mosquera, Paul Mulder, Sonja Munnix **N** Ingrid Naden, Spencer & Mary Beth Nelson, Judy Netherwood, Dori Neubronner, Gillian Newell, Dennis Nilsson, Morten Norjordet, Katharina Nothelfer, Sarah Nouis, Nadja Nys **O** Brent Ohata, Shinji Okitsu, Justin Oliver, Caprice Olsthoorn, Sonja Olszewski, Andrew Oost, Richard M Orona, Celia Ortega, Carlos Ortega Hurtado de Mendoz, Conor Oshea, Pascal Otten, Konrad Ozols **P** Jennifer Pacourek, Elena Parlanti, Trish Patrick, Sabina Pensek, Rebecca Perez, Al Perry, Matt Peters, Matthew Peters, Stephanie Petit, Severine Peudupin, Antonella Piccini, Jason Pielemeier, Melissa Pike, Jennifer Pittman, Steve Pogue, Ryan Pohl, Merce Pons, Sharon Portugal, Crystal Powell, Natasha Pozo, Luis F. Prieto, Juli Puryear **Q** Shahreen Quazi **R** Andre Racine,

Mads Dippel Rasmussen, Charles Regnier, M. Rehorst, John P Reid, Scott Reilly, Karina Reindlmeier, Uta & Heidi Reith, Diana Renard, Meloney Retallack, Jean Claude Rey, Paul Rigg, Romolo Ripini, Romolo & Gessica Ripini, Branden Rippey, Alex Robertson, Eric Robette, Jo Robinson, Jacquie Rodgers, Mike Rodgers, Deborah Rodrigo, Filipe Rodrigues, James Rogers, Elisabeth Rogolsky, Matt Roque, Antoinette & Dey Rose, Francoise Roux, Woody Rubin, Floren Rudy, Dr Shimon Rumelt, Rachel Rumsey, Krzysztof Rybak, Claire Ryder **S** Edwina Sassoon, Thomas Schaffner, Lex Schaling, Christian Schild, Treya Marie Schmitt, Wendy Schneider, Doris Schoch, Martina Schoefberger, Susanne Schoenauer, Marianne Schrotter, Tim Schultz, Seth Seiderman, Elke Selter, Olaf Shaefer, Alexander Sharman, Cynthia Sharon, Jade Shephard, Daniel Sher, Paul Sheridan, Tali Sherman, Amy Shindler, Amit Irit Shwartz, Nadine Sicard, Alen Silva, Michael Simone, Evita Sips, Karen Skibo, Dorkas Sloth, Erica Smith, James Smith, Joseph Smith, Samuel Smith, Timothy J Smith, Vic Sofras, Claudine Solin, Susan Sommer, Heike Sonnberger, Loes Sparwer, Will Staler, Peggy Stauffer, Hendrik Steringa, Mary Kay Stine, Helen Stohlman, Cecilia Stranneby, Ursula Strauss, Beat Stueber, Thomas Stutzer, Marjon Sutherland, Tom Sweeney **T** Masahori Takahashi, Achim Talmon, Jay E Taylor, Robert Taylor, Jeroen Thijs, Nick Thomas, Lynn Tiede, Vanessa Tierney, Klaas Tjoelker, Markus Toepler, Marcello Tomaselli, Shelley Tozer, Andrew Trout **V** Mauro Valentini, Cor & Jenny Valk, Maurits van den Boorn, Judith van den hengel, Ilse van der Veer, Wendy van Driel, Eelco Van Geene, Marly van Horck, Wim van Immerzeel, Peter van Nes, Rutger van Otterlo, Max van Riel, Martine van Rijn, Ron van Rooijen, Leonie van Rossum, Michel van Rossum, Lianne van Someren, Diederik Vanderburg, Todd Varness, Frits Verbeek, Marieke Verboord, Didier Verbruggen, Bart Verlinden, Yves Vervaet, Joerg Viereck, Jesus Villen, Thomas Villette, Marcella Vinciguerra, Rolf Von Behrens **W** Kelsey Wagner, Thomas Wagner, Chow Chung Wah, David Wahl, Heidi Waltz, Gwynn Watkins, Julie Webb, Jamie Weed, Dan & Martha Weese, David Weibel, Andreas Weichert, Mark Weitz, Peggy Wenrick, Sascha Wenzel, Sharon Whatley, Kirsten Wheeler, Jason White, Natalie White, Philip Wiebe, Martin Wielecki, Ellen Wijnand, Paul Wilson, Steve Wilson, Chritopher & Tanda Wilson-Clarke, Thomas Wimmer, Margaret Winn, Emma Wise, Kevin Withers, Stephen Wollmer, Young-Jee Won, Ben Wrigley, Marisa Wyatt **X** Hedy **X Y** Todd Youngs **Z** Dennis Zijlstra, Heidi Zotter, Alexandra Zum Felde, Arjan Zutt

ACKNOWLEDGMENTS

Many thanks to the following for the use of their content:

Mountain High Maps® Copyright © 1993 Digital Wisdom, Inc.

Index

000 Map pages
000 Location of colour photographs

LONELY PLANET OFFICES

Australia
Head Office
Locked Bag 1, Footscray, Victoria 3011
☎ 03 8379 8000, fax 03 8379 8111
talk2us@lonelyplanet.com.au

USA
150 Linden St, Oakland, CA 94607
☎ 510 893 8555, toll free 800 275 8555
fax 510 893 8572, info@lonelyplanet.com

UK
72–82 Rosebery Ave,
Clerkenwell, London EC1R 4RW
☎ 020 7841 9000, fax 020 7841 9001
go@lonelyplanet.co.uk

France
1 rue du Dahomey, 75011 Paris
☎ 01 55 25 33 00, fax 01 55 25 33 01
bip@lonelyplanet.fr, www.lonelyplanet.fr

Published by Lonely Planet Publications Pty Ltd
ABN 36 005 607 983

© Lonely Planet 2004

© photographers as indicated 2004

Cover photographs by Lonely Planet Images: Portrait of girls at sunset, Antigua, Aaron McCoy (front); Temple of the Grand Jaguar, Eric L Wheater (back). Many of the images in this guide are available for licensing from Lonely Planet Images: www.lonelyplanetimages.com.

Printed by SNP SPrint (M) Sdn Bhd, Malaysia